ICSEA 2019

The Fourteenth International Conference on Software Engineering Advances

November 24 - 28, 2019

Valencia, Spain

ICSEA 2019 Editors

Luigi Lavazza, Università dell'Insubria - Varese, Italy

Herwig Mannaert, University of Antwerp, Belgium

Krishna Kavi, University of North Texas, USA

Printed from e-media with permission by:

Curran Associates, Inc.
57 Morehouse Lane
Red Hook, NY 12571

Some format issues inherent in the e-media version may also appear in this print version.

Printed with permission by Curran Associates, Inc. (2020)

International Academy, Research, and Industry Association (IARIA)
412 Derby Way
Wilmington, DE 19810

Phone: (408) 893-6407
Fax: (408) 527-6351

petre@iaria.org

Additional copies of this publication are available from:

Curran Associates, Inc.
57 Morehouse Lane
Red Hook, NY 12571 USA
Phone: 845-758-0400
Fax: 845-758-2633
Email: curran@proceedings.com
Web: www.proceedings.com

Table of Contents

ICSEA 2019

Forward

The Fourteenth International Conference on Software Engineering Advances (ICSEA 2019), held on November 24 - 28, 2019- Valencia, Spain, continued a series of events covering a broad spectrum of software-related topics.

The conference covered fundamentals on designing, implementing, testing, validating and maintaining various kinds of software. The tracks treated the topics from theory to practice, in terms of methodologies, design, implementation, testing, use cases, tools, and lessons learnt. The conference topics covered classical and advanced methodologies, open source, agile software, as well as software deployment and software economics and education.

The conference had the following tracks:

- Advances in fundamentals for software development
- Advanced mechanisms for software development
- Advanced design tools for developing software
- Software engineering for service computing (SOA and Cloud)
- Advanced facilities for accessing software
- Software performance
- Software security, privacy, safeness
- Advances in software testing
- Specialized software advanced applications
- Web Accessibility
- Open source software
- Agile and Lean approaches in software engineering
- Software deployment and maintenance
- Software engineering techniques, metrics, and formalisms
- Software economics, adoption, and education
- Business technology
- Improving productivity in research on software engineering
- Trends and achievements

Similar to the previous edition, this event continued to be very competitive in its selection process and very well perceived by the international software engineering community. As such, it is attracting excellent contributions and active participation from all over the world. We were very pleased to receive a large amount of top quality contributions.

We take here the opportunity to warmly thank all the members of the ICSEA 2019 technical program committee as well as the numerous reviewers. The creation of such a broad and high quality conference program would not have been possible without their involvement. We also kindly thank all the authors that dedicated much of their time and efforts to contribute to the ICSEA 2019. We truly believe that thanks to all these efforts, the final conference program consists of top quality contributions.

This event could also not have been a reality without the support of many individuals, organizations and sponsors. We also gratefully thank the members of the ICSEA 2019 organizing committee for their help in handling the logistics and for their work that is making this professional meeting a success.

We hope the ICSEA 2019 was a successful international forum for the exchange of ideas and results between academia and industry and to promote further progress in software engineering research. We also hope Valencia provided a pleasant environment during the conference and everyone saved some time for exploring this beautiful city.

ICSEA 2019 Steering Committee

Herwig Mannaert, University of Antwerp, Belgium
Mira Kajko-Mattsson, Royal Institute of Technology, Sweden
Luigi Lavazza, Università dell'Insubria - Varese, Italy
Roy Oberhauser, Aalen University, Germany
Elena Troubitsyna, Abo Akademi University, Finland
Radek Koci, Brno University of Technology, Czech Republic
Stephen W. Clyde, Utah State University, USA
Sébastien Salva, University Clermont Auvergne (UCA), Limos, France
Christian Kop, Universitaet Klagenfurt, Austria
Luis Fernandez-Sanz, Universidad de Alcala, Spain
Bidyut Gupta, Southern Illinois University, USA

ICSEA 2019 Industry/Research Advisory Committee

J. Paul Gibson, Telecom Sud Paris, France
Adriana Martin, National University of Austral Patagonia (UNPA), Argentina
Muthu Ramachandran, Leeds Beckett University, UK
Michael Gebhart, iteratec GmbH, Germany

ICSEA 2019 Publicity Chair

Ayman Aljarbouh, University of Grenoble Alpes (UGA) in Grenoble, France

ICSEA 2019

Committee

ICSEA Steering Committee

Herwig Mannaert, University of Antwerp, Belgium
Mira Kajko-Mattsson, Royal Institute of Technology, Sweden
Luigi Lavazza, Università dell'Insubria - Varese, Italy
Roy Oberhauser, Aalen University, Germany
Elena Troubitsyna, Abo Akademi University, Finland
Radek Koci, Brno University of Technology, Czech Republic
Stephen W. Clyde, Utah State University, USA
Sébastien Salva, University Clermont Auvergne (UCA), Limos, France
Christian Kop, Universitaet Klagenfurt, Austria
Luis Fernandez-Sanz, Universidad de Alcala, Spain
Bidyut Gupta, Southern Illinois University, USA

ICSEA Industry/Research Advisory Committee

J. Paul Gibson, Telecom Sud Paris, France
Adriana Martin, National University of Austral Patagonia (UNPA), Argentina
Muthu Ramachandran, Leeds Beckett University, UK
Michael Gebhart, iteratec GmbH, Germany

ICSEA Publicity Chair

Ayman Aljarbouh, University of Grenoble Alpes (UGA) in Grenoble, France

ICSEA 2019 Technical Program Committee

Shahliza Abd Halim, Universiti of Technologi Malaysia (UTM), Malaysia
Tamer Abdou, Ryerson University, Toronto, Canada
Muhammad Ovais Ahmad, University of Oulu, Finland
Iftekhar Ahmed, University of California, Irvine, USA
Jacky Akoka, CNAM & IMT, France
Mustafa Al-Hajjaji, pure-systems GmbH, Germany
Saadia Binte Alam, Advanced Medical Engineering Center (AMEC) | University of Hyogo, Japan
Ayman Aljarbouh, University of Grenoble Alpes (UGA) in Grenoble, France
Abdullah Alqahtani, Imam Abdulrahman Bin Faisal University, Saudi Arabia
Hussein Alrubaye, Rochester Institute of Technology, USA
Mohammad Alshayeb, King Fahd University of Petroleum and Minerals, Saudi Arabia
Zakarya Alzamil, King Saud University, Saudi Arabia
Daniel Andresen, Kansas State University, USA
Gilbert Babin, HEC Montréal, Canada
Doo-Hwan Bae, School of Computing - KAIST, Korea
Aleksander Bai, Norsk Regnesentral, Norway
Jorge Barreiros, ISEC (Instituto Superior de Engenharia de Coimbra) / NOVA-LINCS, Portugal

Bernhard Bauer, University of Augsburg, Germany
Ateet Bhalla, Independent Consultant, India
Mitra Bokaei Hosseini, St. Mary's University, USA
Kenneth Boness, University of Reading, UK
Mina Boström Nakicenovic, NetEnt, Stockholm, Sweden
Nadia Bouassida, Higher Institute of Multimedia and Informatics, Sfax, Tunisia
Uwe Breitenbücher, University of Stuttgart, Germany
Hongyu Pei Breivold, ABB Corporate Research, Sweden
Fernando Brito e Abreu, Instituto Universitário de Lisboa (ISCTE-IUL), Portugal
Georg Buchgeher, Software Competence Center Hagenberg GmbH, Austria
Luigi Buglione, Engineering Ingegneria Informatica SpA, Italy
Carlos Henrique Cabral Duarte, Brazilian Development Bank (BNDES), Brazil
Haipeng Cai, Washington State University, Pullman, USA
Gabriel Campeanu, Mälardalen University, Sweden
José Carlos Metrolho, Polytechnic Institute of Castelo Branco, Portugal
Everton Cavalcante, Federal University of Rio Grande do Norte, Brazil
Antonin Chazalet, Orange, France
Fuxiang Chen, Hong Kong University of Science and Technology, Hong Kong
Federico Ciccozzi, Mälardalen University, Sweden
Marta Cimitile, University Unitelma Sapienza of Rome, Italy
Siobhán Clarke, Trinity College Dublin | University of Dublin, Ireland
Stephen W. Clyde, Utah State University, USA
Methanias Colaço Júnior, Federal University of Sergipe, Brazil
Rebeca Cortazar, University of Deusto, Spain
Monica Costa, Politechnic Institute of Castelo Branco, Portugal
Beata Czarnacka-Chrobot, Warsaw School of Economics, Poland
Yanja Dajsuren, Eindhoven University of Technology, Netherlands
Darren Dalcher, Lancaster University Management School, UK
Yuetang Deng, Tencent, China
Vincenzo Deufemia, University of Salerno, Italy
Daniele Di Pompeo, University of L'Aquila, Italy
Themistoklis Diamantopoulos, Aristotle University of Thessaloniki, Greece
Ivan do Carmo Machado, Federal University of Bahia (UFBA), Brazil
Tadashi Dohi, Hiroshima University, Japan
Lydie du Bousquet, Université Grenoble-Alpes (UGA), France
Jorge Edison Lascano, Universidad de las Fuerzas Armadas - ESPE, Ecuador
Holger Eichelberger, University of Hildesheim, Software Systems Engineering, Germany
Simon Eismann, University of Würzburg, Germany
Younes El Amrani, University Mohammed-V Rabat, Morocco
Diana El Rabih, Monty Holding, Beirut, Lebanon
Gledson Elias, Federal University of Paraíba (UFPB), Brazil
Romina Eramo, University of L'Aquila, Italy
Farima FarimahiniFarahani, University of California - Irvine, USA
Kleinner Farias, University of Vale do Rio dos Sinos, Brazil
Adel Ferdjoukh, University of Nantes, France
Luis Fernandez-Sanz, Universidad de Alcala, Spain
M. Firdaus Harun, RWTH Aachen University, Germany
Jicheng Fu, University of Central Oklahoma, USA

Dieter Landes, University of Applied Sciences Coburg, Germany
Jannik Laval, University of Lyon, France
Luigi Lavazza, Università dell'Insubria - Varese, Italy
Valentina Lenarduzzi, Tampere University of Technology, Finland
Maurizio Leotta, University of Genova, Italy
Zheng Li, University of Concepción, Chile
Panos Linos, Butler University, USA
Peizun Liu, Northeastern University, USA
Yingjun Lyu, University of Southern California, USA
André Magno Costa de Araújo, Federal University of Pernambuco, Brazil
Sajjad Mahmood, King Fahd University of Petroleum and Minerals, Saudi Arabia
Nicos Malevris, Athens University of Economics and Business, Greece
Herwig Mannaert, University of Antwerp, Belgium
Neel Mani, ADAPT Center for Digital Content Technology | Dublin City University, Ireland
Alexandre Marcos Lins de Vasconcelos, Federal University of Pernambuco, Brazil
Alessandro Margara, Politecnico di Milano, Italy
Daniela Marghitu, Auburn University, USA
Beatriz Marín, Universidad Diego Portales, Chile
Adriana Martin, National University of Austral Patagonia (UNPA), Argentina
Célia Martinie, IRIT, University Toulouse 3 Paul Sabatier, France
Vanessa Matias Leite, Universidade Estadual de Londrina, Brazil
Fuensanta Medina-Dominguez, Carlos III University of Madrid, Spain
Mariem Mefteh, University of Sfax, Tunisia
Jose Merseguer, Universidad de Zaragoza, Spain
Vojtech Merunka, Czech University of Life Sciences in Prague / Czech Technical University in Prague, Czech Republic
Sanjay Misra, Covenant University, Nigeria
Md Rakib Hossain Misu, University of Dhaka, Bangladesh
Mohamed Wiem Mkaouer, Rochester Institute of Technology, USA
Óscar Mortágua Pereira, Telecommunications Institute | University of Aveiro, Portugal
Mohammad Reza Nami, TUDelft University of Technology, The Netherlands
Marcellin Nkenlifack, University of Dschang, Cameroon
Marc Novakouski, Software Engineering Institute, USA
Roy Oberhauser, Aalen University, Germany
Shinpei Ogata, Shinshu University, Japan
Pablo Oliveira Antonino, Fraunhofer IESE, Germany
Flavio Oquendo, IRISA (UMR CNRS) - University of South Brittany, France
Muhammed Maruf Öztürk, Suleyman Demirel University, Turkey
Marcos Palacios, University of Oviedo, Spain
Fabio Palomba, TU Delft, The Netherlands
Mike Papadakis, University of Luxembourg, Luxembourg
Fabiano Pecorelli, University of Salerno, Italy
Beatriz Pérez Valle, University of La Rioja, Spain
Pasqualina Potena, RISE SICS Västerås, Sweden
Rahul Purandare, Indraprastha Institute of Information Technology Delhi (IIIT-Delhi), India
Evgeny Pyshkin, University of Aizu, Japan
Rafael Queiroz Gonçalves, Federal University of Santa Catarina, Brazil
Abdallah Qusef, Princess Sumaya University for Technology, Jordan

Claudia Raibulet, Universita' degli Studi di Milano-Bicocca, Italy
Muthu Ramachandran, Leeds Beckett University, UK
Raman Ramsin, Sharif University of Technology, Iran
Catarina I. Reis, School of Technology and Management - Polytechnic of Leiria, Portugal
Gianna Reggio, DIBRIS - Università di Genova, Italy
Fernando Reinaldo Ribeiro, Polytechnic Institute of Castelo Branco, Portugal
Michele Risi, University of Salerno, Italy
Gabriela Robiolo, Universidad Austral, Argentina
Rodrigo G. C. Rocha, Federal Rural University of Pernambuco - UFRPE, Brazil
Daniel Rodriguez, University of Alcalá, Spain
Colette Rolland, University of Paris 1 Pantheon-Sorbonne, France
Álvaro Rubio-Largo, Universidade NOVA de Lisboa, Portugal
Mehrdad Saadatmand, RISE SICS Västerås, Sweden
Gunter Saake, Otto-von-Guericke-Universitaet, Germany
Francesca Saglietti, University of Erlangen-Nuremberg, Germany
Djamel Eddine Saidouni, University Constantine 2 - Abdelhamid Mehri, Algeria
Sébastien Salva, University Clermont Auvergne (UCA), Limos, France
María-Isabel Sanchez-Segura, Carlos III University of Madrid, Spain
Hiroyuki Sato, University of Tokyo, Japan
Sagar Sen, Simula Research Laboratory, Norway
Vesna Sesum-Cavic, Vienna University of Technology, Austria
Istvan Siket, University of Szeged, Hungary
Alberto Sillitti, Innopolis University, Russian Federation
Felipe Silva Ferraz, CESAR School, Brazil
Maria Spichkova, RMIT University, Australia
Fausto Spoto, University of Verona / JuliaSoft Srl, Italy
Sidra Sultana, National University of Sciences and Technology, Pakistan
Mahbubur Syed, Minnesota State University Mankato, USA
Sahar Tahvili, RISE SICS Västerås AB, Sweden
Shigeaki Tanimoto, Chiba Institute of Technology, Japan
Sobhan Yassipour Tehrani, King's College London & Jaguar Land Rover, UK
Valerio Terragni, Università della Svizzera italiana (USI), Lugano, Switzerland
Dhafer Thabet, University of Mannouba, Tunisia
Pierre F. Tiako, Tiako University, USA
Elena Troubitsyna, Abo Akademi University, Finland
Christos Troussas, University of Piraeus, Greece
Mariusz Trzaska, Polish-Japanese Academy of Information Technology, Poland
Masateru Tsunoda, Kindai University, Japan
Sylvain Vauttier, LGI2P - Ecole des Mines d'Alès, France
Colin Venters, University of Huddersfield, UK
Laszlo Vidacs, Hungarian Academy of Sciences / University of Szeged, Hungary
Vinay Vkulkarni, Tata Consultancy Services, India
Stefan Voget, Continental Automotive GmbH, Germany
Song Wang, University of Waterloo, Canada
Hironori Washizaki, Waseda University / National Institute of Informatics / SYSTEM INFORMATION, Japan
Bingyang Wei, Texas Christian University, USA
Dietmar Winkler, Vienna University of Technology, Austria

Copyright Information

An Empirical Study of Mutation-Based Test Case Clustering Prioritization and Reduction Technique

Longbo Li*, Yanhui Zhou*, Yong Yu*, Feiyan Zhao*, Shenghua Wu† and Zhe Yang†
*Department of Computer and Information Science
Southwest University
Chongqing, China
E-mail: {lilongbo iyuyong zfy201809}@email.swu.edu.cn, xiaohui@swu.edu.cn
†Meiyun Zhi Number Technology Co., Ltd.
Guangdong,China
E-mail: {wush18 yangzhe1}@meicloud.com.

Abstract—**Regression testing is an important activity to ensure software quality throughout the software life-cycle. However, due to the expansion of the software scale, a large number of test cases are generated in the regression test. In the actual regression test process, it is impossible for us to execute all the test cases. In order to save time and improve efficiency, we need to prioritize and reduce the test cases. In this paper, we propose a new concept mutation program unit priority that works well in the prioritization and reduction of test cases. To evaluate our approach, we designed the experiment and validated it using the Defects4J data set, which contains the real fault programs. We experimented with 350 real faults and 550254 developer-written test cases for Defects4J. The average reduction rate for test cases is 40%, and the fault detection capability is only reduced by 1.38%. The results show that the mutation-based test case prioritization and reduction method improves the effectiveness of test case prioritization and reduction technique.**

Keywords–test case prioritization; regression test; clustering algorithms.

I. Introduction

A large number of test cases need to be executed during the regression test, which makes the regression test process take a long time. For example, in the era when the application software version is updated frequently, we urgently hope that the regression testing can be executed quickly. A recent study shows that for Apache Geode Test takes 14 hours [1]. Many test case prioritization techniques have been empirically studied [2][3]. Researchers have created a variety of regression testing techniques. These include test case selection [4], test suite minimization [5] and test case prioritization [3].

Most of the existing test cases prioritization technology mainly depends on the code coverage information, code complexity metrics and expert knowledge. In a lot of empirical research, based on the code coverage information measurement was proved to be effective [6]. Using branch, statement, and mutation programs to study the effectiveness of test case prioritization techniques, they found that test case prioritization techniques based on mutation program have the best results [3][6]. We know that the use of hierarchical clustering algorithm (HCA) to cluster test cases based on code coverage information has achieved great results in test case prioritization [7]. Thus, we apply HCA to mutation-based test case prioritization and reduction.

In this paper, we use HCA to prioritize and reduce test cases, focusing on mutation program unit priorities and real fault programs. We believe that the priority of the mutation program unit in the test case prioritization is different. We propose the novel concept of the priority of the mutation program unit and give the calculation method. Based on the result of the mutation test, we generate the mutation program unit kill & priority matrix.

To verify the validity of our method, we use the Defects4J benchmark data set [8], which contains a large number of test cases written by developers, and Defects4J also contains real fault programs. The Defects4J data set [8] is widely used by many researchers in mutation testing, so we use it for our experiments. Our results show that the mutation-based test case prioritization and reduction, and use HCA can improve the effectiveness of test case prioritization and reduction technique.

The empirical research contributions of this paper are as follows:

- We proposed the novel concept of mutation program unit priority. For a large number of mutation programs that has many diverse attributes, and each corresponding mutation program has different priorities.
- Combining prioritization and reduction techniques, we experimented with 350 real fault programs and 550254 developer-written test cases in Defects4J. The test cases after prioritization and reduction are 330166. The average reduction rate for test cases is 40%, and the fault detection capability only lost by 1.38%.

The rest of the paper is organized as follows. Section II provides background for mutation-based test case prioritization and reduction technique. Section III presents a novel definition of the mutation program unit priority and test case prioritization evaluation method. Section IV describes the design of our empirical evaluation. Section V introduces the results of which are presented and analysed. Section VI discusses conclusion and future work.

II. Background

In this section, we will introduce the test case prioritization and test case reduction, and use formally language to describe the problem of research.

A. Test Case Prioritization

The goal of test case prioritization is to find an ideal test case execution order that exposes faults as early as possible. The test case prioritization approach was first mentioned by [9]. Subsequently, many researchers have carried out related research [2][3][10][11]. The test case prioritization problem was formally defined by [3].

Definition 1: Test case prioritization problem

Given:

a test suite,TS

the set of permutations of TS, PTS

a function that gives a numerical score for $T' \in PTS$,f

Problem:

find $T' \in PTS$ such that

$(\forall T'')(T'' \in PTS)(T'' \neq T')[f(T') \geq f(T'')]$

In Definition 1, PTS represents all possible orderings of the given test case in TS, and f represents an evaluation function that calculates an award value for an ordering $T' \in PTS$. Since we can't get the fault message during the regression testing progress, we usually need to consider a surrogate for fault detection based on the historical information of the test case. Hoping that early maximization of a certain chosen surrogate property will result in maximization of earlier fault detection. In a controlled-regression-testing environment, the result of prioritization can be evaluated by executing test cases according to the fault-detection rate [6].

The code coverage information, such as statement coverage and branch coverage are one of used surrogates in test case prioritization [3][12]. For example, a test case covering more statements has higher priority. The mutants are also used as another surrogate for test case prioritization [13][14]. For instance, the work in [3] consider the fault expose potential (FEP)-total approach that prioritize test cases according to the number of mutants killed by individual test cases, they find mutation-based test case prioritization techniques work better. In the process of mutation testing, a large number of mutants were generated. Donghwan et al. consider that these mutation programs have diverse attributes [15]. Based on this research, we propose a novel concept mutation program unit priority. For more details, we will discuss in Section III.

B. Test Case Reduction

The test case reduction is primarily to remove redundant test cases from the test case set, which usually do not change the mutation score in mutation-based test case reduction. For test case reduction problem, we can't reduce a test case set to a minimum set of test cases. The test case set minimization problem is an NP-complete problem. We try to reduce the test case set as much as possible without affecting the mutation score. Mike et al. introduces the relationship between the mutation score and real faults [16]. They believe that achieving higher mutation scores improves significantly the fault detection. Since the redundant mutation program problem is another area beyond the scope of this paper, we will not explain it in follow sections.

More formally, we consider the test suite reduction problem is defined as follows [6]:

Definition 1: Test suite reduction problem

Given:

a test suite, T, a set of test requirements $r_1, \ldots, r_n$, which must be satisfied to provide the desired adequate testing of the program, and subsets of $T, T_1, \ldots, T_n$, one associated with each of the r_is such that any one of the test case t_j belong to T_i can be used to achieve requirement r_i.

Problem:

Find a representative set, T', of test cases from T that satisfies all r_is.

A number of test suite reduction approaches have been proposed in the literature [17]-[19]. Many researchers let statement coverage be the kind of test requirement considered, a reduced test suite that covers the same statements as the original test suite. Recently, a clustering test case reduction approach was proposed that reduced test suites only partially preserve the test requirement of the original test suites [20]. They empirically evaluate this methods that define guidelines for these to get trade-offs between reductions of in test suite size and losses of fault-detection capability. They mainly are concerned with the level of code coverage. In this paper, we use HCA to prioritize and reduce the test cases. We mainly focus on the level of program mutation.

III. EMPIRICAL EVALUATION AND MUTATION PROGRAM UNIT PRIORITY

In this section, we introduce the novel concept of mutation program unit priority, mutation program unit kill & priority matrix, test case prioritization evaluation index and HCA.

A. Mutation Program Unit Kill Matrix

In the study of existing mutation-based test case prioritization problems, all mutation programs are considered to be equally important in test case prioritization process and no analysis of the priority of mutants. The minimum mutation program unit is usually called a mutant. For the mutants generated by the same mutation operator, we call a large mutation program unit. Due to the limited space of the paper, we only discuss the minimum mutation program unit in this paper. In the future work, we analyze and explain the whole mutation program unit theory in detail. Recently, The diversity-aware mutation-based techniques was proposed by [15][21]. They believe that many mutation programs are diverse and require more test cases to distinguish mutation programs, which aims to distinguish one mutant's behaviour from another mutation programs. Obviously, mutation programs have diverse attributes, and each mutation program has different priorities. When perform mutation analysis, the test case is executed into the mutation program unit, it is marked as 1 if the test case kills the mutation program, otherwise it is marked as 0. For example, Table I show mutation program unit kill matrix. $m_0 \cdots m_7$ show mutation program unit name and $T_0 \cdots T_4$ show test case name.

TABLE I. MUTATION PROGRAM UNIT KILL MATRIX

Test Case Name	Mutation Program Unit (MPU)							
	m_0	m_1	m_2	m_3	m_4	m_5	m_6	m_7
T_0	1	0	**1**	0	0	1	0	0
T_1	1	1	**1**	0	1	0	0	0
T_2	0	1	**1**	1	1	1	0	0
T_3	0	0	**1**	0	0	0	1	1
T_4	0	0	0	0	0	0	0	0

In general, in mutation analysis, we estimate the fault detection capability of test cases as measured by how many mutation programs are killed. In test case prioritization process, we might find such a set of sequences using greedy algorithm, for instance $T_2 - T_1 - T_0 - T_3$. Because T_2 kills the most mutation programs, it is chosen first. T_4 did not kill any of the mutants, we removed them in the reduction of the test case. However, we find that m_2 is killed by all test case. No matter how we prioritize it, m_2 will be killed when the first test case is executed. So, only the T_3 is in the first executed in the prioritization, the m_6, m_7 mutation program units are killed. In the prioritization process, mutation program units have different priorities. We should pay attention to mutation programs that are killed by very few test case. This mutation program is more difficult to kill.

TABLE II. MUTATION PROGRAM UNIT PRIORITY MATRIX

Test Case Name	Mutation Program Unit(MPU)							
	m_0	m_1	m_2	m_3	m_4	m_5	m_6	m_7
T_0	0.5	0	**0**	0	0	0.5	0	0
T_1	0.5	0.5	**0**	0	0.5	0	0	0
T_2	0	0.5	**0**	0.75	0.5	0.5	0	0
T_3	0	0	**0**	0	0	0	0.75	0.75

B. Mutation Program Unit Priority

Given a program under test (PUT), after mutation testing, generated m mutation program units, n test cases, we define an $m \times n$ mutation program unit kill matrix H that represents the kill information of the mutation program unit. H_{ij} indicates whether the test case j killed the mutation program unit i. We formally define this mutation program unit priority weight $W_i (0 < W_i < 1)$.

$$W_i = -\frac{\sum_{j=1}^{n} H_{ij}}{n} + 1 \tag{1}$$

As for (1) the value of W_i cannot be taken as 0 and 1 because in the prioritization and reduction we removed the mutation program unit with a value of 0 and 1. We updates mutation program unit kill matrix, Table II show mutation program unit priority matrix and m_2 is a redundant mutants by optimizing the weight calculation. Because m_2 will must be killed no matter how we prioritization. For example, we might find such a set of sequences using greedy algorithm in test case prioritization, $T_2 - T_3 - T_1 - T_0$. Similarly, in Table I, we remove T_4 from the mutation program unit kill matrix because it has no ability to kill all mutants.

C. Average Percentage of Fault-Detection

We usually use the Average Percentage of Fault-Detection (APFD) metric results in test case prioritization [22]. Higher APFD values confirm faster fault-detection rates. It is simply and accurately formalized as follows:

$$APFD = 1 - \frac{TF_1 + \cdots + TF_n}{nm} + \frac{1}{2n} \tag{2}$$

where TF_i is the first test case position in test case prioritization among n test cases which detects the ith fault among m faults. According to mutation program unit priority weight, we formally define the Average Percentage of Weight Fault-Detection (APWFD) as follows:

$$APWFD = 1 - \frac{W_1 \times TF_1 + \cdots + W_n \times TF_n}{\sum_{j=1}^{n} W_i \times n} + \frac{1}{2n} \tag{3}$$

where W_i is a weight as mutation program unit m_i. In order to better help readers understand, we using Table I and II results to clearly and accurately calculate APFD and APWFD. We use greedy algorithm to prioritize test case and based on killed the most mutation program. For example, $T_2 - T_1 - T_0 - T_3$ as for Table I and APFD is 0.5625. $T_2 - T_3 - T_1 - T_0$ as for Table II and APWFD is 0.7279. Only from the value of the result we have at least improved about 16.54%. Because we do not only consider the most mutants that is killed, but also consider the mutants that is hard to kill.

D. Hierarchical Clustering Algorithm

The clustering algorithm is an unsupervised learning algorithm that reveals the intrinsic properties and law of data. We obtain mutation analysis kill information by mutation analysis tool Major [23] and use Algorithm 1 (shown in Figure 2) generate mutation program unit kill & priority matrix. Cluster analysis was performed on the generated mutation program unit kill matrix and priority matrix, and the test case prioritization and reduction results were evaluated use APFD and APWFD. After configure data set Defects4J [8], we firstly checkout our every project program and compile fixed program. Thus, we use test execution framework and mutation analysis our fixed program. In Algorithm 1 (shown in Figure 2), T is contain developer-written test case set. The algorithm takes a developer-written test case set T, a mutation analysis result set of $mutantlog, testMap, killMap, trigger_bug$ as input, and returns a mutation program unit kill & priority matrix. In Algorithm 1 (shown in Figure 2), $killMap$ represents the mutation analysis tool kill information. The value of $testMap$ contain test case ID and name. Matrix information can be generated by use both information, and test cases that trigger faults can also be statistically analyzed. But we not conducted relevant research in this paper.

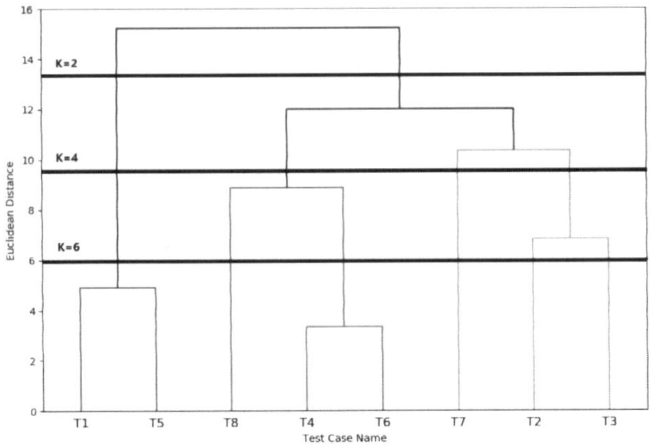

Figure 1. Hierarchical clustering tree.

Similarly, we choose a HCA, which can well control the size of clusters after clustering. HCA has achieved great test case prioritization results in terms of code coverage and expert knowledge [24][25]. Figure.1 shows the hierarchical clustering tree generated by HCA. The x coordinate represents the name of the test case, and the y coordinate represents the average Euclidean distance between test cases. We can easily control the size of the cluster generated by the HCA, according to the size of the test case set. Each vertical represents a cluster. The k is the size of the clusters. We use fast cluster function and improve prioritization and reduction strategy [26]. Recently, in the clustering prioritization and reduction of test cases based on code coverage, Carmen et al.[20] studied the effects of different clustering calculation methods on the test case prioritization and reduction, and found that clustering results are obviously different. Based on their research, our first research question in the experiment explores the impact of different computational methods on mutation-based test case prioritization and reduction.

Algorithm 1 Mutation program unit kill & priority matrix

Input: $mutant\ log, testMap, killMap, trigger\_bug, T$
Output: $kill\ \&\ priority\ matrix$
reading a mutant log M_i ;
$M[\ ] \leftarrow M_i$;
reading a testMap file;
$T\{name, Tid\} \leftarrow testMap$
reading a killMap file;
$K\{Tid, Mid\} \leftarrow killMap$
reading a trigger_bug file;
$F[\ ] \leftarrow trigger\_bug$
while $(M[\ ]\ not\ null)$ **do**
  if F[ ] in T **then**
    Label(1)
  else
    Label(0)
  end if
  if T{name,Tid} in K{Tid,Mid} **then**
    T.containkey(name)
    Label(1)
  else
    Label(0)
  end if
end while
return $kill\ \&\ priority\ matrix$

Figure 2. Algorithm for mutation program unit kill & priority matrix.

IV. EXPERIMENTAL DESIGN

In this section, we conduct empirical evaluation and design experiment that use developer-fixed program, developer-written tests, and real faults. As for empirical evaluation, we investigate the following two main research problems:

- RQ1: Is the different distance calculation methods have different effects on test case prioritization and reduction?
- RQ2: Is the test case prioritization and reduction techniques that outperforms in terms of trade-off between reductions in test suite size and losses in fault-detection capability?

We use benchmark data sets Defects4J [8] that include mutation analysis tool Major [23], developer-fixed program, manually-verified real fault and developer-written test case. Figure 3 shows the overall flow of our experiment. We will introduce our experiment in detail.

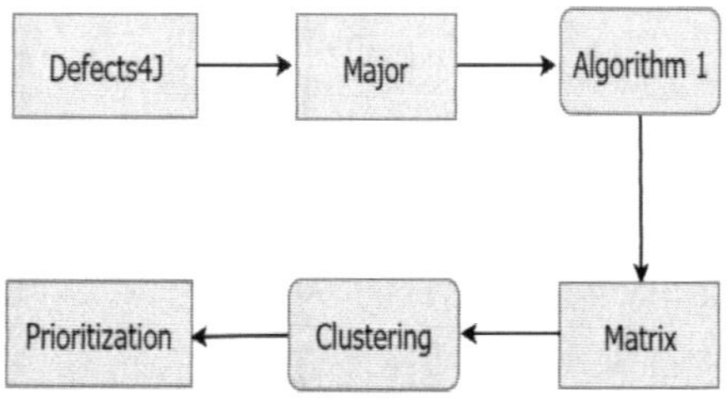

Figure 3. Experiment setup.

A. Experimental Tool

a) Defects4J database: We mainly use test execution framework in Defects4J that contains 438 bugs from the open-source projects. We consider five open-source projects (JFreeChart, Closure compiler, Apache commons-lang, Joda-Time and Apache commons-math) and 350 fixed programs. Because some fixed programs includes seldom developer-written test cases. Therefore we delete some fixed program. For example, fixed program Chart-23 only include five developer-written test cases. One of our goals is to provide a method for prioritization and reduction for a large number of test cases, helping to improve the efficiency of test engineers in regression testing.

b) Major: As for mutation kill information, we use Major mutation analysis tool for generating and executing all mutants to the developer-written test case for each fixed-program. Major includes a set of commonly used mutation operator [27]. For example, Binary operator replacement (BOR), Unary operator replacement (UOR), Constant value replacement (CVR), Branch condition manipulation (BCM), Logical operator replacement, and Statement deletion (STD). Because different mutation operators produce different mutation programs. Therefore, we applied all the mutation operators in mutation analysis.

B. Design Review

We configure Defects4J in Ubuntu18.04 LTS (intel i7-7700 cpu, RAM 8G). For more detailed configuration information, please refer to Defects4J official webpage at [28]. To configure Defacts4J on the Ubuntu18.04 system, we firstly perform "checkout" on all the programs, and then compile. If the test command is executed at this time, the test case written by the tester included in the test case Defects4J is used. Secondly, we use Major to perform mutation analysis on all "checkout" programs. The time of mutation analysis is controlled within one hour, and the program that exceeds the time is deleted. Finally, we use algorithm to generate mutation program unit kill and priority matrix for mutation analysis results, cluster the mutation program unit kill matrix and priority matrix, and use APFD and APWFD to evaluate test case prioritization and

TABLE III. CALCULATION STRATEGY STATISTICAL ANALYSIS.

Program	Calculation method			
	Jaccard	Hamming	Euclidean	Cosine
Chart	20.4816	21.0925	21.0862	20.0210
Closure	127.2672	128.9538	128.9563	123.9185
Lang	52.9445	56.8870	56.8507	47.6511
Math	90.8519	93.7491	93.3974	91.4900
Time	26.4618	26.4767	26.4825	25.5815
Average	0.9085	0.9347	0.9336	0.8819

TABLE IV. TEST CASE PRIORITIZATION AND REDUCTION STATISTICAL ANALYSIS

Program	Analysis index			Analysis index		
	APFD	Cluster time(s)	Test case	APWFD	Cluster time(s)	Test case
Chart	20.0210	2.0764	5693	18.7334	0.1189	3577
Closure	123.9185	1649.2548	440296	123.1317	758.1702	182155
Lang	47.6511	10.0078	11338	48.4177	1.5700	6480
Math	91.4900	165.7274	22688	88.2791	63.9586	9941
Time	25.5815	122.3370	70239	25.2988	71.4638	17935
Average	0.8819	5.5697	-	0.8681	2.5579	-

reduction results. Similarly, we can also use the automatic generation tools that generate a large number of test cases. Exploring the impact of different types of test case sets on test case prioritization and reduction is beyond the scope of this paper. We can delve into this issue in future research work.

V. RESULT AND ANALYSIS

In this section, we discuss the experiment obtained results and answer Section IV two questions.

A. RQ1: Is the different distance calculation methods have different effects on test case prioritization and reduction?

RQ1 explores the impact of different computational s-trategies on clustering results. Because of different clustering results have an impact on code coverage-based test case prioritization. Carmen et al. used code coverage information to study different computational strategies for hierarchical clustering [20]. They point out cluster test case, the use of the cosine and Jaccard-based dissimilarities seems to be more promising than the use of the Euclidean and Hamming.

We use mutation-based information to study different computational strategies for hierarchical clustering. We use four calculation methods(Jaccard, Hamming, Euclidean, Cosine) to conduct experiments. In order to control the experiment, only the calculation method is different, and the other experimental factors are all the same. Figure 4 shows that the x coordinate is the number of each program, and the y coordinate is the value of APFD, and four calculation strategies curve trend results are almost the same on the 350 real fault programs.

Different computing strategies maybe have different clustering effects on mutation-based test case prioritization. We can conclude that in the mutation-based test case prioritization in Figure 4, this strategy has no significant different. We also counted the average of four calculation strategies. Table III shows that cosine similarity method is lower than the other three calculation methods. However the difference is not obvious, the highest to the lowest is only 5.28%. Each column of data is the sum of real fault programs' APFD. For example, the 20.4816 of the $Chart$ program is the sum of the APFD values of all $Chart$ programs. Our experimental results show that there is no significant difference between test case prioritization based on mutation analysis using different calculation strategies for HCA.

B. RQ2: Is the test case prioritization and reduction techniques that outperforms in terms of trade-off between reductions in test suite size and losses of fault-detection capability?

RQ2 mainly explores test case reduction and loss of fault detection capabilities. In order to control the experiment, we use the Cosine dissimilarity distance calculation method. We use the prioritization and reduction strategy to calculate the value of APWFD in this paper. We used the value of APFD in one of the evaluation indicators in the control experiment.

From Table IV, it results that we used the proposed method to reduce and prioritize 550254 test cases. The number of test cases after prioritization and reduction is 330166. The average reduction rate for test cases is 40%. We also analyze the average reduction rate of each program. For example, the average fault reduction rate for the $Chart$, $Closure$, $Lang$,$Math$, and $Time$ programs are 62.82%,41.37%,57.15%,43.81% and 25.53% respectively. We use test case prioritization and reduction methods to make a large number of reductions to test cases. However the fault detection capability is only reduced by 1.38%. The average clustering time for each program is 2.5579s. Clustering time after prioritization and reduction reduced by 45.92%. This is a very interesting discovery, then software test engineers can use the test case prioritization and reduction techniques of clustering method to better manage and optimize regression testing activity. For example, a corporation does not have enough time to run all the test cases, and they still have a better chance of capturing faults.

Our experimental results show that the proposed prioritization and reduction strategy has good consequents in terms of reduction in number, time reduction and fault detection. Test case prioritization and reduction techniques ideal goal mainly is a higher test case reduction rate and a lower fault loss rate.

VI. CONCLUSION AND FUTURE WORK

This paper proposes a new concept mutation program unit priority. We use mutation-based test case prioritization and reduction strategies to prioritize and reduce test cases combine with mutation program unit priority. In the empirical evaluation, we used four different clustering calculation strategies to study the effects of different computing strategies on the results of prioritization test cases. The results show that the computational strategy has little effect on the results after clustering. We also present an empirical study comparing test case prioritization and reduction methods in terms of test case reduction in number and fault detection capability. Our method can reduce the number of test cases by 40%, and the loss of fault detection capability is only 1.38%.

In the future, we will continue to study the impact of different clustering numbers in test case prioritization and reduction. Similarly, we also noticed that there is no empirical analysis of the test cases that triggered the faults in the prioritization and reduction methods. We will analyze and explain the whole mutation program unit theory in detail.

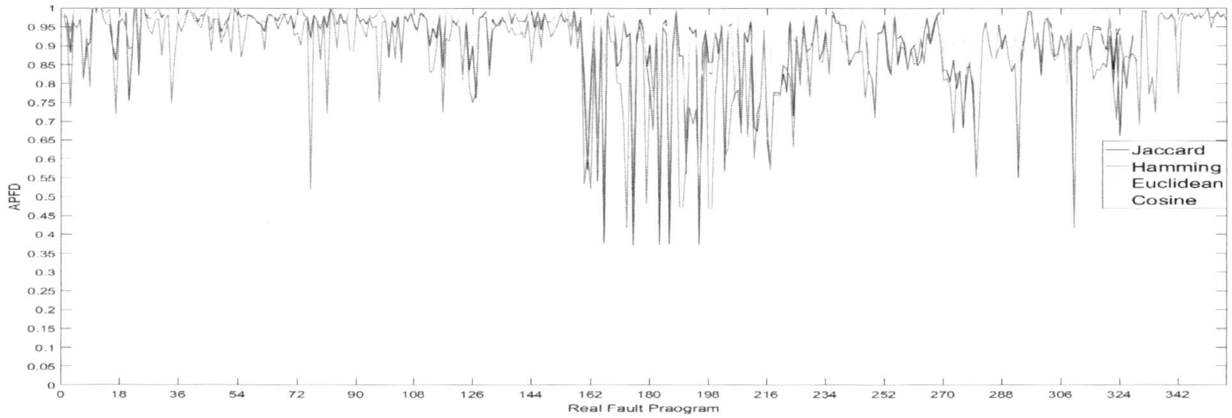

Figure 4. Calculation strategy.

REFERENCES

[1] Apache Geode Nightly Test Report.(2018).https://builds.apache.org/view/E-G/view/Geode/job/Geode-release/lastCompletedBuild/testReport/

[2] H. Do, G. Rothermel and A. Kinneer, "Prioritizing JUnit Test Cases: An Empirical Assessment and Cost-Benefits Analysis," Empirical software engineering, vol. 11, no. 1, 2006, pp. 33-70.

[3] S. Elbaum, A. Malishevsky and G. Rothermel, "Prioritizing Test Cases for Regression Testing," IEEE Transactions on Software Engineering, vol. 27, no. 10, 2001, pp. 924-948.

[4] M. J. Harrold, D. Rosenblum, G. Rothermel and E. Weyuker, "Empirical studies of a prediction model for regression test selection," IEEE Transactions on Software Engineering, vol. 27, no. 3, 2001, pp. 248-263.

[5] J. Jones and M. Harrold, "Test suite reduction and prioritization for modified condition/decision coverage," IEEE Transactions on Software Engingeering, vol. 29, no. 3, 2003, pp. 193-209.

[6] S. Yoo and M. Harman, "Regression testing minimization, selection and prioritization: A survey," Software Testing,Verification and Reliability, vol. 22, (2), 2012, pp. 67-120.

[7] R. Carlson, H. Do and A. Denton, "A clustering approach to improving test case prioritization: An industrial case study," IEEE International Conference on Software Maintenance (ICSM), 2011, pp. 382-391.

[8] R. Just, D. Jalali and M.D. Ernst , "Defects4J: A database of existing faults to enable controlled testing studies for Java programs," In Proceedings of the International Symposium on Software Testing and Analysis (ISSTA), 2014, pp. 437-440.

[9] W. Wong, J. Horgan, S. London and A. Mathur, "Effect of test set minimization on fault detection effectiveness," Software Practice and Experience , 28(4), 1998, pp. 347-369.

[10] A. Srivastava and J. Thiagarajan, "Effectively prioritizing tests in development environment," Proceedings of the International Symposium on Software Testing and Analysis (ISSTA), 2002, pp. 97-106.

[11] H. Do, G. Rothermel and A. Kinneer, "Empirical studies of test case prioritization in a junit testing environment," Proceedings of the 15th International Symposium on Software Reliability Engineering (ISSRE), 2004, pp. 113-124.

[12] L. Zhang, D. Hao, L. Zhang, G. Rothermel and H. Mei, "Bridging the gap between the total and additional test-case prioritization strategies," In Proceedings of the 2013 International Conference on Software Engineering, 2013, pp. 192-201.

[13] H. Do and G. Rothermel, "On the use of mutation faults in empirical assessments of test case prioritization techniques," IEEE Transactions on Software Engineering 2006, 32(9), pp. 733-752.

[14] Y. Lou, D. Hao and L. Zhang, "Mutation-based test-case prioritization in software evolution," In Proceedings of the 26th International Symposium on Software Reliability Engineering (ISSRE), 2015, pp. 46-57.

[15] D. Shin, S. Yoo and D.H. Bae, "A Theoretical and Empirical Study of Diversity-Aware Mutation Adequacy Criterion," IEEE Transactions on Software Engineering, vol. 44, (10), 2018, pp. 914-931.

[16] M. Papadakis, D. Shin, S. Yoo and D.H. Bae, "Are mutation scores correlated with real fault detection? A large scale empirical study on the relationship between mutants and real faults," International Conference on Software Engineering (ICSE), 2018, pp. 537-548.

[17] M. Jean Harrold, R. Gupta and M. Lou Soffa, "A Methodology for Controlling the Size of a Test Suite," ACM Transactions on Software Engineering, 2, 1993, pp. 270-285.

[18] Z. Li, M. Harman and R. M. Hierons, "Search Algorithms for Regression Test Case Prioritization," IEEE Transactions on Software Engineering. 33, 2007, pp. 225-237.

[19] L. Zhang, D. Marinov, L. Zhang and S. Khurshid, "An Empirical Study of JUnit Test-Suite Reduction," In Proceedings of International Symposium on Software Reliability Engineering (ISSRE), IEEE, 2011 pp. 170-179.

[20] C. Coviello, S. Romano, G. Scanniello, A. Marchetto, G. Antoniol and A. Corazza, "Clustering support for inadequate test suite reduction," In Proceedings of International Conference on Software Analysis,Volution and Reengineering, Vol. 00, 2018, pp. 95-105.

[21] D. Shin, S. Yoo, M. Papadakis and D.H. Bae, "Empirical evaluation of mutation-based test case prioritization techniques," Software:testing verification and reliability, Vol. 29, (1-2), 2019, e1695.

[22] S. Elbaum, A. Malishevsky and G. Rothermel, "Test case prioritization: A family of empirical studies," IEEE Transactions on Software Engineering, 28(2), 2002, pp. 159-182.

[23] R. Just, "The Major mutation framework: Efficient and scalable mutation analysis for Java," In Proceedings of the International Symposium on Software Testing and Analysis (ISSTA), ACM, 2014, pp. 433-436.

[24] R. Carlson, H. Do and A. Denton, "A clustering approach to improving test case prioritization: An industrial case study," IEEE International Conference on Software Maintenance (ICSM), 2011, pp. 382-391.

[25] S. Yoo, M. Harman, P. Tonella and A. Susi, "Clustering test cases to achieve effective & scalable prioritisation incorporating expert knowledge," Proceedings of the International Symposium on Software Testing and Analysis(ISSTA), 2009, pp. 201-211.

[26] D. Mllner, "fastcluster: Fast Hierarchical, Agglomerative Clustering Routines for R and Python," Journal of Statistical Software, 53, no. 9, 2013, pp. 1-18.

[27] A. S. Namin, J. H. Andrews and D. J. Murdoch, "Sufficient mutation operators for measuring test effectiveness," in Proceedings of the 30th International Conference on Software Engineering (ICSE), 2008, pp. 351-360.

[28] Defects4J. https://github.com/rjust/defects4j. last accessed on 10/04/19.

A Framework for Robust, Low-Overhead Binary Instrumentation

Amir Majlesi-Kupaei
University of Maryland
Collge Park, USA
email: majlesi@umd.edu

Danny Kim
University of Maryland
Collge Park, USA
email: dannykim32@gmail.com

Kapil Anand
Google Inc.
Mountain View, USA
email: kapilanand2@gmail.com

Aparna Kotha
SecondWrite LLC
Collge Park, USA
email: akotha@secondwrite.com

Khaled Elwazeer
Google Inc.
Mountain View, USA
email: kelwazeer@gmail.com

Rajeev Baura
University of Maryland
Collge Park, USA
email: barua@umd.edu

Abstract—**We have designed and implemented a binary rewriter called RL-Bin, which can rewrite binaries correctly with low overhead. Existing binary rewriters have their challenges: static rewriters do not reliably work for stripped binaries (*i.e.*, those without relocation information), and dynamic rewriters suffer from high base overhead. Because of this high overhead, existing dynamic rewriters are limited to off-line testing, and cannot be used in deployment. RL-Bin differentiates itself from other binary rewriters by having the capability to robustly rewrite stripped binaries with very low overhead (averaging 1.05x for SPECrate 2017, not including the instrumentation cost, compared to 1.16x overhead for DynamoRIO). The overhead added by RL-Bin itself is negligible and it is proportional to the added instrumentation. Hence, lightweight instrumentation can be added to applications that are deployed in live systems for monitoring and analysis purposes.**

Keywords–Program Analysis; Binary Instrumentation; Static and Dynamic Analysis; Testing and Verification; Program Transformation.

I. INTRODUCTION

There are several reasons why it is desirable to instrument or modify the code that is directly executed in deployment. The applications of instrumentation range from resource monitoring, application performance monitoring, security policy enforcement, vulnerability patching, dynamic information flow tracking, and performance optimization. The code modification can be applied either at the level of source code or binary code.

Binary code is the code that executes directly on the hardware using machine code instructions. Binary code can theoretically be produced from any language, but is typically produced not only from older languages like C, C++, Fortran, and COBOL, but is also often produced from popular modern languages, such as Go, Erlang, Visual Basic, Swift, and Objective C.

Binary code is widespread because it offers significant advantages for two types of code: IP-protected code and high-performance code. First, IP-protected code is code that is sold by companies to outside parties. Second, high-performance programs, such as those in the domains of image processing, financial transactions, machine learning, and scientific codes are often deployed in binary code to ensure the highest execution speed. For the aforementioned application areas, it is often needed to be able to instrument or modify the binary code when the source code is unavailable, such as for third-party binaries. To do so, we need a tool named binary rewriter.

A. Criteria and Trade-Offs in Building a Binary Rewriter

There are *two equally important and necessary criteria that a binary rewriter must have: it must be robust, and it must incur low overhead.* First, a binary rewriter must work for different types of binaries, including those produced by commercial compilers from a wide variety of languages, and possibly modified by obfuscation tools. Second, the binary rewriter must be low overhead. Although the *off-line use of programs*, such as in testing and profiling, can tolerate large overheads, the use of binary rewriters in *deployed programs* must not introduce significant overheads; typically, it should not be more than a few percents [1].

Unfortunately, existing methods cannot modify binary code in a manner that is both robust and low overhead. To understand the reason, let us consider that there are two types of binary rewriters: static vs. dynamic. Static rewriting refers to approaches which take an executable binary program as input, and without running it, produce another (rewritten) binary program as output that has the same functionality as the input program, but is enhanced in some way, for example in improving its run-time, memory use, or security. Dynamic rewriters change the binary code during its execution and modify the binary code in memory, either in-place or in a copy of the code memory.

Static rewriters are not robust. Static rewriters can have very low overhead, but are not robust, meaning that they often do not work for certain types of binaries. As our related work section details, 24% of commercial benign programs had dynamically generated code and 1% had obfuscated code, which are the features that static rewriters cannot handle. Several schemes do not even work for simpler programs with indirect branches whose targets cannot be statically determined.

Dynamic rewriters have high overhead. In contrast, dynamic rewriters are robust but have high overhead, usually ranging from 20% to several hundred percents. Dynamic rewriters are robust because they discover all code at run-time. However, they incur high overhead since most of them maintain a code cache, where rewritten copies of code blocks are stored and executed from. As a result of the above drawbacks, binary rewriters are generally not used in deployment today on third-party programs, since for those programs, usually no guarantees can be made on how they were compiled.

Dynamic rewriters, such as DynamoRIO [2], copy all the code that executes into another memory region called a *code cache*. The code cache is useful because it ensures robustness; the program still works if a piece of data is mistakenly assumed to be code and rewritten. The reason is that the code cache was changed and the original copy of the code segment is still unchanged.

The overhead of dynamic rewriters is caused by two factors. First, copying the code into the code cache is expensive at run-time. Second, and more seriously, the target addresses of an indirect Control Transfer Instruction (CTI) must be translated at run-time because the locations of code have changed to be in the code cache instead. Such indirect jumps or calls are very common – they mostly arise from return instructions, function pointer calls, and calls to virtual functions in object-oriented languages, such as C++. This translation process is inevitable for DynamoRIO since the original destination address in the program is different from the address of the rewritten code inside the code cache.

B. Robust, Low-Overhead Binary Instrumentation

Consequent to the needs above, we developed RL-Bin. It supports several types of obfuscation, as well as dynamically generated and self-modifying code. As a result, it is robust enough to be used for benign third-party applications. Also, we have designed and implemented several optimizations, so it has very low overhead. We present the following contributions.

- Design and development of the first low overhead dynamic binary rewriter that can handle stripped binaries without relocation or debug information, containing self-modifying or dynamically-generated code or obfuscation.
- An innovative method that tracks the execution of code dynamically by anticipating future control-flow to the new code, and adding instrumentation and breakpoints to process such new code when discovered.
- Using a novel dynamic method to eliminate the overhead of breakpoints, once the new code is discovered.
- Using Just-In-Time (JIT) dynamic analysis of the discovered code and traditional data flow analysis concepts, to find "Safe" functions and further reduce the overhead by eliminating redundant checks.
- The above design is unlike other dynamic rewriters that translate indirect control transfer addresses to their copies in a code cache.
- The result is the first In-Place dynamic binary rewriter – which does not use a code cache – that combines the robustness and coverage of a dynamic rewriter with the low overhead of a static rewriter.
- Extensive testing and performance comparison with DynamoRIO for SPEC CPU2017 benchmark with over 7 million lines of code in C, C++, and Fortran, compiled with Microsoft Visual Studio, GCC, and ICC compilers.
- Design and implementation of a "Debugging System in Deployment" as a use case of RL-Bin, which enables the developer to find and patch the errors during execution without sharing debug information with the end-user.

RL-Bin will find use in implementing a variety of applications of binary rewriting. For example, researchers have proposed binary rewriting-based methods for securing untrusted code [3], enforcing control flow integrity [4], implementing software transactional memory [5], self-randomizing instruction addresses [6], profiling tools [7], and taint tracking to prevent sensitive data leaks [8].

The paper is structured as follows: Section II discusses the capabilities and limitations of RL-Bin. Sections III and IV describe the base design of RL-Bin and the optimization methods designed to reduce the overhead. In Section V, we demonstrate the results of our evaluation of RL-Bin and compare them to DynamoRIO. Section VI looks into a debugging and patching system as a use-case of RL-Bin. Section VII describes related work. Finally, Section VIII looks ahead at future work and concludes the paper.

II. RL-Bin Capabilities and Limitations

In this section, first, we list some of the troublesome features that may occur in benign programs. These must be handled correctly since our goal is robust binary rewriting. Additionally, we briefly go over binaries with features for which RL-Bin might fail to instrument properly, most of which are found in malicious applications.

A. Handling Complicating Features

Obfuscation is a technique used to mislead attempts to reverse-engineer the code. Here, we are primarily concerned about control-flow obfuscation, which makes it appear that data is code, or vice-versa. There are publicly available applications and research methods which will control-flow-obfuscate a binary application to protect the binary from reverse-engineering, such as the Binary obfuscation project tool [9], and the work by Popov et. al [10].

RL-Bin supports two types of obfuscation techniques that are problematic for binary rewriters: (i) unconditional to conditional branch flow obfuscation, (ii) exception-based obfuscation. In the unconditional to conditional branch obfuscation, an unconditional branch is replaced by a conditional branch, one of its targets is never taken. Instead, the never-taken path contains data, rewriting which will break the program. Another technique is exception-based obfuscation. In this method, a change of control flow is achieved without a CTI, using exceptions instead. For example, the program can deliberately trigger a divide-by-zero exception by using a zero value in the denominator. The program may also register a custom exception handler, which can redirect to any arbitrary location in the program.

Dynamically-Generated Code is common in binary applications. It is mostly used when executing user scripts or any script coming from external sources. Another instance of dynamically-generated code is packed code. Unlike dynamic rewriters, static rewriters cannot disassemble such dynamically generated code.

Self-Modifying Code is similar to dynamically generated code with an important difference: the addresses into which dynamically generated code are stored may already contain instructions that have been executed during the program. This modifies the program's code at run-time.

B. Limitations of RL-Bin

RL-Bin is capable of analyzing and instrumenting most of the common commercial binary files which do not have relocation information, and may have obfuscated, dynamically-generated or self-modifying code. However, RL-Bin is not designed to support adversarial binaries, which can deliberately use methods to prevent their examination by a binary rewriter or a debugger. We will go over certain types of behavior in adversarial binaries that can cause problems for the binary rewriter.

(i) Verifying the memory image by using a checksum. Some adversarial binaries compare the checksum on their memory image against a previously calculated checksum to make sure that the program is not altered by debuggers. The goal is not ensuring integrity, but defeating debuggers. In most commercial binaries, developers know that many users may use debuggers on the software which will not work with such binaries. *(ii) Disabling the debugger.* Binaries can check the presence of a debugger and can try to disable it. As mentioned before, commercial binary applications are intended to support debuggers and binary rewriter can handle them properly. *(iii) Modifying breakpoints inserted by the debugger.* Adversarial binaries attempt to remove breakpoints inserted by debuggers, which can interfere with the operation of rewriters and debuggers. This behavior is limited to only adversarial binaries.

III. BASE DESIGN

In this section, we describe the base unoptimized algorithm that is used by RL-Bin. This algorithm has very high overhead (approximately 5x to 10x the run-time of the un-instrumented program for SPEC CPU2017 benchmarks) but demonstrates the correctness of the method.

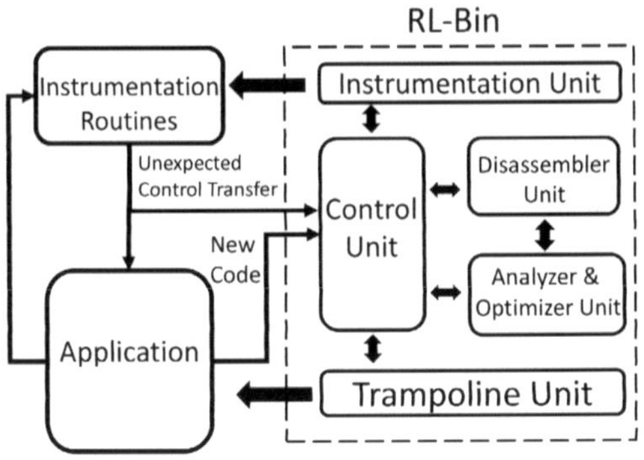

Figure 1. RL-Bin System Overview

The components of RL-Bin are shown in Figure 1. The Control Unit keeps the state of the application and manages other units. The Instrumentation Unit creates and manages instrumentation routines. The Trampoline Unit is responsible for efficiently placing trampolines in the original code to redirect execution to the instrumentation routines.

A. RL-Bin Baseline Algorithm

The main intuition behind RL-Bin is to add instrumentation at run-time that monitors the discovery of the new code. To discover code, our method assumes that a block of memory is code only if we discover an actual control transfer to it during run-time. Our **purely dynamic** disassembly method will begin at the start of a memory block (whose address we call START) once it is proven to be code and follows non-control-transfer instructions one after another, which are all discovered to be code until it reaches a control transfer instruction. Whenever the method reaches a CTI, if that CTI can have more than one possible target, the method ensures that some instrumentation is triggered when the actual target becomes known later during the same run.

Some terminology: All instructions that change the control-flow behavior of a program, such as branches, jumps, and calls, are called *Control-Transfer Instructions (CTIs)*. A *direct CTI* is a CTI whose target is specified by an immediate constant in the instruction. Direct CTIs can be unconditional or conditional. An *indirect CTI* is a CTI whose target is specified in a register or memory location and hence is usually unknown statically.

Here are the steps in RL-Bin's **Disassembly Routine:**

1) Add entry point to the list of instructions to be discovered, let us name it D.
2) Pick an instruction I from list D.
3) Mark the address of instruction I as discovered in the disassembly table.
4) If instruction I is a non-control-transfer instruction,
   4.1. The next instruction must be code as well, so we add it to list D if has not been disassembled before.
5) If instruction I is an unconditional direct CTI,
   5.1. It has only one possible constant target (*i.e.*, it is a direct jump), so we can infer that the target is code as well, so we add the target to list D and disassembly continues from there.
6) If instruction I is a conditional direct branch, (see Figure 2 as an example)
   6.1. We cannot assume that its target (T) and fall-through (F) addresses are both code. As discussed before in Section II-A, because of conditional branch obfuscation, only one of the target or the fall through might be code, but not necessarily both. Hence we insert hardware breakpoints at both the target and fall-through addresses (T and F).
   6.2. Register a custom exception handler for handling these hardware breakpoints. Particularly, when either one of them is executed (say T),
      i) It will register that memory location as code in the disassembly table.
      ii) Then it removes hardware breakpoints at both T and F. (The reason that hardware breakpoints are removed from a block after it is executed is that in most ISAs, only a small number of hardware breakpoints are allowed at a time. In the case of x86, there is a limit of four hardware breakpoints that can be set at a time.)
      iii) Adds trampoline at START (see trampoline (1) in Figure 2), which will transfer to instrumentation routine that adds back the hardware breakpoint at the non-executed address among T and F (say F) (If the code is executed from START again, we do not need to disassemble the code from START again, but just insert the hardware breakpoint at F when at START.)
      Note: In the case of x86, if there are more than four non-executed addresses in the function, extra trampoline(s) will be placed in the middle of the function to remove hardware breakpoints from previous addresses and insert them on the following addresses.
   6.3. Later, as an optimization, if the handler at F also executes, remove the hardware breakpoint, as well as the instrumentation at START. This leads to zero overhead in

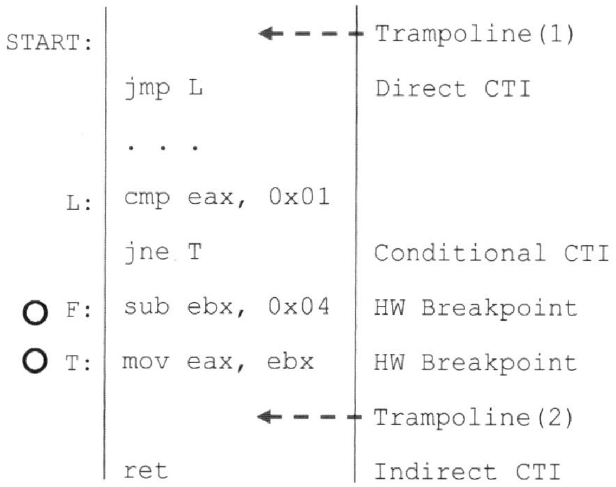

Figure 2. Disassembling a Memory Block

the steady-state after T and F are both proven to be code.

7) If instruction I is an indirect CTI,

7.1. Insert trampolines to an instrumentation routine (see trampoline (2) in Figure 2), just before the indirect CTI to the instrumentation routine which,

i) Computes the target upon reaching that point.

ii) Add it to the list D, if it is not disassembled before.

(The target of indirect CTIs needs to be checked every time because it can change every time the instruction is executed; hence, our trampoline and instrumentation will remain in place to check the target of indirect CTIs to discover new code and handle unexpected control flows.)

8) If D is empty, then exit, otherwise go to Step 2.

The above method works for dynamically-generated code without a special case, since it tracks the CTI into the dynamically-generated code just like any other CTI. It also handles unconditional to conditional branch obfuscation as described above. However, the method needs additional components to handle self-modifying code and exception-based obfuscation. These will be described in the subsections below.

B. Handling Self-Modifying Code

Self-modifying code is handled as follows.

1) To check whether the code has modified itself, write-protect the pages that contain code, so any write to these pages will cause an exception.

2) Register the exception handler to:

2.1. Check the addresses which are being written.

2.2. If they have previously been discovered as code, remove those entries from the disassembly table. (As a result, the newly written code will be treated the same as the code which has never been seen before.)

The above method is very high overhead and it needs to be optimized. The main overhead comes from the fact that every write to the code segment will cause an exception. Such writes will happen if data is stored in the code segment and is written to by the program. To reduce the overhead, we use the following scheme. We add instrumentation code around memory store instructions that trigger the exception for the first time. The instrumentation will turn off write protection, check the addresses being written to, and turn back on write protection after the memory store. In this way, stores to data locations in the code segment will never trigger an exception more than once. As a result, only a small portion of memory store instructions (those that write to the code segment) will be surrounded by our added instrumentation.

C. Handling Exception-Based Obfuscation

This obfuscation happens when an instruction that is not a CTI is used to transfer control of the program. As an example, a divide instruction that deliberately triggers an exception can be used as a CTI. As a result, the memory location following the divide instruction may never be executed. It may contain data and not code. To handle exception-based obfuscation, we follow the following method.

1) Create a stub for every exception handler that is registered. When an instruction triggers the exception it will execute our instrumentation before the actual exception handler.

2) Disassembly routine must stop disassembly at every instruction that can cause an exception that has been registered so far. (In the common case no such exceptions will be registered, thus the overhead will be minimal.)

2.1. If such an exception causing instruction is found (in Step 4 of the baseline algorithm), put a hardware breakpoint on the instruction that immediately follows it.

2.2. After hitting the breakpoint, remove it and start discovering code from that location. (This method ensures that no data is mistakenly assumed to be code.)

Using the algorithm in this section, more and more code is discovered during run-time. This method will ensure that not a single instruction can be executed without first being observed by our binary rewriter, even if the instruction has been generated dynamically or through self-modification. Also, in case there is obfuscation, we would never instrument data inside the code segment since we instrument only the locations that contain code that has been executed during run-time.

D. Handling Multi-Threaded Applications

By the advent of multi-core processors, multi-threaded applications have become very common. As a result, every binary rewriter must handle such applications. The main issue in multi-threading is to make sure that the data structures that are shared between threads are being used correctly. Specifically, they should not be used by a thread while simultaneously being updated by another thread. To avoid the problems regarding concurrent access to RL-Bin data structures, each thread must acquire the lock before being able to modify RL-Bin internal data structures. During this modification, no other threads are allowed to access the same data structure.

IV. OPTIMIZATIONS

This section presents the optimization techniques used in RL-Bin to reduce the overhead. The effectiveness of each optimization will be discussed in Subsection V-C.

OP1. Conditional Branches

As was described in Step 6.3 of the baseline algorithm, if at any point both outcomes of a conditional branch are registered as code, then the instrumentation and hardware breakpoints at that branch can both be removed. In the steady-state, the checks before most direct conditional branches are removed.

OP2. Predicting the Target of Indirect CTIs

The baseline algorithm in Step 7, instruments every indirect CTI to compute its target at run-time and register it as code. This overhead can be reduced by optimization with the following intuition: indirect CTIs usually transfer the control to one of a few constant targets. We will replace this check with a check which takes less time.

As an example, let us assume that function *foo()* is being called from three different call sites. So, the return instruction of the function will return to the instruction after one of these call sites. First, the target will be checked against the most frequent call site. If it matched, the indirect CTI can safely transfer the control flow back to the call site. The same idea would be done for second and third call sites. In the end, if none of the previous checks were true, we would refer to the disassembly table to check whether the target of indirect CTI has been discovered as code before.

There is a trade-off between overhead and the number of frequent call sites that need to be checked before referring to the disassembly table. We use heuristics on the frequency of each target to determine the optimal number of checks.

OP3. Function Cloning

It is often the case in programs that a small function is being called frequently from a call site. The intuition is to remove the check needed before the return instruction (indirect CTI) to the call site. During Step 7 of the baseline algorithm, we selectively clone functions to reduce the overhead and remove the checks needed before their return instructions.

In this method, the function is cloned so that no check is needed if called from that specific call site. First, the function is copied to a new location. The call instruction is modified to a direct jump to the new location. As a result, no return address will be pushed on the stack. Also, the return instructions in the function are replaced by direct jumps to the instruction after the call site.

Again, we face a trade-off here. If we clone every function, it would lead to excessive code bloat. Thus, we must clone functions selectively only for the call sites when doing so will reduce the overhead significantly.

```
Set I = Instructions in the function
Set C = Set of Safety Conditions(Called Functions)
bool Is_Safe(Address Entry_Point)
  Set W={Entry_Point} //Insts waiting to be checked
  While(W ≠ ∅)
    pick inst from W
    if(inst ∈ P) return false
    if(inst ∈ Call_Instructions)
      add Dests(inst) to C
      add Next(inst) to W if(Next(inst) ∉ I)
    else add Dests(inst) to W if(Dests(inst) ∉ I)
    if(stack_height ≠ value assigned before)
      return false
    else
      assign stack_height of Dests(inst)
    if (inst is an indirect write)
      if(Write_Address(inst) = Return_Address)
        return false
    remove inst from W and add it to I
  Let c ∈ C, if(Is_Safe(c) = false) return false
  return true
```

P1 = Set of indirect branch instructions

`jmp dword ptr [eax*4 + 0x0c]`

P2 = Set of instructions that modify the stack pointer to a value that is statically unknown.

`add esp, eax`

`mov esp, dword ptr [ecx]`

Not including

`add esp, 0x4`

(Added value is constant)

P3 = Set of instructions that write to an indirect address which may or may not be the return address of the function

i.e. `mov dword ptr [eax], 0x3c`

`mov dword ptr [esp + ebp*4], eax`

Not including

`mov dword ptr [esp + 0x4], eax`

(Check whether esp+0x4 points to return address)

$$P = \bigcup_{i=1}^{3} Pi$$

Figure 3. The Algorithm to Determine Safety of a Given Function. (None of the instructions in the set P that is defined on the right side, are allowed in a "Safe" function. Dests(inst) returns the targets of CTIs and for non-CTIs, returns the next instruction.)

OP4. Optimizing White-Listed Modules

It often happens that applications load dynamically shared libraries during their execution and then execute functions from them. In most cases, these DLLs are part of the kernel or they are part of the standard library provided by the programming language. It is possible to optimize away the checks needed for some of these DLLs.

The interaction between the main module of the program and the shared libraries happens by calling a function exported by the library. The control will be sent back to the main module after the execution of the function. The only exception is when the library performs a callback and calls a function from the main module. DLLs are analyzed and their callback functions are discovered. If the behavior of the functions and the callback values can be determined before execution, then the analyzed DLL will be white-listed and checks in that module will be optimized away.

OP5. Detecting "Safe" Functions

The most common indirect CTIs are return instructions. The overhead of the checks before return instructions, checks added during Step 7 of the baseline algorithm, can be further eliminated when the function has certain properties. A "Safe" function, can be proven that it cannot modify its return address, hence the return instruction always returns to the instruction after the call site.

We outline in Figure 3 our Just-In-Time (JIT) analysis algorithms, by which the safety of many functions can be established before their execution. For such safe functions, the instrumentation before the return instruction can be removed. The intuition behind the algorithm is to determine the exact addresses of the memory locations on the stack that will be modified by the instructions within the function. If the return address is not modified, then the function will return to the original call site.

"Stack Height" for every instruction, is defined to be the difference between the value of the stack pointer at the entry point of the function and the value of stack pointer at that instruction. For example, a push instruction will reduce the "Stack Height" by four. If the function does not contain any of the instructions defined in Figure 3 as set P, the "Stack Height" of all instructions can be determined before the execution of the function. If there are more than one control flow paths from the entry point to a given address, and "Stack Height" is not the same between different paths, we declare that function as not "Safe" and do not optimize it. This rarely happens in benign code.

The algorithm will determine the "Stack Height" of each instruction and based on the "Stack Height", will determine whether an indirect write rewrites the return address of the function. We also create a list of functions that are called from this function and put them in set C. Later on, after disassembling all instructions in the function, we check the safety of all the functions in set C. If any of the called functions are not safe, the current function will be declared not "Safe". If all the aforementioned checks showed that the return address cannot be modified, the function will be declared "Safe". Note that the algorithm above will be executed only once for each discovered function, thus there will be no overhead in the steady-state.

OP6. Using Data-Flow Analysis to Find "Safe" Functions

OP5 algorithm does not cover some functions, because writing to global or static data, which is not stored on the stack, is frequently done through indirect addressing.

If there is a write to an indirect address, we need to make sure it does not overwrite the return address of the function. Most of the indirect write instructions that write to the stack use stack-derived registers as the base register (in x86, these are esp and ebp registers). So, if the base register is not stack-derived or it is not a copy of these registers, then it cannot modify any value which is previously stored on the stack. As a result, we must ensure the base register is not derived from the stack pointer.

We define the term PNSD, which is short for "Provably Not Stack Derived". If a register value is PNSD, it means that it can be proved during run-time analysis that the current value in the register is not derived from the stack pointer. An indirect write instruction which uses a PNSD register can never write to the stack. We use traditional data-flow analysis to identify all the different definitions that can reach the base register in the write instruction. If all of the definitions of the base register are PNSD, then the base register is also PNSD.

As it is demonstrated in Figure 4, we modify the algorithm in the previous section to check for PNSD variables when there is an instruction, which stores the value to an indirect address. Again, note that the analysis above will be done only once for each discovered function, thus there will be no overhead in the steady-state.

V. Evaluation and Results

We have completed and tested a fully optimized prototype of the above method. Most of the code is written in C++, while there are some functions which are written in x86 assembly, for the sake of optimization. Our experiments are done on a

```
5     if(inst ∈ P) return false
5'    if(inst ∈ P3)
5''   |  if(!Is_PNSD(base register))
5'''  |  |return false
```

P3 = Set of instructions that write to an indirect address which may or may not be the return address of the function.

$$P = \bigcup_{i=1}^{2} Pi$$

`i.e. mov dword ptr [eax + 0x38], 0x3c`

Is_PNSD(eax) returns true if register eax is PNSD

Figure 4. Algorithm Modification to Cover Indirect Write Instructions with PNSD Base Register.

system with Intel Core i7, 3.33GHz CPU with 12 Mb cache and 24.0 GB DDR3 memory on 64-bit Windows 10 OS. We chose the Windows Operating System since most commercial binaries are developed for Windows.

In our experimental setup, we used the SPECrate 2017 Integer and Floating-Point with their reference data sets. SPECrate Integer has 10 benchmarks and all of them are included in our testing. However, we could evaluate 10 out of 13 benchmarks in SPECrate Floating-Point. The other three benchmarks could not be compiled for 32-bit x86 Windows machines, thus *fotonik3d_r*, *cactuBSSN_r*, and *cam4_r* were excluded from the set. This is because our current implementation is for 32-bit Windows binaries; 64-bit binaries can be supported in our theory but are not implemented yet.

Also, we compiled the binaries with three different compilers; Microsoft Visual Studio, GCC, and ICC. The overhead reported for each benchmark is the average of the overhead for binaries compiled with these compilers. In the case that a benchmark could not be compiled with a particular compiler, that compiler is not included in the average.

Comparison with DynamoRIO: Among different dynamic rewriters available, we compared RL-Bin to DynamoRIO. The reason is that DynamoRIO is designed for efficient binary instrumentation. Based on the previous studies [11] [12], Pin and Dyninst have higher overhead in comparison to DynamoRIO.

A. Performance Without Instrumentation

The goal of RL-Bin is to perform only light instrumentation efficiently. Although it can be used to perform heavy instrumentation, such as basic block counting, no binary rewriter can deliver low overhead for such instrumentation, because the added instrumentation itself is heavyweight. Hence such instrumentations are not good use-cases for RL-Bin, whose main motivation is low run-time overhead in deployed code. As a result, we measured the performance overhead of applications running under binary rewriter without added instrumentation. This overhead should be low for use-cases of RL-Bin.

As it is illustrated in Figure 5, RL-Bin outperforms DynamoRIO by a huge margin. In this Figure, A run-time of 100 is the run-time of the original unmodified program without rewriting. (The overhead shown as 107, means the overhead added by the rewriter is 7% without any instrumentation.) In fact, the overhead of DynamoRIO is 1.06x and 1.26x for SPECrate 2017 Floating-Point (Figure 5 (a)) and Integer (Figure 5 (b)) benchmarks respectively (1.16x or 16% on average), whereas the overhead of RL-Bin is 1.015x and 1.09x for the same benchmarks (1.05x or 5% on average). The reason for higher overhead in Integer benchmarks is the higher number of indirect CTIs compared to Floating-Point benchmarks.

B. Performance with Instrumentation

The next experiment measures the overhead added by the rewriters when instrumenting the application to count the number of external calls from the application module to other DLLs. This particular instrumentation is used because the number of locations that need to be instrumented is relatively low. Hence, it is a good use-case of RL-Bin to perform light instrumentation with very low overhead. Figure 6 shows the overhead of RL-Bin ranges from 5% to 130%, with an average of 25% compared to DynamoRIO which

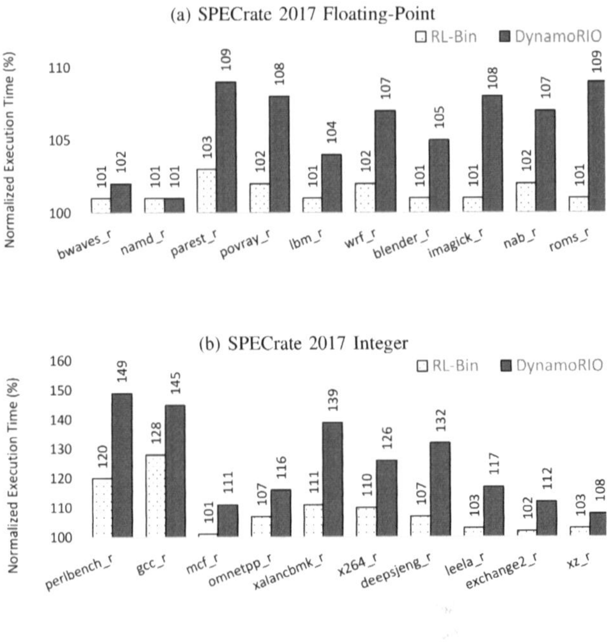

Figure 5. Normalized Run-Time of Rewriters Without Added Instrumentation for SPECrate 2017.

has 56% average overhead (ranging from 4% to 187%). Our experiment demonstrates that RL-Bin can be successfully used to add instrumentation with fairly low overhead compared to DynamoRIO.

C. Optimization Effectiveness

To show the contribution of each optimization method proposed in Section IV, we measured the overhead of SPECrate 2017 Integer with different optimization levels. Figure 7 shows the overhead with six different optimization levels. The overhead is expectedly large (10.25x for *perlbench_r*) without any optimization. Optimizing conditional branches (OP1) will bring the average overhead from 7.24x to 2.93x. Adding target prediction for indirect CTIs will reduce the overhead of remaining checks, thus the average overhead will be 2.02x with OP1+OP2. White-listing modules and cloning functions (OP4 and OP3) will remove lots of the added overhead for checking the target of indirect CTIs and will bring down the average overhead to 1.22x. The last set of optimizations (OP5 and OP6) detect safe functions and remove the check before the return instruction in such functions. Thus, boosting the overhead to just 1.09x on average for SPECrate 2017 Integer benchmarks.

D. Instrumentation Robustness in Commercial Applications

Our last experiment is designed to demonstrate that RL-Bin is robust enough to handle commercial multi-threaded applications that contain dynamically generated and self-modifying code, as well as obfuscation. We aimed to show that RL-Bin fully instruments the binary and it achieves full code coverage, meaning that no instruction is executed without being monitored by RL-Bin. The number of dynamically executed instructions was measured by instrumenting every basic block of the application to add the size of the basic block to the total count.

We tested three popular Microsoft Office tools; Word, PowerPoint, and Excel as well as Adobe Reader, and Apache

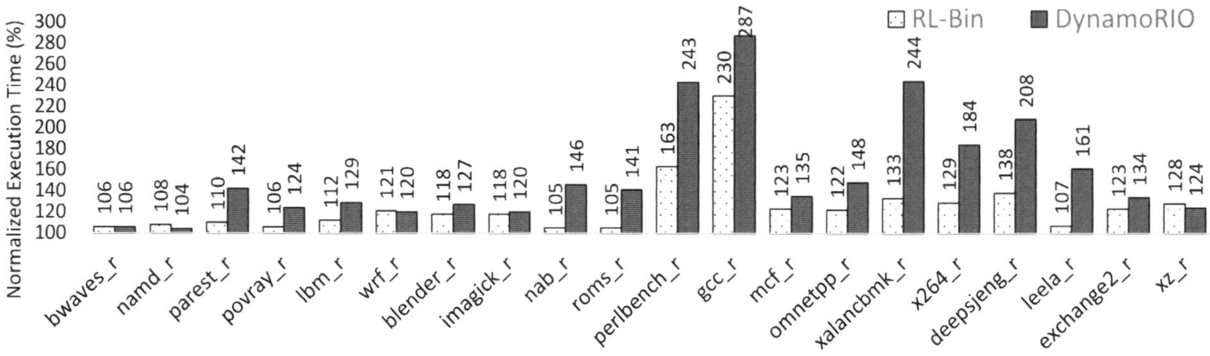

Figure 6. Normalized Run-Time Overhead of Rewriters with Added Instrumentations to Count External Calls for SPECrate 2017

Web Server. In our experiments, in order to have dynamically generated and self-modifying code, we opened documents that contained VBA code in Microsoft Office and JavaScript in Adobe Reader. Apache Web Server heavily uses multi-threading, so this application would appropriately stress test the multi-threading capabilities of RL-Bin.

For commercial programs, we did not measure the overhead, since interaction with users and other uncertain factors, make them unacceptable as benchmarks for measuring the overhead, introduced by RL-Bin. Instead, SPEC CPU 2017 was used for measuring overhead, since they are standardized benchmarks without user interaction, making them suitable for run-time measurement.

The measurements on the number of dynamic instructions were done with both RL-Bin and DynamoRIO. The results showed that the numbers are the same for every application in the set, thus proving that every single instruction is counted by RL-Bin and full code coverage is achieved. As a result, proposed optimization techniques do not result in any loss of coverage, verifying that RL-Bin instrumentation is robust and accurate.

VI. A Use Case: Debugging in Deployment

Making sure that the application is running flawlessly is one of the most arduous tasks in the software development process. In practice, it is often the case that programs face run-time errors, or show unexpected behavior. The main reason is insufficient data sets to test different scenarios. End-user systems will have different resources, and configuration. An error may arise only in certain execution platforms, and never come up in development tests. As a result, debugging is needed even after the development process.

Now, consider the following scenario. The developer has released the software to the end-user, but there is a bug in the software which only happens in the end-user system. The developer cannot reproduce the error in the development environment. There are two existing methods to solve this problem. First, the program may be executed with the presence of a debugger to find where the issue happens. However, almost all commercial binaries are stripped of their debug information to protect their code from being reverse-engineered. As a result, this solution is impractical and the developer will not share debugging information with the user. Another solution is to generate an error log whenever the application crashes and send it to the developer. The log file may contain the current stack and the value of certain attributes of the program. This may be useful to learn more about the issue, however, it is too general, the developer will need extra information. In addition, neither of the methods above would patch the code and solve the issue. Even if the error is found, the user needs to wait for the next release of the application which may take a long time. If the bug is a security concern, it is crucial to patch the program as soon as possible.

Our solution takes as input debugging information of the program and any arbitrary instrumentation that the developer wants to put in the program. We recompile RL-Bin to use the information of the debug file and generate instrumentation that will be inserted in the target application. Based on the debug file, RL-Bin would know where to instrument. The modified

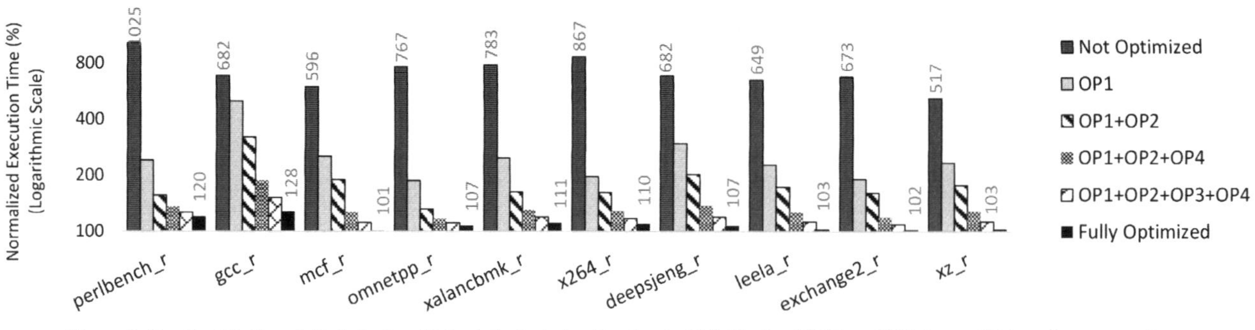

Figure 7. The Contribution of Optimization Methods in Reducing Overhead of RL-Bin for SPECrate 2017 Integer Without Instrumentation

version of RL-Bin, the dynamic debugger, will be sent to the end-user. Added instrumentation will monitor execution and send requested information to the developer. Thus, enabling the developer to pinpoint the problem and fix the issue. This dynamic debugger does not reveal debugging information to the end-user. Only recompiled RL-Bin is sent to the end-user system and the debug information file never gets exposed. Another advantage is that the code can be patched dynamically when the binary is being executed. This is crucial for certain service applications which need to be responsive all the time.

As proof of concept, we developed a simple version of our dynamic debugger. This prototype is capable of parsing PDB file format which stores debugging information of the programs compiled with Microsoft Visual Studio. Our debugger will instrument the program to monitor it during its execution. As an example, instrumentation was added to report the maximum value of the first argument passed to ten random functions. (The purpose of our test was to measure the overhead. The monitored functions and monitoring method depend on the developer and may vary case by case.) Our test results showed that the average overhead was just 6.1% for SPECrate benchmarks, which means that added instrumentation added little extra overhead in comparison to 5% overhead for binaries without instrumentation according to Subsection V-A. This low overhead makes RL-Bin practical for use in deployment.

VII. Related Works

Binary rewriting is a well-researched field of study and during the past thirty years, there have been several major rewriters developed to address the specific needs of the community. [13] thoroughly covers existing works in full depth. In this section, we briefly review existing static and dynamic binary rewriters and compare them against RL-Bin.

RL-Bin [14] represents a very early snapshot of this project published in a non-archival workshop. The current paper is extensively different from [14] by providing a more in-depth analysis, formal definitions of algorithms, more thorough evaluations and experiments that were not part of the earlier paper. As a result of these changes, 72% (about seven out of ten pages) of the material in the current paper is new and never published before.

In particular, [14] presented the initial version of RL-Bin which had high overhead, around 2.5 times the overhead of the current version. The new version has introduced new optimization techniques such as indirect branch target prediction, white-listing external modules, and extending the coverage of safe functions by defining PNSD variables, all of which have helped to achieve overhead of less than 5% on average, indicating that current version can practically be used in deployment. In addition, the earlier paper did not have methods for handling exception-based obfuscation, multi-threaded applications, and self-modifying code. Hence, previously it was only tested for single-threaded applications not containing self-modifying code or exception-based obfuscation. The current version has reached a level of maturity and robustness that can be used for all benign stripped commercial binaries.

A. Static Binary Rewriters

Currently, lots of static rewriting solutions are available including [15]–[19]. SecondWrite project [15] aims to recover compilable source code from binaries, initially output as LLVM IR, which could then further be compiled into rewritten executable code. ATOM [16] provides a flexible interface for code instrumentation which helps in the development of program analysis tools. Diablo [18] aims to provide a framework for link-time program transformation with whole program optimization and instrumentation. Dyninst's version 2007 [12] is an in-place static binary rewriter aiming to provide low-overhead instrumentation capability. Pebil [19] is another static binary rewriter focused on achieving efficient binary instrumentation by using function-level code relocation for inserting control structures.

Static rewriters, including all of the above, face significant limitations due to the lack of run-time information when trying to disassemble and instrument the binary. The first limitation is that they cannot disassemble dynamically generated or self-modifying code. The reason is that these codes are not available before the execution of the program. This will lead to incomplete code coverage.

Dynamically generated code is quite common in benign applications. In a recent study [20], it was observed that 29 out of 120 benign applications contain dynamically generated code, which is used for supporting the execution of user scripts. This means that implementations of security policies that use static binary rewriters would fail for 24% of applications.

The second limitation of static binary rewriting arises from the fact that some benign programs contain data in their code segment. Static disassemblers aim to understand the contents of code segments using two types of disassembly – linear sweep or recursive traversal. Linear sweep ensures high code coverage. However, it cannot distinguish between real code and data in the code segment.

To overcome the problem of data in code segments, another method of disassembly must be used. This method is recursive traversal, which only treats a region of the code segment as code if it can statically prove a control-flow path to it exists. static control flow paths are only known through direct CTIs. For indirect CTIs, the targets are not statically known and the target is only reachable via indirect CTIs.

A third limitation of static binary rewriting is that some benign programs contain obfuscated code, in which case static rewriting can break the program. The relevant kind of obfuscation is control-flow obfuscation whose goal is to mislead disassemblers so that they cannot reverse-engineer binaries.

B. Dynamic Binary Rewriters

There are two main types of dynamic binary rewriters: in-place designs, and code-cache based designs. We will go over them briefly.

In-place designs, such as BIRD [21] have lower overhead in comparison to code-cache based designs by avoiding the high overhead incurred by maintaining the code cache; however, they fail to support some of the features which may happen relatively frequently in benign binaries such as obfuscation, dynamically-generated and self-modifying code. The reason BIRD does not work for obfuscated code is that it assumes both the fall through and destination of a conditional branch are code, which may not be true in obfuscated code. Further, BIRD does not support self-modifying code. The reason is that once they disassemble code from a location, they never change the disassembly even if the code is overwritten.

Unlike static and in-place dynamic rewriters, **code-cache based** dynamic rewriters are robust and can correctly rewrite all programs. However, existing rewriters have high overhead that is generally unacceptable for deployment on live systems. Two of the most popular code-cache based dynamic rewriters are DynamoRIO [2] and Pin [11] with 1.2x and 1.54x run-time overhead, respectively, on average for the full SPEC'06 benchmark suite *even without any instrumentation inserted.* Dyninst's version 2011 [22] is another code-cache based design which has 1.2x overhead for the same benchmark. Vulcan [23] is another dynamic binary rewriter which has a very strong API for adding instrumentation; however, it has very high overhead, around 2x to 3x compared to uninstrumented binaries.

VIII. CONCLUSION

In this paper, we have developed a novel design for a fully optimized, low-overhead binary rewriter which is robust like other dynamic binary rewriters. Due to its low overhead, it is practical to be used in real-time systems. Our experiments show that the overhead of DynamoRIO is 1.16x, whereas the overhead of RL-Bin is 1.05x.

In our future work, we will develop an instrumentation API for RL-Bin that is going to be both efficient and flexible. We aim to have a similar set of APIs to existing tools [24], [25] so that users can adapt to RL-Bin with minimal effort. We are also exploring other adversarial and obfuscation techniques against binary rewriters and the methods to circumvent them. In the near future, we will release RL-Bin's binary for non-commercial uses, similar to how Pin [11] is licensed.

REFERENCES

[1] D. Shackleford, "A new era in endpoint protection," https://go.crowdstrike.com/rs/281-OBQ-266/images/ReportSANSProductReview.pdf, 2017, retrieved: October, 2019.

[2] D. L. Bruening, "Efficient, transparent, and comprehensive runtime code manipulation," Ph.D. dissertation, Massachusetts Institute of Technology, 2004.

[3] R. Wartell, V. Mohan, K. W. Hamlen, and Z. Lin, "Securing untrusted code via compiler-agnostic binary rewriting," in Proceedings of the 28th Annual Computer Security Applications Conference. ACM, 2012, pp. 299–308.

[4] C. Zhang et al., "Practical control flow integrity and randomization for binary executables," in Security and Privacy (SP), 2013 IEEE Symposium on. IEEE, 2013, pp. 559–573.

[5] M. Olszewski, J. Cutler, and J. G. Steffan, "Judostm: A dynamic binary-rewriting approach to software transactional memory," in Proceedings of the 16th International Conference on Parallel Architecture and Compilation Techniques. IEEE Computer Society, 2007, pp. 365–375.

[6] R. Wartell, V. Mohan, K. W. Hamlen, and Z. Lin, "Binary stirring: Self-randomizing instruction addresses of legacy x86 binary code," in Proceedings of the 2012 ACM conference on Computer and communications security. ACM, 2012, pp. 157–168.

[7] A. Roy, S. Hand, and T. Harris, "Hybrid binary rewriting for memory access instrumentation," ACM SIGPLAN Notices, vol. 46, no. 7, 2011, pp. 227–238.

[8] D. Y. Zhu, J. Jung, D. Song, T. Kohno, and D. Wetherall, "Tainteraser: Protecting sensitive data leaks using application-level taint tracking," ACM SIGOPS Operating Systems Review, vol. 45, no. 1, 2011, pp. 142–154.

[9] "Binary obfuscation project tool," https://www.codeproject.com/Articles/856846/Binary-Obfuscation, retrieved: October, 2019.

[10] I. V. Popov, S. K. Debray, and G. R. Andrews, "Binary obfuscation using signals." in USENIX Security Symposium, 2007, pp. 275–290.

[11] C.-K. Luk et al., "Pin: building customized program analysis tools with dynamic instrumentation," in Acm sigplan notices, vol. 40. ACM, 2005, pp. 190–200.

[12] G. Ravipati, A. R. Bernat, N. Rosenblum, B. P. Miller, and J. K. Hollingsworth, "Toward the deconstruction of dyninst," Comput. Sci. Dept., Univ. Wisconsin, Madison, Tech. Rep., 2007.

[13] M. Wenzl, G. Merzdovnik, J. Ullrich, and E. Weippl, "From hack to elaborate technique—a survey on binary rewriting," ACM Computing Surveys (CSUR), vol. 52, no. 3, 2019, p. 49.

[14] A. Majlesi-Kupaei, D. Kim, K. Anand, K. ElWazeer, and R. Barua, "Rl-bin, robust low-overhead binary rewriter," in Proceedings of the 2017 Workshop on Forming an Ecosystem Around Software Transformation. ACM, 2017, pp. 17–22.

[15] K. Anand et al., "A compiler-level intermediate representation based binary analysis and rewriting system," in Proceedings of the 8th ACM European Conference on Computer Systems. ACM, 2013, pp. 295–308.

[16] A. Eustace and A. Srivastava, "Atom: A flexible interface for building high performance program analysis tools," in Proceedings of the USENIX 1995 Technical Conference Proceedings. USENIX Association, 1995, pp. 25–25.

[17] B. Schwarz, S. Debray, G. Andrews, and M. Legendre, "Plto: A link-time optimizer for the intel ia-32 architecture," in Proc. 2001 Workshop on Binary Translation (WBT-2001). Citeseer, 2001.

[18] L. Van Put, D. Chanet, B. De Bus, B. De Sutter, and K. De Bosschere, "Diablo: a reliable, retargetable and extensible link-time rewriting framework," in Signal Processing and Information Technology, 2005. Proceedings of the Fifth IEEE International Symposium on. IEEE, 2005, pp. 7–12.

[19] M. A. Laurenzano, M. M. Tikir, L. Carrington, and A. Snavely, "Pebil: Efficient static binary instrumentation for linux," in Performance Analysis of Systems & Software (ISPASS), 2010 IEEE International Symposium on. IEEE, 2010, pp. 175–183.

[20] D. Kim et al., "Dynodet: Detecting dynamic obfuscation in malware," in International Conference on Detection of Intrusions and Malware, and Vulnerability Assessment. Springer, 2017, pp. 97–118.

[21] S. Nanda, W. Li, L.-C. Lam, and T.-c. Chiueh, "Bird: Binary interpretation using runtime disassembly," in Code Generation and Optimization, 2006. CGO 2006. International Symposium on. IEEE, 2006, pp. 12–pp.

[22] A. R. Bernat and B. P. Miller, "Anywhere, any-time binary instrumentation," in Proceedings of the 10th ACM SIGPLAN-SIGSOFT workshop on Program analysis for software tools. ACM, 2011, pp. 9–16.

[23] A. Edwards, H. Vo, and A. Srivastava, "Vulcan binary transformation in a distributed environment," Microsoft Research, Tech. Rep., 2001.

[24] "Intel pin api," https://software.intel.com/sites/landingpage/pintool/docs/81205/Pin/html/group__API__REF.html, retrieved: October, 2019.

[25] B. Buck and J. K. Hollingsworth, "An api for runtime code patching," The International Journal of High Performance Computing Applications, vol. 14, no. 4, 2000, pp. 317–329.

Automatically Checking Conformance on Asynchronous Reactive Systems

Camila Sonoda Gomes

Computing Department
UEL - State University of Londrina
Londrina, Brazil
Email: camilasonoda@uel.br

Adilson Luiz Bonifacio

Computing Department
UEL - State University of Londrina
Londrina, Brazil
Email: bonifacio@uel.br

***Abstract*—Software testing is an important issue in the software development process to ensure the quality of products. Formal methods have been promising on testing reactive systems, where accuracy is mandatory and any fault can cause severe damage. Systems of this nature are characterized by receiving messages from the environment and producing outputs in response. One of the biggest challenges in model-based testing is the conformance checking of asynchronous reactive systems. The aim is to verify if an implementation complies with its respective specification. In this work, we study conformance checking for reactive systems specified by Input Output Labeled Transition Systems (IOLTS). We develop a practical tool to check the conformance relation between reactive models using the classical ioco relation and a more general theory based on regular languages. In addition, we present some testing scenarios in practical applications and compare them to other tools from the literature using both notions of conformance.**

***Keywords*–model-based testing; conformance testing; automatic verification; reactive systems.**

I. INTRODUCTION

Automatic testing tools have been proposed to support the development process of reactive systems that are characterized by continuous interaction with the environment. In this setting, systems receive external stimuli and produce outputs, asynchronously, in response. In addition, systems of this nature are usually critical and require more accuracy in their development process, especially in the testing activity, where appropriate formalisms must be used as the basis [1]–[3]. IOLTSs [2]–[5] are traditional formalisms usually applied to model and test reactive systems.

In model-based testing, an IOLTS specification can model desirable and undesirable behaviors of an Implementation Under Test (IUT). The aim is to find faults in an IUT according to a certain fault model [1] [6] in order to show if requirements are satisfied regarding its respective system specification. The well-established **ioco** conformance relation [3] requires that outputs produced by an IUT should also be produced by its respective specification. A more recent and general conformance relation [1] specifies desirable and undesirable behaviors using regular languages to define the testing fault model.

In this work, we address the development of an automatic tool for conformance verification of asynchronous reactive systems modeled by IOLTSs. We introduce both notions of conformance in our practical tool to provide a wider application range compare to other tools. JTorx [7], for instance, is a tool from the literature that also implements a conformance testing verification process, but only based on the classical **ioco** relation. Our tool comprises both the classical **ioco** relation and also the more general conformance based on regular languages. We also run some practical scenarios to evaluate aspects related to the effectiveness and usability of both conformance theories and these tools. We show scenarios where the language-based conformance is able to find faults which cannot be detected by the classical **ioco** conformance.

We organize this paper as follows. Section II describes the conformance verification methods using regular languages and the **ioco** relation. The practical tool which implements the more general method of conformance checking is presented in Section III. Some applications and a comparative study are given in Section IV. Section V describes the comparative analysis of tools. Section VI offers some concluding remarks.

II. CONFORMANCE VERIFICATION

The conformance checking task can determine if an IUT complies with its specification when both are modeled by appropriate formalisms. The classical **ioco** conformance relation [3] [5] establishes the compliance between IUTs and specifications when they are specified by IOLTS [2]–[5]. An IOLTS is a variation of the Labeled Transition Systems (LTS) [8]–[11] with the partitioning of input and output labels.

Definition 1: An IOLTS $\mathcal{S}$ is given by (S, s_0, L_I, L_U, T) where: S is the set of states; $s_0 \in S$ is the initial state; L_I is a set of input labels; L_U is a set of output labels; $L = L_I \cup L_U$ and $L_I \cap L_U = \emptyset$; $T \subseteq S \times (L \cup \{\tau\}) \times S$ is a finite set of transitions, where the internal action $\tau \notin L$; and (S, s_0, L, T) is the underlying LTS associated with $\mathcal{S}$.

A transition $(s, l, s') \in T$ indicates that from the state $s \in S$ with the label $l \in (L \cup \{\tau\})$ the state $s' \in S$ is reached in an LTS/IOLTS model. When we have a transition $(s, \tau, s') \in T$ with an internal action, it means that an external observer can not see the movement from state s to state s' in the model.

We may also have the notion of quiescent states. If a state s of an IOLTS has no output $x \in L_U$ and internal action τ defined on it, we say that s is quiescent [3]. When a state s is quiescent we then add a transition (s, δ, s), where $\delta \notin L_\tau$. Note that we denote $L \cup \{\tau\}$ by L_τ in order to ease the notation.

In a real scenario of black-box testing where an IUT sends messages to a tester and receives back responses, quiescence indicates that an IUT could no longer respond to the tester, or it has timed out, or even it is simply slow.

We also need to define the semantics of LTS/IOLTS models. But first, we introduce the notion of paths.

Definition 2: ([1]) Let $\mathcal{S} = (S, s_0, L, T)$ be a LTS and $p, q \in S$. Let $\sigma = l_1, \cdots, l_n$ be a word in $L_\tau^\star$. We say that σ is a *path* from p to q in $\mathcal{S}$ if there are states $r_i \in S$, and labels $l_i \in L_\tau$, $1 \leq i \leq n$, such that $(r_{i-1}, l_i, r_i) \in T$, with $r_0 = p$ and $r_n = q$. We say that α is an *observable path* from p to q in $\mathcal{S}$ if we remove the internal actions τ from σ.

A path can also be denoted by $s \xrightarrow{\sigma} s'$, where the behavior $\sigma \in L_\tau^\star$ starts in the state $s \in S$ and reaches the state $s' \in S$. An observable path σ, from s to s', is denoted by $s \overset{\sigma}{\Rightarrow} s'$. We can also write $s \xrightarrow{\sigma}$ or $s \overset{\sigma}{\Rightarrow}$ when the reached state is not important.

Paths that start from state s are called paths of s, and the semantics of an LTS model is given by the paths that start from their initial state. Now we give the semantics of LTS models.

Definition 3: ([1]). Let $\mathcal{S} = (S, s_0, L, T)$ be a LTS and $s \in S$: (1) The set of paths of s is given by $tr(s) = \{\sigma | s \xrightarrow{\sigma}\}$ and the set of observable paths of s is $otr(s) = \{\sigma | s \overset{\sigma}{\Rightarrow}\}$. (2) The semantics of $\mathcal{S}$ is $tr(s_0)$ or $tr(\mathcal{S})$ and the observable semantics of $\mathcal{S}$ is $otr(s_0)$ or $otr(\mathcal{S})$.

The semantics of an IOLTS is defined by the semantics of the underlying LTS.

Conformance checking can be established between IOLTS models over the **ioco** relation. When we apply input stimuli to both a specification and an IUT, if the IUT produces outputs that are also defined in the specification, we say that the IUT conforms to the specification. Otherwise, we say that they do not conform [3].

Definition 4: ([3]). Let $\mathcal{S} = (S, s_0, L_I, L_U, T)$ be a specification and $\mathcal{I} = (Q, q_0, L_I, L_U, R)$ be an IUT. We say that $\mathcal{I}$ *ioco* $\mathcal{S}$ if, and only if, $out(q_0\ after\ \sigma) \subseteq out(s_0\ after\ \sigma)$ for all $\sigma \in otr(\mathcal{S})$, where $s\ after\ \sigma = \{q | s \overset{\sigma}{\Rightarrow} q\}$ for all $s \in S$ and all $\sigma \in otr(\mathcal{S})$, and the function $out(V) = \bigcup_{s \in V} \{l \in L_U | s \overset{l}{\Rightarrow}\}$.

The more general conformance relation is established over regular languages. This approach provides a wider fault coverage for both LTS and IOLTS models. Basically, desirable and undesirable behaviors are specified by regular languages, D and F, respectively. Given an implementation $\mathcal{I}$, a specification $\mathcal{S}$, and regular languages D and F, $\mathcal{I}$ complies with $\mathcal{S}$ according (D, F), i.e, $\mathcal{I}\ conf_{D,F}\ \mathcal{S}$ if, and only if, no undesirable behavior of F is observed in $\mathcal{I}$ and is specified in $\mathcal{S}$, and all desirable behaviors of D are observed in $\mathcal{I}$ and also are specified in $\mathcal{S}$.

Definition 5: ([1]) Let a set of symbols L, and the languages $\mathcal{D}, \mathcal{F} \subseteq L^\star$ over L. Let $\mathcal{S}$ and $\mathcal{I}$, LTS models, with L as their set of labels, $\mathcal{I} conf_{D,F}\ \mathcal{S}$ if, and only if: (1) $\sigma \in otr(\mathcal{I}) \cap F$, then $\sigma \notin otr(\mathcal{S})$; and (2) $\sigma \in otr(\mathcal{I}) \cap D$, then $\sigma \in otr(\mathcal{S})$.

We remark that an ordinary LTS can be checked using the language-based approach using only the notion of desirable and undesirable behaviors. In this case, we do not need to partition the alphabet into input and output labels, as required by IOLTS models and crucial for **ioco** relation. The next proposition states the language-based conformance checking.

Proposition 1: ([1]). Let the specification $\mathcal{S}$ and the IUT $\mathcal{I}$ be LTS models over L, and the languages $D, F \subseteq L^\star$ over L. We say that $\mathcal{I}\ conf_{D,F}\ \mathcal{S}$ if, and only if, $otr(\mathcal{I}) \cap [(D \cap \overline{otr}(\mathcal{S})) \cup (F \cap otr(\mathcal{S}))] = \emptyset$, where $\overline{otr}(\mathcal{S})$ is the complement of $otr(\mathcal{S})$ given by $\overline{otr}(\mathcal{S}) = L^\star - otr(\mathcal{S})$.

On the other hand, the next lemma shows that the more general notion of conformance relation given in Definition 5 restrains the classical **ioco** conformance relation.

Lemma 1: ([1]). Let a specification $\mathcal{S} = (S, s_0, L_I, L_U, T)$ and an IUT $\mathcal{I} = (Q, q_0, L_I, L_U, R)$ be IOLTS models, we have that $\mathcal{I}$ *ioco* $\mathcal{S}$ if, and only if, $\mathcal{I}\ conf_{D,F}\ \mathcal{S}$ when $D = otr(\mathcal{S})L_U$ e $F = \emptyset$.

Clearly, the **ioco** relation can be given by the more general conformance relation using regular languages.

The conformance checking can be obtained using the automata theory [12] as proposed by Bonifacio and Moura [1]. We transform LTS/IOLTS models into Finite State Automatons (FSAs) and apply union, intersection, and complement operations over regular languages. An FSA is formally given by $\mathcal{A} = (S, s_0, L, T, F)$, where $\mathcal{S} = (S, s_0, L, T)$ is the underlying LTS associated with $\mathcal{A}$. Note that the set of final states in $\mathcal{A}$ is defined by all states of $\mathcal{S}$, i.e., $F = S$. Since the semantics of an FSA is given by the language it accepts, a language $R \subseteq L^\star$ is *regular* if there is an FSA $\mathcal{M}$ such that $L(\mathcal{M}) = R$, where L is an alphabet [12]. Hence, we can effectively construct the automatons $\mathcal{A}_D$ and $\mathcal{A}_F$ such that D and F are regular languages and $D = L(\mathcal{A}_D)$ and $F = L(\mathcal{A}_F)$.

The notions of the test case and test suite according to formal languages are given as follows.

Definition 6: ([1]). Let a set of symbols L, the test suite T over L is a language, where $T \subseteq L^\star$, so that each $\sigma \in T$ is a test case.

If the test suite is a regular language, then there is an FSA $\mathcal{A}$ that accepts it, such that the final states of $\mathcal{A}$ are fault states. The set of undesirable behaviors, defined by these fault states, is called by fault model of $\mathcal{S}$ [1].

A complete test suite can be obtained from an IOLTS specification $\mathcal{S}$ and a pair of languages (D, F) using the Proposition 1. The test suite $T = [(D \cap \overline{otr}(\mathcal{S})) \cup (F \cap otr(\mathcal{S}))]$ is able to identify the absence of desirable behaviors specified by D and the presence of undesirable behaviors specified by F in the specification $\mathcal{S}$. We declare that an implementation $\mathcal{I}$ complies with a specification $\mathcal{S}$ if there is no test case of the test suite T that is also a behavior of $\mathcal{I}$ [1].

We also provide the determinization of models which is useful in this method. Therefore, from a deterministic IOLTS $\mathcal{S}$ we can obtain the automaton $\mathcal{A}_1$ induced by $\mathcal{S}$ that is also deterministic. We write $L(\mathcal{A}_1) = otr(\mathcal{S})$. Hence, we can effectively obtain an FSA $\mathcal{A}_2$ such that $L(\mathcal{A}_2) = L(\mathcal{A}_F) \cap L(\mathcal{A}_1) = F \cap otr(S)$. Also, consider the FSA $\mathcal{B}_1$ obtained from $\mathcal{A}_1$ by reversing its set of final states, that is, a state s is a final state in $\mathcal{B}_1$ if, and only if, s is not a final state in $\mathcal{A}_1$. Clearly, $L(\mathcal{B}_1) = \overline{L(\mathcal{A}_1)} = \overline{otr}(\mathcal{S})$. We can now effectively get an FSA $\mathcal{B}_2$ such that $L(\mathcal{B}_2) = L(\mathcal{A}_D) \cap L(\mathcal{B}_1) = D \cap \overline{otr}(\mathcal{S})$. Since $\mathcal{A}_2$ and $\mathcal{B}_2$ are FSAs, we can construct an FSA $\mathcal{C}$ such that $L(\mathcal{C}) = L(\mathcal{A}_2) \cup L(\mathcal{B}_2)$, where $L(\mathcal{C}) = T$. We can conclude that when D and F are regular languages and $\mathcal{S}$ is a deterministic specification, then a complete FSA $\mathcal{T}$ can be constructed such that $L(\mathcal{T}) = T$.

Next proposition states an algorithm with a polynomial time complexity for the language-based verification.

Proposition 2: ([1]) Let $\mathcal{S}$ and $\mathcal{I}$ be the deterministic specification and implementation IOLTSs over L with n_S and n_I states, respectively. Let also $|L| = n_L$. Let $\mathcal{A}_D$ and $\mathcal{A}_F$ be deterministic FSAs over L with n_D and n_F states, respectively, and such that $L(\mathcal{A}_D) = D$ and $L(\mathcal{A}_F) = F$. Then, we can effectively construct a complete FSA $\mathcal{T}$ with $(n_S + 1)^2 n_D n_F$ states, and such that $L(\mathcal{T})$ is a complete test suite for $\mathcal{S}$ and (D, F). Moreover, there is an algorithm, with polynomial time complexity $\Theta(n_S^2 n_I n_D n_F n_L)$ that effectively checks whether $\mathcal{I} conf_{D,F} \mathcal{S}$ holds.

Next, we obtain a similar result for **ioco** using Lemma 1.

Theorem 1: ([1]) Let $\mathcal{S}$ and $\mathcal{I}$ be deterministic specification and implementation IOLTSs over L with n_S and n_I states, respectively. Let $L = L_I \cup L_U$, and $|L| = n_L$. Then, we can effectively construct an algorithm with polynomial time complexity $\Theta(n_S n_I n_L)$ that checks whether $\mathcal{I}$ **ioco** $\mathcal{S}$ holds.

III. A Testing Tool for Reactive Systems

In this section, we present the automatic checking conformance tool *Everest (conformancE Verification on tEsting ReactivE SysTems)* [13]. Our tool supports the more general notion of conformance based on regular languages and also the classical **ioco** relation when testing reactive systems modeled by LTS/IOLTS. Everest has been developed in Java [14] using the *Swing* library [15], providing a yielding and friendly usability experience through a graphical interface.

Some features provided by the Everest tool are: (i) check conformance based on regular languages and **ioco** relation; (ii) describe desirable and undesirable behaviors using regular expressions; (iii) specify formal models in Aldebaran format [16]; (iv) generate test suites when non-conformance verdicts are obtained; (v) provide state paths, i.e, the sequence of states induced by a test case over the IUT and specification; and (vi) allow the graphical representation of the models.

The tool's architecture is organized into four modules as depicted in Figure 1. The modules are given by rectangles and

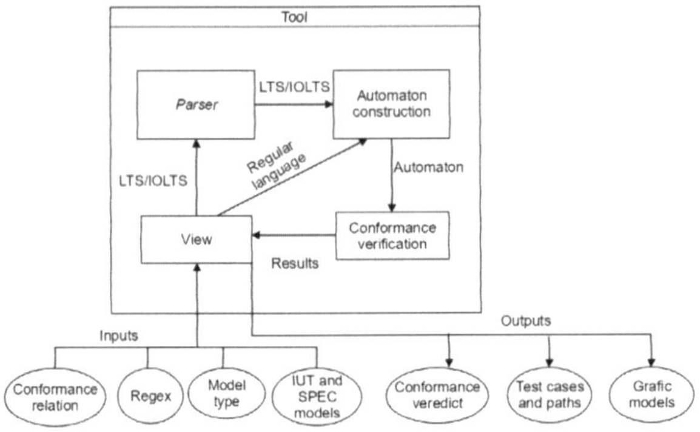

Figure 1. Tool's Architecture

the data flow between them is denoted by the arrows. The input data and the output results are represented by ellipses.

The *View* module implements an intuitive graphical interface with three different views: configuration; **ioco** conformance; and language-based conformance.

The *Parser* module reads the input data with the descriptions of IUT and specification, and turn them into data structures to internally represent their respective models. The *Automaton Construction* module transforms the LTS/IOLTS models into their respective finite automatons which, in turn, are used to construct the fault model together with the automatons obtained by means of regular languages.

The *Conformance Verification* module provides all necessary operations over regular languages such as union, intersection, and complement [12]. This module also constructs the finite automaton that represents the complete test suite and comprises both conformance verification techniques. The conformance checking processes and their essential algorithms are described in [17].

Everest defines a standard representation of LTS/IOLTS models over the Aldebaran [18] format as a set of transitions. Figure 2a presents an example of Aldebaran format and Figure 2b shows its respective IOLTS model. The header $des(s0, 9, 4)$ indicates the initial state, the number of transitions and the number of states. The set of transitions follows the header line by line, where each transition (s, a, q) is defined such that s is the source state, a is the label associated to the transition and q is the target state. Input and output labels can be indicated by the special markers "?" and "!", respectively. But we remark that the special markers just ease the graphical visualization. Everest constructs, internally, a list of input and output labels even if these labels have the special markers or they are settled by the sets of input and output, L_I and L_U, respectively (Figure 2b).

```
des (s0,9,4)
(s0,?a,s1)
(s0,?b,s3)
(s1,?b,s2)
(s1,!x,s2)
(s1,?a,s3)
(s2,?b,s2)
(s2,!x,s3)
(s3,?b,s0)
(s3,?a,s3)
```

(a) $\mathcal{S}$ in Aldebaran format

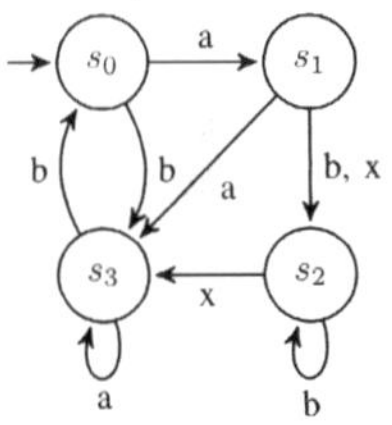

(b) IOLTS specification $\mathcal{S}$

Figure 2. An example of Aldebaran file format

In Figure 3, we can observe the configuration view, where specification and the implementation models are selected, in the Aldebaran format. When the model type is an LTS, the parameters $Label$, $Input\ labels$, and $Output\ labels$ are omitted. If IOLTS models are given then we need to inform how the input/output labels are distinguished (field $Label$), informing below the $Input$ and $Output$ labels or the special markers are assumed in the Aldebaran files, as in Figure 3.

Figure 4 presents the interface for **ioco** conformance verification. Note that in both conformance verification views all information from the configuration view remains visible to ease the reference. Also, the buttons $view\ model$ and $view\ IUT$ allow the graphical visualization of the implementation and specification models. The verdict is displayed by clicking the button $Verify$. In case of non-conformance, the tool presents a set of paths induced by the test suite that detects the faults. The tool also informs incorrectly filled fields in the configuration view in the text box $Warnings$.

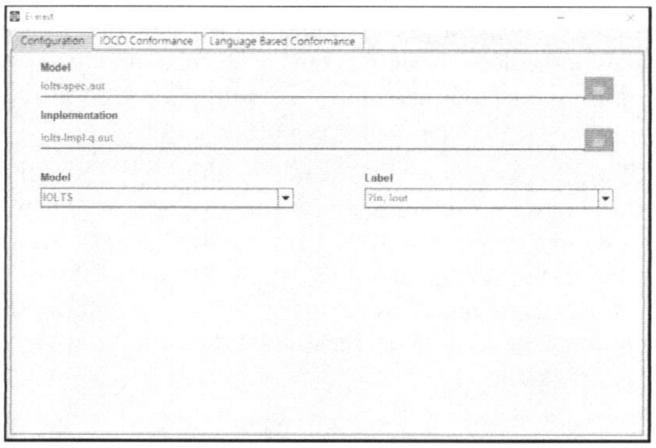

Figure 3. Configuration view

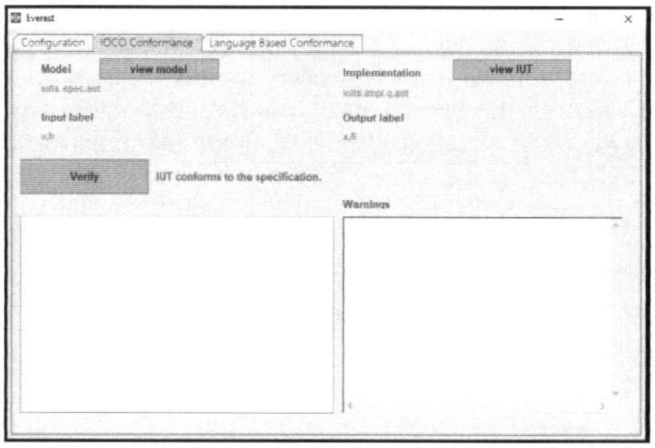

Figure 4. **ioco** verification view

In Figure 5, we present the language-based conformance verification view. *Desirable* and *Undesirable* behaviors must

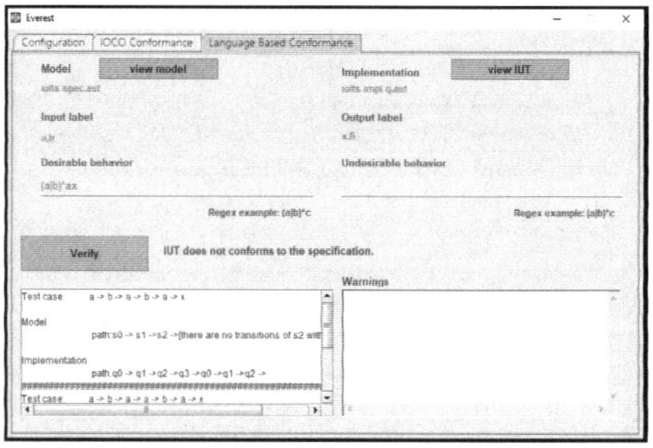

Figure 5. Language-based verification view

be specified by regular expressions. When no regular expression is provided the Kleene closure [12] is assumed over the alphabet to identify faults when models are not isomorphic. After the compliance check, the verdict is displayed similarly to the **ioco** verification conformance.

IV. Practical Application

This section describes some practical testing scenarios applied to the Everest and JTorx tools. Let $\mathcal{S}$ be the IOLTS specification of Figure 2b and let $\mathcal{R}$ and $\mathcal{Q}$ be implementations candidates as depicted in Figures 6a and 6b. Also, let $L_I = \{a, b\}$ and $L_U = \{x\}$ be the input and output alphabets, respectively. All models here are deterministic [19] [20] but we remark that our tool also deals with non-deterministic models.

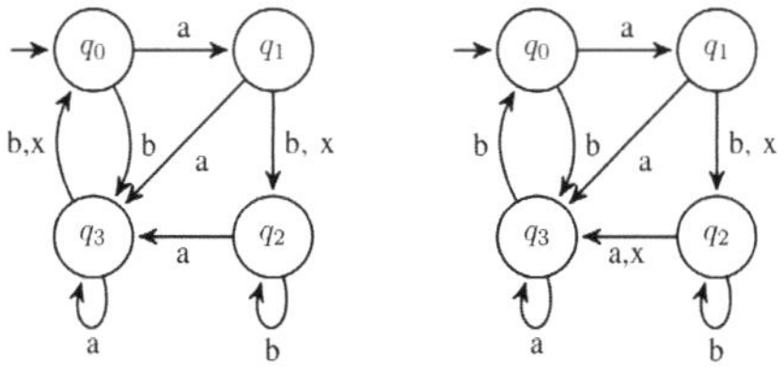

(a) Implementation $\mathcal{R}$ (b) Implementation $\mathcal{Q}$

Figure 6. IOLTS Models

In the first scenario, we check if IUT $\mathcal{R}$ conforms to specification $\mathcal{S}$. Everest tool has returned a non-conformance verdict using **ioco** relation and generated the test suite $\{b, aa, ba, aaa, ab, ax, abb, axb\}$. The subset of test cases $\{b, aa, ba, aaa\}$ induces state paths from s_0 to s_3 in $\mathcal{S}$ and from q_0 to q_3 in $\mathcal{R}$, where the output x is produced by $\mathcal{R}$ but $\mathcal{S}$ does not. Note that s_3 in $\mathcal{S}$ is a quiescent state whence no output is defined on it. The subset $\{ab, ax, abb, axb\}$ induces state paths to state s_2 in $\mathcal{S}$ and q_2 in $\mathcal{R}$. In this case, the output δ is produced by IUT $\mathcal{R}$ whereas $\mathcal{S}$ produces x. That is, a fault is detected according to **ioco** relation. Note that both tools modify the formal models by adding *self-loops* labeled with δ [21] on quiescent states.

The same scenario has been also applied to JTorx tool, resulting in the same verdict, as expected, but it generates the test suite $\{b, ax, ab\}$. Notice that the test suite generated by JTorx is a subset of the test suite generated by Everest. That is, Everest shows all test cases and associated state paths related to each fault according to a transition cover criteria over the specification, differently from JTorx which does not apply transition coverage to test suite derivation. Everest also allows state coverage as criteria to obtain the test suite using only one path per fault when checking conformance over an IUT. But, in this case, we reduce not only the number of test cases, but also the information that might be useful to aid the tester in the fault mitigation process.

In the second scenario (Figure 5), when checking the IUT $\mathcal{Q}$ against the specification $\mathcal{S}$, the language-based conformance verification was able to detect a fault that was not detected by the **ioco** conformance relation (Figure 4). We have obtained the fault model using the regular expressions $D = (a|b)^*ax$ and $F = \emptyset$. Language D clearly expresses behaviors that finish with a stimulus a followed by an output x produced in response. Since the only complete test suite is given by $[(D \cap \overline{otr}(\mathcal{S})) \cup (F \cap otr(\mathcal{S}))]$ and $F \cap otr(\mathcal{S}) = \emptyset$, so we check the condition $D \cap \overline{otr}(\mathcal{S}) \neq \emptyset$, i.e., a fault is detected when behaviors of D are not present in $\mathcal{S}$. Everest then results in a verdict of non-conformance and produces the test suite $\{ababax, abaabax\}$ reaching a fault that is not detected by JTorx using the **ioco** relation.

The specification $\mathcal{S}$ (Figure 2b) and the candidate implementation $\mathcal{Q}$ (Figure 6b) are IOLTS models which, after being converted into underlying automatons respectively, $\mathcal{A}_S$ and $\mathcal{A}_Q$, have all their states defined as final states. Figure 7a displays the complement automaton of the specification.

The **ioco** conformance verification first obtains the underlying automata, $\mathcal{A}_S$ and $\mathcal{A}_Q$, from the IOLTS models. The automaton D (Figure 7b) is constructed to obtain the fault model (Figure 7c) by the intersection of the language $otr(S)L_u$, which is captured by D, and complement language of the specification (Figure 7a). The automaton that represents the test suite (Figure 7d) is obtained by the intersection between the fault model and the $\mathcal{A}_Q$. Since the resulting automaton has no final state, the verdict between models is that $\mathcal{I}$ **ioco** conforms to $\mathcal{S}$.

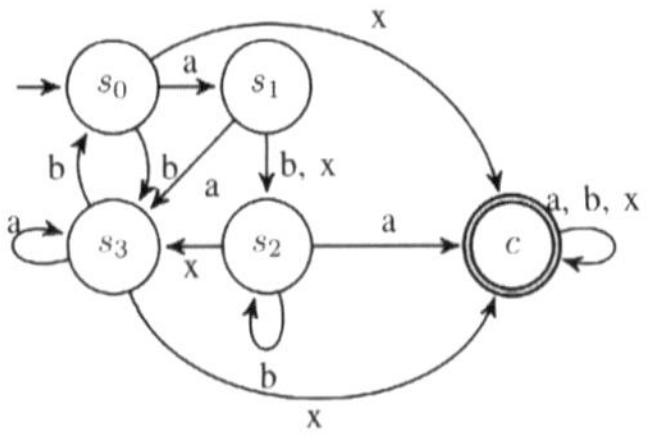

(a) Automaton $\overline{\mathcal{A}_S}$

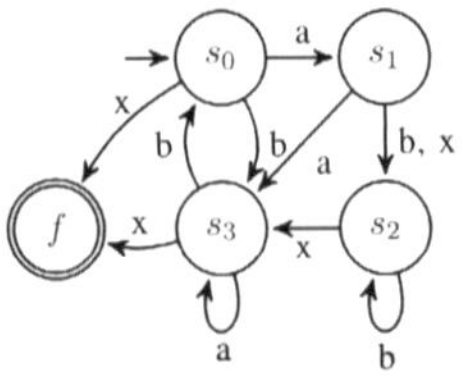

(b) Automaton D

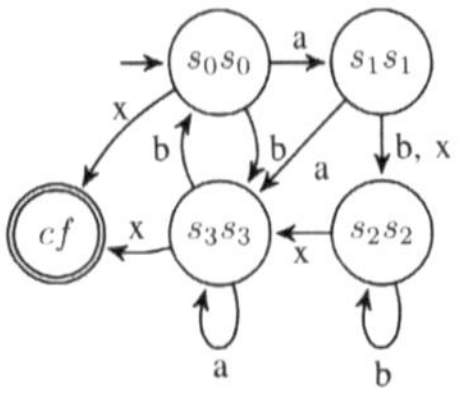

(c) Fault model automaton

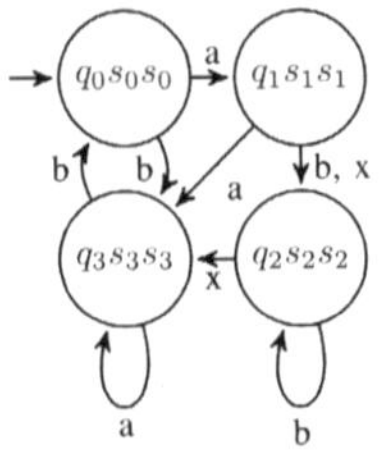

(d) Test suite automaton

Figure 7. Automatons: **ioco** conformance verification

In language-based conformance verification, the underlying automatons, $\mathcal{A}_S$ and $\mathcal{A}_Q$, are also obtained from the IOLTS models depicted in Figures 2b and 6b, respectively. From the regular expression $(a|b)^*ax$ we obtain the automaton (Figure 8a) that accepts the respective language. Since the fault model is given by $[D \cap \overline{otr}(\mathcal{S})] \cup [(F \cap otr(\mathcal{S}))]$ and no undesirable behavior F is defined, then $F \cap otr(\mathcal{S}) = \emptyset$, and the fault behaviors are reduced to $D \cap \overline{otr}(\mathcal{S})$. The automaton that represents the fault model is illustrated in Figure 8b. The automaton that represents the test suite is illustrated in Figure 8c. Note that this automaton contains a final state, indicating that the words accepted by the automaton are part of the test suite that reveals the faults and, consequently, the non-conformity between the models. The test suite generated by the Everest tool is $\{ababax, abaabax\}$.

Also, we have performed a practical study over a simple version, but a real scenario, of a vending machine. The IOLTS specification $\mathcal{N}$ of the vending machine is depicted in Figure 9a. Now consider an IUT $\mathcal{P}$ of this vending machine as given in Figure 9b. The input alphabet is given by $L_I = \{1, 3, 5\}$ which means input stimuli are received from the environment. In this case, labels $1, 3, 5$ represent coins provided by users according to the desired drinks. On the other

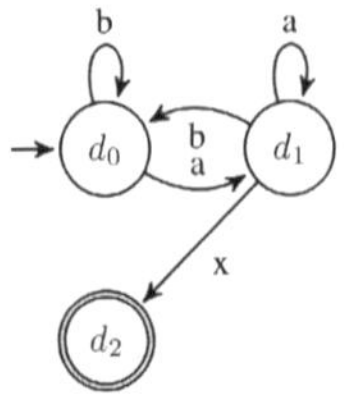

(a) Automaton D

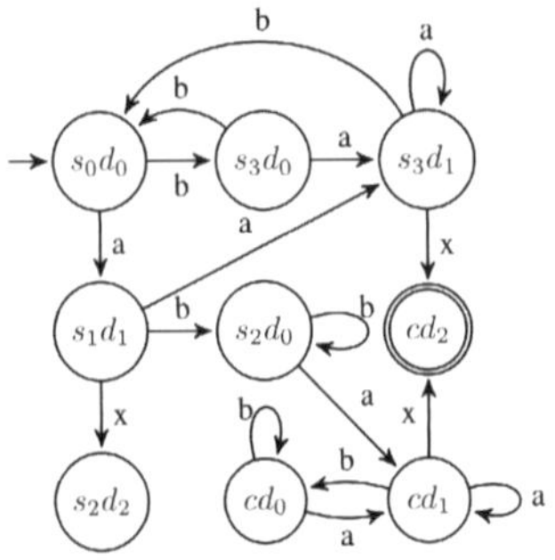

(b) Fault model automaton

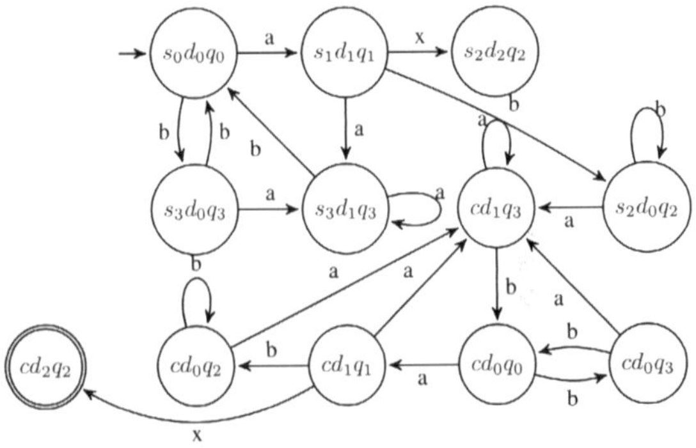

(c) Test suite automaton

Figure 8. Automatons: language-based conformance verification

hand, the output alphabet is defined by $L_U = \{cof, tea\}$, that is, the vending machine gives back to the user the requested drink, a coffee or a tea.

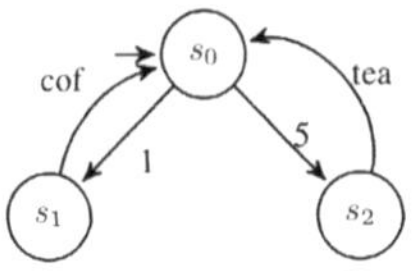

(a) Specification $\mathcal{N}$

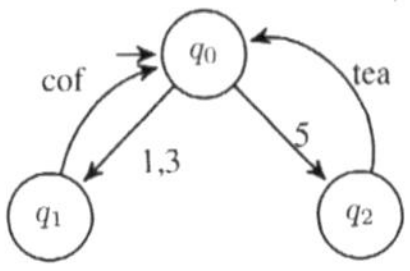

(b) IUT $\mathcal{P}$

Figure 9. Vending machine

When checking whether $\mathcal{N}$ conforms to $\mathcal{P}$ using the language-based method, Everest was able to detect faults that were not detected by JTorx. The desirable behaviors are expressed by $D = 3cof$ and the undesirable behaviors are specified by $F = 1(cof|tea)$. The former expression says that after a user gives the coin 3 the vending machine is supposed to give back a coffee. Similarly, the undesirable expression establishes that after a user gives the coin 1 the vending machine should return neither a coffee nor a tea.

Everest then results in a non-conformance verdict between $\mathcal{N}$ and $\mathcal{P}$, producing the test suite $\{1cof, 3cof\}$. The test case $1cof$ is generated because $\mathcal{N}$ and $\mathcal{P}$ specify that after a coin 1 is provided by the user the vending machine must return a cof which, in turn, is undesirable according to F. The test case $3cof$ reaches a fault because the desirable behavior requires the vending machine gives back a coffee if a coin 3 is inserted into the vending machine. However, this property is not specified on $\mathcal{N}$ and the IUT $\mathcal{P}$ allows such situation.

V. Comparative Analysis of Tools

In this section, we perform a comparative analysis between Everest and JTorx. Both tools implement the conformance verification between a specification and an IUT based on **ioco** theory [3], but only Everest implements the more general conformance relation based on regular languages. Table I summarizes the comparative analysis.

TABLE I. COMPARATIVE ANALYSIS

	JTorx	Everest
Conformance verification		
ioco	X	X
Language-based	-	X
Restrictions over the models		
Support underspecified models	X	X
Require *input-enabledness*	X*	-
Support quiescence	X	X

* JTorx adds self-loops with input labels

The classical **ioco** relation imposes some restrictions and properties over the models, for instance, underspecified models [22] are not allowed on IUT models. In contrast, the language-based conformance relation can deal with specification and implementation models that are not *input-enabled.* Everest implements the language-based conformance relation and also the classical **ioco** relation, which is reduced from the former. We remark that both relations developed in Everest do not require any of these restrictions over the formal models (See Lemma 1). But JTorx requires, for instance, the input enabledness over the IUT models. To overcome the problem of underspecified models, JTorx adds *self-loops* with input labels that are not defined in the states. However, such changes can result in unreliable verdicts since transitions are added to the model, modifying its original behavior. Everest treats underspecified models with no change and keeping the reliability over the original behavior of the models.

Another important issue over underspecified models is quiescence. In this case, Jtorx and Everest add self-loops labeled by δ on states that no output is specified for both specification and implementation models.

VI. Conclusion

Testing of reactive systems is an important and complex activity in the development process for systems of this nature. The complexity of such systems and, consequently, the complexity of the testing task requires high costs and resources in software development. Therefore, automation and accuracy on the testing activity have become essential in this process. Several studies have addressed the testing of reactive systems [23] [24] using model-based testing. More precisely, many works have focused on the conformance checking [1]–[3] between IUTs and specifications to guarantee more reliability.

In this work, we have developed an automatic tool for checking conformance on asynchronous reactive systems. We have implemented not only the classical **ioco** theory but also the more general language-based relation for checking conformance between IOLTS models. We observe by the practical applications that Everest could find faults using the language-based conformance verification process which was not detected by JTorx using the classical **ioco** relation. Everest then gives us an advantage with a wider range of testing scenarios and a full fault detection coverage according to a defined fault model.

There are several tools from the literature that implement conformance checking based on **ioco** relation and its variations [18] [20] [22] [25]–[28]. But, we are not aware of any other tool that implements a different conformance notion, such as the language-based relation. So, the main contribution of this work is the design of Everest tool and its more flexible conformance checking, in addition to its algorithms, the intuitive graphical interface, the practical applications and comparative studies.

A new module of Everest tool is already being developed to provide the test suite generation in a black-box setting. We also intend to perform more experiments using real-world problems with Everest and similar tools from the literature. In this way, we may give a more precise analysis regarding conformance checking for asynchronous reactive models, usability, and performance of these tools.

References

[1] A. L. Bonifácio and A. V. Moura, "Complete test suites for input/output systems," CoRR, vol. abs/1902.10278, 2019, accessed on: 2019-06. [Online]. Available: http://arxiv.org/abs/1902.10278

[2] A. da Silva Simão and A. Petrenko, "Generating complete and finite test suite for ioco: Is it possible?" in Proceedings Ninth Workshop on Model-Based Testing, MBT 2014, Grenoble, France, 6 April 2014., 2014, pp. 56–70, accessed on: 2019-07. [Online]. Available: https://doi.org/10.4204/EPTCS.141.5

[3] J. Tretmans, Model Based Testing with Labelled Transition Systems. Berlin, Heidelberg: Springer Berlin Heidelberg, 2008, pp. 1–38, accessed on: 2019-07. [Online]. Available: https://doi.org/10.1007/978-3-540-78917-8_1

[4] B. K. Aichernig and M. Tappler, "Symbolic input-output conformance checking for model-based mutation testing," Electronic Notes in Theoretical Computer Science, vol. 320, 2016, pp. 3 – 19, accessed on: 2019-06. [Online]. Available: http://www.sciencedirect.com/science/article/pii/S1571066116000037

[5] J. Tretmans, "Testing concurrent systems: A formal approach," in CONCUR'99 Concurrency Theory, J. C. M. Baeten and S. Mauw, Eds. Berlin, Heidelberg: Springer Berlin Heidelberg, 1999, pp. 46–65.

[6] B. K. Aichernig, M. Weiglhofer, and F. Wotawa, "Improving fault-based conformance testing," Electronic Notes in Theoretical Computer Science, vol. 220, no. 1, 2008, pp. 63 – 77, proceedings of the Fourth Workshop on Model Based Testing (MBT 2008). Accessed on: 2019-08. [Online]. Available: http://www.sciencedirect.com/science/article/pii/S157106610800443X

[7] "JTorX a tool for model-based testing," https://fmt.ewi.utwente.nl/redmine/projects/jtorx/wiki/, accessed on: 2018-06.

[8] G. Tretmans, "A formal approach to conformance testing," Ph.D. dissertation, University of Twente, 1992.

[9] P. Daca, T. A. Henzinger, W. Krenn, and D. Nickovic, "Compositional specifications for ioco testing," in 2014 IEEE Seventh International Conference on Software Testing, Verification and Validation, March 2014, pp. 373–382.

[10] F. Zeng, Z. Chen, Q. Cao, and L. Mao, "Research on method of object-oriented test cases generation based on uml and lts," in 2009 First International Conference on Information Science and Engineering, Dec 2009, pp. 5055–5058.

[11] E. G. Cartaxo, F. G. O. Neto, and P. D. L. Machado, "Test case generation by means of uml sequence diagrams and labeled transition systems," in 2007 IEEE International Conference on Systems, Man and Cybernetics, Oct 2007, pp. 1292–1297.

[12] M. Sipser, Introduction to the Theory of Computation, 2nd ed. Course Technology, 2006.

[13] C. Sonoda, "Everest website," https://everest-tool.github.io/everest-site, accessed on: 2019-07.

[14] Oracle, "Java se development kit 8," http://www.oracle.com/technetwork/pt/java/javase/, accessed on: 2019-07.

[15] ——, "Package javax swing," https://docs.oracle.com/javase/7/docs/api/javax/swing/package-summary.html, accessed on: 2019-06.

[16] "AUT manual page," https://cadp.inria.fr/man/aut.html, accessed on: 2019-08.

[17] C. S. Gomes and A. L. Bonifácio, "Automatically checking conformance on asynchronous reactive systems," CoRR, vol. abs/1905.08914, 2019, accessed on: 2019-08. [Online]. Available: http://arxiv.org/abs/1905.08914

[18] J. Calamé, "Specification-based test generation with tgv," Software Engineering Notes, 2005.

[19] J. E. Hopcroft, R. Motwani, and J. D. Ullman, Introduction to Automata Theory, Languages, and Computation (3rd Edition). Boston, MA, USA: Addison-Wesley Longman Publishing Co., Inc., 2006.

[20] B. L. Mark Utting, practical model-based testing a tools approach, 1st ed. Elsevier, 2007.

[21] G. Tretmans, Test Generation with Inputs, Outputs and Repetitive Quiescence, ser. CTIT technical report series. Netherlands: Centre for Telematics and Information Technology (CTIT), 1996, no. TR-CTIT-96-26, cTIT Tecnnical Report Series 96-26.

[22] A. Belinfante, "Jtorx: Exploring model-based testing," Netherlands, 9 2014, iPA Dissertation series no. 2014-09.

[23] B. K. Aichernig, E. Jöbstl, and S. Tiran, "Model-based mutation testing via symbolic refinement checking," Science of Computer Programming, vol. 97, 2015, pp. 383 – 404, special Issue: Selected Papers from the 12th International Conference on Quality Software (QSIC 2012). [Online]. Available: http://www.sciencedirect.com/science/article/pii/S0167642314002329

[24] S. Anand et al., "An orchestrated survey of methodologies for automated software test case generation," Journal of Systems and Software, vol. 86, no. 8, 2013, pp. 1978 – 2001, accessed on: 2019-08. [Online]. Available: http://www.sciencedirect.com/science/article/pii/S0164121213000563

[25] W. Mostowski, E. Poll, J. Schmaltz, J. Tretmans, and R. Wichers Schreur, "Model-Based Testing of Electronic Passports," in Formal Methods for Industrial Critical Systems, M. Alpuente, B. Cook, and C. Joubert, Eds. Berlin, Heidelberg: Springer Berlin Heidelberg, 2009, pp. 207–209.

[26] A. Belinfante, L. Frantzen, and C. Schallhart, 14 Tools for Test Case Generation. Berlin, Heidelberg: Springer Berlin Heidelberg, 2005, pp. 391–438, accessed on: 2019-06. [Online]. Available: https://doi.org/10.1007/11498490_18

[27] P. Bhateja, "A tgv-like approach for asynchronous testing," in Proceedings of the 7th India Software Engineering Conference, ser. ISEC '14. New York, NY, USA: ACM, 2014, pp. 13:1–13:6, accessed on: 2018-05. [Online]. Available: http://doi.acm.org/10.1145/2590748.2590761

[28] C. Jard and T. Jéron, "Tgv: theory, principles and algorithms," International Journal on Software Tools for Technology Transfer, vol. 7, no. 4, Aug 2005, pp. 297–315, accessed on: 2019-08. [Online]. Available: https://doi.org/10.1007/s10009-004-0153-x

An Empirical Evaluation of the Accuracy of NESMA Function Points Estimates

Luigi Lavazza

Dipartimento di Scienze teoriche e Applicate
Università degli Studi dell'Insubria
21100 Varese, Italy
Email: luigi.lavazza@uninsubria.it

Geng Liu

School of Computer Science and Technology
Hangzhou Dianzi University
Hangzhou, China
Email: liugeng@hdu.edu.cn

Abstract—**Functional size measures of software—especially Function Points—are widely used, because they provide an objective quantification of software size in the early stages of development, i.e., as soon as functional requirements have been analyzed and documented. Unfortunately, in some conditions, performing the standard Function Point Analysis process may be too long and expensive. Moreover, functional measures could be needed before functional requirements have been elicited completely and at the required detail level. To solve this problem, many methods have been invented and are being used to estimate functional size based on incomplete or not fully detailed requirements. Using these methods involves a trade-off between ease and timeliness on one side and accuracy on the other side. In fact, estimates are always affected by some error; knowing the magnitude of estimation errors that characterize the estimates provided by a given method is of great importance to people who use size estimates. This paper reports the results of an empirical study devoted to evaluate the accuracy of estimates provides by 'NESMA estimated' and 'NESMA indicative' methods, which are among the best known and most widely used Function point estimation methods. The results of the study show that the NESMA estimated method provides estimates that are accurate enough for practical usage.**

Keywords–Function Points; IFPUG; Function point Analysis; Functional Size Measurement; Functional Size Estimation; NESMA estimated; NESMA indicative; Early Size Estimation.

I. Introduction

The availability of accurate functional size measures can help software companies plan, monitor and estimate development costs, and control software development processes. Among the functional size measurement methods that have been proposed, Function Point Analysis (FPA) [1] is by far the most popular. The International Function Points User Group (IFPUG) took charge of maintaining FPA and publishes the official Function Point counting manual [2].

In some conditions, performing the standard FPA process may be too long and expensive. Moreover, standard FPA can be applied only after the completion of the software requirements elicitation stage, while functional measures could be needed earlier, i.e, before functional requirements have been elicited completely and at the required detail level.

Therefore, many methods were invented and used to provide *estimates* of functional size measures based on less or coarser grained information than required by standard FPA. Among those methods, the NESMA method [3] is the most popular. Actually, the NESMA method was adopted by IFPUG as the election method for early estimation of unction Point size [4].

Inevitably, all the early functional size estimation methods involve some estimation error. Accordingly, project managers need to know—at least approximately—the magnitude of the potential error that affects size estimates. This is especially true for the NESMA method, since it has been proposed as the "official estimation method by IFPUG.

Not surprisingly, several researchers and practitioners evaluated the accuracy of the proposed functional size estimation methods (as described in Section III). However, most evaluations were based on academic software projects or used small datasets, hence most evaluations cannot be considered very reliable, and they are hardly generalizable. In order to assess the actual value for industry of the NESMA method, it is necessary to perform an experimental evaluation based on a large dataset collecting measures from industrial settings.

In this paper, we present the experimental evaluation of the accuracy of NEMSA estimates, based on a dataset that includes data from 479 software development projects in the finance and banking domain. The size of the dataset and the real-life nature of the data make the evaluation presented here the most exhaustive and reliable published evaluation of the NESMA method.

The rest of the paper is organized as follows. Section II briefly describes FPA and the NESMA functional size estimation measurement method. Section III illustrates the related work. Section IV describes the empirical study. Section V discusses the threats to the validity of the study.

Finally, Section VI draws some conclusions and outlines future work.

II. Background

To make the paper easier to read and as self-contained as possible, in this section we outline the fundamentals of Function Point Analysis and the NESMA estimation methods.

A. Function Point Analysis

The basic idea of FPA is that the "amount of functionality" released to the user can be evaluated by taking into account the data used by the application to provide the required functions, and the transactions (or processes) through which the functionality is delivered to the user. Specifically, the data used by the application are classified into Internal Logic Files (ILF) and External Logic Files (EIF), the latter being essentially "read only" for the application being measured. Transactions are classified into External Input (EI), External

Output (EO) and External Queries (EQ), depending on their main purpose.

According to the counting manual [2], the measurement process is organized into the following activities: 1) Determining the type of function point count; 2) Identifying the Counting Scope and Application Boundary; 3) Identifying Data Functions; 4) Identifying Transaction Functions; 5) Weighting data and transaction functions. The latter activity requires that each data and transaction function is analyzed in detail, so that its "complexity" is determined and the corresponding weight can be assigned to the function. Activity 5) is relatively time and effort consuming.

For additional information on Function Point measurement, please see [2]. Unadjusted Function Points have been recognized as an international standard by ISO [5]. In this paper, we always refer to unadjusted function points, even when we do not qualify explicitly measures as unadjusted.

B. The NESMA estimated method

The NESMA method was proposed [3] to get an estimate of the functional size of a given application without analyzing data and transactions in detail.

Actually, there are two NESMA estimation methods: the Indicative NESMA method and the Estimated NESMA method.

The former estimates size (*EstSize*) based on the number of ILF (#ILF) and the number of EIF (#EIF), as follows:

$$EstSize = \#ILF \times W_{ILF} + \#EIF \times W_{EIF}$$

where W_{ILF} is 25 or 35 and W_{EIF} is 10 or 15, depending on ILF and EIF being identified based on a conceptual model in third normal form or not, respectively.

The process of applying the NESMA indicative method involves only identifying logic data and classifying them as ILF or EIF. Accordingly, it requires less time and effort than standard FPA. However, the Indicative NESMA method is quite rough in its computation: the official NESMA counting manual specifies that errors in functional size with this approach can be up to 50%.

The Estimated NESMA method requires the identification and classification of all data and transaction functions, but does not require the assessment of the complexity of each function: Data Functions (ILF and EIF) are assumed to be of low complexity, EI, EQ and EO are assumed to be of average complexity. Hence, estimated size is computed as follows:

$$EstSize = 7\ \#ILF + 5\ \#EIF + 4\ \#EI + 5\ \#EO + 4\ \#EQ$$

IFPUG adopted the NESMA estimated method as the official early function point analysis method [4].

C. Function Point counting and estimation example

In this section, we illustrate IFPUG FP counting and NESMA estimation using a slightly modified version of the Warehouse management software (WMS) by Fetcke [6].

The WMS is used by a company that operates several warehouses, where customers' goods are stored. Customers can deposit items into storage locations in the warehouse. After the items have been kept in the warehouse for some period of time, they can be retrieved by their owners. The customers get billed for the storage service.

The Entity/Relationship diagram representing the entities involved in the WMS is given in Figure 1. The entities and their attributes are described in Figure 2. Attributes `Owner` and `Storage_place` are references to entities `Customer` and `Place`, respectively.

Figure 1. Entity/Relationship diagram of the WMS [6].

The WMS allows the user to perform several operations, such as adding a new customer, deposit an item, receive payment, print the customer item list, and many others. Here we report the specifications of the `Delete_customer` operation, which will be used to illustrate the functional measurement methods. The `Delete_customer` operation removes an instance of `Customer` from the system's repository, given the `Name` attribute of the customer. `Customer` data are removed if the `Amount_due` attribute is zero and the customer does not own any stored items. An error message is displayed, if the record cannot be removed or if there is no instance of `Customer` with the given name.

Based on the given specifications, we can measure the size of `Item` data file and the `Delete customer` transaction, according to IFPUG rules, as follows.

`Item` is an ILF, since it is managed by the WMS application. It has just one RET, since the only type of instance for `Items` is the one shown in Figure 2. According to the same figure, `Item` has 6 attributes, i.e., 6 DETs. Having 1 RET and 6 DETs, `Item` is a low complexity ILF, hence its size is 7 FP [2]. `Delete_customer` is an EI, since its main objective consists in updating a data file, namely the `Customer`. This transaction reads `Item` instances and reads and (possibly) deletes an istance of `Customer`: accordingly, it references 2 types of files (FTR = 2). In the execution of this transaction, only two DETs are moved through the boundaries: the `Name` given in input to identify the customer to be removed, and the error message issued if the deletion cannot be performed. As an EI with 2 FTR and 2 DETs it has low complexity and its size is 3 FP [2].

We can now compute the estimated size of `Item` data file and `Delete_customer` transaction using NESMA methods.

According to the NESMA estimated method, `Item` (an ILF) is assumed to be of low complexity, hence its size is estimated to be 7 FP, `Delete_customer` (an EI) is assumed to be of average complexity, hence its size is estimated to be 4 FP.

Using the NESMA indicative method, we can estimate the

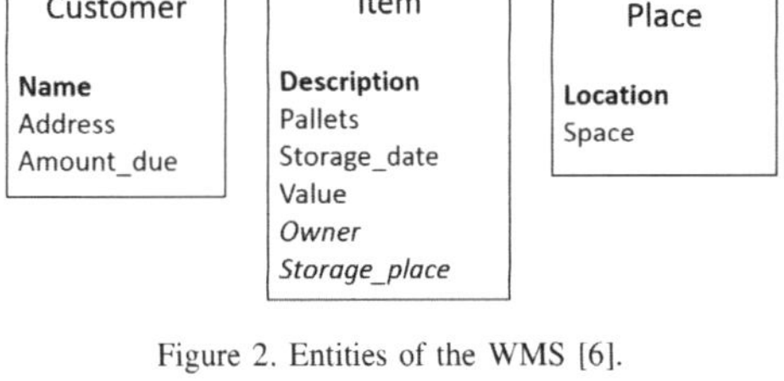

Figure 2. Entities of the WMS [6].

size of the whole WMS: Figure 1 shows that a third-normal fiorm model of data includes 3 ILF and no EIF, hence the expected size of WMS is $3 \times 25 = 75$ FP.

III. Related work

NESMA defined the application of FPA in the early phases of the application life cycle, and recognizes three function point analysis methods: Detailed function point analysis (currently corresponding to IFPUG measurement), Estimated function point analysis, Indicative function point analysis. Using a database of over 100 developed and implemented applications, NESMA empirically evaluated the accuracy of the estimated and indicative FPA approximation methods [10]. The results showed that: size measures of the high-level function point analysis and the detailed function point analysis are very close. Moreover, indicative function point analysis gives a surprisingly good estimate of the size of several applications.

H. S. van Heeringen described the size accuracyas well as the difference in measurement effortof the NESMA estimated and NESMA indicative methods, by measuring 42 projects [3]. The results show that the estimation error of NESMA estimated was in the [-6%, +15%] range, with average 1.5%; the estimation error of NESMA indicative was in the [-15%, +50%] range with average 16.3%. In both cases the estimation error was evaluated with respect to the detailed measurement.

Wilkie et al. [11] utilized five commercial projects used in the research to evaluate the cost-benefit trade-off of size measurement with respect to size estimation; they concluded that whilst the Indicative NESMA method was insufficiently accurate for the involved commercial organization, the NESMA Estimated approach was definitely viable.

IFPUG adopted NESMA methods for early "high-level" size estimation [4]. IFPUG suggested that 1) The High Level FPA method can be used to size an application early in the software development life cycle; 2) The High Level FPA method can also be applied as an alternative to standard FPA estimate (the outcome is not significantly different, while the estimation time is considerably shorter); 3) The indicative FPA method may be used to get a very fast, rough indication of the size of a project or an application, but it is not suited for contractual commitments.

Lavazza et Liu [9] used 7 real-time applications and 6 non real-time applications to evaluate the accuracy of the E&QFP [12] and NESMA with respect to full-fledged Function Point Analysis. The results showed that the NESMA indicative method yields the greatest errors. On the contrary, the NESMA estimated method yields size estimates that are close to the actual size. The NESMA indicative method is generally outperformed by the other methods. The NESMA estimated method proved fairly good in estimating both Real-Time and non Real-Time applications.

Morrow et al. used a dataset of 11 projects to evaluate the quality of sizing estimates provided by NESMA methods [13]. They also adapted NESMA methods' general principles to enhance their accuracy and extent of relevance, and empirically validated such an adapted approach using commercial software projects.

The main limitations of the mentioned research are that most of the research work used small datasets containing data concerning little projects of not industrial nature. In our paper, we evaluate measurement accuracy of the NESMA method with respect to FPA method over a dataset containing data from 479 industrial projects, of which several are above 10000 FP.

IV. The Empirical Study

The empirical study was made possible by the availability of a dataset that includes—for every application—both the measure in IFPUG UFP and the number of ILF, EIF, EI, EO and EQ. Using the latter numbers we were able to compute NESMA estimates, by applying the formulae given in Section II-B. So, having both the NESMA estimates and the IFPUG size for every application, we were able to evaluate the accuracy of estimates.

A. The Dataset

We use a dataset of 479 projects developed and used by a Chinese financial enterprise. The considered projects are all new development projects, that delivered applications to be employed in the financial and banking domain. The measures in the dataset were all computed by expert professionals.

TABLE I. Descriptive statistics of dataset.

			NESMA indicative	
	Standard FP	NESMA estimated	Not Normalized	Normalized
Max	82501	87100	87420	61895
Mean	3567	3435	3456	2438
St. Dev.	6725	6694	7258	5120
Median	1135	1122	985	700

Descriptive statistics of the dataset are given in Table I.

B. The Analysis

To assess the obtained estimates, in Figure 3 we plot the values of the estimates with respect to the actual size measured according to the standard IFPUG counting manual [2]. In Figure 3, we also draw the NESMA estimated = UFP line: if the estimates were perfect, all the points would lie on the line. As a matter of fact, most points are quite close to the line, thus indicating that in general the estimates are close to the actual measures.

To better appreciate the accuracy of estimates, in Figure 4 the situation for projects having size not greater than 20000 UFP is shown. It can be observed that most points are below the y=x line, thus indicating that the NESMA method tends to underestimate.

To verify if and to what extent the NESMA method underestimates the IFPUG size, in Figure 5 a boxplot of NESMA estimation errors is given (errors are defined as the standard IFPUG size measure minus the estimate). For the sake of readability, in Figure 5, errors having magnitude greater than 1000 UFP are not shows. It can be seen that both the median and the mean (shown as a blue diamond) are above the zero error line. Actually, about 75% of the projects are underestimated. We can thus conclude that—in the considered dataset—the NESMA method underestimates functional size.

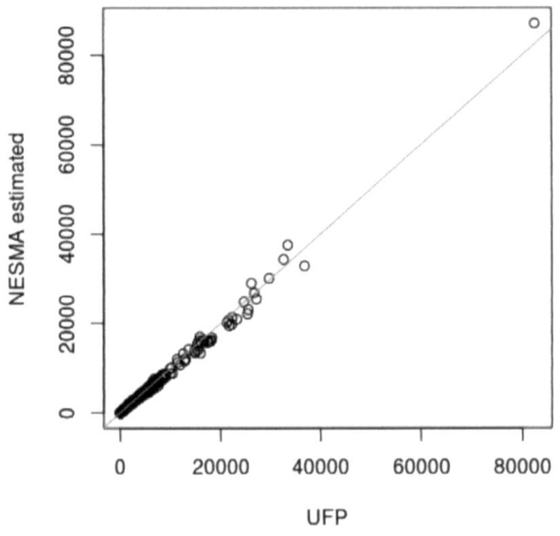

Figure 3. Standard IFPUG UFP measures vs. NEMSA estimates.

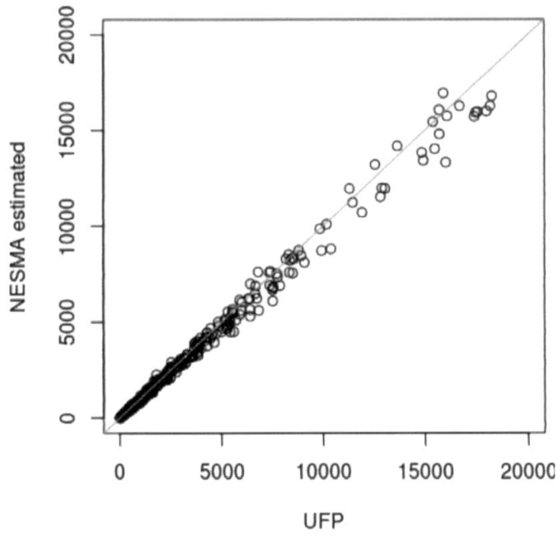

Figure 4. Standard IFPUG UFP measures vs. NEMSA estimates: zoom on projects not greater than 20000 UFP.

C. Accuracy Evaluation

It is now necessary to evaluate quantitatively the accuracy of NESMA estimates. First of all—as suggested by Shepperd and McDonell [7] and by Lavazza and Morasca [8]—we checked whether NESMA estimates perform better than "baseline" models. Shepperd and MacDonell [7] proposed that the accuracy of a given estimation method be measured via the Mean Absolute Residual (MAR): $MAR = \frac{1}{n}\sum_{i=1..n}|y_i - \hat{y}_i|$. Shepperd and MacDonell suggest to use random estimation, based solely on the known (actual) values of previously measured applications, as a baseline model. Shepperd and MacDonell observed also that the value of the 5% quantile of the random estimate MARs can be interpreted like α for conventional statistical inference, that is, any accuracy value

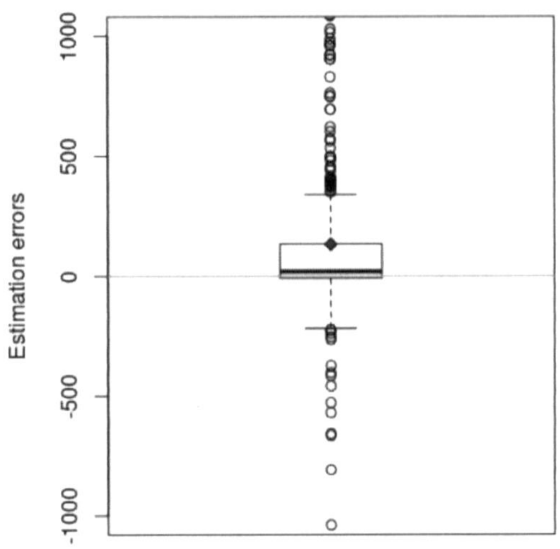

Figure 5. Boxplot of NEMSA estimation errors (no outliers).

that is better than this threshold has a less than one in twenty chance of being a random occurrence. Accordingly, the MAR of a proposed model should be compared with the 5% quantile of the random estimate MARs, to be reasonably sure that the model is actually more accurate than the random estimation.

Lavazza and Morasca [8] proposed to use a "constant model," where the estimate of the size of the ith application is given by the mean size of the other applications.

With our dataset, the MAR of the constant model is 3864 UFP, while the 5% quantile of absolute residuals for random estimates is 4566 UFP. The MAR of NESMA estimates is 246 UFP, much smaller than both baselines. Consequently, we can state that the NESMA method satisfies the necessary conditions for being considered an acceptable estimation method.

Concerning the accuracy of NESMA estimates, in Figure 6 the distribution of absolute errors is given. The blue diamond is the mean, i.e, the MAR of the estimates. The median of absolute residuals is 57 UFP, however the MAR is definitely greater (246 UFP), because of several large errors.

In general, relatively large estimation errors are deemed acceptable in very large projects. To help practitioners appreciate the "importance" of errors with respect to the size of the project, in Figure 7 we give the boxplot representing the distribution of absolute relative errors (the relative error of an estimate is the estimation error divided by the actual size).

Figure 7 shows that the great majority of estimate errors are less than 10%, and in only a few (out of 479) cases, errors are greater than 25%. Considering that NESMA estimates are produced without considering the details of functional requirements, this level of accuracy is likely acceptable by most practitioners.

D. Analysis of the Indicative Method

The analysis reported above concentrated on the NESMA Estimated method, since the NESMA Indicative method is reported to be much less accurate [3],[9].

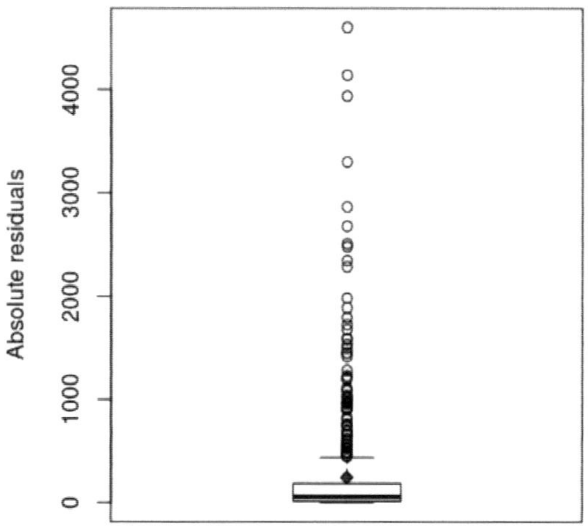

Figure 6. Boxplot of absolute errors.

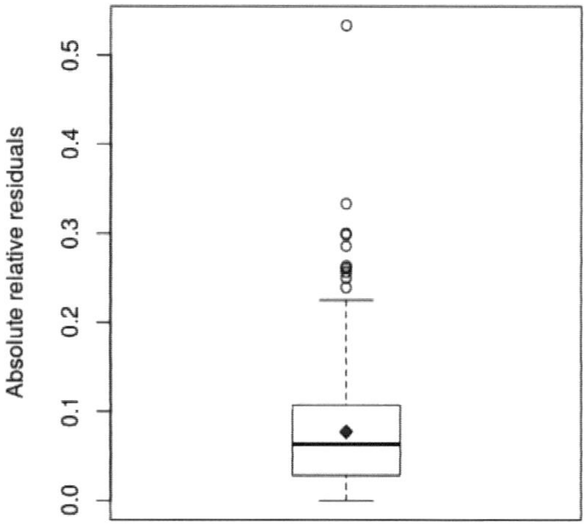

Figure 7. Boxplot of absolute relative errors.

However, we consider necessary to check if the NESMA Indicative method is really less accurate than the NESMA Estimated method. To this end, for each of the 479 project in the dataset, we computed the estimated size according to the NESMA Indicative method. Since we had no reliable information concerning the normalization of the data models used to identify ILF and EIF, we applied the NESMA Indicative method with both the normalized and not normalized weights.

The results we achieved agree with the previously published evaluations. Figure 8 shows the distributions of relative errors of estimates obtained via NESMA Indicative methods in comparison with the NESMA Estimated method. It is quite clear that the NESMA Indicative methods is definitely less accurate than the NESMA Estimated method. This difference in accuracy is even more evident in Figure 9, where the absolute residuals of NEMSA methods are shown (outliers are omitted to keep the figure readable).

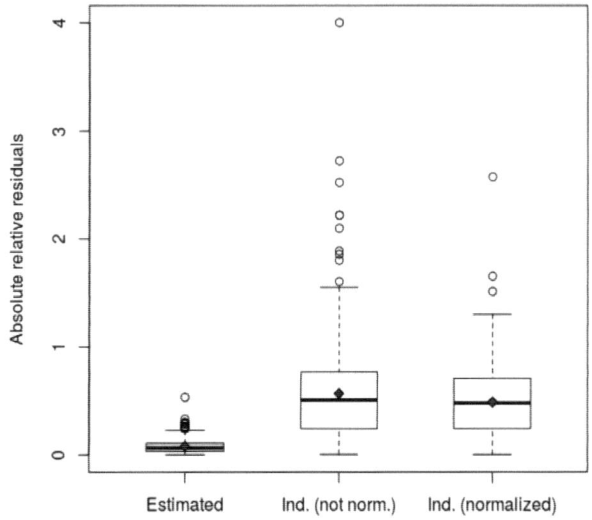

Figure 8. Distributions of absolute relative estimation errors of the NESMA methods.

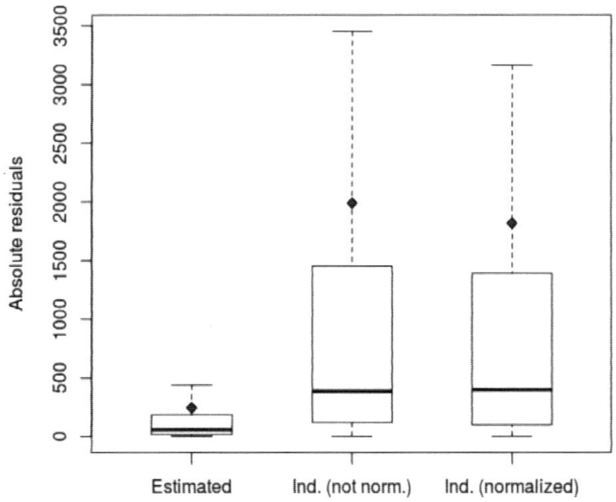

Figure 9. Distributions of absolute relative estimation errors of the NESMA methods.

TABLE II. RESULTS WITH DIFFERENT NESMA METHODS

		Indicative	
	Estimated	Not Norm.	Normalized
Mean AR	264	1989	1817
Median AR	57	386	398
Mean MRE	7.7%	57%	49%
Median MRE	6.3%	51%	48%

The MAR and MMRE obtained with the different NESMA methods are given in Table II.

V. THREATS TO VALIDITY

Given the type of study we presented, there are two main threats to validity that need attention.

First, we should consider the correctness of the given data. In fact, the data in the analyzed dataset were derived from the analysis and measurement of functional requirements: both analysis and measurement could be affected by error, which would end up in the dataset. Concerning this threat, we are reasonably sure that the used data are of good quality, since they were collected by professionals in industrial contexts where functional size measures are quite important, hence great attention is posed in the measurement activities. Evan so, we cannot exclude that some errors are present; however, in such case most errors are expected to affect both IFPUG measures and NESMA estimates, in approximately the same way. Hence, these errors should not be able to affect our results to a large extent.

Second, we need to consider external validity, i.e., whether we can generalize the results of our study outside the scope and context that characterize the considered software projects. On the one hand, our dataset is much larger than the datasets usually involved in software engineering empirical studies; besides, our dataset includes data from fairly large projects (e.g., over 20000 FP). In this sense, our dataset represents a large and varied enough sample. On the other hand, all the considered projects are from the economic, financial and banking domain, hence we cannot be sure that the results of our study apply equally well in other domains. In this respect, readers are reminded that previous studies (e.g., [9]) show some difference in accuracy when estimates concern real-time software applications.

VI. Conclusions

In this paper, we addressed the evaluation of the accuracy of functional size estimates that can be achieved via the NESMA estimation methods. To this end, we compared functional size measures obtained via the standard IFPUG Function Point Analysis process, and estimates obtained via the NESMA indicative and NESMA estimated methods. Both measures and estimates were computed for a dataset containing data from 479 software projects. Based on the results of the analysis, we can draw a few relevant conclusions:

- The NESMA estimated method is definitely more accurate than the NESMA indicative method.
- The NESMA estimated method provides reasonably accurate estimates: the mean absolute residual is 264 FP, quite small, considering that the average size of estimated projects is 3567 FP.
- 75% of applications were estimated by the NESMA estimated method with errors not greater than (or extremely close to) 10%.
- The NESMA method tends to underestimate. This can be dangerous, since at the initial stages of development one could be induced to believe that the development process will be shorter and cheaper than actually required.

Future work includes experimenting with additional estimation methods and investigating whether and how estimation accuracy can be improved.

Acknowledgment

This work was partly supported by the "Fondo di ricerca d'Ateneo" funded by the Università degli Studi dell'Insubria, by Zhejiang Provincial Science Foundation of China under Grant No. LY19F020046 and LY17F020023, and by the Chinese Scholarship Council under Grant No. 201708330399

References

[1] A. J. Albrecht, "Measuring application development productivity," in Proceedings of the joint SHARE/GUIDE/IBM application development symposium, vol. 10, 1979, pp. 83–92.

[2] International Function Point Users Group (IFPUG), "Function point counting practices manual, release 4.3.1," 2010.

[3] H. van Heeringen, E. van Gorp, and T. Prins, "Functional size measurement-accuracy versus costs-is it really worth it?" in Software Measurement European Forum (SMEF 2009), 2009.

[4] A. Timp, "uTip – Early Function Point Analysis and Consistent Cost Estimating," 2015, uTip # 03 (version # 1.0 2015/07/01).

[5] International Standardization Organization (ISO), "ISO/IEC 20926: 2003, Software engineering IFPUG 4.1 Unadjusted functional size measurement method Counting Practices Manual," 2003.

[6] T. Fetcke, "The warehouse software portfolio: A case study in functional size measurement," Département d'informatique, Université du Quebec à Montréal, Tech. Rep. 1999 20, 1999. [Online]. Available: http://citeseerx.ist.psu.edu/viewdoc/download?doi=10.1.1.195.5828&rep=rep1&type=pdf Retrieved: September 2019

[7] M. Shepperd and S. MacDonell, "Evaluating prediction systems in software project estimation," Information and Software Technology, vol. 54, no. 8, 2012, pp. 820–827.

[8] L. Lavazza and S. Morasca, "On the evaluation of effort estimation models," in Proceedings of the 21st International Conference on Evaluation and Assessment in Software Engineering. ACM, 2017, pp. 41–50.

[9] L. Lavazza and G. Liu, "An empirical evaluation of simplified function point measurement processes," International Journal on Advances in Software Volume 6, Number 1 & 2, 2013, 2013, pp. 1–13.

[10] nesma, "Early Function Point Analysis." [Online]. Available: https://nesma.org/themes/sizing/function-point-analysis/early-function-point-counting/ Retrieved: September 2019

[11] F. G. Wilkie, I. R. McChesney, P. Morrow, C. Tuxworth, and N. Lester, "The value of software sizing," Information and Software Technology, vol. 53, no. 11, 2011, pp. 1236–1249.

[12] L. Santillo, M. Conte, and R. Meli, "Early & quick function point: sizing more with less," in 11th IEEE International Software Metrics Symposium (METRICS'05). IEEE, 2005, pp. 41–41.

[13] P. Morrow, F. G. Wilkie, and I. McChesney, "Function point analysis using nesma: simplifying the sizing without simplifying the size," Software Quality Journal, vol. 22, no. 4, 2014, pp. 611–660.

Metaphor Models in Software Education: An Empirical Study

Evgeny Pyshkin
University of Aizu

Tsuruga, Ikki-Machi, Aizu-Wakamatsu, Fukushima, 965-8580, Japan
Email: pyshe@u-aizu.ac.jp

Abstract—**This research contributes to the literature on using metaphors in computing and software education. We examine the major theories of metaphors focusing on linguistic, cognitive and communicational aspects of contemporary discourse on metaphor and the applicability of these theories to the domain of computing, software engineering and education. We investigate the specific characteristics of metaphors used in computer science and software systems and introduce a number of use cases demonstrating how metaphors are used in programming classes while discussing such topics as code organization, code readability, code aesthetics, and software project workflow.**

Keywords–Metaphor; software engineering; education; empirical; readability.

I. Introduction

Exploring metaphors and their use in education received significant attention in research works in various fields of knowledge from philosophy and linguistics on one side of the spectrum to technology and engineering on the other. Convergence of models and approaches used in different subject domains becomes a noticeable trend in present-day technology-related cross-disciplinary research. In the last decade, we can cite a number of efforts to put software engineering and computing discourse into the context of human-centric paradigm [1], humanities [2], social and cognitive sciences [3]. Investigations on crossings between natural, social and technology disciplines [4], centricity of computer science in contemporary liberal arts education [5], digital disruption challenges [6], relationsips between digital humanities, digital society and software study [7] are of much interest for both humanity and engineering researchers.

In linguistics, metaphors are language constructs referring to (or reasoning about) the concepts using words and phrases with the meanings appropriate to different kinds of concepts [8]. Consider the famous William Shakespeare's fragment from the play "As You Like It" [9]: *"All the world's **a stage**, And all the men and women merely **players**: They have their **exits** and their **entrances**."* We find here a direct metaphor: "world as theater stage" using the connected concepts "players", "actor's exit (from the stage)" and "actor's entrance (to the stage)". Persy Bysshe Shelly uses a metaphor of family to describe the cloud, which is itself a metaphor of his romantic hero in the poem "The cloud" [10]: *"I am the **daughter** of Earth and Water, And the **nursling** of the Sky."*

In poetry, the metaphors of empathy are very common; here is one more good example from Paul Verlaine's "L'heure exquise" (1820), where the lune has voice, the willow has a silhouette, and the wind (not a willow!) weeps [11] (Table I shows the original text together with the English direct translation).

TABLE I. VERLAINE'S METAPHORS

Original French Text	*English Direct Translation*
De chaque branche	From every branch
Part une voix	A **voice** goes
Sous la ramé...	To under the ridge
La silhouette	**The silhouette**
Du saule noir	Of the black **willow**
Où le vent pleure...	Where the **wind weeps**...

Metaphors are mental phenomena that could be manifested not only in language, but also in gesture or graphic form; thus, in every form connected to the metaphor's (and human being's) cognitive nature and the metaphor's socio-cultural dimensions [12]. Metaphors do not only assert object similarities; paradoxically, they point up the dissimilarities and contrasts between the objects, and this is equally important for understanding how metaphors work [13].

Apart from linguistics and philosophy, there are numerous metaphor connotations in technology and engineering. Carbonelli, Sánchez-Esguevillas, and Carro pointed out the role of metaphors in understanding the emerging technologies: *"Technologies are not only changing our world in a materialistic and pragmatic way but they are a primary factor in defining our conceptual models, influencing the way we understand and perceive our experience"* [14]. Being a new reality, the technologies are often based on new concepts requiring metaphors for their understanding, such as:

- **"Data as resources"** metaphor in *Data Science* (derived from the earlier resource-based metaphors for electricity, time, transportation systems, etc.);
- **"Software as a construction material"** in *Software-defined Anything* (connected to the earlier metaphor of software design as architecture);
- **"Home as device container"** in *Smart Home technology* (closely related to the IoT metaphors).

Kendall mentioned that successful user metaphors have an impact on the development of successful information systems and their interfaces: *"Invoking a metaphor means opening the door for a listener to use all previous associations in entering the subject in different way"* [15].

In software engineering, requirement elicitation and initial system design need good metaphors in order to facilitate establishing communication between the development team and project stakeholders, to allow both parties interpreting and understanding their languages (see Figure 1). We use the term "languages" in a broader sense, to designate the process of mapping the conceptual core connected to the subject domain to the model used on developer's side.

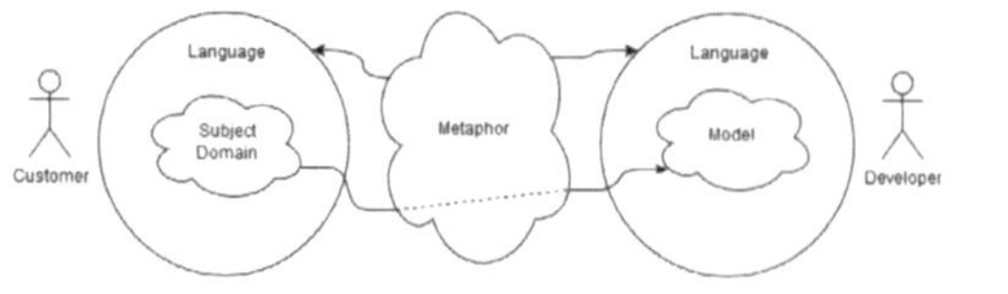

Figure 1. Mapping the customer's domain language to the development team's language.

The remaining text is organized as follows. In Section II, the existing theories of metaphor are introduced at a glance with respect to their mutual dependencies. Section III is focused on using the theories of metaphor in education, with particular emphasis on their applicability to technology disciplines. Section III presents our own experience on introducing metaphors to students attending a programming class.

II. Metaphor Paradigms in Historical Perspective

It is no exaggeration in saying that modern theories of metaphor appeal to a number of ancient views, where the works of Aristotle and Quintilian are the most discussed. Multiple hypotheses of contemporary linguistics are built on revealing the insights and finesse of the analysis of ancient authors [16]. Traditionally, the sources of so-called **Comparison Theory** are attributed to Aristotle, who introduced a metaphor as the *application (ἐπιφορά) of an alien name by transference either from genus ()γένος) to species (εΐδος), or from species to genus, or from species to species, or by analogy* [17]. In contrast to many modern studies of metaphor insisting that Aristotle undervalued metaphor and believed it to be a solely ornamental language feature, Mahon argued that Aristotle held a position on the *ubiquity of metaphor* which supports current views about the omnipresence of metaphors in everyday discourse [18]. Wood claimed that the Aristotle's definition contributes to the relationships between concepts and the processes of metaphor application (thus, from the perspective of software engineering, it is in direction of entity-relationship modeling) [19].

Quintilian, in turn, used a "process-oriented" approach, but emphasized the alteration, or mutation, rather than transferring [20]. Quintilian stated that the alterations arise from the words used metaphorically, and the involved changes *"concern not merely individual words, but also our thoughts and the structure of our sentences"* [21]. Thus, the Quintilian's approach may be considered as a precursor of **Cognitive Theory of Metaphor** by Lakoff and Johnson [22].

Richards introduced, and then Black developed the **Interaction Theory of Metaphor**. In contrast to ancient authors who worked with the transitional concepts of source and target, Richards introduced the technical concepts of **tenor** and **vehicle**, where the former is the thought being described in terms of another (metaphorically), while the latter is the thought, in terms of which the tenor is described [23]. Black described it in his conceptual book "Models and Metaphors": *"A memorable metaphor has the power to bring two separate domains into cognitive and emotional relation by using language directly appropriate to the one as a lens to seeing the other; the implications, suggestions, and supporting values entwined with the literal use of the metaphorical expression enable us to see a new subject matter in a new way. [...] the metaphor itself neither needs nor invites explanations and paraphrase. Metaphorical thought is a distinctive mode of achieving insight, not to be construed as an ornamental substitute for plain thought"* [24]. Thus, metaphors are linked to ontological models connected to the tenor and vehicle.

Lakoff created a **Contemporary Theory of Metaphor** focused on examination of metaphors as not solely language entities, but matters of thought and reason: *"the locus of metaphor is not in language at all, but in the way we conceptualize one mental domain in terms of another. The general theory of metaphor is given by characterizing such cross-domain mappings"* [25]. Such a conceptualization is delivered via finding and creating the ontological correspondences between the target and source domains. There are subject matters that cannot be comprehended, without using metaphors, even in everyday conversational language. Many conceptual metaphors are cross-language metaphors. The famous metaphor **"Love as Journey"** can be described in different languages without losing much of its metaphoric contents. This makes this example extremely successful. Vocabulary related to a journey serves as a frequent source for metaphors used in different knowledge areas. In project management, for example, we use **milestones** to designate the important project stages, **tickets** – to name the tasks assigned to engineers that should be completed by the deadline, project **roadmaps** – to name an overview of the project's goals and deliverable artifacts presented within a project **timeline**, etc.

Steen extended the preceding theories by adding a third, communicative, dimension. He pointed out that though Lakoff's cross-domain mappings may have been required in the history of language and its understanding, *"these mapping have become irrelevant to the thought processes of the contemporary language user, precisely because the metaphorical senses of the words have become equally conventional, and sometimes even more frequent that the non-metaphorical ones"* [26]. Specifically, in technology disciplines, there are frequent cases, when the professional language becomes non-metaphorical, even if many concepts were originally defined using the metaphor constructions, but which are not presently considered as a deliberate use of metaphors. There is also a kind of ontology deformation: when metaphors of **files**, **folders** and **directories** were used to name the interface elements in computer systems (first, command-line, and later – graphical), many people were able to understand the cross-domain mapping between the abstractions of computer storage organization and the concrete example of stationery items. Nowadays, for younger generations, these interface names are not abstract anymore; some have never seen physical files or folders. Thus, they use these words without thinking of their initial metaphorical connotations.

In terms of comparative theory, the source and the target may change roles. In the early years of Internet technology, the concept of electronic mail was explained by mapping the electronic message domain to a traditional letter mail. At that time, people had to explicitly emphasize the fact of sending an electronic message, not a traditional one: "e-mail me", "check your e-mail", etc. Nowadays, when most of communications have been transferred to the domain of computer (e.g., (still) electronic) systems, this "e" prefix became unnecessary and almost disappeared. By saying "mail me", we rather mean sending an electronic message, not a traditional mail. Colburn and

Shute give the following explanation of the above-mentioned phenomena: *"when the target domain becomes so dissimilar to the source through information enrichment that a metaphorical name for the target concept ceases to be metaphorical and becomes a historical artifact"* [27]. Because of technology, there could be even more unobvious cases, when at attempt to use a particular metaphor in its literal sense may generate a metaphorical connection "in opposite direction": nice example is the 2006 American romantic drama by Alejandro Agresti "Lake House", where the heroes used a physical mail box for operations shifted in time. Such operations are possible and even normal for electronic communications (nicely working for the heroes), but seems surrealistic while moved to the physical (neither electronic or virtual) reality.

III. Using Metaphors in Education

A. *From Language Learning to Education in Broad Sense*

In language learning, using metaphors is natural part of introducing new lexical material to learners. Metaphors provide a convenient approach to enhance and organize the learner's vocabulary, as well as to group together the words and synthetic concepts having a metaphorical meaning. Researching a metaphorical use of language constructions within a particular topic may enhance the vocabulary related to the mapped topics. In [28], Lazar gives a number of examples such as using body vocabulary to describe the locations (*in the heart of the city*, *on the foot of a mountain*) or weather vocabulary to describe the human relations (*a warm welcome*, *to freeze somebody out*).

Even the teaching process itself can be described metaphorically with respect to the teacher's roles and responsibilities. Clarken introduced 5 (perhaps, not exhaustive) teaching metaphors: *teachers as parents*, *teachers as gardeners*, *teachers as prophets*, *teachers as pearl oysters*, and *teacher as physicians* [29]. A teacher may operate differently by using different metaphors in different time; finding an appropriate teaching model is an important aspect of making the teaching process efficient and learner-friendly.

B. *Metaphors in Computing and Software*

Computer science and software metaphors are diverse and multi-faceted, they actively exploit different theories of metaphors (including linguistic, cognitive and communication approaches): they all may be concurrently used and cooperate.

Research on the particularities of technology language does not concern the corresponding technological or industrial applications only, but society at large. The aspects of technological and engineering literacy are important for improving educational practices in many areas of knowledge: *"informed citizens need an understanding of what technology is, how it works, how it is created, how it shapes society, and how society influences technological development"* [30]. The language of a particular technology-sensitive domain (such as software engineering) is not only for the domain professionals anymore: all members of contemporary society need a better understanding of this language and its metaphors. What makes software metaphors particularly complex is that they have connotations to abstract entities that we could not physically touch or point to. Johnson describes computer abstractions as *"based not on nature but rather on artificial world created by humans"* [31].

Software architecture exploits the **construction** metaphor with the list of relevant terms such as process **building**, **architectural pattern**, etc. In turn, an appropriate metaphor may improve the process of designing and describing software architectures. The architectures could not be designed only by a group of software engineers, they need more experts. That is why Smolander defined four metaphors referring to the different meanings of architecture, its description and stakeholder environment [32]:

- **Architecture as blueprint** describing the high-level implementation of the system;
- **Architecture as literature** describing the project documentation;
- **Architecture as language** describing the common understanding about the system structure and communication between different stakeholders;
- **Architecture as decision** describing the decisions about the system structure, the required resources and development strategies.

In education, metaphors help to introduce the unknown by using **concrete** examples explaining **abstract** things [29]. However, understanding of what is concrete and what is abstract differs between disciplines. Abstraction in computer science is not the same as in mathematics and linguistics [27]: computer scientists (rightfully) believe that an application control stack is a concrete entity, and its complexity can be explained better with using the inferential structures of abstract domains (like queuing). However, for others, the concept of memory stack seems to be a complete abstraction.

Software works with many abstract concepts, which are largely metaphorical. According to Boyd, software can be considered as a special case of fiction literature, that is why it is essentially metaphorical [33]. The approaches we use to describe the data entities and control structures, memory organization and program workflow, structural patterns and architecture designs actively exploit various metaphors. Some of such metaphors are listed in Table II.

Interestingly, introducing a metaphor to a software domain may lead to further extension of these metaphor within the bag of concepts specific for software design. Figure 2 provides an illustration: a design pattern, describing the object-oriented structure of instance creators, used a metaphor of factory borrowed from the domain of industrial technology.

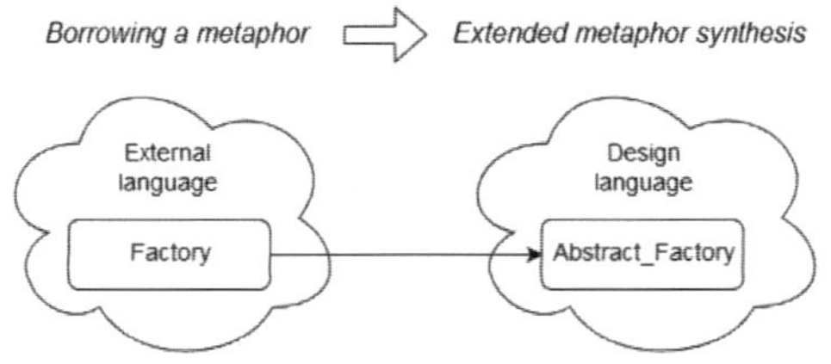

Figure 2. Synthesis of extended metaphor.

A **Factory Method** is for creation instances. It doesn't have compile-time dependencies on the object's type. In turn, for a given set of related interfaces, an **Abstract Factory** provides a way to create objects that implement those interfaces for a matched set of concrete classes (for example, while supporting changing platform's look and feel by selecting an alternative set of widgets as shown in Figure 3).

TABLE II. EXAMPLES OF SOFTWARE METAPHORS

Domain	*Examples*
Program objects	Scope Assignment Lifetime Location
Control structures and program workflow	Selection Loop Thread Lazy computation
Modular structure	Library Package
Interface design	Menu Palette Folder File
Storage containers	Array Map List Queue Tree
Structural and design patterns	Factory method Bridge Observer Visitor
Design process	Waterfall Evolution Agile
Software analysis	Bad smell Refactoring Test mutation
Project flow	Maturing Degradation Evolving

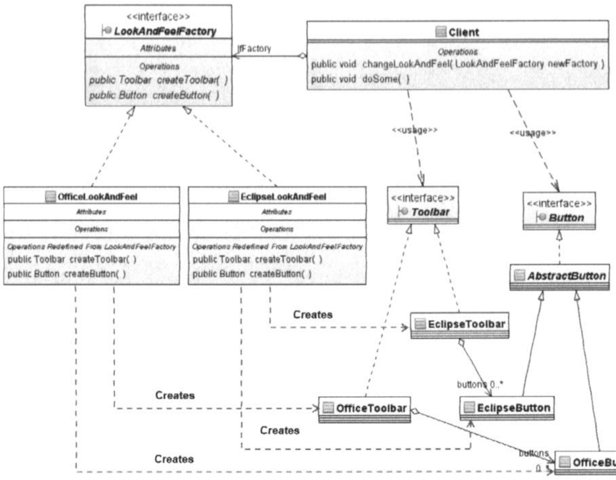

Figure 3. Abstract factory and "Look and Feel" Metaphor.

Indeed, "Abstract factory" could hardly be imagined in real world, however, in computer architectures, it provides a concrete (not abstract!) model of class structure representing the object creation subsystem of extensible and interchangeable sets of multiple object types that should function in a way that is independent on the specific types they are working with.

IV. Using Metaphors in the Programming Class: Study of Experience

Metaphors in education are helpful for many reasons. First, to link students' knowledge to newly introduced concepts and models [34] (experience-based metaphors). Second, to name new concepts in a way we can understand them by using similarity between the source and target domains (comparative metaphors). Finally, they can exploit the ontology mapping (ontological and interactive metaphors).

A. *Software Code Organization Metaphors*

Tomi and Mikko Difva introduced a number of metaphors used in the programming class for beginners that help to understand the different views on code structuring [35]. They defined nine metaphors: **machine**, **organism**, **brain**, **flux and transformation**, **culture**, **political system**, **psychic prison**, **instrument of domination**, and **carnival**. For example, the **Machine** metaphor is used to introduce a code as a sequence of commands, thus, referring an imperative programming paradigm; the **Organism** metaphor is used to introduce a code as a collection of interacting objects, thus, referring to object-oriented models, etc. Such metaphors may be very helpful in discussion on why the different views on system organization are required, and how a particular development process reflects a particular software development approach. Their suggestions are very interesting, but probably need further adjustments. For example, a sequential process probably needs another metaphor, not "Machine", since the contemporary understanding of this concept is more complex: Frank, Roerhrig and Pring define a machine as a **system of intelligence** combining software, hardware and user input. Such a machine is aimed not only at performing a series of control commands, but at improving on its own over time [36].

B. *Form and Contents as a Readability Metaphor*

In my programming class, I sometimes organize an exercise entitled *"The Form inside the Work"*, which is about discussing visual metaphors for introducing multi-faceted software concepts. In particular, we discuss how the code readability concept may be metaphorically expressed and analyzed using the famous artwork masterpieces (see the example of using Van Eyck's "Annunciation" for such an exercise in [37]).

As pointed out by Oosterman et al. in [38], artworks (compared to the photography or textual artifacts) provide less and often inconsistent visual information being an abstract, symbolic or allegorical (often metaphorical) interpretation of reality; therefore, their exact reading and annotation is a challenging problem. Nonetheless, the artworks are still readable, though such readings might naturally give various interpretations. Similarly to literary works, manner and matter are mutually dependent in visual works [39]: structures used by a creator in an artwork (the form) provide the ways making possible the reproduction of creator's intentions, metaphors and messages (the contents) in the beholder's mind. This reproduction implements the artist's program approximately, thus, giving space for many interpretations that can be considered as co-creation acts [40].

Let me illustrate this idea by using the iconic Rembrandt's chez-d-oeuvre "The Night Watch". Rembrandt Harmenszoon van Rijn's "The Night Watch" ("Militia Company of District II under the Command of Captain Frans Banninck Cocq", 1642,

Amsterdam Museum on permanent loan to the Rijksmuseum, Amsterdam, Netherlands) is an exceptional example of huge multi-layer composition portraying a military group. Full of metaphoric symbolism, this masterpiece provides an excellent case to learn "painting reading". Figure 4 graphically demonstrates a possible interpretation.

Figure 4. Possible reading links inside "The Night Watch" by Rembrandt.

As noted by Oliveira in [41], the canvas has visible multilayer structure. "Departing" from the two central characters (representing a cooperation between Protestant and Catholic parties), an eye may follow different ways, but the most likely directions are implicitly embedded inside the picture: a trained soldier close to the captain in the second layer (Figure 4, link 2) demonstrating his shooting skills by cutting the strip of a spear (link 3). The strip virtually points to the drummer (link 4) calling of arms. Close to the drummer, just behind the Catholic lieutenant, we see an aged volunteer and a distressed dog (links 4). From the "drummer's group" the eye moves to the left part of the composition (links 6) with an experienced soldier, making a compositional balance with the less experienced volunteer on the right side. Moving up to the back stage layer, a beholder's attention is caught by the figure of the man (link 7) holding the national flag (link 8). The flag colors call up the similar colors of the military baton held by the Catholic lieutenant (dashed line). In turn, the light-colored figure of the lieutenant is symbolically linked to the bright woman's figure (link 9), being one of the most discussed character of this painting work (Oliveira suggests she is a symbolic interpretation of the motherland).

Of course, the above presented rendition is not the only possible way to rediscover rich symbolism of Rembrandt's masterpiece, which has much more symbolic allusions and enigmatic elements (their detailed analysis is naturally out of scope of this paper). Nevertheless, it clearly shows that the possibilities are somehow "programmed" by the author, though the exact links are not represented. This consideration needs to go back to Aristotle's *Poetics*, where the cognitive meaningfulness of metaphor was emphasized: metaphors require an act of recognition and interpretation from the recipient [17].

In the case of software programs, it is commonly agreed that the code graphics, organization and legibility can be considered as essential aesthetic properties [42]. Meanwhile, the aesthetic values are connected to the quality properties, as it is nicely pointed out by Edmonds: *"if the resulting code is like spaghetti [. . .], it is not highly rated even if it performs its functions perfectly"* [43]. That is why the exercise described here can be considered as a small effort to compensate for relatively minor attention to the problems of understanding programming style and readability in software engineering curricula. Learning parallels between software engineering and art education give interesting insights to improving developers' culture (where, by the way, "culture" can be understood both literally and metaphorically).

In the research presented in [44], the authors describe the empirical code annotation study. They come to a conclusion, which is in partial contradiction to common practices in programming teaching: the source code comments (being an explicit way to explain the meaning of commented solution) affect the notion of code readability only moderately. Although the comments provide the very direct way of communication between the software writer and its reader, the code readability may be increased mostly because of improving the code organization and the used models (i. e., the code properties which do not provide a direct communication intent), and not because of increasing the number of detailed comments.

V. Conclusion

On the basis of analysis of linguistics and cognitive science original sources, this study examines the diversity and multifacetedness of the metaphor concept and its important role in technology and engineering areas. Since the particular focus of this research is on software education, we address a number of practical cases of using metaphors in the programming class by including a brief review of architectural software metaphors, metaphors of code organization, code readability and code aesthetics metaphors.

The above-mentioned cases do not exhaust the rich possibilities of using and exploring metaphors in class-time teaching scenarios. Hence, I expect that further extension of this study in cooperation with the experts from both liberal arts and technology domains might be of significant interest for teaching and research communities. Based on the wide contemporary discourse, we need more systematic analysis of metaphors used in software engineering, in order to classify the published approaches and to make them better visible and shareable among the members of academic community. Learning metaphors is connected to the development of soft skills, which are nowadays considered an important aspect of software engineering education. However, the evaluation whether the use of metaphors significantly improve the learning process still remains an open issue; the empirical analysis of benefits and potential results isn't trivial.

There are many important aspects, which, being out of scope of this paper, requires much attention. These aspects include software visualization and visual metaphors, metaphors of software architectures and design pattern metaphors, software code transformation and restructuring metaphors (such as code smells and refactoring), cooperation and mutual dependencies of different theories of metaphor in their application to technology domains, and transition of metaphors introduced in technology domains back to the non-technology areas.

ACKNOWLEDGEMENT

I would like to thank Professor John Blake from the Center for Language Research of the University of Aizu who kindly read the earlier versions of this study and made very valuable comments.

Many thanks to the anonymous IARIA reviewers for their very constructive suggestions on making more focused and compact concretization of basic ideas described in the initial submission.

The work is supported by the University of Aizu Research Funding.

REFERENCES

[1] M. Niemelä et al., "Human-driven design: a human-driven approach to the design of technology," in IFIP International Conference on Human Choice and Computers. Springer, 2014, pp. 78–91.

[2] G. C. Murphy, "Human-centric software engineering," in Proceedings of the FSE/SDP Workshop on Future of Software Engineering Research, ser. FoSER '10. New York, NY, USA: ACM, 2010, pp. 251–254.

[3] E. Pyshkin, "Liberal arts in a digitally transformed world: Revisiting a case of software development education," in Proceedings of the 13th Central & Eastern European Software Engineering Conference in Russia, ser. CEE-SECR '17. New York, NY, USA: ACM, 2017, pp. 23:1–23:7.

[4] S. Easterbrook, J. Singer, M.-A. Storey, and D. Damian, "Selecting empirical methods for software engineering research," in Guide to advanced empirical software engineering. Springer, 2008, pp. 285–311.

[5] D. Baldwin and A. Brady, "Guest editors' introduction: Computer science in the liberal arts," Trans. Comput. Educ., vol. 10, no. 1, Mar. 2010, pp. 1:1–1:5.

[6] V. Davidovski, "Exponential innovation through digital transformation," in Proceedings of the 3rd International Conference on Applications in Information Technology, ser. ICAIT'2018. New York, NY, USA: ACM, 2018, pp. 3–5.

[7] F. Frabetti, "Have the humanities always been digital? For an understanding of the digital humanities in the context of originary technicity," in Understanding digital humanities. Springer, 2012, pp. 161–171.

[8] J. H. Martin and D. Jurafsky, Speech and language processing: An introduction to natural language processing, computational linguistics, and speech recognition. Pearson/Prentice Hall Upper Saddle River, 2009.

[9] W. Shakespeare, As You Like It. Edward Blount and William and Isaac Jaggard, London, 1623.

[10] P. B. Shelley, The Cloud. Charles and James Ollier, London, 1820.

[11] P. Verlaine, L'heure exquise. Creuzevault, 1936.

[12] L. Cameron, "Operationalising 'metaphor' for applied linguistic research," Researching and applying metaphor, 1999, pp. 3–28.

[13] R. M. Weaver and R. S. Beal, A rhetoric and handbook. Holt, Rinehart and Winston, 1967.

[14] J. Carbonell, A. Sánchez-Esguevillas, and B. Carro, "The role of metaphors in the development of technologies. The case of the artificial intelligence," Futures, vol. 84, 2016, pp. 145–153.

[15] J. E. Kendall and K. E. Kendall, "Metaphors and their meaning for information systems development," European Journal of Information Systems, vol. 3, no. 1, 1994, pp. 37–47.

[16] M. Armisen-Marchetti, "Histoire des notions rhétoriques de métaphore et de comparaison, des origines à quintilien," Bulletin de l'association Guillaume Budé, vol. 49, no. 4, 1990, pp. 333–344.

[17] S. H. Butcher, The poetics of Aristotle edited with Critical Notes and a Translation. Macmillan, 1902.

[18] J. E. Mahon, "Getting your sources right," Researching and applying metaphor, 1999, pp. 69–80.

[19] M. S. Wood, "Aristotle and the question of metaphor," Ph.D. dissertation, Université d'Ottawa/University of Ottawa, 2015.

[20] A. Novokhatko, "The linguistic treatment of metaphor in quintilian," Pallas, vol. 103, 2017, pp. 311–318.

[21] H. E. Butler et al., The Institutio Oratoria of Quintilian. Harvard University Press, 1922, vol. 4.

[22] G. Lakoff and M. Johnson, "Metaphors we live by," Chicago, IL: University of, 1980.

[23] I. A. Richards and J. Constable, The philosophy of rhetoric. Oxford University Press New York, 1965, vol. 94.

[24] M. Black, "Models and metaphors: Studies in language and philosophy." 1962.

[25] G. Lakoff, "The contemporary theory of metaphor," 1993, retrieved: Sep, 2019. [Online]. Available: https://escholarship.org/uc/item/54g7j6zh

[26] G. J. Steen, "The contemporary theory of metaphor – now new and improved!" Review of Cognitive Linguistics. Published under the auspices of the Spanish Cognitive Linguistics Association, vol. 9, no. 1, 2011, pp. 26–64.

[27] T. R. Colburn and G. M. Shute, "Metaphor in computer science," Journal of Applied Logic, vol. 6, no. 4, 2008, pp. 526–533.

[28] G. Lazar, "Exploring metaphors in the classroom," Teaching English, 2006.

[29] R. H. Clarken, "Five metaphors for educators," 1997.

[30] J. Krupczak et al., "Defining engineering and technological literacy," Philosophical and Educational Perspectives in Engineering and Technological Literacy 3, 2012, p. 8.

[31] G. J. Johnson, "Of metaphor and difficulty of computer discourse," Communications of the ACM, vol. 37, no. 12, 1994, pp. 97–103.

[32] K. Smolander, "Four metaphors of architecture in software organizations: finding out the meaning of architecture in practice," in Proceedings International Symposium on Empirical Software Engineering. IEEE, 2002, pp. 211–221.

[33] N. Boyd, "Software metaphors," 2003, retrieved: Sep, 2019. [Online]. Available: https://pdfs.semanticscholar.org/deee/512ab8b7a3753fda248fe99780e3470e6881.pdf

[34] I. N. Umar and T. H. Hui, "Learning style, metaphor and pair programming: Do they influence performance?" Procedia-Social and Behavioral Sciences, vol. 46, 2012, pp. 5603–5609.

[35] T. Dufva and M. Dufva, "Metaphors of codestructuring and broadening the discussion on teaching children to code," Thinking Skills and Creativity, vol. 22, 2016, pp. 97–110.

[36] M. Frank, P. Roehrig, and B. Pring, What to do when machines do everything: How to get ahead in a world of AI, algorithms, bots, and Big Data. John Wiley & Sons, 2017.

[37] E. Pyshkin, "Designing human-centric applications: Transdisciplinary connections with examples," in Cybernetics (CYBCONF), 2017 3rd IEEE International Conference on. IEEE, 2017, pp. 1–6.

[38] J. Oosterman, J. Yang, A. Bozzon, L. Aroyo, and G.-J. Houben, "On the impact of knowledge extraction and aggregation on crowdsourced annotation of visual artworks," Computer Networks, vol. 90, 2015, pp. 133–149.

[39] J. G. McElroy, "Matter and manner in literary composition." Modern Language Notes, 1888, pp. 29–33.

[40] D. Likhachev, "Neskolko mysley o netochnosti iskusstva i stilisticheskikh napravleniyakh," in Philologica. Issledovaniya po yazyku i literature, 1973, pp. 394–401, (Some ideas about uncertainty of arts and stylistic trends – In Russian).

[41] P. M. Oliveira, "The Dutch company," retrieved: Aug, 2019. [Online]. Available: https://www.academia.edu/8579003/_Eng_The_Dutch_Company

[42] S. Gruner, "Problems for a philosophy of software engineering," Minds and Machines, vol. 21, no. 2, 2011, pp. 275–299.

[43] E. Edmonds, "The art of programming or programs as art," Frontiers in Artifical Intelligence and Applications, vol. 161, 2007, p. 119.

[44] R. P. Buse and W. R. Weimer, "Learning a metric for code readability," IEEE Transactions on Software Engineering, vol. 36, no. 4, 2009, pp. 546–558.

A Practical Approach to Teaching Requirements Engineering in Computing Programs

Anderson dos Santos Guerra
Department of Exact and Technological Sciences
Federal University of Amapá
Macapá, Amapá, Brazil, email:
and.guerra@outlook.com

Julio Cezar Costa Furtado
Department of Exact and Technological Sciences
Federal University of Amapá
Macapá, Amapá, Brazil, email:
furtado@unifap.br

Abstract—**This paper aims to contribute to the teaching of Requirements Engineering with a proposal of teaching approach that makes use of student-focused strategies for the development of skills expected by the industry. For this, the work presents the methodology used to create the approach through the identification of the skills expected by a requirement engineer. The results obtained through an experiment are presented, and it shows that the students were more motivated to research and to learn.**

Keywords-Software Engineering; Requirements Engineering; Software Engineering Education; Teaching Methodology.

I. Introduction

Based on study done by Menon et al. [11], although requirements engineering is an area of great importance and helps to avoid failure in systems development, its teaching still does not reach the expected performance of the industry. This occurs often because traditional teaching is used instead of dynamic teaching that prioritizes group activities and the use of creativity to solve problems.

Several researches [10][13][19] reports on the existing lack of qualified professionals to work in the software development industry, and one of the important factors that influences the quality of the professionals is education. This may indicate that the shortage of qualified professionals may be related to the required skills of a requirements engineer not being properly developed during education, making it difficult for the software industry to achieve the skilled workforce. A newly graduated professional will only effectively obtain the necessary knowledge when acting in the market. In this context, the objective of this work is to present a teaching approach to requirements engineering for computer courses that can prepare participants to understand how requirements engineering works in a real environment. For this, the Capability Maturity Model Integration for Development (CMMI-DEV) model [15] was used, which, among its good practices, offers recommendations for the Requirements Engineering process. Through the CMMI-DEV was created a list of skills expected by a professional in the area of requirements engineering, through this list were developed activities and dynamics used in the methodology for teaching Requirements Engineering.

In addition to this introduction, the article is structured as follows: Section 2 presents a review of the definitions of software engineering, requirements engineering and the education landscape of these two items; Section 3 talks about the teaching approach created, from the methodology used to elaborate to the activities used; Section 4 shows the survey created and presented to the students at the end of the course; in Section 5 the analysis of the answers obtained in the survey is made; Section 6 concludes the article.

II. Bibliographic Review

This session discusses a literature review of the concepts used to create the teaching approach, starting with Requirements Engineering and followed by Software Engineering Education.

A. *Requirements Engineering*

The area of Requirements Engineering has a great importance in the development of software because it offers a series of concepts that formalize an adequate elicitation and validation of requirements, ensuring that a certain system can adequately satisfy the needs of the client, reducing so the margin for errors, as well as costs that could be unnecessary and saving time [16].

One of the problems encountered in relation to requirements engineering is the communication barrier between developers and clients [18]. It is necessary to move away from traditional teaching and use more didactic means for teaching requirements engineering, such as Role Playing, which improve the use of communication in projects. The ACM / IEEE [1] states that the curriculum in the area of Software Engineering requires that the classroom training goes beyond the expository.

Since communication between stakeholder and developers may be flawed by several factors, such as the very difference of technical knowledge between the two parties, another problem that occurs is the flaw in the requirements documentation process, research [11] shows that this problem is caused by the lack of preparation of the professionals in the moment of action in activities involving the engineering of requirements.

B. *Software Engineering Education*

In order to find an opinion of professionals in Software Engineering in relation to an area that is approached in the courses of Computer Science, a research was made and there is a lack of attention to some topics of Software Engineering during a class [19], and these topics are taught insufficiently, highlighting the following: project management, software quality assurance, requirements management, and requirements development.

Professionals in the field learn more about these topics at work than in the period of academic training [9]. Regarding the teaching strategy, the curriculum in the area of Software Engineering [1] emphasizes that there is a need to go beyond the expository classroom format. It is important to consider the variation of teaching and learning techniques.

The quality of the software engineering professionals is directly related to the quality of the education they have had, although there are other factors that may contribute to this [13]. The most common approaches to teaching software engineering include lectures, lab classes, with a greater focus on the teacher, as shown in the Table 1 [14].

TABLE I. COMPARISON BETWEEN TEACHER-FOCUSED CLASSES AND STUDENT-FOCUSED CLASSES

Characteristics	Teacher-focused	Student-focused
Teacher's role	Main provider of information; Specialist; Academic performance evaluator.	Facilitator; provides information to help in understanding the information.
Learning climate	Individualistic.	Collective; Focus on group cohesion.
Guidance	Based on the teacher's experience and knowledge.	Based on students' experience and knowledge.
Study program	Defined by the teacher.	Negotiated between teacher and students.
Teaching Objective	Defined by the teacher; default result.	Defined by the students; Different results for each student.
Knowledge Acquisition	Focus on acquisition; Focus on memorization.	Focus on the use and absorption of knowledge focusing on real problems.
Teaching methods	Didactic, Great participation of the teacher.	Methods involving student participation (dynamic techniques)
Focus on education	Educação individual.	Collective education
Evaluation	Performed by Teacher, Traditional Use of Tests and Grades	Students are also responsible for assessing

Research done in [14] states that there are teacher-centered approaches to teaching and student-centered approaches, each with its own peculiarities. The more expository the class, the greater its tendency to be focused on the teacher. However, the more dynamism and practicality in the class, the greater the focus on the student

III. An Approach to Teaching Requirements Engineering

This session explains how the teaching approach was created, from defining the methodology that was used to the practices that were used throughout the approach.

A. *Methodology*

In order to define the content to be taught by the approach, it was necessary to first identify which competences are expected by a professional working in the area, so that the teaching approach can focus on the acquisition and improvement of these skills by participating students. The CMMI-DEV model was used as a reference, since its processes are used as a basis in several areas [15].

The CMMI-DEV model contains a set of guides that covers content for the development of products and services. CMMI for Development includes practices that encompass process management, project management, systems engineering, hardware engineering, software engineering, and other processes used to assist in the development and maintenance of products [15].

A total of 10 competencies were identified for a professional to be able to act in the area of ER in a manner satisfactory to the industry. In CMMI-DEV, Requirements Engineering is seen in the Requirements Development process (in level 3 of the model) and in the Requirements Management area (in level 2 of the model), in Table 2 it is possible to observe the skills and abilities.

TABLE II. EXPECTED SKILLS OF A REQUIREMENT ENGINEERING PROFESSIONAL, BASED ON CMMI-DEV

Skills	CMMI-DEV
Elicit stakeholder needs and expectations for all phases of the product life cycle	RD SG 1 SP 1.1
Turn stakeholder needs and expectations into customer requirements	RD SG 1 SP 1.2
Establish and maintain product requirements, which are based on customer requirements.	RD SG 2 SP 2.1
Identify interface requirements	RD SG 2 SP 2.3
Establish and maintain a definition of required features and quality attributes.	RD SG 3 SP 3.2
Analyze requirements to ensure they are necessary and sufficient	RD SG 3 SP 3.3
Validate requirements to ensure that the resulting product will perform as intended in the end user environment	RD SG 3 SP 3.5
Develop understanding of requirements through who provides the requirement	REQM SP 1.1
Get commitment to requirements from project participants	REQM SP 1.2
Manage changes in requirements throughout the project	REQM SP 1.3
Maintain bidirectional tracking on requirements	REQM SP 1.4
Ensure project plans stay in line with requirements	REQM SP 1.5

The study from [13] was used as a basis for choosing the methods and resources used in this methodology, with the aim of developing the joint adoption of these items, through an iterative cycle that attends the different learning profiles. The teaching model created by Portela [13] is supported by the learning cycle of Kolb [8] and the iterative teaching methodology proposed by Gary et al. [4]. Based on this, the model is aligned primarily in the reading of articles and reports of experiences, practical case discussions, use of simulators and games, besides the execution of projects and reflection by the student about the content that was learned and the exercises that were performed. The course was designed to be run over a semester as an optional topic in the Computer Science course for students who had already taken the basic discipline of Software Engineering, so that they already had the necessary basics. The discipline had a workload of 60h, used by means of 4h weekly.

Table 3 lists the planning of the discipline, where it is possible to observe: the programmatic content, attending the competences planned for the discipline; the teaching strategy, established according to the level of learning that has been estimated for the topic and the expected outcomes; the expected results, what the student can do after the study of the unit; and the level of learning, using a terminology based on Bloom's [20] taxonomy, which consists of knowledge, understanding and application, in which: Knowing means remembering the material that was previously taught; Understanding refers to understanding the information and meaning of the material that has been taught; and Apply, indicates knowing how to use the material learned in new situations.

The first two topics in the discipline agenda, introduction to requirements engineering and requirements discovery, are based primarily on the CMMI-DEV Requirements Development process, while the third topic is mainly based on CMMI-DEV Requirements Management process.

TABLE III. DISCIPLINE AGENDA

Content	Teaching Strategy	Expected results
1. Introduction to Requirements Engineering		
1.1. Course Presentation	Card dynamics for product creation.	The student should be aware of the yearnings, stress and difficulty of project execution when requirements are incorrectly collected.
1.2. The Importance of Requirements Engineering	Reading and class discussion of the support material. Game: Quantum Software	The student should be able to know the importance of the Requirements Engineer for software product quality.
1.3. The Requirements Engineering Process	Reading and class discussion of the support material. Game: A Ilha dos Requisitos	The student should know the steps, roles and activities involved in the requirements engineering process.
2. Requirements Discovery		
2.1. Activities involved	Reading and class discussion of the support material. Requirements Discovery Dynamics	The student should be able to understand the relationships between the activities developed in the requirements discovery.
2.2. Main difficulties	Reading and class discussion of the support material. Seminar on the difficulties encountered in the previous dynamics	The student must understand the main difficulties of requirements discovery and be able to develop ways to mitigate these problems.
2.3. Techniques	Reading and class discussion of the support material. GameMaker Dynamics	The student should be able to understand the various requirements discovery techniques.
3. Specification and Documentation		
3.1. Requirement Types	Reading and class discussion of the support material.	The student must know and identify the types of requirements.
3.2. Ways to document requirements	Reading and class discussion of the support material. GameMaker Dynamics Continuation	The student should be able to understand the various requirements documentation techniques.
4. Final project		
4.1. Practical project	Customer Interview Dynamics	The student must be able to apply the knowledge gained throughout the course and perform the entire requirements engineering process (with teacher supervision)

B. Practices Used

1) Card Dynamics: The dynamics of the cards for product creation are as follows: the class is divided into groups, each group must create the same product based on the requirements requested by the client (the teacher). Throughout the class the client adds or removes a requirement, forcing the groups to make the necessary adjustments to the prototype. In this way, it is possible to provide participants with an initial view of the volatility of the requirements, of the difficulties caused by poor collection of these requirements and the consequences of this throughout a project. The dynamics of the cards were designed to be executed in 45 minutes, with the level of learning classified in knowing;

2) Game: Software Quantum: Quantum Software [7] is a game created to run on the web and simulates the requirements engineering process. It was created with the intention of offering a model that is simple and easy to learn in a few minutes, but at the same time has the ability to convey the main ideas contained in Requirements Engineering. The game does not necessarily cover all the dynamic aspects of software projects, but focuses on the tension between developing a system correctly and developing the right system for the customer [7]. The dynamics with the use of Quantum Software was designed to be executed in 45 minutes, with the level of learning classified in knowing.

3) Game: Ilha dos Requisitos: The game Ilha dos Requisitos [17] has a story in which the protagonist suffers an accident on a trip and ends up on an unknown island. The main objective of the game is to help the protagonist escape from the island along with members of the Nerds tribe before the island is destroyed by a volcano. Throughout the game are presented seven challenges that help the player to better understand the concepts and the requirements engineering process. Throughout the challenges the player can receive immediate feedback of his actions as tips to remember concepts that are related to requirements engineering and results that were obtained at the end of each challenge. A feature of the game is that it seeks to engage the participant in a situation analogous to situations that could be solved through practices related to Requirements Engineering. The challenges are Requirements Engineering Process: the player must order the phases of the requirements engineering process; Validation of requirements: it is necessary to take the requirements to the client so that they are validated before the actual execution of the project; Role of the requirements analyst: the player must correctly identify the skills of a requirements analyst; Analysis of the problem: it is necessary to distinguish between the problems and their possible solutions; Requirements specification: the player must perform the classification of requirements between functional or non-functional; Classification of requirements: it is necessary to classify the requirements presented as functional or non-functional; Requirements Management: The player must order the process of changing the listed requirements and identify the activities that are part of the requirements management. The dynamics with the Game Ilha dos Requisitos was designed to be executed in 30 minutes, with the level of learning classified in knowing.

4) GameMaker Dynamics: GameMaker is a proprietary tool used for game development. The use of GameMaker is based on the teaching of Software Engineering through Game Design [6], which has a fun factor that can engage students to participate more actively in teaching. To perform the activity, the students were instructed so that the classroom teacher is the client and the students would be part of a development team, the client requested requirements to be implemented in the product (the game that was being created in the GameMaker tool) , throughout the activity the participants were able to experiment with a collection of requirements and its implementation in the product under development, as well as to experience the difficulties caused by communication failures and consequently in the collection of requirements. The dynamics with the use of GameMaker was designed to be executed in two 50-minute classes, with the level of learning ranked in understanding

5) Practical project: In the Practical Project, the participants created "companies" that were supposed to interview an external customer to create a product, with weekly meetings and prototype presentations to verify that the project was in line with the client's needs. the requirements engineering process and all the good practices that have been learned throughout the course. The client was the coordinating secretary of the Computer Science course where the main problem that the groups needed to solve was the systematization of the selective process of an extension project. At the end of the project, the groups presented the final software for the client, developed from the requirements, which made the choice of what best served their needs and was put to use by the extension project. The practical project was planned to run over four weeks, with the apprenticeship level.

IV. RESULTS

For the evaluation of the teaching methodology it was used a survey, the target population is characterized by students of computer courses that have subjects related to Software Engineering, the specific group attends the fourth semester of Computer Science in a public institution of teaching. Regarding the design of data collection, it can be considered crosscutting, since the participants inform data related to their past experiences.

The survey used quantitative and qualitative data about the students who participated in the experiment, regarding their individual information and preferences. Thus, for the data collection, a questionnaire was used consisting of objective and subjective questions.

Responses were received from 22 students, all in the undergraduate degree in Computer Science at the Federal University of Amapá, the participants were in the fourth semester of the course and already had a base due to the discipline of Software Engineering that had previously been studied.

A. *The Survey Questions*

The study aims to answer two research questions:

- **Research Question 1 (RQ1):** Was a teaching approach used during the course appropriate to the relevance of content and teaching methods?
- **Research Question 2 (RQ2):** What are the strengths and weaknesses of the teaching approach used?

Based on the references cited in the previous section, the survey questions were defined. Table 4 shows the questions created for the participants of the experiment in order to assess whether the teaching approach used during the course was adequate in relation to the relevance of the content and teaching methods.

TABLE IV. RESEARCH QUESTION 1

Questions	Answer Options
RQ1.1. The content covered by the course was sufficient to understand how Requirements Engineering works in an organization.	Answer performed by the likert scale: • Strongly disagree • Partially Disagree • Neutral • Partially agree • Totally agree
RQ1.2. The approach chosen for the discipline had a good integration of theory and practice.	
RQ1.3. The dynamics / practices were performed in a timely manner.	
RQ1.4. The dynamics / practices had an appropriate level of complexity.	
RQ1.5. The dynamics / practices developed did not restrict students' creativity to think about their own solutions.	
RQ1.6. The dynamics / practices	

made the learning process fun and challenging	
RQ1.7. Throughout the course, the teaching approach kept me motivated to learn	
Formulation: Frequency of distribution of each group variable RQ1	

V. RESULT AND ANALYSIS

In this section, there will be presented the data obtained in the survey that was answered by the academic participants of the discipline proposal.

Regarding the adequacy of the approach to software engineering education (RQ1), relative to RQ1.1 (The content covered by the discipline was sufficient to understand how Requirements Engineering works in an organization), participants responded with a 63.7% approval rate. As to the verification if the approach used in the discipline had a good integration of theory with practice (RQ1.2), 86.3% of the students who participated in the approach responded positively. Taking into account RQ1.3 (The dynamics / practices were carried out in a timely manner), the result was a positive response of 77.3%.

As for RQ1.4 (Dynamics / practices had an adequate level of complexity), 77.3% of respondents gave a positive answer to the question. Regarding RQ1.5 (The dynamics / practices developed did not restrict the students' creativity to think about their own solutions), the question had 63.7% positive answers. Considering RQ1.6 (The dynamics / practices made the learning process fun and challenging), the question is 86.4% approved. Based on RQ1.7 (Throughout the course, the teaching approach kept me motivated to learn), the question had a total of 81.9% positivity

A. *About teaching approaches*

In terms of teaching, 77.3% of respondents said they feel motivated to learn more about Software Engineering content. Regarding the teaching approach, 81.9% of the participants state in full or in part that they felt motivated to learn more about requirements engineering due to the dynamics used in class, it is possible to observe the response graph in Figure 1.

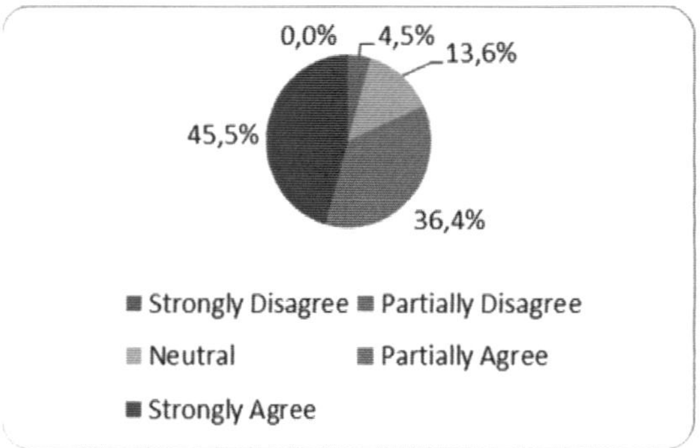

Figure 1. I am motivated to learn more about requirements engineering

This shows that the dynamics adopted throughout the course motivate students to learn more about the content. Added to this, another important fact is that 86.4% of students fully or partially agree that the dynamics / practices have made the learning process fun and challenging, as shown in Figure 2 with the response data.

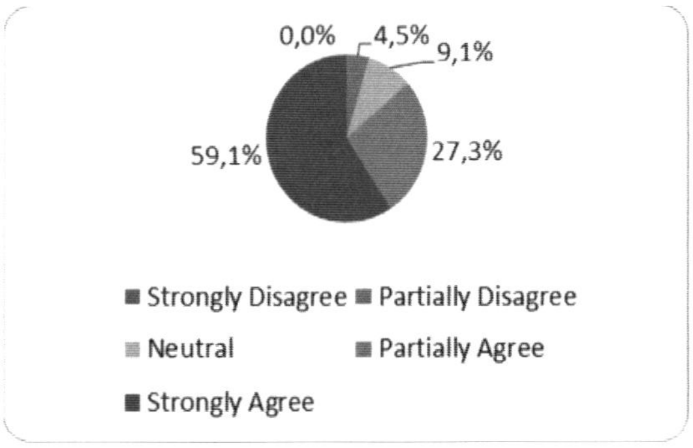

Figure 2. The dynamics / practices made the learning process fun and challenging

From these results, it was possible to show that students prefer more practical teaching approaches that motivate them to practice the content of software engineering, besides the incentive through practices, it is also noticed that through this approach the students can fix a concepts in this area, in addition to fostering learning and participation, as seen in the results of teaching strategies highlighted by [3][13][14]. The dynamics along with the hands-on activities reflect the interest of students who are more motivated to learn more about the subject. This reveals that the Requirements Engineering discipline is much more understood from practical situations than from the conventional teaching mode with only theoretical classes.

Still analyzing the data concerning the teaching approach chosen for the course, it is possible to observe in Figure 3 that 86.3% of the participants totally or partially agreed that the approach chosen for the course had a good integration of theory and practice. This further corroborates how more practical approaches are most effective in the students' learning process in the software engineering discipline.

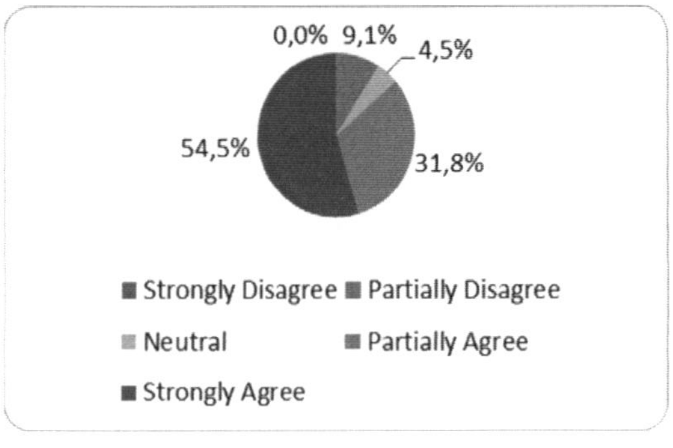

Figure 3. The approach chosen for the discipline had a good integration of theory and practice.

Turning to the analysis of the data obtained through the survey, it is noteworthy that 78.3% of the course participants totally or partially agree that the content taught in the course was relevant, the answer graph can be seen in Figure 4. This is explained by the fact that students, through requirements engineering dynamics and practices, have really understood the real relevance of content. Because they had to work in a reality-simulating environment, they were able to see how crucial this phase is and what it has on the entire development of software, with students better understanding requirements engineering concepts in a number of ways. practical classes significantly lower than theoretical classes, a result similar to that obtained by [3][13], in the teaching strategy that involves the use of recreational activities and games in general.

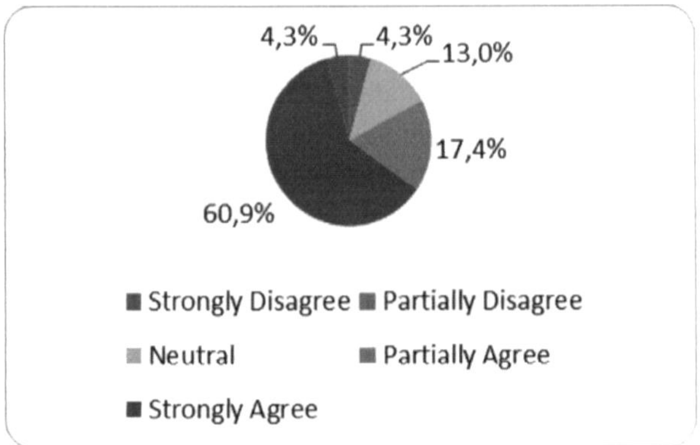

Figure 4. The content taught in the course was relevant.

From this deeper understanding of the content, participants were more aware of how requirements engineering is important in an organizational setting. This was evident when participants were asked if the content covered by the course was sufficient to understand how Requirements Engineering works in an organization, and the answer was that 63.7% of participants fully or partially agreed with this statement while only a total of 9 % disagree with the statement in some way, the remaining 27.3% goes to those who were neutral about the statement, as shown in Figure 5, showing that as much as the experiment used practices that resembled the operation of software engineering In one organization, a considerable number of participants could not confirm this similarity as they did not have the experience of working in the area. Although not such a high percentage, it is still a satisfactory percentage given that understanding how an organizational environment works is not a simple task and also takes some time.

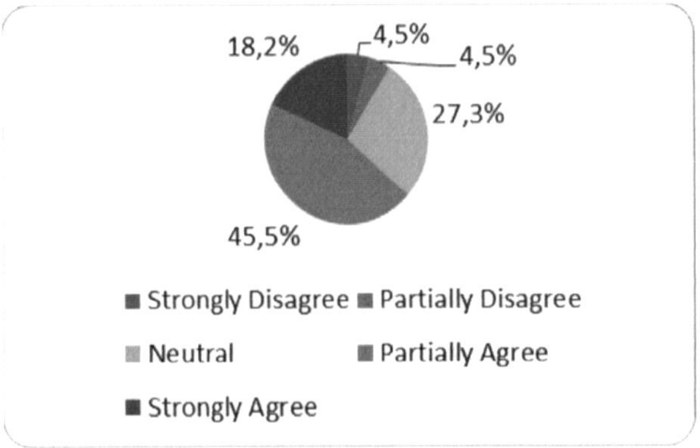

Figure 5. The content covered by the course was sufficient to understand how Requirements Engineering works in an organization.

Figure 6 demonstrates participants' satisfaction by comparing two statements: (i) I am motivated to learn more about requirements engineering; (ii) the dynamics / practices have made the learning process fun and challenging. It can be seen that most students considered the activities appropriate and were motivated to delve deeper into the requirements engineering area.

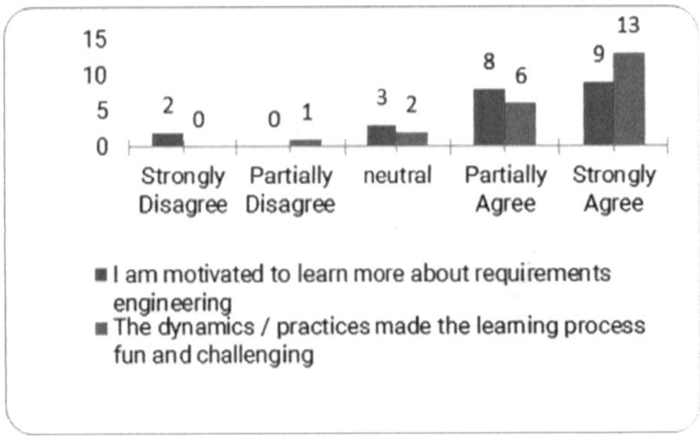

Figure 6. Relationship between learning motivation and learning process to be fun

The main finding with regard to the negative points was not about the approach itself, but about the short time given to the practical activities and theory, given that the experiment lasted one semester. When asked if the dynamics / practices were performed in a timely manner, 77.3% agreed totally or partially with this finding. Even with the short course period being short, the pass rate is still quite satisfactory. Figure 7 shows the response data.

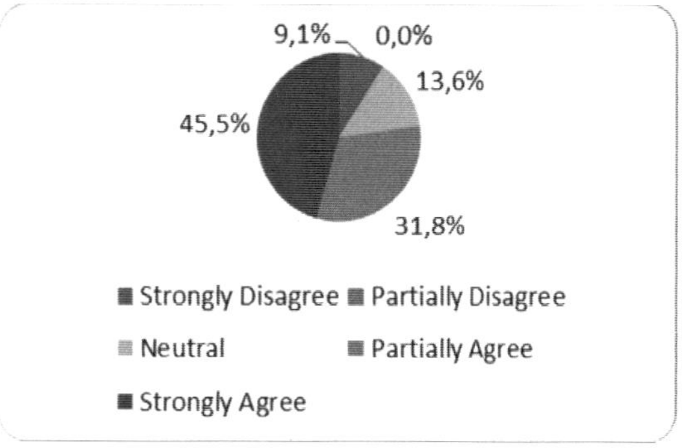

Figure 7. The dynamics / practices were performed in a timely manner.

Another point analyzed by the survey regarding the teaching approach shows us that 77.3% of the participants totally or partially agreed that the dynamics / practices had an adequate level of complexity, this is an important factor, since most students already had had some contact with the subject, mainly through the software engineering discipline, in Figure 8 it is possible to observe the answers given by the students.

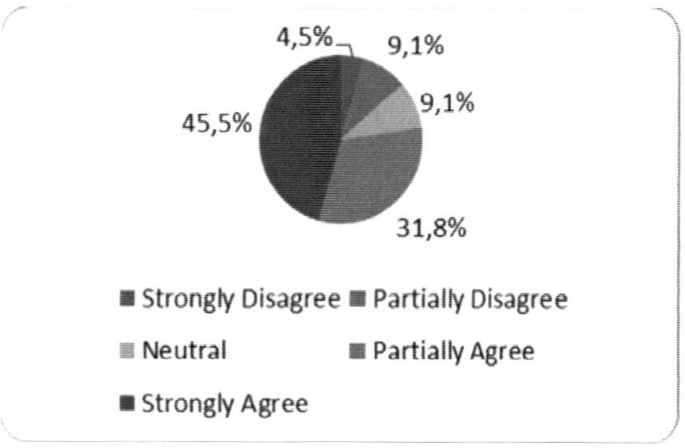

Figure 8. The dynamics / practices had an appropriate level of complexity.

Based on the survey, 63.7% of the participants of this experiment totally or partially agreed that the dynamics / practices developed did not restrict students' creativity to think about their own solutions, which was another very positive point of the approach adopted, as participants could make use of their own ideas for solving some data problems, data relating to this issue can be viewed in Figure 9.

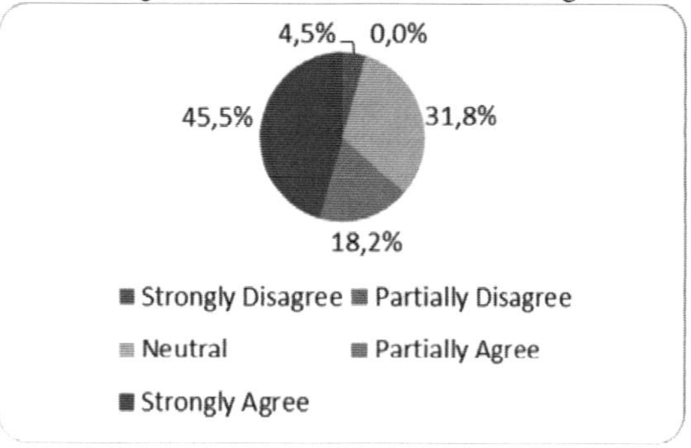

Figure 9. The dynamics / practices developed did not restrict students' creativity to think about their own solutions.

B. *About teaching approaches*

One of the main things about conducting an experiment is knowing how valid its results are. The priority order of the validation types is performed through the objectives that the experiment has. The order of importance of validity applied is: internal, external, construction and conclusion.

1) Internal Validity: Internal validity is used to define whether the relationship between the treatment itself and the result obtained is causal rather than the result of a factor that has not been measured or cannot be controlled. In this experiment, some threats to internal validity can be described as the effect of maturation or even instrumentation. Regarding maturation, it may have occurred through studies and learning activities that were not planned in the scope of the experiment, through the participant's own initiative to search for more content. To alleviate this factor, the students were instructed not to look for questions that were not within the planned activities for the experiment. However there is no way to confirm that the instructions have been properly followed.

2) External Validity: Through external evaluation, conditions are defined that limit the ability to generalize the results obtained to other populations in other contexts. The context of the experiment was academic, so the overall results should be limited by the academic context. Another limiting factor in this regard is that the experiment was conducted with a small sample of participants and, to date, has not been replicated in other populations, groups or universities. The teaching approach used tried to insert the student into the practical application of the concepts learned, however the practical activities were based on simplified real scenarios, so there is no guarantee that the skills obtained will be reflected in a real development environment.

3) Construction Validity: Construction validity considers the relationship between theory and observation, that is, it verifies whether the treatment reflects the cause satisfactorily and the result reflects the effect satisfactorily. During the evaluation of the construction validity, human factors and aspects relevant to the design of the experiment should be highlighted. Thus, it is not possible to state that the participants learned to use this new knowledge in a different context from the one used in the experiment.

4) Validity of Completion: The validity of completion is the ability to reach a correct conclusion about the relationship between treatment and the outcome of the experiment. During the evaluation of this quality it is necessary to take into account concepts such as: the reliability of the measurements; the reliability of the treatment implementation and the choice of the statistical test. Even when grouping all the data, the sample remains small, making it impossible to demonstrate any valid statistical relationship.

VI. Conclusion

This research aimed to analyze the strengths of a student-centered approach to teaching Requirements Engineering. Through a list of competencies obtained using the CMMI-DEV, an approach was created that seeks to achieve the competencies listed satisfactorily, making use of practical activities, dynamics, games and projects, so that at the end of the discipline, the student get a sense of how the requirements engineering process works in an organization.

According to the data obtained by the survey, it was shown that the approach taken in the short course tends to be effective. In addition to the theory, practical aspects of the discipline were approached, allowing the participants a great understanding and a better contact with the Requirements Engineering area. There is an interest of the students in practical and dynamic activities [3][13]. This behavior can also be verified through the results of the survey applied after the short course, because besides the interactions, the participants also felt motivated to study more the topics covered.

Although the results of the approach are significant, further research is needed to assess the actual learning gain that has been achieved by the proposal compared to other models used for teaching Requirements Engineering.

References

[1] ACM/IEEE, Computer Science Curricula 2013: Curriculum Guidelines for Undergraduate Degree Programs in Computer Science, New York, EUA, 2013.

[2] J. Carver, L. Jaccheri, S. Morasca, and Shull, F. "Issues in Using Students in Empirical Studies in Software Engineering Education", Proceedings of the 9th Interna-tional Software Metrics Symposium, IEEE, 2003.

[3] J. C. Furtado and S. R. B. Oliveira, Evaluating Students' Perception of their Learn-ing in a Student-Centered Software Engineering Course – A Experimental Study, In: 13th International Conference on Software Technologies, Porto, Portugal, 2018.

[4] K. Gary, T. Lindquist, S. Bansal, and A. Ghazarian, "A Project Spine for Software Engineering Curricular Design", Proceedings of 26th Conference on Software Engineering Education and Training, 2013.

[5] C. Ghezzi and D. Mandrioli, "The challenges of Software Engineering Education", Proceedings of the 27th international conference on Software engineering, St. Louis, MO, USA, pages 637-638, May, 2005.

[6] K. Claypool and M. Claypool., "Teaching software engineering through game design", In Proceedings of the 10th annual SIGCSE conference on Innovation and technology in computer science education (ITiCSE '05). ACM, New York, NY, USA, 123-127, 2005.

[7] E. Knauss, K. Schneider, and K. Stapel, "A Game for Taking Requirements Engineer-ing More Seriously". In Proceedings of the 2008 Third International Workshop on Multimedia and Enjoyable Requirements Engineering - Beyond Mere Descriptions and with More Fun and Games (MERE '08). IEEE Computer Society, Washington, DC, USA, 22-26, 2008.

[8] D. Kolb. "Experiential Learning: Experience as the Source of Learning and De-velopment", NJ: Prendice-Hall, 1984

[9] T. C. Lethbridge, "What Knowledge is Important to a Software Professional", Journal IEEE Computer Society Press Los Alamitos, CA, USA, pages 44-50, Volume 33 Issue 5, May, 2000.

[10] T. C. Lethbridge, J. Diaz-Herrera, R. Leblanc, and J. Thompson, "Improving software practice through education: Challenges and future trends", Proceedings of the Conference Future of Software Engineering, Minneapolis, 2007.

[11] R. N. Menon, R. B. Ahmad, and S. S. Salim, "Problems in requirement Engineering education: a survey", Proceedings of the 8th International Conference on Frontiers of Information Technology, 2010.

[12] P. Naur, B. Randel, "Software Engineering: Report of a Conference Sponsored by the NATO Science Committee, Garmisch, Germany, 7-11 Oct, 1968, Brussels, Scientific Affairs Division, NATO", 1969.

[13] C. Portela, "Um modelo iterativo para o ensino de engenharia de software baseado em abordagens focadas no aluno e práticas de capacitação da indústria", Centro de Informática, Universidade Federal de Pernambuco, Recife, 2017.

[14] R. Prikladnicki, A. Albuquerque, C. G. Wangenheim, and R. Cabral, "Ensino de Engenharia de Software: Desafios, Estratégias de Ensino e Lições Aprendidas", 2009.

[15] SEI, CMMI® for Development, version 1.3, CMU/SEI-2010-TR-033 ESC-TR-2010-033. Software Engineering Institute-SEI, Carnegie Mellon University: 561, 2010.

[16] I. Sommerville, Engenharia de Software, 9ª ed., Pearson Education do Brasil, 2011.

[17] M. Thiry, A. Zoucas, and R. Gonçalves, "Promovendo a Aprendizagem de Engenharia de Requisitos de Software Através de um Jogo Educativo". Simpósio Brasileiro de Informática na Educação, Brasil, 2010.

[18] D. Zowgui and S. Paryanim, "Teaching requirements engineering through role playing: lessons learnt", Proceedings. 11th IEEE International Requirements Engineering Conference, Monterey Bay, CA, USA, 2003.

[19] C. G. Wangenheim and D. A. Silva, "Qual conhecimento de engenharia de software é importante para um profissional de software?", 2009, Fórum de Educação em Engenharia de Software, Fortaleza.

[20] B. S. Bloom, Taxonomy of Educational Objectives: The Classification of Educational Goals, Handbook I, Cognitive Domain: Longmans, 1956.

Economic Impact of Cloud Computing in the Health System: A Systematic Mapping

Jonathan Santos[1] and Felipe Ferraz[1 2]

[1]*CESAR School,* [2]*CESAR - Recife Center for Advanced Studies and Systems*
Recife, Brazil

{jcas,fsf}@cesar.school, fsf@cesar.org.br

***Abstract*- Cloud computing has become one of the most widely used technologies today, bringing positive impacts to its adopters and changing the way many areas work, impacting their solutions in the market. The healthcare system can enjoy the same benefits brought by the adoption of this technology, improving its infrastructure, reducing its costs tremendously and speeding up processes. With that in mind, what are the economic impacts of adopting cloud computing on healthcare environments? This paper conducts a systematic mapping in order to depict the economic and other impacts of cloud computing in the healthcare system and solutions, analyzing aspects that go beyond the technological issues.**

Keywords* - *Cloud computing; economic impacts; health; challenges.

I. INTRODUCTION

Cloud computing is one of the most impactful technologies of recent times. Not surprisingly, large companies are embracing this infrastructure paradigm with significant economic gains. Highly discussed technologies such as blockchain, conversational platforms, and artificial intelligence have in common the use or need for cloud computing [1].

According to the National Institute of Standards and Technology (NIST), Cloud computing is a model for enabling ubiquitous, convenient, on-demand network access to a shared pool of configurable computing resources that can be rapidly provisioned and released with minimal management effort or service provider interaction. Comparing with the traditional Information Technology (IT) model, cloud computing presents a fundamental change in the way IT services are developed, deployed, maintained and paid for.

As global population increases, life expectancy rises, and living standards improve, causes of death across the world are changing [2]. Heart disease and cancer are the leading causes of death. The health system, like any other, needs continuous and systematic innovation to deliver high quality, safe and cost-effective services. A well-adopted cloud gives a lot of advantages to the organization such as easy and pervasive access to data and applications, increases cost-effectiveness [3].

The purpose of this article is to study the economic impacts of the use of cloud computing in the health area. This work is organized as follows: first, in Section 2, basic concepts related to cloud computing and the methodology used will be presented together with the objectives of the study. Then, in Section 3 the methods, processes, and protocols applied in the elaboration of systematic mapping will be described. Finally, in Section 4, we will present the results obtained, conclusions and plans for future work.

II. APPLIED PROTOCOL

Based on the guidelines for developing systematic software engineering reviews in software engineering described by Kitchenham [4], a new methodology for revision was created. The purpose of this review is to identify primary studies that focus on the use and benefits of cloud computing adoption based on the following question:

- *What is the economic impact on cloud computing adoption in health/healthcare environments?*

This main question intends to focus not only on the technological impacts of using cloud computing, but also to conduct research on related, but not limited, topics such as economics, time-saving, improved treatment, and other non-technological factors. However, it is expected that, during the analysis features, such as security, privacy, complexity, and others, appear as factors that may limit the adoption and use of cloud computing.

From this central question, secondary questions were created to help in understanding and comprehension of the problem:

1. What areas of health can benefit from using Cloud Computing?

2. What is the economic impact of Cloud Computing on disease control and treatment?
3. What are the main challenges and opportunities for using cloud computing in health environments?

A. Inclusion and Exclusion Criteria

For this review, we considered studies that depict information and data related to cloud computing adoption, usage, positive and negative impacts. This review limited the examined studies to the ones published starting from year 2015.

Were also excluded:

- Studies whose focus was only on technical aspects;
- Studies not published in the English language;
- Studies that were unavailable online;
- Studies not based on research and that are not full papers;
- Call for works, prefaces, conference annals, handouts, summaries, panels, interviews, and news reports.

B. Search Strategies

The databases considered in the study is on the list below:

- ACM Digital Library;
- IEEE Xplore;
- Science Direct;

Combinations of terms were created to guarantee that relevant information would not be excluded when querying different search engines and databases. As a result, four search strings were created:

1. (Cloud Computing) AND (Economic OR Economy OR Business OR Benefits) AND (Health);
2. 2. (Cloud Computing) AND (Adoption OR Migration) AND (Health);
3. (Cloud Computing) AND (Challenges OR Opportunities) AND (Health);

In the process of extracting information from the databases, the search strings were used separately on each database. The searches were performed restricting the years between 2015 and 2019. The results of each search were grouped together according to the database and were, later, examined closer in order to identify duplicity.

C. Studies Selection Process

This section describes the selection process from the beginning: from an initial search using the Search Strategies described below to the identification of primary studies. In the first step, the studies that were obtained from the databases were gathered and added to a management citation tool, the authors' choose Mendeley. Next, once the initial studies were selected, the titles of all works selected were analyzed to determine its relevance in this systematic review. In this stage, an initial filter is conducted removing works that did not present relevant topics for this research. When the works' titles were vague or unclear, they were put aside to be analyzed in the next step. Since the main intention was to analyze aspects not specifically related to technology, works that mentioned security or big data, and others, were selected for further analysis during the abstract reading. At the end of this stage, 5138 citations were excluded, thus remaining 142 items for further analysis.

In the third step, all abstracts of the Works found in the previous one were assessed. Once more, many were eliminated from the study due to them not conforming to the scope of cloud computing and topics not related only to technologies. One of the difficulties found in this step was related to the quality of the abstract, a portion of the abstract was not clear about the main topic addressed by the work. When that happened, the authors did a deeper analysis reading introduction and conclusion looking for topics and sentences related to this research. Because of this phase, 103 studies were excluded, thus remaining 39 to be analyzed more closely. Table 1 presents the amount of studies filtered in each step
of the selection process.

TABLE I. AMOUNT OF STUDIES FILTERED IN THE SELECTION PROCESS

	ACM Digital Library	IEEE Explore	Science Direct	Total
Initial	593	1656	3031	5280
Title	39	65	38	142
Abstract	8	20	11	39

For qualitative and quantitative assessment, seven questions were used to assist in quality assessment. The questions are:

1. Does the study examine impacts and/or economic aspects related to cloud computing adoption in healthy environments?
2. Does the study present aspects related to solutions that use cloud computing?

3. Does the study present aspects related to challenges or opportunities in health?
4. Is the study based on research - not merely on specialist's opinions?
5. Is the context of the study adequately described?
6. Were the research results adequately explained and described?
7. Does the study contribute to the research of cloud and health in any way?

The research process that was developed resulted in 39 primary studies. They were written by 119 institution-related authors and were published between 2015 and 2019. As described in the previous Section, each of the primary studies was evaluated according to 7 quality criteria regarding the rigor and credibility of the research in addition to relevance to the topic addressed. Brought together, these 7 criteria provide a measure of reliability for the conclusions that a particular study can bring to the review. The classification for each of the criteria used a scale of positives (1) and negatives (0) and is presented in Table 2.

TABLE II. EXTRACTION OF QUALITY ANALYSIS OF PRIMARY STUDIES STUDY

Study	Q1	Q2	Q3	Q4	Q5	Q6	Q7	Total
{5}	1	1	1	1	1	1	1	7
{6}	1	1	1	1	1	1	1	7
{7}	1	1	1	1	1	1	1	7
{8}	1	0	1	1	1	1	1	6
{9}	1	1	1	0	1	1	1	6
{10}	1	1	1	1	1	1	0	6
{11}	1	1	0	1	1	1	1	6
{12}	1	1	1	1	1	1	0	6
{16}	1	0	1	1	1	1	1	6
{20}	1	1	1	0	1	1	0	5
{21}	1	1	0	1	1	0	1	5
{22}	1	1	1	1	0	1	0	5
Total	12	10	10	10	11	11	8	

From the primary articles, {5} {6} and {7} scored on all questions raised, these articles deal with models and cloud adoption in health/care environments, therefore, are aligned with the research objectives and realize that the survey, a priori, brought work that aggregated in the analyzes made.

The qualitative and quantitative assessment analyzed all 39 studies selected as primary studies. Table 2 presents a portion of the studies and highlights the studies that had 5 or more points.

III. DISCUSSION

After analyzing and extracting data in the primary studies, it was possible to identify some aspects related to cloud computing in health environments with economic impacts, opportunities, and challenges. According to Ferraz [3], it is possible to conclude that the adoption of cloud computing in the development of a new solution or business has a great impact on the economy of companies and industries. It is noteworthy that this article does not intend to study only the impacts related to healthcare. However, it was observed during the research, a large number of studies related to this theme and the possible implications on the use of cloud computing.

A. Economic Health.

Adopting cloud computing can bring health benefits, both economically and help institutions fight and prevent disease as quickly as possible. According to the study by Chang and Zhu [5], in modern and current hospitals, the use of cloud computing becomes more centralized data management, making hardware and software maintenance more convenient. Hospital environments that adopt physical servers need to invest large amounts in IT, staff responsible for the infrastructure, maintenance and security of the machines used. In addition, over time, the model becomes increasingly obsolete and costly. This is the fundamental change brought about by the cloud, the virtualization of resources without the need to maintain an expensive on-site infrastructure [3].

As seen in [6] biomedicine labs can enjoy positive financial impacts, significant flexibility and benefits to their administration by using a cloud architecture. This brings new solutions that can transform the hospital economy [7], and business models begin to emerge with a new vision in their solutions. Because all infrastructure can be abstracted by the cloud, those involved in creating solutions can be more focused on the problem to be solved, bringing innovative solutions that change the way the economy of these solutions works.

B. Cloud Treatments.

The benefits of cloud computing adoption go far beyond financial impacts and cost savings. Although the impact of cloud computing adoption has generated around the economic sphere, major advances in medicine can be seen in the use of this and other technologies together.

As can be seen here [8], the authors presents the Disease Diagnosis and Treatment Recommendation System

(DDTRS) which uses big data and cloud computing to generate diagnoses and treatment recommendations efficiently and assertively, improving the response time of diagnosis.

Another medical cloud use [9] promotes blood pressure monitoring in a patient with hypertension. Since monitoring is done in real-time, the number of data generated is huge and requires an IaaS structure framework for management.

The academic field also benefits from using cloud computing, whether in data storage, infrastructure or processing power. Complex studies at the forefront of medicine using the latest theoretical chemistry in the treatment of cancer [10] generate huge amounts of data and require enormous computational power for data processing. Research, such as [11] that simulates electron-nuclear dynamics of proton cancer therapy reactions, depending on the system studied, may take months to present the results. Therefore, cloud computing benefits by lowering its costs as infrastructure and the use of data science can generate great insights of the studied subject.

C. Health Cloud Challenges.

Based on the previous Sections and the studies analyzed, three major sectors and specific areas were identified as cloud computing and health research challenges and opportunities. They are security and privacy, chronic disease and cloud, cancer treatment and prevention. In the first area, the need to ensure the security, privacy, and authenticity of the information was identified. Any information that may lead to the identification of the user by an unauthorized party during authentication or data processing is a breach of privacy [12]. Because most data is stored on cloud servers, which is susceptible to threats and breaches, there is an imminent need to protect against unauthorized access. There are many challenges to protecting the privacy of cloud patient data; some models have been proposed [13][14]. Even so, it is clear, including several studies, that this area is extremely important for the future of the use of cloud as a whole not only limited to health.

The second specific area is shown in the development of solutions for chronic diseases. The emergence of emerging technologies demonstrates opportunities and challenges [15]. Most of these technologies have in common the need to use cloud computing in their development. Therefore, further studies and innovative solutions can change the way we treat these diseases in a few years.

Finally, studies and solutions that advance cancer treatment and diagnosis deserve attention as they can generate major economic impacts on cancer treatment and prevention. The American Cancer Society (ACS) estimates that 606,880 Americans will die of cancer by 2019, or nearly 1,700 deaths a day. This area generates a huge amount of data for storage and requires very large data processing power [11]. The search for cancer prevention combined with innovative solutions and cloud computing should be a priority area of study, considering the numbers presented by ASC. The development of SaaS or IaaS solutions is a great opportunity for the area.

IV. CONCLUSION

The main objective of this work was to conduct research that analyzed areas related to cloud computing, specifically in the health environment, deepening how this technology impacts health and solutions for this market. To achieve the objective, a systematic mapping was performed, first analyzing 5280 articles and deeply analyzing more than 100 articles in order to discuss topics not only related to the technology itself, but how its adoption impacts the health area and the economy of its own solutions.

During the analysis phases, it was clear the benefit of adopting cloud computing and how the combination of technologies can bring disruptive solutions to the market and society. Biomedicine labs and research centers also benefit from adoption, reducing response times for exams or surveys that require extensive processing and storing data. As future work, further analysis of solutions can be developed, facilitating better technical understanding to identify more efficient approaches. Further work can be done to ensure data privacy and security, and how governments will ensure privacy in public health policies.

REFERENCES

[1] K. Panetta.:Gartner, Top 10 strategic technology trends for 2018. Gartner Top 10 strategic technology trends for 2018, 3 October 2018. Gartner . https://www.gartner.com/smarterwithgartner/gartner-top-10-strategic-technology-trends-for-2018

[2] Global Burden of Disease Collaborative Network. Global Burden of Disease Study 2017 (GBD 2017) Results. Seattle, United States: Institute for Health Metrics and Evaluation (IHME), 2018.

[3] F. Ferraz, F. Ribeiro, W. Lima, and C. Sampaio, "A Disturbing Question: What is the Economical Impact of Cloud Computing? A Systematic Mapping," IEEE Int. Conf. Cloud Comput. CLOUD, vol. 2018-July, pp. 853–856, 2018.

[4] B. Kitchenham and S. Charters,"Guidelines for performingSystematic Literature reviews in Software Engineering Version 2.3," Engineering, vol. 45, no. 4ve, p. 1051, 2007

[5] C. Chang and Y. Zhu, "A Study on the Application of Cloud Computing Platform in Hospital Information Construction," pp. 280–282, 2018

[6] A. Rosenthal, P. Mork, M. H. Li, J. Stanford, D. Koester, and P. Reynolds, "Cloud computing: A new business paradigm for biomedical information sharing," J. Biomed. Inform., vol. 43, no. 2, pp. 342–353, 2010.

[7] C. Venkatesan, P. Karthigaikumar, and S. Satheeskumaran, "Mobile cloud computing for ECG telemonitoring and real-time coronary heart disease risk detection," Biomed. Signal Process. Control, vol. 44, pp. 138–145, 2018.

[8] J. Chen, K. Li, H. Rong, K. Bilal, N. Yang, and K. Li, "A disease diagnosis and treatment recommendation system based on big data mining and cloud computing," Inf. Sci. (Ny)., vol. 435, pp. 124–149, 2018.

[9] B. Yip et al., "Blood Pressure Management with Data Capturing in the Cloud among Hypertensive Patients: A Monitoring Platform for Hypertensive Patients," Proc. - 2015 IEEE Int. Congr. Big Data, BigData Congr. 2015, pp. 305–308, 2015.

[10] C. Stopera, T. V. Grimes, P. M. McLaurin, A. Privett, and J. A. Morales, Some recent developments in the simplest-level electron nuclear dynamics method. Theory, code implementation, and applications to chemical dynamics, 1st ed., vol. 66. Elsevier Inc., 2013.

[11] E. Teixeira et al., "Electron nuclear dynamics simulations of proton cancer therapy reactions: Water radiolysis and proton-and electron-induced DNA damage in computational prototypes," Cancers (Basel)., vol. 10, no. 5, 2018.

[12] M. Dawoud and D. T. Altilar, "Cloud-based e-health systems: Security and privacy challenges and solutions," 2nd Int. Conf. Comput. Sci. Eng. UBMK 2017, pp. 861–865, 2017.

[13] M. S. Elsayed and M. A. Azer, "Health Records Privacy Issues in Cloud Computing," 1st Int. Conf. Comput. Appl. Inf. Secur. ICCAIS 2018, pp. 1–6, 2018.

[14] H. Wang, "Security and Privacy-preserving Challenges of e-Health Solutions in Cloud Computing," IEEE Access, vol. 7, pp. 74361–74382, 2019.

[15] D. Gu et al., "Discovering and Visualizing Knowledge Evolution of Chronic Disease Research Driven by Emerging Technologies," IEEE Access, vol. 7, pp. 1–1, 2019.

[16] M. D. Assunção, R. N. Calheiros, S. Bianchi, M. A. S. Netto, and R. Buyya, "Big Data computing and clouds: Trends and future directions," J. Parallel Distrib. Comput., vol. 79–80, pp. 3–15, 2015.

[17] F. Gao, S. Thiebes, and A. Sunyaev, "Rethinking the meaning of cloud computing for health care: A taxonomic perspective and future research directions," J. Med. Internet Res., vol. 20, no. 7, pp. 1–16, 2018.

[18] F. Gao and A. Sunyaev, "Context matters: A review of the determinant factors in the decision to adopt cloud computing in healthcare," Int. J. Inf. Manage., vol. 48, no. July 2018, pp. 120–138, 2019.

[19] A. Jemal, R. Siegel, E. Ward, T. Murray, J. Xu, and M. J. Thun, "Cancer Statistics, 2007," CA. Cancer J. Clin., vol. 57, no. 1, pp. 43–66, 2007.

[20] M. Chen et al., "Wearable 2.0: Enabling Human-Cloud Integration in Next Generation Healthcare Systems," IEEE Commun. Mag., vol. 55, no. 1, pp. 54–61, 2017

[21] B. B. Rad, M. E. Rana, and T. Diaby, "Cloud computing adoption : a short review of issues and challenges," Int. Conf. E-commerce, E-bus. E-Government, pp. 51–55, 2017.

[22] K. K. F. Tsoi, Y. H. Kuo, and H. M. Meng, "A Data Capturing Platform in the Cloud for Behavioral Analysis among Smokers: An Application Platform for Public Health Research," Proc. - 2015 IEEE Int. Congr. Big Data, BigData Congr. 2015, pp. 737–740, 2015.

[23] L. Leong, G. Petri, B. Gill, and M. Dorosh, "Magic Quadrant for Cloud Infrastructure as a Service, Worldwide," Gartner, no. August, pp. 1–36, 2017.

[24] D. Chen, and H. Zhao, 2012. Data Security and Privacy Protection Issues in CC. IEEE International Conference on Computer Science and Electronics Engineering (ICCSEE).

[25] Z. Tang., X. Wang, J. Li, X. Zhang, and W. Man, 2012. Study on Data Security of Cloud Computing. IEEE Spring Congress on Engineering and Technology (S-CET).

[26] R. Asija, and N. Rajarathnam. "A Survey on Security and Privacy of Healthcare Data." Conference Paper · July (2014).

[27] A. Abbas , K. Bilal , L. Zhang , S.U. Khan , A cloud based health insurance plan recommendation system: a user centered approach, Futur. Gener. Comput. Syst. 43–44 (2015) 99–109 .

[28] M.S. Hossain, Cloud-supported cyber-physical localization framework for patients monitoring, IEEE Syst. J. 11 (2017) 118–127

[29] Q. Wang et al., "Remote analysis of myocardial fiber information in vivo assisted by cloud computing," Futur. Gener. Comput. Syst., vol. 85, pp. 146–159, 2018.

[30] J. Yang, "Cloud computing for storing and analyzing petabytes of genomic data," J. Ind. Inf. Integr., no. April, pp. 0–1, 2019.

[31] N. Sultan, "Discovering the potential of cloud computing in accelerating the search for curing serious illnesses," Int. J. Inf. Manage., vol. 34, no. 2, pp. 221–225, 2014.

SIMON: Semantic Inference Model for Security in Cyber Physical Systems using Ontologies

Rohith Yanambaka Venkata, Rohan Maheshwari and Krishna Kavi
Department of Computer Science and Engineering
University of North Texas
Denton, Texas-76207
Email: {rohithyanambakavenkata, rohanmaheshwari}@my.unt.edu and krishna.kavi@unt.edu

Abstract—**Cyber Physical Systems (CPS) are an integration of computational and physical processes, where embedded cyber systems monitor and control physical processes. Cyber attacks largely target components in the cyber domain with the intention of disrupting the functionality of the components in the physical domain. In this paper, we present SIMON, an Ontological design and verification framework that captures the intricate relationship(s) between cyber and physical components in CPS by leveraging standard specification Ontologies and extending the NIST CPS framework. We demonstrate the capabilities of SIMON using two vehicle to infrastructure (V2I) safety applications. In addition, we also investigate introducing resiliency measures that will ensure compliance of physical systems with their design specifications.**

Keywords–CPS Security; Ontology; CPS Privacy, CPS Resiliency.

I. INTRODUCTION

CPS systems can be considered as electronic or computer systems that control physical systems. These systems use sensors to collect information about the physical system and possibly other situational inputs, process these inputs to determine appropriate decisions and affect these decisions on the physical system via actuators. The data collection and transmission of actions may involve the use of communication networks. Thus, CPS systems contain sensors, actuators, electronic/processing components and communication networks, explosing CPS systems to cyber attacks. These cyber attacks will likely impact the physical operation of the system and may also impact the physical world these systems reside in. Thus, it is essential to understand the inter-relationships between the functions of the physical systems and the cyber (or electronic) systems and how an attack on one affects the other.

We advocate the use of Ontologies to model CPS systems and the relationships between their constituent subsystems. An Ontology is a formal description of knowledge as a set of concepts within a domain and the relationships that hold between them [1]. To enable such a description, we need to formally specify components such as individuals (instances of objects), classes, attributes, and relations as well as restrictions, rules, and axioms. Ontologies not only enable a shareable and reusable knowledge representation but, can also add new knowledge about a domain [1]. Our approach extends NIST CPS framework [2] by differentiating between an abstract realization and a concrete realization levels. The abstract level translates the conceptual requirements of CPS systems (such as functional, timing, trustworthiness requirements) into responsibilities and roles of system components (such as sensors, actuators, processing elements, communication systems, computational algorithms). The concrete realization defines specific products used to implement the abstract responsibilities and functionalities (such as selecting a specific IoT system, or a communication device). Our Ontologies allow for common vocabularies to describe concepts and properties of CPS systems at various levels of the design framework. This permits for adapting best design practices of one domain to the design of systems in another domain.

In this paper, we present our preliminary work in vulnerability assessment and design validation of CPS systems. Our prior work on using Ontologies in vulnerability assessment in cloud systems [3] [4] enables us to extend those Ontologies to address security concerns in CPS systems. Using the NIST CPS framework as a basis for SIMON allows for a broad and integrated view of CPS and positions trustworthiness among other aspects of CPS design. Furthermore, using standard Ontologies like SOSA will help streamline the process of secure CPS design by considering the properties of a CPS system like sensing and actuation.

The rest of the paper is organized as follows. Section III describes SIMON, our proposed CPS framework. This section also describes the various standard Ontologies, as well as some of our new Ontologies used in our framework. Section IV includes two case studies to show how SIMON can be used for the design and validation of CPS systems. We show some examples of cyber attacks and use reasoners to identify potential compromise of design goals associated with the physical system.

II. RELATED WORK

Extensive research has been done in applying Ontologies to either identify or validate the security posture of CPS or IoT systems. Mozzaquatro et al. [5] proposed a framework that employs a model-driven approach to designing secure CPS systems. While this may be prudential in some domains, it fails to account for concerns from various stakeholders in a CPS system. This is addressed by the NIST CPS framework.

Fenz et al. [6] and Settas et al. [7] proposed Ontological frameworks that are complemented by Bayesian networks to predict threat probabilities in cloud systems. The key competencies of these contributions is vulnerability assessment and threat modeling for cyber systems in the cloud.

SIMON aims to bridge the gap between design validation using cyber threat data from multiple sources. We believe that this approach will help in the design of secure CPS systems.

III. THE FRAMEWORK

The proposed framework combines (and extends) existing standard specification Ontologies such as Semantic Sensor Networks (SSN), and new ones as required by the domain of interest. Let us take a closer look at some of the Ontologies and frameworks used in our research.

A. NIST CPS Framework

National Institute of Standards and Technology (NIST) has developed a framework that provides guidance in designing, building and verifying complex CPS systems [2]. The framework captures generic functionalities that CPS provide, the activities and artifacts needed to support conceptualization, realization and assurance of CPS design [2]. Designing a CPS system involves:

- **Conceptualization** - Capturing all activities related to high-level goals, functional requirements and organization of CPS as they pertain to what the CPS is supposed to do. It provides a conceptual model of the CPS system under consideration.
- **Realization** - Capturing all activities surrounding the detailed engineering, design, production, implementation and operation of the desired systems. However, to facilitate comparing Ontological models of CPS systems, we propose bifurcating the overarching realization phase described in the NIST CPS framework into the following sub-phases.
  - **Abstract Realization** - In this phase, design goals are broken down into roles and responsibilities and delegated to subsystems and interfaces. For example, we may identify that the network communications needed in the system will be handled by a wireless data communication application but not provide details on either the specific hardware device or communication protocols. We use Ontologies to capture the Abstract Realization.
  - **Concrete Realization** - The roles and responsibilities identified during the abstract realization phase need to be implemented by specific products. For example, a Cisco ASR1002-10G-HA/K9 is selected as the wireless data communication application identified in the Abstract Realization phase. We use Ontologies to relate the products used for various functions and roles identified in the Abstract Realization.
- **Assurance** - The assurance phase deals with obtaining confidence that the system built in the realization phase satisfies the model developed in the conceptualization phase [2]. In our case, we use reasoners to infer and derive assurances (or violations) of the goals and functional requirements are met. We use additional Ontologies to capture cyber threat data so that vulnerabilities, cyber attacks and possible mitigations can be related to the products identified in Concrete Realization; we rely on NIST Common Platform Enumeration (CPE) identities with specific products for this purpose.

SIMON can be used to modify the CPS design at any of the various phases to address any design violations discovered by our reasoners.

Figure 1 describes an abstract view of our framework for the design and verification of CPS systems, focusing on security and trustworthiness. We use different Ontologies in our framework to describe the concepts, properties and restriction associated with CPS systems at each of the design phases described in the previous section.

B. Sensor-Observation-Sampling-Actuator Ontology (SOSA)

The Sensor-Observation-Sampling-Actuation Ontology (SOSA), a subset of the Semantic Sensor Network (SSN) Ontology presents a conceptualization of all entities, activities and properties that typically constitute a CPS. SOSA is a World Wide Web Consortium (W3C) standard specification.

The *core structure* of SOSA Ontology encompasses all of the three modeling perspectives; the activities of observing, sampling, and actuating [8]. Each activity targets a feature of interest by either changing its state or revealing its properties by following a designated procedure. All activities are carried out by an object, also called an agent.

SOSA aims to strike a balance between the expressivity of the underlying description logic, the ease of use of language features and the expectations of the target audience, while accommodating a broad range of domains and applications [8].

C. Cyber Threat Information Ontology

The activities of observing and sampling must be followed by communicating the data and processing to interpret the observations and making decisions on the actions. These actions are then used to control physical systems through actuation. The communication and processing subsystem, which is not directly included in the SOSA ontology can expose the cyber and physical components of the CPS to security attacks. Thus, SOSA must be extended to describe the processing and communication subsystems. This allows us to relate cyber threat data from multiple sources to obtain insights into the security posture of a CPS system under consideration. We have defined an Ontology that captures Cyber Threat Information (CTI) from three sources:

- **The National Vulnerability Database (NVD)** - A U.S. government repository of standards based vulnerability management data [9].
- **Exploit Database** - An archive of public exploits and corresponding vulnerable software, developed for use by penetration testers and vulnerability researchers [10].
- **Metasploit** - A framework for developing, testing and executing software exploits [11].

Our Ontology can easily be extended to capture CTI from ohter sources. The cyber threat Ontology is underpinned by the STIX structured language, that enables organizations to share, store and analyze CTI in a consistent manner, allowing security communities to better understand what computer-based attacks they are most likely to see and to anticipate and/or respond to those attacks more effectively [12]. The STIX Ontology utilizes twelve core concepts: Attack pattern, Campaign, Course of Action, Identity, Indicator, Intrusion Set, Malware, Observed Data, Report, Threat Actor, Tool and Vulnerability.

Attack Pattern describes ways that threat actors attempt to compromise targets and *Campaign* categorizes malicious activities that occur over a period of time by identifying their intended targets. *Vulnerability* describes a flaw in software (or hardware) that can be exploited by a *Threat Actor* to breach a target.

Our objective in defining the CTI Ontology is to unify information from three sources (described earlier in this section) and facilitate logical reasoning about the security of CPS using *Axioms*. Axioms are rules that are used by a reasoner to infer additional information that may be hard to define using a knowledge representation language. To provide a perspective

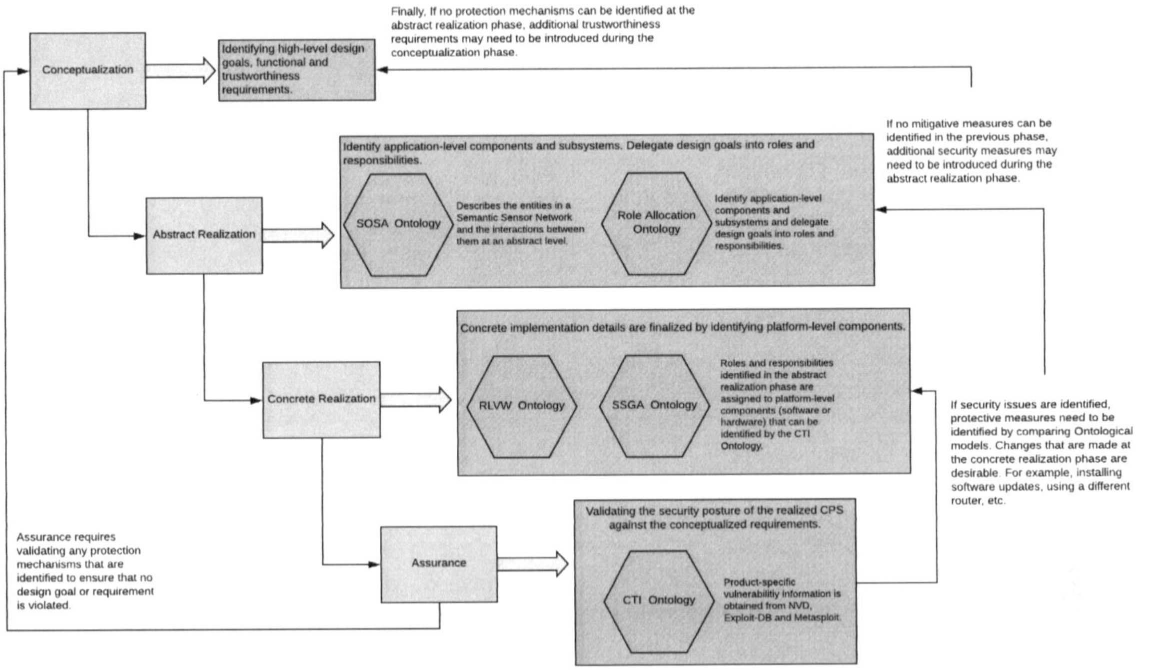

Figure 1. The SIMON Ontological Framework.

of the complexity of CTI Ontology, it includes 6657 axioms that describe CTI data. In addition to STIX, the CTI Ontology also inherits characteristics from two additional Ontologies:

- **Cyber Observable Expression (CybOX)** - A standardized language for encoding and communicating information about cyber observables [12]. Using CybOX language, relevant observable events or properties pertaining to an attack pattern can be captured.
- **Common Attack Pattern and Enumeration (CAPEC)** - Provides a dictionary of known patterns of attack employed by adversaries to exploit known weaknesses in cyber-enabled capabilities.[13].

Here is a brief look at some of the important characteristics of our CTI Ontology:

- **Attack:** This feature is mapped to the *Indicator*, *Observed Data* classes in the STIX Ontology and the *Observation, FeatureOfInterest and ObservableProperty* classes in the STIX Ontology. This characterizes a cyber attack by identifying a pattern, set of adversarial behaviors or information observed on a system in the network.
- **Exploit:** Mapped to the *Vulnerability* and *Intrusion set* classes in the STIX Ontology and the *Sensor, Actuator* and *Sample* classes in the SOSA Ontology, the Exploit feature enumerates a flaw in a platform (Software or Hardware with a CPE entry in the NVD) that can be leveraged by an adversary to compromise a CPS system.
- **Ramification:** Incident response teams often desire to know the consequences/objectives of potential adversaries to prioritize responses to cyber attacks. In a similar vein, threat modeling at the design phase of a CPS system will equip CPS designers to understand the outcome of cyber attacks and design more secure or resilient systems. At present, threat classification is based on the Spoofing, Tampering, Repudiation, Information disclosure, Denial of Service and Elevation of Privilege (STRIDE) classification model [14], where each type of threat is assigned its own class. The *Ramification* feature maps to a class in the STRIDE based on the nature of the threat. In addition, it also maps to the *ThreatActor, CourseOfAction* and *Vulnerability* classes in the STIX Ontology and the *Actuation, Observation, Procedure, FeatureOfInterest, Platform* and *ObservableProperty* classes in the SOSA Ontology.

Thus, our framework allows users to identify and enumerate cyber threats that affect a CPS system of interest. We rely on Ontologies because of the following benefits they offer:

- **Knowledge Representation:** The primary benefit of using an Ontology is it's ability to define a semantic model of data, within the context of an associated domain knowledge and this can be leveraged to achieve knowledge sharing and more importantly, knowledge reuse, which is discussed in the next section.
- **Modularity:** Our framework facilitates modularity by allowing CPS designers to use domain-specific properties (Ontologies like SOSA). Users have the option of using additional vocabulary, in addition to the W3C specification to model proprietary systems.
- **Extensibility:** CPS systems are constantly evolving. Advances in networking and embedded system technologies like system-on-chip (SoC) and wireless transceivers result in the emergence of new CPS applications. The structure of SIMON, coupled with its modular design supports integrating or modifying CPS characteristics, and

to reason about the security posture of a system.

IV. Vehicle To Infrastructure (V2I) Wireless Data Interface Ontology: A Case study

As a case study to show the use of our framework, we use the Red Light Violation Warning (RLVW) safety application as described in the US Department of Transportation document [15]. The Red Light Violation Warning (RLVW) application enables a connected vehicle approaching an instrumented signalized intersection to receive information from the infrastructure regarding the signal timing and the geometry of the intersection. The application in the vehicle uses its speed and acceleration profile, along with the signal timing and geometry information to determine if it appears likely that the vehicle will enter the intersection in violation of a traffic signal. If the violation seems likely to occur, a warning can be provided to the driver.

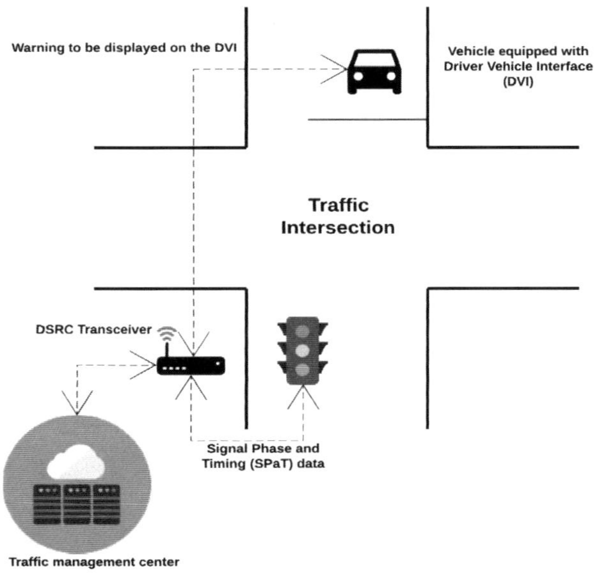

Figure 2. The RLVW system

Figure 2 depicts the RLVW system. To identify the most vulnerable areas in this system, it is vital to understand the flow and origin of data (i.e., sensing and observation aspects of the system). We have developed an Ontology for the Vehicle To Infrastructure or Infrastructure To Vehicle (V2I/I2V) Wireless Data Interface through which all vehicular and infrastructure data is exchanged. The ontology highlights the cyber and physical components comprising the wireless data interface portion of the V2I system and distinguishes between the physical components that produce the data and the cyber components that transmit the data. The flow of data in the ontology has revealed that the Infrastructure Wireless Data System (IWDS) and the Vehicle Wireless Data System (VWDS) which are connected through the V2I Wireless Data Interface are the most vulnerable regions of the entire V2I CPS because data flows on a completely open network when traversing through these cyber components. With the source and destination IP addresses of data packets unprotected, this can lead to numerous threats from any third party with a V2X communication handler. Before classifying the immediate threats that can occur with data flowing on this presumed 5G open network, the Ontology also describes the various types and origins of data to understand the impact of a cyber attack.

Accurately modeling a CPS system is vital in identifying and mitigating security issues. The Ontological framework described in Section III helps achieving this because it offers the following features.

- **CPS Framework:** Perhaps the most important characteristic that enables comparison between Ontologies is sharing a common underlying framework that ensures similarities in structure. The NIST CPS framework is an ideal candidate because it addresses cross-cutting concerns that are crucial to identifying design flaws or vulnerabilities that could be introduced due to interaction between cyber components. Ontologies needs to be modeled using the CPS framework to be compared.
- **Cyber Threat Ontology:** Using an Ontology that is optimized for identifying, obtaining and organizing cyber threat data for CPS systems is invaluable in identifying potential mitigation measures that will ensure compliance with design goals of a CPS system.
- **Domain-specific Properties:** Identifying and expressing domain-specific properties is imperative in accurately modeling CPS systems. This helps correctly identify aspects (such as Functional, Human, Timing, etc.) and concerns (such as Physical security, Predictability, Dissociability, etc.). These properties contribute to identifying design flaws/vulnerabilities that are unique to the CPS system under consideration. For example, the SOSA Ontology used in this framework helps identify design goals such as latency and timing requirements that are unique to sensor networks. This helps identify pertinent mitigation measures that ensure compliance with the design goals. If no such measure(s) can be found, a change in the design of a CPS system may be required.

Sharing a common underlying framework enables knowledge-reuse by providing a shared conceptualization of a domain of interest. Therefore, it stands to reason that Ontologies describing similar CPS systems, sharing the same semantic structure can be compared to investigate protection mechanisms that could protect against security threats. With this in mind, let us consider a CPS model that was developed using the framework described in Section III.

A. *Infrastructure Data Types and Significance*

Starting with the Infrastructure, its physical components consists of the signalized intersection sensor systems that capture two main types of data [15].

1) SPaT: SPaT data (Signal Phase and Timing) contains information about the behavior of the traffic controllers regarding the state of the signal (viz., red, green or yellow), how long that state will remain, and time until next phase change.

2) Driving Conditions: The physical component of the infrastructure also produces data that characterizes the environmental conditions approaching vehicles may face. This data consists of weather data, visibility data and road conditions for the vehicle to incorporate in its decision making computations to improve precision in judgement as approaching the intersection.

B. *Vehicle Data Types and Significance*

The vehicle's physical components consists of the position and stability systems, actuators, and telematic sensors that transmit Differential GPS (DGPS) and Dynamic Telematic Data (DTD) [15].

1) Differential GPS: DGPS data contains map data of the vehicle's position relative to the approaching signalized intersection. The vehicle data systems transmit DGPS to the infrastructure in order to alert the traffic controllers of the instantaneous distance the vehicle is from the intersection.

2) Dynamic Telematic Data: DTD consists of information regarding the vehicle's speed, position and reveals how the vehicle is behaving internally. This data is combined with DGPS, and incoming SPaT data for the vehicles to calculate using DVI equations and algorithms in order to make precise judgement of whether the driver should increase or decrease speed to avoid traffic violations and or accidents at the intersection.

C. *Stop Sign Gap Assist (SSGA)*

As a reference for investigating the reuse of protection mechanisms that are currently in place, we use the Stop Sign Gap Assist (SSGA) system in the Department of Transportation V2I specifications [15]. The SSGA Infrastructure Application component delivers roadside advisory, alert, and warning messages to the driver, based upon infrastructure-based sensor systems placed on the major roadway that detect the speed and location of approaching remote vehicles. It is intended to improve safety at non-signalized intersections where only the minor road has posted stop signs [16]. This application includes both on-board (for connected vehicles) and roadside signage warning systems (for non-equipped vehicles) [16]. The application will help drivers on a minor road stopped at an intersection understand the state of activities associated with that intersection by providing a warning of unsafe gaps on the major road. The SSGA application collects all available sensor information (major road, minor road, and median sensors) data and computes the dynamic state of the intersection in order to issue appropriate warnings and alerts [16].

Intuitively, it is easy to recognize the similarities in the design goals of the RLVW and SSGA applications, the distinction being that signalized intersections are replaced by a stop sign in the SSGA system.

The CPS framework ensures that concepts of two Ontologies being compared are aligned. Comparing the relationship of each aligned concept with its neighbors in the Ontologies being compared yields the differences in interpretation. The abstract realization phase of the framework deals with identifying, defining and delegating design goals identified in the conceptualization phase into roles and responsibilities for system components and interfaces at an abstract level. This provides a good basis to determine if the conceptualized concepts and their relationships are aligned.

D. *Identifying Security Threats and Protection Mechanisms*

In this section, let us consider a few vulnerabilities in the RLVW system that can be addressed by reusing mitigation measures employed in a distinctly different CPS system, viz., the SSGA application, by comparing their Ontological models. Now that the baseline for the V2I WDI region is set, we can analyze the proposed ontology to classify potential threats in the flow of data.

1) V2X Remote DSRC Interjection Threat: The IWDS and VWDS communicate through the V2I WDI over a bidirectional DSRC network [15]. While DSRC provides a robust and low latency connection for short distance communication [17], its security protocol only prevents Distributed Denial of Service (DDoS) attacks from a short distance. Therefore, a third party with V2X communication handlers can interject data transmission remotely through Internet Protocol and Domain Name Service (IP/DNS) Spoofing attacks to reroute outgoing Differential GPS (DGPS) data and Dynamic Telematic Data (DTD) from the vehicle. With this data in their possession, unauthorized V2X handlers can track drivers and read into vehicle logs which creates privacy issues for the victim. The NIST Vulnerability Database highlights a similar issue with the configuration *cpe:2.3:a:cisco:application-policy-infrastructure- controller:8.31s6:*:*:*:*:*:*:** [9]. Existence of this vulnerability suggests that this simple attack is highly probable if correct mitigation is not in place. A potential start for resolving this issue may involve ITS developers implementing a SSL certificate with outgoing data which requires V2X handlers to have a certain cryptographic key in order to access the contents of the data packets [18].

The RLVW and SSGA systems share some design goals. Furthermore, comparing their abstract realization phases reveals that they share the same WDI. This is further evidenced by comparing their concrete realization phases, which reveals that they use the same DSRC transceiver and network communication subsystem. It may be worthwhile to compare the two Ontologies to determine if protection mechanisms employed in the SSGA application can be reused in the RLVW system.

```
The Ontology is consistent
Road side equipment CPE : cpe:2.3:a:cisco:application-policy-infrastructure-controller:8.31s6:*:*:*:*:*:*:*
Adversary may leverage CVE-2017-12352 to gian elevated privileges
Adversary may tamper with the RLVW warning data that is broadcast to vehicles
(Warning) Potential violation of functional requirement 1.1.5 of the Road side equipment
(Inferred) Potential violation of functional requirement 1.2.4.7 of the RLVW system
(Inferred) Potential violation of functional requirement 1.2.5.2 of the RLVW system
(Inferred) Potential violation of functional requirement 1.1 of the Driver Interface system
```

Figure 3. RLVW Inference.

The CTI Ontology obtains vulnerability information for components identified in the concrete realization phase using NIST CPE (Common Platform Enumeration) identifications. In this example, let us consider one vulnerability that can be exploited for a privilege escalation with NIST Common Vulnerability Enumeration(CVE) identification, *CVE 2017-12352*, associated with the CISCO router with *cpe:2.3:a:cisco:application-policy-infrastructure-controller:8.31s6:*:*:*:*:*:*:** [9]. An adversary can exploit this vulnerability in certain system script files on Cisco Application Policy Infrastructure Controllers to gain elevated privileges and execute arbitrary commands with root privileges on an affected host operating system [19]. The vulnerability is due to insufficient validation of user-controlled input that is supplied to script files of an affected system [19]. A simple fix would be to install a software update for the application policy infrastructure controller. However, to demonstrate the capabilities of Ontological modeling and reasoning, we will assume that no software patches are available for this component.

Figure 3 shows how the CTI Ontology uses semantic reasoning to link vulnerabilities to the design goals identified during the conceptualization phase. While an elevation of privilege attack can lead to catastrophic failure of the affected system, we will focus on adversaries potentially spoofing their identities in this example.

The SSGA system uses Extensible Authentication Protocol (EAP), a certificate-based authentication scheme to validate the V2X handler that issues requests for DGPS and DTD data. This prevents most spoofing attacks.

```
The Ontology is consistent
Distinction identified between SSGA and RLVW VWDS
(Asserted) SSGA uses wireless message authentication scheme
(Inferred) EAP introduces latency
(Inferred) Potential violation of requirement 1.3.1 of the Driver Interface System
(Inferred) Potential violation of requirement 1.5.2.2 of the RLVE system
```

Figure 4. Comparing the Ontologies

Figure 4 illustrates how the message authentication scheme used in SSGA is capable of preventing the spoofing attack identified by the CTI Ontology. However, this scheme introduces latency, which may impact the timing requirement listed in the conceptualization phase of RLVW. Let us investigate if message authentication scheme is a viable solution for RLVW.

```
(Asserted) Timing Requirements 1.3.4.1 needs to be met
(Inferred) RLVW zone needs to be extended to 100 meters
(Asserted) DSRC radio has a maximum range of 120 meters
(Inferred) Additional requirements need to be added at abstract realization
```

Figure 5. Testing compliance

As evidenced from Figure 5, the Ontology determines that the RLVW requirement to warn drivers well in advance of a red light violation, to provide ample stopping distance may be violated by the latency that is introduced by the authentication scheme. Furthermore, the Ontology also infers that the components used in this system are capable of supporting the timing requirement as the DSRC transceiver has a range of 120 meters. To address this, the Ontology recommends that the warning zone be increased from 80 meters before the intersection to 100 meters, which should provide ample time for EAP to authenticate the communication. A requirement needs to be added in the abstract realization phase to include an authentication scheme that also includes fail-safe measure if authentication is inconclusive. A domain expert needs to be consulted to ensure that all design goals are accurately captured in the SIMON framework.

2) V2X Handler Elevation of Priviledge Threat: Unfortunately, DSRC communication between V2I WDI and VWDS is not the only insecurity of the WDI region. The performance requirements set by the DoT do not mention any form of security over the functionality of the IWDS and VWDS [15]. In this section, we investigate the possibility of improving the resiliency of a CPS system against privilege escalation attacks by implementing a fail-safe mechanism. The proposed ontology outlines the path of data through the Infrastructure Application component (IAC) and platform (IAP) that reveals no form of encryption on data produced by the physical components or verification when that data is transmitted through the cyber components. Therefore, V2X Handlers with identical communication functionality and IP address can replace the role of the IWDS in the TCP handshake and give false acknowledgement to the IAP. V2X Handlers can then tamper with outbound SPaT and road data which results in the vehicle application component producing false metrics. These metrics may result in a red light traffic violation or even roadside accidents. A similar vulnerability issue is noted with the configuration *cpe:2.3:o:cisco:ios-xe:16.10.1:*:*:*:*:*:** in the NIST Vulnerability Database [9], thus, indicating the possibility of this threat occurring roadside. A general solution to this vulnerability can involve ITS developers implementing an ingress filtering protocol that requires the VWDS to check incoming data packets for their source headers to ensure it matches the one of the origin and to reject the packet if it does not [18].

The SSGA application uses Public Key Infrastructure (PKI) encryption for communication between the components. This requires a Certifying Agency (CA) to generate and assign a public key to each component in the system. The CA is maintained by the DoT. The messages are authenticated using Message Authentication Code (MAC). PKI is a comprehensive security and authentication scheme requiring all entities to ensure confidentiality, integrity, non-repudiation and end-to-end monitoring and key life cycle management.

The CTI identifies the configuration of the V2X handler and maps it to *cpe:2.3:o:cisco:ios-xe:16.10.1:*:*:*:*:*:**. It is able to identify vulnerability *CVE 2019-1756* that can be leveraged by adversaries to launch an elevation of privilege attack to breach the communication channel between the IAC and IAP. A vulnerability in Cisco IOS XE Software could allow an authenticated, remote attacker to execute commands on the underlying Linux shell of an affected device with root privileges [20]. The vulnerability occurs because the affected software improperly sanitizes user-supplied input. An attacker who has valid administrator access to an affected device could exploit this vulnerability by supplying a username with a malicious payload in the web UI and subsequently making a request to a specific endpoint in the web UI. A successful exploit could allow the attacker to run arbitrary commands as the root user, allowing complete compromise of the system [20].

```
The Ontology is consistent
Road side equipment CPE : cpe:2.3:o:cisco:ios-xe:16.10.1:*:*:*:*:*:*
Adversary may leverage CVE-2019-1756 to gian elevated privileges by code injection
Adversary may tamper with SPaT data
(Asserted) Potential violation of functional requirement 1.1.5 of the Road side equipment
(Inferred) Potential violation of functional requirement 1.2.4.7 of the RLVW system
(Inferred) Potential violation of functional requirement 1.2.5.2 of the RLVW system
(Inferred) Potential violation of functional requirement 1.1 of the Driver Interface system
(Inferred) Potential violation of functional requirement 1.1.6 of the RLVW system
```

Figure 6. Elevation of Privilege Threat Inference

The potential impact of this vulnerability being exploited is shown in Figure 6. The framework is able to infer that the primary design goals of the RLVW application and the roadside equipment may be violated as a direct result of this vulnerability.

As discussed in the previous example, SSGA uses message authentication and EAP. The same measures can be used in this example to protect the RLVW system. However, we are interested in identifying possible resiliency measures that can be employed by the RLVW system to protect against privilege escalation attack. To identify activities that can be used in the vehicle to detect spurious data from the infrastructure, let us consider an autonomous vehicle that is capable of perceiving the world around it.

We have defined a simple Ontology that models approximately 3118 attributes of an autonomous vehicle that includes driving actions like stop and go, a collision warning system, a lane change detection system and so on The insights provided by this Ontology can be used to prevent attacks like those discussed above by introducing resiliency into the design of the CPS system. The inference engine compares the RLVW system against three principles of a fully autonomous vehicle.

- **Sensing the world** - It is imperative for autonomous vehicles to possess the ability to perceive the world around them.
- **Conveying intent** - Assuming that other autonomous vehicles are present in the immediate vicinity, conveying intent such as lane change or impending change in driving action to other vehicles (and possibly pedestrians) is required.
- **Situational awareness** - Assigning a context to the information obtained by sensing the world is essential in making an informed decision. Comprehending events in the environment with respect to time and space is crucial.

```
1. Ensure vehicle meets requirement for sensing the world (1.2.1.1)
            - Cameras in the front windshield to detect traffic lights (Refer to requirement 1.3.3.2)
```

Figure 7. Measure to introduce resiliency into the RLVW system

The Ontology limits the inference to the design principle of sensing the world for the RLVW system as the other principles do not apply to it. Applying all three principles will negate the role of the infrastructure elements in this V2I system. To that end, the insights provided by the Ontology are shown in Figure 7.

While this is only a preliminary design of a specific region of the V2I CPS, the potential of an Ontology-based model is shown through the vulnerabilities it can classify. By describing various components through their roles, data types, and functionality, the Ontology can reason about new threats or vulnerabilities upon the addition of an unknown component to the system. If the properties of the unknown component, which in this case study is a V2X handler, become known, the ontology can use reasoners to infer where this new component may interject by comparing properties of the new component with existing components in the CPS. When a match is found, the ontology will classify the new component in a certain instance of the CPS. This knowledge can be used to implement new levels of security and mitigation in existing components to make it difficult for V2X handlers to either interject the CPS, or play the role of a component in the CPS [21].

V. Conclusion and Future Work

In this paper, we have presented an argument for modeling CPS using Ontologies. We also presented SIMON, a framework that is based on the NIST CPS framework, but extends it in several ways. We use Ontologies during each design phase of the framework to check for compliance and provide recommendations by reusing knowledge. Increased traction in CPS adoption, their growing complexity, and heterogeneous nature necessitates accuracy in capturing the relationship between various components in a CPS. Reasoning about a CPS realization and validating that the realization does not violate functional as well trustworthiness goals is essential in improving the security posture of a CPS system. The SIMON framework can aid in this process. We have only described the framework at a very high level and we plan to integrate various Ontologies and reasoning engines in the near future. Although Ontologies are used extensively for knowledge representation in domains such as healthcare and bioinformatics, we aim to leverage their capabilities to define a domain agnostic framework that can be extended to various CPS domains by attributing domain-specific properties (like SOSA). We are also developing tools for automatically (or semi-automatically) convert CPS designs using NIST framework to SIMON framwork.

Acknowledgement

This research is supported in part by the NSF Net-centric Industry-University Cooperative Research Center at UNT and the industrial members of the Center.

References

[1] "What are ontologies?." URL: https://ontotext.com/knowledgehub/fundamentals/what-are-ontologies/ [accessed: 2019-06-11] .

[2] D. A. Wollman, M. A. Weiss, Y. Li-Baboud, E. R. Griffor, and M. J. Burns, "Framework for cyber-physical systems," *Special Publication (NIST SP) - 1500-203*, 2017.

[3] P. Kamongi, M. Gomathisankaran, and K. Kavi, "Nemesis: Automated architecture for threat modeling and risk assessment for cloud computing," 12 2014.

[4] P. Kamongi, S. Kotikela, K. Kavi, M. Gomathisankaran, and A. Singhal, "Vulcan: Vulnerability assessment framework for cloud computing," in *Proceedings of the 2013 IEEE 7th International Conference on Software Security and Reliability*, SERE '13, (Washington, DC, USA), pp. 218–226, IEEE Computer Society, 2013.

[5] B. Mozzaquatro, C. Agostinho, D. Goncalves, J. Martins, and R. Jardim-Goncalves, "An ontology-based cybersecurity framework for the internet of things," *Sensors*, vol. 18, p. 3053, Sep 2018.

[6] S. Fenz, "An ontology- and bayesian-based approach for determining threat probabilities," in *Proceedings of the 6th ACM Symposium on Information, Computer and Communications Security*, ASIACCS '11, (New York, NY, USA), pp. 344–354, ACM, 2011.

[7] D. Settas, A. Cerone, and S. Fenz, "Enhancing ontology-based antipattern detection using bayesian networks," *Expert Systems with Applications*, vol. 39, no. 10, pp. 9041 – 9053, 2012.

[8] K. Janowicz, A. Haller, S. J. D. Cox, D. L. Phuoc, and M. Lefrançois, "SOSA: A lightweight ontology for sensors, observations, samples, and actuators," *CoRR*, vol. abs/1805.09979, 2018.

[9] "National Vulnerability Database." URL: https://nvd.nist.gov/ [accessed: 2019-06-11].

[10] "Exploit-DB." URL: https://www.exploit-db.com [accessed: 2019-06-20].

[11] "Metasploit-penetration testing framework." URL: https://www.metasploit.com/ [accessed: 2019-06-20].

[12] S. Barnum, "Standardizing cyber threat intelligence information with the structured threat information expression (stix)," *MITRE*, 2014.

[13] "Common Attack Pattern Enumeration and Classification (CAPEC)." URL: https://capec.mitre.org/ [accessed: 2019-07-02].

[14] Microsoft Corporation, "The STRIDE threat model." URL: https://docs.microsoft.com/en-us/previous-versions/commerce-server/ee823878(v=cs.20) [accessed: 2019-07-08].

[15] Department of Transportation, "Performance Requirements, Vol. 3, Red Light Violation Warning (RLVW)," *Vehicle-to-Infrastructure (V2I) Safety Applications*, pp. 1–68, 2015.

[16] D. Stephens, J. Schroeder, and R. Klein, "Vehicle-to-infrastructure (v2i) safety applications - stop sign gap assist (ssga)," *FHWA-JPO-16-254*, vol. 7, 2015.

[17] "Dedicated Short Range Communications (DSRC) Service," 2019. URL: https://www.fcc.gov/wireless/bureau-divisions/mobility-division/dedicated-short-range-communications-dsrc-service [accessed: 2019-06-11].

[18] "DDoS Glossary," 2019. URL: https://www.cloudflare.com/learning/ddos/ glossary/ [accessed: 2019-06-11].

[19] Cisco, "Cisco application policy infrastructure controller local command injection and privilege escalation vulnerability," 2017. URL: = https://tools.cisco.com/security/center/content/CiscoSecurityAdvisory/cisco-sa-20171129-apic [accessed: 2019-07-22].

[20] Cisco, "Cisco ios xe software command injection vulnerability," *Cisco security advisory*, 2019. URL: = https://tools.cisco.com/security/center/content/CiscoSecurityAdvisory/cisco-sa-20190327-iosxe-cmdinject [accessed: 2019-07-22].

[21] R. Y. Venkata and K. Kavi, "An Ontology-Driven Framework for Security and Resiliency in Cyber Physical Systems," *The Thirteenth International Conference on Software Engineering Advances*, pp. 4–6, 2018.

OpenCL-Generated Optimizing Compiler for FPGA Using ROSE Compiler Infrastructure

Yuichiro Aoki
Research and Development Group, Center for Technology Innovation - Digital Technology
Hitachi, Ltd.
1-280, Higashi-Koigakubo, Kokubunji, 185-8601, Tokyo, Japan
e-mail: yuichiro.aoki.jk@hitachi.com

Abstract— **Many researchers are investigating deep learning because it can recognize pedestrians for automatic driving and/or criminals to prevent crimes on the street. A promising device for such tasks in deep learning is a Field Programmable Gate Array (FPGA). However, the conventional manual FPGA programming and optimizations are complicated and take a long time. Thus, FPGA development time needs to be decreased. In this paper, we propose an OpenCL-generated optimizing compiler based on the ROSE Compiler Infrastructure. OpenCL is a C-extended programming language for heterogeneous computing, such as an FPGA and a Central Processing Unit (CPU). We add simple pragmas to the C program, and our compiler generates the optimized OpenCL program for FPGA. The preliminary evaluation using the deep learning framework Caffe shows that our compiler decreases to about 1/16 of the conventional development time.**

Keywords-FPGA; OpenCL; compiler; parallel programming.

I. INTRODUCTION

Many researchers are investigating deep learning because it can recognize pedestrians for automatic driving [1][2] and/or criminals to prevent crimes on the street [3]. However, deep learning takes a long time to learn data. For example, training large data may take a week or more. Shortening this long training time can help make deep learning more practical and make its hyper-parameters easier to tune.

A Field Programmable Gate Array (FPGA) is a promising device for deep learning because it does not have unused circuits to be connected and consumes low power. The conventional development process of the FPGA involves the use of Hardware Description Languages (HDLs), such as Verilog HDL and/or VHDL, which are strongly hardware-dependent programming languages. Thus, development steps, such as writing and optimizing the FPGA programs, incur high cost. To address this problem, a new programming language called Open Computing Language (OpenCL™) [4] has been developed for FPGAs [5][6].

OpenCL is an extended C-style language that can be used to write host (Central Processing Unit (CPU)) and device

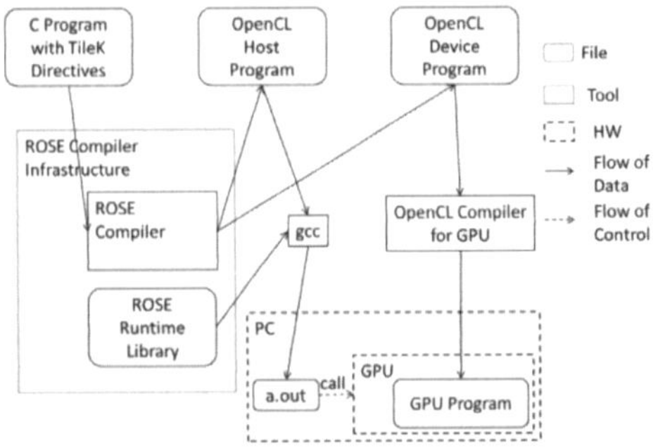

Figure 1. ROSE compiler infrastructure overview.

(FPGA) programs. Thus, programmers can write and optimize C-style OpenCL more easily than HDLs. However, they must write the communications between the host program and the device program manually. Some examples are data transfer function calls between a CPU and an FPGA. Sometimes they have a few hundred lines. In addition, programmers have to optimize the device program for the FPGA manually, which is a hard task.

In this paper, we propose an OpenCL-generated optimizing compiler from the C program with specific pragmas based on the ROSE Compiler Infrastructure. This is a preliminary study. However, no other compiler generates the optimized OpenCL program for FPGA.

The rest of the paper is organized as follows: In Section II, we review related study. In Section III, we describe ROSE Compiler Infrastructure. In Section IV, we explain how to modify ROSE for FPGA. We show the preliminary evaluation results in Section V. In Section VI, we discuss OpenCL optimization candidates for FPGAs, followed by conclusion and future study in Section VII.

II. RELATED WORK

ROSE Compiler Infrastructure [8][9] was developed by the Lawrence Livermore National Laboratory. Its input is C/C++ with the original pragmas, and its output is OpenCL. RoseACC [10] is an extended module of ROSE and can compile C program with OpenACC pragmas to the OpenCL.

OpenARC Compiler [11][12] is developed by the Oakridge National Laboratory on the basis of the Cetus

Parallelizing Compiler [13]. Its input is C/C++ with OpenACC pragmas, and its output is OpenCL or CUDA.

IPMACC [14] compiles C program with OpenACC pragmas into the OpenCL program. The status of optimization implementation is unknown.

Grewe et al. [15] complied C program with OpenMP pragmas into a multiversion program using OpenMP and OpenCL. Memory access optimizations, such as register promotion for CPU are implemented.

MATISSE [16] compiles a MATLAB program with the original pragmas into OpenCL program. Type inference optimization and variable shape inference optimization are implemented.

Habanero-Java [17] compiles an extended Java program into OpenCL program. To treat Java's exception handling functions, two versions of the program are generated.

Gaspard2 [19] compiles UML into OpenCL. The communication optimization which removes unnecessary data transfer between CPU and GPU is implemented.

PyOpenCL [20] compiles Python program into OpenCL program. CU2CL [18] and Swan [21] compiles CUDA program into OpenCL program. Firepile [7] compiles Scala program into OpenCL program. They do not optimize the output OpenCL program.

In addition, the target device of all the compilers described above is GPU. FPGA-specific code generation and optimizations are not implemented yet. Our compiler generates and optimizes the OpenCL device program for FPGA.

III. ROSE COMPILER INFRASTRUCTURE

In this section, we give an overview of the ROSE Compiler Infrastructure [8][9]. It is an open-source tool for analyses and source-to-source program transformations developed by the Lawrence Livermore National Laboratory. Its characteristics are as follows:

(i) Its input is C/C++ programs with TileK pragmas.

(ii) ROSE transforms the input program into the OpenCL host and device program for Graphics Processing Unit (GPU).

(iii) The generated OpenCL device program is not optimized.

Figure 1 shows the overview of the ROSE Compiler Infrastructure. C program with TileK pragmas is inputted to the ROSE, and it outputs the OpenCL host program and device program. Gcc compiles the OpenCL host program and generates a.out. The OpenCL compiler for a GPU compiles the OpenCL device program and outputs the GPU program. Then, a.out calls the GPU program.

Figure 2 shows a TileK pragma example. TileK is a ROSE original pragma manually inserted in front of the target loop. The target loop is offloaded to the GPU if the pragma exists.

```
#pragma tilek kernel data(x[0:N])
for (i=0; i<N; i++) {
  x[i] = i;
}
```

Figure 2. TileK pragma example.

The clause of the pragma, such as data(x[0:N]), means that the array x[0]...x[N-1] is sent to the GPU just before GPU offloading and sent back to the CPU just after GPU offloading.

IV. OUR PROPOSAL TO MODIFY ROSE FOR FPGA

In this section, we point out the problems of the ROSE Compiler Infrastructure when it is applied to the FPGA, and propose new functionalities for it. The current ROSE Compiler Infrastructure is not appropriate for the FPGA. Among its characteristics described in Section III, (i) and (ii) indicate that it can output the OpenCL host and device programs from the input C/C++ program. However, (ii) states that its target device is a GPU, not an FPGA. In addition, (iii) shows that the output OpenCL device program is not optimized. Thus, the current output OpenCL device program may run on an FPGA but are not optimized for the FPGA. We thus have to modify the ROSE Compiler Infrastructure for FPGA.

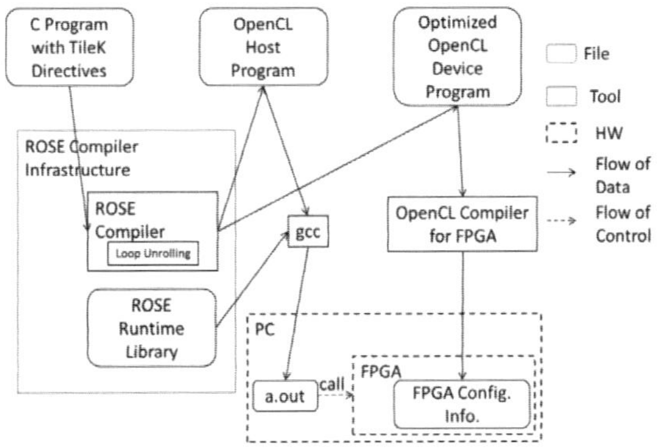

Figure 3. Modified ROSE compiler infrastructure.

```
for traverse loopnest
  if the loopnest is offloaded by TileK pragma
    get innermost loop of the loopnest
    insert loop unrolling pragma
      in front of the innermost loop
  endif
endfor
```

Figure 4. Algorithm of inserting loop unrolling pragma.

```
#pragma unroll
for (it_0 = 0; it_0 <= N - 1; it_0 += 1) {
  x[it_0] = it_0;
}
```

Figure 5. Example of generated loop with unrolling pragma.

First, we create a new environment variable ROSE_OPENCL_PLATFORM. It uses a device name as a clause. This environment variable selects appropriate OpenCL functions for the device. For example, for an FPGA, the host program calls the clCreateProgramWithBinary function, instead of clCreateProgramWithSource for GPU.

Second, we add a new FPGA optimization function to the ROSE. The new optimization is loop unrolling because it increases the parallelism of the OpenCL device program for FPGA. Thus, it can decrease the execution time on an FPGA if the OpenCL compiler for FPGA can utilize the parallelism. In this case, we automatically insert the loop unrolling pragma to the innermost loops of the OpenCL device program for FPGA.

Figure 3 depicts the modified ROSE Compiler Infrastructure. The ROSE outputs the OpenCL host program and the optimized OpenCL device program for FPGA. In addition, a.out calls FPGA, instead of GPU.

Figure 4 shows the loop unrolling algorithm. It traverses loopnests and find if the loopnest is offloaded by the TileK pragma. If so, it gets the innermost loop of the loopnest and inserts the loop unrolling pragma in front of the innermost loop.

Figure 5 shows an example of the output OpenCL device program that is inserted in the loop unrolling pragma. Intel FPGA SDK for OpenCL Compiler [5] and Xilinx SDAccel Compiler [6] support similar pragmas for FPGA.

V. Preliminary Evaluation

In this section, we evaluate the validity of our proposal. First, we interviewed skilled HDL programmers about how long they take to make the HDL program for FPGA manually. Second, we manually made an OpenCL host and device program and measured how long it took. Third, we used TileK pragma and generated the OpenCL host program and optimized device program for FPGA automatically. Thus, we compared the development times among manual HDL, manual OpenCL, and ROSE-Generated OpenCL.

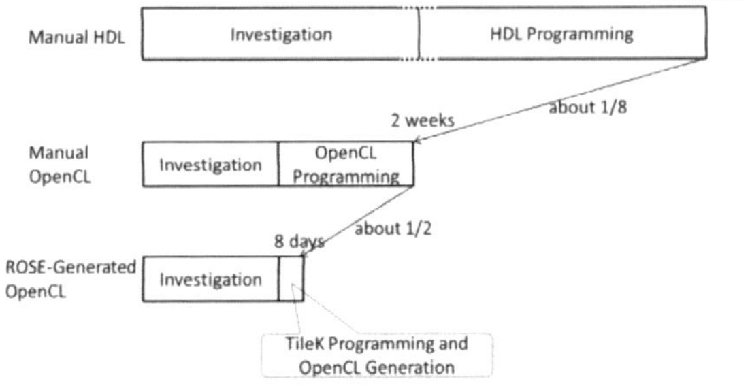

Figure 6. Comparison of development time.

The example application program is Caffe, a deep learning framework written in C++ and developed by the Berkeley Artificial Intelligence Research at the University of California, Berkeley. It has many layers for deep learning, and we use the pooling layer for the development time evaluation because it is one of the most widely used and one of the most time-consuming layers in deep learning.

Figure 6 compares development times. In manual HDL, both the investigation of the program (pooling layer) and the HDL programming for an FPGA take about two months. Thus, the development takes about four months. In manual OpenCL, both the investigation and the OpenCL programming are reduced to one week each. Thus, the development takes about two weeks. In ROSE-Generated OpenCL, the investigation takes seven days and TileK programming and automatic OpenCL generation takes one. Thus, development time is only about eight days. Thus, the OpenCL-generated optimizing compiler reduces the development time of Caffe's pooling layer for FPGA to 1/16 of the conventional HDL development time.

Caffe's pooling layer has 6 multiple loop nest. Using our optimization, the loop unrolling pragma is inserted to the innermost loop automatically. Thus, the maximum FPGA pipeline pitch predicted by the FPGA compiler (Altera® SDK for OpenCL™ v15.0.0) decreases from 487 cycles to 1 cycle. It suggests that the optimized pooling layer may run much faster on FPGA. Execution time, accuracy, and power consumption comparison among other devices (CPU, GPU) will be a future study.

VI. Discussion

In this section, we discuss the OpenCL optimization candidates for FPGA. Besides the loop unrolling we implemented, there are several optimization candidates suitable for FPGA. One is the use of the OpenCL's vector type. OpenCL has original vector types, such as float2, float4, float8, and float16. For example, a variable with type float4 is processed in a group of four in parallel. These types are useful in parallel processing for FPGA.

Another optimization candidate is to copy the global memory data to the local memory. An FPGA has two kinds of memory: global (DRAM) and local (SRAM). The global memory has large capacity but large latency, whereas the local memory has small capacity but small latency. In addition, we have to use the global memory to store the CPU's main memory data via a PCI Express(R) between the CPU and FPGA. If there are multiple global memory accesses for the same variable, the performance might degrade. Thus, the global memory data should be copied to the local memory.

The other optimization candidate is to align the data to the 4-byte boundary. If the data in FPGA is not aligned to the 4-byte boundary, the OpenCL compiler for FPGA may generate a low-speed program [5]. Thus, we will insert the padding to the data to align it to the 4-byte boundary.

Our loop unrolling in this paper is the first step to implement the OpenCL optimizations for the FPGA.

VII. CONCLUSION

To reduce the development time of the OpenCL host and device program, we developed an OpenCL-generated optimizing compiler on the basis of the ROSE Compiler Infrastructure.

Our compiler compiles a C/C++ program with TileK pragmas into the OpenCL host program and the OpenCL optimized device program with loop unrolling pragmas automatically. Preliminary evaluation shows that our compiler decreases the development time of the OpenCL host and device program to 1/16 of the conventional development time with manual HDL.

In the future, we will implement other optimizations to our compiler to generate more optimized OpenCL device programs for FPGA easily and evaluate the execution time, accuracy, and power consumption compared to CPU and GPU.

ACKNOWLEDGMENT

The author thanks Dr. Tsuyoshi Tanaka for his support in writing this paper.

REFERENCES

[1] Toyota Motor Corporation, "Toyota to Make Additional Investment in Preferred Networks, Inc.," Aug. 4, 2017, [Online]. Available: https://newsroom.toyota.co.jp/en/detail/18012355, Accessed on: Sep. 18, 2019.

[2] NVIDIA, "Automotive Innovators Motoring to NVIDIA DRIVE," Jan. 4, 2016, [Online]. Available: http://blogs.nvidia.com/blog/2016/01/04/automotive-nvidia-drive-px-2/, Accessed on: Sep. 18, 2019.

[3] NTT Communications, "NTT Com's New AI Technology Identifies Specific Human Motions with High Accuracy," Oct. 7, 2015, [Online]. Available: http://www.ntt.com/release/monthNEWS/detail/20151007_4.html, Accessed on: Sep. 18, 2019.

[4] Khronos Group, "The open standard for parallel programming of heterogeneous systems," [Online]. Available: https://www.khronos.org/opencl/, Accessed on: Sep. 18, 2019.

[5] Intel Corporation, "Intel FPGA SDK for OpenCL, " [Online]. Available: https://www.intel.com/content/www/us/en/software/programmable/sdk-for-opencl/overview.html, Accessed on: Sep. 18, 2019.

[6] Xilinx Inc., "SDAccel Development Environment," [Online]. Available: https://www.xilinx.com/products/design-tools/software-zone/sdaccel.html, Accessed on: Sep. 18, 2019

[7] N. Nystrom, D. White, and K. Das, "Firepile: Run-time Compilation for GPUs in Scala," In Proc. of the Tenth International Conference on Generative Programming and Component Engineering, Portland, OR, USA, pp. 107-115, 2011.

[8] D. Quinlan and C. Liao, "The ROSE Source-to-Source Compiler Infrastructure," The Cetus Users and Compiler Infrastructure Workshop, Galveston Island, Texas, USA, 2011.

[9] Y. Yan, P.-H. Lin, C. Lio, B. R. Supinski, and D. J. Quinlan, "Supporting Multiple Accelerators in High-Level Programming Models," In Proc. the Sixth International Workshop on Programming Models and Applications for Multicores and Manycores, San Francisco, CA, USA, pp.170-180, 2015.

[10] T. Vanderbruggen and J. Cavazos, "Generating OpenCL C kernels from OpenACC," The International Workshop on OpenCL 2013 & 2014, Bristol, United Kingdom, 2014.

[11] S. Lee and J. S. Vetter, "OpenARC: Extensible OpenACC Compiler Framework for Directive-Based Accelerator Programming Study," In Proc. of the First Workshop on Accelerator Programming using Directives, New Orleans, LA, USA, pp.1-11, 2014.

[12] S. Lee and J. S. Vetter, "OpenARC: Open Accelerator Research Compiler for Directive-Based, Efficient Heterogeneous Computing," In Proc. the 23rd ACM Symposium on High-Performance Parallel and Distributed Computing, Vancouver, BC, Canada, pp.115-120, 2014.

[13] S.-I. Lee, T. A. Johnson, and R. Eigenmann, "Cetus -- An Extensible Compiler Infrastructure for Source-to-Source Transformation," in Proc. the 16th International Workshop on Languages and Compilers for Parallel Computing, in Lecture Notes in Computer Science 2958, Springer Verlag, 2003, pp. 539-553.

[14] A. Lashgar, A. Majidi, and A. Baniasadi, "IPMACC: Translating OpenACC API to OpenCL," The 3rd International Workshop on OpenCL, Palo Alto, CA, USA, 2015.

[15] D. Grewe, Z. Wang, and M. F. P. O'Boyle, "Portable Mapping of Data Parallel Programs to OpenCL for Heterogeneous Systems," In Proc. of the 2013 International Symposium on Code Generation and Optimization, Shenzhen, China, pp.1-10, 2013.

[16] J. Bispo, L. Reis, and J. M. P. Cardoso, "Multi-Target C Code Generation from MATLAB(R)," In Proc. the ACM SIGPLAN International Workshop on Libraries, Languages and Compilers for Array Programming, Edinburgh, United Kingdom, pp.95-100, 2014.

[17] A. Hayashi, M. Grossman, J. Zhao, J. Shirako, and V. Sarkar, "Accelerating Habanero-Java Programs with OpenCL Generation," In Proc. the International Conference on Principles and Practices of Programming on the Java Platform: virtual machines, languages, and tools, Cracow, Poland, pp.124-134, 2014.

[18] G. Martinez, M. Gardner, and W.-c. Feng, "CU2CL: A CUDA-to-OpenCL Translator for Multi- and Many-core Architectures," In Proc. the 17th IEEE International Conference on Parallel and Distributed Systems, Tainan, Taiwan, pp.300-307, 2011.

[19] A. Wendell O. Rodrigues, F. Guyomarc'h, and J.-L. Dekeyser, "An MDE Approach for Automatic Code Generation from UML/MARTE to OpenCL," Computing in Science & Engineering, January/February 2013, pp. 46-55, 2013.

[20] A. Klöckner, et al., "PyCUDA and PyOpenCL: A scripting-based approach to GPU run-time code generation," Parallel Computing, vol. 38, no. 3, pp. 157-174, 2012.

[21] M. J. Harvey, "Swan: A tool for porting CUDA programs to OpenCL," Computer Physics Communications, vol. 184, issue 4, pp. 1093-1099, 2011.

From a Subset of LTL Formula to Büchi Automata

Bilal Kanso

Lebanese University
Faculty of sciences (V), Computer Science Department
Email: bilal_kanso@hotmail.com

Ali Kansou

Lebanese University
Faculty of sciences (V), Computer Science Department
Email: ali.kansou@gmail.com

***Abstract*—We present a fragment of Linear Temporal Logic (LTL) together with an polynomial translation of formula from this LTL fragment into equivalent Büchi automata. The translation is completely implemented based on Java Pluging Framework in GOAL Tool as a plugin. The implementation is mainly based on pre-proven theorems such that the transformation works very efficiently. In particular, it runs in polynomial space in terms of the length of the given formula. The main application of this transformation could be in model checking area which consists in obtaining a Büchi automaton that is equivalent to the software system specification and another one that is equivalent to the negation of the property. The intersection of the two Büchi automata is empty if the model satisfies the property. Furthermore, the experiments are performed with three sets of LTL formula, which is commonly used in the literature and the result shows that our proposed LTL fragment covers most of them.**

Keywords–Linear Temporal Logic; Büchi automata; Model checking; Compositional modeling.

I. Introduction

The Linear Temporal Logic (LTL) [1] becomes increasingly one of the most important formalisms to model system properties which are widely used in different areas such as model checking [2][3], testing [4][5], reasoning event in time, *etc.* It is equivalent to first-order logic over finite and infinite words. It is well-known that model checking and satisfiability for LTL are PSPACE-complete and in most all cases the model checking problem is equivalent to a satisfiability-checking problem. This justifies why the satisfiability problem for LTL and its fragments has received so much attention. By way of illustration, model checking based on LTL formalism is PSPACE-hard [6][7]. This complexity arises from the translation step of the negation of a property (described as a LTL formulæ) into Büchi automata. Indeed, the Büchi automaton of a property is constructed in exponential space in the length of this property. This makes verification methods hard or even impossible to be implemented in practice and makes the scalability of the LTL model checking limited, which commonly referred to as the state explosion problem [8].

The question we handled is there some LTL fragments that are feasible in practice. In this paper, we contribute to finding a subset of LTL properties that can be converted polynomially into Büchi automata. A fragment called, *FLTL Logic*, is defined and how formula in this fragment can be transformed into Büchi automata whose the state space size is linear is shown. This fragment is identified by looking for natural subclasses of LTL formula for which complexity decreases and by deep understanding of what makes the converting into Büchi automata PSPACE-complete. Thanks to the structure of our fragment *FLTL* formulæ, the proposed algorithm can be compositional in the sense that the target Büchi automaton associated to a given formulæ is obtained by developing a sub-automaton for each sub-formulæ of the principal formulæ. Hence, the basic idea for developing the final automaton for a FLTL formulæ φ is that φ can be recursively decomposed into a set of sub-formula, arriving at sub-formula that can be completely handled. Composition is then used for assembling different sub-automaton and then forming larger ones. Such a composition can be seen as an operation taking sub-automata for sub-formula, as well as the FLTL operator to provide a new more complex automaton. Furthermore, we showed by experiments that the fragment coverage average is 65.531% which is acceptable and slightly high and the use of such fragments seems promising. The experiments are based on three common sets of LTL formula widely used in the literature. For each set, we identify the formula which can be described in the extension and generate its equivalent automata using the proposed algorithm.

The rest of this article is organized as follows: Section II briefly describes Büchi automata. In Section III, we describe our fragment of LTL logic and the reasons to choose it. In Section IV, we present for each formulæ in our fragment LTL, its equivalent Büchi automata. Section V shows the final algorithm that generates to any formulæ in our fragment an equivalent Büchi automaton. Section VI represents the experiments we conducted to compute the coverage average of our LTL fragment. Section VII presents the related work and Section VIII presents the conclusion and some future works.

II. Büchi automata

A Büchi automaton is variant of non-deterministic finite-state automata on infinite inputs [9]-[10]. A word is accepted if the automaton goes through some designated "accept" states infinitely often while reading it. Formally, a **Büchi automaton** is defined by a 5-tuple $A = (S, s_0, F, \Sigma, \delta)$ where S is a finite set of states, $s_0 \in S$ is the initial state, Σ is a non-empty set of atomic propositions, $F \subseteq S$ is a finite set of accepting states and $\delta : S \times \Sigma \longrightarrow 2^S$ is a transition function. A **run** of A on $\sigma = \sigma(0)\sigma(1)\sigma(2)\cdots \in \Sigma^\omega$ is an infinite sequence of states $s_0 s_1 s_2 \cdots \in S^\omega$ starting with the initial state s_0 of A such that $\forall i, i \geq 0, s_{i+1} \in \delta(s_i, \sigma(i))$. A run $s_0 s_1 s_2 \ldots$ is **accepting** by an automaton A if A goes through accepting states (i.e $\in F$) infinitely often while reading it. The *accepted language* of a Büchi automaton A, denoted by, $\mathcal{L}_\omega(A)$ is then defined by $\mathcal{L}_\omega(A) = \{\sigma \in \Sigma^\omega \mid \text{there is an accepting run for } \sigma \text{ in } A\}$. The union of two Büchi automata A_1 and A_2 is formally defined as follows:

Definition 1 (Buchi automata union): Let $A_1 = (S_1, s_{10}, F_1, \Sigma, \delta_1)$ and $A_2 = (S_2, s_{20}, F_2, \Sigma, \delta_2)$ be two Büchi automata. The **union** $A_1 \cup A_2$ of A_1 and A_2 is the Büchi automaton $A = (S, s_0, F, \Sigma, \delta)$ defined as follows:

- $S = S_1 \cup S_2 \cup \{s_0\}$
- $s_0 \in S$ is the initial state
- $F = F_1 \cup F_2$
- the transition relation δ is defined as follows:

$$\delta(s,p) = \begin{cases} \delta_1(s,p) \text{ if } s \in S_1 \\ \delta_2(s,p) \text{ if } s \in S_2 \\ \delta_1(s_{10},p) \cup \delta_2(s_{20},p) \text{ if } s \text{ is the initial} \\ \text{state } s_0 \end{cases}$$

In Definition 1, we add a new initial (nonaccept) state s_{new} to the union set of states of both A_1 and $A_2$and the transitions $s_{\text{new}} \xrightarrow{p} s$ if and only if $s^0_{A_1} \xrightarrow{p} s$ and $s_{\text{new}} \xrightarrow{p} s$ if and only if $s^0_{A_2} \xrightarrow{p} s$ to the union set of transitions of both A_1 and A_2.

The construction of the intersection automaton works a little differently from the finite state automata case. One needs to check whether both sets of accepting states are visited infinitely often. Consider two runs r_1 and r_2 and a word σ where r_1 goes through an accept state after $\sigma(0), \sigma(2), \ldots$ and r_2 enters accept state after $\sigma(0)\sigma(3) \ldots$. Thus, there is no guarantee that r_1 and r_2 will enter accept states simultaneously. To overcome this problem, we need to identify the accept states of the intersection of the two automata. To do so, we create two copies of the intersected state space. In the first copy, we check for occurrence of the first acceptance set. In the second copy, we check for occurrence of the second acceptance set. When a run enters a final state in the first copy, we wait for that run also enters in an accept state in the second copy. When this is encountered, we switch back to the first copy and so on. We repeat jumping back and forth between the two copies whenever we find an accepting state.

Definition 2 (Buchi automata intersection): Let $A_1 = (S_1, s_{10}, F_1, \Sigma, \delta_1)$ and $A_2 = (S_2, s_{20}, F_2, \Sigma, \delta_2)$ be two Büchi automata. The intersection $A_1 \cap A_2$ of A_1 and A_2 is the Büchi automaton $A = (S, s_0, F, \Sigma, \delta)$ defined as follows:

- $S = S_1 \times S_2 \times \{1, 2\}$
- $s_0 = (s_{10}, s_{20}, 1)$
- $F = S_1 \times F_2 \times \{2\}$
- The transition function δ is defined as follows:

$$\delta((s_1, s'_1, 1), p) = \begin{cases} (s_2, s'_2, 1) \text{ if } s_2 \in \delta_1(s_1, p), \\ s'_2 \in \delta_2(s_2, p) \text{ and } s_1 \notin F_1 \\ (s_2, s'_2, 2) \text{ if } s_2 \in \delta_1(s_1, p), \\ s'_2 \in \delta_2(s_2, p) \text{ and } s_1 \in F_1 \end{cases}$$

$$\delta((s_1, s'_1, 2), p) = \begin{cases} (s_2, s'_2, 2) \text{ if } s_2 \in \delta_1(s_1, p), \\ s'_2 \in \delta_2(s_2, p) \text{ and } s'_1 \notin F_2 \\ (s_2, s'_2, 1) \text{ if } s_2 \in \delta_1(s_1, p), \\ s'_2 \in \delta_2(s_2, p) \text{ and } s'_1 \in F_2 \end{cases}$$

Theorem 1: Let $\psi = \varphi_1 \vee \varphi_2$ (resp. $\psi = \varphi_1 \wedge \varphi_2$) be a LTL formulæ and A_{φ_i} be the Büchi automaton equivalent to φ_i for $i = 1, 2$. Let A_ψ be the LTL automaton built according to Definition 1 (resp. Definition 2). Then, $\mathsf{Words}(\psi) = \mathcal{L}_\omega(A_\psi)$ (See Proof in Appendix)

III. Flat LTL Logic

In this section, we introduce our subset of LTL logic that we call *FLTL Logic*. This fragment will be used to express temporal properties and then translate them into Büchi automata in linear size. The syntax of our FLTL logic adds to usual boolean propositional operators $\neg$ (negation) and $\wedge$ (conjunction), some modal operators that describe how the behavior changes with time. **Next**: $\mathsf{X}\varphi$ requires that the formula φ be true in the next state. **Until**: $\varphi_1 \mathsf{U} \varphi_2$ requires that the formula φ_1 be true *until* the formula φ_2 is true, which is required to happen. **Eventually**: $\Diamond\varphi$ requires that the formula φ be true at some point in the future (starting from the present) and it is equivalent to $\Diamond\varphi \equiv \mathsf{true} \; \mathsf{U} \; \varphi$. **Always**: $\Box\varphi$ requires that the formula φ be true at every point in the future (including the present). **Release**: $\varphi_1 \mathsf{R} \varphi_2$ requires that its second argument φ_2 always be true, a requirement that is *released* as soon as its first argument φ_1 becomes true. It is equivalent to $\varphi_1 \mathsf{R} \varphi_2 \equiv \neg(\neg\varphi_1 \mathsf{U} \neg\varphi_2)$.

A. Our fragment LTL logic

Definition 3 (FLTL formulæ): **The set of FLTL formulæ** $\mathcal{L}_f$ is given by the following grammar:

$$\varphi{:=}\Theta \;|\Box\Theta \;|\Theta \;\mathsf{U}\; \varphi \;|\varphi \;\mathsf{R}\; \Theta \;|\mathsf{X}\varphi \;|\neg\Delta \;|\varphi_1 \wedge \varphi_2 \;|\varphi_1 \vee \varphi_2$$

where Θ is a propositional formula defined by: $\Theta{:=}\mathsf{true} \;|p \;|\neg\Theta \;|\Theta_1 \wedge \Theta_2$ and Δ is the formula defined by: $\Delta{:=}\Delta \;\mathsf{U}\; \Theta \;|\Theta \;\mathsf{R}\; \Delta \;|\mathsf{X}\varphi \;|\neg\Delta$ with $p \in \Sigma$.

For the sake of brevity and the lack of space, we only discuss here why the fragment $\Theta \mathsf{U} \varphi$ is included within our LTL fragment to the detriment of both formula $\varphi_1 \mathsf{U} \varphi_2$ and $\varphi_1 \mathsf{U} \Theta$. It is well-known the size of an Büchi automaton $\overline{A}$ that recognizes the complement language $\mathcal{L}_\omega(\overline{A})$ of the language accepted $\mathcal{L}_\omega(A)$ by an automaton A is exponential [11], [12]. Suppose we have separately built an automaton A_1 for φ_1 and an automaton A_2 for φ_2, and let us then try to compositionally obtain the resulting automaton A for φ. According to the until operator's semantics, it is required that φ *holds at the current moment, if there is some future moment for which* φ_2 *holds and* φ_1 *holds at all moments until that future moment.* That means constructing the automaton for $\varphi = \varphi_1 \mathsf{U} \underline{\varphi_2}$ firstly requires constructing of the intersection of A_1 and $\overline{A_2}$. As stated previously, computing $\overline{A_2}$ is exponential and therefore, constructing the Büchi automaton for $\varphi \mathsf{U} \varphi_2$ is exponential. To avoid this kind of formula, we choose the formulæ $\Theta \mathsf{U} \varphi$ to be a part of our LTL subset where the construction of the Büchi automaton associated to it, does not need to complement any Büchi automaton.

B. Positive Normal Form (FPNF)

As LTL formula, FLTL formula can be transformed into the so-called *Positive Normal form (FPNF)*. This form is characterized by the fact that negations only occur adjacent to atomic propositions. All negation symbols of the given LTL formula have to be pushed inwards over the temporal operators.

Definition 4 (FPNF): **The set of FLTL Positive Normal Form (FPNF) formulæ** $\mathcal{L}_{FPNF}$ is given by the following grammar:

$$\varphi{:=}\mathsf{true} \;|p \;|\neg p \;|\varphi_1 \wedge \varphi_2 \;|\varphi_1 \vee \varphi_2 \;|\Box\Theta \;|\Theta \;\mathsf{U}\; \varphi \;|\varphi \;\mathsf{R}\; \Theta \;|\mathsf{X}\varphi$$

Each formulæ $\varphi \in \mathcal{L}_f$, can be transformed into a formulæ $\varphi\prime \in \mathcal{L}_{FPNF}$. This is done by pushing negations inside, near to atomic propositions. To do this, we use the following transformation rules:

$\neg\text{true} \rightsquigarrow \text{false}, \neg\neg\varphi \rightsquigarrow \varphi, \neg(\varphi_1 \wedge \varphi_2) \rightsquigarrow \neg\varphi_1 \vee \neg\varphi_2, \neg\mathsf{X}\varphi \rightsquigarrow \mathsf{X}\neg\varphi, \neg(\varphi \ \mathsf{U}\ \Theta) \rightsquigarrow \neg\varphi \ \mathsf{R}\ \neg\Theta, \neg(\Theta \ \mathsf{R}\ \varphi) \rightsquigarrow \neg\Theta \ \mathsf{U}\ \neg\varphi$.

Theorem 2: For any FLTL formulæ $\varphi \in \mathcal{L}_f$, there exists an equivalent LTL formula $\varphi\prime \in \mathcal{L}_{FPNF}$ $|\varphi\prime| = \mathcal{O}(|\varphi|)$.

C. Semantics

The semantics of FLTL formulæ is defined over infinite sequences $\sigma : \mathbb{N} \longrightarrow 2^{\Sigma}$ (2^{Σ} is the power set of Σ). In other words, a model is an infinite sequence $A_0A_1\ldots$ of subsets of Σ. The function σ, called *interpretation function*, describes how the truth of atomic propositions changes as time progresses. For every sequence σ, we write $\sigma = (\sigma(0),\ldots,\sigma(n),\ldots)$. Thus, $\sigma(\mathbf{i})$ denotes the state at index i and $\sigma(i:j)$ the part of σ containing the sequence of states between i and j. $\sigma(\mathbf{i}\ldots) = \mathbf{A_i A_{i+1} A_{i+2}}\ldots$ denotes the suffix of a sequence $\sigma = A_0A_1A_2\cdots \in (2^{\Sigma})^{\omega}$ starting in the $(i+1)$st symbol A_i where ω denotes *infinity*. We also write $\sigma(i) \models \varphi$ to denote that "*φ is true at time instant i in the model σ*". This notion is defined inductively, according to the structure of φ.

The FLTL formula are interpreted over infinite sequences of states $\sigma : \mathbb{N} \longrightarrow 2^{\Sigma}$ as follows:

Definition 5 (Semantics of FLTL): Let $\sigma : \mathbb{N} \longrightarrow 2^{\Sigma}$ be an interpretation function and $\varphi \in \mathcal{L}_{FLTL}$. σ **satisfies** φ, noted $\sigma \models \varphi$,is inductively defined over the construction of φ as follows:

- $\varphi = \text{true}$, then $\sigma \models \text{true}$
- if $\varphi = p$, then $\sigma \models p$ iff $p \in \sigma(0)$
- if $\varphi = \mathsf{X}\varphi'$, then $\sigma \models \mathsf{X}\varphi'$ iff $\sigma(1) \models \varphi'$
- if $\varphi = \Box\Theta$, then $\sigma \models \Box\Theta$ iff $\forall i \geq 0, \sigma(i) \models \Theta$
- if $\varphi = \Theta \ \mathsf{U}\ \varphi$, then $\sigma \models \Theta \ \mathsf{U}\ \varphi$ iff $\exists i, i \geq 0, \sigma(i,\ldots) \models \varphi$ and $\forall j, 0 \leq j < i, \sigma(j\ldots) \models \Theta$
- if $\varphi = \varphi \ \mathsf{R}\ \Theta$, then $\sigma \models \varphi \ \mathsf{R}\ \Theta$ iff $\exists i, i \geq 0, \sigma(i,\ldots) \models \varphi$ and $\forall j, j \geq 0, \sigma(j\ldots) \models \Theta$ or $\exists i, i \geq 0$ $(\sigma(i\ldots) \models \varphi \wedge \forall k, k \leq i, \sigma(k\ldots) \models \Theta)$
- if $\varphi = \neg\varphi'$, then $\sigma \models \neg\varphi'$ iff $\sigma \not\models \varphi'$
- Propositional connectives are handled as usual

The semantics of a FLTL formulæ can be also seen as the language Words(φ) that contains all infinite words over the set of atomic propositions (*i.e.* alphabet) 2^{Σ} that satisfy φ. Thus, the language Words(φ) for a FLTL formulæ φ is formally defined by Words(φ) $= \{\sigma \in (2^{\Sigma})^{\omega} \mid \sigma \models \varphi\}$.

Proposition 1: Two FLTL formula φ_1 and φ_2 are *equivalent*, denoted $\varphi_1 \equiv \varphi_2$, if Words($\varphi_1$) =Words($\varphi_2$).

IV. Construction of Büchi automata for FLTL logic

In the sequel, we explain for each subformulæ in our fragment LTL logic how its equivalent Büchi automaton can be obtained.

A. Büchi automata for Θ formula

The Büchi automaton associated to a propositional formulæ Θ is obtained by creating two states s_0 and s_1 and two transitions tr_1 and tr_2. s_0 is the only initial state while s_1 is the only final state. tr_1 is the transition from s_0 to s_1 labeling with Θ while the transition tr_2 is a loop labeled with true over the state s_2.

Definition 6 (Θ automaton): Let Θ be a propositional formulæ. The **automaton** $A_\Theta = (S_\Theta, s^0_\Theta, F_\Theta, \Sigma, \delta_\Theta)$ associated to Θ is defined as follows:

- $S_\Theta = \{s_0, s_1\}$, $s^0_\Theta = s_0$, $F_\Theta = \{s_1\}$
- The transition function δ is defined as follows:

$$\delta_\Theta(s_0,\Theta) = \{s_1\} \text{ and } \delta_\Theta(s_1,\text{true}) = \{s_1\}$$

B. Büchi automata for $\Theta \ \mathsf{U}\ \varphi$ formula

The automaton associated to $\Theta \ \mathsf{U}\ \varphi$ is obtained by adding a new initial (nonaccept) state s_{new} to the state set of A_φ, a loop over the added state s_{new} labeled with the propositional formula Θ and transitions $s_{\text{new}} \overset{p}{\longrightarrow} s$ if and only if and only if $s^0 \overset{p}{\longrightarrow} s$ with s^0 is the initial state of A_φ. All other transitions of A_φ, as well as the accept states, remain unchanged. s_{new} is the single initial state automaton, is not accept, and has no incoming transitions except the loop one.

Definition 7 ($\Theta \ \mathsf{U}\ \varphi$ automaton): Let Θ be a propositional formula and φ be an LTL flat formulæ. Let $A_\varphi = (S_\varphi, s^0_\varphi, F_\varphi, \Sigma, \delta_\varphi)$ be the automaton associated to φ. The **automaton** $A_\psi = (S_\psi, s^0_\psi, F_\psi, \Sigma, \delta_\psi)$ associated to $\psi = \Theta \ \mathsf{U}\ \varphi$ is defined as follows:

- $S_\psi = \{s_{\text{new}}\} \cup S_\varphi$
- $s^0_\psi = s_{\text{new}}$, $F_\psi = F_\varphi$
- The transition function δ_ψ is defined as follows:

$$\delta_\psi(s,p) = \begin{cases} \delta_\varphi(s,p) \text{ if } s \in S_\varphi \ (A_\varphi \text{ transitions}) \\ \delta_\varphi(s^0_\varphi,p) \text{ if } s = s_{\text{new}} \\ \text{(Connection initial state to } A_\varphi) \\ \{s_{\text{new}}\} \text{ if } s = s_{\text{new}} \text{ and } p = \Theta \\ \text{(Loop over the new initial state)} \end{cases}$$

Example 1: Figure 1 illustrates the composition definition of $\Theta \ \mathsf{U}\ \varphi$. Figure 1a shows the Büchi automaton associated to $(\Diamond b)\ \mathsf{R}\ c$. To construct the Büchi automaton associated to $(a \ \mathsf{U}\ (\Diamond b \ \mathsf{R}\ c))$, we add a new state s_{new} that we consider as initial state. Then, for each transition outgoing from s_{new} with label l and goes to state s, we add a transition from s_{new} to the state s with a label l. Finally, we then add a loop labeled with the atomic proposition a over the added state.

Theorem 3: Let $\psi = \Theta \ \mathsf{U}\ \varphi$, A_φ be the Büchi automaton equivalent to φ and A_ψ be the automaton built according to Definition 7. Then, Words(ψ) $= \mathcal{L}_\omega(A_\psi)$.

C. Büchi automata for $\mathsf{X}\varphi$ formula

The automaton associated to $\mathsf{X}\varphi$ is obtained by adding two new states s_{new} (neither initial state or accept state) and s_{init} (considered as the initial state) to the state set of A_φ with the following two transitions (1) add for any transition in A_φ which starts from the initial state s^0 to a state s, a transition from s_{new} to s; (2) add a transition from the initial state s_{init} to the s_{new} labeled with true. All other transitions of A_φ remain

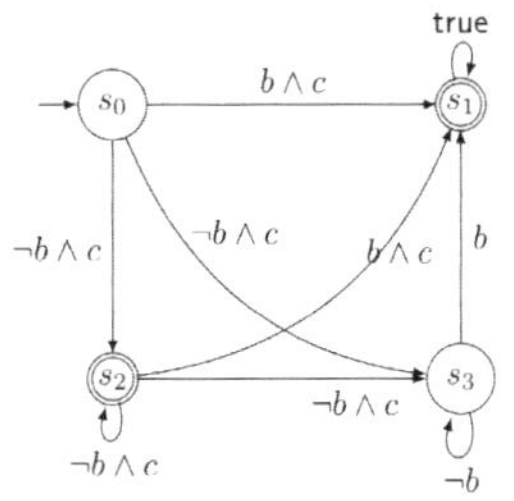

(a) $(\Diamond b)$ R c

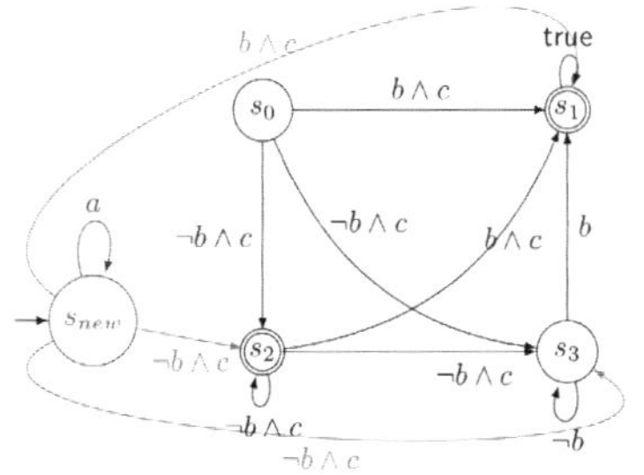

(b) a U $(\Diamond b$ R $c)$

Figure 1. Example of composition: Θ U φ

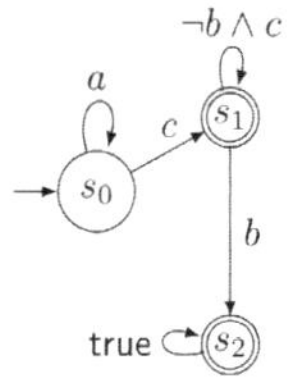

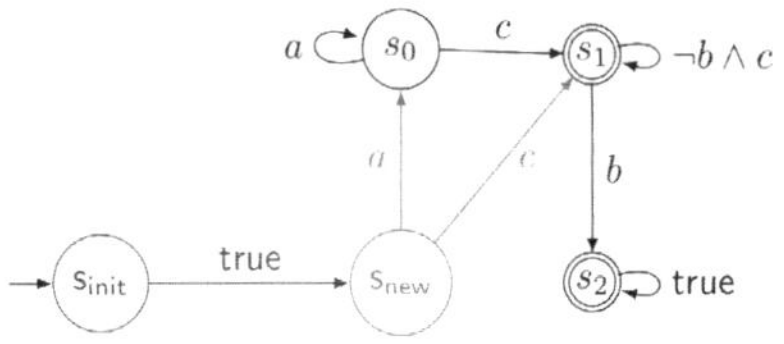

(a) a U (Xb R c) (b) X(a U (Xb R c))

Figure 2. Example of composition: Xφ formula

unchanged and final states of A_φ become accept ones of A_ψ and initial state of A_ψ become the state s_{init}.

Definition 8 (Xφ automaton): Let φ be an Flat LTL formulæ. Let $A_\varphi = (S_\varphi, s_\varphi^0, F_\varphi, \Sigma, \delta_\varphi)$ be the automaton equivalent to φ. The **automaton** $A_\psi = (S_\psi, s_\psi^0, F_\psi, \Sigma, \delta_\psi)$ equivalent to $\psi =$ Xφ is defined as follows:

- $S_\psi = S_\varphi \cup \{s_{\text{new}}, s_{\text{init}}\}$
- $s_\psi^0 = s_{\text{init}}$, $F_\psi = F_\varphi$
- The transition function δ is defined as follows:

$$\delta_\psi(s,p) = \begin{cases} \delta_\varphi(s,p) \text{ if } s \in S_\varphi \ (A_\varphi \text{ transitions}) \\ \delta_\varphi(s_\varphi^0, p) \text{ if } s = s_{\text{new}} \\ (\text{Connection } s_{\text{new}} \text{ to initial state of } A_\varphi) \\ \{s_{\text{new}}\} \text{ if } s = s_{\text{init}} \text{ and } p = \text{true} \\ (\text{Connection } s_{\text{init}} \text{ to } s_{\text{new}}) \end{cases}$$

Example 2: Figure 2 illustrates the definition of Xφ. Figure 2a shows the Büchi automaton associated to the formulæ a U (Xb R c). To construct the Büchi automaton equivalent to X(a U (Xb R c)), we add a new state s_{new} and for each transition tr starting from the initial state s_φ^0 to a state s, a transition from s_{new} to s with the same label. Finally, we add the state s_{init} that we consider as initial and we connect s_{init} to s_{new} with a transition labeled with the true label.

Theorem 4: Let $\psi =$ Xφ, A_φ be the Büchi automaton equivalent to φ and A_ψ be the LTL automaton built according to Definition 8. Then, Words(Xφ) $= \mathcal{L}_\omega(A_\psi)$.

D. Büchi automata for φ R Θ formula

The formulæ φ R Θ informally means that Θ is true until φ becomes true, or Θ is true forever. Thus, the construction of a Büchi automaton for φ R Θ can be done by construction the Büchi automaton associated to the fact that Θ is true until φ becomes true and the construction of a Büchi automaton associated to the fact that Θ is true forever. Finally, make the union between the two constructed Büchi automata. Consequently, to build the Büchi automaton for φ R Θ, we need to add two new states s_i and s_f to the set of states of the automaton A_φ. s_i becomes the single initial state of the resulting automaton and s_f is added to set of final states of the resulting automaton. The following transitions are added to the set of transitions of the resulting automaton:

- Transitions $s_i \xrightarrow{p \wedge \Theta} s$ if and only if and only if $s^0 \xrightarrow{p} s$ where s^0 is the initial state of A_φ.
- A loop over the added state s_i labeled with the propositional formula Θ
- A loop over the added state s_f labeled with the propositional formula Θ
- A transition $s_i \xrightarrow{\Theta} s_f$

All other transitions of A_φ, as well as the accept states, remain unchanged.

Definition 9 (φ R Θ automaton): Let Θ be a propositional formula and φ be an LTL flat formulæ. Let $A_\varphi = (S_\varphi, s_\varphi^0, F_\varphi, \Sigma, \delta_\varphi)$ be the automaton associated to φ. The **automaton** $A_\psi = (S_\psi, s_\psi^0, F_\psi, \Sigma, \delta_\psi)$ associated to $\psi = \varphi$ R Θ is defined as follows:

- $S_\psi = \{s_i, s_f\} \cup S_\varphi$
- $s_\psi^0 = s_i$, $F_\psi = F_\varphi \cup \{s_f\}$
- The transition function δ is defined as follows:

$$\delta_\psi(s,p) = \begin{cases} \delta_\varphi(s,p) \text{ if } s \in S_\varphi \ (A_\varphi \text{ transitions}) \\ \delta_\varphi(s_\varphi^0, p\prime) \text{ if } s = s_i \text{ and } p = \Theta \wedge p\prime \\ (\text{Connection } s_i \text{ to initial state of } A_\varphi) \\ \{s_i, s_f\} \text{ if } s = s_i \text{ and } p = \Theta \\ (\text{Loop over } s_i \text{ or connection } s_i \text{ to } s_f) \\ \{s_f\} \text{ if } s = s_f \text{ and } p = \Theta \\ (\text{Loop over } s_f) \end{cases}$$

Example 3: Figure 3 illustrates the composition definition of φ R Θ. Figure 3a shows the Büchi automaton associated to the formulæ c U $\Diamond b$. To construct the Büchi automaton associated to the LTL formulæ ((c U $\Diamond b$) R a), we add a state s_i that we consider as the only initial state and a state s_f that we consider as a final state. We add a loop labeled with the atomic proposition a over the two added states. Finally, for each transition outgoing from the initial state of the automaton φ with label l and goes to state s, we add a transition from the added state s_i to the state s with a label $l \wedge a$. We also add a transition labeled with a from the state s_i to the state s_f.

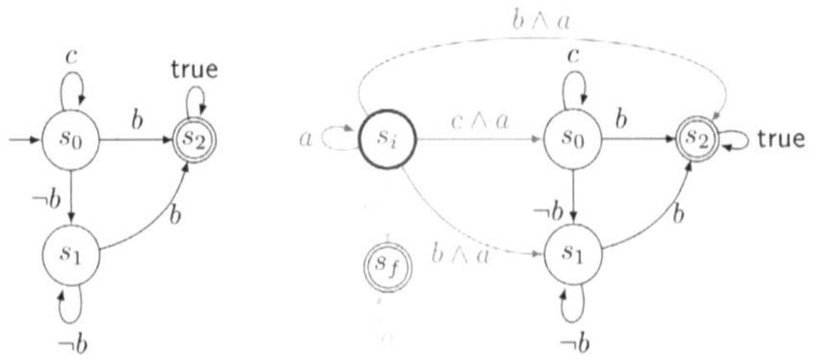

(a) c U $\Diamond b$ (b) $(c$ U $\Diamond b)$ R a

Figure 3. Example of composition: φ R Θ

Theorem 5: Let $\psi = \varphi$ R Θ, A_φ be the Büchi automaton equivalent to φ and A_ψ be the LTL automaton built according to Definition 9. Then, Words(φ R Θ) $= \mathcal{L}_\omega(A_\psi)$.

E. Büchi for $\Box\Theta$ formula

The Büchi automaton associated to formulæ $\Box\Theta$ is obtained by creating one state s_0 and a loop over s_0 labeling with Θ.

Definition 10 ($\Box\varphi$ automaton): Let Θ be an propositional formulæ. The automaton associated to $\Box\Theta$ is defined as $A_{\Box\Theta} = (\{s_0\}, s_0, \{s_0\}, \text{Prop}, \delta_{\Box\Theta})$ where $\delta_{\Box\Theta}$ is defined as follows: $\delta_{\Box\Theta}(s_0, \Theta) = \{s_0\}$

V. Our Algorithm and its Implementation

Our algorithm to build Büchi automata from FLTL formula is compositional in the sense that the final Büchi automaton is obtained by developing a sub-automaton for each subformulæ of the principal formulæ . Hence, the basic idea for developing the final automaton for a FLTL formulæ φ is to explore the formulæ φ in a preorder traversal. That is to say, we visit the root operator of φ first, then recursively do a preorder traversal of the left sub-formula, followed by a recursive preorder traversal of the right formulæ . Algorithm 1 allows us to build a Büchi automaton for a positive FLTL formula φ and uses the following five functions:

- BuchiProp(Θ): takes as input a propositional formula Θ and returns the automaton as defined in Definition 6 (Section IV);
- BuchiNext(BA): takes as input an Büchi automaton BA and returns a Büchi automaton defined according to Definition 8 (Section IV);
- BuchiEventuelly(BA): takes as input an Büchi automaton BA and returns a Büchi automaton defined according to Definition 7 (Section IV);
- BuchiBinary(op, BA_l, BA_r): that takes as input $\wedge$ or $\vee$ operator and two Büchi automata BA_l and BA_r and returns a Büchi automaton defined according to definitions of $\wedge$ and $\vee$ given in Section II;
- BuchiUntil(Θ, BA): that takes as input a propositional formula Θ and a Büchi automaton BA and returns the automaton as defined in Definition 7 (Section IV);
- BuchiRelease(Θ, BA) that takes as input a propositional formula Θ and a Büchi automaton BA and returns the automaton as defined in Definition 9 (Section IV).
- BuchiAlways(Θ): takes as input a propositional formula Θ and returns the automaton as defined in Definition 10 (Section IV);

Algorithm 1: Generating Büchi automata: **GenerateBA(φ)** for a FLTL formula

```
Name : GenerateBA
Input: a positive FLTL formulæ φ
Output: a Büchi automaton A;
if φ instance of U then
    return BuchiUntil(Left (φ),
     GenerateBA(right (φ)));
else if φ instance of R then
    return BuchiRelease(right (φ),
     GenerateBA(Left (φ)));
else if φ instance of X then
    return BuchiNext(GenerateBA(right
     (φ)));
else if φ instance of □ then
    return BuchiAlways(φ);
else if φ instance of ◇ then
    return
     BuchiEventuelly(GenerateBA(right
     (φ)));
else if (φ instance of ∨) or (φ instance of
 ∧) then
    if isPropositionnal (Left (φ)) and
     isPropositionnal (right (φ) then
        return BuchiProp(φ) ;
    else if isPropositionnal (Left (φ)) then
        return BuchiBinary(BuchiProp(Left
         (φ)),GenerateBA(right (φ)) ;
    else if isPropositionnal (right (φ)) then
        return BuchiBinary(GenerateBA(Left
         (φ),BuchiProp(right (φ))) ;
    else
        return BuchiBinary(BuchiProp(Left
         (φ)),BuchiProp(right (φ))) ;
```

The proposed translation algorithm is very efficient where we can translate any FLTL formula φ of length n in time $O(n)$ with $O(n)$ states. The trick is to eliminate from our translation each step that could be exponential. As Büchi automata complementation is exponential [11][12], our transformation prohibit the use of complement Büchi automata operation and requires to use only LTL formula with negation pushed to atomic propsitions.

Theorem 6: For any FLTL formulæ $\varphi \in \mathcal{L}_f$, there exists an Büchi automaton A_φ with $|A_\varphi| = O(|\varphi|)$ and if A_ψ is the Büchi automaton generated by Algorithm 1, then: $Words(\psi) = \mathcal{L}_\omega(A_\psi)$.

We implemented our algorithm within the Graphical Tool for Omega-Automata and Logics (GOAL) tool that is an adequate graphical tool for defining and manipulating common variants of omega-automata, in particular Büchi automata, and temporal logic formula [13]. GOAL supports the translation of temporal formula such as Quantified Propositional Temporal Logic (QPTL) into Büchi automata where many well-known translation algorithms are implemented. It also provides language equivalence between two Büchi automata, automata

TABLE I. BENCHMARK FORMULA FOUND IN [14]

Formula	$\in \mathcal{L}_{FLTL}$
p U (q U □r)	yes
p U (q ∧ X(r U s))	yes
p U (q ∧ X(r ∧ (◇(s ∧X(◇(t ∧ X(◇(u ∧ X◇v))))))))	yes
◇(p ∧ X□q)	yes
◇(p ∧ X(q ∧ X◇r))	yes
◇(q ∧ X(p U r))	yes
(◇□q) ∨ (◇□p)	yes
◇(p ∧ X◇(q ∧ X◇(r ∧ X◇s)))	yes
□◇p ∧ □◇q ∧ □◇r ∧ □◇s ∧ □◇t	yes
(p U q U r) ∨ (q U r U p) ∨ (r U p U q)	yes
□(p → (q U (□r ∨ □s)))	no
□(p → (q U r))	no

complementation, automata union, automata intersection and emptiness algorithms. It has extensions covering common translation algorithms (*e.g.*, LTL2BA [8], Tableau algorithm, LTL2AUT, *etc.*). As the recent implementation of GOAL is based on the Java Plugin Framework, it can be properly extended by new plug-ins, providing new functionalities that are loaded at run-time. We implemented our composition algorithm within an independent plug-in. The automata generated by our algorithm are simplified by several simplification methods (*e.g.*, simulation, Delayed simulation, Faired simulation, reducing unreachable/dead states) by taking advantage from GOAL tool which implements all these methods.

VI. COVERAGE AVERAGE OF FLTL FRAGMENT

In this section, we present the experiments that we conducted to show the coverage average of our fragment *FLTL* formula. Three sets LTL formula which commonly considered in the literature are performed. The experiments on the one hand, emphasis the performance of our implementation algorithm and, on the other, demonstrates that a wide range of LTL formula can be covered by our approach and translating polynomially and properly using our GOAL plug-in. The process we applied for each formula φ in our experiments can be summarized as follows:

1) Checking whether φ belongs to *FLTL* fragment by building the finite syntax tree of φ.
2) Using the well-known algorithm LTL2BA to generate a Büchi automaton equivalent to φ (called A_1)
3) Using our GOAL plugin to generate the Büchi automaton A_2 according to rules defined in our algorithm (*i.e.*, Algorithm 1)
4) Runing the GOAL Büchi automata equivalence to check the equivalence between A_1 and A_2.

The first set contains 12 formula and can be found in [14]. The experiments for this set show that only two formula do not belong to our grammar as shown in Table I. The coverage average for this set is then 83.334%.

The second set contains 27 formula and can be found in [15][16]. The results show that the *FLTL* fragment fails to express only 11 formula as shown in Table II. The coverage average for this set is then 59.259%.

The third set contains 50 formula and can be found in [17]. Indeed, the authors in [17] have proposed a pattern-based approach which uses specification patterns that, at a higher abstraction level, capture recurring temporal properties. The main idea is that a temporal property is a combination of one **pattern** and one **scope**. A scope is the part of the system

TABLE II. BENCHMARK FORMULA FOUND IN [15][16]

Formula	∈	Formula	∈
p U q	yes	¬ □(p → X(q R r))	yes
p U (q U r)	yes	¬ (□◇p ∨ ◇□q)	yes
¬ (p U (q U r))	no	◇p ∧ ◇¬ p	yes
□◇p → □◇q	yes	(□(q ∨ □◇p) ∧ □(r ∨ □◇¬p)) ∨ □q ∨ □r	no
¬ (◇◇p ↔◇p)	yes	(□(q ∨ ◇□p) ∧ □(r ∨ ◇□¬p)) ∨ □q ∨ □r	no
¬ (□◇p → □◇q)	yes	¬ ((□(q ∨ □◇p) ∧ □(r ∨ □◇¬p)) ∨ □q ∨ □r)	yes
¬ (□◇p ↔ □◇q)	yes	¬((□(q ∨ ◇□p) ∧ □(r ∨ ◇□¬p)) ∨ □q ∨ □r)	yes
p R (p ∨ q)	yes	□(q ∨ X□p) ∧ □(r ∨ X□¬ p))	no
(Xp U Xq) ∨ ¬ X(p U q)	yes	□(q ∨ (Xp ∧ X¬ p))	no
(Xp U q) ∨ ¬ X(p U (p ∧ q))	yes	(p U p) ∨ (q U p)	yes
□(p → ◇q) ∧ ((Xp U q) ∨ ¬ X(p U (p ∧ q)))	no	◇p U □q	no
□(p → ◇q) ∧ ((Xp U Xq) ∨ ¬ X(p U p))	no	□p U q	no
□(p → ◇q)	no	□(◇p ∧ ◇q)	yes
(Xq ∧ r) R X(((s U p) R r) U (s R r))	no		

TABLE III. COVERAGE DWYER'S PATTERNS/SCOPES BY OUR LTL FRAGMENT

Scope/Pattern	Globally	Before r	After q	Between q and r	After q until r
Absence	yes	yes	yes	yes	yes
Universality	yes	yes	yes	yes	no
Existence	no	no	yes	yes	yes
Precedence	yes	yes	yes	no	yes
Response	yes	yes	no	no	no
s, t precedes p	yes	yes	yes	no	no
p precedes s, t	yes	yes	yes	no	no
p responds s t	no	yes	no	no	no
s, t responds p	no	yes	no	no	no
s, t without z responds to p	no	yes	no	no	no

execution path over which a pattern holds. For more details about patterns and scopes can be found in [17]. They proved that the patterns dramatically simplify the specification of temporal properties, with a fairly complete coverage where they collected hundreds of specifications and they observed that 92% of them fall into this small set of patterns/scopes. A translational semantics have been proposed to Dwyer's properties by mapping each pattern/scope combination to a corresponding LTL formula. As Dwyer's and *al.* propose 5 scopes and 10 patterns, the total number of involved LTL formula is then 50. The results of the comparison are given in Table III and show that our LTL fragment covers 27 formula from 50 formula associating by Dwyer to scopes/patterns. The coverage average for this set is then 54%.

The covering average of each set is accepted and slightly high. This shows that our fragment covers more than 65.531%, which is considered very good enough due to the importance of LTL formalism in modeling area. Such a result could be a promising direction to explore LTL-based model checking techniques in which system properties are first expressed in LTL formula then converted into Büchi automata.

VII. RELATED WORK

Translation from LTL formula to Büchi automata has been extensively studied in the literature. Authors in [1][18] constructed Büchi automata whoses states are sets of subformula of the considered LTL formula. This translation is of order $2^{O(n)}$ where n is the length of the LTL formula in input. [19] proposed to build Büchi automata by a bottom-up traversal through the syntax tree of the considered LTL formula. This translation has been proved in order of $2^{O(nlog(n))}$. [20] presented an efficient translation by means of alternating ω-automata. The translation from LTL formula to alternating ω automata is linear in terms of the length of the considered LTL formula, but the translation of the resulting alternating ω-automaton to the target Büchi automata is exponential. [21]-

[22] proposed on-the-fly translation of so-called generalized Büchi automata (Büchi automata with multiple acceptance conditions) which then linearly converted into Büchi automata.

There are several fragments of LTL that have been proposed in the literature. [3] has proved that converting any formula in which the only allowed modality is the until operator U or the only allowed modality is X or $\Diamond$ to Büchi automata is PSPACE. The formula that uses only the $\Diamond$ operator is coNP-Complete. The formula that uses only the X operator is coNP-Complete [23]. The formula that uses only the $\Diamond$ operator in the form $\Box\Diamond$ is co-NPComplete [24]. In [23], the authors used the term Flat LTL to express formula that use the U operator whose the left-hand side does not contain any temporal combinator, but the right-side can contain only formula with the U operator (or its negation). Translation from this fragement to Büchi automata has been proved NP-Complete. Several simple cases with a lower worst-case complexity are handled in [23][24].

VIII. Conclusion and Future Work

This paper presented a compositional algorithm for generating Büchi automata from a fragment of LTL logic. First, we proposed the grammar of this fragment and then built for each formulæ φ, its equivalent Büchi automata. Second, we showed theoretically how to compositionnally build from Büchi automata associated to each sub-formulæ, the Büchi automaton of the target formulæ. Third, we implemented our approach in GOAL tool as a plugin and showed the complexity and the correctness of our Büchi automata generation method. Fourth, we demonstrated the interest of our method by computing coverage average of the fragment FLTL using three sets of well-known LTL formulas as benchmarks.

Several research lines can be continued from the present work. First, some temporal operators such as always, precedes or since are not considered in this paper, as an immediate perspective, we will study how to include these operators in our LTL fragment. Second, it will be interesting to study whether our fragment LTL is minimalist and whether there is possibility to more expand it by identifying what makes it smallest. A good direction for this point is to study whether there is a subset of Dwyer's pattern/scope from which all other patterns/scopes can be deduced. Third, it would be interesting to connect the proposed language to usual model checking tools.

Acknowledgment

This project has been jointly funded with the support of the National Council for Scientific Research in Lebanon CNRS-L and Lebanese University.

References

[1] O. Lichtenstein and A. Pnueli, "Checking that finite state concurrent programs satisfy their linear specification," in Proceedings of the 12th ACM SIGACT-SIGPLAN Symposium on Principles of Programming Languages. New York, NY, USA: ACM, 1985, pp. 97–107.

[2] C. Baier and J. Katoen, Principles of Model Checking (Representation and Mind Series). The MIT Press, 2008.

[3] A. Sistla and E. Clarke, "The complexity of propositional linear temporal logics," J. ACM, vol. 32, no. 3, july 1985, pp. 733–749.

[4] R. Hierons and al., "Using formal specifications to support testing," ACM Comput. Surv., vol. 41, February 2009, pp. 9:1–9:76.

[5] S. Gnesi, D. Latella, M. Massink, V. Moruzzi, and I. Pisa, "Formal test-case generation for UML statecharts," in Proc. 9th IEEE Int. Conf. on Engineering of Complex Computer Systems. IEEE Computer Society, 2004, pp. 75–84.

[6] E. Clarke, O. Grumberg, and K. Hamaguchi, "Another look at LTL model checking," in Formal methods in system design. Springer-Verlag, 1994, pp. 415–427.

[7] M. Vardi, "Branching vs. linear time: Final showdown," in Proceedings of the 7th International Conference on Tools and Algorithms for the Construction and Analysis of Systems. London: Springer, 2001, pp. 1–22.

[8] P. Gastin and D. Oddoux, "Fast LTL to Büchi automata translation," in Proceedings of the 13th International Conference on Computer Aided Verification (CAV'01), ser. LNCS, vol. 2102. Paris, France: Springer, jully 2001, pp. 53–65.

[9] V. King, O. Kupferman, and M. Vardi, On the Complexity of Parity Word Automata. Springer Berlin Heidelberg, 2001, pp. 276–286.

[10] E. A. Emerson, "Handbook of theoretical computer science (vol. b)," J. van Leeuwen, Ed. Cambridge, MA, USA: MIT Press, 1990, ch. Temporal and Modal Logic, pp. 995–1072.

[11] S. Safra, "On the complexity of omega-automata," in 29th Annual Symposium on Foundations of Computer Science, White Plains, New York, USA, 24-26 October 1988, 1988, pp. 319–327.

[12] A. Sistla, M. Vardi, and P. Wolper, "The complementation problem for büchi automata with applications to temporal logic," in Automata, Languages and Programming. Springer Berlin Heidelberg, 1985, pp. 465–474.

[13] Y.-K. Tsay, Y.-F. Chen, M.-H. Tsai, K.-N. Wu, and W.-C. Chan, "Goal: A graphical tool for manipulating büchi automata and temporal formulae," in Tools and Algorithms for the Construction and Analysis of Systems. Springer Berlin Heidelberg, 2007, pp. 466–471.

[14] K. E. and G. Holzmann, "Optimizing Büchi automata." Springer, 2000, pp. 153–167.

[15] M. Daniele, F. Giunchiglia, and M. Vardi, "Improved automata generation for linear temporal logic," in In 11th International Conference on Computer Aided Verification, ser. CAV '99. London, UK: Springer, 1999, pp. 249–260.

[16] F. Somenzi and R. Bloem, "Efficient büchi automata from ltl formulae," in Computer Aided Verification, E. A. Emerson and A. P. Sistla, Eds. Berlin, Heidelberg: Springer, 2000, pp. 248–263.

[17] M. Dwyer, G. Avrunin, and J. Corbett, "Patterns in property specifications for finite-state verification," in Proceedings of the 21st International Conference on Software Programming, 1999, pp. 411–420.

[18] P. Wolper, "On the relation of programs and computations to models of temporal logic," in Temporal Logic in Specification, B. Banieqbal, H. Barringer, and A. Pnueli, Eds. Springer Berlin Heidelberg, 1989, pp. 75–123.

[19] G. G. de Jong, "An automata theoretic approach to temporal logic," in Computer Aided Verification, K. G. Larsen and A. Skou, Eds. Berlin, Heidelberg: Springer Berlin Heidelberg, 1992, pp. 477–487.

[20] M. Y. Vardi, An automata-theoretic approach to linear temporal logic. Berlin, Heidelberg: Springer, 1996, pp. 238–266.

[21] J.-M. Couvreur, "On-the-fly verification of linear temporal logic," in FM'99 — Formal Methods, J. M. Wing, J. Woodcock, and J. Davies, Eds. Springer, 1999, pp. 253–271.

[22] S. Schwoon and J. Esparza, "A note on on-the-fly verification algorithms," in Tools and Algorithms for the Construction and Analysis of Systems, N. Halbwachs and L. D. Zuck, Eds. Springer Berlin Heidelberg, 2005, pp. 174–190.

[23] S. Demri and P. Schnoebelen, "The complexity of propositional linear temporal logics in simple cases," Information and Computation, vol. 174, no. 1, 2002, pp. 84 – 103.

[24] E. A. Emerson and C.-L. Lei, "Modalities for model checking: branching time logic strikes back," Science of Computer Programming, vol. 8, no. 3, 1987, pp. 275 – 306.

Towards Component-Based Development of Textual Domain-Specific Languages

Andreas Wortmann

Software Engineering
RWTH Aachen University
Aachen, Germany
http://www.se-rwth.de/

***Abstract*—Software-intensive systems are developed with the help of experts of different domains. This requires reifying their domain expertise in software, which raises the need for Domain-Specific Languages (DSLs) to bridge the gap between the problem space of the experts' experience and software development. Developing suitable DSLs still is prohibitively complex due to the lack of pervasive concepts for DSL reuse. Existing concepts either give rise to a conceptual gap between their abstractions and language definition constituents or are tied to specific technological spaces. To mitigates this, we present a novel conceptual model for the systematic reuse of textual DSLs. This technology-independent model promotes modularity and reusability based on language families that exhibit specific reuse interfaces. To realize these concepts, we conceived an extensible modelling infrastructure that supports the engineering of reusable textual DSLs using the MontiCore language workbench. This enables systematic reuse of textual DSLs for compatible technological spaces from which DSL engineers in many domains can greatly benefit.**

***Index Terms*—Software Language Engineering, Textual Languages, Language Components**

I. Introduction

Society increasingly depends on systems developed by experts from various domains using their own Domain-Specific Languages (DSLs) [1]. DSLs have become innovation drivers in many disciplines, including automotive, avionics, civil engineering, Industry 4.0, robotics, and software engineering itself. This, *e.g.,* led to the engineering of over 120 DSLs for software architectures [2] used in different domains and various technological spaces [3]. All of these need to be developed, maintained, and evolved on their own, which is costly, error-prone, and hinders progress in the multi-domain engineering of modern software-intensive systems.

Research in Software Language Engineering (SLE) [4] investigates the efficient and reliable engineering, maintenance, deployment, use, and evolution of DSLs to support software engineers and domain experts in efficiently developing future systems. Despite attempts to a systematic SLE, many DSLs are engineered ad-hoc, for very specific challenges, and very limited purposes only [5]. Hence, research has produced a multitude of solutions to facilitate creating DSLs. These include on metamodels [6], grammars [7], or abstract data types [8], interpreters [9] or code generators [10], and well-formedness rules defined in metalanguages [8] or programming languages [11]. For these, the SLE community has proposed various reuse techniques, based on experiences from general software reuse (*e.g.,* polymorphic [12] and parametric [13] reuse, composition [7] or variability [14]). Although these techniques address a wide range of scenarios, most support specific parts of DSL definitions (*e.g.,* abstract syntax or code generators) only and are limited to specific technological spaces. This complicates the engineering and customization of real-world DSLs for different usage scenarios, which ultimately hinders systems engineering by domain experts.

To mitigate this, we present the COLD4TXT conceptual model for component-based language development of textual DSLs that implement behavior with code generators (txtDSLs). In this model, *language components* with explicit interfaces of required and provided grammar rules, well-formedness rules, and code generators are the principal elements of reuse. Feature models arrange these components, according to their required and provided extension points, in language families. Thus selecting features governs how the language components are composed. Based on this model, we present a systematic method to describe and resolve the component's variability, as well as their customization.

As the technical realizations of composing grammars, well-formedness rules, and code generators have been presented already [10], [15], this contribution illustrates their conceptual framework consisting of:

1) The COLD4TXT conceptual model for reusable txtDSL components featuring explicit interfaces of required and provided elements.
2) A systematic method for engineering languages based on reusable txtDSL components.
3) A realization of both with the MontiCore language engineering workbench.

With these, reusing language components in different language families can greatly facilitate engineering DSLs.

In the following, Section II motivates our method by example. Afterwards, Section III presents txtDSL language components and Section IV our method to reuse theses for efficient txtDSL engineering. Ultimately, Section V debates observations, Section VI discusses related work, and Section VII concludes.

II. Example

Consider using Architecture Description Languages (ADLs) [2] – DSLs for the specification of software

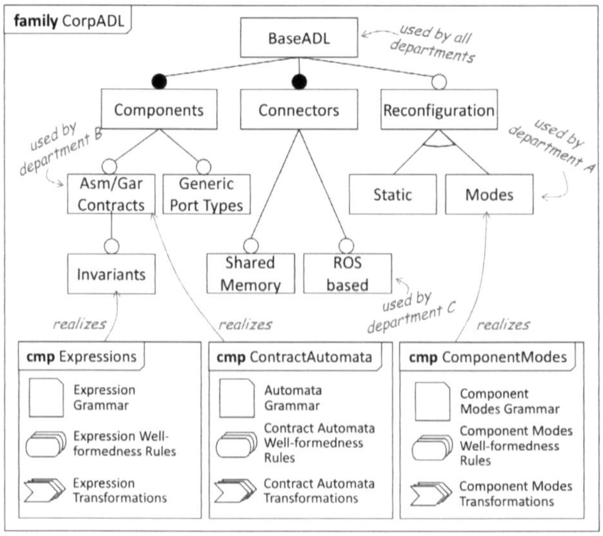

Fig. 1. A language family comprising features of language components that can fulfill the requirements of all three departments.

architectures – for the different departments of a large corporation. In each of these departments, some developers occasionally, maybe once a week, (re-)model parts of a specific software architecture (*e.g.,* of a train, a factory, or a mobile service robot). Instead of learning overly generic ADLs and operating with complex modeling guidelines that describe how to properly model with these, modelers of each department should be able to use their specific terminology and learn only the modeling elements required for their specific application.

Hence, while in general, these ADLs require some notion of components, ports, and connectors, each department has domain-specific requirements for the ADLs to be used:

- Department A (trains) requires components that support dynamic reconfiguration via components modes [16] to enable switching components related to country-specific technology when the train crosses a border.
- Department B (smart factories) demands components with assumption/guarantee contracts [17] that facilitate correct integration of new components when the factory reconfigures.
- Department C (robotics) demands novel connectors that support bridging architecture models with the robot operating system (ROS) [18].

Developing a general ADL that captures all of these concepts is not feasible as it complicates modeling in departments where only some of these modeling elements are required. Alternatively developing three specific ADLs – each with their specific infrastructure (*e.g.,* parsers, model checkers, code generators) – independently is costly and inefficient.

Instead, building suitable language components and combining these as required can significantly reduce the effort of fulfilling the departments' requirements. For our example, consider the language family of Figure 1: this family contains the language features required by the different departments and each feature is implemented by a language component comprising a combination of grammar, well-formedness rules, and code generators. By developing independent language components that implement the different features and by leveraging variability modeling techniques, the configuration of the base ADL for the different departments only requires selecting the appropriate language components and (semi-)automatically integrating these. If no appropriate features are available, developing and integrating novel language components and integrating these into existing language families reduces the effort of building a suitable ADL.

Our method to engineer and reuse language components considers both, planned variability and opportunistic reuse, and supports semi-automated composition of language component constituents in the technological space of the MontiCore [11] language workbench.

III. COLD4TXT LANGUAGE COMPONENTS

The conceptual model of COLD is a vision of language reuse that requires concretization. For txtDSLs, we have developed the COLD4TXT variant of COLD which realizes variability, explains how resolving variability affects the language components, how variability and customizability interact, how variability, customizability, the language facets' artifacts relate, and provides modeling techniques to realize this. At its core, COLD4TXT resolves variability and customizability through the additive composition of language components according to their explicitly provided and required extension points.

To enable this, COLD4TXT differs from COLD: In COLD4TXT, *language families* and *language components* replace language concerns and language facets of COLD, respectively: The language concerns of COLD provide both variability and customizability. This entails that they provide the complete customizability of their intrinsic language product line and express this towards the user despite only a small subset of customization options being available in the language product derived from the product line (namely these provided by the features selected for the product). In contrast, customizability should express means for tailoring languages that are not resolved by variability. Therefore, the language component comprising the derived language product provides customizability options instead. Moreover, to enable the proper composition of language components based on a feature selection, the COLD4TXT language components yield interfaces themselves. These interfaces guide and restrict their use in the variation interface's feature model and enable composing two language components (semi-)automatically, with only the implementation of adapters for generator composition requiring manual interaction [10]. To explain the effects of resolving variability and customizability in COLD4TXT, a *language component* consists of a

- one language component interface,
- one customization interface,

- up to one grammar artifact,
- arbitrary many well-formedness rule artifacts, and
- arbitrary many code generator artifacts.

The language component interfaces explicitly provide or require language grammar productions, well-formedness rules, or code generators. Also, they may yield constraints between these (*e.g.*, representing whether an extension point is optional or mandatory, or to express that selecting a provided code generator entails selecting a grammar production as well). The provided extension points for grammar rules identify productions of the contained CFG that are meant for reuse (*e.g.*, expressions of an imperative modeling language, method signatures of a class diagram language, *etc.*). The required extension points for grammar productions explicate productions that demand (optional or mandatory) extension for the contained syntax to be completed.

Specifying required well-formedness rules within the interface either demands complete specifications of the required well-formedness rules behavior (*i.e.*, their implementation) or demands conditions under which an independently provided well-formedness rule is suitable for the required rule (*i.e.*, some form of acceptance tests). The former entails having a specification that is precise enough to become a implementation automatically and the latter testing rarely would be complete. Hence, we decided to consider the set of well-formedness rules of a language component as its extension point. Thus, a language component can provide arbitrary many well-formedness rules that may or may not be used by other components, but it cannot (yet) describe that it requires additional well-formedness rules. Specifying the semantics of required well-formedness rules is subject to ongoing work. For code generators, language components leverage the notions of producer interface and product interface as introduced in [10]. Hence, language components may provide and require extension points that declare exactly one producer interface and one product interface. The customization interfaces of language interfaces comprise parameters of well-formedness rules and generators that are not meant to be resolved through the closed variation of language families but enable open customization instead. Such customization could be the numbers of initial states supported in models of a language component for an automaton DSL or the path a generator should produce artifacts in.

The language interfaces ground their required and provided extension points in the artifacts of their language components as illustrated in Figure 2. Here, the red concepts (solid lines) represent the language components and the yellow concepts (dashed lines) highlight their customization interface parts. The language components are part of language families. Aside from at least one language component, a *language family* contains a variation interface comprising a single feature model and a mapping that relates features to language component interfaces. By transitivity of language interface extension points, this also identifies one language component per feature. The feature model of the variation interface is developed by a

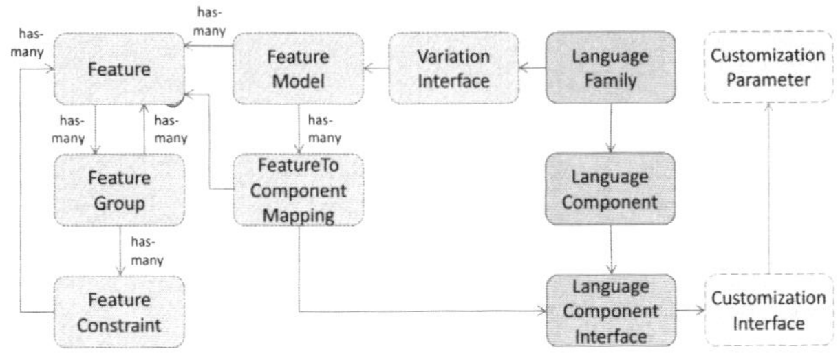

Fig. 2. Conceptual model for txtDSL reuse focusing on language families and their variation interfaces.

```
01 language family CorpADL {                       available language components
02   components
03     MontiArc, ContractAutomata, ComplexPortTypes, Expressions;
04   variation interface root BaseADL {
05     mandatory Components {
06       optional AsmGarContracts { optional Invariants; }   variation interface
07       optional GenericPortTypes;
08     }
09     // additional features relations
10   }
11   root feature BaseADL uses MontiArc;
12   abstract feature Components;
13   feature AsmGarContracts uses ContractAutomata {
14     binds production Automaton to Components.ArcElement;
15     binds generator Automaton2Java to Components.BehaviorGenerator;
16     binds wfrs NonHierarchical;
17   }          feature definition
18   feature Invariants uses Expressions {
19     binds production Expression to AsmGarContracts.Expr.
20     binds Expression.All;
21     binds generator Expressions2POJO to AsmGarContracts.Guard2Java;
22   }                                    feature to component mappings
23   // additional features definitions
24 }
```

Fig. 3. Textual model of the `CorpADL` language family of Figure 1.

language family designer that intends to derive similar DSLs of joint buildings blocks. As such, the designer models the selection of a specific child feature implementing the extension points of its parent feature and specifies constraints between features in the `Feature2ComponentMappting`.

The language components are composed based on the arrangement of language components in the variation interfaces' feature model. From this, a new language component comprising their (possibly composed) artifacts together with a derived interface are synthesized. If there are required extension points not fulfilled by the selected features, these become part of the new component's interface.

COLD4TXT is realized as a language engineering framework using the MontiCore language workbench. To this end, we have developed modeling languages for language families, language components, feature configurations, and customization configurations as well as a toolchain that supports resolving variability and customizability.

The language family `CorpADL` of our example (*cf.* Figure 1) can be represented as illustrated in Figure 3. This family describes which language components it comprises (ll. 2-3), its variation interface in terms of a feature model (ll. 4-10), and defines its features (ll. 11-24). A feature either is a root feature (at most one), an abstract feature solely for grouping other features (such as the feature `Component`),

```
language component ContractAutomata {
  grammar mc.automata.ca.ContractAutomata;

  provides production ConractAutomatonMain;                              ┐ provided
  provides AsmAutomaton for production AssumptionAutomaton;             ├ grammar
  provides GarAutomaton for production GuaranteeAutomaton;              ┘ productions
  requires mandatory Expr for production IGuardExpression;
provided generator ↘        ↖ required grammar production
  provides generator Automaton2Java for ContractAutomatonMain {
    producer IAutomatonGen;
    product IAutomatonPairRealization;
  }              ↙ required generator
  requires generator Guard2Java for IGuardExpression {
    producer IGuardExpressionGenerator;
    product IGuardExpression
  }

  provides wfrs Hierarchical {                    ┐
    mc.automata.ca.coco.base.*;                   │
    mc.automata.ca.coco.hierarchical.*;           │ provided sets of
  }                                               ├ well-formedness
  provides wfrs NonHierarchical {                 │ rules
    mc.automata.ca.coco.base.*;                   │
    mc.automata.ca.coco.NoHierarchy;              ┘
  }
                 ↙ customization parameters
  parameters {
    int max for mc.automata.cocos.NumHierarchyLevels.initialize;
    String prefix for IAutomatonGen.generate;
  }
}
```

Fig. 4. Model of the `ContractAutomata` component of Figure 1.

```
language component Expressions {
  grammar mc.basic.expressions.Expressions;
  provides production Expression;
  provides wfrs All { mc.basic.expressions.*; }

  provides transformation Expressions2POJO for Expression {
    producer IExpressionJavaGenerator;
    product IExpression;
  }
}
```

Fig. 5. Model of the `Expression` component of Figure 1.

or is realized by a language component. Each feature of the latter kind defines how the provided extension points of its language component are mapped to the required extension points of its parent feature. For instance, selecting the feature `Invariants` entails that (1) its production `Expression` will be embedded [15] into the extension point `Expr` of the language component `AsmGarContracts` (l. 21); (2) its well-formedness rules provided via the extension point `All` will be reused (l. 22); and (3) its code generator provided via the extension point `Expressions2POJO` will be embedded into the code generator `Guard2Java` of language component `AsmGarContracts` (l. 23). The well-formedness rules of the language family ensure that these mappings are valid w.r.t. the language components illustrated in Figure 4 and Figure 5.

IV. Deriving Languages

Modeling language families with COLD4TXT first demands its instantiation for a specific technological space by providing modules for (1) analysing the compatibility of COLD4TXT models with the referenced technology space artifacts and (2) composing these artifacts according to COLD4TXT specifications as depicted in Figure 6. The former modules, for instance, check whether a well-formedness rule provided by a language component exists or whether a grammar production declared as an extension point indeed is an interface production. The latter modules take composition instructions (the binding mappings) and related artifacts, and compose these accordingly. For MontiCore, these modules are provided. Language engineers than can use this instance of COLD4TXT to engineer language components. Language family developers can reuse these in different contexts through arranging these in the variation interfaces. Language family users select the desired language features matching their requirements and use the COLD4TXT instance to synthesize a suitable language component. If this language component is incomplete w.r.t. its mandatory required extension points or parameters, it cannot be used as a DSL yet. In this case, the language family user has to specify the missing customization configuration, before a fully configured language component and the artifacts for a DSL in the corresponding technological space are derived.

For MontiCore, these artifacts are a synthesized CFG, the union of the selected well-formedness rules, and a code generator composed along its producer and product interfaces. These artifacts can be processed by MontiCore to produce a DSL that is completely independent of language families and language components. Moreover, the (possibly incomplete) language components derived from resolving variability and customizability can be used as parts of other language families again, which facilitates their reuse.

Based on a feature configuration, the COLD4TXT framework composes the language components associated with the selected features pairwise and top-down. The resulting component yields the provided extension points of the parent and child components. For each mandatorily required extension point (*e.g.*, `Expr` of language component `ContractAutomata`), if an implementation is defined by the binding mappings in the variation interface's feature model, then this extension point becomes optional and is copied to the interface of the new component as well. The sets of well-formedness rules from the parent component and the ones from the selected provided extension point of the child component are merged and provided as a new extension point in the new component. For the CFGs, COLD4TXT expects the responsible modules of the specific technology space to produce combined CFGs and adapters between the participating code generators accordingly.

For instance, selecting the features "Asm/Gar Contracts" and "Invariants" depicted in Figure 1 with the variation interface specified in Figure 3 entails combining the language components `ContractAutomata` (Figure 4) and `Expressions` (Figure 5) accordingly. The resulting language component is given in Figure 7. This component uses a synthesized CFG featuring contract automata and expressions (l. 2), the union of selected well-formedness rules, and the composed code generators. Its interface reduces the cardinality of the required grammar extension point `Expr` to optional (l. 7), adds the provided extension point `Expression` (l. 8), as well as the code generator for expressions (ll. 14-17)

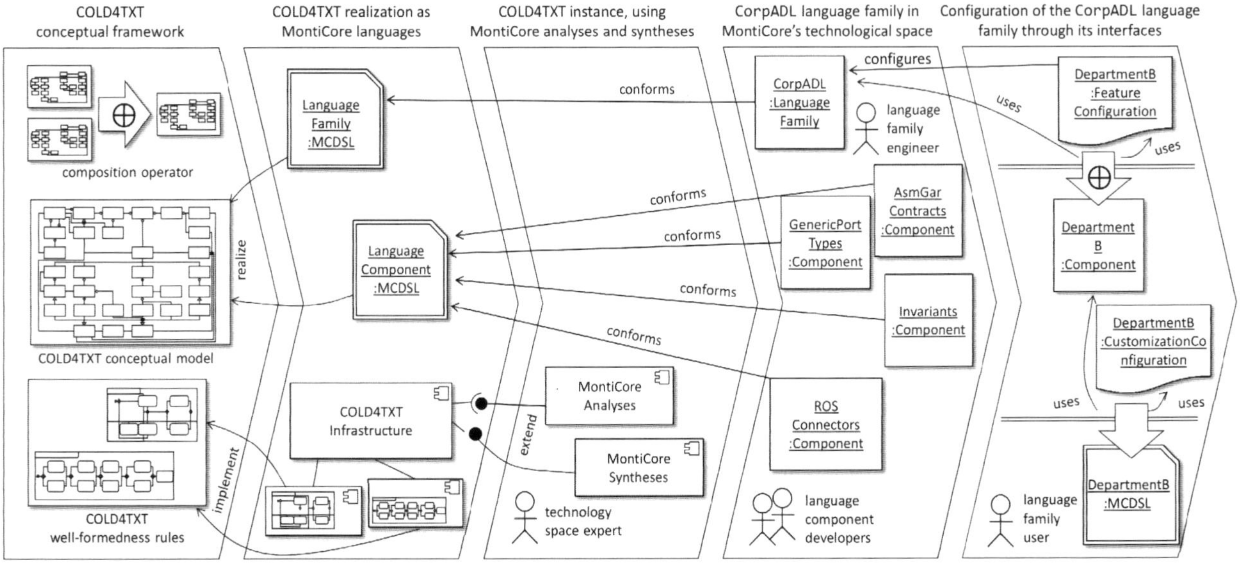

Fig. 6. After tailoring CORE4TXT for a specific technological space, developers can engineer language components to be used by language family developers to facilitate creating DSLs.

```
01 language component ContractAutomataWithExpresssions {
02   grammar mc.automata.ca.ContractAutomataWithExpressions;
03
04   provides production ConractAutomatonMain;                      synthesized
05   provides AsmAutomaton of production AssumptionAutomaton;        grammar
06   provides GarAutomaton of production GuaranteeAutomaton;
07   requires optional Expr for production IGuardExpression;
08   provides production Expression;     added                  became optional
09
10   provides transformation Automaton2Java for ContractAutomatonMain {
11     producer IAutomatonGen;
12     product IAutomatonPairRealization;
13   }                                                               added
14   provides transformation Expressions2POJO for Expression {
15     producer IExpressionJavaGenerator;
16     product IExpression;
17   }
18                            synthesized set of well-
19   provides wfrs All {           formedness rules
20     mc.automata.ca.coco.base.*;
21     mc.automata.ca.coco.NoHierarchy;
22     mc.basic.expressions.*;
23   }
24
25   parameters {
26     int max for mc.automata.cocos.NumHierarchyLevels.initialize;
27     String prefix for IAutomatonGen.generate;
28   }
29 }
```

Fig. 7. Language component synthesized as result from selecting the features "Asm/Gar Contracts" and "Invariants" of Figure 3.

from the `Expressions` language component of Figure 5, and provides a new set of well-formedness rules (ll. 19-23). As this component does not require further extension, specifying values for its parameters enables MontiCore to derive a complete DSL from it.

V. DISCUSSION

In contrast to the purely conceptual models of DSL reuse [19], [20], COLD4TXT supports capturing all DSL definition constituents at a sufficient level of abstraction to support the precise explanation of the effects of composing these, binding their variability, and resolving their customizability on its own.

The conceptual model of COLD4TXT aims to be independent of technological spaces as long as these enable to (1) identify grammar extension points; (2) compose grammars, sets of well-formedness rules, and code generators without eliminating the extension points in the process; (3) describe code generators and the generated products in terms of their interfaces; (4) identify parameters of well-formedness rules and code generators in an object-oriented fashion. While these are strong assumptions, we currently investigate applying COLD4TXT and its realization within the technological spaces of Neverlang [7] and Xtext [21]. Moreover, it currently only supports embedding in the sense of [10], whereas there are various other composition operators for txtDSLs. Whether and how supporting these is possible, also is ongoing research.

In the future, we aim to extend the notion of language components to feature additional constituents (*e.g.,* model-to-model transformations or editor fragments), support other forms of composition (*e.g.,* coordination or aggregation), and make the constraints of required well-formedness rule extensions more explicit.

VI. RELATED WORK

Research on Language product lines (LPLs) [15], [22], [23] is scattered across different kinds of DSL definition constituents and technological spaces. And while we developed a notion of LPLs for the technological space of MontiCore [15] in particular, there currently is no actionable understanding of the variability of complete txtDSLs (*i.e.,* encompassing all four kinds of constituents). Moreover, (closed) variation rarely is connected with (open) customization to systematically reuse

DSLs in general. There are only a few solutions that consider either txtDSL variation or customization across different kinds of DSL definition constituents. These include a few language workbenches [24], such as Argyle [23], Neverlang [7], or the combination of SDF and FeatureHouse [22].

In Argyle [23], DSLs are constructed from language assets that resemble concerns and comprise syntax, data types, and code generation templates. A feature model arranges assets according to their dependencies, which demands their white-box apriori composition that hinders the reuse of facets. In contrast, COLD4TXT will be based on our exploratory work [15] that makes extension points of concerns explicit and supports the black box composition of their artifacts through the generation of suitable adapters between these.

SDF and FeatureHouse realize variability based on compositional language modules containing grammar rules, typing rules, and evaluation rules [22]. It also focuses on the white-box composition of artifacts and interpretation. Similar partial solutions towards variation or customization of selected kinds of DSL definition constituents are available from a variety of language workbenches. For instance, ableC [25] is an extensible C language that leverages attribute grammars to reuse syntax and semantics, MPS [21] enables reuse of projectional languages with views and model transformations, and Spoofax [8] supports reuse of textual, interpreted languages. All of these concepts for (partial) DSL reuse focus on specific technological spaces. and lack support for integrated reuse across variation and customization.

VII. Conclusion

We have presented the novel COLD4TXT conceptual framework to facilitate reusing textual DSLs through systematic variability and customizability. In COLD4TXT, language families capture txtDSL variability as feature models and realize it via composition of language components according to their interfaces. Composing language components yields new language components that may demand further extension or customization before these can be translated into complete DSLs for specific contexts. Making the interfaces of language components explicit enables reusing these in different language families. This facilitates engineering textual DSLs for different contexts and fosters the application of DSLs.

References

[1] M. Voelter, B. Kolb, K. Birken, F. Tomassetti, P. Alff, L. Wiart, A. Wortmann, and A. Nordmann, "Using language workbenches and domain-specific languages for safety-critical software development," *Software & Systems Modeling*, pp. 1–24, 2018.

[2] I. Malavolta, P. Lago, H. Muccini, P. Pelliccione, and A. Tang, "What Industry Needs from Architectural Languages: A Survey," *IEEE Transactions on Software Engineering*, vol. 39, no. 6, pp. 869–891, 2013.

[3] I. Kurtev, J. Bézivin, and M. Aksit, "Technological spaces: An initial appraisal," *CoopIS, DOA*, vol. 2002, 2002.

[4] K. Hölldobler, B. Rumpe, and A. Wortmann, "Software Language Engineering in the Large: Towards Composing and Deriving Languages," *Computer Languages, Systems & Structures*, vol. 54, pp. 386–405, 2018.

[5] J. Whittle, J. Hutchinson, and M. Rouncefield, "The State of Practice in Model-Driven Engineering," *Software, IEEE*, vol. 31, no. 3, pp. 79–85, 2014.

[6] T. Kühne, "Matters of (meta-) modeling," *Software & Systems Modeling*, vol. 5, no. 4, pp. 369–385, 2006.

[7] E. Vacchi and W. Cazzola, "Neverlang: A framework for feature-oriented language development," *Computer Languages, Systems & Structures*, vol. 43, pp. 1–40, 2015.

[8] G. H. Wachsmuth, G. D. P. Konat, and E. Visser, "Language Design with the Spoofax Language Workbench," *IEEE Software*, vol. 31, no. 5, pp. 35–43, 2014.

[9] E. Bousse, J. Corley, B. Combemale, J. Gray, and B. Baudry, "Supporting efficient and advanced omniscient debugging for xDSMLs," in *Proceedings of the 2015 ACM SIGPLAN International Conference on Software Language Engineering*. ACM, 2015, pp. 137–148.

[10] A. Butting, R. Eikermann, O. Kautz, B. Rumpe, and A. Wortmann, "Modeling Language Variability with Reusable Language Components," in *International Conference on Systems and Software Product Line (SPLC'18)*. ACM, 9 2018.

[11] K. Hölldobler and B. Rumpe, *MontiCore 5 Language Workbench Edition 2017*, ser. Aachener Informatik-Berichte, Software Engineering, Band 32. Shaker Verlag, December 2017. [Online]. Available: http://www.se-rwth.de/phdtheses/MontiCore-5-Language-Workbench-Edition-2017.pdf

[12] T. Degueule, B. Combemale, A. Blouin, O. Barais, and J.-M. Jézéquel, "Safe model polymorphism for flexible modeling," *Computer Languages, Systems & Structures*, vol. 49, pp. 176–195, 2017.

[13] J. de Lara and E. Guerra, "Generic Meta-modelling with Concepts, Templates and Mixin Layers," in *Model Driven Engineering Languages and Systems*, D. C. Petriu, N. Rouquette, and Ø. Haugen, Eds. Berlin, Heidelberg: Springer Berlin Heidelberg, 2010, pp. 16–30.

[14] T. Kühn, W. Cazzola, and D. M. Olivares, "Choosy and picky: configuration of language product lines," in *Proceedings of the 19th International Conference on Software Product Line*. ACM, 2015, pp. 71–80.

[15] A. Butting, R. Eikermann, O. Kautz, B. Rumpe, and A. Wortmann, "Systematic composition of independent language features," *Journal of Systems and Software*, vol. 152, pp. 50–69, 2019.

[16] P. H. Feiler and D. P. Gluch, *Model-Based Engineering with AADL: An Introduction to the SAE Architecture Analysis & Design Language*. Addison-Wesley, 2012.

[17] M. Broy and K. Stølen, *Specification and development of interactive systems: focus on streams, interfaces, and refinement*. Springer Science & Business Media, 2012.

[18] K. Adam, K. Hölldobler, B. Rumpe, and A. Wortmann, "Modeling Robotics Software Architectures with Modular Model Transformations," *Journal of Software Engineering for Robotics (JOSER)*, vol. 8, no. 1, pp. 3–16, 2017.

[19] T. Clark, M. v. d. Brand, B. Combemale, and B. Rumpe, "Conceptual Model of the Globalization for Domain-Specific Languages," in *Globalizing Domain-Specific Languages*, ser. LNCS 9400. Springer, 2015, pp. 7–20.

[20] B. Combemale, J. Kienzle, G. Mussbacher, O. Barais, E. Bousse, W. Cazzola, P. Collet, T. Degueule, R. Heinrich, J.-M. Jézéquel, M. Leduc, T. Mayerhofer, S. Mosser, M. Schöttle, M. Strittmatter, and A. Wortmann, "Concern-oriented language development (COLD): Fostering reuse in language engineering," *Computer Languages, Systems & Structures*, vol. 54, pp. 139–155, 2018.

[21] M. Völter, S. Benz, C. Dietrich, B. Engelmann, M. Helander, L. C. L. Kats, E. Visser, and G. Wachsmuth, *{DSL} Engineering - Designing, Implementing and Using Domain-Specific Languages*. dslbook.org, 2013. [Online]. Available: http://www.dslbook.org

[22] J. Liebig, R. Daniel, and S. Apel, "Feature-oriented language families: a case study," in *VaMoS*, 2013.

[23] C. Huang, A. Osaka, Y. Kamei, and N. Ubayashi, "Automated DSL construction based on software product lines," in *2015 3rd International Conference on Model-Driven Engineering and Software Development (MODELSWARD)*. IEEE, 2015, pp. 1–8.

[24] S. Erdweg, T. Van Der Storm, M. Völter, L. Tratt, R. Bosman, W. R. Cook, A. Gerritsen, A. Hulshout, S. Kelly, A. Loh, and Others, "Evaluating and comparing language workbenches: Existing results and benchmarks for the future," *Computer Languages, Systems & Structures*, vol. 44, pp. 24–47, 2015.

[25] T. Kaminski, L. Kramer, T. Carlson, and E. Van Wyk, "Reliable and automatic composition of language extensions to C: the ableC extensible language framework," *Proceedings of the ACM on Programming Languages*, vol. 1, no. OOPSLA, p. 98, 2017.

An Intermediate Model for Code Generation from the Two-Hemisphere Model

Konstantins Gusarovs, Oksana Nikiforova
Department of Applied Computer Science
Riga Technical University
Riga, Latvia
email:{konstantins.gusarovs, oksana.nikiforova}@rtu.lv

Abstract—**Nowadays, models are widely used in software engineering. By using different types of models, it is possible to present business requirements, system architecture, test strategies, etc. It is also possible to use models as an input to an automated or semi-automated method that will produce other types of artifacts – other models, statistics, or even software code specified in a programming language. The authors of the present paper work in the area of Model-Driven Software Development (MDSD) by constantly improving the so-called two-hemisphere model that can be used for system modelling and later transformed into several types of artifacts, including Unified Modelling Language diagrams. The goal of the paper is to define an intermediate representation (or model) that can be used for code generation. The present research is the extended and expanded version of the authors' previous work.**

Keywords - two-hemisphere model; model transformation; code generation; model-driven software development.

I. INTRODUCTION

Model-Driven Software Development (MDSD) is one of the advanced approaches to the software development process that is still being developed and adopted by several researchers and enterprises. It seems that nowadays it is possible to distinguish two main groups of MDSD users: those treating models as an analytical tool that can help in better understanding of a problem domain, requirements, etc. [1], as well as those who see models as a high level executable ones that can be further used to produce a programming language code on a target platform [1]. This task can be achieved by using model transformation and code generation techniques, which can be done in an automatic [2] or a semi-automatic way.

The authors of the current paper also treat models as a source for producing the software definition in a chosen programming language and for a chosen platform. While several researchers undertake their efforts to produce a software code from the Unified Modelling Language (UML) [3] defined diagrams (for example, [2][4][5]), the current research is based on another approach to code generation, which is called the two-hemisphere model that has been developed by the authors [6]-[8].

The role of models in Software Development is still unclear, and it can be explained by the fact that MDSD is still at high level of vision [9], and while UML is de-facto industry standard [5], it can be hard for a business analyst, who is not a software engineer, to develop a set of UML diagrams. Even more, most UML diagrams describe the architecture of the system that conforms to object-oriented principles. As an example, the UML class diagram defines a set of classes that form the system, and the UML sequence diagram defines how use cases can be implemented using this set of classes, while the UML communication diagram defines relations between classes from a communication perspective – how classes (or their instances) interact with each other, and what information is passed, etc. It is possible to see that this set of diagrams used as a system analysis model basically corresponds to the core elements of code written in object-oriented programming language.

Nowadays, it is possible to find multiple tools that can be used to transform the system analysis model into the code. The main condition for code generation is that the model should contain both aspects of the system (i.e., static and dynamic), and both should be supported in code generation. Despite several limitations in code generation, which are mainly limitations of the tools rather than the transformation abilities [10], a lot of studies performed since 1980s demonstrate different sets of transformation rules for code generation from UML and mention exactly the dynamic aspect as the primary problem in code generation [11]. Therefore, the authors indicate that by creating a set of UML diagrams, one basically carries out the coding work. In addition, one also has to overcome the difficulties caused by UML usage. As the two-hemisphere model provides an ability to generate UML diagrams, which is enough for code generation, the authors of the paper assume that the two-hemisphere model already contains all the necessary information to get all the required constructions specified in the programming language. That is why in the present research the authors move further away from complex models specified in UML and use their own model. The research also attempts not to focus on the static aspects of the system, i.e., data structures and domain models, but rather on defining the dynamic capabilities of the system by the so-called intermediate model, which, in general, is like the adoption of the two-hemisphere model for the task of code generation.

The goal of the paper is to define an intermediate artifact that will serve as a "bridge" between the initial model (two-hemipshere model) and the target model (source code). Although UML can be used to cover this area, and there are the methods to generate UML diagrams from the two-hemisphere model, the authors would like to mention once again that most UML diagrams cover object-oriented architecture. This raises a need for the intermediate model that is target-architecture-agnostic and can be used to describe both static and dynamic aspects of the system. This model should also serve as a source model for the code generator, which means, it should cover necessary elements of the source code.

The paper is structured as follows. Section II gives an insight into related work. Section III provides a high-level overview of the two-hemisphere model. Section IV discusses the target model, which in this case is a code written in some programming language. Section V describes what is required to define the data structures for the system being built. Section VI covers the definitions that can be used for describing the capabilities of the dynamic system. Section VII provides examples of various applications of the proposed intermediate model along with the analysis of the respective applications. A short demonstration of intermediate model application is presented in Section VIII. Finally, Section IX concludes the paper, as well as provides an insight into the future research to be conducted in this area.

II. Related Work

Having defined requirements for the intermediate model, the authors performed an analysis of the existing approaches to code generation in the MDSD area. Full analysis of the published articles is an area for a separate research itself; therefore, in this article the authors provide a brief overview of related studies.

The first example under consideration is [12]. Its authors propose an extensible intermediate model for code generation from UML sequence diagrams. The article describes metamodel and its possible extensions. The authors claim that their model can be used with different target languages; however, such languages must be object-oriented.

Another example is [13], where the author develops an intermediate model, called Hierarchical Syntax Char (HSC), which is used for the UML activity diagram conversion to the source code. Here, the author has chosen the Java programming language [14] as a target model. The HSC developed by the author once again recognizes the necessity for the object-oriented target language.

Authors of [15] also target object-oriented languages in their research. Even more, the approach described in [15] also defines the architecture of generated code by listing specific components of the system to be generated. Again, an intermediate model is developed to support multiple target platforms.

It is possible to find more studies in this area; however, it seems that they mostly aim at improving the code generation techniques from different types of UML diagrams. For example, studies [2][4][5] focus on code generation from UML diagrams, targeting at object-oriented languages. It should be noted that researchers usually target the object-oriented languages, which could probably be explained by the use of UML, since it already defines basic components of an object-oriented system. This, in turn, leads to limited coverage of target languages that do not support an object-oriented paradigm by the existing methods. Examples of such languages are provided in Section V of this paper. The authors consider that the current state of code generation from models is somehow limited to support only one paradigm, and, therefore, propose the intermediate model described in the paper.

III. The Two-Hemisphere Model: A High-Level Overview

One of the MDSD tasks is transformation from the source model to the target model. The task itself describes a need for at least two models – one that is defined in the beginning and is called the source model. This is an initial artifact that can be produced, for example, by a business analyst, while performing a requirement analysis. Another one is a target model, which can be almost everything, starting with the set of UML diagrams and ending with the software code defined in some programming language.

The authors of the present paper define the two-hemisphere model [6] as a source artifact. The model itself was first introduced in 2004 with the goal of describing the business requirements with as minimal set of diagrams as possible for an object-oriented system analysis. It introduces an idea of joining both static and dynamic aspects of the system in the model that consists of two diagram types. Later, several improvements were introduced to it, enriching the model and precising its elements in [7] and [8], and working on the supporting tool in [16]. The notation of the two-hemisphere model is presented in Figure 1.

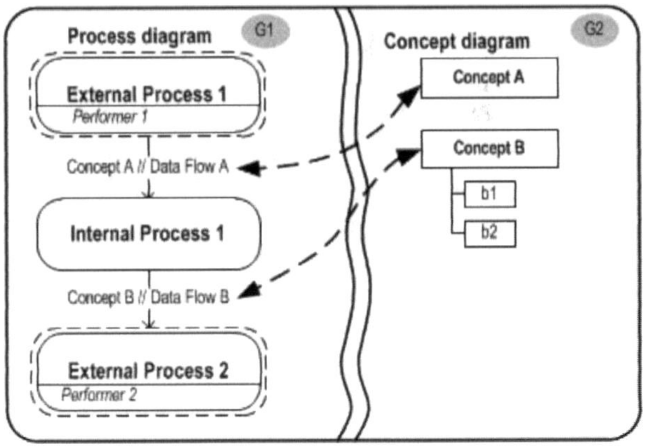

Figure 1. Two-Hemispher model notation.

The two-hemisphere model contains two diagrams:

- Concept model (labeled G2) is a set of concepts or datatypes used throughout the system or a given use case. Each concept has at least its name and a set of 0-n attributes. Each attribute consists of a name and data type, where data type might be a primitive value, such as a number, string literal, boolean type, etc., another concept or array/collection of the aforementioned. The notation of the concept model is similar to the one used for Entity-Relationship (ER) diagram [17], but relationships among concepts is not used as far as they are not meaningful at this level of abstraction and are generated automatically at the level of UML class diagram.

- Process model (labeled G1) is based upon the notation of Data Flow Diagram (DFD) [18] and is composed of two types of elements – processes and data flows. Processes show units of work inside the system. Data flows, in turn, interconnect processes, both defining the sequence of process execution and the data each process receives and produces. Here, data might be 0-n of the same data types, concept attribute use. Thus, the data flow might carry no data at all or a complex set of data. This way both diagrams are interconnected, i.e., concepts appear as the data flow content.

It is possible to see that the definition of the two-hemisphere model does not require specific software engineering knowledge – basically to create it, one has to analyze what business processes take place in the system being built, what data they consume and produce, and in which order it might be executed. Moreover, the two-hemisphere model can be obtained directly from the business domain, where business processes and data flows are somehow or other structured and supported in the form of the model specified in the analogical notation for business issues. Thus, the authors of the paper see this model as a great candidate for the MDSD source model, since the model only describes how the system works, rather than how the system should be built.

After the choice of the source model is performed, it is necessary to define what type of artifact is targeted. Little information on the chosen target model is provided in the next section. This model is nothing else, but the software code written in the chosen programming language, in other words, computer program.

IV. Computer Program: Definition

In order to define the concept of computer program, the authors would like to mention several definitions from ISO/IEC 2382:2015 standard [19] and analyze what is required to transform the source model to it.

First, it is necessary to define what a computer program is at a glance. In ISO/IEC 2382:2105, it is defined as a "syntactic unit that conforms to the rules of a particular programming language and that is composed of declarations and statements or instructions needed to solve a certain function, task, or problem". By analyzing this definition, it is possible to see that a computer program should consist of the two main parts:

- Declarations that are used to describe data structures and variables that are used to solve the given task.
- Statements or instructions needed for the given task or problem solution. It is also possible to further analyze the standard and conclude that these elements are used to compose the algorithm – "finite ordered set of well-defined rules for the solution of a problem".

By combining and analyzing these definitions and common knowledge about software engineering, it is possible to define the target model that consists of the two main parts:

- Data structure and variable definitions – to cover the static aspect of the system in development.
- Sequence of instructions or statements that use former part to cover the dynamic aspect of the developed system.

Again, it is possible to see that the chosen source model already provides an insight into these two aspects with the concept model being focused on the data structure definition and the process model describing the dynamic capabilities of the system, i.e., how data are transformed during the system operation, and in which order processes are invoked performing these transformations.

Thus, to transform the two-hemisphere model into the computer program, it would be necessary to transform every element (or a set of elements) of it to the appropriate element (or a set of elements) of the target model and to preserve the linkage between them based on the specific algorithm defined by the authors.

V. Converting Concepts To Data Structures

Data structures describe the static aspect of the system that is being analyzed and built. According to [19], data structure can be defined as "physical or logical relationship among units of data and the data themselves". This definition can be linked to the concept model of the two-hemisphere model: by representing data types in form of units of data and defining the necessary relationship by utilizing already defined concepts, it is possible to extract all the necessary information to the form required for code generation.

In order to be programming language-agnostic, it is necessary to analyze how data structures might be represented in different programming languages and what information is shared between these representations.

The first case is object-oriented programming languages – here, it is possible to define data structure as a class with appropriate attributes. Each attribute can be described by its name and data type.

Some programming languages, for example, ECMAScript [20], are sometimes called object-based. While the latest ECMAScript standard allows for the definition of classes, it is also possible to use the so-called prototypes for the object blueprint definition. Prototype here is an object that has a set of fields and methods that can be used by all the other objects that are referencing this prototype. In a way, this is like the class in stricter object-oriented languages; however, prototypes usually do not support inheritance. In case of the static aspect description, a prototype should contain a set of fields, where each field has a name and data type.

Next, there are programming languages that are not object-oriented, for example, C programming language [21], where data structures are commonly represented with a `struct` syntax construction. Structure in C language can be viewed as a "weak class" – it is a set of data that consists of fields that are like class attributes. Each of them has a name and data type. However, structures in C language do not have methods (it is possible to reference the function via the pointer, which is a field of structure; however, it still will be a field, but not a method).

Other non-object-oriented programming languages, such as Erlang [22], can have different ways of representing the data structures. For example, in Erlang it is possible to define it as a `record`, which is similar to structure in C language and consists of fields of given types, or it is also possible to define it as a tuple, which can be viewed similar to the array. In case of record, each element has a name and can have a data type. In case of tuple, a name is omitted and replaced by an index; a data type, in turn, can be preserved.

Even using low-level assembly languages, it is usually possible to define the data structures. For example, one of the modern assemblers – flat assembler [23] – provides a way of defining the so-called structures consisting of a field, where each of them has a name and data type definition.

To sum up, it is possible to see that most programming languages require a data structure to have its own type (or name) and a set of fields/attributes, each of them having its own name and data type. Even considering some exclusions, such as Erlang tuples, where names are not preserved, it is possible to define an intermediate representation of a data structure that can be later used to generate a code in different programming languages.

This intermediate representation is provided in (1). Here, the data structure definition is described by its name and a set of attributes, each having its name and data type. Basically, one can notice that such a representation corresponds to the concept definition in a concept model of the two-hemisphere model. Thus, obtaining the data structure information from the source model is a simple task.

$$DS\,Def = \begin{pmatrix} Name \\ (\langle Attr_1|Type_1\rangle \ldots \langle Attr_k|Type_k\rangle) \end{pmatrix} \tag{1}$$

Data structure information is the first part of the proposed intermediate model that can be used for code generation. The second part is the information that can be used for describing the behavioral capabilities of the code. Definition of such a model is provided in the subsequent section.

VI. DEFINITIONS OF SYSTEM BEHAVIOR

System behavior in the two-hemisphere model is described with the help of the process model that provides the information on the processes that are executed inside the analyzed system, the data exchanged by these processes, and the sequence of execution. In order to convert this information to the code defined in a programming language, it is necessary to define a model that is capable of the programming language code description and can represent such a code.

One of the ways to represent the target model, i.e., programming language syntax constructions, is to use Abstract Syntax Tree (AST) [24]. This approach is widely used in the compilers, which translate textual representation of the code into ASTs and then build the machine instruction set out of them. Thus, AST is one of the possible intermediate models that can be used for code generation.

As mentioned above, AST is used to generate the machine instruction set that, in turn, can be represented in a way of the so-called Assembly Language [25], which is human readable representation of the machine instructions. Obviously, it is possible to use a similar approach when defining the dynamic part of the intermediate code representation. However, assembly languages for the modern processors can contain a lot of instructions, for example, x86-64 instruction set consists of ~1000 instructions [26], which would make the intermediate model complex to define correctly, while easy to transform to the appropriate code.

Yet another option to analyze is to look at cross-platform languages, such as Java [14] and .NET [27]. These languages are compiled into the so-called bytecode that can be defined as a "lightweight assembly". Bytecode provides an alternative to more complex assembly languages by defining a reduced instruction set, for example, Java Virtual Machine (JVM) bytecode consists of ~200 instructions [28].

It is possible to use these representations to define the logic encapsulated in the process model and describe the dynamic aspect of the system under analysis. Though, at first, the use of AST seems to be a correct approach, the authors would like to note that ASTs usually define the syntax of a particular language. Therefore, AST defined for the Java language [14] will probably not be suitable for language such as Erlang [22], since the syntaxes of two are different. However, it might be used for code generation in JavaScript [20] or C [21].

Thus, the authors propose defining the intermediate model by using ideas that define the bytecode – use a reduced set of instructions in order to accomplish the task. It is necessary to define such instructions in a way that they can be used to cover the maximum number of possible target languages.

For this purpose, it is necessary to analyze the two-hemisphere model once again. It is possible to see that the dynamic aspect of the system under analysis is described by processes, each of which might accept and produce data flows. Data flows, in turn, can carry data in form of concepts or primitives. Therefore, the main logical element here is process. Processes can be turned into methods, functions, predicates, etc., depending on the chosen target language. Common characteristic of these targets is that they can have inputs and outputs, which correlate well with the process consuming and producing data flows.

Therefore, it is possible to define an intermediate representation of the process: it should have an identifier (it, for example, can be a name), a set of consumed data, which can be empty, and a set of produced data, which can also be empty. Transformation to such representation from the target model is straightforward – it is necessary to use the process name and collect all the possible data elements from the incoming and outgoing data flows to define the representation shown in (2).

$$P\ Def = \begin{pmatrix} Name \\ (\langle Input_1|Type_1\rangle \dots \langle Input_k|Type_k\rangle) \\ (\langle Output_1|Type_1\rangle \dots \langle Output_k|Type_k\rangle) \end{pmatrix} \quad (2)$$

In this representation, each process is transformed into a three-element tuple that consists of name, inputs and outputs. Both inputs and outputs are defined as sets of name-type tuples, where a name is a logical name of the input/output, i.e., parameter name, and a type is a data structure, primitive or array/collection of former types mixed in any way.

Such a representation allows for a wide range of possible target languages – it does not define whether the target language element is a class method or a free function, or any other kind of data processing primitive. It does not enforce a way on how parameters are passed – there are languages, for example, C# [27] or Python [29] that can allow returning multiple data structures from the function/method. Otherwise, it is possible to combine the outputs into a special data structure to guarantee a single returned item.

The authors propose calling this representation a "logical unit", since it corresponds to a single process being executed inside a system; however, its target representation may vary.

In order to define the interaction between the logical units, it is necessary to analyze what might happen inside the system and how processes might interact with each other.

The simplest case is sequential invocation of processes, which takes the data produced by the first processes and passes it to the next one in the logical chain. To cover this case, it is necessary to define storage units for data process exchange – when doing further transformation, these definitions can become local or global variables, virtual or physical machine registers, etc. It is also necessary to be able to invoke any logical unit by passing its parameters to it and storing its result.

Next case is branching – branching in programming languages can be represented by various syntax constructions, starting with `if..else`, `switch` and ending with loops that, in turn, may contain premature exit conditions. It is also necessary to note that loops can be defined in several ways – a loop may have its condition checked before the next iteration execution, or after it. Despite different ways of branching, it is possible to analyze lower-level languages, such as assembly language [25], and different byte code implementations (for example, JVM [28] bytecode and .NET [27] intermediate language) to see that it should be possible to implement the necessary branching support by using several definitions. It should be possible to define labels, which can mark different states (or points) in the execution flows and instructions that would allow passing the control to these labels, i.e., branching instructions. Branching, in turn, can be conditional and non-conditional. In the first case, when the execution flow reaches an appropriate instruction, the so-called jump is performed to the appropriate label, which means a change in the next executed instruction. Conditional branching requires first performing the condition check and then, depending on the result of this check, performing or not performing the "jump".

By analyzing the possible logical unit execution flows, one can see that these two cases are enough to cover all the possible process execution sequences in the initial model. Thus, it is possible to define additional elements that are described further to be generated for the intermediate model.

First of these elements is label definition instruction. It is shown in (3). Here, the label is defined by its name, which can be any kind of symbolic identifier – numeric or textual.

```
Label<Name>
```
(3)

Next elements are branching instructions that are used with the labels. The first branching instruction is non-conditional branching that is shown in (4).

```
Jump<Label>
```
(4)

Non-conditional jump transfers the execution to the label defined in it, so it can be defined by a jump instruction followed by a label to be "jumped" to.

Next two instructions are conditional branching instructions, and they are presented in (5). Both instructions are similar, with only difference in the situation when branching should happen – when the condition is met or is not met.

```
JumpIf<Var, Label>
JumpIfNot<Var, Label>
```
(5)

These instructions require the boolean type variable to be checked. This variable is defined via its name, which will be discussed later. Otherwise, both instructions contain labels to be "jumped" to, depending on the value of this variable.

It is possible to see that conditions here are not the part of the branching instruction; instead branching instructions use variables that contain the result of the condition check. This means the necessity for the condition checking instruction, which is given in (6).

```
Check<Var, Condition>
```
(6)

This instruction has two parameters – a variable to store the condition check result and the condition to be checked. Here, the condition is a free-text phrase or a sentence.

It is possible to see that condition checking requires a variable to store the result, which later will be used by a conditional branching instruction. Therefore, it is necessary to be able to define the variable, which is supported by variable definition instruction presented in (7).

```
Var<Name, Type>
```
(7)

This instruction has two arguments – the name of variable and its type, which is the same as for data structures.

Last necessary instruction is the process invocation instruction. It is presented in (8).

```
Invoke<Process, Inputs, Outputs>
```
(8)

Here, the instruction has three parameters defined in it – the name of the process to be executed, its inputs, which are an array of appropriate variable names, and its outputs defined in the same way.

As it will be shown in the next section, these instructions are enough to define all the types of branching and possible execution flows, at least in the context of code generation from the two-hemisphere model.

VII. Examples of the Proposed Model Applications

In order to prove that the developed model is feasible and can be used for code generation, the authors propose analyzing several examples of its application.

The first example is sequential invocation of processes. In case of the Java [14] programming language, such a code can be written in a form shown in Figure 2.

```
c = f1(a, b);
d = f2(c);
```

Figure 2. Sequential process invocation in Java.

Here, method `f1` is invoked with arguments `a` and `b`, its invocation result is stored in variable `c`, and then used to invoke method `f2`. It is possible to define such an invocation sequence in the proposed intermediate model notation, which, in turn, is shown in Figure 3.

```
Invoke<f1, [a, b], [c]>
Invoke<f2, [c], [d]>
```

Figure 3. Sequential process invocation in the proposed model.

One can realize that the proposed model corresponds to the Java code, and it is possible to perform transformations from one to another.

Next example is presented in Figure 4. Here, several branching definitions are given – first, there is simple branching with only single condition check, which defines if method `f1` should be executed. Next, there is more complex `if..else` branching, and finally – branching using `switch`.

The same branching instructions are presented in Figure 5. Again, by studying both representations, it is possible to see their equality and ability to transform from one to another.

```
if (a == b) {
    f1();
}

if (c < d) {
    f2();
} else if (c == d) {
    f3();
} else {
    f4();
}

switch (e) {
    case 1:
        f5();
        break;
    case 2:
        f6();
        break;
    default:
        f7();
}
```

Figure 4. Branching in Java.

```
Check<Cond1, "a == b">
JumpIfNot<Cond1, L1>
Invoke<f1, [], []>

Label<L1>
Check<Cond2, "c < d">
Check<Cond3, "c == d">
JumpIfNot<Cond2, L2>
Invoke<f2, [], []>
Jump<L4>
Label<L2>
JumpIfNot<Cond3, L3>
Invoke<f3, [], []>
Jump<L4>
Label<L3>
Invoke<f4, [], []>
Label<L4>

Check<Cond4, "e == 1">
JumpIfNot<Cond4, L5>
Invoke<f5, [], []>
Jump<L7>
Label<L5>
Check<Cond5, "e == 2">
JumpIfNot<Cond5, L6>
Jump<L7>
Invoke<f6, [], []>
Label<L6>
Invoke<f7, [], []>
Label<L7>
```

Figure 5. Branching in the intermediate model.

Last situation to be covered by the proposed intermediate model is loops in the code. To show that these cases can also be covered, the authors propose considering the Java code provided in Figure 6. The appropriate intermediate model representation is given in Figure 7.

Here, three types of loops are presented. The first loop is `for loop`, which repeats for a given amount of time. This is controlled via a local loop variable `i`. The second loop is a loop with precondition, while the last one is a loop with post-condition. The second loop also involves possible premature exit via checking local variable `c` value.

It is possible once again to see that all the necessary cases are covered by the intermediate model with a single exception of incrementing the loop variable value in case of the loop with fixed iteration count. This, however, can be improved by adding additional instructions to the model. It is also worth noting that the two-hemisphere model notation does not allow defining such loops now, so this case is not covered fully.

```
for (int i = 1; i < 5; i++) {
    f1();
}

while (a < b) {
    if (c > 0) {
        break;
    }

   f2();
}

do {
    f3();
} (while e > 1);
```

Figure 6. Loops in Java.

It is possible to see that the proposed intermediate model allows covering all the possible cases that might be encountered in the initial model, as well as presents a solid way to enable code generation in various programming languages.

VIII. An Example of the Proposed Model Application

In order to demonstrate how the proposed model can be used in conjunction with the two-hemisphere model, the authors refer to the diagram first presented in [30]. Due to the fact that the research described here is still underway, the authors do not present a full system. Instead, the authors demonstrate only part of it that was used to evaluate the approach. As in the original work, only a process diagram is analyzed here. It is presented in Figure 8.

```
Label<L1>
Check<Cond1, "i < 5">
JumpIfNot<Cond1, L2>
Invoke<f1, [], []>
Jump<L1>
Label<L2>

Label<L3>
Check<Cond2, "a < b">
JumpIfNot<Cond2, L4>
Check<Cond3, "c > 0">
JumpIf<Cond3, L4>
Invoke<f2, [], []>
Jump<L3>
Label<L4>

Label<L5>
Invoke<f3, [], []>
Check<Cond4, "e > 1">
JumpIfNot<Cond4, L6>
Jump<L5>
Label<L6>
```

Figure 7. Loops in the intermediate model.

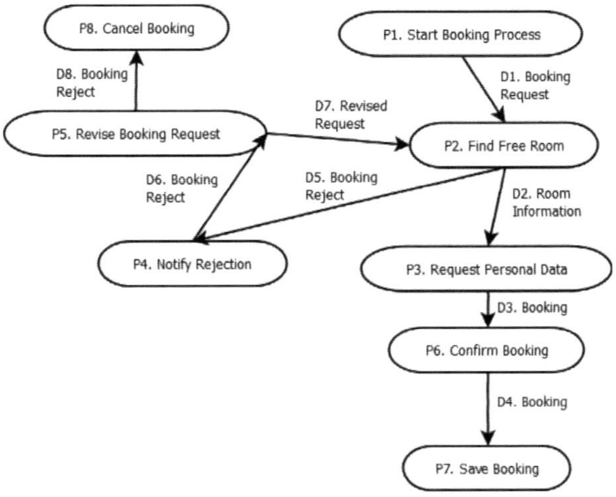

Figure 8. Example of the two-hemisphere model.

Here, the model describes a booking process in the hotel that starts with receiving a booking request with room preference details. After that there are two options: either room that fits the request is found or not (for example, due to the fact that rooms do not meet the criteria, or non-availability of the rooms in the given dates). If no room is found, a user is advised to revise the information and submit a new request. At this point, a user can also cancel the booking. If a room is found and request can be served, a user is asked to provide additional information, which is used to create the booking and store it in the database. Here, all elements are marked with identifiers – processes are marked P1…P8, dataflows – D1…D8. These identifiers are later used in the intermediate model that is presented in Figure 9. Here, it is possible to see how the intermediate model would look after transformation of the initial process model. It is also possible to see that additional information is required to produce it – such as conditions for branching.

```
Invoke<P1, [], [D1]>

Label<L1>
Invoke<P2, [D1, D7], [D2, D5]>
Check<Rejected,
      "booking is rejected">
JumpIfNot<Rejected, L2>
Invoke<P4, [D5], [D6]>
Invoke<P5, [D6], [D7, D8]>
Check<Canceled, "User canceled">
JumpIf<Canceled, L3>
Jump<L1>

Label<L2>
Invoke<P3, [D2], [D3]>
Invoke<P6, [D3], [D4]>
Invoke<P7, [D4], []>
Jump<L4>

Label<L3>
Invoke<P8, [D8], []>

Label<L4>
```

Figure 9. Example of the intermediate model.

It is also possible to trace the intermediate model back to the initial one and see that processes are invoked in the same sequence as defined by the initial business process analysis. This task could also be automated – it is possible to create a graph of all the possible branching and compare it with the initial model in order to check, if the defined process invocation sequence is preserved. Such a graph definition would allow verifying the correctness of the generated model. However, the algorithm to define such a verification graph is out of scope of this paper. However, it should be noted that it has already been developed and currently is under testing.

IX. CONCLUSIONS AND FUTURE WORK

Previous research conducted by the authors on the use of the two-hemisphere model for generation of different types of UML diagrams, such as use case, sequence, communication, state or class diagrams, has demonstrated that the two-hemisphere model contains quite enough information to obtain the static elements of the system analysis model, as well as dynamic ones. The received UML model, according to the main statement of MDSD, provides an ability to generate a code as well. So far, as we have a transformation chain: the two-hemisphere model → UML diagrams → code, the authors can assume that the direct transformation, i.e., the two-hemisphere model → code is also feasible. In this paper, the authors have presented the intermediate model that can be used to enable direct code generation from the two-hemisphere model. The proposed model allows for code generation in different programming languages – object-oriented, object-based, procedural, etc.

While this paper describes how the model should look like and what artifacts it consists of, it is also necessary to define algorithms for transformation of the initial model to the intermediate one. This is the first part of future work. It might also be necessary to enrich the model itself to cover more cases, as well as develop algorithms for transforming this model into an actual code. This is also part of future research in this area.

Since the intermediate model described here is still being developed and the research about its definition and application is still being carried out, the authors define the evaluation of the proposed approach and additional validation of the achieved results as another part of future work. The goal is to test this model with a completely developed system and identify the possible gaps and improvement areas.

So far, the goal has been to develop the intermediate model as a basis for code generation. The proposed model covers both static and dynamic aspects of the system and should be compatible not only with the two-hemisphere model, but also with other types of the source model, since the model itself is simple enough to be generated from any type of initial data. The authors also consider the proposed model to be useful for code generation in different programming languages, since it does not enforce any paradigm to be applied and can be used to generate data structures and invocation flows of different types.

REFERENCES

[1] B. Perisic, "Model Driven Software Development – State of the Art and Perspectives", Invited Paper, INFOTEH 2014, Proceedings Vol. 13, pp. 1237-1248, 2014.

[2] F. Daniel and M. Matera, "Model-Driven Software Development," in Mashups. Data Centric Systems and Applications, 1st ed., Berlin: Springer-Verlag Berlin Heidelberg, pp. 71-93, 2014.

[3] OMG® Unified Modeling Language® (OMG UML®), OMG [Online]. Available: https://www.omg.org/spec/UML/ [retrieved: September, 2019]

[4] M. K. Shiferaw and A. K. Jena, "Code Generator for Model-Driven Software Development Using UML Models" 2018 Second International Conference on Electronics, Communication and Aerospace Technology (ICECA), pp. 1671-1678, 2018.

[5] H. D. Gurad and V. S. Mahalle, "An Approach to Code Generation from UML Diagrams", IJESRT - International Journal of Engineering Sciences & Research Technology, pp. 421-423, 2014.

[6] O. Nikiforova and M. Kirikova, "Two-hemisphere model Driven Approach: Engineering Based Software Development", Scientific Proceedings of CAiSE 2004 (the 16th International Conference on Advanced Information Systems Engineering), pp. 219-233, 2004.

[7] O. Nikiforova, "Two Hemisphere Model Driven Approach for Generation of UML Class Diagram in the Context of MDA",

e-Informatica Software Engineering Journal - Volume 3, Issue 1, pp. 59-72, 2009.

[8] O. Nikiforova, "System Modeling in UML with Two-Hemisphere Model Driven Approach", Proceedings of The 50th Scientific Conference of Riga Technical University, Computer Science, Applied Computer Systems, pp. 37-44, 2010

[9] A. Noureen, A. Amjad, and F. Azam, "Model Driven Architecture - Issues, Challenges and Future Directions," JSW, vol. 11, No. 9, pp. 924-933, 2016.

[10] J. Sejans and O. Nikiforova, "Practical Experiments with Code Generation from the UML Class Diagram", Proceedings of MDA&MDSD 2011, 3rd International Workshop on Model Driven Architecture and Modeling Driven Software Development In conjunction with the 6th International Conference on Evaluation of Novel Approaches to Software Engineering, pp. 57-67, 2011.

[11] O. Nikiforova, "Object Interaction as a Central Component of Object-Oriented System Analysis", Proceedings of the 2nd International Workshop „Model Driven Architecture and Modeling Theory Driven Development" (MDA&MTDD 2010), pp. 3-12, 2010.

[12] E. B. Omar, B. Brahim, and G. Taoufiq, "Automatic code generation by model transformation from sequence diagram of system's internal behavior", International Journal of Computer and Information Technology Vol. 01 Issue 02, pp. 129-146, 2012.

[13] Z. Wang, "A JAVA Code Generation Method based on XUML", IOP Conference Series: Materials Science and Engineering, pp 1-8, 2019.

[14] Java | Oracle [Online]. Available: https://java.com/ [retrieved: September, 2019]

[15] A. Lasbahani, M. Chhiba, and A. Tabyaoui, "A UML Profile for Security and Code Generation", International Journal of Electrical and Computer Engineering (IJECE), pp 5278-5291, 2018.

[16] O. Nikiforova, U. Sukovskis, and K. Gusarovs, "Application of the Two-Hemisphere Model Supported by BrainTool: Football Game Simulation", Proceedings of the 4th Symposium on Computer Languages, Implementations and Tools, organized within the International Conference of Numerical Analysis and Applied Mathematics (ICNAAM 2014), pp. 1-4, 2014

[17] P. Chen, "The Entity-Relationship Model - Toward a Unified View of Data", ACM Transactions on Database Systems, pp. 9-36, 1976.

[18] W. Stevens, G. Myers, and L. Constantine, "Structured Design". IBM Systems Journal. 1974, vol.13, no.2, pp.115-139, 1974.

[19] *ISO/IEC 2382:2015 Information technology -- Vocabulary*. [Online]. Available from: https://www.iso.org/obp/ui/#iso:std:iso-iec:2382:ed-1:v1:en [retrieved: September, 2019]

[20] *Standard ECMA-262* [Online]. Available: https://www.ecma-international.org/publications/standards/Ecma-262.htm [retrieved: September, 2019]

[21] D. M. Ritchie and B. W. Kernighan, The C Programming Language, Second Edition. - USA: Prentice Hall, 1988.

[22] *Erlang Programming Language* [Online]. Available: https://www.erlang.org/ [retrieved: September, 2019]

[23] *flat assembler* [Online]. Available: https://flatassembler.net/ [retrieved: September, 2019]

[24] D. Grune and C.J.H Jacobs, Parsing Techniques – a Practical Guide. - USA: Prentice Hall, 1988.

[25] D. Salomon, Assemblers and Loaders. - USA: Prentice Hall, 1993.

[26] Intel® 64 and IA-32 Architectures Software Developer Manuals | Intel® Software [Online]. Available: https://software.intel.com/en-us/articles/intel-sdm [retrieved: September, 2019]

[27] .NET | Free. Cross-platform. Open Source. [Online]. Available: https://www.microsoft.com/net/ [retrieved: September, 2019]

[28] The Java® Virtual Machine Specification [Online]. Available: https://docs.oracle.com/javase/specs/jvms/se12/html/index.html [retrieved: September, 2019]

[29] Welcome to Python.org [Online]. Available: https://www.python.org/ [retrieved: September, 2019]

[30] K. Gusarovs and O. Nikiforova, "Workflow Generation from the Two-Hemisphere Model", Applied Computer Systems, Vol.22, pp. 36-46, 2017.

Augmenting Fiat Currency with an Integrated Managed Cryptocurrency

Peter Mell
National Institute of Standards and Technology
Gaithersburg MD, USA
peter.mell@nist.gov

***Abstract*—In this work, we investigate how the governance features of a managed currency (e.g., a fiat currency) can be built into a cryptocurrency in order to leverage potential benefits found in the use of blockchain technology and smart contracts. The resulting managed cryptocurrency can increase transparency and integrity, while potentially enabling the emergence of novel monetary instruments. It has similarities to cash in that it enables the general public to immediately transfer funds to a recipient without intermediary systems being involved. However, our system is account-based, unlike circulating bank notes that are self-contained. Our design would allow one to satisfy know your customer laws and be subject to law enforcement actions following legal due process (e.g., account freezing and fund seizure), while mitigating counterparty risk with checks and balances. Funds can thus be transferred only between approved and authenticated users. Our system has on-chain governance capabilities using smart contracts deployed on a dedicated, permissioned blockchain that has different sets of control mechanisms for who can read data, write data, and publish blocks. To enable the governance features, only authorized identity proofed entities can submit transactions. To enable privacy, only the block publishers can read the blockchain; the publishers maintain dedicated nodes that provide access controlled partial visibility of the blockchain data. Being permissioned, we can use a simple consensus protocol with no transaction fees. A separate security layer prevents denial of service and a balance of power mechanism prevents any small group of entities from having undue control. While permissioned, we ensure that no one entity controls the blockchain data or block publishing capability through a voting system with publicly visible election outcomes.**

***Index Terms*—Blockchain, Cryptocurrency, Digital Cash, Fiat Currency, Smart Contract**

I. INTRODUCTION

Bitcoin is a protocol for a permissionless distributed ledger that was designed to provide non-reversible transactions with direct account-to-account fund transfers where no third party needs to be trusted [1]. It leveraged blockchain technology to enable a form of non-sovereign digital currency that was previously not possible. It and subsequent cryptocurrencies introduced smart contracts and new kinds of decentralized governance models that have significant organizational and political implications (e.g., having no relationship with any government). With respect to these systems, [2] points out that cryptocurrencies can enable users to remain anonymous, can have permissionless access, and thus usually do not support know your customer (KYC) and anti-money laundering (AML) laws at the protocol level by design. In this work, we investigate how to leverage some of the novel benefits provided by blockchain technology and smart contracts to enable a new form of managed cryptocurrency that has built-in support for KYC and AML laws with system governance mechanisms along with a balance of power structure. Note that we are not suggesting that such a cryptocurrency should necessarily be issued, as that decision involves policy and economic factors outside of the scope of this work. Instead, we are proposing a technical architecture that could lead towards the technical ability to do so.

We investigate how the governance features of a managed currency (e.g., a fiat currency) can be built into a cryptocurrency in order to leverage potential benefits found in the use of blockchain technology and smart contracts. It is designed to be compatible with and augment a partner managed currency, the users being able to freely exchange one for the other. The resulting managed cryptocurrency can increase transparency and integrity, while potentially enabling the emergence of novel monetary instruments. It has similarities to cash in that it enables the general public to immediately transfer funds to a recipient without intermediary systems being involved and the associated counterparty risks (a single transaction to the system transfers funds). This is accomplished through a distributed multi-party managed cryptocurrency system providing guarantees similar to Bitcoin style cryptocurrencies. However unlike circulating bank notes, our system is account-based and all recipients are identity proofed and authorized. Our design thus supports the satisfaction of KYC and AML laws at the protocol level. Entities distinct from the platform and currency managers can register as identity providers, ensuring fund transfers only to identity proofed and authenticated recipients while maintaining openness to the private sector and competition. Accounts would also be subject to law enforcement actions following legal due process to include the freezing of accounts and fund seizure.

Our system has on-chain governance capabilities using smart contracts deployed on a dedicated, permissioned blockchain that has different sets of control mechanisms for who can read data, write data, and publish blocks. To enable the cryptocurrency to have built-in governance roles along with KYC/AML checks, only authorized identity proofed entities can submit transactions. To support user privacy features, only the miners (referred to henceforth as validators) can read the blockchain. Validators then maintain dedicated nodes that provide access controlled partial visibility of blockchain data to users (e.g., their account balance, transaction history, and system management transactions). Being permissioned, we can use a lightweight consensus protocol. The protocol could be as simple as the dirty round robin used in Multichain [3]. The use of a security layer that prevents denial of service attacks (which works since all accounts must be pre-authorized and can easily be filtered) can enable a no transaction fee system where the validators are paid by the currency issuer to maintain the currency. Lastly, the architecture contains a balance of power mechanism to prevent any small group of entities from having undue control over the blockchain data or publication of new blocks. While it is a permissioned system, there is not a single entity that decides which accounts can publish blocks. Instead, the existing group of validators vote to determine changes to validator eligibility, with the outcomes being made publicly visible. No one entity controls the blockchain data or block publishing capability.

We implemented our architecture using smart contracts written with the Solidity programming language and made the code open source under a public domain license. It has functions for fund tracking, fiat-to-cryptocurrency fund conversion, transaction logging, account creation, voting scenarios, a bootstrapping mode, role assignment, and the ability of accounts to take special actions given their roles (e.g., law enforcement account freezing and central bank fund creation). A set of initial parameters are used to bootstrap the initial governance options but afterwards a voting system is used for multiple accounts with various roles to collectively manage different aspects of the cryptocurrency.

Research economists seem divided about the effectiveness of central bank issued cryptocurrencies. Some, like in [4], point out the potential economic viability of such assets. Others are more critical: [2] for instance states that there is a 'non-case' for a central bank cryptocurrency; their rationale for this was based on perceived immutable features of cryptocurrencies that would make them useless as alternatives to digital currency. In this work, we want to show that these features, considered immutable, can be altered through changing technical fundamentals about how a cryptocurrency blockchain works; this could enable sovereign cryptocurrencies with fiat currency style governance. Non-sovereign cryptocurrencies started the discussion on how to use blockchain to make the global financial system more stable and distributed; we hope that our work on sovereign cryptocurrencies will further facilitate that discussion.

The remainder of this paper is organized as follows. Section II discusses the foundational technology that underlies the design of our cryptocurrency platform. Section III presents our cryptocurrency architecture while section IV explains the account roles within that architecture. Section V discusses how to instantiate our cryptocurrency to integrate it with a fiat currency. Section VI analyzes the security model of our approach and Section VII discusses our implementation. Section VIII summarizes related efforts and section IX concludes.

II. Foundational Technology

Our managed cryptocurrency leverages existing approaches and borrows concepts from other technologies. This includes the cryptocurrency role system, on-chain governance of validator nodes, on-chain voting, and the decoupling of the validation and execution of transactions.

Our managed currency relies upon each cryptocurrency account being assigned a set of roles; these roles enable the management and use of the currency. Assigning roles to cryptocurrency accounts was initially introduced in [5].

On-chain governance is used to manage the set of validators through the assignment of 'validator' roles to accounts, those allowed to participate in a consensus algorithm to publish blocks. This concept of on-chain validator governance can be found in the Proof of Authority (PoA) consensus model. Here, block creation is distributed among different allowed nodes over time while offering Byzantine fault tolerance. PoA with smart contract based validator governance is implemented in the Ethereum client Parity (through the Aura consensus algorithm [6]) and by POA Network [7]. Another example of a PoA implementation can be found in the Microsoft Azure Blockchain system [8].

To manage the set of validators as well as other system functions, our managed cryptocurrency smart contracts must implement voting mechanisms which add or remove roles, as well as to approve or disapprove system security actions such as fund transfer reversals. Various standards and projects provide blockchain technology for decentralized voting [9]; the Ethereum standard EIP-1202 [10] offers for example an interface for implementing voting within smart contracts. As another example, the open-source project Aragon [11], built on Ethereum, allows token holders to cast a vote on protocol upgrades by signing a specific transaction. The Delegated Proof of Stake (DPoS) consensus algorithm, used for instance in BitShares [12], is another illustration of an on-chain voting structure. In BitShares, users vote by staking tokens into another account (called 'delegate'); the delegate account is then allowed to execute certain actions on behalf of its stakeholders (such as producing blocks and voting on protocol upgrades).

Lastly, our cryptocurrency introduces the concept of a 'Security Gateway'. A list of gateways linked to their associated validators, maintained at the smart contract level, are charged with pre-processing incoming transactions. This decouples the execution and validation of transactions. The Hyperledger Fabric, a permissioned blockchain, also has a similar decoupling [13]. Note that any mention of commercial products in this paper is for information only; it does not imply recommendation or endorsement.

III. Cryptocurrency Architecture

A cryptocurrency platform providing the benefits described in Section I and leveraging technology from Section II can be built using the following architecture. Figure 1 shows the overall architecture from the perspective of a single validator.

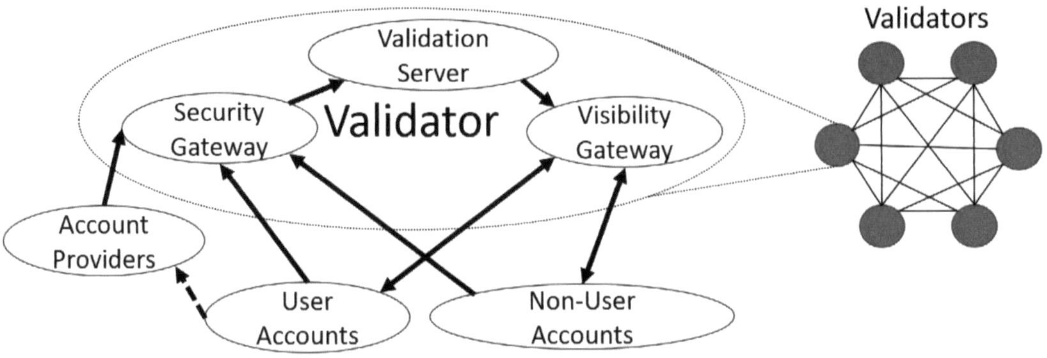

Fig. 1. Interactions of an Individual Validator

A. Platform Architecture

The architecture requires a permissioned smart contract cryptocurrency platform, such as PoA-based Ethereum. It should be configured to not charge transaction fees or gas for sending transactions to the smart contracts. The native cryptocurrency mechanisms of the platform will not be used and instead the cryptocurrency will be stored within the smart contracts (similar to token based ERC-20 [14] compliant smart contract currencies but running on a dedicated platform). Without gas and transaction fees, validators will be rewarded either off-chain or will participate through being inherently motivated to support the cryptocurrency. This is tractable because our use of a lightweight consensus model makes the execution of a validator node less expensive (it is done this way currently by other permissioned blockchain platforms such as Hyperledger Fabric).

The set of smart contracts will be fixed to a small set used to maintain the cryptocurrency. Being a permissioned system, the block publishing software must determine which validators are allowed to participate in the publication of new blocks. This set of permitted validators is managed at the smart contract layer and can be retrieved from the blockchain. In this way our architecture marries what are usually isolated governance layers, the protocol layer which manages the validator node permissions and the smart contract layer which executes code on behalf of system users.

B. Security Gateway

Also managed at the smart contract layer is the list of gateways that each validator maintains to accept proposed transactions from the users of the system. These security gateways pre-process incoming transactions to ascertain their validity. Transactions must be properly formatted and are only accepted from accounts that have roles. Security gateways also keep track of the rate of transactions issued by each account. Accounts with an unusually high rate can be throttled as a form of denial of service protection and to prevent any particular account from taking too large a percentage of system resources. It is possible to white list accounts that have a valid reason to issue a high throughput of transactions.

C. Visibility Gateway

A final platform level resource managed and made visible at the smart contract layer is the set of visibility gateways. Each validator independently maintains a set of such gateways to provide controlled blockchain read access for the account holders. The read access capabilities will be encoded as smart contract view functions (a view function is one that provides read only access and is highly efficient as it is executed locally and not propagated among validators nor included within a block like a normal transaction). However, unlike with typical view function responses, for security reasons (discussed in section VI) the responses will be signed by the associated validator account. The full blockchain is kept private by the validators and user read access is only available through the visibility gateways.

D. Smart Contracts

The smart contract layer, besides managing the authorized platform level resources listed previously, implements the managed cryptocurrency. The smart contracts maintain the list of authorized accounts, the roles granted to each account with associated features, and the balance in each account. We use the account/balance model as opposed to the unspent transaction output (UTXO) model (e.g., in Bitcoin) to avoid the unnecessary complexity (found in [5]) of having to label each unspent transaction with roles. The roles define a set of permissions that enable certain accounts to manage the cryptocurrency and are discussed in the following section.

E. Digital Wallets

Identity proofing results in the participants' identifiers being added to a global on-chain registry controlled by the account providers. As described in [15], the identifiers can be held in custodial, semi-custodial, or non-custodial digital wallets that can be integrated into existing applications, browsers, and operating systems.

IV. Managed Cryptocurrency Roles

The management features and integration with an associated fiat currency are enabled through accounts with various roles. This account and role capability is instantiated on top of the previously described platform and implemented within the fixed set of smart contracts. Section V will describe how these roles can be used in real world systems.

A. Platform Managers

An account with the platform manager role sets the policy for the cryptocurrency system and creates accounts and assigns them non-user roles. Policy can be set to be permanent, temporary, or have a timed expiration. Permanent policies cannot be changed once set (assuming the integrity of the blockchain itself is not compromised). They may be used to instantiate a particular architecture that the cryptocurrency will adopt. Alternately, they may be used to provide confidence to the user base that certain features or settings are guaranteed even though the cryptocurrency is managed by a set of privileged entities. Temporary policies can be changed at any time by a currency manager. Timed expiration policies are considered permanent until a published time at which they become temporary. The system may be set up with only one platform manager, a group of accounts that must vote to make changes, or a hierarchical system where higher priority managers can override policies from lower level managers (as in [5]). This latter design can be used as a security feature in case a currency manager account was compromised; higher priority accounts whose keys are stored in physical vaults could be used to override the compromised account and restore the system.

The policies available to be set can include enabling/disabling features within other roles, setting blockchain parameters such as the size and frequency of blocks, adjusting any fees charged (if any), and setting parameters on how voting will be performed (since the system requires groups to vote to perform certain actions).

During the bootstrapping phase for the cryptocurrency, within some fixed number of blocks, the platform manager defines the initial set of validators. Once the bootstrapping phase is over, the accounts with the platform manager role may not modify the validator roles (thus limiting their authority and creating a balance of power).

B. Account Providers

An account with an account provider role has been authorized by the platform manager(s) to manage user accounts. They identity proof users off-chain, receive a list of the users not yet authorized accounts, and add the user role to those accounts to authorize them. It is important that the users demonstrate ownership of each provided account through proving possession of the associated private key. Each account provider then keeps an internal record of which users are associated with which accounts; this record is not published or shared. This allows KYC and AML laws to be supported at the account provider level (rather than at the entire platform level), which may enhance security and user privacy.

C. System Security

An account with the system security role has the ability to control other accounts for system security purposes. Such accounts can freeze and unfreeze other accounts. They can also move funds between accounts to confiscate funds or reverse transactions. In the latter case we note that the relevant accounts simply need to be debited and credited funds due to our system being account-based (as opposed to following Bitcoin's UTXO model). We also note that since all accounts are identity proofed, system security actions can take place off-chain using existing legal frameworks.

To limit unauthorized actions, policy can be set by the platform manager requiring an on-chain voting mechanism for certain system security transactions. In addition, the platform manager(s) can limit or disable any of the powers of the system security role through policy settings.

D. Users

An account with the user role is one that can be used to receive, store, and send value in the form of tokens maintained by the smart contracts. A single user may have multiple accounts and may use multiple account providers to do so (note that every account must be identity proofed by an account provider).

Each account is labelled within the smart contract with its associated public key. A user maintains use of an account through possession of the associated private key (possibly stored on a hardware token for greater security). If a user loses a private key or suspects that their private key has been stolen, they need a way to retake possession of the account. This is accomplished by swapping out the account's original public key with a new one within the smart contract. When creating their account, users can choose what method they prefer to enable this action; there are at least three options. They can trust their account provider to do this for them and simply re-identity proof to their account provider. They could authorize a set of other accounts to validate the public key swap (using accounts they own or accounts of trusted individuals). Or they could require the involvement of system security along with their account provider, necessitating re-identity proofing with both entities.

E. Currency Managers

An account with the currency manager role has the ability to control the money supply through direct actions or ongoing policy. This includes fund creation, deletion, and the provision of interest. The currency manager accounts vote to set monetary policy or initiate an action (for example the creation of funds to be lent to other entities).

F. Validators

An account with the validator role is an account that represents an authorized block publisher. Validator accounts vote to add/remove the validator role to/from other accounts. Other than block publishing, the validators manage their respective security and visibility gateways. On their visibility gateways, they make visible all cryptocurrency management transactions to provide full transparency to all users.

Each validator account posts on the smart contract the Internet Protocol (IP) addresses of their security and visibility gateways. The visibility gateways then make the security and visibility gateway addresses visible to all users and the validation server addresses visible to other accounts with the validator role. This latter publication facilitates the peer-to-peer permissioned networking between validators used for transaction propagation and block publication.

Each validator account publishes on the blockchain a publicly visible special public key associated with the signed responses from its visibility gateways. This key is different from the public key for the validator account itself. It also publicly publishes contact information (e.g., an email address) for reporting any problems. This is essential for security reasons discussed in Section VI.

V. Integration with Fiat Currencies

The architecture presented in sections III and IV is designed to be integrated with a fiat currency and traditional bank deposits. A government administration could instantiate the cryptocurrency and act as the platform manager. The directors of the government's independent central bank could act as the currency managers. The government law enforcement agencies could act in the system security role. This creates a balance of power where no one organization 'controls' the blockchain. To further promote this, government entities separate from the administration can act as the validators (e.g., a set of states). The national standards body can define the specification for the supporting cryptocurrency software and independent laboratories can test compliance of that software. Note that multiple developers should be used, especially for the validator software, for security purposes and the code should be developed open source and made available publicly. This way a single developer cannot maliciously or unintentionally violate the specification and enable non-protocol compliant blocks to be published and accepted.

Financial institutions (e.g., commercial banks, cryptocurrency exchanges, and other fintech companies) could be made account providers, among other entities, since they already must identity proof their customers. They would keep their mapping of identity proofed users to account numbers private and only reveal select information to fulfill a court order (thus supporting KYC and AML laws while still maintaining user privacy). They can modify their banking software to simultaneously show users their bank deposit balances and cryptocurrency balances (since they established each user's accounts). The financial institution itself would not have access to the user's cryptocurrency balance and transactions but their banking application, on behalf of the user, could retrieve this information from the visibility gateways. These applications could then enable the conversion of bank deposits to cryptocurrency and vice versa (also often referred as on-ramp/off-ramp). The application could send cryptocurrency to the financial institution and have the institution deposit traditional money into the user's bank accounts (and vice versa). The application could also transfer funds between the user's different cryptocurrency accounts using a bank owned account as an intermediary to hide any linkage between the user's accounts from appearing on the blockchain. Note that the financial institution obtains cryptocurrency through its existing fiat accounts with the central bank: the institution sends the central bank fiat currency and the central bank sends it cryptocurrency. If users are allowed to interact directly with the central bank, users can perform this operation themselves.

The central bank, as the currency manager, unifies the fiat and cryptocurrency by enabling the exchange between both. The cryptocurrency could be maintained as a separate line item on the central bank balance sheet. The central bank can create and destroy both currencies and thus can implement a cryptocurrency monetary policy in a similar fashion as when managing solely its fiat currency. Note that offering two forms of currency, with different characteristics and risk profiles, can have significant economic implications that are out of scope for this paper.

VI. Security Analysis

In this section we analyze the security and functionality provided by our architecture using the three traditional computer security pillars of confidentiality, integrity, and availability.

A. Confidentiality

Our architecture provides accounts/transactions that are pseudonymous for the validators and confidential to the rest of the users. We note that there is a possibility of user confidentiality being lifted when necessary to support KYC and AML laws (e.g., through a court order for validators to reveal transactions and the respective account providers to divulge account ownership). Users choose which account provider they trust to know which accounts they own. The account provider keeps this private unless required to reveal it. Furthermore, the account provider can distribute user funds between the user's accounts such that there is no linkage on the blockchain between the multiple accounts from the same user.

The transactions on the blockchain are kept private and only shared within the set of validators. The visibility gateways only reveal blockchain transactions to the parties involved in those transactions. A downside of this is that it would appear then that accounts with the platform manager, system security, and currency manager roles can issue transactions without oversight. However, the validators are independent entities that make these transactions publicly visible through their visibility gateways. This offers transparency for all management transactions but confidentiality for user fund transfers.

The IP addresses of the validating servers are stored on the blockchain but the visibility gateways make this information visible only to the validator accounts. Thus, the validation servers themselves are kept confidential. If this information was leaked, a single transaction could be used to update a revealed server to a new IP address (to discourage denial of service (DoS) attacks). The security gateways and visibility gateways' addresses are made public. The visibility gateways operate independently with only a copy of the blockchain and thus can be replicated at scale to counter possible DoS attacks.

Likewise, a validator may have multiple security gateways to provide load balancing and DoS protection.

B. Integrity

The use of a group of independent validators ensures the integrity of the newly published blocks. No validator will accept a block from another validator that does not follow the established protocol. Each block and the transactions therein must be of the proper form and have the necessary digital signatures. As is the norm with blockchains, each block contains a hash of the previous block to enable detection of any changes with previously published blocks. However unlike public blockchain systems, the users themselves cannot verify the retained integrity of the blockchain and so another mechanism must exist to hold individual validators accountable.

For this, user software will query multiple visibility gateways when retrieving user blockchain data. Any discrepancy between the visibility gateways owned by different validators reveals a problem with one of the validators. An exception is for very recent transactions that have not yet been posted by all validators and thus there should thus be an agreed-upon time delay before taking any action. In the case of a discrepancy, an event transaction is triggered and sent to all validators to describe the discrepancy. As long as at least one validator is honest, the discrepancy will be published. Note that this is considered a 'management' type transaction and thus is made publicly visible to all users. Note that since the visibility gateways sign their responses, the user can prove that multiple visibility gateways provided different answers. As long as a majority of the validators remain honest, the honest ones can vote out any validators that provide incorrect results.

If a set of the validators decide to overtly violate the cryptocurrency protocol (e.g., to change a permanent policy or take control away from the platform or currency managers), this will fork the blockchain as happens with other cryptocurrency systems. The non-violating validators would inform participating parties using off-chain methods and, like other cryptocurrency forks, the resolution would take place off-chain. Given that the cryptocurrency will be tied to a fiat currency, investigations and legal action may be taken against the violating validators. Note that only if 100 percent of the validators collude can they make changes without being noticed. Also, note that our cryptocurrency leverages the fact that it is a sovereign currency, existing within an off-chain legal framework.

C. Availability

There are two types of availability that need to be considered: the availability of the cryptocurrency system as a whole and the availability of a particular account to conduct transactions.

The cryptocurrency platform itself has robust availability because it is a distributed system with no central point of failure. Many of the validation servers may fail, even the majority of them, and the system can still continue to function. Note that individual validation servers can be run efficiently due to the use of a lightweight consensus algorithm, permitted by the permissioned blockchain configuration. Also, each security and visibility gateway can be implemented as a cluster of servers to reduce susceptibility to DoS attacks and individual server failures.

Individual accounts are not dependent upon a particular validator and user applications should issue transactions to multiple systems simultaneously (this includes both write transactions to the security gateways and read transactions to the visibility gateways). Using multiple security gateways ensures that no validator could decide to unilaterally block a particular account (note that account ownership is pseudonymous to the validators making this less likely). Using multiple visibility gateways, as discussed above, addresses integrity concerns.

VII. IMPLEMENTATION

We implemented our managed cryptocurrency as smart contracts using the Solidity programming language. It is available as open source software on Github at https://github.com/usnistgov/managed_token under a public domain license. In this proof-of-concept prototype, we implemented the core functions of the managed cryptocurrency. This includes fund tracking, fiat to cryptocurrency fund conversion, transaction logging, account creation, voting scenarios, bootstrapping mode, role assignment, and the ability of accounts to take special actions given their roles (e.g., law enforcement account freezing and central bank fund creation). Certain aspects are simplified, such as monetary policy options, as our goal was not to create a production system but to demonstrate that this managed architecture approach is feasible. We tested our code by deploying it to a local Ethereum test environment.

A couple of money creation schemes are provided in our system as examples. Schemes are provided to vote and carry out money creation in arbitrary accounts (following a top-down approach) as well as in all user accounts in the form of interests (following a bottom-up approach). Furthermore, these schemes can be either push-based or pull-based. In the push-based model, the money creation function creates funds in the recipient(s) account without any action being required from the recipient(s). In the pull-based model, the currency managers set rules through a single transaction to give the right to the recipient(s) to create their own funds according to this set of rules. This can provide scalability gains as users do not have to claim their allowance right away, and instead, may wait until they need it without any risk of not receiving it. In the case of periodic funds creation (e.g. interests, dividends), a user might be able to skip claiming funds between period X and period X + Y, and then, withdraw funds at period X + Y + 1 for all of the periods between X and X + Y + 1 combined. Finally, a set of view functions allows one to selectively control the visibility of monetary creation and other on-chain fund data, both at the user level and at the currency management level (e.g., global supply indicators).

Note that our implementation did not cover the off-chain aspects of our cryptocurrency architecture. In particular, we did not build the security or visibility gateways (although we did write the smart contract view functions to support the latter). We also did not modify the Ethereum mining software to only publish blocks in collaboration with the validators specified by the smart contracts (but we did implement the smart contract code to enable a set of validators to use the on-chain data to manage themselves).

VIII. Related Work

Most of the existing work related to managed cryptocurrencies consists in studies and pilots on blockchain-based central bank digital currencies (CBDC), as well as research and development of protocols for stablecoins, algorithmic currency management, and privacy-preserving KYC/AML checks.

The literature distinguishes two main categories of CBDCs: wholesale and retail. As explained by the Bank for International Settlements (BIS) in their money taxonomy [16], a wholesale CBDC is only available to financial institutions and mainly intended for inter-bank transactions whereas a retail CBDC is globally accessible and usable by the general public. Our managed cryptocurrency architecture is geared towards retail CBDCs, although it could also be launched as a wholesale CBDC, at least initially.

We have developed our architecture to change how cryptocurrencies usually work to enable support for retail CBDCs. As stated earlier, this does not mean that we are necessarily claiming that one should be created; we are simply providing some of the technical capability to do so. That said, the subject of state or central bank issued cryptocurrencies has been one of considerable interest. A BIS poll in 2018 showed that more than 70 percent of central banks worldwide were already engaged in CBDC work [17]. Some central banks, such as the central bank of Canada (project Jasper [18]), the Monetary Authority of Singapore (project Ubin [19]), or the Bank of Thailand [20] have focused their research on wholesale CBDC. Also, the European Central Bank and the Bank of Japan are conducting joint research on wholesale CBDCs with Project Stella [21]. Others, such as the Ecuadorian Central Bank ('Dinero Electronico' [22]), the People's Bank of China [23], and the Government of Venezuela (Petro [24]) aim at developing a CBDC for retail use. It should be noted, however, that many central bank efforts do not use (nor plan to use in the future) distributed ledger technologies (DLT); for example the Sveriges Riksbank from Sweden [25] stated that they currently deemed DLT too inefficient for use in a retail CBDC. An example of a non-DLT retail electronic currency is the e-Peso [26]. This is a pilot from the Central Bank of Uruguay that was launched as complement to physical cash but relied on a central registry for ownership recording.

Aside from efforts from governments and central banks, several other blockchain-based research projects have entered the field of managed cryptocurrencies. For example, RScoin [27] provides a cryptocurrency framework using a UTXO model where generation of the monetary supply is controlled by a central authority and transaction processing is handled by dedicated institutions, called 'mintettes'; ultimately, the central authority handles the creation and posting of new blocks. Our system differs from this approach in that currency managers do not influence the block creation process nor benefit from special viewing rights over the content of the blockchain. Another example of a managed cryptocurrency system can be found in Fedcoin [28], which builds upon RScoin's framework by providing a Node.js implementation, KYC rules that enable a central bank to blacklist users, and improved anonymity features. However, unlike our proposal, it does not natively offer the ability for accounts to be assigned roles; this leaves the central bank as the sole entity involved in the identity provider, management, and system security functions (e.g., identity-proofing new accounts, freezing unlawful users, and coin production).

'Decentralized Finance' projects, many of which are currently built with smart contracts deployed on the public Ethereum blockchain or as second layer solutions atop Bitcoin, are also being developed for stablecoins and decentralized currency management where money supply is governed algorithmically (such as Dai [29]). In our system, unlike reserve-backed stablecoins (such as Libra [30], USD Coin [31], and J.P. Morgan Coin [32]) that are pegged one-to-one with the asset(s) that they represent, there is a built-in currency manager role that can develop monetary instruments and vote for monetary policies to increase and decrease the currency supply. Since it is programmable, novel, potentially more flexible monetary instruments may be implemented.

From a security point of view, efforts are being made to offer security standards, toolsets, and services for cryptocurrencies. For example, EIP-1080 [33] is an Ethereum standard that offers an interface geared towards charge back and theft prevention/resolution for ERC-20 tokens [14]. Also, more loosely related is that the Enterprise Ethereum Alliance (EEA) Legal Industry Working Group [34] intends to standardize law-compliant smart contract designs.

Our system provides user privacy through use of a permissioned blockchain that supports roles with different responsibilities and data visibility (e.g., block publishers cannot see account owners' identities). However, cash transactions offer an ideal for anonymity and attempts to achieve this ideal for electronic currencies have been the subject of much research. The development of some privacy-preserving technologies, such as zero-knowledge protocols, has assisted in this objective. For example, Chaum introduced eCash [35] in 1983, one of the first attempts at anonymizing electronic money transactions via the use of blind signatures; Zcash [36] is an example of cryptocurrency that relies on a type of zero-knowledge proof called zk-SNARKs for keeping transactions private; and ChainAnchor [37] offers a method based on the 'Enhanced Privacy ID' zero-knowledge protocol for controlling access to a permissioned blockchain while allowing users to transact pseudonymously and maintain transaction unlinkability.

IX. Conclusion

Most cryptocurrencies and cryptocurrency research efforts focus on providing cryptocurrencies with strong anonymity and privacy guarantees in a robust distributed system that is not owned or managed by any single entity or group. We do not dispute the importance of such efforts and the emergence of the associated new social constructs, but point out that research in managed cryptocurrencies integrated with our current institutions has been sorely lacking. This is unfortunate as all people live under the laws of their respective countries and it is thus important to research cryptocurrencies that can explicitly support those laws.

In recent years, central banks have been interested in this area, but some of their researchers have discounted cryptocurrency solutions because the foundational technology appears incompatible with central bank goals, especially the support for KYC and AML laws. In this work, we showed how the foundational elements of a cryptocurrency can be rethought to support central bank goals and to explicitly support the laws that apply to electronic fiat currencies. We hope to convince the reader that this type of approach is technically feasible and that cryptocurrencies can be developed that integrate with an associated fiat currency and explicitly support the laws of the respective government.

References

[1] S. Nakamoto, "Bitcoin: A peer-to-peer electronic cash system," 2008. [Online]. Available: https://bitcoin.org/bitcoin.pdf

[2] A. Berentsen and F. Schar, "The case for central bank electronic money and the non-case for central bank cryptocurrencies," 2018. [Online]. Available: https://doi.org/10.20955/r.2018.97-106

[3] G. Greenspan, "Multichain private blockchain," *White paper*, 2015. [Online]. Available: https://www.multichain.com/download/MultiChain-White-Paper.pdf

[4] J. Barrdear and M. Kumhof, "The macroeconomics of central bank issued digital currencies," 2016. [Online]. Available: https://www.bankofengland.co.uk/working-paper/2016/the-macroeconomics-of-central-bank-issued-digital-currencies

[5] P. Mell, "Managed blockchain based cryptocurrencies with consensus enforced rules and transparency," in *2018 17th IEEE International Conference On Trust, Security And Privacy In Computing And Communications/12th IEEE International Conference On Big Data Science And Engineering (TrustCom/BigDataSE)*. IEEE, 2018, pp. 1287–1296.

[6] Parity, "Parity tech documentation - validator sets webpage," Retrieved on 2 July 2019 from https://wiki.parity.io/Validator-Set.htmlreporting-contract.

[7] P. Network, "Proof of authority: consensus model with identity at stake," 2017. [Online]. Available: https://medium.com/poa-network/proof-of-authority-consensus-model-with-identity-at-stake-d5bd15463256

[8] Microsoft, "Ethereum proof-of-authority consortium," 2019. [Online]. Available: https://docs.microsoft.com/en-us/azure/blockchain/templates/ethereum-poa-deployment

[9] Anonymous, "Governing decentralization: How on-chain voting protocols operate and vary," 2018. [Online]. Available: https://cointelegraph.com/news/governing-decentralization-how-on-chain-voting-protocols-operate-and-vary

[10] E. EIP-1202, "Voting standard," 2018. [Online]. Available: https://github.com/ethereum/EIPs/blob/master/EIPS/eip-1202.md

[11] Aragon, "Aragon website," Retrieved on 10 June 2019 from https://aragon.org/.

[12] Bitshares, "Bitshares website," Retrieved on 3 July 2019 from https://bitshares.org/.

[13] M. Vukolić, "Rethinking permissioned blockchains," in *Proceedings of the ACM Workshop on Blockchain, Cryptocurrencies and Contracts*. ACM, 2017, pp. 3–7.

[14] F. Vogelsteller and V. Buterin, "Erc-20 token standard," 2015. [Online]. Available: https://eips.ethereum.org/EIPS/eip-20

[15] L. Lesavre, P. Varin, P. Mell, M. Davidson, and J. Shook, "A taxonomic approach to understanding emerging blockchain identity management systems (draft)," National Institute of Standards and Technology, Tech. Rep., 2019.

[16] M. L. Bech and R. Garratt, "Central bank cryptocurrencies," *BIS Quarterly Review September*, 2017.

[17] C. Barontini and H. Holden, "Proceeding with caution-a survey on central bank digital currency," *Proceeding with Caution-A Survey on Central Bank Digital Currency (January 8, 2019). BIS Paper*, no. 101, 2019.

[18] B. of Canada, "Fintech experiments and projects," Retrieved on 26 June 2019 from https://www.bankofcanada.ca/research/digital-currencies-and-fintech/fintech-experiments-and-projects/.

[19] M. A. of Singapore, "Project ubin: Central bank digital money using distributed ledger technology," Retrieved on 25 June 2019 from https://www.mas.gov.sg/schemes-and-initiatives/Project-Ubin.

[20] B. of Thailand, "Public vs private blockchain in a nutshell," 2019. [Online]. Available: https://www.bot.or.th/Thai/PressandSpeeches/Press/News2562/n562e.pdf

[21] E. C. B. . B. O. Japan, "Boj/ecb joint research project on distributed ledger technology," 2018. [Online]. Available: https://www.boj.or.jp/en/announcements/release_2019/rel190604a.htm

[22] J. Campuzano, G. Cruz, and G. Jr. Y Maza Iñiguez, "El fracaso del dinero electrónico en ecuador," vol. 7, pp. 82–101, 08 2018.

[23] W. Knight, "Mit technology review - china's central bank has begun cautiously testing a digital currency," 2017. [Online]. Available: https://www.technologyreview.com/s/608088/chinas-central-bank-has-begun-cautiously-testing-a-digital-currency

[24] G. of Venezuela, "Petro webpage," Retrieved on 28 June 2019 from https://www.petro.gob.ve/eng/home.html.

[25] S. Riksbank, "E-krona webpage," Retrieved on 26 June 2019 from https://www.riksbank.se/en-gb/payments–cash/e-krona/, 2019.

[26] I. M. Fund, "Uruguay : 2018 article iv consultation-press release; staff report; and statement by the executive director for republic of uruguay," 2019. [Online]. Available: https://bit.ly/2SkS7pE

[27] G. Danezis and S. Meiklejohn, "Centrally banked cryptocurrencies," *arXiv preprint arXiv:1505.06895*, 2015.

[28] S. Gupta, P. Lauppe, and S. Ravishankar, "Fedcoin: A blockchain-backed central bank cryptocurrency," 2017. [Online]. Available: https://zoo.cs.yale.edu/classes/cs490/16-17b/gupta.sahil.sg687

[29] Maker, "Dai website," Retrieved on 18 June 2019 from https://makerdao.com/en/dai/.

[30] Libra, "Libra white paper," 2019. [Online]. Available: https://libra.org/en-US/wp-content/uploads/sites/23/2019/06/LibraWhitePaper_en_US.pdf

[31] Coinbase, "Usdc webpage," Retrieved on 18 June 2019 from https://www.coinbase.com/usdc.

[32] J. Morgan, "J.p. morgan creates digital coin for payments," 2019. [Online]. Available: https://www.jpmorgan.com/global/news/digital-coin-payments

[33] E. EIP-1080, "Recoverable token," 2018. [Online]. Available: https://github.com/ethereum/EIPs/blob/master/EIPS/eip-1080.md

[34] E. E. Alliance, "Eea legal industry working group press release," 2017. [Online]. Available: https://entethalliance.org/ethereum-enterprise-alliance-legal-industry-working-group-press-release-2/

[35] D. Chaum, "Blind signatures for untraceable payments," in *Advances in cryptology*. Springer, 1983, pp. 199–203.

[36] E. C. Company, "Zcash webpage," Retrieved on 20 June 2019 from https://z.cash/.

[37] T. Hardjono, N. Smith, and A. S. Pentland, "Anonymous identities for permissioned blockchains," 2014. [Online]. Available: https://petertodd.org/assets/2016-04-21/MIT-ChainAnchor-DRAFT.pdf

Blockchain Use Cases: A Systematic Study

Thiago Lopes da Silva
Professional Master Program
CESAR School
Recife, Brazil
e-mail: tls@cesar.org.br

Felipe Silva Ferraz
Professional Master Program
CESAR School
Recife, Brazil
e-mail: fsf@cesar.school

Francisco Icaro Ribeiro
Professional Master Program
CESAR School
Recife, Brazil
e-mail: finr@cesar.school

Abstract—**The emergent blockchain technology has become even more widely used in various areas, apart from financing, where bitcoin is already a great success. Fully secure, highly available and with many consensus algorithms on the network, the use of this technology, as well as any emergent one, offers challenges and opportunities that need to be explored. This paper proposes a systematic mapping of challenges, opportunities and common problems in many areas.**

Keywords-blockchain; Systematic Mapping; Challenges; Smart Contracts

I. INTRODUCTION

From a survey developed by Mettler [1], it was identified that until 2025, about 10% the Gross National Product will be provided from the use of blockchain technology. That was an important data to encourage big companies to invest more than half billion dollars in 2015, in search for new approaches and challenges to using this technology. The great interest in blockchain is due to the fact that it withstands a safe and distributed network with inviolable lodgers, as well as the fact that there is no authorized dealer [2] that interferes in the result and data control.

Blockchain technology has been drawing attention in the market because of its good acceptance with cryptocurrency, such as bitcoin. It is an electronic payment system peer-to-peer in which the algorithm proof-to-work is used to ensure an irreversible transaction history [2]. Several areas, such as healthcare [34][39], IoT [5][10], chain of supplies [16][17], energy [6] and public sector [18][41] are developing cases of use with blockchain technology to create new business opportunity, decrease of costs, audit data, integrate with stakeholders basis, improve generation process and increase security of transmitted data.

However, with the adoption of new technologies in projects, challenges, problems, characteristics and opportunities appear in the analysis of the pre-project or during the development through blockchain technology in projects.

According to Nakamoto [2], blockchain is a public distributed timestamp server that registers every transaction that happens and allows data storage, verification and audit of those. Blockchain consists in an array of blocks composed of many transactions and every block is linked to another, as a chained list. The authenticity to each transaction is verified by a digital signature based in Elliptic Curve Cryptography (ECC).

Another concept to be considered is the use of smart contract. They are customized scripts that perform the necessary logic to provide a complex service, like management of state and controlling verification of credentials [26]. It contains the business logics that may interact with other contracts, make decisions, store data and send cryptocurrency to another recipient [7].

This paper aims to answer these questionings in the context of adopting this technology in projects.

This study is divided in 4 sections. In the first one, it will be explained how the blockchain technology works. In Section 2, it will be explained how the research protocol will be developed. In Section 3 a thorough examination will be carried out from primary studies. Finally, the conclusion will be in the fourth section.

II. PROTOCOL APPLICATION

Based on Kitchenham's work [4], a well-defined outlining protocol stage is necessary to reduce the researcher bias. The following protocol was divided in stages. In the first one, it was made a main survey question with secondary ones, aiming a broader research. The second stage is the criteria protocol definition for insertion or exclusion of papers. The third stage is the application of primary studies selection protocol. The fourth stage will be checklist generation in order to verify research quality. The fifth and last stage will be the analysis whether the present research is relevant.

A. Survey Questions

- How to analyze the viability of blockchain in projects?

From the main survey, secondary questions were formulated with the aim of helping understand the problem.

- *Which challenges and opportunities are there with blockchain solutions?*
- *Which characteristics are more present in blockchain solutions?*
- *Which are the most common problems found in blockchain projects?*

B. Insertion and Exclusion Criteria

In order to reduce researcher bias, it was created a criterion through a well-defined protocol. For this research, only studies which aim to present characteristics and challenges in the adoption of blockchain technology in projects will be considered. This systematic mapping will be limited to verify studies which were published from 2016 on.

The following exclusion criteria were used.

- Studies not published in English.
- Studies which are unavailable online.
- Studies not based on this present research or unpublished.
- Preface, brochure, interviews and reports.

C. Search Strategy

The following virtual libraries were used:

- IEEE Xplore;
- Sciencedirect;
- ACM DL

Combinations of strings were created to guarantee that relevant information would not be excluded when querying different search engines and databases. As a result, three search strings were created

- ((blockchain AND challenges) OR (blockchain AND opportunity));
- ((blockchain) AND (solution OR characteristics OR application));
- ((blockchain) AND issues);

With the creation of search strings in each virtual library, the option advanced search was used on September 30th, 2018 and some papers published from January 2016 until 2018 were included. The result of each respective digital library, which were later removed to avoid duplicate of papers by Mendeley tool, was grouped according to their respective virtual library as shown in Table 1.

TABLE I. THE AMOUNT OF STUDIES FOUND IN EACH VIRTUAL LIBRARY

Library	Number of articles
IEEE Xplore	1001
Science Direct	104
ACM DL	183

The combination of strings showed a result of 183 research articles from Science Directory Library. In IEEE Xplorer there, were a total of 1001 research articles. Finally, the ACM DL Library generated 104 papers as shown in Table 1.

D. Choice of Studies Process

In this section, the process of choice of primary research articles will be outlined by using a protocol of insertion and exclusion.

In the first stage, 1288 research articles were found from virtual libraries. After the removal of duplicates, there were 906 distinct files left. For this process, Mendeley software was used along with Zotero.

Within the developed protocol, in the second stage, each research article was verified whether they were in the context of the research or not, with the analysis of artefacts titles.

However, certain studies, after a thorough analysis of titles, could not be conclusive regarding their relevance to this study. Due to that, a third stage was added: abstract verification.

In the fourth stage, the introduction and conclusion of the work were analyzed to verify relevance of the state of art approached in this paper.

Lastly, a qualitative analysis will be made from the reading of all articles left, excluding, this way, artefacts that are not relevant to this research.

After the execution of the stages of the protocol, 1249 studies were removed, and a total of 39 artefacts were analyzed.

E. Quality Control

In order to evaluate this research quality, it is necessary the primary studies to be analyzed critically. All in all, a protocol was developed and executed to minimize the amount of initial studies. Based on that, a following stage was deemed necessary, in which, it was made the reading of the research articles. Six secondary questions were then created with the purpose of evaluating the credibility and relevance of each artefact.

The three initial questions were used to investigate how blockchain technology is generally being used in projects, as criteria for excluding unrelated artefacts. The other questions were used to evaluate if the paper approaches themes that add value to the use of blockchain in projects, as well as if the paper found does not approach only blockchain.

The questions that will help assess the quality of the research are:

1. Were the challenges and opportunities of blockchain technology use clear in the article?
2. Were the characteristics of blockchain technology well-approached in the research?
3. Were the common problems with the blockchain approached?
4. Was a survey developed with the user about the implementation of blockchain project?
5. Was the article not restricted to just discussing blockchain?
6. Does the paper make an analogy of the use of blockchain adding value in the final product?

After the analysis and extraction of articles chosen, based on the protocol, there were a total of 39 files left, which were approved in the quality control. The process of quality control will be explained in the next section. It will focus in remaining 39 artefacts.

III. Results

Based on the execution of the developed protocol, 39 primary studies were selected [2] and [4] – [41]. It was identified the use of blockchain in different areas, as described below.

According to the selected primary studies, it was observed a higher demand in the use of blockchain technology in the IoT, healthcare, cryptocurrency, government, energy and voting, respectively.

In the next section, a quantitative and qualitative analysis of the primary studies was held.

A. Quantitative Analysis

The research showed a total of 39 primary researches by 126 different authors and they were published from 2016 to 2018. It was identified a total of 229 keywords related to blockchain.

In regards to frequency of publishing, it had a growth of interest for blockchain's. In 2016, it had 2 publishing. followed by 17 in 2017 and 20 in 2018. The large amount of publishing across the years show up a huge interessing for blockchain.

From the primary studies, the interest in blockchain was identified in the areas of IoT, healthcare, supply chains, government, big data, design, cloud computing and digital property.

Among 39 primary articles found, 229 keywords were found. The most found keywords were: internet of things (7), bitcoin (5), iot (4), government (4), smart contracts (6), cryptocurrency (3), iot security (3), cloud computing (3), trust (3), decentralized iot (2), consensus protocols (2), blockchain challenges (2), voting (2), food safety (2), data integration (2), egovernment (2), finance (2), distributed ledger (2), business (2), voter (1), big data (1), food chain (1), and smart agriculture (1).

It has been observed with keywords in the research that the use of blockchain can be applied in diverse areas that go beyond Nakamoto [1] in cryptocurrency. That is a fact of relevance to this research.

B. Qualitative Analysis

The result of the qualitative analysis will be displayed in this section from 39 primary studies, taking into consideration six criteria, to evaluate the credibility and quality of the studies. The classification of artefacts will be either positive (1) or negative (0) and there will be a reference to the article.

TABLE II. QUALITATIVE ANALYSIS OF PRIMARY STUDIES

Study	Q1	Q2	Q3	Q4	Q5	Q6	Total
[5]	1	1	1	1	1	1	6
[6]	1	1	1	1	1	1	6
[7]	1	1	1	1	1	1	6
[8]	1	1	1	1	1	1	6
[9]	1	1	1	1	1	1	6
[10]	1	1	1	0	1	1	5
[11]	1	1	1	0	1	1	5
[1]	1	1	0	1	1	1	5
[12]	1	1	1	0	1	1	5
[13]	1	1	1	0	1	1	5
[14]	1	1	0	1	1	1	5
[15]	1	1	0	1	1	1	5
[16]	1	1	1	0	1	1	5
[17]	1	1	1	0	1	1	5
[18]	1	1	1	0	1	1	5
[19]	1	1	1	0	1	1	5
[20]	1	1	1	0	1	1	5
[21]	0	1	1	1	1	1	5
[22]	1	1	1	0	1	1	5
[23]	0	1	1	0	1	1	4
[24]	1	0	1	0	1	1	4
[25]	1	0	1	0	1	1	4
[26]	1	1	0	0	1	1	4
[27]	0	1	1	0	1	1	4
[28]	1	1	0	0	1	1	4
[29]	1	1	1	0	1	0	4
[3]	1	1	1	0	1	0	4
[30]	1	0	1	0	1	1	4
[31]	0	1	1	0	1	1	4
[32]	1	0	1	0	1	1	4
[33]	0	0	1	0	1	1	3
[34]	0	0	1	0	1	1	3
[35]	1	0	0	0	1	1	3
[36]	1	0	1	0	1	0	3
[37]	0	0	1	0	1	1	3
[38]	0	0	1	0	1	1	3
[39]	1	1	0	0	1	1	3
[40]	1	1	0	0	1	0	3
[41]	1	0	0	0	1	1	3
Total	31	28	30	9	39	35	171

Based on the results as shown in Table 2 it was observed from the first question, there is, indeed, a great tendency for blockchain use to generate opportunities and challenges in many areas. Among the 39 selected articles, 28 described that the characteristics of the use of blockchain can help in projects. Analyzing the third question, related to common problems, the primary articles showed high rate of problems in the adoption of blockchain in projects. Analyzing the result of the fourth question, it was observed that the use of surveys was not relevant as a tool to support decision and generate new opportunities. The fifth question is focused on quality assessment, since it analyzes whether the articles are restricted to describing blockchain only. Thus, the sixth question is related to verifying whether blockchain adds value to the final product. In conclusion, from 39 selected articles, 35 use blockchain as an addition to the final product.

IV. DISCUSSION

The following subjects will be approached in the primary studies according to the questions used in the quality control assessment. It will be taken into account the studies involving IoT, government and healthcare, once these are the most recurrent subjects.

1. Which challenges and opportunities are there with blockchain solution?

In IoT, according to [5], it was identified that the blockchain network can help in Iot area to keep data safely and immutable. This way, generating opportunity to track data that was once generated by different devices. One of the greatest challenges in integrating data generated by devices and network is due to the fact that these devices have already delivered corrupt data. Therefore, it is necessary that the devices to be tested before is put in the network, besides of being allotted, in order to avoid physical alteration.

Reyna et al. [5] comments about the value that blockchain brings, providing a network where information is traceable, immutable and highly safe. In cases which the data is provided by devices, blockchain will play an important role integrating the parts.

Elsden et al. says in his article [21] that the outcome of the survey resulted in the use of blockchain in IoT, as a way of keeping the devices interoperable and safe for sharing and exchanging messages.

To the author Smith, the safety in IoT with integration in blockchain networks is challenging due to the limitations in processing, being necessary a smaller precision in the algorithm proof-of-state, used on the network. This approach can generate attacks in blocks with bigger reputation, generating new blocks with invalid data.

As opportunity, Kahn and Salah [10] defend that blockchain technology, based on smart contracts, can be used to manage, control and, the most important, keep IoT devices safe. Another point raised is the possibility of using a public key of 160-bit form blockchain generated by Elliptic Curve Digital Signature algorithm (EDCSA) instead of 128 bits from IPV6. blockchain can generate and allocate addresses offline for around 1.46 ∗ 1048 IoT devices., removing needs of an entity internet Assigned Numbers Authority (IANA) central authorizer of devices.

In article [26] it reports that the possible use of blockchain in the network can track millions of connected devices, process transactions and coordinate devices, allowing connection peer-to-peer to send messages and allowing blockchain to control the devices connected through smart contracts.

Regarding healthcare, Jiang et al. [39] verified that great part of the products developed that used blockchain recorded only data generated in EMR (electronic medical records), ignoring data from PHD (personal healthcare data). In the article [13] the author debates the necessity of not manipulating data generated from EHRS (electronic health records). It can entail manipulation of data, and consequently, problems to patients.

The use of blockchain, along with smart contracts, will help keep the integrity, safety and immutability of network data. This way, a greater collaboration among hospitals and clinics will help save 93 billion dollars in 5 years' time in the USA from the safe mass data sent from blockchain [13].

According to Mettler [1] the possibility to create a shared infrastructure among researchers and doctors comes from data generated by patients using blockchain. This will allow further analysis of wasted resources, operational problems and improvement of user service. The author comments about the challenges in patient's data privacy, and about the possibility to create a new platform, where users would be in control of their data.

At last, there is an opportunity for the user to be compensated for allowing access to their data in the blockchain. Alhadhrami [36] exposes that the data privacy in the blockchain network is a challenge due to public data. Therefore, it is necessary to take some precautions in the moment of sending data to the network. In article [26] it comment about the opportunity of using public blockchain as a way of centralizing data from patients with the challenge of patronizing the data inserted.

In government, Antipova [32] describes the opportunity of using blockchain to help audit data, removing the need for a centralizing entity and avoid fraud, since these transactions in the network are inviolable.

There are challenges in the area of public blockchain. The need for attention in anonymous transaction in the network, deems necessary the supervision of a third-party with the intention to avoid possible alterations in the result and audit. Batubara [41] comments that there are challenges in the adoption of blockchain in e-governments. She mentions the creation of new governmental models, as well as acceptance, since the creation of a platform needs the cooperation of multiple institution and stakeholders.

As seen in [12] it portrays the opportunity to use blockchain as an integration tool among different governmental database. In article [18] it is mentioned that the use of blockchain in governmental solutions will help reduce costs, frauds payment error and the transparency of shared data between government and citizens.

2. Which characteristics are more present in blockchain solutions?

In the IoT area, Karafiloski and Mishev [26] describe the use of blockchain smart contracts along with smart lockers connected to the network, to create a renting system without the need of a third party. The network consensus is the tax agent. Khain and Salah [10] argue that the data transmitted from the devices to blockchain will always be encrypted and signed by the sender. That guarantees authentication and integrity of the data sent.

Another feature is the possibility of audit transmitted data form devices in the network and smart contracts, as a decentralized authenticator with simple logic rules and multi-party. That would have minor complexity to the devices, if we compare the traditional authorization protocol in which Role Based Access Management, OAuth 2.0, OpenId, IMA DM and OMA Lightweight M2M are used.

According to Alketbi et al. [18] the change from a centralized architecture to a distributed P2P will remove flaws, throughput and raise in scalability of the system. Blockchain will favor in setup management of devices, storage of sensitive data and to enable micro payment.

Regarding healthcare, Alketbi et al. [18] sees the use of blockchain as a facilitator for sharing files among users and doctors, insurance agencies and others, with privacy in focus, and smart contracts, so that the user is in control of the data. Shae and Tsai [13] argue about the need of not manipulating the data in clinical trials in order to avoid health problems in the patients. In this article, blockchain is described as a solution to this problem, since the data in the network are safe, transparent, available in real time and inviolable. Consequently, contributing to a greater precision in the report.

The research articles [26] and [34] describe the need of choice in which the used data must be sent to the blockchain network. It is proposed the insertion of user metadata, such as visitor ID, provider ID and payer ID with a linkage to an external database.

In government area, Antipova [32] exposes the need for government standardization of database in the blockchain, to maximize compatibility, interoperability, repeatability and quality.

The possibility to audit the data inside the blockchain network in real time is a very important characteristic that will help the government to identify fraud swiftly.

According to [12] using blockchain in government area will help unify different public service base to allow user improve their data understanding through authorized smart contracts. Olnes e Jansen [9] analyzed that digital ID management, safe records maintenance of digital files are more adequate cases for government inside the blockchain.

From T. D. Smith's survey result [11], it was found the use of Ethereum as a widely used platform.

3. Which characteristics are more present in blockchain solutions?

In IoT, Karafiloski and A. Mishev describe [26] that the limitation in processing devices and mining timing transactions will limit the number of devices to do that in the network. Billions of devices in the network can lead to a crash. In their research article, Khan and Salah [10] report that even if blockchain provides a robust safety to IoT, there is still a mechanism problem of consensus, upon mining hashing power which can be compromised, allowing the invader to be the network owner. Equally, private key generated in the network are dynamically limited, allowing the attacker to compromise some account in the network.

In healthcare, the articles [34][11] relate the issue of keeping all the healthcare database in the network due to its high operational costs and the possible security breach in public blockchain encrypting. Shae and Tsai [13] mention that data coming from clinical trials sent to blockchain can entail problems in final reports, since they are shown and updated in real time.

In government, Hou [12] comment that the use of blockchain in governmental solutions involve the integration with various systems, different organizations and problems with time and expenses that hinder solution. The use of blockchain as a way of keeping long term unused data, since it guarantees data reliability. The author defends that data should be recorded in blockchain as well as in third-party. In the article [18] summons that blockchain can be attacked by Dos(Denial of Service) causing and impact in processing legitimate pending transactions to miners leading to slowness in the network.

Olnes and Jansen [9] created a survey with the main people in the public sector in 2018, observing emerging technologies: Robotics, Blockchains, Artificial Intelligence and Virtual Reality. As a result, the majority answered that blockchain is immature and not ready to be used in the public.

4. How to analyze the viability of blockchain use in projects?

From this present research, it has been observed that there are challenges and problems in adopting an emergent technology such as blockchain. Once the viability of using blockchain in projects, some characteristics must be observed according to some points below.

Safety:

- In projects which there is the need of keeping sensitive data in the network, some precautions should be taken to avoid data to be read by others [36]. It is necessary the adoption of a routine of cryptography before the data is involved in the network.
- A. Reyna et al. [5] mentions that recorded data in the network are inalterable, which gives more security in projects that require reliability. The case described is in IoT.
- For solutions which require the need for integration among many parts involved, A. Reyna et al. [5] mentions that the network will help keep data integrity, if there is the necessity for every transaction to be signed by the sender.

Data Integration:

- A. Reyna et al. [5] observes that blockchain will help with the integration of data provided by different devices safely, once all data is signed by the sender. This will help with more critical projects which need data integration, transparently and safely.

Auditing:

- For projects in which there is the need for assessment in real time. Antipova [32] describes that blockchain network will help avoid fraud and increase transparency of data, due to the fact that every transaction is public and inalterable.

Data availability:

- In projects which require high availability of data, Nakamoto [2] describes that blockchain will help keep high availability of data connected via peer-to-peer with respective duplicate in blockchain network

Removal of Centralizing Entity:

- Kshetri and Voas [3] write that the removal of a centralizing entity will help create in not manipulating of results, as well as in controlling data. This will help projects to remove a centralizing entity in controlling data, as well as not manipulating data.

Smart Contract:

- Khan and Salah [10] defend that blockchain based in smart contracts can be used to manage, control, and the most important, to keep IoT devices safe. This matter, raised by the author, can help projects to create smart contracts as self-manageable micro services with business rules in the blockchain network.

Data Uniformity:

- Karafiloski and Mishev [26] mention the opportunity of using blockchain network as a centralizer of public data from patient, creating a standardization of data inserted and this project usually involves stakeholders. It is necessary that the parts involved create a protocol of data before sending the transaction to the blockchain network.

Limitations:

- For Smith [11] in IoT, the integration with blockchain network is challenging due to the fact that devices have limited processing, being necessary a smaller precision in the consensus proof-of-state used by network. That can result in a massive attack on account of the consensus being reduced. This limitation is taken into consideration in projects which there is the need for mining of micro processed transactions or devices with limited processing.

V. Conclusion and Future Work

This paper aimed to identify opportunities, problems and challenges in the use of the emergent blockchain technology in many areas. It has been found 906 initial studies, with a total of 39 primary artefacts left.

To assure quality of the evaluated primary research articles, a protocol was developed composed by four stages, resulting in a great interest for using blockchain in areas such as healthcare, IoT and government. In each area, there is the interest of assuring safety of data, integration of data and scalability of services through blockchain.

Regarding viability of blockchain use in many areas that do not involve finance, there are still problems and challenges in diverse areas that have been presented. It is necessary a deeper research per area in order to mitigate risks in the adoption of and emergent technology in small and big projects.

This works presents a important summarization of blockchains aspects such as problems, challenges and opportunities of technology adoption in projects and it adds important set of information for the area, as for now, the amount of works presenting consolidated ideas related to blockchain are not common and are important in a theme that can be explored in a variety of ways.

As a future work, guidelines are to be created to provid projects and engineers with means to better choose the adoption of blockchain technology in several areas.

References

[1] M. Mettler, "Blockchain technology in healthcare: The revolution starts here," *2016 IEEE 18th International Conference on e-Health Networking, Applications and Services, Healthcom 2016*, pp. 16–18, 2016.

[2] S. Nakamoto, "Bitcoin: A Peer-to-Peer Electronic Cash System," Www.Bitcoin.Org, p. 9, 2008.

[3] N. Kshetri and J. Voas, "Blockchain-Enabled E-Voting," IEEE Softw., vol. 35, no. 4, pp. 95–99, 2018.

[4] B. Kitchenham and S. Charters, "Guidelines for performing Systematic Literature reviews in Software Engineering Version 2.3," Proc. Est. Acad. Sci. Eng., vol. 45, no. 4ve, p. 1051, 2007.

[5] A. Reyna, C. Martín, J. Chen, E. Soler, and M. Díaz, "On blockchain and its integration with IoT. Challenges and opportunities," Future Gener. Comput. Syst., vol. 88, pp. 173–190, Nov. 2018.

[6] Andoni et al., "Blockchain technology in the energy sector: A systematic review of challenges and opportunities," Renewable Sustainable Energy Rev., vol. 100, pp. 143–174, Feb. 2019.

[7] V. Brilliantova and T. W. Thurner, "Blockchain and the future of energy," Technol. Soc., Nov. 2018.

[8] T. Ahram, A. Sargolzaei, S. Sargolzaei, J. Daniels, and B. Amaba, "Blockchain technology innovations," in 2017 IEEE Technology Engineering Management Conference (TEMSCON), 2017, pp. 137–141.

[9] S. Olnes and A. Jansen, "Blockchain Technology As Infrastructure in Public Sector: An Analytical Framework," in Proceedings of the 19th Annual International Conference on Digital Government Research: Governance in the Data Age, 2018, pp. 77:1–77:10.

[10] M. A. Khan and K. Salah, "IoT security: Review, blockchain solutions, and open challenges," Future Gener. Comput. Syst., vol. 82, pp. 395–411, May 2018.

[11] T. D. Smith, "The blockchain litmus test," in 2017 IEEE International Conference on Big Data (Big Data), 2017, pp. 2299–2308.

[12] H. Hou, "The application of blockchain technology in E-government in China," in 2017 26th International Conference on Computer Communications and Networks, ICCCN 2017, 2017.

[13] Z. Shae and J. J. P. Tsai, "On the Design of a Blockchain Platform for Clinical Trial and Precision Medicine," in 2017 IEEE 37th International Conference on Distributed Computing Systems (ICDCS), 2017, pp. 1972–1980.

[14] P. Tasatanattakool and C. Techapanupreeda, "Blockchain: Challenges and applications," in 2018 International Conference on Information Networking (ICOIN), 2018, pp. 473–475.

[15] F. Wessling, C. Ehmke, M. Hesenius, and V. Gruhn, "How Much Blockchain Do You Need? Towards a Concept for Building Hybrid DApp Architectures," 2018 IEEE/ACM 1st International Workshop on Emerging Trends in Software Engineering for Blockchain (WETSEB), pp. 44–47, 2018.

[16] F. Tian, "An agri-food supply chain traceability system for China based on RFID amp;amp; blockchain technology," in 2016 13th International Conference on Service Systems and Service Management (ICSSSM), 2016, pp. 1–6.

[17] D. Tse, B. Zhang, Y. Yang, C. Cheng, and H. Mu, "Blockchain application in food supply information security," in 2017 IEEE International Conference on Industrial Engineering and Engineering Management (IEEM), 2017, pp. 1357–1361.

[18] A. Alketbi, Q. Nasir, and M. A. Talib, "Blockchain for government services — Use cases, security benefits and challenges," in 2018 15th Learning and Technology Conference (L T), 2018, pp. 112–119.

[19] T. Aste, P. Tasca, and T. Di Matteo, "Blockchain Technologies: The Foreseeable Impact on Society and Industry," Computer , vol. 50, no. 9, pp. 18–28, 2017.

[20] L. Mertz, "(Block) Chain Reaction: A Blockchain Revolution Sweeps into Health Care, Offering the Possibility for a Much-Needed Data Solution," IEEE Pulse, vol. 9, no. 3, pp. 4–7, 2018.

[21] C. Elsden, A. Manohar, J. Briggs, M. Harding, C. Speed, and J. Vines, "Making Sense of Blockchain Applications: A Typology for HCI," in Proceedings of the 2018 CHI Conference on Human Factors in Computing Systems, 2018, pp. 458:1–458:14.

[22] J. Lin, Z. Shen, A. Zhang, and Y. Chai, "Blockchain and IoT Based Food Traceability for Smart Agriculture," in Proceedings of the 3rd International Conference on Crowd Science and Engineering, 2018, pp. 3:1–3:6.

[23] J. F. Galvez, J. C. Mejuto, and J. Simal-Gandara, "Future challenges on the use of blockchain for food traceability analysis," Trends Analyt. Chem., vol. 107, pp. 222–232, Oct. 2018.

[24] C. Xie, Y. Sun, and H. Luo, "Secured Data Storage Scheme Based on Block Chain for Agricultural Products Tracking," Proceedings - 2017 3rd International Conference on Big Data Computing and Communications, BigCom 2017, pp. 45–50, 2017.

[25] N. Fotiou and G. C. Polyzos, "Smart Contracts for the Internet of Things: Opportunities and Challenges," in 2018 European Conference on Networks and Communications (EuCNC), 2018, pp. 256–260.

[26] E. Karafiloski and A. Mishev, "Blockchain solutions for big data challenges: A literature review," in IEEE EUROCON 2017 -17th International Conference on Smart Technologies, 2017, pp. 763–768.

[27] C. F. Liao, S. W. Bao, C. J. Cheng, and K. Chen, "On design issues and architectural styles for blockchain-driven IoT services," 2017 IEEE International Conference on Consumer Electronics - Taiwan, ICCE-TW 2017, pp. 351–352, 2017.

[28] B. A. Tama, B. J. Kweka, Y. Park, and K. Rhee, "A critical review of blockchain and its current applications," in 2017 International Conference on Electrical Engineering and Computer Science (ICECOS), 2017, pp. 109–113.

[29] S. Porru, A. Pinna, M. Marchesi, and R. Tonelli, "Blockchain-oriented software engineering: Challenges and new directions," Proceedings - 2017 IEEE/ACM 39th International Conference on Software Engineering Companion, ICSE-C 2017, pp. 169–171, 2017.

[30] D. K. Tosh, S. Shetty, X. Liang, C. Kamhoua, and L. Njilla, "Consensus protocols for blockchain-based data provenance: Challenges and opportunities," in 2017 IEEE 8th Annual Ubiquitous Computing, Electronics and Mobile Communication Conference, UEMCON 2017, 2018, vol. 2018-Janua, pp. 469–474.

[31] T. Moura and A. Gomes, "Blockchain Voting and its effects on Election Transparency and Voter Confidence," pp. 574–575, 2017.

[32] T. Antipova, "Using blockchain technology for government auditing," Iberian Conference on Information Systems and Technologies, CISTI, vol. 2018-June, pp. 1–6, 2018.

[33] I. Makhdoom, M. Abolhasan, H. Abbas, and W. Ni, "Blockchain's adoption in IoT: The challenges, and a way forward," Journal of Network and Computer Applications, vol. 125, pp. 251–279, Jan. 2019.

[34] P. Zhang, M. A. Walker, J. White, D. C. Schmidt, and G. Lenz, "Metrics for assessing blockchain-based healthcare decentralized apps," in 2017 IEEE 19th International Conference on e-Health Networking, Applications and Services (Healthcom), 2017, pp. 1–4.

[35] N. Rifi, E. Rachkidi, N. Agoulmine, and N. C. Taher, "Towards using blockchain technology for eHealth data access management," in 2017 Fourth International Conference on Advances in Biomedical Engineering (ICABME), 2017, pp. 1–4.

[36] Z. Alhadhrami, S. Alghfeli, M. Alghfeli, J. A. Abedlla, and K. Shuaib, "Introducing blockchains for healthcare," in 2017 International Conference on Electrical and Computing Technologies and Applications (ICECTA), 2017, pp. 1–4.

[37] N. Fabiano, "Internet of things and blockchain: legal issues and privacy. The challenge for a privacy standard," in Proceedings - 2017 IEEE International Conference on Internet of Things, IEEE Green Computing and Communications, IEEE Cyber, Physical and Social Computing, IEEE Smart Data, iThings-GreenCom-CPSCom-SmartData 2017, 2018, vol. 2018-Janua, pp. 727–734.

[38] S. R. Niya, S. S. Jha, T. Bocek, and B. Stiller, "Design and implementation of an automated and decentralized pollution monitoring system with blockchains, smart contracts, and LoRaWAN," IEEE/IFIP Network Operations and Management Symposium: Cognitive Management in a Cyber World, NOMS 2018, pp. 1–4, 2018.

[39] S. Jiang, J. Cao, H. Wu, Y. Yang, M. Ma, and J. He, "BlocHIE: A BLOCkchain-Based Platform for Healthcare Information Exchange," in 2018 IEEE International Conference on Smart Computing (SMARTCOMP), 2018, pp. 49–56.

[40] M. Foth, "The Promise of Blockchain Technology for Interaction Design," in Proceedings of the 29th Australian Conference on Computer-Human Interaction, 2017, pp. 513–517.

[41] F. R. Batubara, J. Ubacht, and M. Janssen, "Challenges of blockchain technology adoption for e-government: A systematic literature review," in ACM International Conference Proceeding Series, 2018.

Denoising Autoencoder with Dropout based Network Anomaly Detection

Safa Mohamed
Research Team in intelligent Machines
National Engineering School of Gabes Tunisia
Omar Ibn El Khattab, Avenue Zrig 6072
e-mail: safamohamed280@yahoo.fr

Ridha Ejbali, Mourad Zaied
Research Team in intelligent Machines
National Engineering School of Gabes Tunisia
Omar Ibn El Khattab, Avenue Zrig 6072
e-mail: ridha_ejbali@ieee.org, mourad.zaied@ieee.org

***Abstract*—A Network Intrusion Detection System (NIDS) plays an important role in ensuring information security. It helps system administrators identify and detect malicious activities in their companies. Many techniques have been devised by researchers to achieve reliable detection of anomalies. It is thus a challenging task to determine a network anomaly more accurately. To solve this problem, we propose a Denoising-Autoencoder (DAE) with a Dropout based network anomaly detection method because it forces the extraction of intrinsic features so as to increase the detection accuracy. A popular NSL-KDD dataset is used for the training and evaluation of our approach. The performance of our approach takes into consideration different metrics such accuracy, precision, recall, f-measure values and the detection rate. Experimental results show that our approach performs better than other detection methods, especially when we use a single hidden layer with 8 neurons.**

Keywords-Anomaly detection; NIDS; Denoising Autoencoder; NSL-KDD.

I. INTRODUCTION

The advent of networks offers immense services to users. Because these services are subject to several attacks and security mechanisms, it is necessary to protect them. Intrusion detection is one major research problem in network security, aiming at identifying unusual access or attacks to secure internal networks. In fact, an intrusion refers to any unauthorized access or misuse of information resources.

There are various systems designed to block attacks. We particularly cite the Network Intrusion Detection System (NIDS). A NIDS is security tools that, like other measures such as antivirus software, firewalls and access control schemes, are intended to strengthen the security of information and communication systems. It monitors and analyzes the network traffic entering into or exiting from the network devices of a company and raises alarms if an intrusion is observed [1].

Based on the methods of intrusion detection, NIDS can be classified into 2 types: Signature based NIDS (SNIDS) and Anomaly detection based NIDS (ADNIDS) [2].

The SNIDS, e.g. Snort (www.snort.org), is used to identify attacks in a form of signature or pattern. It uses the known pattern to detect attacks; the main disadvantage is that it fails to identify any unknown attacks to the network or system. In contrast, ADNIDS determines a normal network activity like the sort of bandwidth generally used, the protocols used, the ports and devices that generally connect to each other and alert the administrator or user when an anomalous (not normal) traffic is detected and it requires an understanding of what "normal" is [2]. However, they have the disadvantage of having high false positive rates, which can make the detector useless in practical areas. Analyzing and detecting anomalies is important because it reveals useful information about the characteristics of the generation process data.

Many NIDSs perform a feature selection task to extract a subset of relevant features from the traffic. Dimensionality reduction based anomaly detection method is one of the popular detection methods. It is based on the assumption that the features of normal data are correlated with each other [3]. In this respect, Principal Component Analysis (PCA) based methods belong to this method of detecting anomalies [4]. However, PCA is a linear transformation, which fails to capture the non-linear correlations between features [5].

With an increasing amount of features, the data have supplementary complicated nonlinear structures. As a solution to this weakness, Kernel Principal Component Analysis (KPCA) is used to generalize PCA to nonlinear dimensionality using techniques of kernel methods [6].

Recently, the Autoencoder (AE) is a novel dimensionality reduction method that uses unsupervised neural networks. It can find the optimal subspace, which captures the non-linear correlations between features [1]. For this reason, we propose a Denoising Autoencoder with Dropout based network anomaly detection of an extension of the basic AE and represent a stochastic version of it used to perform dimensionality reduction and force the extraction of intrinsic features. We use the NSL-KDD [7] dataset, with a separate training and testing set to evaluate their performances.

The rest of this paper is organized as follows: Section 2 presents the context of our work. In Section 3, we present our approach or methodologies. In Section 4, we present the evaluation and analyze the results. Section 5 concludes and suggests future works to be adopted later.

II. LITERATURE REVIEWS

Anomaly detection is applied in traffic detection, Card fraud detection, abnormal crowd behavior detection and network intrusion detection [8]. The widely-used anomaly detection methods can be divided into the following categories: Classification based methods, nearest neighbor-based methods, Clustering based methods, Statistic based methods and Dimensionality Reduction based methods [3][8].

Classification based methods learn a model from labeled data and then classify testing data into one of the classes using the learnt model. Nearest neighbor based methods show that normal data have relatively more neighbors than the anomalous data requiring a distance measurement to evaluate the resemblance between a testing sample and its neighborhoods. Clustering based methods group homogenous data into one cluster and suppose the outliers far away from their closest cluster center. Statistics based methods shape well a statistical model using the given training data and then apply a statistical inference to decide whether an unseen instance is an outlier or not. Dimensionality reduction based methods utilize the reconstruction error to classify the anomalies. PCA are an effective preprocessing method before anomaly detection [9].

Lakhina et al. [10] proposed a new hybrid algorithm; Principal Component Analysis Neural Network Algorithm (PCANNA) is used to reduce the number of computer resources, both memory and CPU time required to detect attacks. Ibraheem et al. [11] presented an intrusion detection model based on PCA and MLP to recognize an attack from normal connections. Ikram et al. [12] developed an intrusion detection model by using PCA as the dimensionality reduction technique and SVM as the classifier. Elkhadir et al. [6] compared the performance between (PCA) and (KPCA) in order to construct robust IDS with the highest anomaly detection rate. Experimental results showed that KPCA are more efficient than PCA. Paula et al. [13] proved that the AE can detect delicate anomalies and linear PCA fails to detect without corrupting the quality of the detecting performance. Sakurada et al. [4] proposed a comparison between the use of AE, PCA and KPCA in the anomaly detection task. Experimental results showed that AE is the most efficient and it can increase their accuracy by extending them to DAE.

For improved dimensionality reduction and better detection rate, we propose to use DAE with a Dropout that makes more objective and principled anomaly score than the reconstruction error of PCA and KPCA based method.

III. PROPOSED METHODOLOGIES

In this section, we present the different steps followed to reach our approach.

A. AE to DEA

AE is a specific type of feedforward neural networks where the input is the same as the output. AE aims to learn a compressed representation of data with minimum reconstruction loss [14]. It consists of 3 components: encoder, code and decoder [15]. The encoder compresses the input and produces the code; the decoder then reconstructs the input only by using this code (see Figure 1).

Keeping the code layer forced our AE to learn an intelligent representation of the samples. There is another way to force the AE to learn useful features. It is adding random noise to its inputs and making it recover the original noise-free data. This way the autoencoder can't simply copy the input to its output because the input also contains random noise. We order it to subtract the noise and produce the underlying meaningful data. This is called a DAE [9] (see Figure 2).

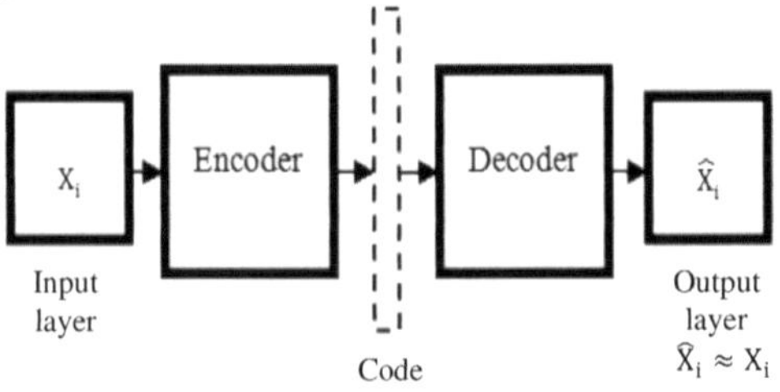

Figure 1. Autoencoder.

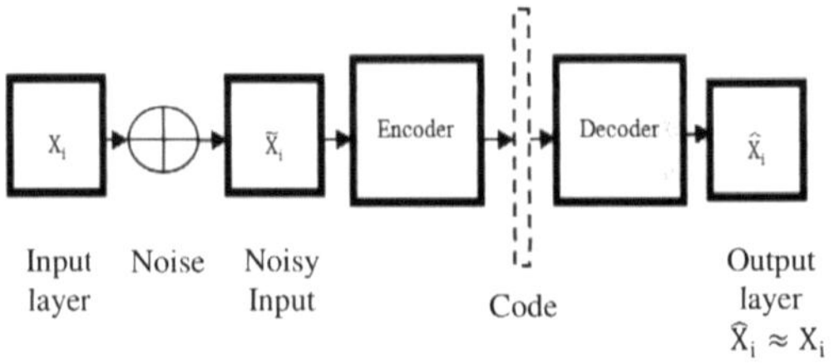

Figure 2. Denoising Autoencoder.

B. DEA with Dropout- Based Anomaly Detection

"Dropout" is a technique that aims to discourage brittle co- adoptions of hidden unit feature detectors. It can also be interpreted as a way of regularizing a neural network by adding noise to its hidden units [16]. The choice of which units to drop is random. In the simplest case, each unit is retained with a fixed probability p independent of other units, where p can be chosen using a validation set or can simply be set at 0.5 [17]. In our method, the Dropout (noise) is applied to the input layer of the Denoising Autoencoder.

We propose using a DEA with Dropout based anomaly detection method for only intrusion detection that is a deviation base anomaly detection method whose training here only contains instances for the normal instances of traffic without labeling. It uses the reconstruction error as the anomaly score. Our NSL-KDD dataset used consists of different steps such as the Numericalization and Normalization. These two steps were performed for both NSL-KDD train and test datasets. Later, the train dataset is used to train the DEA with Dropout. Our method is tested with test dataset and the results were analyzed (see Figure 3). The detailed development process is provided in the following sub-section.

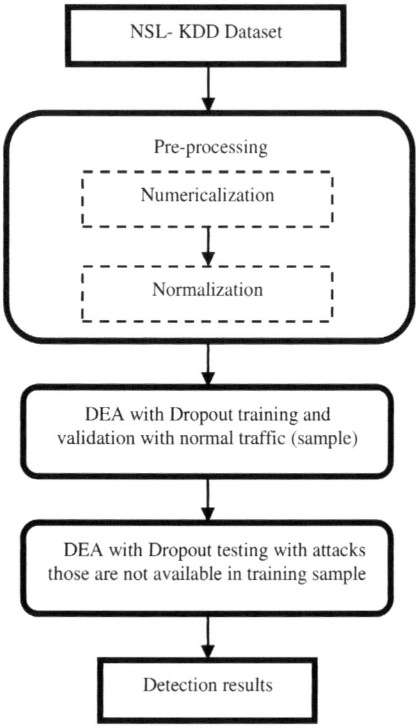

Figure 3. Denoising Autoencoder with Dropout-based anomaly detection method.

C. NSL-KDD Dataset

NSL-KDD is an improved and reduced version of the KDD Cup 99 dataset. The KDD Cup dataset was prepared using the network traffic captured by 1998 DARPA IDS evaluation program [13]. It is continuously an index which is used to compare the NIDS models in common researches [7]. In the latest literature, all the researchers use the NSL-KDD as the benchmark dataset [18]. It includes 125,973 network traffic samples in the KDDTrain+ Dataset and 22,554 network traffic samples in the KDDTest+ Dataset. In each record, there are 41 attributes unfolding different features of the flow and a label is assigned to each sample either as an attack type or as a normal type. The features include 10 basic features (1- 10), 12 content features (11 - 22), and 18 traffic features (23 -.41) as shown in (Table I).

Apart from normal data, records for 39 different attack types exist in NSL-KDD dataset. All these attack types were grouped into four attack classes:

- **DOS (Denial of Service):** an attacker tries to prevent legitimate users from using a service.
- **Probe:** an attacker tries to find information about the target host.
- **U2R (User to Root):** an attacker has local account on victim's host and tries to gain the root privileges
- **R2L (Remote to Local):** an attacker does not have local account on the victim host and try to obtain it.

The summary of the attack classes and their attack types is given in (Table II).

TABLE I. FEATURES IN NSL-KDD [19]

Type	Features
Nominal	2,3,4
Binary	7,12,14,15,21,22
Numeric	1,5,6,9,10,11,13,16,17,18,19,20,23,24,25,26,27,28, 29,30,31, 32, 33,34,35,36,37,38,39,40,41

TABLE II. ATTACK TYPES IN NSL –KDD DATASET [20]

Attack Class	Training Set	Testing Set
DOS	Back, Land, Neptune, Pod, Smurf, , Teardrop	Back, Land, Neptune, Pod, Smurf Teardrop, **mailbomb, Apache 2, Udpstorm, Processtable, Worm**
R2L	Guess_Password, Ftp_write, Imap, Phf, Multihop, Waremaster, Warezclient, Spy	Guess_Password, Ftp_write, Imap, Phf, Multihop, Waremaster, Spy, **Xlock, Xsnoop, Snmpguess, Snmpgetattack, Httptunnel, Sendfmail, Named**
U2R	Buffer_overflow, Loadmodule, Perl, Rotkit	Buffer_overflow, Loadmodule, Rotkit, Perl, **Sqlattack, Xterm, Ps**
PROBE	Satan, Ipsweep, Nmap, Portsweep	Satan, Ipsweep, Nmap, Portsweep, **Mscan, Saint**

D. Pre-processing

Before proceeding to experimental work, the NSL-KDD data sets first went through a data preprocessing operation and attribute a type of conversion by following the steps described in the following part:

1) Numericalization: The features 2, 3 and 4 namely the protocol_ type, service and flag were non-numerical. The input value of the Denoising AE should be a numeric matrix. We must convert these features into numeric form in the train and test data set. 'tcp','udp'and 'icmp'and its numeric values are encoded as binary vectors (1, 0, 0), (0, 1, 0) and (0, 0, 1). Similarly, the feature 'service' has 70 types of attributes, and the feature 'flag' has 11 types of attributes. Continuing in this way, we obtain a 41 dimensional feature map into 122 dimensional features after transformation.

2) Normalization: The values obtained after the operation of the numericalization are very varied and constitute a big interval. Some attributes take great values (1, 5 and 6) (duration, src_bytes, dst_bytes) while others take only small values. To help them accord to same features, we apply the logarithmic scaling method. Finally, the value of every feature is mapped to the [0, 1] using min-max where max denotes the maximum value and min denotes minimum value for each feature.

$$x_i = \frac{x_{i-min}}{max-min} \quad (1)$$

E. Methodology

In this approach, we implemented a DEA with Dropout on the inputs. It consists of an input layer of 122 neurons due to the fact that the number of features for each sample is 122 followed by a Dropout layer with a fixed probability p= 0.5 and a single hidden layer with different number of neurons such as (8, 16, 24 and 32) units so the hidden representation of the autoencoder has a compression ratio of 122 to (8, 16, 24 o and 32) forcing it to learn interesting patterns and relations.

Finally, there is an output layer of 122 units; the activation of both the hidden layer and the output layer is the "Relu" function.

The training set has 125973 rows, but the DEA was trained using only the samples labeled "Normal" to capture the nature of normal behavior , and this was accomplished by training the model to minimize the mean squared error between its output and its input. We use 67343 samples labeled "Normal" with 60608 are used for training. The model is trained for 20 epochs using an Adam optimizer with a batch size of 150. Furthermore, we held out 6735 for validation that refer to 10% of the normal training samples to validate the model.

IV. Evaluation and Result Analysis

The model performs anomaly detection by calculating the reconstruction error of samples since the model was trained using normal data samples. Only the reconstruction error of samples that represent attacks should be relatively high compared to the reconstruction error of normal data samples. This intuition allows us to detect attacks by setting a threshold for the reconstruction error. If a data sample has a reconstruction error higher than the preset threshold then the sample is classified as an attack. Otherwise, it's classified as normal traffic.

A. Evaluation Based on Training and Data Validation

For the choice of a threshold, two values can be helpful to guide the process. Concerning the model loss over the training data and over the validation data, we found by experiment that a choice around these values produces acceptable results. For our experiments, we use the model loss over the training data as a threshold.

In Table III, we present the val_loss for 3 epochs using a single hidden layer with different neurons.

TABLE III. Val_ Loss in 3 Epochs

Single hidden layer	Epoch 1/20	Epoch 2/20	Epoch 3/20
32 neurons	loss: 0.0334 val_loss: 0.014	loss: 0.0128 val_loss: 0.0094	loss: 0.0102 val_loss: 0.0077
24 neurons	loss: 0.0316 val_loss: 0.0133	loss: 0.0124 val_loss: 0.0091	loss: 0.0101 val_loss: 0.0075
16 neurons	loss: 0.0335 val_loss: 0.0160	loss: 0.0139 val_loss: 0.0103	loss: 0.0096 val_loss: 0.0073
8 neurons	loss: 0.0339 val_loss: 0.0184	loss: 0.0160 val_loss: 0.0127	loss: 0.0129 val_loss: 0.0107

B. Evaluation Based on Test Data

In the section, we evaluate the performance over the test dataset which includes 22543 rows, 37 different attacks and one normal label that refers to 12832 for normal samples and 9711 for attack samples. The calculated losses are a helper function that accepts the original features and the predicted features and relies on the reconstruction loss of each data sample. Afterwards, each data sample is classified according to its reconstruction error and the preset threshold.

The nature of this approach is purely for anomaly detection. We evaluate the performance of DEA based anomaly detection on the following metrics

- Accuracy (A): Defined as the percentage of correctly classified records over the total number of records.

$$A= \frac{TP+TN}{TP+TN+FP+FN} \quad (2)$$

- Recall (R): Defined as the % ratio of number of true positives records divided by the sum of true positives and false negatives (FN) classified records.

$$R = \frac{TP}{(TP+FN)} \times 100\% \quad (3)$$

- Precision (P): Defined as the % ratio of the number of true positives (TP) records divided by the sum of true positives (TP) and false positives (FP) classified.

$$P = \frac{TP}{(TP+FP)} \times 100\% \quad (4)$$

- F-measure (F): The harmonic average F combines recall and precision in a number between 0 and 1.

$$F = \frac{2.P.R}{(P+R)} \quad (5)$$

TABLE IV. EVALUATION METRICS

Single hidden layer	Accuracy	Recall	Precision	F-measure
32 neurons	89.13%	94.07%	87.72%	90.78%
24 neurons	89.65%	95.66%	87.36%	91.32%
16 neurons	89.90%	**96.61%**	87.07%	91.59%
8 neurons	**90.32%**	95.04%	**88.12%**	**91.85%**

From Table IV, we can see that our results have demonstrated that our approach offers high levels of accuracy, recall, precision and F-measure especially when we use a little number of neurons (8 neurons) in a hidden layer. In addition, in the 4 metrics, our method is evaluated according to a Detection rate (see Table V).

TABLE V. DETECTION RATE

Single hidden layer	Normal	DOS	R2L	U2R	PROBE
32 neurons	17.40%	92.48%	93.72%	77.61%	**99.95%**
24 neurons	18.29%	93.07%	99.11%	**100%**	99.87%
16 neurons	18.95%	94.60%	**99.26%**	**98.50%**	99.91%
8 neurons	**22.27%**	**95.80%**	**98.85%**	**100%**	99.91%

Table V illustrates the detection rate for every type of attacks (DOS, U2R, R2L and PROBE) and normal data. The process of detecting anomalies using our Denoising autoencoder with dropout method produced a high detection rate. We can see that for testing data, U2R attack is detected with a rate of 100% using 8 and 24 neurons in a hidden layer. Also, we can note that DOS and PROBE attacks are highly detected with a rate of 95.80% (8 neurons) and 99.95 %.(32 neurons). R2L is also well identified as attacks with 99.26% (16 neurons). In contrast, the normal data are not well detected with a maximum rate of 22.27%.

These detection rates were better that the results produced by Elkhadir et al. [6] when using PCA and KPCA for detection of anomalous connection in NSL- KDD dataset (see Table VI).

TABLE VI. ATTACK'S DETECTION RATE OF PCA AND KPCA [6]

Method	DOS	R2L	U2R	PROBE
PCA	90.35%	93.6%	87.2%	85.15%
KPCA	90.2%	92.6%	87.25%	85.45%

Finally, according to the 5 metrics previously mentioned to evaluate the performance of DEA based anomaly detection; the best result is obtained when we used a single hidden layer with 8 neurons.

V. CONCLUSION AND FUTURE WORK

In this approach, we attempted to develop a Denoising Autoencoder with Dropout-based network anomaly detection method for improving intrusion detection. This method was trained only using normal traffic. The strength of this approach is its simplicity. It consists of only a single hidden layer with different neurons making it very easy to train. In terms of detection rates, our approach outperforms many methods in the existing literature.

In future work, we can build and evaluate a model with many hidden layers.

ACKNOWLEDGMENT

The authors would like to acknowledge the financial support of this work by grants from General Direction of Scientific Research (DGRST), Tunisia, under the ARUB program.

REFERENCES

[1] A. Javaid, Q. Niyaz, W. Sun, and M. Alam, "A deep learning approach for network intrusion detection system," In Proceedings of the 9th EAI International Conference on Bio-inspired Information and Communications Technologies (formerly BIONETICS), (ICST (Institute for Computer Sciences, Social-Informatics and Telecommunications Engineering), pp. 21-26, 2016.

[2] B. C. Rhodes, J. A. Mahaffey, and J. D. Cannady, " Multiple self-organizing maps for intrusion detection," In Proceedings of the 23rd national information systems security conference, pp. 16-19, 2000.

[3] Z. Chen, C. K. Yeo, B. S. Lee, and C. T. Lau, "Autoencoder-based network anomaly detection," Wireless Telecommunications Symposium (WTS), pp. 1-5, 2018.

[4] M. Sakurada and T. Yairi, "Anomaly detection using autoencoders with nonlinear dimensionality reduction," Proceedings of the MLSDA 2014 2nd Workshop on Machine Learning for Sensory Data Analysis, ACM, 2014.

[5] S. Heni, R. Ejbali, M. Zaied, and C. B. Amar, "A Neural Principal Component Analysis for text based documents keywords extraction,"3rd International Conference on Next Generation Networks and Services (NGNS), pp. 112-115, 2011.

[6] Z. Elkhadir, K. Chougdali, and M. Benattou, "Intrusion Detection System Using PCA and Kernel PCA Methods," IAENG International Journal of Computer Science, 2016.

[7] S. Revathi, and A. Malathi, "A detailed analysis on NSL-KDD dataset using various machine learning techniques for intrusion detection," International Journal of Engineering

Research & Technology (IJERT), vol. 2, no 12, pp. 1848-1853, 2013.

[8] D. Hou, Y. Cong, G. Sun, J. Liu, and X.Xu, "Anomaly detection via adaptive greedy model," Neurocomputing, vol. 330, pp. 369-379, 2019.

[9] P. Vincent, H. Larochelle, I. Lajoie, Y. Bengio, and P. A. Manzagol, "Stacked denoising autoencoders: Learning useful representations in a deep network with a local denoising criterion," vol.11, no Dec, pp. 3371-3408, 2010.

[10] S. Lakhina, S. Joseph, and B. Verma, "Feature Reduction Using Principal Component Analysis for Effective Anomaly–Based Intrusion Detection on NSL-KDD," International Journal of Engineering Science and Technology ,Vol. 2(6), pp.1790-1799, 2010.

[11] N. B. Ibraheem , M. M. Jawhar, and H. M. Osman, "Principle Components Analysis and Multi Layer Perceptron Based Intrusion Detection System," AL-Rafidain Journal of Computer Sciences and Mathematics, vol. 10, no 1, pp.127-135, 2013

[12] S.T Ikram and A. K. Cherukuri, "Improving accuracy of intrusion detection model using PCA and optimized SVM," Journal of computing and information technology, vol. 24, no 2, pp. 133-148, 2016.

[13] E. L. Paula, M. Ladeira, R. N. Carvalho, and T.Marzagao, "Deep learning anomaly detection as support fraud investigation in brazilian exports and anti-money laundering," In 2016 15th IEEE International Conference on Machine Learning and Applications (ICMLA), pp. 954-960, 2016.

[14] M. Gnouma, A. Ladjailia, R. Ejbali, and M. Zaied, "Stacked .sparse autoencoder and history of binary motion image for human activity recognition," Multimedia Tools and Applications, vol. 78, no 2, pp .2157-2179, 2019.

[15] S. Said et al. ,"Deep wavelet network for image classification," IEEE International Conference on Systems, Man, and Cybernetics (SMC), 2016.

[16] A. ElAdel, R. Ejbali, M. Zaied, and C. B. Amar, "Fast deep neural network based on intelligent dropout and layer skipping," IEEE International Joint Conference on Neural Networks (IJCNN), pp. 897-902, 2017.

[17] G. E. Dahl, T. N. Sainath, and G. E. Hinton, "Improving deep neural networks for LVCSR using rectified linear units and dropout," IEEE International Conference on Acoustics, Speech and Signal Processing, pp. 8610-8613, 2013D. Kornack and P. Rakic, "Cell Proliferation without Neurogenesis in Adult Primate Neocortex," Science, vol. 294, Dec. 2001, pp. 2127-2130, doi:10.1126/science.1065467.

[18] Y. Ding and Y. Zhai, "Intrusion Detection System for NSL-KDD Dataset Using Convolutional Neural Networks," In Proceedings of the 2018 2nd International Conference on Computer Science and Artificial Intelligence, pp. 81-85, 2018.

[19] C.YIN, Y. Zhu, J. Fei, and X. He, "A deep learning approach for intrusion detection using recurrent neural networks, " Ieee Access, vol. 5, pp. 21954-219, 2017.

[20] T. A. Tang, L. Mhamdi, D. McLernon, S. A. R. Zaidi, and M.Ghogho,"Deep learning approach for network intrusion detection in software defined networking," IEEE International Conference on Wireless Networks and Mobile Communications (WINCOM), 2016.

i* (iStar) Security Hierarchy for Cloud Computing

Fiza Saher Faizan
National University of Sciences and Technology (NUST),
Islamabad, Pakistan
fiza.saher@yahoo.com

Seemab Latif
National University of Sciences and Technology (NUST),
Islamabad, Pakistan
seemab.latif@seecs.edu.pk

Athar Mohsin Zaidi
National University of Sciences and Technology (NUST),
Islamabad, Pakistan
athar@mcs.edu.pk

Abstract— **The world is advancing with the Cloud Computing technology. The aim of Cloud Computing is to provide improved usage of distributed resources like networks, servers, storage applications, and services. With the advancement, there are some risks involved as well. Whenever a cloud-system is being developed, an entity should be there, which looks-after security threats that may arise for the system. This entity is proposed in this research work and named as "Guard". A framework is proposed, which can elicit functional requirements, as well as security requirements of the system. Online-banking case study is used to verify the proposed framework. To accomplish the task, a survey is also conducted and then results are analyzed from survey to propose a framework. The evaluation result of the proposed framework shows that the system will be protected from multiple security risks of cloud computing.**

Keywords- Requirement Engineering; Cloud Computing; iStar.

I. INTRODUCTION

Banking is the term that is used everywhere nowadays. With the huge involvement of banking in the period of technology, the think-tankers of every bank are trying to cope with the technology to beat their competitors. Therefore, moving towards cloud computing is the new era in the field of banking i.e., online-banking, as well as a great challenge for financial institutions because there are many issues that need to be resolved in cloud computing such as security issues [1].

Security is a major concern in the field of cloud computing [2]. Security leads towards the loss of cloud customer's trust on cloud providers as Forrester Research Consultants did survey of 11 merchant companies offering cloud services concluded that most cloud customers or stakeholder's needs do not meet with the result of the cloud service provider, which causes the loss of customer or stakeholder trust [3][4]. Therefore, if good requirement engineering is performed when transforming the traditional system to the cloud system then security issues can be predicted and resolved during development [5][6].

This paper proposes a framework to identify security issues that can be faced by the developers of the cloud system. The rest of this paper is organized as follows. Section II describes the literature review. Section III describes the research methodology. Section IV presents proposed iStar Security hierarchy. Section V presents results and analysis. And finally research is concluded in Section VI with the future work.

II. LITERATURE REVIEW

According to the Cloud Security Alliance (CSA) reports, security is the major concern in cloud computing [8][9][10]. Figure 1 shows the statistics of these reports.

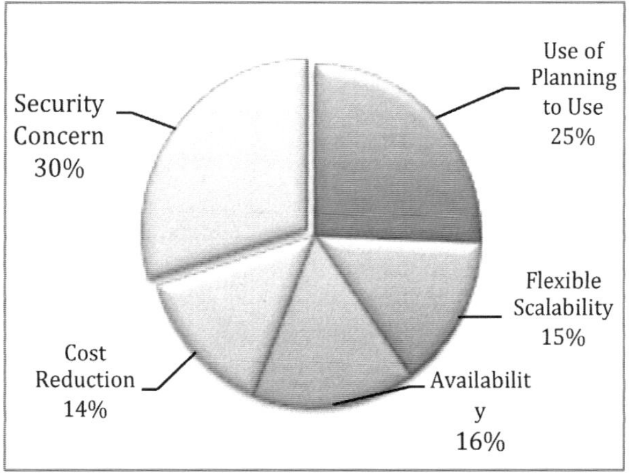

Figure 1: Statistics on Spotlight Reports by CSA

By keeping these reports in view, those techniques are considered in the literature review, which falls in the following four factors:

1) Focused on functional requirements
2) Focused on non-functional requirements
3) Elicits security requirements
4) Inconsistency in technique, which means that technique, persists only for the defined domain.

Therefore, 11 requirements engineering techniques/ methodologies are identified during the literature review and hence they are compared with each other using the above-mentioned factors. This comparative analysis is shown in Table 1.

TABLE I: COMPARATIVE ANALYSIS OF REQUIREMENT ENGINEERING TECHNIQUES FOR CLOUD COMPUTING

Frameworks/Techniques	1	2	3	4
Crowd-Centric RE [11]	✓	×	×	×
UML based Structure [12]	✓	✓	✓	×
Improved RE Framework [6]	✓	×	×	×
Fuzzy Galois Lattice [13]	✓	×	×	×
i* (iStar) [14]	✓	×	×	✓
Security Requirement Engineering and Mechanism [15]	×	✓	✓	✓
Cloud Framework [16]	✓	×	×	×
Security Requirement Elicitation Technique [17]	×	✓	✓	×
Cloud Framework [18]	×	✓	✓	×
Modeling Non-functional Requirements Technique [19]	×	✓	×	✓
RE for Developing Business Process Model Technique [5]	✓	×	×	✓

It is concluded from the literature review that requirement engineering has a very significant role in gathering security requirements for cloud-based systems. For instance, a framework and/or technique is required to elicit security requirements. Traditional requirement engineering techniques are not adequate to elicit the security requirements of cloud-based systems [4]. Hence, this research work is conducted to develop a framework used to elicit the security requirements of cloud-based systems.

III. Research Methodology

This research work is based on qualitative research methodology that includes descriptive and case study research methodologies.

To accomplish this research work, a literature review has been conducted to identify all RE techniques and methods used in cloud system development. This literature review is based on the methodology described by Kitchenham [7]. From the literature review, research questions are identified and according to the identified research questions, existing techniques are analyzed to accomplish this research work. After analyzing techniques, an on-ground survey has been performed in which multiple banks are involved to gather the information. The results of the survey are then merged into i* hierarchy and hence the proposed framework is obtained.

The proposed framework has been implemented in a case study. The existing RE techniques and the proposed framework are compared with respect to the factors, which will be discussed in the Section 5. These factors are considered according to domain area of research i.e., requirement elicitation technique to resolve security issues in the cloud-based system, which may arise after the execution of the system.

IV. ISECURITY HIERARCHY

The proposed framework is grounded on two techniques i* Hierarchy and Security Requirement Elicitation and Assessment Mechanism (SecREAM) [14][15]. SecREAM is used to find the security threats, which can weaken the cloud system that is being developed for banking. The results are then merged into i* hierarchy, which shows the elicitation of functional, as well as security requirements for online banking. Figure 2 shows the main i* Security Hierarchy. In i* hierarchy three layers are involved as shown in Figure 2. According to the case study, banks and cloud providers are the main actors of the hierarchy, and a guard is the new actor introduced in this research work and plays a vital role because the purpose of this actor is to locate security requirements with functional requirements at each layer.

On the layer of directors, the goal of Guard is to provide security to online banking. On the manager layer, its goal is to provide security requirements to the bank operational manager and cloud provider manager, as well as an actor working parallel to it at the administration layer. At this layer, the guard finds the assets of the system then finds what security parameters belong to these assets. Afterward, it generates misuse cases against parameters and stores them in the security pool so that the system would be secure. Table 2 gives indicated requirements by these parameters, and these are the result of SecREAM.

TABLE II: PARAMETERS AND SECURITY REQUIREMENTS

Parameters	Security Requirements
Authentication	How do account details access? How do account is protected from unauthorized access?
Authorization	The customer views his account details. What things he has allowed? What if he tries to view other things?
Availability	How much downtime is allowed for the system? When the downtime prolongs then what system should do?
Maintainability	Does a system backup it's data? When the last up-gradation of account details has been done? Which architecture is provided by the service provider?
Configurability	How did an online-banking service provide to the customers either through mobile applications or web services?
Scalability	Does the system allow upgrading to meet technological changes?
Integrity	Does data encrypt? Who will decrypt the data and how? Is digital signature allowed customers to add on their account?

With respect to the case study, the assets of online banking are data storage and data processing and their parameters are authentications, authorization, availability, maintainability, configuration, scalability, and integrity. Forouzan says that these are the security parameters of any system, which may be targeted by an attacker hence security requirements are derived from these parameters [20]. Figure 3 illustrates the working of Guard at the manager's layer. On the administrator layer, its goal is to provide security parameters to the respective actors to be deployed. The working of an actor guard at the administration layer is elaborated in Figure 4. It analyzes what security parameters according to the requirements are deployed on the system and then fetches new security parameters from the pool to be deployed.

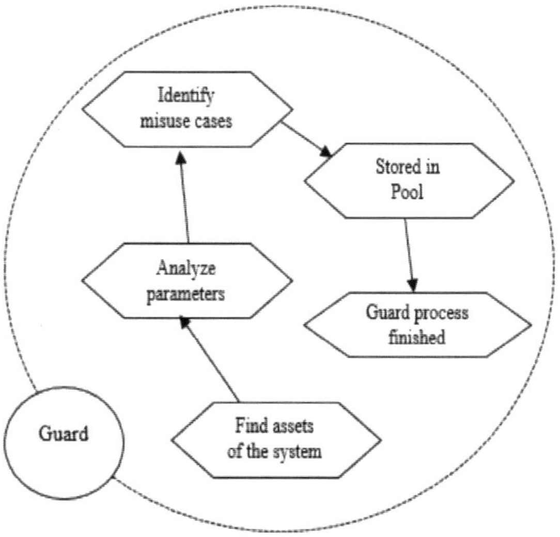

Figure 3: i* Hierarchy "Strategic Rationale of Guard at Manager Layer"

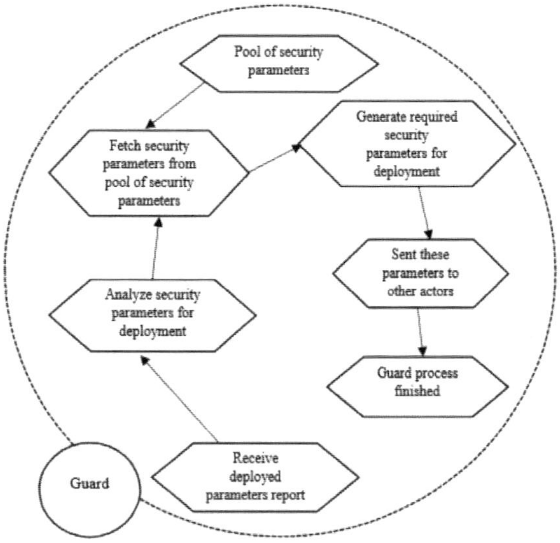

Figure 4: i* Hierarchy "Strategic Rationale of Guard at Administration Layer"

i* hierarchy is goal-oriented and SecREAM is asset-based methodology when combine they can elicit requirements more deeply. SecREAM declares that an asset of the online-banking system is data storage with security parameters mentioned in Table 2. i* evaluate these parameters according to the goal of an actor Guard. For example, at the manager's layer Guard finds that authentication is the most critical security parameter for data storage then it identifies misuse cases for authentication like "How do account details access? and How to do account is protected from unauthorized access?". Similarly, for scalability "Does system allow to upgrade to meet technological changes?". At the layer of administration, the Guard assures that "How the system will behave when a fake person access data with authentic information?" and "What security measures are taken for software viruses when system upgraded?

V. RESULTS AND ANALYSIS

By comparing CSA report discussed in Section 2 and security parameters gathered in Table 2, it can be derived that those security issues can be targeted during the initial stage of system development i.e., requirements elicitation. Table 3 shows security threats that are targeted by security parameters to resolve security issues that might be faced after the execution of the system.

TABLE III: PARAMETERS AND TARGETED SECURITY THREATS

Parameters	Security Threat
Authentication	Verification and Permission issues
Authorization	Usage and Data Protection from Leakage
Availability	Denial of Service
Maintainability	Veracity (Accuracy), privacy and backups
Configurability	Web Browsers, Protocols, Remote connections
Scalability	Technological issues
Integrity	Malicious attacks

Hence, the proposed framework secures the system from data loss, account hijacking, denial of services, inside attacks and shared technology issues.

The comparison has been taken between existing techniques, discussed in the Section 2, and the proposed framework with respect to the following factors that are derived based on the research area.

F1. The technique is a traditional methodology.
F2. The technique is used for cloud-based systems.
F3. The technique is focused on functional requirements for cloud systems.
F4. The technique is focused on non-functional requirements for cloud systems.
F5. The technique is specifically proposed to elicit security requirements for cloud computing.

These factors are recorded as following and then recorded in Table 4:

1) ✓ (Yes), score points = 1, if paper considered the factor.
2) ✗ (No), score points = 0, if paper does not consider the factor.

TABLE IV: COMPARISON OF FRAMEWORKS

Sr.	Techniques	F1	F2	F3	F4	F5	SP
T1	Crowd Centric Requirement Engineering	✓	✓	×	×	×	2
T2	UML based Structure	✓	✓	✓	×	×	3
T3	Improved RE Framework for Cloud	×	✓	✓	×	×	2
T4	Requirement Elicitation Cloud Framework	✓	✓	✓	×	×	3
T5	Software Security RE and Management as an Emerging cloud Service	×	✓	✓	×	✓	3
T6	Proposed Framework	✓	✓	✓	×	✓	**4**

Hence, it is derived that a traditional technique can be modified to elicit requirements for cloud-based systems. The proposed framework focused on functional and non-functional requirements specifically security requirements. In Figure 5, statistics shows that Techniques 1 and 4 satisfy two factors and hence secure 2 score points whereas Techniques 2, 3 and 5 satisfy three factors and hence secure 3 score points. The proposed framework satisfies four factors and hence secure 4 score points, which are the highest score in comparison. The proposed framework also satisfies the factor F4 to some extent because security issues categorized as a non-functional requirement.

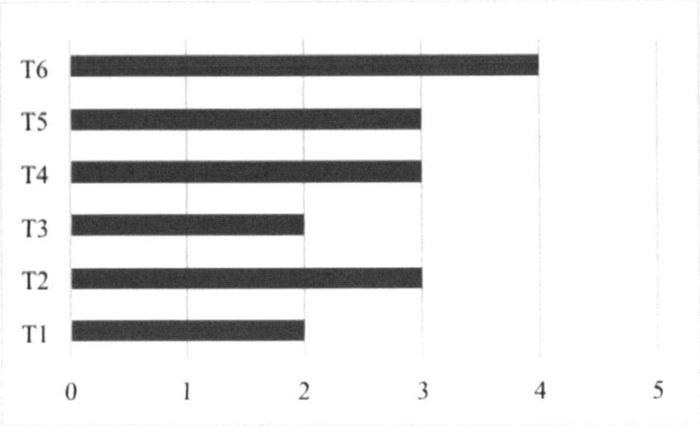

Figure 5: Statistics of Comparison

VI. CONCLUSION AND FUTURE WORK

The proposed framework is based on i* hierarchy and SecREAM and named as "i* Security Hierarchy", which helps to elicit functional requirements with the most demanding requirement i.e., security requirements. An online-banking case study is used to manipulate this work. This framework elicits both functional and non-functional requirements as security is in the non-functional requirements category. The proposed framework concentrates on the requirement elicitation process; hence, it is not involved in all processes of requirement engineering. The proposed framework also proves the flexibility of based techniques.

In the future, the proposed work will be applied to different domains and make it appropriate to involve all processes of requirement engineering, which are (i) requirement analysis, (ii) requirement prioritization and (iii) requirement specification.

REFERENCES

[1] N. Ikram, S. Siddique, and N. F. Khan, "Security Requirement Elicitation Techniques: The Comparison of Misuse Cases and Issue-Based Information Systems", pp. 36-43, IEEE 2014.

[2] A. Alshammari, S. Alhaidari, A. Alharbi, and M. Zohdy, "Security Threats and Challenges in Cloud Computing", International Conference on Cyber Security and Cloud Computing, pp. 46-51, IEEE 2017.

[3] Forrester, TechRadar for infrastructure & operations professionals, Cloud Computing, Forrester, 2009.

[4] H. Schrodl, and S. Wind, "Requirements Engineering for Cloud Computing", Journal of Communication and Computer Vol. 8 pp. 707-715, 2011.

[5] M. Nosrati, "Exact requirements engineering for developing business process models," 2017 3th International Conference on Web Research (ICWR), 2017, pp. 140-147.

[6] M. E. Rana, J. Dauren, and S. Kumaran, "An improved Requirements Engineering framework for cloud based application development," 2015 IEEE Student Conference on Research and Development (SCOReD), 2015, pp. 702-709.

[7] B. A. Kitchenham, "Guidelines for performing Systematic Literature Reviews in Software Engineering", 2007.

[8] H. Schulze, "Cloud Security", Spotlight Report powered by Cloud Passage Information Security Community on LinkedIn, 2015.

[9] H. Schulze, "Cloud Security", Spotlight Report powered by Cloud Passage Information Security Community on LinkedIn, 2016.

[10] H. Schulze, "Cloud Security", Spotlight Report powered by Cloud Passage Information Security Community on LinkedIn, 2017.

[11] R. Snijders, F. Dalpiaz, M. Hosseini, A. M. Shahri, and R. Ali, "Crowd-Centric Requirements Engineering", IEEE/ACM International Conference on Utility and Cloud Computing, 2014, pp. 614-615.

[12] M. Ficco, F. Palmieri, and A. Castiglione, "Modeling Security Requirements for Cloud-based System Development", Special issue Paper, 2014, pp. 2107-2124.

[13] I. T. Koitz, and M. Glinz, "A Fuzzy Galois Lattices Approach to Requirements Elicitation for Cloud Services," in IEEE Transactions on Services Computing, vol. 11, no. 5, pp. 768-781, 1 Sept.-Oct. 2018.

[14] Sandfreni, N. R. Oktadini, and K. Surendra, "Requirement Engineering for Cloud Computing Using i* (iStar) Hierarchy Method", International Journal of Information Science and Applications, 2015, pp. pp 885-890.

[15] R. Goel, M. C. Govil, and G. Singh, "Security Requirements Elicitation and Assessment Mechanism (SecREAM)", IEEE

International Conference on Advances in Computing, Communications and Informatics (ICACCI), 2015, pp. 1862-1866.

[16] J. Vijayashree, P. U. Ivy, and J. Jayashree, "Requirement Elicitation Framework for Cloud Applications", International Journal of Engineering Research and General Science, Vol. 3, Issue 1, 2015, pp. 729-733.

[17] M. Ramachandran, "Software Security Requirements Management as an Emerging Cloud Computing Service", International Journal of Information Management, 2016, vol. 36, pp 580-590.

[18] S. A. Aljawarneh, A. Alawneh, and R. Jaradat, "Cloud Security Engineering: Early Stages of SDLC", International Journal of Future Generation Computer Science, 2016, pp. 385-392.

[19] S. Devata, and A. Olmsted, "Modeling Non-Functional Requirements in Cloud Hosted Application Software Engineering", International Conference on Cloud Computing, GRIDs, and Virtualization, 2016, pp. 47-50.

[20] S. Harbajanka, and P. Saxena, "Survey Paper on Trust Management and Security Issues in Cloud Computing", IEEE Symposium on Colossal Data Analysis and Networking (CDAN), 2016, pp. 1-3.

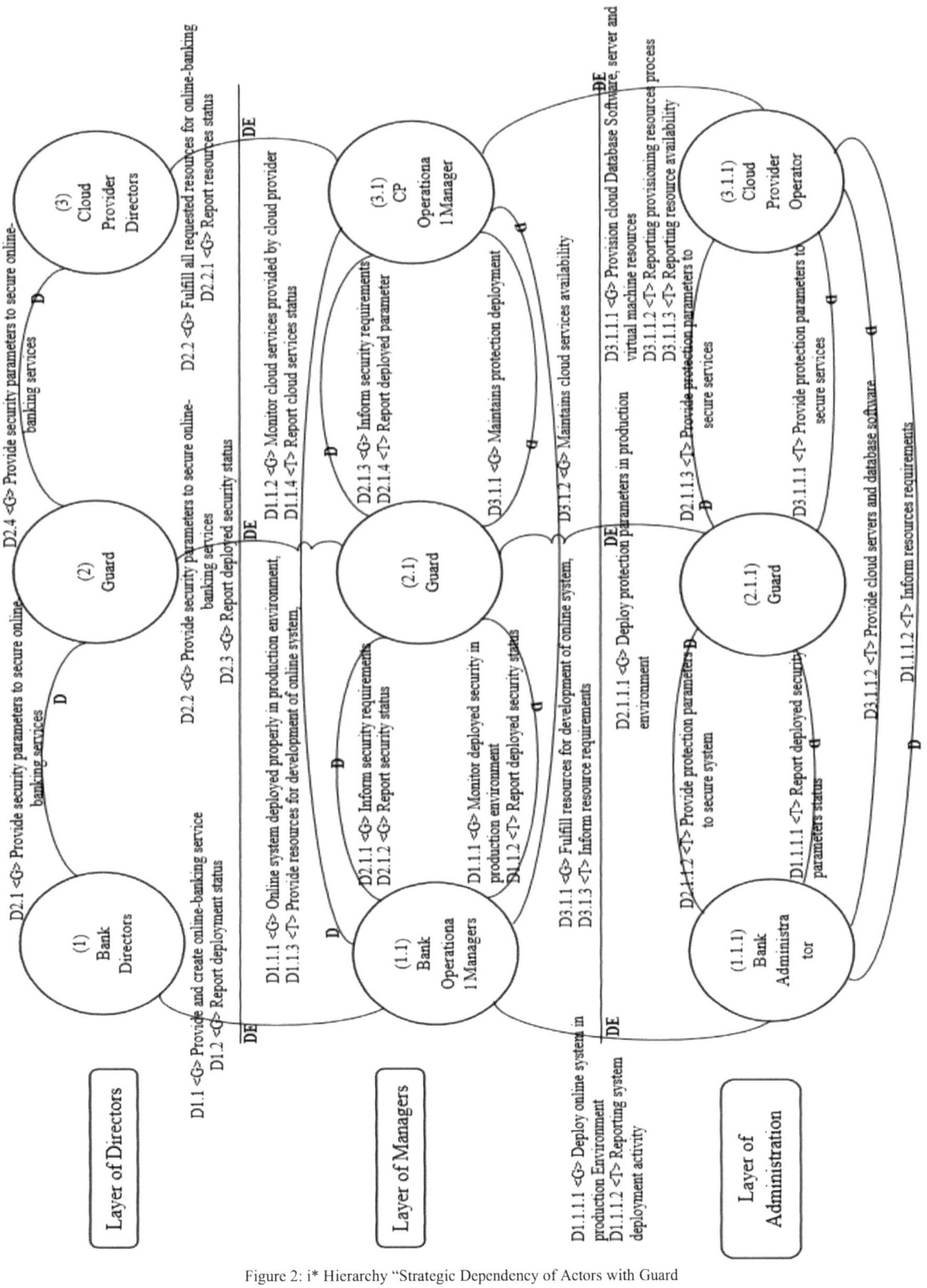

Figure 2: i* Hierarchy "Strategic Dependency of Actors with Guard

Implementing a Protocol Native Managed Cryptocurrency

Peter Mell
National Institute of Standards and Technology
Gaithersburg MD, USA
peter.mell@nist.gov

Aurelien Delaitre
Prometheus Computing
New Market MD, USA
aurelien.delaitre@nist.gov

Frederic de Vaulx
Prometheus Computing
New Market MD, USA
frederic.devaulx@nist.gov

Philippe Dessauw
Prometheus Computing
New Market MD, USA
philippe.dessauw@nist.gov

***Abstract*—Previous work presented a theoretical model based on the implicit Bitcoin specification for how an entity might issue a protocol native cryptocurrency that mimics features of fiat currencies. Protocol native means that it is built into the blockchain platform itself and is not simply a token running on another platform. Novel to this work were mechanisms by which the issuing entity could manage the cryptocurrency but where their power was limited and transparency was enforced by the cryptocurrency being implemented using a publicly mined blockchain. In this work we demonstrate the feasibility of this theoretical model by implementing such a managed cryptocurrency architecture through forking the Bitcoin code base. We discovered that the theoretical model contains several vulnerabilities and security issues that needed to be mitigated. It also contains architectural features that presented significant implementation challenges; some aspects of the proposed changes to the Bitcoin specification were not practical or even workable. In this work we describe how we mitigated the security vulnerabilities and overcame the architectural hurdles to build a working prototype.**

***Index Terms*—Fiat Currency, Cryptocurrency, Bitcoin**

I. Introduction

The United States National Institute of Standards and Technology developed an architecture for a managed cryptocurrency that has many of the features of electronic fiat currencies and includes a governing entity [1]. It is intended to combine the strengths of both fiat currencies and cryptocurrencies. In doing this, it deviates from the goals of most cryptocurrencies by introducing concepts such as central banking, law enforcement, and identity proofed accounts. It also deviates from a government controlled fiat currency world in denying the currency administrator absolute power over financial controls. It enables a currency administrator to enact policy to create a specific cryptocurrency instance from the architecture, usually with immutable configurations that even the administrator cannot violate. This can promote public trust in the currency since the limits to the administrator's power are immutably recorded on the associated blockchain. The architecture uses a public permissionless blockchain approach whereby the administrator's actions are completely transparent. Furthermore, a public set of miners maintaining the blockchain can prevent the administrator from performing unauthorized actions. At the same time, the cryptocurrency is designed to prevent the public miners from taking control from the administrator or from preventing the administrator's transactions from being processed. This architecture thus creates a 'balance of power' between the administrator and the public miners. Additional features include adding role attributes to cryptocurrency accounts that represent fiat currency entities (e.g., commercial banks, central banks, and law enforcement) such that there is created a tree based hierarchy of nodes with roles for all users of the cryptocurrency.

A major limitation to the approach is that it was presented only as a theoretical architecture. It demonstrated what might be possible to create through modest forks to existing cryptocurrencies, specifically using Bitcoin [2] [3] [4] as an example. The empirical work was limited to proposing changes to the implicit Bitcoin specifications in [5] and [6] to add the features necessary for this 'balance of power' managed cryptocurrency approach. No code was developed and no implementation was tested. The ability of [1] to modify the Bitcoin specification to add the needed features indicated that a managed cryptocurrency might be able to be built through a modest fork of an existing cryptocurrency, but it lacked a proof-of-concept prototype built as a protocol native implementation.

In this work, we set out to build such a prototype as an applied research endeavor. We tested whether or not such a managed cryptocurrency system could be built through modest modifications to the code base of an existing cryptocurrency. In this way we explored how to create a protocol native managed cryptocurrency built into the blockchain platform itself and explore the advantages of this approach. This was non-trivial as we did not simply create a token on top of another cryptocurrency. We also wanted to see if this could be done efficiently, with only a modest amount of programming effort (we scoped using half a person year, in part due to resource constraints). We chose to use Bitcoin since [1] described their theoretical model through proposing changes to Bitcoin. We wanted to discover the complexity of modifying Bitcoin to require identity proofing of accounts, establish accounts with roles, enable law enforcement functions, enable central banking functions, and create and visualize a hierarchy tree of accounts that specifies the scope of control of the various management and law enforcement nodes.

An unattributed quote says that 'theory is when you know everything but nothing works.' Yogi Berra said, 'in theory there is no difference between theory and practice. But, in practice, there is.' We found these statements to be true with regard to our implementation of the theoretical work. We discovered that the theoretical model contains several vulnerabilities and security issues that needed to be mitigated. It also contains architectural features that presented significant implementation challenges; some aspects of the proposed changes to the Bitcoin specification were not practical or even workable. We thus had to augment the material in [1] in order to achieve a functional and secure system, especially in areas such as preserving the balance of power, law enforcement powers, management node powers, bootstrapping the system, and the needed movement of accounts within the node hierarchy (e.g., when an account holder changes their account manager). We also encountered difficulties using the Bitcoin code base which necessitated design changes not foreseen in [1]. However, in the end we discovered that it was possible to modestly modify Bitcoin to implement this 'balance of power' managed cryptocurrency approach and to do it with a relatively low amount of programming effort.

In summary, we showed that the theoretical architecture provided by [1] works and can be implemented efficiently. However, we had to change, refine, and augment the original design in order to make it function. This paper describes these changes and the final prototype implementation which we have made publicly available on GitHub (any mention of commercial products is for information only; it does not imply recommendation or endorsement). Note that due to resource constraints, our prototype is not a full implementation. The largest limitation is that the cryptocurrency policy configuration is static, while the full design in [1] permits dynamic policy changes. While not all features were implemented, the core functionality was enabled to provide confidence that the system could be efficiently constructed.

The rest of this paper is organized as follows. Section II presents the theoretical architecture from [1] and discusses relevant Bitcoin architectural features. Section III discusses the vulnerabilities and security issues we discovered in the architecture. Section IV discusses the architectural hurdles that we had to overcome. Section V outlines how we created our prototype system and Section VI presents the related work. Section VII discusses our future plans for the system and Section VIII concludes.

II. Theoretical Architecture

The research in [1] provides an architecture that can be instantiated into a cryptocurrency instance through specifying a specific policy configuration. The policy parameters enable or disable feature sets while specifying parameters for cryptocurrency operation. The financially related parameters are just examples of what could be (e.g., limits on money production) and are not intended to be exhaustive given that the identification of financial controls is a related but separate research area. In this architecture, anyone can create an account, but an account cannot do anything unless it is granted one or more roles. The initial block on the blockchain has a 'genesis transaction' that grants roles to the root administrator account and all future role assignments spring from this initial root account. The root account grants roles to other accounts, and those accounts in turn may grant roles to accounts. This sets up a hierarchy of accounts in a tree structure with the root account (or node) being the most authoritative.

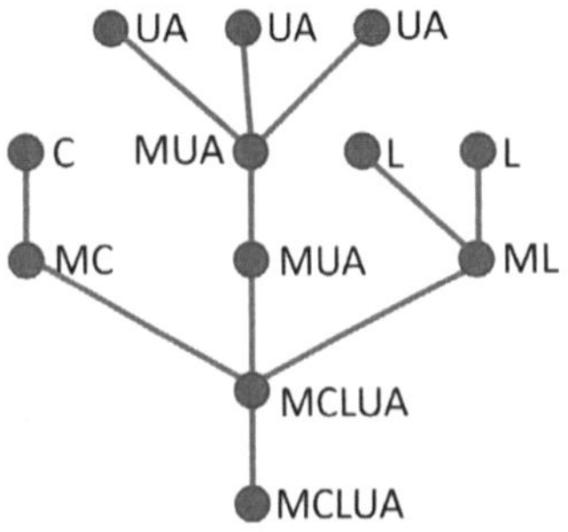

Fig. 1. Example Managed Cryptocurrency Hierarchy (from [1])

The initial root node is given all possible roles so that it can propagate these roles to other accounts. Of particular import is the 'M' currency manager role that enables an account to give its roles to other accounts (or withdraw granted roles) and to modify cryptocurrency policy. Other roles include 'U' user, 'A' account manager, 'C' central banker, and 'L' law enforcement. Their abilities are summarized in [1] as follows:

- 'The U role enables an account to receive and spend coins. An account for which the U role has been removed has its funds frozen.
- The A role enables a node to create accounts with the U role (and only the U role). It may also remove the U label for its descendants.
- The C role enables the creation of new coins (apart from the block mining rewards).
- The L role enables an account to forcibly move funds between accounts, to remove the U label, and to restore a previously removed U label. However, these actions can only be performed against nodes with the same or greater distance from the root.'

Note that in this model the currency administrator controls the root manager node and thus controls the privileges of all other nodes participating in the system. It can thus ensure that the A nodes perform identity proofing of U nodes (if desired). This can enable law enforcement, at least with a court order, to identify individuals within the system. This goes counter to the trend in cryptocurrencies where privacy and non-traceability are key objectives. An example node hierarchy tree with role assignments is shown in Figure 1.

There are three types of transactions that enable accounts with roles to perform their functions: coin transfer mode, role change mode, and policy change mode. A large portion of [1] specifies how to modify the nValue field in Bitcoin (which normally specifies the amount of coin to transfer) to enable the role and policy change functionality while still enabling coin transfer (but now only between accounts with the U role).

Lastly, there are two possible security models. There is an independent mining model where the miners are truly independent from the currency administrator, but they could then as a group deny the inclusion of management transactions (i.e., role changes and policy changes). This would be similar to a 51 % attack [7] being launched against Bitcoin. To prevent this there is also a dependent mining model where the miners must include a certain number of management transactions every so many blocks. This can prevent a large group of miners from being able to revolt and exclude management transactions as with the independent mining model. However, it shifts the balance of power slightly towards the currency administrator by allowing them to convey a small financial advantage to preferred miners. This risk can be arbitrarily diminished through making certain permanent policy settings.

The theoretical architecture defined in [1] proposed modifying Bitcoin for its implementation. The original Bitcoin whitepaper is available at [2] while detailed explanations can be found in [3], [4], and [5]. Of import to this work is that Bitcoin transfers coins using transactions. The coins are not stored in user accounts but are linked to the transactions themselves. Thus, each transaction has one or more inputs (Vin fields) that bring unspent coins into the transaction and one or more outputs (Vout fields) that declare who can next spend those coin outputs. As shown in Figure 2, a Vin field from some transaction x brings in an unspent Vout field from some transaction y. Figure 3 shows the format of a Bitcoin transaction.

III. Discovered Vulnerabilities and Security Issues

We discovered vulnerabilities and security issues in the theoretical architecture that needed to be mitigated in order to implement the prototype system. The vulnerabilities enabled violations of the balance of power, replay attacks, and attacks against miners. The security issues included improper scoping of manager and law enforcement powers as well as insecure bootstrapping for establishing cryptocurrency policy.

A. Preserving the Balance of Power

The research in [1] contains a 'dependent mining model' where the manager can specify that x number of management transactions must be included within each interval of y blocks. One can set x and y through issuing policy transactions. The idea is that this model forces the miners to periodically include management transactions.

However, we have discovered a vulnerability in which the manager can use this feature to take over the blockchain. The manager can initially set y to be high and wait for the community to fully adopt and use the cryptocurrency. Once a significant amount of value has been invested in the cryptocurrency, the manager can issue a policy transaction changing y to be very low. The manager then could, for example, require management transactions to be issued with every block and only send those management transactions to miners whom they favor or control. The miners receiving those transactions would then not propagate them to other miners, preventing the other miners from mining any blocks (since per policy all blocks would have to contain a management transaction). This way, only miners that the manager favored or controlled could publish blocks and the manager could effectively take over the blockchain with effects similar to that of a 51 % attack [8].

Our mitigation is to simply limit how tightly a manager can set y. If the specification and developed code reject policy transactions that set y values below some threshold, then the manager is prevented from using this method to take control of the blockchain. The manager could also voluntarily set a minimum threshold for these values using permanent policy transactions issued by the root manager node in order to create public confidence in the cryptocurrency. Even with minimums set, it should be noted that the manager can still implement this attack periodically, favoring their own miners every y blocks if they refuse to issue management transactions in the intervening blocks. This would give a periodic financial advantage to manager favored miners but would be highly visible to the community and would not result in the manager controlling the blockchain. To minimize the impact of this residual attack possibility, y should be required to be high enough to make the financial advantage minuscule. An alternative is to use the independent mining model discussed in II, but this opens up the possibility for the miners to revolt against the manager.

B. Preventing Replay Attacks

The research in [1] modifies the Bitcoin transactions to support roles because the architecture requires that all transactions include roles. They are brought into the transaction using a modified Vin field; in Bitcoin Vin fields are only used to bring coin into a transaction. Both uses of the Vin field use the same cryptographic protections and one would assume that they would inherit the same security properties. However, this is not the case and it results in a vulnerability in the architecture.

Since roles are spent like coins but never get used up (since you don't lose a role through using it), they can be spent an infinite number of times. This means that transactions that use a role might be able to be replayed. For the typical transactions also transferring coin (e.g., to pay a transaction fee), this is not a problem as the replayed transaction will be rejected because the coin would already have been spent. However, if the transaction does not involve coin it could be replayed. This might happen if the manager owns miners servers and issues management transactions without transaction fees with the intention that their miners will publish them. In this case, there would be no barriers to performing a replay attack. This might result in a situation where law enforcement unlocks an account but can never securely lock it again because the original unlocking transaction can be replayed by anyone.

There are several possible solutions. One approach is to require that all transactions pay some transaction fee while requiring transaction signatures to sign the entire transaction. In our attempt to modify Bitcoin as little as possible, our approach was to change the theoretical model to truly spend roles as if they were coin; once spent they can't be spent again. However, whenever we spend a role by including it in a Vin field we also re-create the same role in one of the Vout

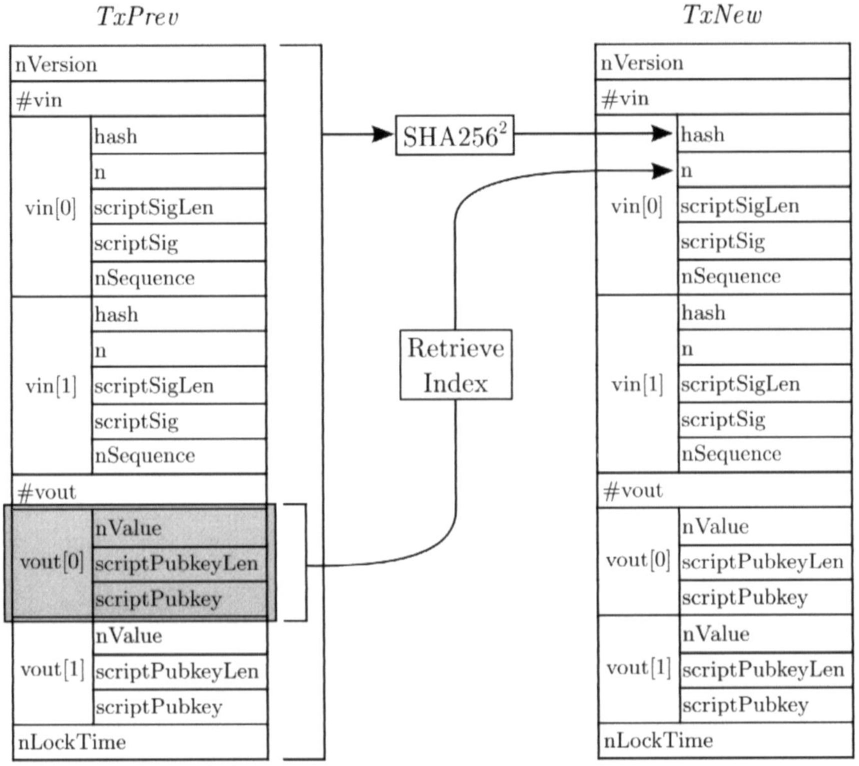

Fig. 2. Bitcoin Vin[] Field Reference to a Previous Transaction (copied from [5]).

Field name		**Type (Size)**	**Description**
nVersion		int (4 bytes)	Transaction format version (currently 1).
#vin		VarInt (1-9 bytes)	Number of transaction input entries in *vin*.
vin[]	hash	uint256 (32 bytes)	Double-SHA256 hash of a past transaction.
	n	uint (4 bytes)	Index of a transaction output within the transaction specified by *hash*.
	scriptSigLen	VarInt (1-9 bytes)	Length of *scriptSig* field in bytes.
	scriptSig	CScript (Variable)	Script to satisfy spending condition of the transaction output (*hash*,n).
	nSequence	uint (4 bytes)	Transaction input sequence number.
#vout		VarInt (1-9 bytes)	Number of transaction output entries in *vout*.
vout[]	nValue	int64_t (8 bytes)	Amount of 10^{-8} BTC.
	scriptPubkeyLen	VarInt (1-9 bytes)	Length of *scriptPubkey* field in bytes.
	scriptPubkey	CScript (Variable)	Script specifying conditions under which the transaction output can be claimed.
nLockTime		unsigned int (4 bytes)	Timestamp past which transactions can be replaced before inclusion in block.

Fig. 3. Bitcoin Transaction Format for Sending Bitcoin (BTC), copied from [5].

fields. The effect is that an account keeps a role when it is spent but the transaction containing the active version of their role can change. Probably the most elegant approach would be to implement the architecture using a cryptocurrency with an accounts based model so that roles are not stored within transactions, but instead within a record associated with each account (discussed more below).

C. Preventing Managers from Attacking Miners

In [1] all accounts must have the U role for them to receive or spend coin. The purpose is to force all participants in the cryptocurrency to be identity proofed by an account manager in order to receive the U role. This in turn supports 'know your customer' laws, which have been a challenge for most cryptocurrencies [9]. However, this also creates a vulnerability. The manager could keep track of the accounts receiving block rewards and remove the U role from those accounts (thus freezing the funds). The public miners would then have no financial incentive to mine and then the manager's own mining servers could take over the majority of mining. This would give the manager the ability to launch a 51 % attack [8] and to a large degree control the blockchain.

Our solution is to enable miners to deposit block rewards into any account, regardless of whether or not it has been registered in the system or has any roles. Also, we handle the coin from these coinbase transactions (the mining reward transactions) specially such that it can be sent without the owning account needing the U role. This prevents the currency administrator from freezing the mining reward coinbase funds. However, once coinbase coin is sent away from the original account it becomes normal coin subject to the normal requirements (it can't be spent without the associated account having the U role).

D. Scoping Law Enforcement Powers

In [1] law enforcement powers are both too limited and too relaxed. They are too limited in that law enforcement can only lock accounts through removing the U label. Law enforcement nodes can't prevent an account using its other roles (M, C, A, or L). This is a major issue in the event that an account is stolen. On the other hand, law enforcement powers are too relaxed in that law enforcement nodes can effect any node higher in the account hierarchy tree regardless of whether or not it is on the same branch. This effectively gives law enforcement nodes a global reach (which is especially problematic if a law enforcement node is compromised).

Our solution is to reflect account locking not through the removal of the U role but by setting a locked flag. We use one of the unused bits in the nValue field for role change mode to set this flag. If the flag is set it temporarily disables all roles, not just the U role. This stops all activity by the targeted account, giving law enforcement the powers it needs to freeze stolen accounts. At the same time, we put additional restrictions on law enforcement nodes by only giving them authority over nodes farther from the root on the same branch of the node hierarchy tree. More precisely, we define the scope of control of a law enforcement node by traversing backwards until the first node is found with the manager role and then by performing a breadth first search to reveal all nodes within scope. This enables law enforcement nodes to 'hang' off of manager nodes in the tree (they don't have to be inline on each branch).

E. Management Node Powers

In [1] management nodes also had powers that were too relaxed. They were required to have any role that they would want to grant. This resulted in management nodes having powers that they had no intention of using. Also, their scope of control was the same as law enforcement giving each M node low down in the hierarchy tree an almost global reach.

Our solution was to limit their scope to nodes reachable by breadth first search and to limit management nodes to only having the M role. However, in our approach management nodes can add any role to other nodes. This gives more power to a manager node (which might be seen as decreasing security) but it limits that power to a more narrow scope creating what we believe is a rational compromise.

F. Policy Bootstrapping

In [1], it is not stated how the initial policy is defined for an instantiated cryptocurrency. It is implied that some configuration file, apart from the blockchain, must exist that provides the original parameter settings. These settings may or may not then be subsequently overridden through policy transactions on the blockchain. The result may be that some policy is defined on the blockchain and some through an original configuration file. Given that the configuration file wouldn't have the same cryptographic protections as blockchain transactions, the distributor of the node software for maintaining the blockchain could conceivably change policy using software updates through modifying the configuration file.

Our solution is to eliminate the need for the unsecured initial configuration file. We do this by specifying that all policy is initially defined as permissive as possible. We then require that all policy parameters be defined explicitly on the blockchain within the first x blocks (as defined in the full node software distribution). Thus early in the blockchain, ideally prior to it being released publicly, the manager will have to explicitly record all possible policy parameters within cryptographically secured blocks.

We also discovered that the original root management node should not be used to set the initial policy (except for policy settings intended to be permanent). This is because, per [1], management nodes closer to the root are more authoritative; any root manager node policy decisions will prevent any other management node from changing that policy. Also, the root management node account ideally should never be used after the initial few blocks and its keys should be physically stored in a vault to eliminate the possibility of it being compromised. Thus, if the root node is used to set policy it should only be used to set permanent policy that, by design, will never be changed.

IV. Architectural Challenges

Apart from mitigating vulnerabilities in the original design, we encountered several architectural challenges where it was not practical or even possible to directly implement the theoretical architecture. In this section we describe the primary challenges, how we modified the theoretical design to overcome them, and how we implemented those changes.

A. Dual Signature Requirements for Coin Transfer Transactions

In [1] an account must have the U role to both spend and receive coin. It specifies that these roles must be brought into each coin transfer transaction using two separate Vin fields. However, this requires both the sender and receiver to sign the transaction which would require off blockchain coordination and some unspecified infrastructure to support this.

This could be resolved by including the coin transfer recipient only in the Vout field (not the Vin) and requiring full nodes to check the U role on the account listed in the Vout field (without explicitly bringing it into the transaction using a Vin field), at the cost of additional tracking overhead. Our mitigation was to only require the U role for spending coin. Any account then can receive coin, but may not be able to spend it. This results in only a single account needing to sign coin transfer transactions and eliminates additional overhead.

B. Node Movement

In [1] there is no mention of how accounts can change position within the node hierarchy graph once they have been created. This is necessary, for example, for users that want to use different account managers. Besides moving nodes, edges in the graph may need to be moved in order to cut out compromised nodes but leave the rest of the node hierarchy intact.

To implement the needed functionality, we created the idea that if a node adds roles to an account that has no roles, this creates an edge in the node hierarchy graph from the node adding the roles to the node representing the account gaining the roles. If an edge already existed to the node gaining the roles (which would happen if an account received roles and then deleted them), the prior edge will be deleted in order to preserve the required tree structure.

To prepare a node to be moved, the relevant account can unilaterally remove its own roles or else a manager whose scope covers the node can remove the roles. Using this paradigm, nodes can be moved around the node hierarchy tree. It also doesn't require explicitly coding edge creation and deletion within the modified Bitcoin protocol, which would have been unnecessarily complicated. A drawback is that node movement requires a two step process: one transaction to remove roles and another to add them back in (thus removing the old edge and creating the new edge). In our future work we will design a format where a single transaction does this atomically. Complicating this may be the need for dually signed transactions to prevent security violations (which we are trying to avoid, see section IV-A). Our current two step approach ensures that the role removal, node movement, and edge addition only happens through transactions issued by nodes authorized to perform those activities.

C. Determining Transaction Types

The theoretical architecture in [1] uses the most significant bits of an nValue field to determine the type of transaction being processed: role change, policy change, or coin transfer. The nValue fields, in the original Bitcoin, specify the amount of coin to be spent. Using the leftmost bits as control bits is conceivably risky because a bug in the code might interpret the leftmost control bits as value bits for moving or create large amounts of coin. More problematic though is that the Bitcoin implementation uses the leftmost bit of the nValue field as a signed bit.

For these reasons, we chose to deviate from [1] and not use the leftmost bits of the nValue field to determine the type of transaction. Instead, we determined the type of transaction using the transaction version number; this then determines how the nValue fields within a transaction are handled. We created three transaction version numbers, each of which correspond to the three different modes for evaluating nValue fields (role change, policy change, and coin transfer). Lastly, we also changed to using the nValue low order bits for specifying roles and policy change types in case those nValue fields ever got interpreted as coin transfer fields through some bug or attack. This would then limit the damage done by having fewer coin inadvertently transferred or created.

D. Transaction Fees

Since we determine transaction type (role change, policy change, or coin transfer) through the transaction version number, it means that the mode of all the nValue fields in the Vout fields are determined by that number. However, it is usually necessary to pay a transaction fee for most transactions and there is usually change that must be sent back to the sender. This is not possible then for the role and policy change transactions because the nValue fields of the Vout fields change roles/policies; they don't send coin as in the original Bitcoin specification. We solved this simply by specifying which Vout field is always the change sent back to the originator of the transaction (which may be 0 coin on occasion).

V. Developed Prototype

Our prototype was developed publicly through Github and is available within the project 'usnistgov/managed-cryptocurrencies-bitcoin'. We built our prototype through forking and modifying the C++ Bitcoin codebase available on Github at 'bitcoin/bitcoin'.

For flexibility, efficiency, and portability we ran our modified bitcoin peer-to-peer network for development and testing on a local virtualized environment. For our testing, we thus had a single virtual machine (VM) executing the entire distributed Bitcoin network. We used the Vagrant virtual machine manager with Virtualbox as the VM provider. Within the VM, we used the Docker Engine to run a set of containers to represent the nodes on the modified Bitcoin network. This enabled us to simultaneously run five Bitcoin miners within a single VM to maintain our test blockchain. Note that we artificially reduced the mining difficulty to enable quick block production for testing and demonstration purposes. Lastly, we used the GraphViz library to enable us to visualize the node hierarchy tree. To make access control decisions for role and policy change transactions, it was inefficient to look up individual node roles using the tree. Thus, we separately maintained an associative array mapping node names to a list of their roles. The tree was only necessary for determining the scope of control of one node over others (e.g., for the law enforcement and manager nodes).

An example output tree is shown in Figure 4. Within each node in parenthesis is listed the roles activated for that node and its state (locked or unlocked). The labels are deciphered as follows: M-manager, C-central banker, L-law enforcement, U-registered user, A-account manager, D-disabled account) Node 0 is the root node created in the genesis block. It should normally never be used directly for security reasons and so Node 1 was created as the 'active' manager. Node 3 is the central banker; it could have hung off of Node 1 but it was useful for our example to have it as a child under Node 0. Node 2 is law enforcement with the scope of all that is reachable from Node 1 (all nodes except 0, 3, and 11). Nodes 4 and 5 are account managers. Node 6 is a user account that has been disabled by law enforcement. Nodes 7, 8, and 10 are ordinary users. Node 9 is a node who has had all its roles removed (either done by Node 9 itself, its account manager Node 5, or one of the manager nodes 0 or 1). This might have been done because Node 9 was compromised or because it is being prepared to move to another part of the tree under a different account manager. Node 11 is a node that has been active in the cryptocurrency but has no roles and has never had any roles (due to their being no edge to it). It represents an account created by a miner to store coinbase coins, that can be spent without needing any roles.

VI. Related Work

To our knowledge, [1] is the only work proposing a managed cryptocurrency that has a balance of power where the public can hold the manager accountable. There have been many government cryptocurrencies proposed but these differ in that they are often not managed, don't use roles, or don't have a balance of power.

Multichain [10] is a system that might appear to be similar in that it contains management features. However, Multichain enables a permissioned chain where what is managed is which entities have the privilege of mining. This is opposite of our prototype that enables open mining. That said, we may explore modifying Multichain to implement [1] while leveraging a permissioned chain whose membership is defined by the current members (not the manager).

There are many government cryptocurrencies proposed and in development (for example [11], more citations are in [1]). However, none of these have yet come to fruition except the Venezuelan Petro [12], which to our knowledge is the only existing government issued cryptocurrency.

There is research proposing a Fedcoin [13], a cryptocurrency that would support central banks with a permissioned blockchain that complies with 'know your customer' laws [9]. It is based on RS—Coin [14], one of many cryptocurrencies advertised to support central and commercial banks with international transaction handling. Others argue that central banks don't need a cryptocurrency, but instead a new form of electronic money [15]. There are also concerns with the amount of power a government could leverage through creating a Fedcoin [16].

VII. Future Work

There are two major changes to be made in future iterations of the implementation: using an account model and better handling of compromised nodes.

A. Using an Account Model

Bitcoin uses an unspent transaction output (UTXO) model. Coin is not stored within user accounts but within the transactions themselves. All transactions have outputs (representing coin) and any unspent output may be spent by another transaction. Who may spend a given output is determined by a script that usually specifies the public key of a particular account. There is no single data structure on the blockchain that shows the coin associated with a particular account.

This works well for Bitcoin, but immediately became awkward for the implementation of our managed cryptocurrency prototype. In the theoretical architecture, accounts have roles that specify their privileges in the system and these roles are specified in nValue fields. Without a central data structure for each account, the roles had to be treated like coin and be spent repeatedly as an account used those roles. In our system, an account's roles are transaction outputs and the active copy (the one that hasn't yet been spent) is temporarily in one particular transaction. We simplified this, compared to the theoretical architecture, by requiring that any role additions and removals repeat the remaining roles. Thus, all of an account's roles are always designated within a single transaction, not spread out among many transactions as would have occurred through a direct implementation of the theoretical architecture.

Our future approach will be to implement the system through forking cryptocurrency code that uses an account model instead of an UTXO model. This is possible because the theoretical architecture is not tied to any particular cryptocurrency. A likely candidate replacement cryptocurrency would be Ethereum due to its maturity, but this choice would bring in the added complexity of a codebase that supports smart contracts. A mature Bitcoin-like cryptocurrency without smart contract capabilities that uses an account model might be better suited.

B. Handling Compromised Nodes

In section III-D we expand the law enforcement powers to disable all the roles of an account to handle the case where

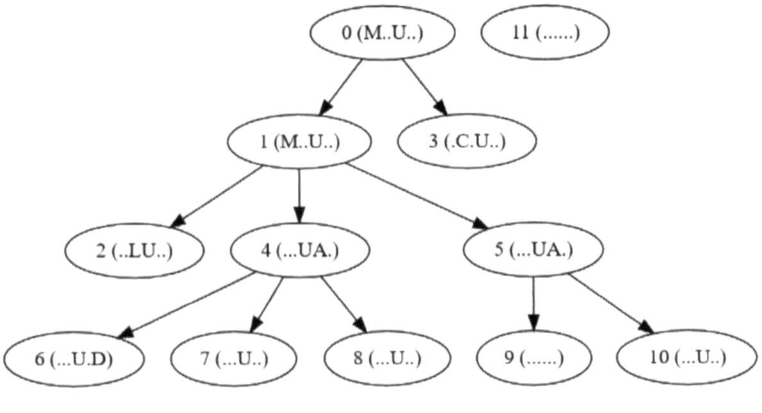

Fig. 4. Example Output Showing a Node Hierarchy.

a node is compromised (in [1] only the ability to send and receive coin was disabled). However, this does not allow the compromised node to be recovered. To do this, we propose that all nodes should have two sets of cryptographic key pairs. The first set is used for the daily signing of transactions for the associated account. The second set is stored offline and is used only to replace the first set. This enables account owners to unilaterally re-establish control over their accounts without having to involve a manager node (one with the M or A role). However, it will require the development and implementation of a new transaction type to enable this resetting of the first key pair.

VIII. Conclusion

The theoretical managed cryptocurrency architecture proposed in [1] can be efficiently developed from an existing cryptocurrency codebase and deployed (despite the many implementation issues that had to be overcome). An important result of this is that we have shown that the novel balance of power concept, whereby a manager and public miners jointly control a cryptocurrency, is a feasible mechanism to be explored for future cryptocurrencies. Another result of our work is to show the practicability of adding roles to cryptocurrency accounts and the capabilities that can be achieved through these roles (in particular for mimicking fiat currency mechanisms). Lastly, we note that building such a protocol native managed cryptocurrency within a blockchain platform itself was non-trivial but we showed that it could be accomplished with only a modest cost in programming effort.

In summary, we have shown that the theoretical system in [1] can be implemented in such a way as to not just leverage many of the strengths of modern cryptocurrencies, but also leverage the capabilities of traditional fiat currencies. While this goes against the goals and directions of most cryptocurrency efforts which are promoting greater privacy and autonomy from managing institutions, this result may be useful for large institutions (e.g., governments) investigating future electronic currency approaches. We do not necessarily believe that the architecture in [1] provides the answer for such a use case, but it and our applied research in this work may open up new research directions to better support large institutions issuing their own managed cryptocurrencies.

References

[1] P. Mell, "Managed blockchain based cryptocurrencies with consensus enforced rules and transparency," in *2018 17th IEEE International Conference On Trust, Security And Privacy In Computing And Communications/12th IEEE International Conference On Big Data Science And Engineering (TrustCom/BigDataSE)*. IEEE, 2018, pp. 1287–1296.

[2] S. Nakamoto, "Bitcoin: A peer-to-peer electronic cash system," 2008. [Online]. Available: https://bitcoin.org/bitcoin.pdf

[3] J. Bonneau, A. Miller, J. Clark, A. Narayanan, J. A. Kroll, and E. W. Felten, "Sok: Research perspectives and challenges for bitcoin and cryptocurrencies," in *Security and Privacy (SP), 2015 IEEE Symposium on*. IEEE, 2015, pp. 104–121.

[4] A. Narayanan, J. Bonneau, E. Felten, A. Miller, and S. Goldfeder, *Bitcoin and Cryptocurrency Technologies: A Comprehensive Introduction*. Princeton University Press, 2016.

[5] K. Okupski, "Bitcoin developer reference," 2016. [Online]. Available: https://lopp.net/pdf/Bitcoin_Developer_Reference.pdf

[6] "bitcoinwiki protocol documentation," accessed: 2017-12-29. [Online]. Available: https://en.bitcoin.it/wiki/Protocol_documentation

[7] J. Yli-Huumo, D. Ko, S. Choi, S. Park, and K. Smolander, "Where is current research on blockchain technology? a systematic review," *PloS one*, vol. 11, no. 10, p. e0163477, 2016.

[8] S. Barber, X. Boyen, E. Shi, and E. Uzun, "Bitter to betterhow to make bitcoin a better currency," in *International Conference on Financial Cryptography and Data Security*. Springer, 2012, pp. 399–414.

[9] M. Staples, S. Chen, S. Falamaki, A. Ponomarev, P. Rimba, A. Tran, I. Weber, X. Xu, and J. Zhu, "Risks and opportunities for systems using blockchain and smart contracts," 2017. [Online]. Available: https://publications.csiro.au/rpr/download?pid=csiro:EP175103dsid=DS2

[10] G. Greenspan, "Multichain private blockchainwhite paper," 2015. [Online]. Available: https://www.multichain.com/download/MultiChain-White-Paper.pdf

[11] L. Coleman. An inside look at chinas government controlled cryptocurrency project. [Online]. Available: https://www.ccn.com/an-inside-look-at-chinas-government-controlled-cryptocurrency-project

[12] D. B. Alexandra Ulmer, "Enter the 'petro': Venezuela to launch oil-backed cryptocurrency," Reuters, Dec. 2017.

[13] S. Gupta, P. Lauppe, and S. Ravishankar, "A blockchain-backed central bank cryptocurrency," 2017. [Online]. Available: https://zoo.cs.yale.edu/classes/cs490/16-17b/gupta.sahil.sg687

[14] G. Danezis and S. Meiklejohn, "Centrally banked cryptocurrencies," *arXiv preprint arXiv:1505.06895*, 2015.

[15] A. Berentsen and F. Schar, "The case for central bank electronic money and the non-case for central bank cryptocurrencies," 2018. [Online]. Available: https://doi.org/10.20955/r.2018.97-106

[16] T. Aube. The terrifying future of fedcoin. [Online]. Available: https://hackernoon.com/the-terrifying-future-of-fedcoin-ddcbef2b9592

A Joint Encryption-Compression Technique for Images Based on Beta Chaotic Maps and SPIHT Coding

Najet Elkhalil *, Rim Zahmoul†, Ridha Ejbali‡, and Mourad Zaied§
* †‡§ Research Team in Intelligent Machines, National Engineering School of Gabes,
6072 Gabes, Tunisia
Email: najet.elkhalil@ieee.org rima.zahmoul@gmail.com ridha_ejbali@ieee.org mourad.zaied@ieee.org

Abstract—**In this paper, we propose a new joint compression-encryption system based on Discrete Wavelet Technique (DWT) and Set Partitioning in Hierarchical Trees (SPIHT) coding for the compression part, and the chaotic standard system (Beta Chaotic Map) for the encryption process. Through the experimental results, the system proposed in this paper has an excellent statistical and cryptographic properties: it resists against common cryptanalytic attacks and provides high picture quality of the reconstructed image.**

Keywords–joint compression-encryption; SPIHT coding; Chaotic systems; Beta Chaotic Map.

I. INTRODUCTION

Recently, information storage and security have received a lot of attention. In image processing, for proving security to an image, several cryptography techniques are proposed. However, most of the Encryption techniques mask some quantity of knowledge to the source image that invariably will increase the dimensions of images, therefore, its storage and transmission time, and from that comes the necessity of data compression.

In literature, researchers try to propose new methods that guarantee the strength of the encryption process and preserve the quality of the compressed image. Arunkumar and Prabu [1] proposed a combination of the Rivest-Shamir-Adleman (RSA) encryption method and the lossless compression technique using SPIHT coding. This combination allows partial data access on the part of the decoder so it produces a better efficiency and less computational complexities. Ou et al. [2] developed an Image Compression Encryption Scheme using DWT, orthogonal wavelet family type Haar and Significance-Linked Connected Component Analysis encoder. For the encryption process, the AAdvanced Enceyption Standard (AES) method is used. The test results show that the reconstructed image has a high quality, and the method used for the encryption is efficient. Xiang et al. [3] proposed a Joint compression and selective encryption based on SPIHT (JCSE-SPIHT). The basic idea of the proposed approach is embedding encryption into SPIHT algorithm. The simulation results show that the proposed method has a high immunity against inherent attacks. To overcome the security issues in some previous works, we have proposed a novel joint Encryption-Compression algorithm.

This paper is organized as follows: Section 2 presented previous related works. In Section 3 DWT and SPIHT coding are described in detail. In Section 4 Beta chaotic map and the encryption process were detailed. Performance and security analysis are given in section 5. Finally, a brief conclusion is drawn in Section 6.

II. RELATED WORKS

In order to achieve better security level, chaos theory was frequently used in image cryptography combined with different compression algorithms. In what follows, some of those works were reviewed. Hamdi et al. [4] proposed a new selective encryption-compression scheme based on SPHIT coding and Chiricov Standard Maps. This scheme aims to integrate the encryption part into the compression one, so simultaneously they obtain an encrypted-compressed image. The approach was divided into three steps: The first step was generating three keys for the encryption process using the Chirikov Standard Map algorithm. The next step was to perform a DWT transformation. The third step is permutation after SPIHT coding. The Simulation results obtained in this approach are 99.91% the NPCR average and 33.51% UACI average. Gupta and Silakari [5] presented a chaos-based compression and encryption scheme using a cascading 3D cat map and standard map. The image is first compressed using curvelet transformation and then encrypted using the chaos 3D cat map. The simulation results show that the PSNR values are over 30dB, the NPCR average is over 99% and the UACI average is below 33%. Goel et al. [6] proposed a compression technique using Discrete Cosine Transform (DCT) and Huffman coding and symmetric cryptosystem technique using the Logistic Map. The experimental results of the proposed method. Also, the method has a high sensitivity key.

All this researches used chaotic maps and several compression techniques. We adopt this approach to create our new algorithm for joint image encryption-compression technique. Our scheme allows to improve image compression quality and security against different attacks.

III. COMPRESSION PART

To achieve better compression result, we combined the DWT and the SPIHT coding algorithm.

A. Discrete Wavelet Transform

The wavelet-based compression technique was created to beat the disadvantages of the discrete cosine transform [7]. The uses of DWT have become very popular within the image and video compression and it is a replacement standard for JPEG 2000 images compression [8][9]. The DWT transforms the plain text images into frequency bands, known as sub-bands LL, HL, LH and HH using filters. For one level decomposition, the DWT represents the image in the form of four sub-bands of lower resolution, one represents the approximation image and the three others show the details of the image with horizontal, vertical, and diagonal orientations as shown in the first part in

Figure 1, the other parts in the Figure show examples of other level decomposition.

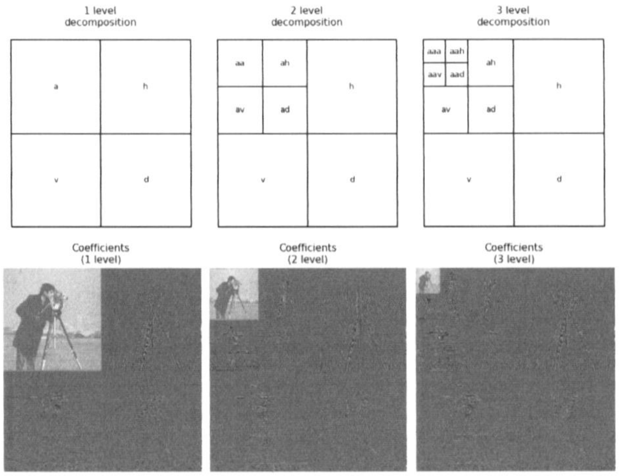

Figure 1. Wavelet Level Decomposition.

B. SPIHT Coding

Once the wavelet transform decomposition is done, several quantization algorithms are used. We decide to work with SPIHT coding because it is an efficient and computationally very fast technique for image compression [10]. The result of the SPIHT coding is an embedded bitstream from which the most effective images are reconstructed. The algorithm of SPIHT coding is defined by steps throughout every state is outlined by a bit-plane that contains an indication of wavelet coefficients that are quantified by the structure in a hierarchical tree. Every coefficient in all spatial orientation tree are then increasingly coded from the Most Significant Bit-plane (MSB) to the Least Significant Bit-plane (LSB), beginning with the coefficients possessing the highest magnitudes within the lowest pyramid levels [11][12]. In every bit-plane SPIHT coding computes a threshold Tp and assign it to one or more of the tree lists bellow:

- List of insignificant pixels (LIP): It contains all the coefficients that have a smaller magnitude than Tp(thresholds).
- List of significant pixels (LSP): It is a list of coefficients of pixels that have a grater magnitude than the Tp.
- List of insignificant sets(LIS): It contains groups (set) of coefficients that are defined by tree structures and they have magnitudes greater than Tp.

The steps of SPIHT coding are mentioned below:

1) Step 1: Initialization
First of all, initialize the threshold Tp and order coefficients in LL sub-band to LIP, all the trees are moved to LIS and the LSP is empty.
2) Step 2: Sorting Pass
This step aims to encode the important coefficient of the current bit. There are two main steps:
    a) Step1: verify the contained coefficients in List of significant pixels to check if they are significant coefficients:
        - If they are important, then output 1 and the sign bit of the wavelet coefficients are represented by 1 and 0 (positive or negative), and then remove the wavelet coefficient from LIP and add to the LSP.
        - If they are not important we do not need to remove them from the LIP and the output then will be"0".
    b) Step 2: Verify all the important set in the LIS.
3) Step 3: Refinement Pass
The aim is output but not the improving position of important factor that was generated in the process of scanning. For all coefficient (i,j) in LSP, if (i,j) is not added in the scanning step, then $|i,j|$of the coefficient will be transmitted.
4) Step 4: Update the threshold
Updating the threshold by decrements n by 1 and (back to step 2). Variable n defines the maximum number of bits needed to represent the largest coefficient in the spatial orientation tree : $n = |log_2 cmax|$,$cmax$ is the higher value of coefficient.

IV. Encryption Part

In this section, we will detail the chaotic encryption and clarify the steps of the Beta chaotic encryption.

A. Chaotic Encryption

We called Chaotic maps all nonlinear maps that display chaotic behavior, they generate pseudo-random sequences, which are used during the encryption process [13]. Many fundamental concepts in chaos theory, such as mixing and sensitivity to initial conditions and parameters are the same in cryptography. The only difference is that encryption operations are defined on limited sets of integers while chaos is defined on real numbers.

B. Beta Chaotic Encryption

In the recent years, chaotic maps have been used in different ways in cryptography, they have attracted the attention of many researchers and have been widely used in diverse applications [14][15], especially those related to security, in which they have shown excellent performance. The Chaotic system proposed, in the design of our new image compression-encryption algorithm, is based on the Beta Chaotic Map. The Beta Chaotic Maps discovered by professor Mourad Zaied, are inspired from the Beta function it is polynomial mapping and it reflects an example of how complex, chaotic behavior can appear from a simple non-linear dynamical equation [16]-[20]. It is chosen for its efficiency in front of different attacks and it is very suitable with the chosen image compression technique. The steps below describe the encryption process of our scheme:

- Step 1: Resizing the image
In this step, we resize the chosen image into square dimension.
- Step 2: Generating the chaotic sequences

After making many combinations of Beta chaotic maps, generate two completely different pseudo-random sequences, the sensitivity of the beta chaotic maps to the simple variation of the initial condition gives us the possibility to generate several random sequences.

- Step 3: Permutation stage
  In this step, we shuffle the plaintext images rows and columns using the Beta random sequences (Q1 and Q2) generated in the previous step.
- Step 4: Substitution stage
  At this point, dividing the resulting matrix into four blocks of equal size. After that, translating each one to a random matrix W where each matrix will be transformed using the functions (1) (2) (3) (4)given below:

$$f_N(d) = T(d) mod G \quad (1)$$

$$f_R(d) = T \left\lfloor (\sqrt{d}) \right\rfloor mod G \quad (2)$$

$$f_S(d) = T(d^2) mod G \quad (3)$$

$$f_D(d) = T(2d) mod G \quad (4)$$

And the matrix function is given bellow:

$$W = \begin{bmatrix} f_N(B_{1,1}) & f_R(B_{1,2}) & f_D(B_{1,3}) & f_S(B_{1,4}) \\ f_S(B_{2,1}) & f_D(B_{2,2}) & f_R(B_{2,3}) & f_N(B_{2,4}) \\ f_D(B_{3,1}) & f_N(B_{3,2}) & f_S(B_{3,3}) & f_R(B_{3,4}) \\ f_R(B_{4,1}) & f_S(B_{4,2}) & f_N(B_{4,3}) & f_D(B_{4,4}) \end{bmatrix} \quad (5)$$

Function T: is a truncation of a decimal to form an integer for every number of the resulting matrix W. G: is the image type, (G=256) and (G=2) for respectively 8-bit gray image and binary image. Here we got a new random integer matrix I. So, we can now determine the encrypted image C using the following equation:

$$C = (P + I) mod G$$

And the decrypted image P by:

$$P = (C - I) mod G$$

- Step 5: Diffusion stage

The main idea of the diffusion stage is to disappear the redundancy in the statics and the information containing in the original image in the encrypted one. It is done by changing each pixel in the original image over the finite field GF(2^8).

To resume, the steps of our encryption-compression algorithm are presented in the flowchart Figure 2:

V. Simulations Results And Comparisons

In this section, different tests are made to evaluate the simulation results: statistical tests: histogram analysis and security tests against a differential attack including calculus of the number of pixel change rate (NPCR) and the unified average changing intensity (UACI). Figures 3 and 4 represent the simulation experiment on Cameraman and Airplane image.

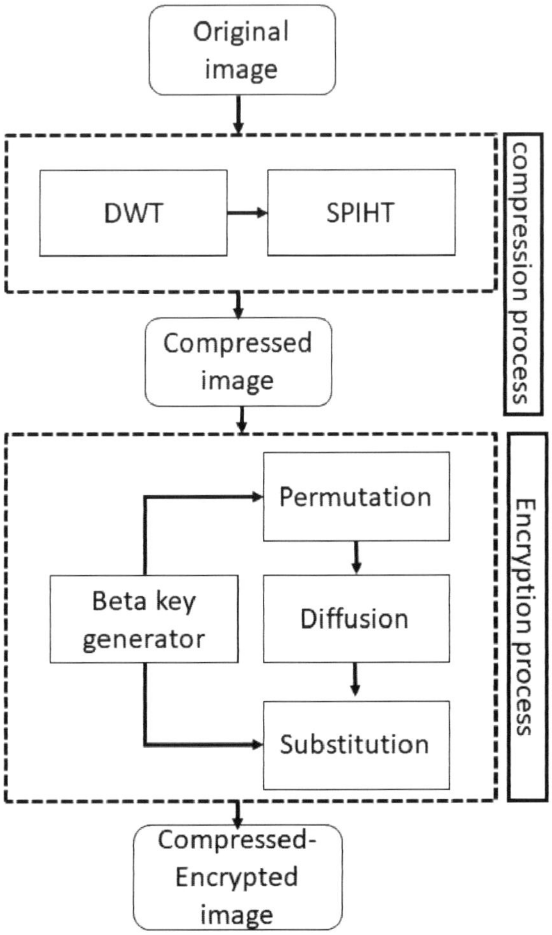

Figure 2. proposed scheme flowchart

Figure 3. Images of simulation experiment on Cameraman: Cameraman original image, Cameraman compressed-encrypted image, cameraman decrypted image.

Figure 4. Images of simulation experiment on Airplane: Airplane original image, Airplane compressed-encrypted image, Airplane decrypted image.

A. Histogram Analysis

To avoid the access of data from attackers, it is very important to make sure that the encrypted and the original images are totally different and do not have any statistical similarities. We analyzed the histograms of many cyphered images also as their original images as shown in Figures 5 and 6. The histograms are totally different. The histogram of the original image has massive spikes and its tilted. However, the histogram of the ciphered image is uniform, very flat, and bears no statistical resemblance to the plaintext image. Therefore, by comparison, the histograms of each encrypted-compressed and decrypted images, we tend to conclude that the encrypted images are random-like. Also, it does not give any chance to use any statistical attack on the proposed image encryption scheme.

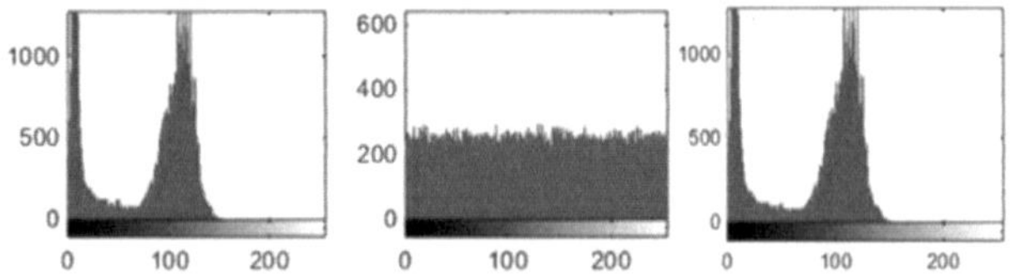

Figure 5. Histograms of experimental image Cameraman:Original image, Compressed-Encrypted image, The decrypted image.

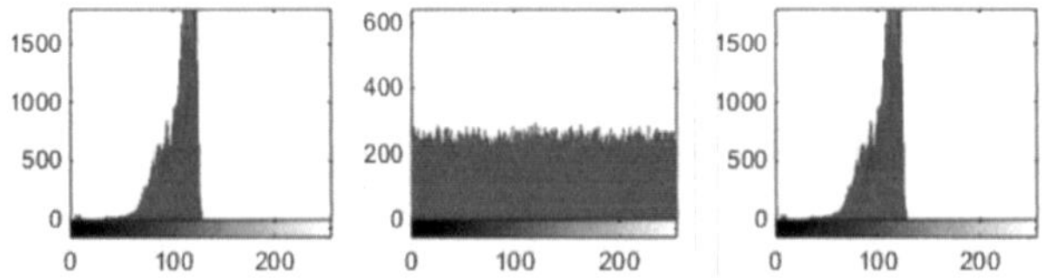

Figure 6. Histograms of experimental image Airplane: Original image, Compressed-Encrypted image, The decrypted image.

B. NPCR And UACI Tests

In order to test the fact of one-pixel change on the original and the encrypted image, two measures can be done: Number of Pixels Change Rate (NPCR) and Unified Average Changing Intensity (UACI). The NPCR measures the percentage of different pixel numbers between the plaintext image and the cipher image however the UACI measures the average intensity of differences between them [21]. We obtained NPCR and UACI for a large variety of images by using our proposed algorithm and other algorithms, their testing results are shown in Tables 1,2 and 3. Also, we compared the NPCR and UACI of the proposed scheme and also the schemes in [4][22] in Table 2 and 3.

C. Mean Square Error

Mean Square Error (MSE) is the cumulative squared error between the encrypted and the original image. It is one of the error metrics used to evaluate the efficiency of various image encryption techniques. It is defined by the equation below:

$$MSE = \frac{1}{MN}\sum_{y=1}^{M}\sum_{x=1}^{N}[I(x,y) - I'(x,y)]^2$$

Where I(x, y) is the original image pixel, I(x, y) is the encrypted image pixel and M and N are the size of the original or the encrypted one. Our experimental results are shown in Table 4. In case of image encryption, MSE should be as high as possible which means more immunity to attacks.

D. Peak Signal To Noise Ratio Analysis

PSNR (Peak Signal to Noise Ratio) of encrypted image and original image is computed as in Table 4. It is defined by:

$$PSNR = 10_{10}\left[\frac{R^2}{MSE}\right]$$

TABLE I. NPCR AND UACI OF ENCRYPTED IMAGES USING OUR SCHEME.

Image name	NPCR	UACI
Lena (512x512)	99.5666	33.3384
Lena(256x256)	99.6368	33.3886
House	99.5910	33.4736
Boat(522x512)	99.6322	33.3720
Barbara	99.6368	33.5151
Lake	99.6337	33.3384

TABLE II. THE UACI OF ENCRYPTED IMAGES FOR OUR APPROACH AND ALGORITHMS IN [4,22].

Image name	UACI (our approach)	Ref[4]	Ref[22]
Lena (512x512)	33.33	33.51	33.36
Lena(256x256)	33.38	33.69	-
House	33.47	33.96	-
Boat(522x512)	33.37	33.73	-
Barbara	33.51	33.49	-
Lake	33.33	33.49	-

TABLE III. THE NPCR OF ENCRYPTED IMAGES FOR OUR APPROACH AND ALGORITHMS IN [4,22].

Image name	NPCR (our approach)	Ref[4]	Ref[22]
Lena (512x512)	99.56	99.91	99.61
Lena(256x256)	99.63	99.88	-
House	99.59	98.99	-
Boat(522x512)	99.63	99.61	-
Barbara	99.63	99.36	-
Lake	99.63	99.02	-

TABLE IV. MSE AND PSNR OF ENCRYPTED IMAGES USING OUR SCHEME.

Image name	MSE	PSNR
Lena (512x512)	10610.07	7.87
Lena(256x256)	11870.38	7.39
House	6986.46	9.69
Boat(522x512)	7648.06	9.30
Barbara	9645.17	8.29
Lake	9190.15	8.50

The high value of MSE and the low value of PSNR cause the resulting encrypted image more randomness.

VI. CONCLUSION

In this paper, we have proposed a high level secure system of image joint compression-encryption based on SPIHT coding and Beta Chaotic Map. As regards to diverse evaluation metrics, some performance and security analysis has been performed on our scheme. The results of the differential analysis indicate that the proposed encryption-compression algorithm is highly sensitive to small changes in original images. Therefore, it is very resistive against the differential attacks.

ACKNOWLEDGMENT

The authors would like to acknowledge the financial support of this work by grants from General Direction of Scientific Research (DGRST), Tunisia, under the ARUB program.

REFERENCES

[1] M. Arunkumar and S. Prabu, "Implementation of Encrypted Image Compression using Resolution Progressive Compression Scheme," International Journal of Computer Science and Mobile Computing (IJCSMC), vol. 3, no. 6, pp. 585590, 2014.

[2] S.-C. Ou, H.-Y. Chung, and W.-T. Sung, "Improving the compression and encryption of images using FPGA-based cryptosystems," Multimedia Tools and Applications, vol. 28, no. 1, pp. 522, Jan. 2006.

[3] T. Xiang, J. Qu, and D. Xiao, "Joint SPIHT Compression and Selective Encryption," Applied Soft Computing, vol. 21, pp. 159170, Aug. 2014.

[4] M. Hamdi, R. Rhouma, and S. Belghith, "A Selective Compression Encryption of Images Based on SPIHT Coding and Chirikov Standard Map," Signal Processing, vol. 131, pp. 514526, Feb. 2017.

[5] K. Gupta and S. Silakari, "Novel Approach for Fast Compressed Hybrid Color Image Cryptosystem," Advances in Engineering Software, vol. 49, no. 1, pp. 2942, Jul. 2012.

[6] N. Goel, B. Raman, and I. Gupta, "Chaos Based Joint Compression and Encryption Framework for End-to-End Communication Systems," Advances in Multimedia, vol. 2014, pp. 110, 2014.

[7] Z. Xiong, K. Ramchandran, M.T. Ochad, and Ya-Qin Zhang, "A Comparative Study of DC And Wavelet-Based Image Coding," IEEE Transactions on Circuits and System for Video Technology, vol. 9, no. 5, 1999.

[8] S. Grgic, K. Kers and M. Grgic, "Image Compression Using Wavelet," IEEE Transactions, ISIE99-Bled, Slovenia.

[9] M. Zaied, S. Said, O. Jemai, and C. Ben Amar, "A novel approach for face recognition based on fast learning algorithm and wavelet network theory," International Journal of Wavelets Multiresolution and Information Processing, 2011.

[10] E. Christophe, C. Mailhes, and P. Duhamel, "Hyperspectral image compression: adapting SPIHT and EZW to anisotropic 3-D wavelet coding," Image Processing: IEEE Transactions on, vol. 17, no. 12, pp. 2334-2346, 2008.

[11] A. Said and W.A. Pearlman, "A new, fast, and efficient image codec based on set partitioning in hierarchical trees, Circuits and Systems for Video Technology," IEEE Transactions on, vol. 6, no. 3, pp. 243-250, 1996.

[12] AG. Kadam and N. Pingle, "overview of spiht based image compression algorithm,": ijesrt,international journal of engineering sciences research technology, February, 2018.

[13] Y. Wang, et al., "A colour image encryption,algorithm using 4-pixel Feistel structure and multiple chaotic systems," Nonlinear Dynamics. vol. 81, no. 1, pp. 151-168.

[14] X. Wang, W. Zhang, W. Guo, and J. Zhang, "Secure chaotic system with application to chaotic ciphers,"Inform. Sci. vol. 221, no. 7, pp.555-570, 2013.

[15] W. Xu, Z. Geng, Q. Zhu, and X. Gu, "A piecewise linear chaotic map and sequential quadratic programming based robust hybrid particle swarm optimization," Inform. Sci. vol. 218, pp. 85-102, 2013.

[16] R. Zahmoul, R. Ejbali, and M. Zaied, "Image encryption based on new Beta chaotic maps," Optics and Lasers in Engineering vol. 96, pp. 39-49.

[17] R. Zahmoul and M. Zaied, "Toward new family beta maps for chaotic image encryption," 2016 IEEE International Conference on Systems, Man, and Cybernetics (SMC).

[18] M. Zaied, C. Ben Amar and A.M. Alimi, "Award a New Wavelet Based Beta Function,"Second International Conference on Signal,System, Decision and information technology IEEE, SSD03, pp. 185-191, Sousse-Tunisia Mars 2003.

[19] R. Zahmoul, A. Abbes, R. Ejbali, and M. Zaied, "A watermarking scheme based on DCT, SVD and BCM," International Joint Conference: 12th International Conference on Computational Intelligence in Security for Information Systems (CISIS 2019) and 10th International Conference on EUropean Transnational Education (ICEUTE 2019)Optics and Lasers in Engineering, pp. 97-104, 2019.

[20] H. Souden, R. Ejbali, and M. Zaied, "Beta Chaotic Map Based Image Steganography," IEleventh International Conference on Machine Vision, (ICMV) , v. 11041, pp. 1104-1113, 2018.

[21] W. Yue, JP. Noonan, and S. Agaian, "NPCR and UACI randomness tests for image encryption,"Cyber J: Multidiscip J Sci Technol J Sel Areas Telecommun (JSAT) 2011:318.

[22] C. Fu, J.J. Chen, H. Zou, W.H. Meng, Y.F. Zhan and Y.W. Yu, "A chaos-based digital image encryption scheme with an improved diffusion strategy," Optics Express. vol. 20, no.3, pp. 2363-2378, 2012.

Requirements Traceability in Cyber Physical Systems using Semantic Inference

Rohith Yanambaka Venkata, Rohan Maheshwari and Krishna Kavi

Department of Computer Science and Engineering
University of North Texas
Denton, Texas-76207
Email: {rohithyanambakavenkata, rohanmaheshwari}@my.unt.edu and krishna.kavi@unt.edu

Abstract—**The distinguishing feature of Cyber Physical Systems (CPS) is the coupling of computational and physical systems, where embedded cyber systems monitor and control physical processes. CPS is responsible for an important role in critical infrastructure, and everyday life. They include smart networked systems with embedded sensors, processors and actuators that sense and interact with the physical world and support real-time, guaranteed performance in safety-critical applications. The cyber-physical nature, coupled with safety-critical application greatly increases the attack surface and the impact of cyber attacks. Understanding the interaction between various subsystems in a CPS is vital in evaluating its security posture and identifying the measures to mitigate threats. To that end, the ability to trace a CPS design from the requirements elicitation phase to the implementation phase, otherwise known as requirements traceability may prove to be invaluable. This paper presents an Ontological approach to requirements traceability in CPS by building upon our previous work on defining the Semantic Inference Model for Security in CPS using Ontologies (SIMON), a design framework for CPS systems.**

Keywords–CPS Security; Ontology; CPS Privacy, CPS Resiliency.

I. INTRODUCTION

CPS systems are increasingly benefiting from the expanding IoT network as they are implemented in the infrastructure. Their role in Industrial Control Systems puts upon a heavy load of data transmission between their cyber and physical components [1]. They face an increasingly difficult challenge across domains as the relationship with the infrastructure heightens in complexity. Independently, cyber and physical systems have developed a resiliency towards outsider threats since the structure of these systems have not required adaption [2]. However, the rapid integration of these systems as a single unit has brought upon changes in architecture that implies vulnerabilities [3].

In an age where the relationship between cyber and physical systems are conflating to create new applications of IoT, the ramifications of security threats are more severe than before. The intertwining of existing communication and information technologies with physical systems such as power plants, healthcare systems, and transportation has increased the autonomous capability to the infrastructure. The implementation of software in these domains has resulted in increased risk of unauthorized access to these newly integrated systems. Consequently, cyber attacks are more severe when the gained privileges cover access to a larger system.

Cyber and physical systems follow a framework that characterizes the path that data takes from a physical to application layer. When considering the amalgamation of these two systems, it can be inferred that new transmission phases will be implemented in order for CPS systems to communicate internally. Therefore, the encryption protocols over the current stages will not cover the introduced vulnerabilities in the layers connecting the cyber and physical components of a system. Therefore, data traveling between these respective planes will be vulnerability to outside attacks and manipulation. The outcome of which can compromise the functionality of the additional components now involved.

Vulnerabilities in CPS systems increase the amount of possible access nodes in both the cyber and physical sub domains. As new components are added in the CPS domain to bridge the cyber and physical components, the region of attack becomes unclear and difficult to mitigate. In fact, because CPS systems require connectivity and reliability on a larger scale than sub domain systems such as the internet, their security protocols contain a higher level of complexity [3]. The increased attack surface calls for threats to be identified in two categories: Infrastructure Security and Information Security. In order to do so, it is important to develop a new framework that can account for threats and vulnerabilities in the increased connection points, data transmission phases, and components involved in CPS systems.

With a plethora of functional requirements, data paths, and components involved in CPS networks, Ontologies provide a reliable technique to visualizing these concerns. Ontologies are a system of components that are connected through the semantic web. Relationships between components and their functionality are described using logical axioms, taxonomies, and other classification tools. These relationships along with objective ruling systems and characteristics of CPS components allow Ontologies to reason about possible vulnerabilities as well the attack path taken to compromise the system. When considering a new CPS domain, Ontologies provide a systematic methodology to understanding the internal communication systems as well as identifying and classifying security threats.

In this paper, we propose a role application framework in which we dissect security threats and vulnerabilities relative to the layer they are violating. In our previous work [4], we presented a semantic inference framework that supplemented the NIST CPS framework [5] divided CPS engineering into three layers as follows: Conceptualization, Abstract Realization, and Concrete Realization [4].

In the Conceptualization Phase, we will organize design goals and top priority functional requirements that describe the CPS system's overarching goals. This way, it will be apparent how individual threats impact the capabilities of the CPS system.

Moving into the Abstract Realization Phase, the supporting functional requirements will be denoted in the order they assist the execution of the design goals. Each requirement will be broken down into roles and responsibilities that are to be met by the CPS components. In addition to listing the objectives of the requirements, there will also be security properties that define the level of resiliency required to ensure reliability in the component. This process will occur recursively until all components are assigned roles. At this stage, we can proceed into the next layer.

In the Concrete Realization Phase, the components organized in the Abstract Realization Phase will be divided into the individual hardware and software components that allow for functionality of the CPS component. The technical identification and mitigation of security threats in the CPS domain will occur here. Once an issue is located in the CPS system, the traceability of the requirements and all linked quantities can be used to identify where a change in the system needs to be made.

The rest of the paper is organized as follows. Section II outlines the structure of the Semantic Inference Model for Security in Cyber Physical Systems using Ontologies (SIMON) framework. In addition, the main contribution of this paper, the role allocation Ontology is also discussed in this section. Section III demonstrates the capabilities of the role allocation framework using the Red Light Violation Warning System (RLVW) as a case study.

II. SIMON Framework

In a companion paper in this conference, we presented the SIMON framework [4] that combines (and extends) existing standard specification Ontologies, such as Semantic Sensor Networks (SSN), and new ones as required by the domain of interest. For the sake of completeness, we will replicate some key aspects of SIMON in this paper. First, we will review some of the Ontologies and frameworks used in our research and then, present a role allocation procedure that enables requirements traceability.

A. NIST CPS Framework

National Institute of Standards and Technology (NIST) has developed a framework that provides guidance in designing, building, verifying, and analyzing complex CPS systems [5]. The framework captures generic functionalities that CPS provide, the activities and artifacts needed to support conceptualization, realization and assurance of CPS design [5]. Designing a CPS system involves:

- **Conceptualization** - Capturing all activities related to high-level goals, functional requirements and organization of CPS as they pertain to what a CPS should be and what they are supposed to do. It provides a conceptual model of the CPS system under consideration.
- **Realization** - Capturing all activities surrounding the detailed engineering, design, production, implementation and operation of the desired systems. However, to facilitate comparing Ontological models of CPS systems, we propose bifurcating the overarching realization phase described in the NIST CPS framework into the following sub-phases.
  - **Abstract Realization** - In this phase, design goals are broken down into roles and responsibilities and delegated to subsystems and interfaces. No implementation details pertaining to products (components and sub-components) are identified. For example, we may identify that the network communications needed in the system will be handled by a wireless data communication application but not provide details on either the specific hardware device or communication protocols. We use Ontologies to capture the Abstract Realization.
  - **Concrete Realization** - The roles and responsibilities identified during the abstract realization phase need to be implemented by specific products. For example, a Cisco ASR1002-10G-HA/K9 will be used as an edge router that functions as the wireless data communication application identified in the Abstract Realization phase. We use Ontologies to relate the products used for various functions and roles identified in the Abstract Realization.
- **Assurance** - The assurance phase deals with obtaining confidence that the CPS built in the realization phase satisfies the model developed in the conceptualization phase [5]. This includes evaluating claims, argumentation and gathering evidence required to address important requirements of design, policy, law and regulation [5]. In our case, we use reasoners to infer and derive assurances (or violations) of the goals and functional requirements are met. We use additional Ontologies to capture cyber threat data so that vulnerabilities, cyber attacks and possible mitigative measures can be related to the products identified in Concrete Realization; we rely on NIST Common Platform Enumeration (CPE) identities with specific products for this purpose.

B. Role Allocation

Requirements traceability is an essential property in identifying changes/modifications to components that will improve the security posture of a CPS system. Delegating the overarching design goals from the conceptualization phase into roles and responsibilities for entities identified in either of the realization phases will help achieve this property.

The abstract realization phase involves identifying application-level components, sans the implementation details. Each system identified in this phase can be used to define a role that defines a set of conceptualized functional requirements for the underlying sub-systems to realize. In addition, each role may define a set of security requirements to be fulfilled. In the concrete realization phase, a detailed example is presented in Section III.

The trustworthiness requirements as described by the NIST CPS Framework can be categorized as:

- **Privacy:** Privacy requirements address concerns pertaining to the prevention of entities gaining access to data stored in, created by or transiting through a CPS system or its components [5].
- **Reliability:** Address concerns related to the ability of a CPS to deliver stable and predictable performance in the expected conditions [5].
- **Resilience:** Address concerns related to the ability of a CPS to withstand instability, unexpected conditions, and gracefully return to predictable, but possibly degraded performance [5].
- **Security:** Concerns related to the ability of the CPS to ensure that all of its processes, mechanisms, both physical and cyber, and services are afforded internal or external protection from unintended and unauthorized access, change, damage, destruction, or use [5]. Security can best be described through three lenses:

- **Confidentiality:** Preserving authorized restrictions on access and disclosure.
- **Integrity:** Guarding against improper modification or destruction of system, and includes ensuring non-repudiation and authenticity
- **Availability:** Ensuring timely and reliable access to and use of a system.

SIMON can be used to modify the CPS design at any of the various phases to address any design violations discovered by our reasoners. We use different Ontologies in our framework to describe the concepts, properties and restriction associated with CPS systems at each of the design phases described in the next section.

C. Sensor-Observation-Sampling-Actuator Ontology (SOSA)

The Sensor-Observation-Sampling-Actuation Ontology (SOSA), a subset of the Semantic Sensor Network (SSN) Ontology presents a conceptualization of all entities, activities and properties that typically constitute a CPS. SOSA is a World Wide Web Consortium (W3C) standard specification that provides a formal, general-purpose framework for modeling the interactions between various entities involved in the functions of *observation, sampling and actuation* in SSNs [6].

The *core structure* of SOSA Ontology design pattern encompasses all of the three modeling perspectives; the activities of observing, sampling, and actuating [6]. Each activity targets a feature of interest by either changing its state or revealing its properties by following a designated procedure. All activities are carried out by an object, also called an agent.

D. Cyber Threat Information Ontology

The SOSA Ontology outlined in the previous section helps capture the intricacies of the coupling between the cyber and physical elements in CPS systems. The activities of observing and sampling must be followed by communicating the data and processing to interpret the observations and making decisions on the actions. These actions are then used to control physical systems through actuation. The communication and processing subsystem, which is not directly included in the SOSA ontology can expose the cyber and physical components of the CPS to security attacks. Thus, SOSA must be extended to describe the processing and communication subsystems. This allows us to relate cyber threat data from multiple sources to obtain insights into the security posture of a CPS system under consideration. We have defined an Ontology that obtains and contextualizes Cyber Threat Information (CTI) from three sources:

- **The National Vulnerability Database (NVD)** - A U.S. government repository of standards based vulnerability management data [7].
- **Exploit Database** - An archive of public exploits and corresponding vulnerable software, developed for use by penetration testers and vulnerability researchers [8].
- **Metasploit** - A framework for developing, testing and executing software exploits [9].

The cyber threat Ontology is underpinned by the STIX structured language, that enables organizations to share, store and analyze CTI in a consistent manner, allowing security communities to better understand what computer-based attacks they are most likely to see and to anticipate and/or respond to those attacks faster and more effectively [10].

Our objective in defining the CTI Ontology is to unify information from three sources (described earlier in this section) and facilitate logical reasoning about the security of CPS using *Axioms*. Axioms are rules that are used by a reasoner to infer additional information that may be hard to define using a knowledge representation language. To provide a perspective of the complexity of CTI Ontology, it includes 6657 axioms that describe CTI data. In addition to STIX, the CTI Ontology also inherits characteristics from two additional Ontologies:

- **Cyber Observable Expression (CybOX)** - A standardized language for encoding and communicating information about cyber observables [10]. Using CybOX language, relevant observable events or properties pertaining to an attack pattern can be captured.
- **Common Attack Pattern and Enumeration (CAPEC)** - Provides a dictionary of known patterns of attack employed by adversaries to exploit known weaknesses in cyber-enabled capabilities.[11].

III. Case Study: Red Light Violation Warning System (RLVW)

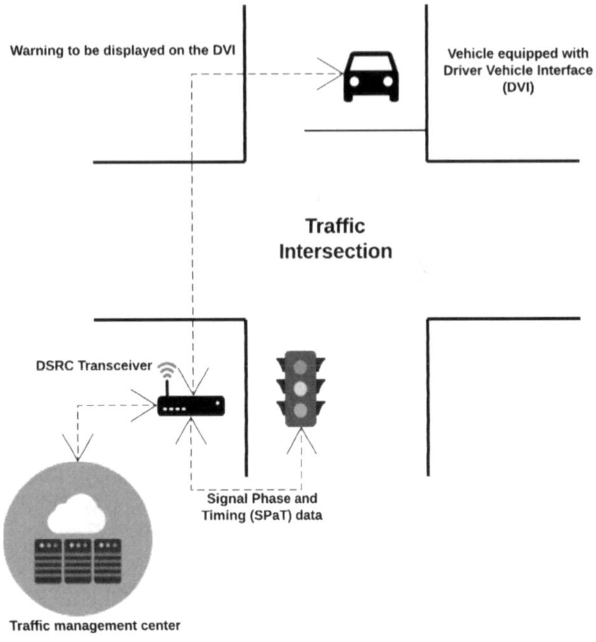

Figure 1. The RLVW system

As a case study to show the use of our framework, we use the Red Light Violation Warning (RLVW) safety application as described in the US Department of Transportation document [12]. The RLVW application enables a connected vehicle approaching an instrumented signalized intersection to receive information from the infrastructure regarding the signal timing and the geometry of the intersection. The application in the vehicle uses its speed and acceleration profile, along with the signal timing and geometry information to determine if it appears likely that the vehicle will enter the intersection in violation of a traffic signal. If the violation seems likely to occur, a warning can be provided to the driver. Figure 1 shows an overview of the RLVW system.

The SIMON framework describes three layers of threat identification by classifying design goals, subsystems that support those goals, and hardware/software that enable functionality of the subsystems. The number of nodes used in this model can demonstrate the complexity of CPS. The more nodes and edges established in this system, the more intermediate layers are formed between the CPS Model layers. In doing so, more vulnerabilities are introduced into the system due to larger access points throughout the CPS. To mitigate this, it is desirable to assign roles and responsibilities to components in the abstract and concrete realization phases based on functional and security requirements. Such an approach will provide requirements traceability, which will aid in increasing resiliency by reducing the attack surface.

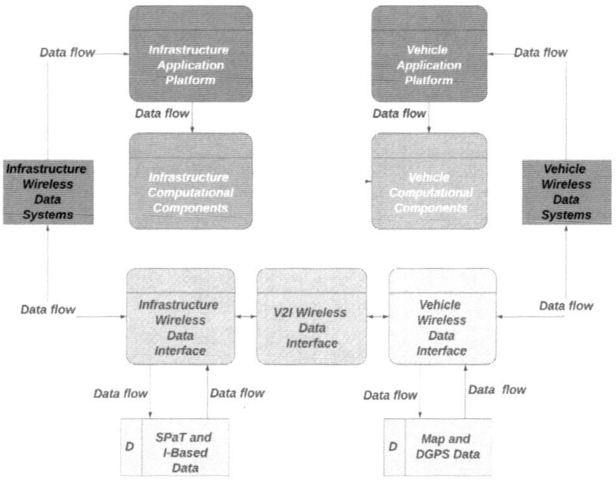

Figure 2. The V2I Wireless Data Systems Network

A. *Conceptualization Phase*

The design goal of the Vehicle to Infrastructure (V2I) Wireless Data Interface (WDI) system is to communicate relevant data between the Infrastructure and Vehicle application components through their respective WDI and Application Platforms (APs). The V2I WDI incorporates algorithms and data exchanged to perform calculations to recognize high-risk situations in advance. This inference results in issuing driver alerts and warnings through specific protocols. The most primitive and fundamental goal of the V2I WDI is to calculate and communicate Signal, Phase and Timing (SPaT) information to the vehicle with support of driving advisories and warnings [12]. The system is also responsible for maintaining authenticity of transmitted data through security measures. Corrupted data can result in compromising driver safety and their informations privacy. The three primary design goals of the V2I WDI system are:

- **Verify Incoming Data (VID):** Since the system serves as a bridge between the vehicle and infrastructure domains, its main design goal revolves around transmitted data between both components. Therefore, a key requirement of this system is to verify the authenticity of incoming data from either side of the system to avoid Phishing and other instances of fraudulent data transfer. This should be accomplished through ingress filtering protocols set in place to verify packet source headers and IP addresses.
- **Verify Outbound Data (VOD):** The WDI system is also responsible for generating advisories and alerts tailored to each nearby vehicle. With this in mind, a supporting requirement for this design goal must be to implement Secure Socket Layer (SSL) protocols or an alternative cryptographic key to ensure outbound data is not tampered with before reaching its destination.
- **Data Routing to Proximate Vehicles (DRPV):** Because this system is involved with establishing multiple connections between the infrastructure and vehicles, there is no generic set of messages purposed for all vehicles. Each advisory is calculated using metrics provided by each vehicle, thus creating a functional requirement to ensure that each message is sent to the appropriate vehicle. Failure of this requirement can serve fatal if metrics are sent to the incorrect vehicle which results in traffic violations or accidents.

B. *Abstract Realization Phase*

The functional requirements listed in the conceptualization phase are purposed to describe the theoretical capabilities of a CPS. When moving into the application layer components that quantitatively satisfy the aspirational properties of the V2I WDI System, it is important to categorize each component into the respective requirement it resolves. This way, in the assurance phase, it can be tested how well the design goal of each component meets its dedicated functional requirement. Each component in the abstract realization phase will be assigned its own role.

Since the V2I WDI system is only a portion of the entire V2I domain, its design goal only covers data transmission. Therefore, only the transmission capabilities and roles of the categorized components will be discussed. Additionally, it is important to note that the sub components of both the infrastructure and vehicle contain similar components with only slightly varying goals. When working with Cyber Physical Systems, the cyber and physical aspect of this CPS can be made resilient independently. However, the current issue that Intelligent transportation system (ITS) developers face is maintaining that level of security when combining both sides of the system. This is because the integration of optimal designs when forming the system can lose the resiliency of both the cyber and physical aspects. So to understand these challenges, we form a general hierarchy of the V2I WDI network that maps each component to the requirement it fulfils [12]. This will unravel the group of threats associated at each layer of the system. Figure 2 shows an overview of the V2I wireless data interconnect.

1) VID Associated Components:

- **Infrastructure Wireless Data Systems (IWDS):** The Infrastructure Wireless Data Interface (IWDI) is responsible for sending and receiving data to/from nearby vehicles via the V2I Wireless Data Interface (VWDI). Its main design goal is to validate passing data by making sure position accuracy of incoming vehicles is up to the DoT standards. Additionally, the system calculates SPaT and Differential Global Positioning System (DGPS) metrics to be deployed to nearby vehicles via the IWDI.

The IWDI role helps realize all activities related to communication with vehicles equipped with a VWDI. In other words, all three conceptual design goals are supported by the IWDI role. The conceptual design goals mandate the security, privacy, resiliency requirements be associated with the IWDI role.

- **Infrastructure Application Platform (IAP):** The IAP is the computational platform which hosts the Infrastructure Application Component and provides the necessary hardware and software interfaces enabling communication with Infrastructure Wireless Data Systems, Infrastructure Data Systems, Roadside Signage System, Traffic Signal Controller, and Local/Back Office User Systems. Its main design goal is to channel all data gathered by sensors and physical systems to the cyber components. It can be considered the bridge between the cyber and physical components of the infrastructure side of the CPS, thus making it one of the least resilient and most vulnerable parts of the CPS.

  The IAP role is perhaps one of the most important in the RLVW system. It facilitates the interaction between the constituent systems in the infrastructure and the vehicle. It is apparent from the conceptual goals that the IAP role must meet the security, privacy, resiliency and reliability requirements.

- **Vehicle Wireless Data Systems (VWDS):** Receives messages from the Vehicle Application Component through the Vehicle Application Platform, formats and processes messages to be received by infrastructure components. This system also transmits data from the Vehicle Wireless Data Interface to the deeper hardware of the vehicle. This system also obtains GPS location and time. It may include a processor for GPS differential correction. Its main design goal is to convey information from the capture point at the Vehicle Wireless Data Interface to the internal components below and vice versa.

  The VWDS role is essential in ensuring communication between the sensors in the infrastructure space and the innards of VDWI. Hence, it must support the security and resiliency requirements outlined in the previous section.

- **Vehicle Application Platform (VAP):** The Vehicle Application Platform is the computational platform which hosts the Vehicle Application Component and provides the necessary hardware and software interfaces enabling communication with Vehicle Wireless Data Systems, Vehicle Data Systems, and the Driver Warning Systems. Its main design goal is to channel all data gathered by vehicle sensors, actuators, and On-Board Diagnostics (OBD) data to the vehicular cyber components for processing and calculations. It can be considered the bridge between the cyber and physical components of this side of the CPS, thus making it one of the least resilient and most vulnerable parts of the CPS.

  The VAP role is equivalent to the IAP role previously discussed. Since they are very similar in the conceptual goals they support, it stands to reason that the VAP role should support security, privacy, resiliency and reliability requirements.

2) VOD Associated Components:

- **Infrastructure Wireless Data Interface:** The IWDI is responsible for sending and receiving to nearby vehicles via the V2I Wireless Data Interface. Its main design goal is to refresh data transmission frequency at a configurable pace. It is also required to be equipped with countermeasures in case of corrupt or tampered data transmission. In these cases, it should issue warning messages to nearby vehicles to terminate data transmission and calculations using any information that comes from the Infrastructure.

  IWDI defines the functional requirements pertaining to communication with VWDI. The functional requirements of IWDI dictate that it should support security and resiliency.

- **Vehicle Wireless Data Interface:** The VWDI is responsible for sending and receiving to nearby Industrial Control Systems such via the V2I Wireless Data Interface. Its main design goal is to validate incoming data and request new packets from the infrastructure at a configurable frequency. It is also required to correct map and DGPS data for the infrastructure application component to produce the most precise RLVW metrics. In the case of inaccurate or corrupt data, the VWDI is required to terminate data transmission and issue alerts to the driver information interface

  VWDI is the vehicle-side equivalent of IWDI. So, Intuitively, this role should support the same security requirements as IWDI, which would be security and privacy.

3) DRPV Associated Components:

- **V2I Wireless Data Interface:** Acts as a bridge for data transmission between the entire Infrastructure and Vehicle components. It receives raw data from the Infrastructure and vehicle components. This communication is functional over a bi-directional Dedicated Short Range Communication (DSRC) network. Therefore, its security protocol is effective within 1000 meters of any attacker. Beyond that, connectivity is loose and vulnerable. Its main design goal relative to the RLVW application is to ensure secure data transmission between approaching vehicles and signalized intersections.

  It is evident from the description of this application that it sustains all three design goals of the RLVW system. Its vital importance means that this role should support privacy, reliability, resilience and security.

C. Concrete Realization Phase

Now that the baseline for the design goals and supporting components are established, we can identify technical aspects of the identified components to understand how these functional requirements are met. Mapping the hardware and software to their respective components will help unravel the classification of security threats since it is at this phase where the core data transmission occurs. Up until now, the above layers cover high-level understandings of the V2I WDI System. Now, we will classify core hardware and software that is generalized for both sides of the system to understand the mechanics behind V2I data transmission.

- **DSRC On Board Unit (OBU):** The DSRC OBU is the dedicated communication device installed on V2X connected vehicles. This hardware is responsible for establishing and receiving SPaT and Roadside data at a configurable frequency between 5.8 GHz -5.9 GHz. It utilizes the widely adaptive ThreadX RTOS operating system designed specifically for Internet of Things (IoT) applications. The DSRC OBU assists in enabling the capabilities of the Vehicle Wireless Data Interface [13].

The OBU resides in vehicles and is responsible for implementing the VWDS, VAP and VWDI roles from the abstract realization phase. All of the security requirements associated with each constituent abstract-level component is required to be supported by the OBU. However, multiple roles/responsibilities may be fulfilled by a single realization. For example, using an encrypted communication channel will fulfill both privacy and confidentiality requirements mandated by the roles that this component supports.

- **DSRC Roadside Unit (RSU):** The RSU unit performs identical functions but on the other end of the V2I wireless network. It is responsible for receiving SPaT and Roadside data from the infrastructure technical systems, verifying the data, and transmitting it upon data request from nearby vehicles. The RSU unit enables the capabilities of the V2I Wireless Data Interface, acting as the cyber bridge between the Vehicle and Infrastructure cyber components.

  The RSU is responsible for supporting the roles of IWDS, IAP, and IWDI. The security requirements associated with each of the three roles need to be supported by the RSU.
- **Wireless Sensor Network (WSN):** The WSN is the sensor network on the infrastructure side that captures road conditions data, Infrastructure based vehicle detection, Road conditions, Speed data, Visibility data, and weather data. It utilizes sensors and actuators for the detection aspect of the hardware and standard transceivers, antennas, and receivers for the communication aspect of the hardware [14]. The Infrastructure Wireless Data Systems are supported by this WSN network, acting as the source of raw data that is formatted and processed into metrics by the Data Systems.

The WSN resides in the intersection between infrastructure and vehicle subsystems and facilitates communication between the IWDI and VWDI systems. It is required to support the security requirements associated with these two roles.

D. Assurance Phase

The assurance phase deals with obtaining confidence that the CPS system built in the concrete realization phase satisfies the models described in the abstract realization and conceptualization phases. Validating the concrete CPS system involves ensuring that it meets the functional and security requirements associated with the roles that each component supports. Figure 3 illustrates the hierarchy of role allocation in SIMON.

Evaluating the security posture of a CPS system requires current CTI data from multiple sources. To that end, SIMON's CTI Ontology discussed in sectionII-D provides pertinent information.

Let us consider the example of an OBU running ThreadX RTOS. The OBU is responsible for sustaining the VWDS, VAP and VWDI roles, which necessitate the support of privacy,

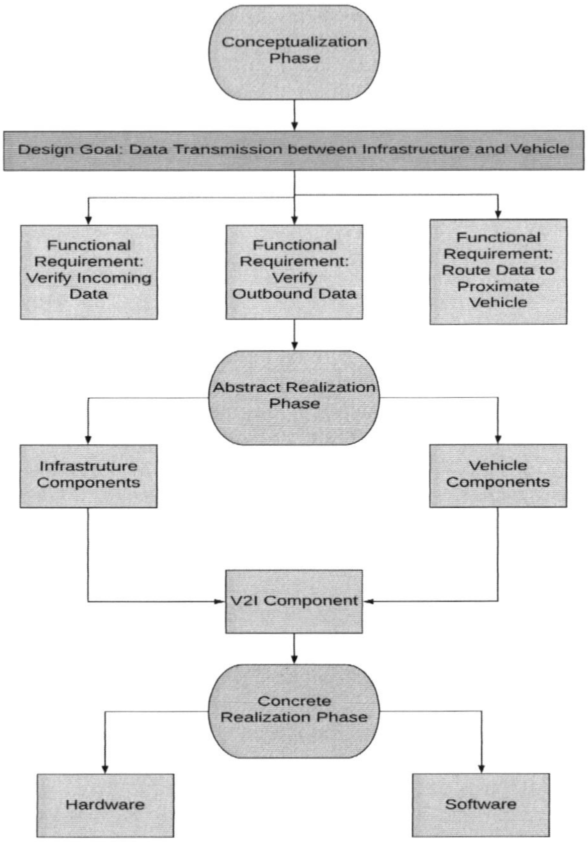

Figure 3. Role allocation hierarchy

security and resiliency requirements. CTI is able to formulate a CPE identifier for this system using information obtained from the NVD. CPE:2.3:o:marvell:88w8997_firmware:-:*:*:*:*:*:*:* identifies the ThreadX-based firmware on a Marvell Avastar WiFi device. The Common Vulnerability Scoring System (CVSS) metrics from the NVD for this CPE indicate that the attack vector for a threat that exploits this vulnerability would be adjacent, which means that any infected devices in a local network could potentially compromise other devices in the network. Furthermore, the high severity score from the CVSS metrics indicates that a an attack that leverages this vulnerability could be catastrophic. If the system were to be affected by CVE-2019-6496 [15], an adversary may be able to launch a denial of service attack on the OBU. The vulnerability allows remote attackers to execute arbitrary code or cause a denial of service (block pool overflow) via malformed WiFi packets during identification of available WiFi networks. Exploitation of the WiFi device can lead to exploitation of the host application processor in some cases, but this depends on several factors including host OS hardening and the availability of DMA.

To understand the impact of this vulnerability on the CPS system, the requirements traceability property offered by SIMON must be leveraged. This would show how the impact of a potential exploitation of this vulnerability would propagate up the three stages of design processes. Figure 5 shows various inferences that the reasoner makes in providing the insights presented below.

- In the concrete realization phase, a vulnerability in the OBU would violate the functional requirements of both the DSRC roadside unit and the OBU. It is desirable to implement mitigative measures in the concrete realization phase because it wouldn't require a complete overhaul or re-engineering of systems previously implemented.
- In the abstract realization phase, all the roles fulfilled by the OBU and DSRC transceiver, VWDS, VAP, VWDI, IWDS, IAP, IWDI are violated. The corresponding security requirements pertaining to availability are affected. CVE-2019-6496, being a vulnerability exploited for DoS, confidentiality and integrity requirements may not be impacted.
- In the conceptualization phase, all three requirements (VOD, VID and DRPV) are affected by the unavailability of the OBU. thereby impacting the primary design goal of the RLVW system, which is to prevent roadway fatalities by ensuring date transmission between the infrastructure and vehicles.

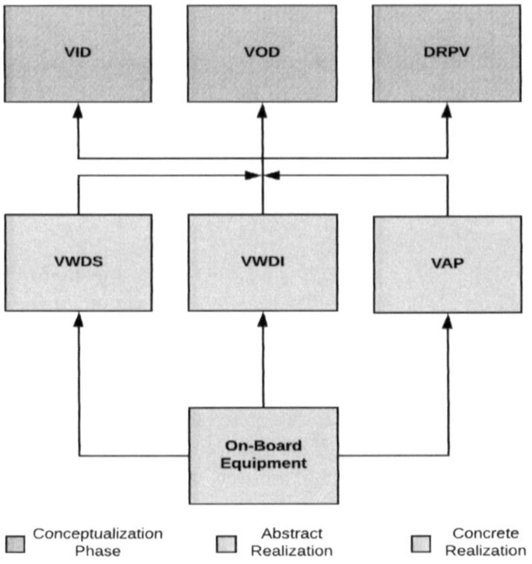

Figure 4. DoS attack on the OBU

A DoS attack on the OBU would violate the availability requirement for all three roles supported by the OBU (VWDS, VAP and VWDI), thereby violating the DRPV design principle of the CPS system. Figure 4 shows the how the design goals of the RLVW system will be affected by such an attack on the OBU. The knowledge reuse property of SIMON can be used to compare various CPS systems to identify mitigative measures from other domains that can be reused in the CPS system under consideration. We have presented multiple examples in our prior work [4]. These insights would be invaluable to CPS system designers.

```
The Ontology is consistent
On-Board Unit (OBU) CPE : cpe:2.3:o:marvell:88w8997_firmware:-:*:*:*:*:*:*:*
(Asserted) OBU uses ThreadX OS
(Inferred) CVE-2019-6496 could be exploited
(Inferred) Potential violation of requirement 1.2.1 of the VWDS System
(Inferred) Potential violation of requirement 1.5.2.2 of the VAP system
(Inferred) Potential violation of requirement 1.4.2 of the VWDI system
```

Figure 5. DoS attack inference

IV. Conclusion and Future Work

In this paper, we have presented an extension to our previous work on CPS design validation using semantic inference. Reasoning about a CPS realization and validating that the realization does not violate functional as well trustworthiness goals is essential in improving the security posture of a CPS system. Currently, the SIMON framework is not capable of automatically translating design goals into Ontological models. However, we are exploring the possibility of extending our work to support this function in the future.

We demonstrated that the role allocation ontology is capable of delegating the functional and security requirements among subsystems at various design stages of a CPS system. It offers requirements traceability to understand the impact of a security threat in CPS. An RLVW system was used a case study to demonstrate the role allocation ontology's capabilities. In the future, we intend to investigate other CPS domains.

Acknowledgement

This research is supported in part by the NSF Net-centric Industry-University Cooperative Research Center at UNT and the industrial members of the Center.

References

[1] A. A. Cardenas, S. Amin, B. Sinopoli, A. Giani, A. Perrig, and S. Sastry, "Challenges for Securing Cyber Physical Systems," *Center for Hybrid and Embedded Software Systems*, pp. 1–3, 2009.

[2] F. AlDosari, "Security and Privacy Challenges in Cyber-Physical Systems," *Scientific Research Publishing*, pp. 4–6, 2017.

[3] B. Li and L. Zhang, "Security analysis of cyber-physical system," *AIP Conference Proceedings*, pp. 1–4, 2017.

[4] R. Y. Venkata, R. Maheshwari, and K. Kavi, "SIMON: Semantic Inference Model for Security in CPS using Ontologies," *ICSEA*, pp. 1–2, 2019.

[5] D. A. Wollman, M. A. Weiss, Y. Li-Baboud, E. R. Griffor, and M. J. Burns, "Framework for cyber-physical systems," *Special Publication (NIST SP) - 1500-203*, 2017.

[6] K. Janowicz, A. Haller, S. J. D. Cox, D. L. Phuoc, and M. Lefrançois, "SOSA: A lightweight ontology for sensors, observations, samples, and actuators," *CoRR*, vol. abs/1805.09979, 2018.

[7] "National vulnerability database." URL: https://nvd.nist.gov/ [accessed: 2019-06-11].

[8] "Exploit-DB." URL: https://www.exploit-db.com [accessed: 2019-06-20].

[9] "Metasploit-penetration testing framework." URL: https://www.metasploit.com/ [accessed: 2019-06-20].

[10] S. Barnum, "Standardizing cyber threat intelligence information with the structured threat information expression (stix)," 2014.

[11] "Common Attack Pattern Enumeration and Classification (CAPEC)." URL: https://capec.mitre.org/ [accessed: 2019-07-02].

[12] Department of Transportation, "Performance Requirements, Vol. 3, Red Light Violation Warning (RLVW)," *Vehicle-to-Infrastructure (V2I) Safety Applications*, pp. 1–68, 2015.

[13] "Vehicle to Infrastructure interaction (V2I)," 2019. URL: http://www.mogi.bme.hu/TAMOP/jarmurendszerek$_i ranyitasa_a ngol/math-ch09.html[accessed : 2019-09-19]$.

[14] D. Snchez-lvarez, M. Linaje, and F.-J. Rodrguez-Prez, "A Framework to Design the Computational Load Distribution of Wireless Sensor Networks in Power Consumption Constrained Environments," *Sensors(Basel)*, pp. 2–5, 2018.

[15] "National Vulnerability Database." URL: https://nvd.nist.gov/vuln/detail/CVE-2019-6496 [accessed: 2019-06-11].

The Matching Lego(R)-Like Bricks Problem: Including a Use Case Study in the Manufacturing Industry

Martin Zinner*, Kim Feldhoff*, Rui Song†, André Gellrich†, Wolfgang E. Nagel*
* Center for Information Services and High Performance Computing (ZIH)
Technische Universität Dresden
Dresden, Germany
E-mail: {martin.zinner1, kim.feldhoff, wolfgang.nagel}@tu-dresden.de
† Technical Information Systems
Technische Universität Dresden
Dresden, Germany
E-mail: {rui.song, andre.gellrich}@tu-dresden.de

***Abstract*—We formulate and transform a real-world combinatorial problem into a constraint satisfaction problem: choose a restricted set of containers from a warehouse, such that the elements contained in the containers satisfy some restrictions and compatibility criteria. We set up a formal, mathematical model, describe the combinatorial problem and define a (nonlinear) system of equations, which describes the equivalent constraint satisfaction problem. Next, we use the framework provided by the Apache Commons Mathematics Library in order to implement a solution based on genetic algorithms. We carry out performance tests and show that a general approach, having business logic solely in the definition of the fitness function, can deliver satisfactory results for a real-world use-case in the manufacturing industry.**

***Keywords*–Constraint satisfaction problem; Combinatorial problem; Genetic algorithm; Crossover; Mutation.**

I. Introduction

We formulate a new real-world combinatorial problem, the motivation for our study. Initially, we describe succinctly the real-world problem as it has been identified at a semiconductor company and present the general strategy to solve it. In order to avoid the technical difficulties related to the industrial application, we present the equivalent problem based on LEGO® bricks. To conclude this chapter, we present the outline of the paper.

A. Motivation

Some time ago we were facing a strategic problem at a big semiconductor company. The company produces Integrated Circuits (ICs), also termed *chips*, assembles them to modules on a circuit board according to guidelines and specifications, and ships the modules as the final product to the customer. The ICs are stored in bins before the last technological process (cleaning) is performed.

The difficulties arise due to technical limitations of the tool that assembles the ICs to modules. The tool can handle at most five bins at once. This means in particular, that the ICs required to fulfill an order from the customer have to be in not more than five bins. Once the bins have been identified, the modules are assembled and shipped to the customer. If it is not possible to identify five bins in connection with a customer order, then either cost-intensive methods (rearranging the content of some bins) or time-intensive methods (waiting some days till the production process delivers new ICs) have to be applied. Hence, identifying the bins necessary to fulfill an order is crucial for the economic success of the company.

B. Current State and Challenge

There has been a selection algorithm in place, based primarily on heuristics and inside knowledge regarding the patterns of the specifications of the modules. Although the existing selection algorithm delivered satisfactory results in most of the cases, it runs for days in some cases and is not flexible enough, in particular, it cannot handle slight deviations from the existing specification patterns.

To circumvent the above inconvenient, the main aim of our study is to determine alternative selection methods, which always deliver satisfactory results within an acceptable time frame, and which are easy adaptable to meet future requirements. Our main objective is to identify and formalize the industrial problem as a mathematical model and to transform the occurring Combinatorial Problem (CP) into a Constrained Satisfaction Problem (CSP). The exact method using MATLAB did not deliver results within a satisfactory time frame. A suitable heuristic method – including Simulated Annealing (SA), Ant Colony Optimization (ACO), Genetic Algorithms (GA), etc. – to solve the CSP within the requirements had to be identified and appropriate algorithms had to be developed, which satisfy both the accuracy and performance demands.

If the general task is to find optimal solution to a set of constraints, we speak about Constrained Optimization Problem (COP). The primarily purpose of the industrial problem is to find a satisfactory solution, since from the technical perspective undercutting the requirements of the specifications does not lead to better quality. However, a straightforward extensions of the CSP towards COP is mentioned later.

C. Problem Description

The following example is artificial, it does not occur in *real life* in this manner, although it is very close to it. It is used to best describe the problem without burden the reader with the technical details of a concrete "real life" example. Later on, we will present a "real life" example from the industry and specify the respective mappings between the two models.

We describe the problem succinctly by using an analogy of building structures out of LEGO®-like pieces (bricks).

LEGO®-like pieces (also termed *blocks* or *bricks*) can be assembled to build sophisticated structures (in the following termed *objects*) like buildings, etc. Figure 1 shows how two bricks can be pooled together. The manufacturer of the bricks

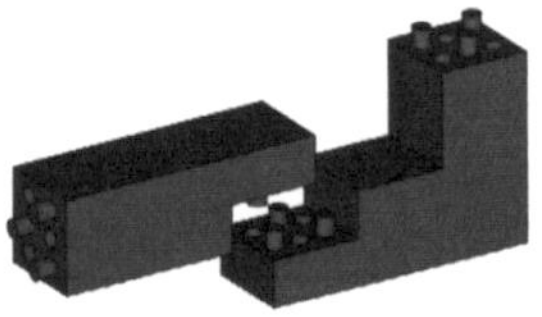

Figure 1: Illustration how two bricks, one of them a corner brick, can be pooled together.

wants to facilitate and simplify the assembling of the bricks to the final objects as well as to cut manufacturing costs and establishes a two phases strategy when designing the layout plans of the final objects. The final object is parsed into components (termed *modules* or *assemblies*) in a straightforward way, such that these modules can also be reused to assemble other objects. This strategy of representing the final object as a composition of modules is very similar to the construction of buildings out of prefabricated structural components, i.e., modules. This way, by using a modular approach, the description and the design plans of quite sophisticated objects can be kept relatively simple and manageable and the complexity and the difficulty of building the final object is delegated to the assembly of the modules. Hence, the building specification of the final object is split into two guidelines, one regarding how to assemble the required modules, one regarding how to put together the modules to form the final object.

Each brick has numerical and non-numerical characteristics. A non-numerical attribute is, for example, a unique ID which characterizes the bricks like shape, approximate dimensions, number and the arrangement of the inner tubes, etc. Another non-numerical attribute is the color of the bricks, etc. There are very tight requirements in order to be able to assemble two or more bricks. In order to cut costs the technological process to manufacture the bricks is kept simple and cost-effective to the detriment of interchangeability. Thus, the pieces are measured after the production process and the measurement values are persisted in adequate storage systems.

In order to be able to assemble the bricks, they have to fit together, i.e., some measurement values (see Figure 2 for an example) have to fulfill some constraints. The respective

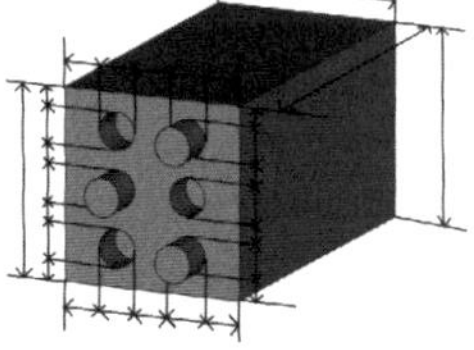

Figure 2: Exemplification of the measurements of a brick.

measurement values must match in order that the bricks can be assembled. For example, putting four bricks together, side by side and on top of each other, strict restrictions concerning perpendicularity and planarity tolerance, have to be satisfied, such that for example, the overall maximum planarity error is 0.05 mm and the maximum perpendicularity error is 0.1 angular degree. Unfortunately, these restrictions can only be evaluated when all the measurement values of the bricks chosen to build the module are at the builder's disposal. Corresponding calculation prescription are available.

Once, the modules have been assembled, the object can be put together out of the pre-assembled modules with no limitations. Furthermore, all the modules are interchangeable with similar ones.

The manufacturing of the bricks is continuous, the bricks are packed into bins after the measuring process occurred and stowed in a warehouse. The ID, the non-numerical attributes and the numerical measurement values are stored in a database and associated to the bin ID. This way, the manufacturer knows exactly the content of each bin. In order to keep the manufacturing costs low, the bins are never repacked, after a bin is full and in the warehouse.

The assembly plan for a particular structure (for example as in Figure 3) is not univocal, i.e., the number and the type of the bricks to build the envisaged structure is not unequivocally specified, the assembly plan contains more alternatives. Since

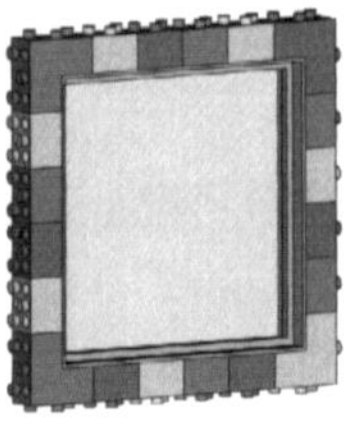

Figure 3: A frame with window as an example for a module.

the manufacturer provides detail information in digital form regarding each brick contained in the bins offered for sale, a computer program could easily verify that a house as given in Figure 4 could be built up from a particular set of bins. Unfortunately, identifying the set of bins necessary to build an

Figure 4: House as exemplification of an order composed of modules.

object (for example the house as in Figure 4) turns out to be a very hard task to accomplish. In order to keep costs down, the number of the bins to be purchased, has to be limited to the necessary ones.

Let us suppose that the order can be assembled out of 5 bins, and the manufacturer offers 1000 bins for sale on his home page. Regrettably, the computer program can only verify if a particular set of five bins contains the bricks necessary to build the house. The brute force method to verify each set of 5 bins out of 1000 does not deliver a practical solution as elementary combinatorics show. Thus, other methods have to be applied.

D. Outline

The remainder of the paper is structured as follows: Section II gives an overview about existing work related to the described problem. Section III introduces the mathematical model and describes how the combinatorial problem can be transformed into a constrained satisfaction problem. Section IV applies the proposed selection algorithm based on genetic algorithms to an industrial use case and shows the performance of an implemented solution which is based on genetic algorithms. A short investigation regarding multi-objective optimization is considered in Section V, whereas Section VI concludes this paper and sketches the future work.

II. Related work

Generally speaking, combinatorial optimization problems are considered as being difficult [1] [2], which stimulated the development of effective approximate methods for their solutions. Combinatorial optimization problems appear in a multitude of real world applications, such as routing, assignment, scheduling, cutting and packing, network design, protein alignment, and in many fields of utmost economic, industrial, and scientific importance. The techniques for solving combinatorial optimization problems can be exact and heuristics. Exact algorithms guarantee optimal solutions, but the execution time often increases dramatically with the size of the underlying data, such that only small size of instances can be exactly solved. For all other cases, optimality is sacrificed for solvability in a limited amount of time [3].

The concept of a constraint satisfaction problem has also been formulated in the nineteen seventies by researchers in the artificial intelligence. Characteristic CSPs are the n queens problem, the zebra puzzle, the full adder circuit, the crossword puzzle, qualitative temporal reasoning, etc. Typical examples of constrained optimization problems are the knapsack problem and the coins problem [4]. Further examples of combinatorial optimization problems [5] are: bin packing, the traveling salesman problem, job scheduling, network routing, vehicle routing problem, multiprocessor scheduling, etc.

For the last decades, the development of theory and methods of computational intelligence regarding problems of combinatorial optimization was of interest of researchers. Nowadays, a class of evolutionary methods [6]–[9] is of particular interest, like simulated annealing, ant colony optimization, taboo search, particle swarm optimization, to which genetic algorithms belong [10]–[13]. Recent publications in this direction [14]–[20] prove the efficacy of applying genetic and other evolutionary algorithms in solving combinatorial optimization problems.

A genetic algorithm is an adaptive search technique based on the principles and mechanism of natural selection and of the survival of the fittest from the natural evolution. The genetic algorithms evolved from Holland's study [21] of adaptation in artificial and natural systems [5].

Typical examples of using evolutionary algorithms are the genetic algorithm approach to solve the hospital physician scheduling problem and an ant colony optimization based approach to solve the split delivery vehicle routing problem [22].

The report [23] offers an approach to use genetic algorithms to solve combinatorial optimization problems on a set of euclidean combinatorial configuration. The euclidean combinatorial configuration is a mapping of a finite abstract set into the euclidean space using the euclidean metric. The class of handled problems includes a problem of balancing masses of rotating parts, occurred in turbine construction, power plant engineering, etc.

III. The Formal Model

In the following, we will formalize the description of the combinatorial problem by introducing a mathematical model. This way, we use the advantages of the rigor of a formal approach over the inaccuracy and the incompleteness of natural languages. First, we introduce and tighten our notation, then we present the formal definition of the constraints which are considered in our formal model and which are the major components in the definition of the fitness function used to control and steer the genetic algorithm. Concluding, the combinatorial problem is defined as a constraint satisfaction problem.

A. Notation

Let $\mathfrak{V}$ be an arbitrary set. We notate by $\mathcal{P}(\mathfrak{V})$ the power set of $\mathfrak{V}$, i.e., the set of all subsets of $\mathfrak{V}$, including the empty set and $\mathfrak{V}$ itself. We notate by $\mathrm{card}(\mathfrak{V})$ the cardinality of $\mathfrak{V}$. We use a calligraphic font to denote index sets, such that the index set of $\mathfrak{V}$ is notated by $I^{\mathcal{V}}$.

The finite sets of bricks, bins, (non-numerical type of) attributes, (numerical type of) and measurements are denoted as follows:

$$\mathfrak{S} := \{s_i \mid i \in I^{\mathcal{S}} \text{ and } s_i \text{ is a brick (stone)}\},$$
$$\mathfrak{B} := \{b_i \mid i \in I^{\mathcal{B}} \text{ and } b_i \text{ is a bin (carton)}\},$$
$$\mathfrak{A} := \{A^i \mid i \in I^{\mathcal{A}} \text{ and } A^i \text{ is an attribute}\},$$
$$\mathfrak{M} := \{M^i \mid i \in I^{\mathcal{M}} \text{ and } M^i \text{ is a measurement}\}.$$

Let $i \in I^{\mathcal{A}}$, $j \in I^{\mathcal{M}}$, and $k \in I^{\mathcal{S}}$. We denote by a_k^i the value of the attribute A^i of the brick s_k and by m_k^j the value of the measurement M^j at the brick s_k. We denote the list of assembly units (modules) by

$$\mathfrak{U} := \{U^i \mid i \in I^{\mathcal{U}} \text{ and } U^i \text{ is an assembly unit (module)}\}.$$

The construction (guideline) plan for a module $U \in \mathfrak{U}$ contains

a) the (three dimensional) design plan description, i.e., the position of each brick within the module,

b) the non-numerical attribute values for each brick and

c) prescriptions regarding the measurement values.

Analogously, by

$$\mathfrak{O} := \{O^i \mid i \in I^{\mathcal{O}} \text{ and } O^i \text{ is an object}\}$$

we denote the list of objects for which there exists construction plans.

The non-numerical attributes values of the selected bricks have to match the corresponding values in the guideline plan.

We denote by

$$\mathfrak{R} := \{R^i \mid i \in I^{\mathcal{R}} \text{ and } R^i \text{ is a requirement (specification)}\}$$

the list of the requirements (specifications) of the objects.

B. Transformation of the CP into a CSP

Let $O \in \mathfrak{O}$ an order. Then, according to the specifications, there exists *(proxy) modules* $\hat{M}^{l_1}, \hat{M}^{l_2}, \ldots, \hat{M}^{l_k}$, such that O is an ordered list of modules, i.e., $O = (\hat{M}^{l_1}, \hat{M}^{l_2}, \ldots, \hat{M}^{l_k})$. The term *proxy* is used to denote an abstract entity according to the specifications. Analogously, each module $\hat{M}^i$ with $i \in \{l_1, l_2, \ldots, l_k\}$ is an ordered list of *proxy bricks* (stones), i.e., $\hat{M}^i = (\hat{s}_{i_1}, \hat{s}_{i_2}, \ldots, \hat{s}_{i_m})$. Hence, each module can be represented by an ordered list of proxy bricks, i.e., $O = (\hat{s}_{k_1}, \hat{s}_{k_2}, \ldots, \hat{s}_{k_n})$. This representation will be used later to define the individuals within the context of the genetic algorithms.

Let $O = (\hat{s}_{k_1}, \hat{s}_{k_2}, \ldots, \hat{s}_{k_n})$ be a module. We say that the ordered list $(s_{k_1}, s_{k_2}, \ldots, s_{k_n})$ with $s_i \in \mathfrak{S}\ \forall i \in \{k_1, k_2, \ldots, k_n\}$ is an assignment (embodiment) of O. This means especially that the abstract unit of the specification is materialized within the production process. We set

$$\mathfrak{E} := \{E^i \mid i \in I^{\mathcal{E}} \text{ and } E^i \text{ is an assignment (embodiment)}\}.$$

Let $R \in \mathfrak{R}$ be a requirement (specification) of a specific module $U \in \mathfrak{U}$ and let $\{\hat{s}_1, \hat{s}_2, \ldots, \hat{s}_n\}$ be the proxy bricks of the specification. The design plan of the specification provides the three-dimensional assembly plan of the proxy bricks. Additionally, the specifications provide information regarding the restriction the bricks have to fulfill in order to be eligible. For each $j \in \{1, 2, \ldots, n\}$ the specifications contain the values $\{\hat{a}^i_j \mid i \in I^{\mathcal{A}}\}$ of the attributes $\mathfrak{A} := \{A^i \mid i \in I^{\mathcal{A}}\}$ at the proxy brick $\hat{s}_j$. We use the symbol $\hat{a}^i_j$ to denote the value of the attribute a^i of the proxy (placeholder) brick $\hat{s}_j$.

This means especially, that the brick s_j can substitute the proxy brick $\hat{s}_j$ if the values of the corresponding attributes coincide, i.e., $a^i_j = \hat{a}^i_j$ for all $i \in I^{\mathcal{A}}$.

More formally, the attributes must satisfy certain constraints:

$$C_A : \mathfrak{A} \times \mathfrak{S} \to \{yes, no\},$$
$$\{s^i_j \mid i \in I^{\mathcal{A}},\ j \in I^{S}\} \mapsto C_A(a^i_j).$$

$C_A(a^i_j) = yes$ if the attribute constraint is satisfied for the brick s_j i.e., $a^i_j = \hat{a}^i_j$, else $C_A(a^i_j) = no$.

On the other side, the (numerical) measurement values must also satisfy certain constraints (restrictions). For example, the standard deviation of the respective measurement values for some bricks of a specific module should not surpass some given limits. Formally, C_M can be represented as:

$$C_M : \mathfrak{M} \times \mathfrak{U} \to \{yes, no\},$$
$$\{m^i_j \mid i \in I^{\mathcal{M}},\ j \in I^{\mathcal{U}}\} \mapsto C_M(m^i_j).$$

$C_M(m^i_j) = yes$ if the constraint is satisfied for the bricks belonging to the module U^j, else $C_M(m^i_j) = no$.

In order to be able to reduce the constraints to brick level, i.e., to be able to decide whether the constraint is satisfied for a specific brick or not, we use the restriction C^S_M of C_M namely $C^S_M := C_M\big|_S$ such that $C^S_M(s^i_j) = yes$ if $s_j \in U^j$ and $C_M(m^i_j) = yes$; else $C^S_M(m^i_j) = no$. Let $U \in \mathfrak{U}$ be a module. The above means especially, that the measurement constraint on brick level is satisfied for $s \in U$ if the measurement constraint is satisfied (on module level) for U.

Since the measurement values do not really characterize the modules (they must only fulfill the requirements regarding the constraints), we introduce equivalence classes on the set of modules. Two modules belong to the same class if

a) they have both the same design plan,

b) the component bricks fulfill the same (non-numerical) attributes and

c) the prescriptions regarding the measurement values are satisfied for both modules.

Accordingly, two modules belonging to the same equivalence class are interchangeable.

Hence, all the bricks needed for a module must be selected in order to be able to finally decide if the constraints are satisfied or not.

As already mentioned, each object $O \in \mathfrak{O}$ should be assembled out of bricks contained in a reduced number of bins. We set $MaxB^O$ for the maximum number of bins as mentioned above.

Let $i \in I^{\mathcal{B}}$, $j \in I^O$, let $\{s_{i_1}, s_{i_2}, \ldots, s_{i_k}\}$ be the content of the bin b_i and let $\{s_{j_1}, s_{j_2}, \ldots, s_{j_l}\}$ be an assignment of $O^j \in \mathfrak{O}$. We set $b^j_i := 1$ if $\{s_{i_1}, s_{i_2}, \ldots, s_{i_k}\} \cap \{s_{j_1}, s_{j_2}, \ldots, s_{j_l}\} \neq \emptyset$ else 0. This means especially, that $b^j_i := 1$ if the bin contains bricks belonging to the respective assignment of O^j.

Analogously, the constraints regarding the bins (cartons) can be regarded formally as:

$$C_B : \mathcal{P}(\mathfrak{B}) \times \mathfrak{O} \to \{yes, no\},$$
$$\{\mathbb{B} \in \mathcal{P}(\mathfrak{B}),\ O^j \in \mathfrak{O}\} \mapsto C_B(\mathbb{B}, O^j).$$

Let $\mathbb{I}$ an index set, such that $\mathbb{B} = \{b_i | i \in \mathbb{I}\}$. Then $C_B(\mathbb{B}, O^j) = yes$ if

$$\sum_{i \in \mathbb{I}} b^j_i \leq MaxB^{O^j},$$

i.e., the bricks of the order O^j are contained in no more than $MaxB^{O^j}$ bins. Additionally, $C_B(\mathbb{B}, O^j) = no$ if the above condition is not satisfied.

Similar to the measurement constraint C_M, we reduce C_B to brick level. Let $\mathbb{S} := \{s_{i_1}, s_{i_2}, \ldots, s_{i_k}\}$ be an assignment of O^i. Let $\mathbb{B} = \{b_{l_1}, b_{l_2}, \ldots, b_{l_n}\}$ be a set of bins, such that each bin contains at least one $s \in \mathbb{S}$ and there is no brick $s \in \mathbb{S}$ which is not contained in one of the bins of the set $\mathbb{B}$. In this sense, $\mathbb{B}$ is minimal regarding the assignment $\mathbb{S}$. Then, for the restriction C^S_B on S of C_M we have $C^S_B(s) = yes$ if $C_B(\mathbb{B}, O^i) = yes$, i.e., all the bricks of the assignment $\mathbb{S}$ are stored in no more than $MaxB^{O^j}$ bins. Additionally, $C^{S,U}_B(s) = no$ if $C_B(\mathbb{B}, O^i)$ is not satisfied.

Until now, we considered the constraints related to the architecture of the object, i.e., related to the attributes of a particular brick, the measurement values of the bricks belonging to a module, and the restrictions regarding the bins which contain the bricks. We can condense the constraints mentioned above, such that they relate only to bricks. This means especially, that the measurement constraint are satisfied for a brick, if there is a group of bricks (module, or order), such that the given measurement constraint is satisfied as described above. We set accordingly:

$$\mathfrak{C} := \{C^i \mid i \in I^C \text{ and } C^i \text{ is a distinct constraint}\}$$

the list of distinct constraints.

The constraints can be considered as a function. Please recall that I^S is the index set of $\mathfrak{S}$.

$$C : \mathfrak{S} \times I^C \to \{yes, no\},$$
$$\{s_k^i \mid i \in I^C,\, k \in I^S\} \mapsto C(s_k^i).$$

Please consider, that the above representation can be misinterpreted, such that the constraint is exclusively a property of the respected brick. This is not the case, for example the measurement constraints fulfilled or not for the bricks assigned to a module. Hence, if one brick is changed, then the constraints of all the bricks belonging to a module can be invalidated.

We define now formally the weights, (i.e., w is a weight if $w > 0$) which are necessary to be able to model the importance of the constraints within the genetic algorithm. We set

$$\mathfrak{W} := \{w_i \mid i \in I^C \text{ and } w_i \text{ is a weight}\}$$

the list of weights. This means especially, that each constraint has an associated weight.

The fitness function [24] characterizes the quality of an assignment of an order, such that a value closer to 1 means a better quality. It plays an important role in the decision, whether an assignment fulfills the specifications or not.

The purpose of the following function inv is purely technical, it is used to switch the values of the boolean values 1 and 0 to be used in the definition of an example of the fitness function, i.e., $inv : \{yes, no\} \to \{0, 1\}$ such that $inv(yes) = 0$ and $inv(no) = 1$.

Please find below an example for the fitness function. Let $I^{\mathbb{S}} \subset I^S$ and let $w_i \in \mathfrak{W}$ for all $i \in I^C$. Then:

$$F : \mathfrak{C} \times I^C \to (0, 1],$$
$$\{s_k^i \mid i \in I^C,\, k \in I^{\mathbb{S}}\} \mapsto \frac{1}{1 + \sum\limits_{i \in I^C, k \in I^{\mathbb{S}}} w_i \cdot inv(C(s_k^i))}. \quad (1)$$

Problem formulation (Combinatorial problem)

Let $O \in \mathfrak{O}$ a given object and let $n \in \mathbb{N}$.

Choose n bins from the warehouse, such that the object can be assembled out of the bricks contained in these bins according to the existing construction plans.

The construction plan for an object $O \in \mathfrak{O}$ specifies the lists of (non equivocally determined) modules, including the design plan, such that the object can be build out of these modules. Hence, it can be unambiguously decided, whether the n cartons contain the necessary bricks to assemble them to modules, which can be put together to form the required object. Let us suppose that $n \ll \mathrm{card}(\mathfrak{C})$, i.e., the number of bins in the warehouse exceeds the number of bins to be chosen by orders of magnitude. The difficulties of solving the problem in a straightforward way lie in the very large number of possibilities to combine n bins out of $\mathrm{card}(\mathfrak{B})$. Therefore, other strategies have to be used.

To summarize: the specification of an object (for example a house composed of bricks), contains very strict requirements regarding the components. The assembly plan specifies the strict order in which the bricks have to be assembled. Hence, the bricks must satisfy some attributes (like shape, type, color, etc., in order to satisfy the requirements of the construction plans. Moreover, some bricks have to fit together (for example the window frame) so they can be assembled in the order given by the construction plans. If the above requirements are satisfied for all the units (modules), the object can be assembled. Furthermore, the selected bricks have to be selected from a restricted number of bins (cartons). The latter makes the task so difficult.

From a formal point of view, the associated constraint satisfaction problem of the combinatorial problem can now be formulated:

Problem formulation (Constraint satisfaction problem)

Let $O \in \mathfrak{O}$ be an order with the representation $O = (\hat{s}_1, \hat{s}_2, \ldots, \hat{s}_k)$. Set $w_i = 1$ for all $i \in I^C$.

Find an index set $\{l_1, l_2, \ldots, l_k\} \subset I^S$ such that $(s_{l_1}, s_{l_2}, \ldots, s_{l_k})$ is an assignment of O, having $F((s_{l_1}, s_{l_2}, \ldots, s_{l_k})) = 1$.

IV. USE CASE: AN EXCERPT

In the following, we present a real-life use case [25] we came across at an international semiconductor company. We describe the problem by using the specific terminology in the semiconductor industry, utilizing them with care and only when it is inevitable and undeniable necessary. We describe the fundamentals of the genetic algorithms and show the way it is used to solve our problem. Finally, we conclude by presenting some performance tests.

A. Problem Description

The company manufactures integrated circuits (ICs, also termed chips), which are subsequently assembled on circuits boards to salable entities, termed modules. In order to keep production cost low, the specification of the ICs do not impose very tight constraints on the attributes of the ICs, such that the same IC can be used for different types of modules. On the contrary, the specification regarding the modules are very stringent, in order that the module should be fully functional at the customer side. As soon as the ICs are manufactured, a good dozen of electrical properties are measured and persisted in a data repository.

Usually, four to six ICs are assembled on the module. The specification of the modules contains the design (i.e., number and positioning) of the ICs on the integrated circuit board, the type of the IC (article, number of pins, etc.), and several constrains regarding the interaction of the ICs of the module. In order for the module to be fully functional, the corresponding measurement values of the ICs have to be in a narrow range. For example, for a specific measurement, the values of the voltage of the ICs have to be between 2.1 volt and 2.5 volt in order that the IC is not scrapped and can be used for further processing. Unfortunately, not all the ICs having the corresponding measurement value in the range as described above, can be assembled to a module. The values differ too much from each other, and the module will not work properly at the customer side. To circumvent this impediment further constraints are needed. These constraints apply on all ICs of the module or just on a subset of it. For example, an often used constraint is limiting the standard deviation of the voltage to 0.1 within one module.

The ordering unit (termed *work order*) contains the description of the modules, the customer expects to be shipped together at once. There are no additional constraints on the ICs regarding the work order.

As soon as the manufacturing process of the ICs has been finished, the ICs are packed in boxes. That way the cleaning of the ICs can be performed and the ICs can be assembled to modules. The boxes are then transferred to the warehouse.

The difficulties of the semiconductor company to honor each the order in general are also due to technological restrictions, since the tool that assembles the ICs can handle at most five boxes, i.e., all the ICs necessary to fulfill a work order should be located in five boxes. Due to the fact that the work orders always contain the same number of ICs, independent of the specification of the modules, the minimal number of boxes which are needed to meet the requirement of the work order is four with 9 percent surplus of ICs. If we rephrase the above in a more concise form, the challenge is: Find five boxes in the warehouse, such that it contains the ICs needed to fulfill the requirements for a work order.

B. Used Methods

Simple combinatorics show that the brute force method, i.e., go through all the possibilities and check if the selected boxes fulfill the requirements, is not implementable for practical systems. Fortunately, there is an implementation in place for the selection strategy, based on heuristics, local optimum, and inside knowledge of the pattern of the modules. This way, we have a very good way to compare the results of the genetic algorithm with alternative solutions. Regretfully, our attempt to deliver exact solutions on the problem using MATLAB were not crowned by success due to the large amount of data and to the restricted computing power of the machines we used. The disadvantages of the already existing solution for the selection strategy were partly also the issues that made it possible to set up such a solution:

a) the unpredictability that the selection strategy delivers a solution within the expected time frame;
b) the inflexibility to even minor changes in the design and specifications of the modules, thus, the unpredictability that the software can be used in the future;
c) heavy maintenance efforts due to the sophisticated and architecture and implementation;
d) lack of the proprietary knowledge and documentation of the implementation on the low level side;
e) impossibility to reuse the existing code with reasonable efforts for further development and enhancements.

The concepts of the genetic methods are straightforward and easy to understand. The main idea is that we start with an initial population of individuals, and as time goes by, the genes of the descendants are improved, such that at least one individual satisfies the expectations. The individual incorporates the requirements of the problem. The expectation in the end is that these requirements are finally satisfied. Each individual owns genes, part of it is inherited by his descendants.

We define the individuals as an abstraction of the work order, such that each gene of the individual is the abstraction for an IC of the warehouse. Accordingly, the individual satisfies the requirements if the ICs can be assembled to modules, such that the corresponding work order is fulfilled. The initial population is randomly generated out of the ICs in the warehouse. The criterion, which determines to what degree the individual fulfills the requirement of the associated work order, is the fitness function. The fitness function takes values between 0 and 1, a greater value means that the individual is more close to fulfill the specification of the work order. To achieve a value of 1 is the ultimate goal. It means that the corresponding individual satisfies the requirements to fulfill the associated work order. Hence, the definition of the fitness function is one of the most sensible parts of the genetic algorithms and the setup of this function should be considered very carefully.

Actually, the strategy of the genetic algorithm resembles very much to the evolution of the mankind. People marry, have children by passing their genes to them, divorce and remarry again, have children, and so on and so forth. The expectation is that the descendants have more "advantageous genes", regardless of how the term "advantageous genes" is defined.

Establishing the fitness function is one of the most important strategical decision to be taken when setting up the genetic algorithm. In our case, there are a few constraints (more than one) which affect the quality of the individuals. Implementations which try to find a Pareto optimal state [26], [27] (i.e., a state from which it is impossible to make an individual better, without making at least one individual worse) use strategies as tournament selection [28] or the improved Pareto domination tournament [27].

As already mentioned, the starting population is selected aleatorically. Once, the first generation is constituted, the preparations to generate the next generation are met. Unfortunately, the Apache Commons Mathematics Library does not support multi-objective optimization problems, hence our algorithms cannot use the strategy of the *Niched Pareto Genetic Algorithm* (NPGA) [27].

Instead, for each individual, the fitness function is calculated such that the suitability to fulfill the expectations, is evaluated for each individual. The higher the computed value is, the better fitted are the individuals. Let us suppose, that the initial population is composed of 500 individuals. We use some of the concepts provided by Apache Commons Mathematics Library in our implementation, among others the *elitism rate,* which specifies the percentage of the individuals with the highest fitness value to be taken over / cloned to the new generation. We use an elitism rate of 10 percent, i.e., the 50 best individuals will be taken without any changes of the genes to the new generation.

The population of each generation remains constant in time. In order to choose the remaining 450 individuals (parents) to generate the next generation, we use the *tournament selection* [28] including the implementation of the Apache Commons Mathematics Library. The tournament strategy can be configured by the *arity* of the tournament strategy, which specifies the number of individuals who take part in the tournament. For our purpose, five individuals in the tournament proved to be efficient. Accordingly, five individuals are selected randomly out of the total population of 500 individuals to take part in the tournament. Out of the individuals taking part in the tournament, the fittest individual is selected as a parent for the new generation. This way, 500 parents are selected out of a population of 500 individuals. These parents are paired aleatorically and they always have two descendants. This way, the next generation is created. Accordingly, the size of each generation remains constant.

We use two major strategies in order to improve the quality of the genes of the descendants, the *crossover strategy* described in [29] and the *mutation strategy*. Generally speaking, during the crossover phase, the two descendants receive the partly interchanged genes of their parents. Additionally, some particular genes can suffer mutations. The general strategy to generate the descendants is based on random decisions.

We describe in brief the creation strategy of the new generation. Some parameters are freely configurable, in order to assure best performance. Thus, the *crossover rate,* i.e., the threshold of the probability that a crossover is performed, has to be set in advance. Then, a crossover is performed if a randomly generated number is less than the crossover rate. Same is true regarding the mutation rate.

The crossover policy is quite straightforward. The position and length of the genes to be crossed over are randomly generated and the two descendants have receive the interchanged genes of their parents. In our case, this policy has been improved, such that by in the end, the number of the bins of at least one descendant is using, is lower than (or if this is not possible equal to) the number of the bins of their parents. This way, the reduction of the number of bins an individual is using, is enforced by the crossover policy itself.

The mutation policy is also very intuitive. In addition to the mutation rate, which defines in the end, whether mutation is applied after the crossover phase or not, the exchange rate indicates whether a slot (IC) is to be renewed. Analogously, the mutation policy can be configured such that the number of bins the descendant is using is reduced or in worst case, kept constant.

C. *Performance Results*

The benchmarks were performed on a Intel® Core^{TM} i5-6500 CPU (quad core CPU 3.2 GHz, 16 GB RAM) running on Windows 10 and Eclipse 3.7.0 using Java SE Runtime Environment 1.6.0_22. The genetic algorithm was implemented using the Apache Common Library, version 3.0. The test data is a subset of the production environment and contained 5518 ICs in 261 boxes, having 28 measurements on average. The restricted test data is a subset of the production environment and contained 27,590 ICs in 1,305 boxes. Due to the incomplete set of production data, only the two most critical modules are considered for selection. After taking into account the attributes corresponding to the specifications of the two modules regarding the ICs (article, number of pins, etc.) only eleven boxes contain ICs to be considered for the selection process. We term *pre-selection* the method to restrict the number of boxes by excluding those boxes which do not contain selectable elements. In this way, the search area can be drastically reduced and thus, the performance of the selection algorithm can be substantially improved.

We use a generation size of 500 individuals, an elitism rate of 10 percent and an arity value of 5. The number of generation is limited to 1000 and the runtime of the selection algorithm is limited to 300 seconds. The other parameters like the crossover rate and the mutation rate are configured on a case by case basis. Regarding the fitness function, the following configuration parameters have proved themselves as good choice: attribute weight = 1; measurement weight = 2; bin weight = 5. This means especially, that fulfilling the bin constraints is the most difficult one. In summary, we use the configuration parameters given in Table I for the performance tests.

TABLE I: SETTINGS OF CONFIGURATION PARAMETERS.

Configuration parameter	Value
Population limit	500 individuals
Generation limit	1000 generations
Crossover policy	Bin reduction
Crossover rate	78 %
Mutation rate	13 %
Runtime limit	300 seconds

The prediction of the results of the selection algorithm is hardly possible, since we use random strategies to generate the initial population, to select the parents for the next generation, to determine the crossover and mutation policy. Moreover, parameters like the elitism rate and the arity have to be configured. Hence, the interaction between many factors that can influence the success and performance of the selection algorithm is not obvious.

It is not the aim of this study to deliver the possible best solution in an acceptable time frame and to improve the performance of the algorithm. Instead, our objective is to deliver an acceptable solution, i.e., a solution that fulfills the required constraints, for the industry to a crucial problem regarding their production problems. For example, there is no technological benefit of tightening the measurement constraints; the bin constraint was set up in such a way that seeking a lower value is not possible due to the fixed number of ICs of a work order and to the maximal capacity of the bins. Hence, the acceptable solution is also the best possible solution.

Nevertheless, we tried to improve the selection algorithm by testing the influence of the parameters, we find out to be decisive. This was also the case for the parameters of the fitness function as described above.

As already mentioned, we have an algorithm in place, which can find

a) a suboptimal solution in a heuristic way,
b) determine exactly whether the group of bins contain ICs which satisfies the specification of a particular work order.

Figure 5 shows that the selection algorithm using pre-selection delivers the expected results, finding individuals having 19 modules. The *success rate,* i.e., the probability that the selection algorithm reaches with an individual the given number of modules, is over 60 percent and thus, high enough for practical systems. The pre-selection strategy is very straightforward and easy to implement. Thus, no practical system would renounce to it. Nevertheless, when neglecting the benefit of reducing the search space by using pre-selection, the results of the genetic algorithm are not always as promising as with pre-selection. In order to evaluate worst-case scenarios, we used work that posed a lot of difficulties to select with the heuristic algorithm in place. As illustrated in Figure 5, the success rate to select 19 modules as in the previous case, is at 60 percent. This means especially, that the successful run of the genetic algorithm heavily depends on the random numbers that were generated.

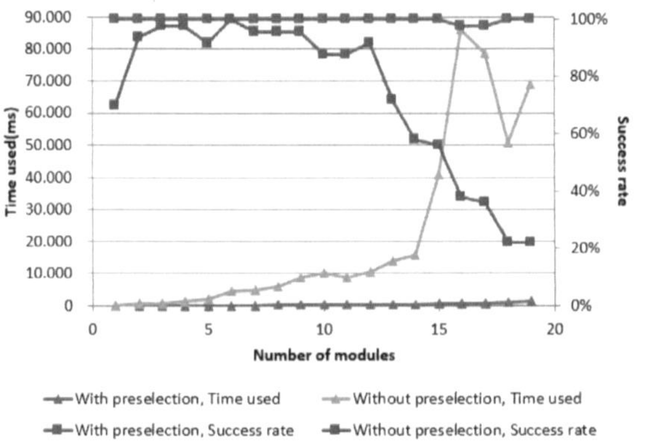

Figure 5: Success rate and time used depending on the number of modules with and without pre-selection.

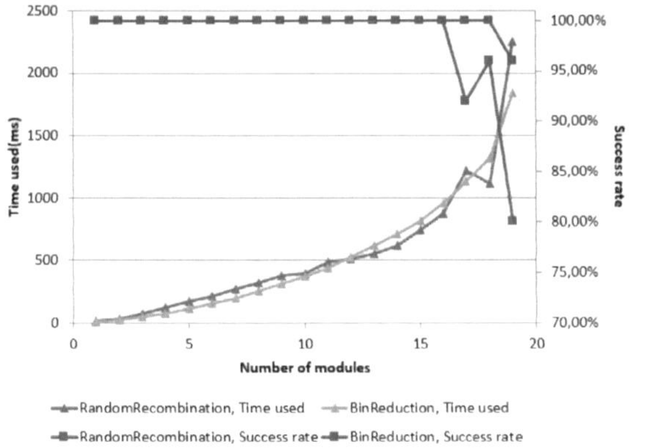

Figure 6: Success rate and time used when selecting the random recombination crossover policy or the bins reduction policy.

Figure 6 shows the difference between the random recombination crossover policy and the bins reduction policy. The boxes reduction crossover policy tries to reduce the number of boxes of the new individuals by focusing on the common bins of the parents. As a conclusion, using business logic over general approach, the general approach is as expected slower and has a lower success rate. This is the price to pay for using a more general solution over a customized one.

Figures 7 and 8 show the influence of the crossover rate and

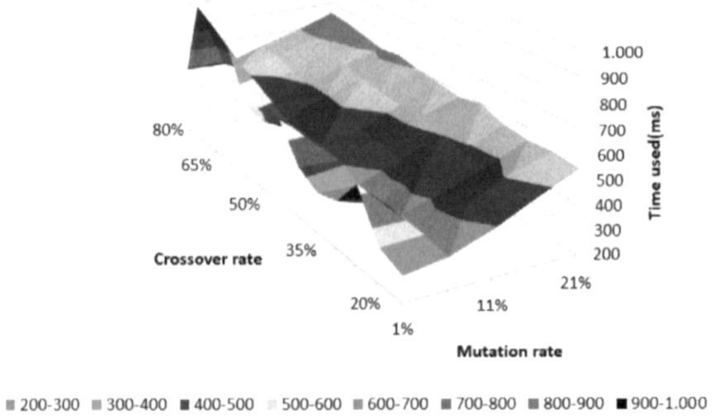

Figure 7: Time used depending on the crossover rate and the mutation rate.

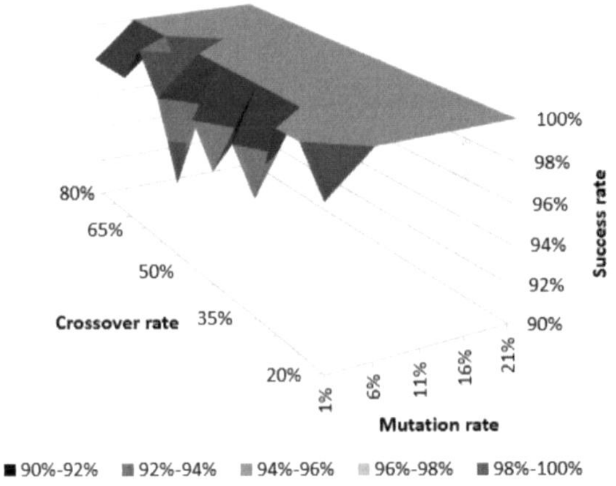

Figure 8: Success rate depending on the crossover rate and the mutation rate.

the mutation rate to the success rate and the wall clock time. As not obvious at first glance, a smaller crossover rate and a higher mutation rate gives better values for the success rate. Keeping the crossover rate and the mutation rate low, better run time performance is achieved. Generally speaking, high mutation rate can destroy the structure of good chromosomes, if used randomly [30]. The above remark does not hold in our case, since we do not exchange ICs randomly, but according to our strategy to minimize the number of bins.

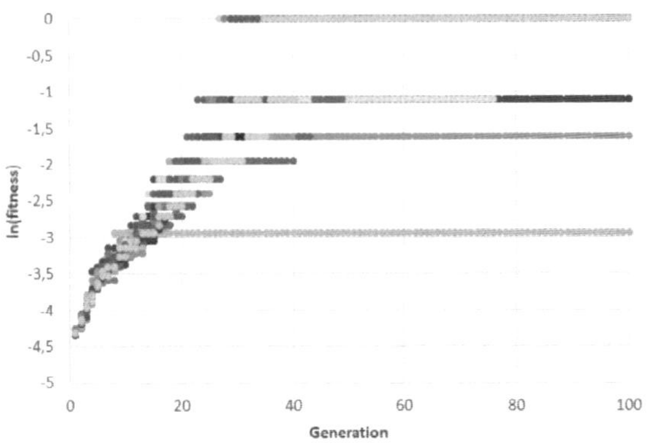

Figure 9: Logarithmic representation of the values of the fitness function depending on the number of generations (50 attempts).

The tendency of the convergence of the fitness function is visualized in Figure 9. The graph shows that in the end all 50 threads converge after some generations, but only a subset to the envisaged value. Recall that the maximum value of the fitness function is per definition equal to 1, the higher the value of the fitness function, the better the solution. The values of the fitness functions are discrete, $\{1, \frac{1}{2}, \frac{1}{3}, \frac{1}{4}, \frac{1}{5}, \ldots\}$.

V. RESUMING ON MULTI-OBJECTIVE OPTIMIZATION

Our preferred implementation framework is *Apache Commons Mathematics Library*, version 3.0 [31]. However, a very similar combinatorial grouping problem, the *Bin Packing Problem (BPP)* is investigated [32], by using the off the shelf *jMetal* framework [33]. The (one-dimensional) BPP [34] is defined as follows: given an unlimited number of bins with an integer capacity $c > 0$ each, a set of n items, $N = \{1, 2, ..., n\}$, and an integer weight $w_i, 0 < w_i \leq c$ for each item $i \in N$ assign each item to one bin, such that the total weight of the items in each bin does not exceed c and the number of bins used is minimized.

Luo et al. [32] extends the base implementation of jMetal to problems with dynamic variables. This was necessary, since the number of the genes in chromosomes is fixed in the base implementation of jMetal. However, the number of the genes in the specific implementation of the chromosomes for BPP – termed group based representation – is fluctuating; they vary in length depending on how many bins are used in every solution. Accordingly, the adopted implementation of BPP includes specific adaptations and enhancements of the basic primitives of jMetal, including those for chromosomes, crossover and mutation. The need for dynamic variables is justified by difficulties to use other solutions due to the fitness function.

In order to evaluate the performance of their algorithms – termed GABP –, Luo et al. [32] use public bench data as well as self-created big data sets. The performance of GABP does not differ very much from some of the known implementation of BPP. The main benefit of GABP is the implementation in a generic framework. However, the problem described in this article, the *Matching Lego(R)-Like Bricks Problem (MLBP)* is new to our knowledge, we are now aware of any implementation of a similar problem. The nearest problem to the MLBP seems to be BPP.

It seems that Luo et al. [32] used the fitness function as given below (termed cost function) [35] for their *group-based encoding scheme*:

$$f_{BPP} = \frac{1}{N_u} \cdot \sum_{i=1}^{N_u} (\frac{fill_i}{c})^k \tag{2}$$

with N_u being the number of bins used, $fill_i$ the sum of sizes of the objects in the bin i, c the bin capacity, and k a constant, $k > 1$. In other words, the cost function to maximize is the average over all bins used, of the k-th power of the bin's utilization of it's capacity. The authors state that experiments show that $k = 2$ gives good results. As Falkenauer and Delchambre [35] point out that one of the major purpose of the fitness function is to guide the algorithm in the search.

Although, both BPP and MLBP yield a reduction of the number of bins, the fitness function of the algorithms are different. The strategy at BPP is to pack the bins as full as possible, i.e., a bad use of the capacity of the bins leads to the necessity of supplementary bins [35]. On the contrary, the suggestion for the fitness function for MLBP is given by the need to fulfill the constraints.

By comparing the formula (1) for the fitness function of MLBP with the formula (2) as above, it is obvious that both formulas are very similar, both are expected to be maximized, contain summation over parameters of the respective problems and the possibility to optimize the execution time of the respective algorithms through clever setting of constants. In this respect, both MLBP and BPP substantially benefit from an ingeniously designed fitness function to ensure fast convergence towards the optimization goals [35].

Although, in concept MLBP is merely a constraint satisfaction problem, the implementation as described in this article, can be easily adapted to simulate an optimization problem. Within the current algorithm, the number of required bins is fixed. This assumption is perfectly reasonable from an industrial perspective, since the number of the objects in the bins is more or less the same and as the number of objects needed for a work order is known, the minimal number of bins necessary to fulfill the work order is thus determined. Besides, the maximum number of bins that can be accessed by a machine is fixed, less beans means just a vacant working place. However, by setting the bin constraints to a lower value, – while keeping the other constraints unchanged – and by modifying the exit criteria accordingly, the algorithm will loop – delivering better solutions according to the guidelines of the fitness function – until the new exit criteria are met. Thus, a local extremum relating to the fitness function is found. The local extremum is not automatically a solution to the constraint satisfaction problem, this has to be validated. The exit criteria only ensure that the best local value of the fitness function and corresponding physical entities are found. In this respect, the MLBP and BPP are closely related problems.

There are other systems, which provide frameworks of evolutionary algorithms, such as EvA2, OPT4j, ECJ, MOEAT, for a discussion and bibliography see [35]. Moreover, a remarkable attempt to obtain a deeper understanding of the structure of the BPP by using Principal Component Analysis and repercussions on the performance of the heuristic approaches to solve them, was undertaken [36].

The aim of jMetal was to set up a Java-based framework in order to develop meta heuristics for solving Multi-objective Optimization Problems (MOP). jMetal provides a rich set of Java classes as base components, which can be reused for the implementation of generic operators, thus making a comparison of different meta heuristics possible [37] [38].

Unfortunately, the Apache Commons Mathematics Library deployed in our use case, does not support multi-objective optimization mechanisms. This means especially, that multi-objective optimization have to be simulated by single-objective optimization. For example, optimization criteria for MLBP are a) reducing the number of bins, b) fulfillment of the measurement constraints, c) fulfillment of the attribute constraints. These criteria are independent of each other and ideally within the multi-objective optimization they can be optimized independently, such that an improvement of a criterion does not lead to a degradation of another one. For practical purposes, the fitness function, see formula (1), can be used for simulating multi-objective optimization by choosing adequate weight function. Thus, by choosing the values $w = 5$ for the criterion (a), $w = 2$ for criterion (b) and $w = 1$ for criterion (c) we achieve fast convergence and hence reduced execution time, but for example by improving criterion (a) we cannot avoid the degradation of criterion (b) or (c). By using frameworks which support multi-objective mechanism, better convergence of the genetic algorithm is expected.

The jMetal project was started in 2006 [37] and since then it underwent significant improvements and major releases [39], such that the redesigned jMetal should be useful to researchers of the multi-objective optimization community, such as evolutionary algorithm, evolution strategies, scatter search, particle swarm optimization, ant colony optimization, etc., [40]. Improvements regarding a new package for automatic tuning of algorithm parameter settings have been introduced [41] in order to facilitate accurate Pareto front approximations.

In addition, jMetal in conjunction with Spark – which is becoming a dominant technology in the Big Data context – have been used to solve Big Data Optimization problems by setting up a software platform. Accordingly, a dynamic bi-objective instance of the Traveling Salesman Problem based on near real-time traffic data from New York City has been solved [42] [43].

VI. Conclusion and Future Work

The main challenge, which led to the results of this paper, was to investigate whether a real-life combinatorial problem, which popped up at a semiconductor company, can be solved within a reasonable time. Moreover, the solution should be flexible, such that the solution is not restricted to the existing specification of the modules.

We established an abstract formal model, such that the implementation of the use case is fully functional within the boundaries of this model. In this sense, new constraints can be added to the existing ones, no inside knowledge regarding the structure of the module is needed, as it is the case for the heuristic algorithm in place.

We set up a genetic algorithmic approach based on the Apache Commons Mathematics Library, implemented it and validated the results. Some decisive policies like the crossover and mutation policy have been additionally implemented and new optimizations like the bin reduction crossover policy have been set up to improve the convergence of the genetic algorithm. The performance results were satisfactory for an industrial application.

The current implementation does not combine good genes (taking into account all the constraints, like measurement, etc.) of the parents. Instead, the crossover strategy is based on random decisions. Additional research is necessary in this direction to find a good balance between a more general suitability (random decisions) and good convergence (adjusted crossover policy). For the time being, only the fitness function contains proprietary information regarding the production process, any other decision is aleatoric.

The implemented basic framework is very flexible, it has many configuration possibilities like the elitism rate and the arity. As a consequence of the random variables, many convergence tests with various configuration assignment have to be performed, in order to ensure satisfying results. Furthermore, of crucial importance for the successful completion of the algorithm is the design of the fitness function, especially the values of the weights.

The convergence tests show that not every execution will succeed to find the best solution delivered, this is due to the random numbers used through out the genetic algorithm. This is exemplified by the success rate. Thus, the selection algorithm based on genetic strategies always delivers local maxima, which may substantially differ from the global one. Our attempt to find the optimal solution using MATLAB for a reduced set of ICs failed due to the long execution time.

As already mentioned, the fitness function plays an outstanding role during the selection of the best candidates for the next generation. This means especially, that two candidates having the same value of their fitness function are considered of the same quality. This assertion is not accurate enough, due to the use of three different weights, whose interdependence can hardly be anticipated. Each weight represents the significance of one aspect of the quality of a candidate. To circumvent this dilemma, Pareto optimality [27] can be used to solve the challenge of the multi-objective function. In this case, a new framework [37] is needed, since Apache Commons Mathematics Library does not support multi-objective mechanism. Genetic algorithms, if configured properly, can be used to solve our constraint satisfaction problem. The delivered solution may substantially differ from the optimal one.

The current problem is not defined as an optimization problem, the constraints of a work order are either satisfied or not. Accordingly, two different solutions of the same work order, which satisfy the constraints, are of the same quality. However, the genetic algorithm is based internally on an optimization process – the higher the value of the fitness function, the better the solution. The constraints are used as exit criterion for the genetic algorithm. In this way, the optimization is stopped arbitrarily, considering that a better solution is out of scope.

Moreover, during the production process multiple work orders have to be honored simultaneously. The current strategy at the semiconductor company adopted a sequential one. We can reformulate the problem as an optimization problem: Given a list of work orders, find the maximum number of work orders that can be satisfied simultaneously.

The elapsed time till the genetic algorithm of MLBP converges is in range of seconds, by all means satisfactory for the investigated industrial application. As expected, not all the execution threads converge to the same solution, and not all the threads find an optimal solution, as shown in some cases less than 60 percent. Therefore, starting a bunch of threads within the genetic algorithm increases the chance towards better solutions.

Acknowledgment

We acknowledge the assistance and helpful comments of the anonymous referees.

REFERENCES

[1] B. Korte and J. Vygen, Combinatorial Optimization: Theory and Algorithms, ser. Algorithms and Combinatorics. Springer Berlin Heidelberg, 2018.

[2] P. M. Pardalos, D.-Z. Du, and R. L. Graham, Handbook of Combinatorial Optimization. Springer, 2013.

[3] J. Puchinger and G. Raidl, "Combining Metaheuristics and Exact Algorithms in Combinatorial Optimization: A Survey and Classification," Lecture Notes in Computer Science, vol. 3562, 06 2005, pp. 41–53, doi: 10.1007/11499305_5.

[4] Krzysztof Apt, Principles of Constraint Programming. Cambridge University Press, 2003, Retrieved: October 2019. [Online]. Available: https://doi.org/10.1017/CBO9780511615320

[5] A. L. Corcoran, Using LibGA to Develop Genetic Algorithms for Solving Combinatorial Optimization Problems. The Application Handbook of Genetic Algorithms, Volume I, Lance Chambers, editor, pages 143-172 CRC Press, 1995.

[6] E. Andrés-Pérez et al., Evolutionary and Deterministic Methods for Design Optimization and Control With Applications to Industrial and Societal Problems. Springer, 2018, vol. 49.

[7] D. Greiner et al., Advances in Evolutionary and Deterministic Methods for Design, Optimization and Control in Engineering and Sciences. Springer, 2015, vol. 1, no. 1.

[8] D. Simon, Evolutionary Optimization Algorithms. John Wiley & Sons, 2013.

[9] A. Pétrowski and S. Ben-Hamida, Evolutionary Algorithms. John Wiley & Sons, 2017.

[10] O. Kramer, Genetic Algorithm Essentials. Springer, 2017, vol. 679.

[11] T. Bäck, D. B. Fogel, and Z. Michalewicz, Evolutionary Computation 1: Basic Algorithms and Operators. CRC press, 2018.

[12] R. K. Belew, Adaptive Individuals in Evolving Populations: Models and Algorithms. Routledge, 2018.

[13] T. Bäck, D. B. Fogel, and Z. Michalewicz, Evolutionary Computation 2 : Advanced Algorithms and Operators. CRC Press, 2000, Textbook - 308 Pages.

[14] K. Hussain, M. N. M. Salleh, S. Cheng, and Y. Shi, "Metaheuristic Research: a Comprehensive Survey," Artificial Intelligence Review, 2018, pp. 1–43.

[15] T. Jiang and C. Zhang, "Application of Grey Wolf Optimization for Solving Combinatorial Problems: Job Shop and Flexible Job Shop Scheduling Cases," IEEE Access, vol. 6, 2018, pp. 26 231–26 240.

[16] H. Zhang, Y. Liu, and J. Zhou, "Balanced-Evolution Genetic Algorithm for Combinatorial Optimization Problems: the General Outline and Implementation of Balanced-Evolution Strategy Based on Linear Diversity Index," Natural Computing, vol. 17, no. 3, 2018, pp. 611–639.

[17] X. Li, L. Gao, Q. Pan, L. Wan, and K.-M. Chao, "An Effective Hybrid Genetic Algorithm and Variable Neighborhood Search for Integrated Process Planning and Scheduling in a Packaging Machine Workshop," IEEE Transactions on Systems, Man, and Cybernetics: Systems, 2018.

[18] I. Jackson, J. Tolujevs, and T. Reggelin, "The Combination of Discrete-Event Simulation and Genetic Algorithm for Solving the Stochastic Multi-Product Inventory Optimization Problem," Transport and Telecommunication Journal, vol. 19, no. 3, 2018, pp. 233–243.

[19] J. C. Bansal, P. K. Singh, and N. R. Pal, Evolutionary and Swarm Intelligence Algorithms. Springer, 2019.

[20] G. Raidl, J. Puchinger, and C. Blum, "Metaheuristic hybrids," Handbook of Metaheuristics, Vol. 146 of International Series in Operations Research and Management Science, 09 2010, pp. 469–496, doi: 10.1007/978-1-4419-1665-5_16.

[21] J. Holland, Adaptation in Natural and Artificial Systems. University of Michigan Press, Ann Arbor. 2nd Edition, MIT Press, 1992.

[22] G. P. Rajappa, "Solving combinatorial optimization problems using genetic algorithms and ant colony optimization," 2012, PhD diss., University of Tennessee, Retrieved: October 2019. [Online]. Available: https://trace.tennessee.edu/utk_graddiss/1478

[23] S. Yakovlev, O. Kartashov, and O. Pichugina, "Optimization on Combinatorial Configurations Using Genetic Algorithms," in CMIS, 2019, pp. 28–40.

[24] T. Weise, "Global Optimization Algorithms – Theory and Application," 2009, Retrieved: October 2019. [Online]. Available: http://www.it-weise.de/projects/book.pdf

[25] Rui Song, "Substrate Binning for Semiconductor Manufacturing," Master's thesis, Dresden University of Technology, Faculty of Computer Science, Institute of Applied Computer Science, Chair of Technical Information Systems, 2013.

[26] K. Deb, A. Pratap, S. Agarwal, and T. Meyarivan, "A Fast and Elitist Multiobjective Genetic Algorithm: NSGA-II," IEEE transactions on evolutionary computation, vol. 6, no. 2, 2002, pp. 182–197.

[27] J. rey Horn, N. Nafpliotis, and D. E. Goldberg, "A Niched Pareto Genetic Algorithm for Multiobjective Optimization," in Proceedings of the first IEEE conference on evolutionary computation, IEEE world congress on computational intelligence, vol. 1. Citeseer, 1994, pp. 82–87.

[28] B. L. Miller, D. E. Goldberg et al., "Genetic Algorithms, Tournament Selection, and the Effects of Noise," Complex systems, vol. 9, no. 3, Champaign, IL, USA: Complex Systems Publications, Inc., 1995, pp. 193–212.

[29] R. Poli and W. B. Langdon, "A New Schema Theorem for Genetic Programming with One-Point Crossover and Point Mutation," Cognitive Science Research Papers-University of Birmingham CSRP, 1997.

[30] F.-T. Lin, "Evolutionary Computation Part 2: Genetic Algorithms and Their Three Applications," Journal of Taiwan Intelligent Technologies and Applied Statistics, vol. 3, no. 1, 2005, pp. 29–56.

[31] M. Andersen et al., "Commons Math: The Apache Commons Mathematics Library," URL http://commons. apache. org/math/, online, 2011, Retrieved: October 2019.

[32] F. Luo, I. D. Scherson, and J. Fuentes, "A Novel Genetic Algorithm for Bin Packing Problem in jMetal," in 2017 IEEE International Conference on Cognitive Computing (ICCC). IEEE, 2017, pp. 17–23.

[33] J. J. Durillo and A. J. Nebro, "jMetal: A Java Framework for Multi-Objective Optimization," Advances in Engineering Software, vol. 42, no. 10, Elsevier, 2011, pp. 760–771.

[34] K. Fleszar and C. Charalambous, "Average-Weight-Controlled Bin-Oriented Heuristics for the One-Dimensional Bin-Packing Problem," European Journal of Operational Research, vol. 210, no. 2, Elsevier, 2011, pp. 176–184.

[35] E. Falkenauer and A. Delchambre, "A Genetic Algorithm for Bin Packing and Line Balancing," in Proceedings 1992 IEEE International Conference on Robotics and Automation. IEEE, 1992, pp. 1186–1192.

[36] E. López-Camacho, H. Terashima-Marín, G. Ochoa, and S. E. Conant-Pablos, "Understanding the Structure of Bin Packing Problems Through Principal Component Analysis," International Journal of Production Economics, vol. 145, no. 2, Elsevier, 2013, pp. 488–499.

[37] J. J. Durillo, A. J. Nebro, F. Luna, B. Dorronsoro, and E. Alba, "jMetal: A Java Framework for Developing Multi-Objective Optimization Metaheuristics," Departamento de Lenguajes y Ciencias de la Computación, University of Málaga, ETSI Informática, Campus de Teatinos, Tech. Rep. ITI-2006-10, 2006.

[38] A. J. Nebro and J. J. Durillo, "jMetal 4.3 User Manual," Available from Computer Science Department of the University of Malaga, 2013, Retrieved: October 2019. [Online]. Available: http://jmetal.sourceforge.net/resources/jMetalUserManual43.pdf

[39] A. J. Nebro, J. J. Durillo, and M. Vergne, "Redesigning the jMetal Multi-Objective Optimization Framework," in Proceedings of the Companion Publication of the 2015 Annual Conference on Genetic and Evolutionary Computation. ACM, 2015, pp. 1093–1100.

[40] J. J. Durillo, A. J. Nebro, and E. Alba, "The jMetal Framework for Multi-Objective Optimization: Design and Architecture," in IEEE Congress on Evolutionary Computation. IEEE, 2010, pp. 1–8.

[41] A. J. Nebro-Urbaneja et al., "Automatic Configuration of NSGA-II with jMetal and irace," ACM, 2019.

[42] J. A. Cordero et al., "Dynamic Multi-Objective Optimization with jMetal and Spark: a Case Study," in International Workshop on Machine Learning, Optimization, and Big Data. Springer, 2016, pp. 106–117.

[43] C. Barba-González, J. García-Nieto, A. J. Nebro, and J. F. A. Montes, "Multi-objective Big Data Optimization with jMetal and Spark," in EMO, 2017.

Business Intelligence Based Tool Development

Libni Almeida Neves
Visual Display Manaus
SIDIA
Manaus, Amazonas
libni.neves@sidia.com

Eric da Silva Ferraz
Visual Display Manaus
SIDIA
Manaus, Amazonas
eric.ferraz@sidia.com

Alipio de Sales Carvalho
Visual Display Manaus
SIDIA
Manaus, Amazonas
alipio.c@sidia.org.br

Abstract — **Software applications, technologies and methodologies that perform data analysis describes the domain of Business Intelligence (BI), which is defined as a set of strategies that involves data analysis and decision-making processes. In this way, it aims to create an environment where the company can easily find, evaluate, collaborate, understand and act from high value information. BI collaborates with increasing employee awareness of the company, enabling process disclosure, feedback collection and organizational data capture to be presented to decision makers a harmonized way. This project addresses the study of BI for a tool development to assist in analyzing data at a mobile device factory in its handset return control. The methodology used in this work was an exploratory study to collect the requirements for the development of the tool, in which it was developed and presented to the users. The tool was well accepted and meets the main needs for process analysis, however to be more comprehensive, new features will be added so that the system provides maturity for decision making and contributes to the process and its medium and long term strategies.**

Keywords-*business intelligence; tool; development.*

I. INTRODUCTION

Currently, companies daily generate and process a large volume of data from a variety of business activities and processes, including procurement, manufacturing, retail, marketing, sales, and distribution. This data is often processed by a wide range of applications on the computer and has a significant importance for business entities for effective and efficient decision making. However, the main disadvantage is that they often suffer from the lack of reliable, accurate and timely information to have a meaningful purpose for decision makers.

The value of information grows exponentially with the addition of each domain of data, information or knowledge properly integrated with it. The raw data cannot provide relevant and up-to-date information about company performance to their managers. For competitive companies that want to be ahead of the competition there is a critical need for up-to-date decision-making information and to optimize critical business processes [1].

Business Intelligence (BI) is a system that integrates multiple sources of information to define strategies of differentiation and performance of the company. The use of information should help organizations understand their strategies and allow the monitoring of organizational objectives throughout the planning horizon [2]. BI is an information technology that aims to centralize multiple sources of information, using large amounts of data, stored in systems for managing databases with flexibility in access and structuring of information [3]. Business is a set of activities that lead to a goal and intelligence is the ability to understand the relationships between the facts and use that understanding as a guide that guides the actions towards a desired goal [5].

BI applications provide reports to decision makers who want to perform more in-depth strategic analysis from huge amounts of data that have expanded over a wide range of time, from various applications and productions [4].

Another aspect to be considered in relation to BI relates to the use of its tools and processes in the most different fields. In the modern competitive environment, analyzing data and predicting market trends in order to improve organizational performance is an essential business activity that requires companies in general, and among them retailers, to process and analyze large quantities of data and turn them into profits [6].

The present work seeks to develop a BI tool to collect data, allow analysis and help in decision making in a mobile device manufacturing company, which has a process of monitoring the return of defective devices to the factory.

This paper is organized as follows: In Section 2 the proposed method is presented; Section 3 introduces the tool; The partial results are described in Section 4. Finally, the conclusions are summarized in Section 5.

II. METHODOLOGY

For this research, the following steps were executed (Figure 1):

1. Parallel review of the literature with the exploratory study to collect the requirements for the software.
2. Development of the initial proposal.
3. Verify if tool is satisfactory to accomplish deployment.

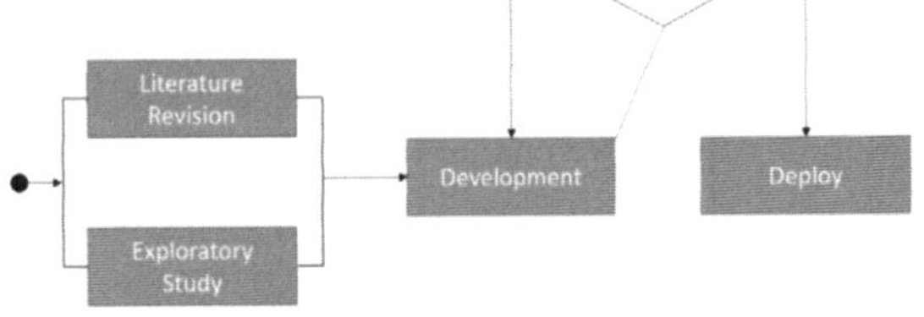

Figure 1. Methodology Overview.

In order to better understand the need to develop the tool, an exploratory study about defective device was carried out in the Quality Department of a mobile device factory. Then, it was noticed that every month there are a massive data accumulation generated by manually data comparisons carried out during the management of the return process of defective devices in which it starts from the exit of the products of the store until the return to factory. The data is analyzed through spreadsheets and manually through paid software.

In addition, other characteristics relevant to the collection of requirements were identified, which allowed the modeling of the software. It was observed that it is important to display the main information of the data, such as:

- Regions with higher rate of return;
- Classification of models with higher defect rate;
- Store classification;
- Classification of defects.

III. Initial proposal

For the development of the tool, visits were made to the company, when information was collected through interviews on the return process of the mobile devices, number of devices, time to return to the factory and periodicity in evaluating the data. During one of the visits, it was noticed that due to the accumulation of data, the person in charge of analyzing the data and generating reports spends a lot of time and effort to do this because they do it manually, and a management dashboard can be looked at as an executive tool whose sole purpose it to make information easier to read.

In the planning stage of this software, it was possible to determine the scope of work required and the best technologies for the development, to identify possible technical problems and to find solutions for them. For the development of this software was used Python and IDE PyCharm, consuming the Pandas library. This technology was selected due the consideration of the license and information sharing restrictions.

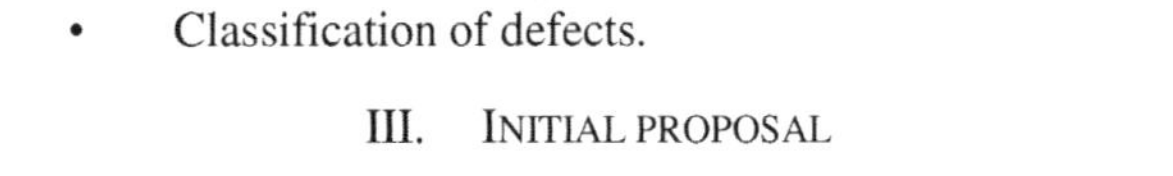

Figure. 2. Software Interface.

The tool has an interface in which the first step is the insertion of the worksheet (Figure 2). It must have the Comma-Separated Values (CSV) extension. The software reads the worksheet and displays the labels (the names of the first row), so the user selects the data to generate graphs (Figure 3).

The application sums up the values that have the most occurrences and displays the top five data (using Pandas library). These requirements were collected due to the need of the quality department as a strategy to analyze the quantity of devices.

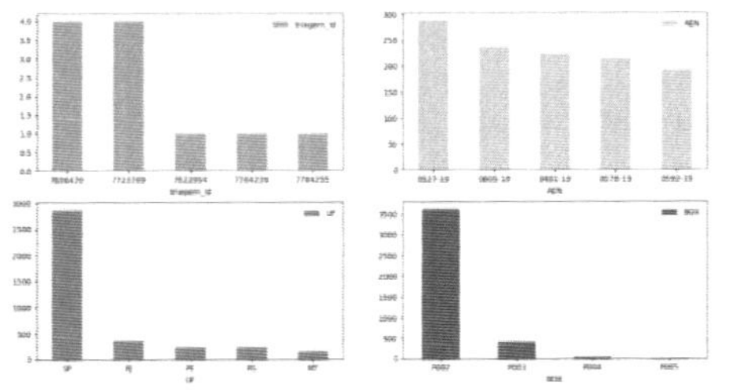

Figure 3. Graphs Generated by the Tool.

IV. Partial Results

The proposal was presented to the quality team and follows the main requirements to display graphs quickly and intuitively with predefined data. The software reads raw data and provides fields for the user to select information, making the tool customizable as needed. Previously, the data analyst needed to view the entire spreadsheet to collect the data. It has been set to display four different graphics with different colors and captions. Up to this work stage, the tool provides the sum of the data because the quality team needs to manage the total quantity. However, some improvements have been suggested, such as the customization of the graphics in which the user can choose the type of graph to be displayed. Another suggestion was to relate the columns; for example, select which models had the most defects and in which city. Another enhancement option was to add average calculation, display the top five values and the bottom five.

V. Conclusion

This work presented a tool designed to assist in data analysis in the Quality Department of a mobile device factory, thus providing the most relevant defect information. It also provides organized and personalized reading and visualization of data in graphical format optimizing information visualization and replacing manual analysis. For the next stage of this work, new functionalities will be developed an exploratory and applicability study of the tool in other departments or different areas.

References

[1] K. E. Sveiby, The new organizational wealth: Managing & measuring knowledge-based assets. Berrett-Koehler Publishers, 1997.

[2] C. Barbieri, Introdução ao Conceito de BI. _. Business Intelligence. BI–Business Intelligence Modelagem & Tecnologia. Rio de Janeiro: Axcel Books do Brasil Editora, 2001.

[3] R. A. Khan, and S. M. K Quadri. Business intelligence: an integrated approach. Business Intelligence Journal, v. 5, n. 1, 2012.

[4] K. C. Laudon, and J. P. Laudon, Sistemas de informação gerenciais. 11ed. São Paulo. Pearson Education do Brasil, 2014.

[5] H. P. Luhn, *A business intelligence system*. IBM Journal of research and development, 2(4), pp. 314-319, 1958.

[6] B.S Sahay and J. Ranjan. Real time Business Intelligence in supply chain analytics. Information Management & Computer Security, 2008.

Training Project Managers to Acquire GSD Soft Skills: A Serious Game

Rubén Márquez
Alarcos Research Group
University of Castilla-La Mancha
Ciudad Real, Spain
Ruben.Marquez@uclm.es

Aurora Vizcaíno
Alarcos Research Group
University of Castilla-La Mancha
Ciudad Real, Spain
Aurora.Vizcaino@uclm.es

Félix Oscar García
Alarcos Research Group
University of Castilla-La Mancha
Ciudad Real, Spain
Felix.Garcia@uclm.es

***Abstract*—A good project manager should develop a set of hard and soft skills if they wish to manage any kind of software project. However, when the team members are geographically distributed, several new skills should be taken into account. Aware of this fact, in this paper we describe the skills and competences that a manager of Global Software Development projects should master, and we sketch out a serious game that can be used to train some of these soft skills, which are grouped under the 3Cs (Communication, Coordination and Control). With this approach we place the focus on the project manager role and seek an immersive and engaging training experience.**

Keywords—Global Software Development; Project Management; Soft Skills; Serious Game.

I. Introduction

Software engineering is an important area of computing, which searches for solutions to complex problems; to reach these solutions, however, it is necessary for software engineers to master a set of knowledge and skills [1]. In the field of software engineering, a new development model has emerged, one which is more offshore than the conventional model, due to the growth of globalization [2]. This development model is called Global Software Development (GSD); it is a term which has come to stay, because it is growing quickly and can be considered an increasing trend in work on software projects [3]. GSD can thus be defined as the development of a software project that involves several work teams, which may belong to different cities or countries [2].

In terms of GSD, the project tasks are separated, and delivered as different jobs. This means that managing GSD project is not a simple task; distance, language and cultural barriers affect Coordination, Communication and Control, thereby increasing the complexity of the management [4]. A variety of problems can therefore occur, such as: strategic and cultural issues, inadequate communication and lack of knowledge among workers, as well as project and process management problems. Future engineers need to be aware of all these potential difficulties, if they are to be prepared for the new world of software development [3].

The points above are supported by a number of articles, which point out that the lack of skills and competences in project managers is the main cause of much project failure [5], especially in GSD projects. This is why many companies explain the need to teach the technical and non-technical skills required in GSD or co-located projects to recently-graduated and newly-qualified Project Management (PM) professionals. Those skills will enable them to manage these kinds of projects effectively, and produce qualified professionals with this expert knowledge [5], [6].

In many domains, games are used to teach and train different aspects of a given field. Educational games simulate an environment, which help the students to feel motivated, thus improving the teaching-learning process [5]. Games can be therefore be justifiably considered to be a way for future project managers to fill in the gaps in the practical information they possess [1]. Some examples of serious games used to teach GSD and PM are [5], [7].

Taking this fact into account, we have been developing Global Skills Game, a serious game designed to help project managers to develop some skills that are advisable to have when managing a GSD project.

The rest of the paper is organized as follows. In Section II a set of useful soft skills for working in GSD project and in Section III for working in PM are specified. In Section IV describe our approach, Global Skills Game along with its characteristics. Finally, in Section V, the conclusion and future work are given.

II. Skills and Abilities for GSD

Anyone who works on a software project must have a set of skills that work towards the success of the project, since, as previously stated, many of the failures in software projects are due to a lack of skills and competences on the part of those working on the project. In a GSD project in particular, the members really must possess certain specific skills.

First of all, and according to [3], some of the most useful skills for software development are being able to *speak the English language*, *local cooperation* and *decision making*. Nevertheless, those abilities that provide the greatest benefit in distributed environments are, in addition to the very important *speak the English language: remote cooperation*, *intercultural cooperation* and *cooperation with clients*.

Besides, and according to [6] some skills which must be provided in training for a GSD are *to be aware of all possible problems*, mastering *communication protocols* (especially using computers), *oral and written communication through a common language* and *codes of ethics* and *time management*.

In [8], the authors indicate that the important skills that should be taught to students of GSD are *regular communication with distributed team members*, *team dynamics*, *working in culturally diverged teams*, *managing time* and *using collaborative technologies*.

Moreover, a framework to teach several GSD skills is described in [9]; the main skills considered are: *computer mediated communication*, *iterative development in remote client-developer relationships* and *distributed PM*.

The competence model specified in [10] indicates what the general competences for GSD teams are, dividing them into four groups depending on the roles that are involved in a GSD team (software engineer, team leader, project manager and organizational unit manager). The abilities that are pointed out as being necessary in the training of any software engineering who is working in GSD are *synchronous and asynchronous communication*, *identification and management of requirement*, *technical problem solution*, *share knowledge management*, *advanced techniques for distributed communication*, *self-learning capacity*, *international relationship ability*, *use of communication and information technologies*, *ability to work in a global setting* and *oral and written communication in English*.

III. SKILLS AND ABILITIES FOR PM

Once we have carried out an analysis of GSD, listing the skills and competences which are needed in this type of development environment, in this section we are going to focus on the competences for PM.

First of all, the authors in [11] state that risk is one of the most important parts of PM. It is thus highlighted that a distributed software development project manager has to take into account areas of risk such as *time zone*, *cultural*, *geographical* and *language differences*, as well as the processes of *Coordination*, *Communication* and *Control*.

In addition to these considerations, the research in [12] offers a range of skills which must be acquired by the project manager in software development if he or she is to successfully achieve the project goals. The skills that are proposed are: *communication skills* (the project manager should listen to the team workers, promote trust relationships and understand the personality differences between its members, with the aim to improve the work process, reduce conflict between workers, and strengthen cooperation); *team building skills* (the project manager must ensure there are strong links formed between other team members and other teams); and *problem-solving skills* (the project manager has to visualize and solve complex problems, making decisions which may have a certain impact on the project cost, quality and productivity).

Finally, the skills that are proposed in [10] as necessary for a project manager in a distributed environment are *decision taking* (the choice between different alternatives in different aspects of PM), *meeting management* (holding meetings with different workers to talk about PM), *establishment of rules to work with shared data* (due to the fact that data is shared between different work teams, rules must be established for its use), *collecting, analysing and interpreting information* (all the necessary project documentation must be processed in order to take the right decisions), *positive attitude and capacity for motivating others* (in this way the project workers also have a positive attitude and their productivity increases), *organization and planning capacity* (the project manager has to carry out the organization and planning of the different tasks of the project), *initiative and leadership* (the project manager is the key component in a distributed project; hence, he or she must have an attitude of leadership and initiative for decision taking), *interpersonal conflict resolution* (since there are many work teams in a distributed project, it is not uncommon for different workers to have conflicts, so the project manager has to solve these by taking the right decision), *identification of competence and CV* (the project manager should be able to know the skills and competences of workers, so as to assign the workstation correctly, and *requirement estimation and prioritization* (the project manager must know the requirements of the project and carry out the prioritization of each one according to the needs of the client).

To sum up, the above study (an overview of the soft skills needed when working in GSD and PM) has helped us to decide which competences we want to implement in our serious game.

IV. THE GAME

In the previous sections we have presented a study of the current literature on the skills needed to work in a distributed software environment, and on those skills needed to perform the activities of a project manager.

In this section our serious game is presented, indicating in detail what it consists of, what particular skills our player will learn, and how he or she will face with different elements to advance towards the successful development of a distributed software project.

Before we start implementing our game, we should first of all reach a decision about which skills from Section II and III will be taught and improved by playing it. It should be noted that the goal of this game is to train individuals for management of software projects in distributed environments, so both GSD and PM skills should be included. Taking that into account, in Table I a set of soft skills which will be implemented in our game is presented, indicating in each case whether it is a skill that concerns Global Software Development (GSD), or Project Management (PM), or both (BTH); the table also shows how the soft skill will be implemented, and how the player will be able to acquire it.

As we can see in the table below, we are going to introduce several skills into our game; however, there are many other GSD and PM skills that have been left out for some reason. These include such skills as those to do with codes of ethics, since these almost always depend on the particular kind of the project, companies, and even countries involved, so their implementation would be too complex. Another not supported skill is that of establishing rules to work with shared data; due to like the previous skill, it will depend on the particular company(ies) involved in the project. As far as the skills positive attitude, capacity to motivate others, or initiative and leadership are concerned, these are considered as very personal skills that will depend on the disposition of the person involved. Therefore, we are going to implement some strategies to develop those skills, or at least to make the player aware of the importance of having them. However, it can be a challenge for a serious game to evaluate them.

TABLE I. SOFT SKILLS IMPLEMENTED IN GLOBAL SKILLS GAME

Soft Skill	Type	Implementation
Time management	GSD	There will be some information in the game about the evolution of the project being managed; this information will be the current budget, time-to-delivery, and the current progress. The player will thus be able receive training in how to conduct the time management of the project, since he/she will also be able to carry out activities designed to optimize the above information.
Intercultural cooperation	GSD	Some of the events that will occur will have certain characteristics that are specific to a given culture; in this way the player will learn how these features affect intercultural cooperation between globally-divided work teams, and they will be able to try to improve the cultural relationship between the members of the project.
Cooperation with client	GSD	Other events will be directly or indirectly involved with the needs of the client of the project, thus enabling the player to learn how to cooperate with the customer in such a way that the project meets their expectations. Furthermore, the player will be able to communicate with the client and request them to answer any queries that may arise.
Communication skills	PM	One of the types of event that will come up in the game will be communication events, in which the player will learn the characteristics that are involved in the communication between the members of a distributed software project; these events will train the ability to improve that communication.
Coordination skills	PM	Another type of event that will occur in the game will be coordination events, in which the player will learn the characteristics that are involved in the coordination of the project, and this will train their ability to carry out different project coordination activities.
Control skills	PM	Control events will be another kind of event in the game; in these, the player will learn how to control the project, and receive training in how to solve a problem, should one occur.
Decision making and problem-solving	BTH	Throughout the execution of the game different events will appear in which some problem arises; the player must decide what is the best way to maintain the execution of the project and work out how to solve the problem.

Once we decided the skills that players will learn and receive training in by playing our game, we designed and implemented the game's graphical interfaces. The first interface is the general menu of the serious game.

After choosing the context of the game project, the player will have to configure different game parameters which will affect the simulation of the game. The parameters with which the player will be able to interact will be both the general aspect of the project, such as the number of sites, the country where the client is located, the common language for communication between sites, and the specific aspects of each site. These details include the number of workers, the country where the site is located, the knowledge of the common language, or whether the site is the main one or not. In addition, the player will be able to choose the type of communication between the different sites and the client. While the project is being configured by the player, the game will show a set of important success factors that are involved in, and characterize, the development of a distributed project, as collected by [13]; some of these success factors are "Working time overlap", "Language difference", "Cultural difference", "Communication" or "Sites number". Finally, and by means of the above factors, the game will calculate a level of difficulty, from low to very high, and will represent the difficulty that the distributed project has to face with, taking into account the current configuration of the player. This screen will enable the player to begin to become familiar with the aspects and factors involved in a distributed project and learn from the feedback, as these factors can have an important influence on the project.

Finally, and once the distributed project that we are going to simulate is configured, the graphic interface of the game where the simulation of the game is to take place will appear. This screen (Figure 1) is divided into two parts; the bottom strip in which the player, through progress bars, will find information that will evolve throughout the simulation of the game. This includes information such as the level of stress, the remaining budget, the time until the delivery of the project and the progress of the project. There will also be general information on the project, such as its difficulty, initial budget and duration. At the bottom of this screen we can find information on each of the sites, such as the level of motivation, communication with other sites, or workload. Turning now to the upper part of the screen, in which the graphic game will be found, this will consist of the static map of an office, along with the character of the player, who will be able to move about with total freedom.

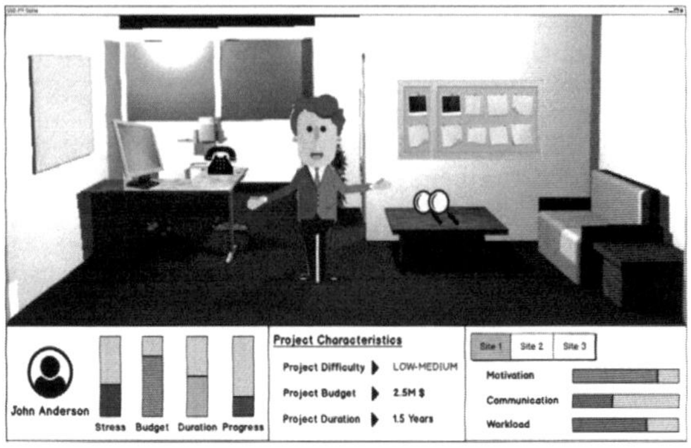

Figure 1. Global Skills Game Graphic Interface

The simulation of the game will consist in the dropping of different objects onto the screen (where the speed of the drop will depend on the difficulty of the project). These objects will be a telephone, a note and a magnifying glass, and each of them will represent an event that has occurred in the simulation of the project, identifying the particular type of event according to the 3Cs, Communication, Coordination and Control, respectively. When an object drops, the player will be able to interact with it so that the description of the event and what has happened appears; in this way the player will be able to train ability in each one of the 3Cs and understand how each one of these affects the evolution of a distributed project. In addition, some of the events will have certain cultural characteristics which will help the player to understand the intercultural cooperation of a distributed project and train in how to deal with this. Other events will have the client of the project as the main actor. This will help the player to understand cooperation with the client and train their skill in this area. The events with which the player interacts will have an impact on the execution of the project, affecting the budget, duration or even the stress of the player; this impact may be felt in any of the different sites, and it may be positive or negative, depending on the particular type of event. Negative events will consist of problems which the player as project manager will have to tackle by taking certain decisions to solve the problems in the best possible way. These decisions can be made in two ways; either by choosing a solution from the whole range that is offered (if offered) or by interacting with the computer and by performing an activity that solves the problem. The user will be able to use the computer to carry out different activities to try to improve the execution of the project; these include tasks such as hiring and firing personnel, giving extra payments or holding a face-to-face meeting.

The project simulation will continue until several possible results occur: the player has overcome the stress level; the project has run out of budget; the project has not met the deadline. In those cases, the player has lost the game. If the project has finished successfully on time and within budget the player has won the game.

V. CONCLUSION AND FUTURE WORK

This paper presents a study carried to find out what soft skills a project manager needs to learn when working on a GSD project. Taking this study as a basis, we then went on to develop a serious game to train future project managers. The fact that it is a serious game offers the advantage of its being much more entertaining than other traditional training methods.

As future work we will focus on testing our serious game on students of software engineering, in order to evaluate it. We will also test it on practitioners, in the quest to make possible improvements.

ACKNOWLEDGMENTS

This work has been funded by the G3SOFT project (Consejería de Educación, Cultura y Deportes de la Junta de Comunidades de Castilla La Mancha, y Fondo Europeo de Desarrollo Regional FEDER, SBPLY/17/180501/000150) and by the BIZDEVOPS-GLOBAL project (Ministerio de Ciencia, Innovación y Universidades, y Fondo Europeo de Desarrollo Regional FEDER, RTI2018-098309-B-C31).

REFERENCES

[1] M. Kosa, M. Yilmaz, R. V. O'Connor, and P. M. Clarke, 'Software engineering education and games: A systematic literature review', *Journal of Universal Computer Science*, vol. 22, no. 12, pp. 1558–1574, 2016.

[2] A. Vizcaíno, F. García, I. G. R. De Guzmán, and M. Á. Moraga, 'Evaluating GSD-aware: A serious game for discovering global software development challenges', *ACM Transactions on Computing Education*, vol. 19, no. 2, pp. 1–23, 2019.

[3] I. Bosnić, I. Čavrak, and M. Žagar, 'Assessing the impact of the distributed software development course on the careers of young software engineers', *ACM Transactions on Computing Education*, vol. 19, no. 2, pp. 1–27, 2019.

[4] I. Richardson, S. Moore, D. Paulish, V. Casey, and D. Zage, 'Globalizing software development in the local classroom', presented at the Software Engineering Education Conference, Proceedings, 2007, pp. 64–71.

[5] J. E. N. Lino, M. A. Paludo, F. V. Binder, S. Reinehr, and A. Malucelli, 'Project management game 2D (PMG-2D): A serious game to assist software project managers training', presented at the Proceedings - Frontiers in Education Conference, FIE, 2015, vol. 2014, pp. 1–8.

[6] M. J. Monasor, A. Vizcaíno, and M. Piattini, 'Training Global Software Development skills through a simulated environment', presented at the ICSOFT 2010 - Proceedings of the 5th International Conference on Software and Data Technologies, 2010, vol. 2, pp. 271–274.

[7] J. Noll, A. Butterfield, K. Farrell, T. Mason, M. McGuire, and R. McKinley, 'GSD Sim: A Global Software Development Game', presented at the Proceedings - International Computer Software and Applications Conference, 2014, vol. 18-21-August-2014, pp. 15–20.

[8] M. Paasivaara, C. Lassenius, D. Damian, P. Räty, and A. Schröter, 'Teaching students global software engineering skills using distributed Scrum', in *2013 35th International Conference on Software Engineering (ICSE)*, 2013, pp. 1128–1137.

[9] D. Damian, A. Hadwin, and B. Al-Ani, 'Instructional design and assessment strategies for teaching global software development: A framework', presented at the Proceedings - International Conference on Software Engineering, 2006, vol. 2006, pp. 685–690.

[10] J. Saldaña-Ramos, A. Sanz-Esteban, J. García, and A. Amescua, 'Skills and abilities for working in a global software development team: A competence model', *Journal of Software: Evolution and Process*, vol. 26, no. 3, pp. 329–338, 2014.

[11] J. M. Verner, O. P. Brereton, B. A. Kitchenham, M. Turner, and M. Niazi, 'Risks and risk mitigation in global software development: A tertiary study', *Information and Software Technology*, vol. 56, no. 1, pp. 54–78, 2014.

[12] K. Sutling, Z. Mansor, S. Widyarto, S. Lecthmunan, and N. H. Arshad, 'Understanding of Project Manager Competency in Agile Software Development Project: The Taxonomy', in *Information Science and Applications*, Berlin, Heidelberg, 2015, pp. 859–868.

[13] A. Vizcaíno, F. García, J. C. Villar, M. Piattini, and J. Portillo, 'Applying Q-methodology to analyse the success factors in GSD', *Information and Software Technology*, vol. 55, no. 7, pp. 1200–1211, Jul. 2013.

Antecedents To Achieve Kanban Optimum Benefits In Software Companies

Muhammad Ovais Ahmad
Faculty of Electronics, Telecommunications and Informatics, Department of Software Engineering, Gdansk University of Technology, Poland.
Department of Mathematics and Computer Science, Karlstad University, Sweden

Anna Rohunen
Center for Ubiquitous Computing, University of Oulu, Oulu, Finland

Päivi Raulamo-Jurvanen
M3S Research Unit, University of Oulu, Finland.
Oulu, Finland
e-mail: firstname.lastname@oulu.fi

Abstract— **In 2004, Kanban successfully entered the Agile and Lean realm. Since then, software companies have been increasingly using it in software development teams. The goal of this study is to perform an empirical investigation on antecedents considered as important for achieving optimum benefits of Kanban use and to discuss the practical implications of the findings. We conducted an online survey with software professionals from the *Lean Software Development* LinkedIn community to investigate the importance of antecedents of using Kanban for achieving optimum benefits. Our study reveals that subjective norm, organizational support, ease of use, Kanban use experience and training are the antecedents for achieving expected benefits of Kanban. The potential benefits of Kanban use can only be realized when the key antecedents are not only identified, but also infused across an organization. When managing the transition to or using Kanban, practitioners need to adapt their strategies on the extent of various antecedents, a few identified in this study.**

Keywords- Agile; Lean; Kanban; Software Development.

I. INTRODUCTION

It has been more than ten years since the use of Kanban in software engineering was suggested. During the last decade, there has been significant adoption of Kanban in domains such as aeronautics, healthcare, retail clothing, human resources, and software development [1]. Kanban was emerged as part of Toyota Production System. The idea was to work effectively under pressure and market situation. Kanban literal meaning is signboard [1].

Toyota, used Kanban due to three reasons: reduction in information processing cost, rapid and precise acquisition of facts, and limiting surplus capacity of preceding shops or stages [10]. In 2004, David Anderson introduced Kanban to a software development team in Microsoft. "Kanban (capital K) is an evolutionary change method that utilizes a kanban (small k) pull system, visualization, and other tools to catalyse the introduction of Lean ideas... the process is evolutionary and incremental" [1]. Anderson identified five key properties, which Boeg called principles: Visualise the workflow, Limit Work In Progress, Measure and manage flow, Make process policies explicit, Improve collaboratively (using models and the scientific method) [1].

The annual State of Agile VersionOne [3] reported that from "2016 to 2017 the use of Kanban grew from 50% to 65% in software companies". The most recent systematic mapping study on applying Kanban in software engineering reports a variety of benefits with the use of Kanban in their work [1]. The study distilled various Kanban benefits under three broad categories [1]:

- Process - Improved visibility and transparency, Better control of project activities and tasks, Identification of impediments to flow, Improved prioritisation of products and tasks.
- People - Improved communication and collaboration, Improved team motivation, Improved team building and cohesion, Increased customer satisfaction.
- Organization - Promotion culture of continuous learning and strategic alignment.

These benefits are achieved by using Kanban in two broad knowledge areas: Software engineering process management and economics [1]. Despite the positive evidence supporting the success of Kanban in software organizations, the industry is still facing recurring problems (with, e.g., customer satisfaction, organizational culture or poor knowledge management) [1]. To achieve the optimum benefits of agile and lean approaches there is lack of sufficient theoretical foundations. However, a few studies have focused on a set of potential factors that impact perceived success or 'acceptance' of agile practices where success is measured using outcomes such as quality, time, and cost [4], agile software solution framework [6] and assimilation of practices [7]. The existing suggested various antecedents which contribute to the effective use of Agile methods (e.g., support from organization, positive change culture, formal training and developers' perception about the difficulty or ease of use regarding method, practice or tool) [1][8][9][11]-[13].

There is a need for detailed studies on agile software development to provide credible advice to software companies regarding its use [13]. Kanban also comes under the agile realm and is still in its infancy in software engineering. Currently, there is lack of empirical evidence regarding Kanban antecedents and use benefits. It is important to investigate the importance of organizational support, training, experience, subjective norms, and perceived ease of use against Kanban claimed benefits. Such evidence will help in the generalization of results, and in confirming or refuting anecdotal evidence. Further, it will provide practical guidelines that can assist software practitioners regarding decisions in their selection of software development approaches. The goal of this study is to investigate various antecedents considered important for achieving optimum benefits of Kanban use.

RQ1. What antecedents make software industry achieve the optimum benefits of Kanban from its use?

To answer RQ1, we conducted a web survey in the summer of 2017, targeted LinkedIn practitioners' group: "*Lean Software Development*" - one of the largest LinkedIn communities of professionals whose members are using and researching Lean and Kanban.

The paper is organized as follows. Section II elaborates conceptualization of the antecedents. Section III describes the survey design, while Section IV presents the methods used for analysing the data. Section V presents the results before moving to discussion about the findings in Section VI. Section VII presents the threats to validity and, Section VIII concludes the paper with recommendations for practice and researchers.

II. ANTECEDENTS CONCEPTUALIZATION

In general, software and system development methodologies are adaptable. Senapathi and Srinivasan [11] claim that agile methods lack a strong theoretical base. The information systems literature extensively tested models, e.g., the diffusion of innovation, planned behaviour, technology acceptance model and information systems implementation research [11]. These models generated interest in the agile research community [7][11]. To investigate software developers' acceptance of methodologies, Riemenschneider et al. [8] compare the existing five theoretical models. Dybå et al. [12] added the construct of organizational support to the four constructs presented by Riemenschneider et al. [8] i.e., perceived ease of use, perceived compatibility, perceived usefulness and subjective norms. Similarly, Senapathi and Srinivasan [11] identify other constructs pertinent to post-adoptive usage of agile practices, namely relative advantage, team attitude and technical competence, championing, and top management support. Ahmad et al. [9] discussed aspects that Kanban practitioners perceived to be important (i.e., organizational support and social influence). We took Dybå et al. [12] model factor as baseline for our study:

Organizational support is the extent to which change agents promote or support efforts, as a factor in explaining an innovation's (e.g., Kanban as a new working method) rate of adoption [9]. Coaching and support is a key to the success of facilitating and sustaining organizational learning and knowledge creation. Iivari and Huisman [16] identified that organizational culture contributes in the espousal of software development methodologies. Kaemar [17] reported that, diffusion of software process effect could be arbitrated by perceived organizational usefulness. Therefore, we believe, Kanban benefits can be achieved by providing organizational support.

Training, in the form of formal training, of any methodology is important for its successful implementation. Chan and Thong [4] exhibit that training has a positive effect on individuals' beliefs and perceived compatibility of an innovation. In Agile methodologies, training and coaching play an important role in the successful use and reap of the benefits [4]. In the light of existing studies [21][22], formal training plays an important role in the use and successful implementation of any methodology. Thus, we believe that Kanban benefits can be reaped by providing formal training.

Experience means individuals with the attitude and experience to embrace new practices (e.g., Agile) easily and fast, whereas high level of team experience contributes to increased productivity [23]. High level of experience, technical knowledge and self-organizing working style within a team affect the successful usage of agile practices. Experience can be considered as a positive or negative aspect in using agile methods and practices. Salo and Abrahamsson [24] present that experienced users of agile methods and practices have positive views about its usefulness. Laanti et al. [5] found a positive connotation between the length of agile experience and attitudes towards its usefulness. Whereas Vijayasarathy and Turk [2] found no evidence.

Subjective norms refer to a person's perception that most people who are important to him/her think he/she should or should not perform the behaviour in question [8][20]. The software companies are encouraging their developers to work collaboratively in teams. To some extent, teamwork creates social pressure on individuals. Subjective norms are significant in methodologies acceptance [4][8] while a few found it insignificant [12][20]. Therefore, we can say that, the stronger subjective norms, the more likely practitioners reap Kanban use benefits.

Ease of use can be described as "*The degree to which a person believes that using a particular system would be free of effort*" Davis [19]. It explains whether a method or tool is easy to use or not, and how they are perceived in relation to the claimed benefits. According to Kaemar et al. [17] the perceptions of development methodology challenges are negatively associated with perceived ease of use. Riemenschneider et al. [8] in turn, claim that ease of use construct has insignificant role in the acceptance of software methodologies. However, other studies recur that ease of use is a significant determinant of adoption behaviour [9][12][19]. Therefore, we believe Kanban's ease to use is an important aspect in achieving the optimum Kanban benefits.

Self-efficacy is about "*belief in one's capabilities to organize and execute the courses of action required to produce given attainments*" [18]. Self-efficacy is to predict positive attitude towards a specific job, technology, training proficiency and job performance [18]. Therefore, we believe self-efficacy is an important aspect in achieving the optimum Kanban benefits.

III. SURVEY DESIGN AND DATA COLLECTION

To reach a global population of Kanban practitioners, we sent out a web survey to "*Agile and Lean Software Development*" community of practitioners in LinkedIn. At the time of the study, the population of "Agile and Lean Software Development" was about 138,460 software practitioners.

Prior to the actual survey launch, we piloted and pre-tested the survey with four relevant field researchers from University of Oulu and five software professionals from the software industry. In the light of the feedback, received from both the researchers and software professionals, we revised and clarified the questions and wordings of the statements accordingly. The survey welcome page provided a clear description of the study purpose and researchers information. The survey remained open for two months (June and July 2017) and had three sections:

- Background information, Kanban use experience and type of Kanban training attended.
- Benefits of using Kanban: We based the questions on literature [1] and asked the respondents to rate the significance of each Kanban benefit for their organization using a five-point Likert-type scale (from 1 strongly disagree to 5 strongly agree). The respondent can also explain the obtained Kanban benefits in more detail, in the form of open-ended questions.
- Antecedents for achieving optimum Kanban benefits: Similarly, with the help of literature [9][20][19], we adapted the questions for the antecedents. For rating, we used a five-point Likert-type scale.

IV. DATA ANALYSIS

In our analysis, we divided the respondents into groups with respect to their reported level of received organizational support, perception of ease of use, training, subjective norm, and experience. These groups were compared to find out whether there are differences in the perceived benefits between the groups. Such comparison provides insight into relationships between perceived benefits of Kanban usage and its antecedents.

Comparisons were conducted through Student's t-test, Welch's t-test, analysis of variance or Welch's ANOVA, depending on the number of groups to be compared and whether the assumption of group-wise variances' homogeneity was met or not. These tests help to investigate whether there are statistically significant differences with respect to the perceived benefits between the groups. We carried out our analysis with the significance level (α) of 0.05, i.e., we decided whether to reject the null hypotheses (no differences between the groups) with the risk level of 5 %.

V. RESULTS

The collected data set included 67 responses. Majority of the respondents were from organizations developing software (n=45), while the rest were working in IT services (n=14), telecommunication (n=2) and hardware manufacturing (n=6).

We categorized all the organizations reported by the respondents, based on small and medium-sized enterprises. Most respondents were working in a small organization (n=30, number of employees between 10–49), the rest worked in large organizations (n=17, more than 250 employees) and middle size organizations (n=14, number of employees between 50–249). Only 6 respondents were from start-up company. Respondents' main organizational roles involved first level management (n=20) and development teams (n=17). Other reported positions were middle management (n=16) and top-level management (n=7). The remaining 7 roles were operation & support staff.

Almost all the respondents understood Kanban. The majority (n=35) of the respondents considered themselves as advanced beginners using Kanban in a local project. However, having said that, only 5 respondents purely used it for distributed projects. Table 1 shows, how the respondents rated the significance of Kanban use benefits and a few explained more in open-ended questions.

The top three benefits are improved visibility of work, reduction in work in progress and improved development flow; which are the key pillars of Kanban. It was also highlighted that Kanban helps to *"visualize tasks in progress" and "highlight the bottlenecks"* in the flow as well as has the *"ability to analyse outliers within the standard deviation of cycle or lead time,* Kanban allows for *"just-in-time prioritization"* and has *"moved the team from a sprint to finish coding to continually deliver excellent software".*

TABLE I. RESPONDENTS RATE KANBAN BENEFITS

Kanban benefits	**Average**
Improved visibility of work	3.67
Reduction in work in progress	3.15
Improved development flow	3.00
Faster time to delivery	2.88
Improved team collaboration	2.63
Improved understanding of whole value stream	2.58
Improved team communication	2.51
Improved team motivation	2.45
Increased productivity	2.42
Reduced cycle time	2.42
Better meeting of customer needs	2.27
Improved software quality	2.21
Enhance customer satisfaction	2.25

Table II shows the internal consistency of antecedent factors using Cronbach's alpha [15]. The items in each variable are grouped together for statistical tests. Cronbach Alphas value for all the items varied between 0.64 and 0.83, suggesting a relatively high internal consistency, based on the 0.7 threshold recommended by Nunnally [15].

Cronbach's alpha was below 0.7 only for OS2 variable that measured the respondents' perceived availability of written instructions on Kanban in their organizations. However, the overall OS internal consistency is 0.83. With respect to the SN and PEOU factors, we did not identify any items whose removal would have increased the internal consistency [15]. Based on the high internal consistency of these items, we calculated the sum variables of all items for each factor and used those for statistical tests in subsequent stages of the study.

TABLE II. CRONBACH'S ALPHAS

Factors	Variables	Cronbach's alpha (α)	
Organizational Support (OS)	OS1	0.83	0.83
	OS2	0.64	
	OS3	0.83	
Subjective Norms (SN)	SN1	0.79	0.88
	SN2	0.79	
Perceived Ease of Use (PEOU)	PEOU1	0.82	0.85
	PEOU2	0.82	
	PEOU3	0.79	
	PEOU4	0.82	

Organizational support: The respondents were divided into two groups based on the value of the organizational support sum variable (the mean of separate items): respondents provided with no support or weak support only (sum variable value less than 3), and respondents with moderate or strong support (sum variable value 3 or higher). Using Student's t-test, a statistically significant difference was found between the groups (p=0.000) with the means of the perceived benefits presented in Table III. The PS mean was higher in the group with moderate or strong support.

TABLE III. MEANS OF PERCEIVED BENEFITS WITH RESPECT TO OS

Group (n=67)	Mean of perceived benefits
No support or weak support (n=53)	2.363
Moderate or strong support (n=14)	3.699

We analysed the respondents' organizational position against the Kanban perceived benefits. The respondents were divided into three groups based on their organizational position: management (including top-level management, middle level management, and first level management), support (including IT/operations/support staff, and sales/marketing personnel) and development. Using ANOVA, a statistically significant difference was found between the groups (p=0.016) with the means of the perceived benefits shown in Table IV. The mean for perceived benefits was lowest in the Development group and highest in the Management group.

TABLE IV. MEANS OF PERCEIVED BENEFITS WITH RESPECT TO ORGANISATIONAL POSITION

Group (n=67)	Mean of perceived benefits
Management (n=43)	2.890
Support (n=7)	2.388
Development (n=17)	2.118

The result indicates that the respondents with the organizational position *management* perceive benefits of Kanban usage higher than the ones with the organizational positions *development* and *support*. Additionally, we investigated association between organizational position and organizational support. In this way, we aimed to find out whether the support received by the respondents' varied among the organizational position groups. Table V shows cross tabulation of these variables. Based on the calculation of Pearson's Chi-Square test of independence, the differences in organizational support between the organizational position groups were statistically significant (χ^2=6.019, df=2, p=0.049). The cross tabulation shows, none of the respondents with the organizational position *development* reported that they had received moderate or strong support.

TABLE V. CROSS TABULATION OF POSITION AND OS

Organizational support (N=67)	Position		
	Management	Development	Support
No support or weak support provided	31	17	5
Moderate or strong support provided	12	0	2

Ease of use: The respondents were divided into two groups based on the value of the perceived ease of use sum variable: respondents with lower level of perceived ease of use (sum variable value less than three), and respondents with higher level of perceived ease of use (sum variable value three or higher). Using Welch's two sample t-test, a statistically significant difference was found between the groups (p=0.000) with the means of perceived benefits presented in Table VI. The mean of perceived benefits was higher in the group with higher perceived ease of use.

TABLE VI. MEANS OF PERCEIVED BENEFITS WITH RESPECT TO PEOU

Group (n=67)	Mean of perceived benefits
Lower perceived ease of use (n=41)	2.099
Higher perceived ease of use (n=26)	3.497

Kanban training: The respondents were divided into two groups based on their Kanban training, i.e., respondents with no training or self-studying, and respondents with formal training (including peer mentoring, and education with the duration of at least one day). Using Student's t-test, no statistically significant difference was found between the groups with respect to their perceived benefits (p=0.854, the means for the groups with No Kanban training or self-studying and with Formal Kanban training as 2.620 and 2.665, respectively).

In order to obtain better insight into the dependence of the perceived benefits on Kanban competence, we investigated Kanban knowledge against benefits. We divided respondents into two groups based on their Kanban knowledge: respondents with lower knowledge (assessed themselves as advanced beginners), and respondents with higher knowledge (assessed as competent or experts). Using Welch's two sample t-test, a statistically significant difference (p=0.000) was found between the groups with the means of the perceived benefits. The mean of perceived benefits was higher in the group with the higher knowledge.

TABLE VII. MEANS OF PERCEIVED BENEFITS WITH RESPECT TO KANBAN TRAINING

Group (n=67)	**Mean of perceived benefits**
No training or self-studying (n=35)	2.620
Formal training (n=32)	2.665

Further, we investigated the association between Kanban training and Kanban knowledge. Pearson's Chi-Square test of independence indicated that there is a statistically significant association between the variables (χ^2=7.81, df=1, p=0.005). Although our analysis does not indicate a dependence between Kanban training and perceived benefits, there still seems to be a relation of some sort between Kanban competence and perceived benefits. As expected, respondents' Kanban knowledge was also dependent on their length of experience in Kanban usage as a statistically significant association was observed between these variables (χ^2=24.396, df=2, p=0.000).

TABLE VIII. MEANS OF PERCEIVED BENEFITS WITH RESPECT TO KANBAN KNOWLEDGE (N=67)

Group	**Mean of perceived benefits**
Lower knowledge (n=40)	2.170
Higher knowledge (n=27)	3.341

Subjective norms: The respondents were divided into two groups based on the value of subjective norms sum variable: the respondents with lower level of subjective norms (sum variable value less than three), and the respondents with higher level of subjective norms of use (sum variable value three or higher). Using Student's t-test, a statistically significant difference was found between the groups (p=0.000) with the means of the perceived benefits presented in Table IX. The mean of perceived benefits was higher in the group with higher subjective norms.

TABLE IX. MEANS OF PERCEIVED BENEFITS WITH RESPECT TO SUBJECTIVE NORMS (N=67)

Group	**Mean of perceived benefits**
Lower subjective norms (n=43)	2.289
Higher subjective norms (n=24)	3.274

Kanban experience: The respondents were divided into three groups based on their Kanban experience: respondents with short experience (one year or less), moderate experience (two years or less), long experience (more than two years; in practice, up to five years). Using ANOVA, a statistically significant difference (p=0.002) was found between the groups with the means of the perceived benefits presented in Table X. Perceived benefits tend to increase along increased Kanban experience.

TABLE X. MEANS OF PERCEIVED BENEFITS WITH RESPECT TO KANBAN EXPERIENCE (N=67)

Group	**Mean of perceived benefits**
Short experience (n=27)	2.35
Moderate experience (n=24)	2.47
Long experience (n=16)	3.38

VI. DISCUSSION

A quantitative survey was performed to investigate antecedents, which help to achieve optimum Kanban use benefits. The study shows that Kanban practitioners experienced various benefits which are claimed in the existing literature, i.e., enhanced visibility of tasks, limit the work in progress at given time, smoothly develop and deliver various tasks continuously. For example, the visibility of various tasks improves team motivation, communication and collaboration.

The ease of use of any method and tool is important for achieving positive effects. Ease of use is an important antecedent for achieving optimum benefits of Kanban. The ease of use is significant to CASE tool usage [21]. Previous studies support that learning and using software development methods or tools does not require much of mental efforts [6][22][20]. In this study, perceived benefits seem to depend on ease of use of Kanban. Therefore, it should be considered that how to make Kanban use easier. The teams need to be free, in order to select the type of Kanban board (physical or virtual) [1][9].

When choosing and adopting to use any new tool, method or process "software professionals can be expected to be motivated by others who are important to them and whose opinions they value" [2]. Our findings highlight that perceived Kanban benefits depend on the level of subjective norms, and the level of perceived benefits tends to increase along with the increased subjective norms. The existing studies support the role of subjective norm in the prediction of innovation use among individuals [2]. Kanban experience has positive relationships with the perceived benefits. The perceived benefits tend to increase along increased Kanban experience. This suggests that with the passage of time, practitioners get experience using Kanban and achieve the optimum benefits which are claimed in existing literature [8][20].

The organizational support is a highly significant antecedent of Kanban perceived benefits. This is also in accordance with prior studies of Kanban use, development processes and software engineering methodologies [1][8][11]. Organizational support should be provided throughout the departments to make Kanban adoption more efficient. Management support is important in the decision of adopting a new technique for eliciting user requirements. A recent systematic mapping study [1] suggested that training and allowing teams to experiment with Kanban in a specific context is a type organizational support. Our findings regarding the dependence between Kanban training and perceived benefits are somehow ambiguous. Specific attention is required, when about the way training is carried out; in order to provide the personnel with skills that really promote their Kanban learning and competence. The organizations provide customized training to various groups (e.g., development or management) and allow them to experiment and adopt Kanban principles based on their own requirements [20]. Studies support that organizational support (aka. training and consultation), play significant role in the use of Agile methodologies including Kanban [4][9].

VII. THREATS TO VALIDITY

We followed the guidelines for threats to validity presented by Runeson and Höst [14]. A common threat to web surveys is that questions might be misunderstood. To handle this threat, we piloted the survey with five researchers and four industry experts. After piloting, we rephrased a few survey questions to provide more clarity. Additionally, we designed survey questions using existing literature. Several questions were used in parallel for measuring many of the studied variables. As part of internal validity, a critical point is need to be taken in consideration that, this study is exploratory in nature and we are not empirically validating any model. We expect that there could be many additional factors, which could affect the actual use of Kanban.

We distributed web survey on LinkedIn, which is prone to external validity threat (i.e., the general applicability of the results) as the sample size was relatively small (n=67). However, the survey was conducted with the global population of practitioners, instead of a random sample or a convenience sample (those both considered as weaker data collection approaches). The respondents were individuals from various organizations. Therefore, it is difficult for individuals to answer on behalf of the whole organization. Further, respondents in diverse positions may have different opinions and familiarity about the organizational practices. Thus, different views could affect the reliability of the results to some degree.

We purposely chose the "Lean Software Development" LinkedIn community as the population, to get an apt data sample. As they have an appropriate understanding and experience of using Kanban. LinkedIn groups and professionals are considered as good source of data collection from all seniority levels of researchers and practitioners [9]. However, the population of this type may cause positive biasness in the results. It is also possible that many of the respondents were the ones with high-level interest in Kanban and open to try new methods in general.

VIII. CONCLUSION

Kanban has many success stories in software engineering. It is a good tool for visualizing work within and between teams. It helps team members to avoid burdening multitasking by limiting to work in progress. Such actions indirectly enable continuous delivery to the customers. The goal of this study was to examine the antecedents of successful Kanban usage to achieve optimum benefits from it.

Our results exhibit that enabling antecedents (such as organizational support, experience, training, ease of use, and subjective norm), play a vital role in the context of software development innovations' adoption as well as pertinent in realizing Kanban benefits. The findings of our study are aligned with earlier studies [8][11][20] which have identified the importance of these antecedents with respect to acceptance and usage of software development methods. The greater the organizational support the more benefits of Kanban use are achieved by the practitioners. This is also reflected in subjective norm and training, which have correlation with achieving optimum benefits of Kanban. It is beneficial for companies, when they find their influential individuals who have adopted Kanban and/or endorse its use.

This study highlights the importance of Kanban training; however, it is essential to allow Kanban experimentation in specific context(s). Once a team adopts Kanban to their work, they will achieve its benefits. The study shows that management experiences more benefits, therefore the assumption is that they have more freedom to adopt Kanban based on their circumstances, needs and nature of work. Practitioners need to monitor and evaluate realization of the antecedents which are reported in this study. Constant evaluation and observing will aid to sustain good Kanban use and achieve maximum benefits.

In the future, similar studies are required to investigate these antecedents in more detail. Further studies need to be carried out to replicate the study, on different teams and different organizations, to accept or refute the findings and to help in the generalizability.

REFERENCES

[1]. M.O. Ahmad, D. Dennehy, K. Conboy, and M. Oivo, "Kanban in software engineering: A systematic mapping study". Journal of Systems and Software, 137, 96-113. 2018.

[2]. L. Vijayasarathy, and D. Turk, "Drivers of agile software development use: Dialectic interplay between benefits and hindrances". J. Info. and Software Tech. 54(2),137-148. 2012.

[3]. VersionOne, The 12th Annual State of Agile Survey Annual State of Agile Survey. 2018.

[4]. F. K. Y. Chan, and J.Y.L. Thong, "Acceptance of agile methodologies: a critical review and conceptual framework". Decision Support Systems 46, 803–814. 2009.

[5]. M. Laanti, O. Salo, and P. Abrahamsson, "Agile methods rapidly replacing traditional methods at Nokia: a survey of opinions on agile transformation", Information and Software Technology. 53 (3), 276-290. 2011.

[6]. A. Qumer, & B. Henderson-Sellers, "A framework to support the evaluation, adoption and improvement of agile methods in practice". Journal of Systems and Software 1899–1919. 2008.

[7]. M. Pikkarainen, X. Wang, and K. Conboy, "Agile practices in use from an innovation assimilation perspective: a multiple case study". International Conf. on Information Syst. 2007.

[8]. C. K. Riemenschneider, B. C. Hardgrave, & F.D. Davis, "Explaining software developer acceptance of methodologies: a comparison of five theoretical models". IEEE Transactions on Software Engineering. 28 (12), 1135-1145. 2002.

[9]. M. O. Ahmad, J. Markkula, and M. Oivo, "Insights into the perceived benefits of Kanban in software companies: Practitioners' views". In Agile Conference 156-168.

[10]. M. O. Ahmad, J. Markkula, M. Oivo, and P. Kuvaja, "Usage of Kanban in software companies: an empirical study on motivation, benefits and challenges". International Conference on Software Engineering Advances. 2015.

[11]. M. Senapathi, and A. Srinivasan, "Understanding post-adoptive agile usage: An exploratory cross-case analysis". Journal of Systems and Software, 85(6), 1255-1268. 2012.

[12]. T. Dybå, T, N.B. Moe, and E.M. Mikkelsen, "An empirical investigation on factors affecting software development acceptance and utilization of Electronic Process Guides". International Symposium on Software Metrics. 220–231.

[13]. T. Dybå, and T. Dingsøyr, "Empirical studies of agile software development: a systematic review", Information and Software Technology, 50, pp. 833-859. 2004.

[14]. P. Runeson, & M. Höst, "Guidelines for conducting and reporting case study research in software engineering". Empirical Softw. Eng. 14(2), 131–164. 2009.

[15]. J. C. Nunnally, "Psychometric Theory". 2nd ed. New York, NY, USA: McGraw-Hill, 1978, pp. 229- 246. 1989.

[16]. J .Iivari, and M. Huisman, "The relationship between organizational culture & the deployment of systems development methodologies". MIS Quarterly, 35-58. 2007.

[17]. C.J.Kaemar, D.J.McManus, E. W. Duggan, J.E. Hale, & D.P. Hale, "Software development methodologies in organizations: field investigation of use, acceptance, and application". J. Information Resources Management, 22 (3), 16-39. 2009.

[18]. A. Bandura, "Self efficacy: The exercise of control". New York: Freeman. 1997.

[19]. F. Davis, "Perceived Usefulness, Perceived Ease of Use, and User Acceptance of Information Technology". MIS Quarterly, vol. 13, no. 3, pp. 318-339. 1989.

[20]. B.C. Hardgrave, and R.A. Johnson, "Toward an information systems development acceptance model: the case of object-oriented systems development". IEEE Trans. Eng. Manage. 50(3), 322–336. 2003.

[21]. J. Drobka, D. Noftz, and R. Raghu, "Piloting XP on four mission-critical projects". IEEE Software, 21 (6). 2004.

[22]. T.L. Roberts, & C.T.Hughes, "Obstacles to implementing a system development methodology". J. Syst. Manage. 47(2), 36–40. 1996.

[23]. L. Williams, L. Layman, and W. Krebs, "Extreme Programming Evaluation Framework for Object-Oriented Languages Version 1.4", NCSU Technical Report. 2004.

[24]. O. Salo, and P. Abrahamsson, "Agile methods in European embedded software development organisations: a survey on the actual use and usefulness of Extreme Programming and Scrum". IET software, 2(1), 58-64. 2008.

A Critical Review of the Use of Spikes in Agile Software Development

Hussein Al Hashimi[1] and Andrew M Gravell [2]

[1,2] *University of Southampton, Southampton, UK*
[1] *King Saud University, Riyadh, KSA*
email: hah2n17@soton.ac.uk, amg@ecs.soton.ac.uk

***Abstract* – Spikes can be an essential component in the agile development cycle since they assist teams in both technical and functional issues in order to obtain the information required to reduce technical risk, understand requirements or enhance the accuracy of a story estimate. Spike is a time-boxed activity to explore and investigate a significant uncertainty and various technical approaches in order to obtain a demonstrable and estimable user story. This paper reviews the uses of spikes through findings in different software development domains to showcase the implementation of spikes in agile software development and their impact on the understanding, consistency, and reliability of the story estimate. The paper provides a critical review of the use of spikes in various software projects and it concludes that limited studies have been conducted on the use of spikes in different software development domains.**

Keywords* - *Agile; Spikes; Risk management; Uncertainty.

I. INTRODUCTION

Spike usage in agile software development was initially defined in the Extreme Programming (XP) approach because spikes represent prototyping, exploration, and investigation, design, and research activities [14]. At the end of the iteration, the spikes in agile are demonstrated and estimated as similar to other stories [26]. Furthermore, they are also responsible for providing the workflow and protocol that are used by the Agile Release Trains (ARTs). The ARTs were developed by Scaled Agile Framework (SAFe). The ARTs are virtual institutions (between 50-125 people) where all persons constitute a self-organising team of experts needed to determine and deliver value by preparing, engaging, and implementing. ARTs help determine the viability and feasibility of epic user stories [23]. The major goal of integrating spikes in agile is to increase the possibility of user story estimation and to minimise technical problems [26]. Spikes can be defined as a particular type of story for the purpose of performing several activities such as research, investigation, exploration, prototyping, and design with the purpose of reducing or driving out uncertainty or the technical risk associated either with the user story or with a project facet [26]. For instance, spikes are required when the agile team needs to resolve a specific technical problem or when they do not have enough information for user story estimation [26].

There are two major types of spikes, functional and technical spikes [26]. Functional spikes are utilised particularly when there is a significant degree of uncertainty. This uncertainty is defined in terms of a lack of understanding of how the system should interact with the user to attain the required benefit. The best way to evaluate the functional spikes is to utilize the prototyping levels by using the user interface mockups, page flows, and the wireframes. However, the other techniques are also utilized in order to get the potential feedback from stakeholders or customers. On the other side, the technical spikes are used for the purpose of conducting technical approaches with respect to the solution domain [26].

Spikes are used for driving out risk and uncertainty in agile software development. There has been a marked shift from traditional software development towards agile methodologies. However, it is important to note that spikes are never really followed in their original forms. Most software developers agree that there is a need for advanced professional skills before a spike can be implemented in software development [26].

At the level of the agile team, spikes are important for extending the runway and thus prioritising other stories. This makes software development visible, accountable and demonstrable at every iteration boundary. This is significant because spikes are used by system architects, product owners, and agile tech leaders to determine what needs to happen and when. Spikes are also important in situations where the story is too large or complex, or the implementation is poorly understood. A technical or functional spike can be built to resolve this impasse. Then based on the result, the stories are split.

Spikes were invented by XP, and are used to remove risk and uncertainty in a user story. Spikes may be used for research, educating the team about new technology, analysing implied behaviour in a large story before it is split into manageable parts, or for prototyping to identify significant risks in a story before committing the user story to some future time box [26]. However, spikes do not provide direct user value, and therefore should be adopted with caution and used carefully in software development. Moreover, it is important to study the use of spikes because the output from spikes is used for information rather than the working code that a typical story will derive. Spikes are important for delivering sufficient, useful information about the story to the agile team. They give visibility to the software development effort, are demonstratable, build collective ownership, and the responsibility for key decisions taken is shared. Therefore, a spike story is usually reserved for larger critical unknowns. A spike is an uncertainty in one or more potential stories; a problem may arise when the spike and the accompanying story are planned in the same iteration. This should be avoided [26][41].

Agile software development is an approach that is currently being adopted by technological- and interactive-based software programming languages. In the course of examining spike usage, this paper begins with a discussion of relevant background and related works in Section II. In Section III, the paper focuses on the application of spikes within the domains of the agile software development approach. Section IV reflects on the influence of spikes on quality in agile software development. In Section V, IT-related security issues are outlined, followed with a discussion about the identified facts in Section VI alongside recommendation and potential future work in Section VII.

II. Background and Related Works

Agile is a philosophy and a method for building and releasing software products. Agile is a group of software engineering methodologies made on similar rules and principles and provides a platform for helping teams, giving a continuously changing functional and technical environment. A focus on fast delivery of business value is maintained [29]. As a result, this approach reduces the risks associated with software development. Agile software development is a blanket term for a group of processes and techniques based on the principles and values described within the Agile Manifesto [5].

A. Agile Methodologies

There are several agile methodologies. The most widely used agile methodologies are Extreme Programming (XP), Scrum, Dynamic System Development Methodology (DSDM), Lean, Crystal, Feature Driven Development (FDD) and Kanban [29].

XP is a disciplined approach to producing high-quality software instantly and consistently. Extreme programming supports high customer engagement, instant feedback loops, consistent planning, consistent testing and production of working software at regular intervals and within very short periods of time. Clients work in partnership with the development team to define and prioritise user stories [6].

Scrum is a framework in persons which identify and resolve adaptive problems that are complex, while creatively and effectively making products that have supreme value. The Scrum framework is usually a Scrum Team with its affiliated functions, rules, artifacts and regular events that put them together with each other [17].

Kanban is a Japanese word and its meaning linked to a time theory, "just in time" created by Toyota in its manufacturing process and applied to software development. The basic concepts of the Kanban method are visualising the flow of work, reducing work in progress, and enhancing the flow of work. The Kanban method matches Scrum in many ways. Both of them are agile, having transparency across the development, and use pull scheduling. Both of them limit the amount of work in progress, the Kanban method at task level and Scrum at sprint level. Both Scrum and the Kanban method focus on early delivery of the releasable software built and require splitting the work into pieces, which is divided into self-organising teams. In both methods, the release plan is also continually optimised depending on empirical data [28].

B. Roles in Agile

An agile team is a multi-functional team of professionals with the necessary resources for the development of a working, properly tested release of a product. In Scrum, the second most significant role is that of the Scrum Master; this individual is responsible for the proper execution of the Scrum methodology as well as removing any potential obstacles that may be encountered by the development team. Accordingly, the Scrum Master is a servant-leader for the team and is not only responsible for promoting and supporting Scrum, but assisting everyone on the team to understand the Scrum theory, practices, value and rules [42]. The Scrum master tracks the project's progress and each individual's input and ensures the conduct of Scrum meetings, planned meetings, demos, reviews, and retrospective meetings [17]. Another role—the product owner—drives the product from the business angle by defining the requirements, evaluating their priority, and determining the date and contents of that release. This person takes an active role in planning the iteration and release meetings as the client's voice. The product owner also accepts and evaluates user stories that meet the defined acceptance criteria and those definitions of done [27]. An agile team is self-sufficient with five to nine members who have an average working experience of around 6 to 10 years. Typically, a team comprises three or four developers, a tester, a technical lead, a product owner, and a Scrum master. The agile team uses its expertise to work on tasks and to decide and plan the scope of work [17].

C. Agile Spikes

Spikes in agile are stories that are estimated only after a development team completes a time boxed investigation. A time box is a defined period of time to accomplish a task in agile. Defined initially in XP, these spikes represent activities such as prototyping, design, research, investigation, and exploration. The purpose behind using spikes is to gather the information needed to better understand the requirement, lower the project risk, and make the story estimate more reliable. Spikes also provide a mutually decided workflow and protocol. At the end of each iteration, spikes are estimated and demonstrated like any other agile story [26]. Spikes are put into the team backlog to fit in to the iteration. The output of a spike is demonstrable, acceptable, and quantified for both the team and any other stakeholders [26]. Planning a spike and the resulting story in the same iteration is risky; however, every user story has uncertainty and risk, so it is necessary for an agile team to learn how to address uncertainty in each iteration using spikes [26][37].

A spike can be described as an investigation that aims to gather information about a project that would otherwise be unavailable. This makes the project more predictable and therefore easier to plan. However, spikes are short in duration, and as a result, spikes may lead to an outcome that is different from what was predicted. A Proof of Concept (POC) is similar to spikes in that it is also an activity that aims to provide more information to developers prior to planning. The only difference between the two is that a spike is focused on discovering complexities, while a POC is used to determine whether a project is worth undertaking [24]. Similar to spikes, the POC also runs for a short period of time because of the deadline that limits it in order to show that the system will successfully run. A POC is also important because it provides information that gives assurance that more investment in the project is not a waste of resources and will lead to positive results. Lastly, the Minimum Viable Product (MVP) aims to test the most basic business hypothesis. This makes MVP the product while Spikes and POCs are tools and techniques used to create the product. The MVP can also be described as a prototype or the first functional version of the product, in most cases, the MVP is used to provide evidence that the product is viable and that it has the potential to solve the problems that it was meant to solve. Most importantly, an MVP can be used to get user opinions and insights about how the product needs to be improved so that it can be perfected and made ready for use. When considering spikes, POCs and MVPs in software development, it is worthwhile to note that the spike is more related to the principles of agile development than either of the other terms; it can be considered a reconnaissance mission to gain a better understanding of a particular aspect of the software development process [43][44].

D. Agile Risk Management

In the software world, risk is the factor that influences the project's success. Due to the many risk factors that can contribute to the working of software, risk management is required in software engineering and development [10].

For projects on agile approaches, formal documentation and meetings are not required for Risk Management. Instead risk management is split into Scrum roles, artifacts and events. It can easily eliminate so many risks in the agile projects by following the principles of agile. These principles significantly mitigate and eliminate the risks that can lead to project challenges and future failures [29].

In the Agile methodology, the spike is used for identifying an issue and providing a short confirmation of an idea to examine an issue further. Spikes also incorporate testing distinctive strategies to accomplish a similar outcome, just like testing to affirm that the ideal outcome is achievable through the present ventured approach. For instance, a group may play out a spike to check whether they can code an application in one language rather than another. A risk-based spike is completed in light of a known risk or openings for project risks [30]. The group may discover that using an alternative programming language can accelerate advancement, or they may discover that they cannot use the one they originally wanted to use. These spikes are added to the backlog as alleviation activities [12].

Risk-based spikes help the agile team eliminate or minimise major risks. Risk-based spikes are used with consideration of fast failure, i.e., if any spike fails for every available approach, the project goes into fast failure, which costs much less than failing late [12].

III. Spikes in Agile Software Development Domains

In agile development spikes are used by the software teams for investigating, closing gaps, and reducing risks. In agile development, the spike is the story that cannot be estimated specifically when the development team is running the time-boxed investigation. The result of the spike is the estimate with respect to the original story. The spike is the "time-boxed" technical investigation that is responsible for generating the answers in accordance to some acceptance criteria on Product Backlog Items (PBIs). These product backlog items are prioritised in the upcoming sprints [34]. In addition, spikes originated in extreme programming where they are considered the special story type that is used specifically for driving out uncertainty and risky elements in either a project facet or user story [26]. Table I shows the agile spike uses in various software domains. It makes evident the limited information available about spike usage.

A. Agile Development for Big Data

Big data is converting business landscapes as the most significant technology in academic ecosystems and business since the dramatic growth of the digital economy and the Internet. Big data refers to data sets that are too enormous or complex for traditional data-processing application software to deal with adequately [12]. According to the Big Data Software Engineering (BIGDSE) workshop, big data systems pull out high-value information to enhance decision-making in Business, science, and society [8]. Performing big data analytics by using agile development methodologies is fairly new and needs wary adaptation as big data analytics are intensely different from "small" data analytics. The requirements of big data analytics require capabilities beyond traditional relational data warehouses [12].

In agile development, spikes can play a major role in data development as it integrates guidelines to make sure that user stories and data are quantifiable, demonstrable, and acceptable. Big data represents parallel processing and data distribution to make sure that data analytics, algorithms, storage lifecycle are not separated from the big data technologies. For such a reason, architecture-supported agile spikes were introduced to make sure that rapid technology changes and new requirements are addressed effectively [15].

B. Agile Development for Data warehouse

The traditional data warehouse projects follow the waterfall development model where they have to complete all six phases—gathering requirements, designing, developing, testing, deploying, and stabilising. In this model, both the technology and business requirements are complex and critical in nature, and approximately six to nine months are required to complete the traditional waterfall model to ensure full implementation. After advances in technology or changes in requirements, it becomes difficult and challenging for the software team to incorporate all the changes without changing the basic architecture of the software system, resulting in frustrated development teams and disappointed stakeholders. On the other side, agile development integrates the solution in an iterative fashion for which it is also known as the "60% solution" [32]. The agile approach assists in delivering the client needs in previous releases with refinements on the subsequent routine release series. To accommodate this task, the agile data warehousing approach improves successful implementation within budget and on time. For data warehouses, the incorporation of spikes may boost agile development by increasing efficiency and functionality.

C. *Agile Development for Computer Science Education*

Just like software project teams use agile spikes to reduce risks, close gaps, and investigate in software development, computer science education can benefit by doing the same while incorporating the techniques of agile development. When practicing the agile development approach stages, software development teams can identify and define the concealed aspects to help determine the steps that need to be covered for related gaps. Spikes include the production and development of the working piece of the software project to address the particular issue. The spike metaphor represents the very specific complete or end-to-end solution. Software projects produced this way are either discarded or simply not used as the final product [38].

In information and communication technology, computer science education is considered a fundamental platform for enhancing the programming skills of students [38]. The agile software development process has a collective nature in which the software team resolves the typical issues in conventional software development processes. In the software industry, the Agile Manifesto is considered the appropriate introduction to the agile approaches [8][38].

Woodward, Montgomery, Vasa, and Cain [38] suggested that spikes are not suitable for freshman students in campus because, at a pre-existing stage, the overhead of the compound skills (e.g., the software development approaches) with respect to spikes prevails over the possible potential benefits.

D. *Agile Development for Blockchain*

The agile methodologies are integrated in adaptive planning because it provides potential support in continuous improvement, which allows the life cycle to respond to changes easily and quickly. These procedures depend on key principles that are organised in different phases [27]. The decentralised technologies and blockchain approach together allow for new possibilities in offering the value of digital and software products to users. Agile development involves integration and transition, whereas blockchain offers a wide variety of possibilities especially when it involves system designs [19]. This creates a platform of uncertainty when a company incorporates the new technology; however, the involvement of spikes may be revoking the level of insecurity. Agile development involves conducting different tests to ascertain how different components involved in the implementation stage would work with software. The involvement of spikes could verify the uncertainty by providing information about the risk a company is bound to encounter through the integration of blockchain and agile development.

E. *Agile User Experience Design (UX)*

The agile and user experience (UX) methods can coexist well only if the management of the organisation supports and understands user experience work, user experience practitioners spend time and show leadership in reaching out to their colleagues, the agile workflows provide flexibility for accommodating user experience needs, and the product teams are composed of user experience professionals, where they can build rapport and respect with the developers [13]. On the other hand, lean UX is an essential technique that is used in projects which utilise the agile development method. Lean UX depends on teamwork; its main aim is to ensure that feedback is received at the earliest possible time. This makes it possible to make quick decisions that match the rapid nature of agile development. Lean UX differs from traditional UX as it focuses on detailed deliverables; the developer's priority is to make changes that make the product better at the current time [45].

Spikes in agile can be used to incorporate user experience design work or monitor user research; however, their main purpose is to handle risk issues in the implementation solutions. Normal planning in spikes should easily predict and anticipate design and research events. Spikes should be responsible for managing risk issues, such as a design task that needs an enquiry into available technology before it can be estimated or any uncertainty that occurs and requires user research to be well defined [9].

F. *Agile Development in Cloud Computing*

The agile methodology is used in software development to cope with the issues of traditional project management where the entire project is preplanned regardless of scope for changing requirements and the assumption that cost and time variables are fixed issues. Agile methodology succeeds by focusing more on collaborative effort to achieve results rather than a predefined process. It is an iterative effort.

The concern solved by agile methodology is the provision of a safe framework for the sharing of information. In cloud computing, there is massive data generation, and through software development, applications are developed to manage these data. Therefore, by design, the aspect of information sharing is considered. The technology provides mechanisms for easily blocking the interception of information while it is in transit, courtesy of the inbuilt application security control capabilities [46]. Effective implementations of the agile methodology help development teams respond to sprints [39]. With the latest advancements, cloud computing has gained popularity, and many entrepreneurs and organisations have adopted cloud hosting services because computing has the advantage of providing a platform for organisations to manage their activities more efficiently [21]. By adopting cloud hosting services, the organisations have been able to respond to the evolving needs in the information technology sector accordingly.

TABLE I: AGILE SPIKES IN DIFFERENT DOMAINS

Spike's Theme	Research paper	Purpose of Study	Conclusion
Risk-based spike	Chen, Kazman, and Haziyev (2016)	To use spikes for addressing the risks of a project by breaking down the story into smaller components	Using an alternate programming language can accelerate advancement, or reveal that the language chosen cannot be used. These spikes would be added to the excess as alleviation activities.
	Albadarneh (2015)	To use spikes in testing to affirm that the ideal outcome is achievable	Spikes incorporate testing distinctive strategies to accomplish a similar outcome, just like testing to affirm that the ideal outcome is achievable through the present ventured approach.
Spikes in agile development for big data	Arndt (2018)	To implement agile approaches on big data for better handling and mutual enrichment	Big data analytics and techniques can help improve the software engineering process.
	Chen, Kazman, and Haziyev (2016)	To effectively implement Agile approaches on big data projects for reducing the risk exposure	Existing agile analytics development methods have no architecture support for big data analytics, but they can help to tame project complexity, reduce uncertainty, and hence reduce project risk.
	Larson and Chang (2016)	To apply agile methodologies and principles to BI delivery and explore how agile has changed with the evolution of BI	Spikes are applicable as the principles of agile can be implemented to BI because agile addresses many problems found in BI projects.
Spikes in agile development for data warehousing	Rahman, Rutz, and Akhter (2013)	To follow agile approaches on data warehousing projects and incorporate all the changes without changing the basic architecture of the software system	Agile methodologies are best known for identifying the inefficient areas for each phase in a data warehousing project. Finding different ways for reducing redundancy, wasted time, and inefficiency can be best serviced with system metrics development.
Spikes in agile development for computer science education	Woodward, Montgomery, Vasa, and Cain (2013)	To take a potential benefit for computer science education by incorporating the techniques of agile development	Spikes are not suitable for fresher students due to the overhead of compound skills at that early stage.
	Bergin, Kussmaul, Reichlmayr, Caristi, and Pollice (2005)	To emphasise the formal processes and detailed documentation that are linked with compliance for computer science education	For application of agile in computer science education, students need to be introduced to agile practices in the right way while preparing them for all kinds of projects.
Spikes in agile development for blockchain	Lenarduzzi, Lunesu, Marchesi, and Tonelli (2018)	To incorporate the potential advantage of the strengths of a blockchain to augment the vulnerability of the Agile/Lean approaches	Agile blockchain might be a good way to record the workflow and to track the enhancements of the product under work as well as the productivity of developers by using Smart Contracts as a payment support.
Spikes in agile development for UX design	Da Silva, Silveira, Maurer, and Hellmann (2012)	To establish a framework for incorporating agile and user experience.	The framework proposed aims at addressing different aspects of this integration, providing alternatives to the UX designer inserted in the agile context.
Spikes in agile development for cloud computing	Younas, Jawawi, Ghani, Fries, and Kazmi (2018)	To ascertain the methods used in a cloud computing platform that are appropriate for agile development using systematic literature review.	Of the studies in the SLR, the techniques using existing tools were reported in 35%, simulations in 20%, and applications developed in 15%.
	Kalem, Donko, and Boskovic (2013)	To illustrate the association between agile methods for software development with the cloud computing platform.	Software development with agile methods is compared with software development with agile methods using cloud computing. All advantages of the second approach are pointed out.
Spikes in agile development for IoT	Cheng, Zhao, Niu, and Chen (2018)	To showcase service communication of agile IoT and orchestration platform using an event-driven service-oriented architecture (SOA) paradigm	The demo shows that the IoT service communication and orchestration platform responds quickly to the dynamic changes in the physical world.
Spikes in agile development for security implementation	Rindell, K., Hyrynsalmi, S. and Leppänen, V.(2017)	To understand benefits and drawbacks of using agile software methodologies in security sensitive development environments.	In order to reduce on overhead costs and uncertainties during agile software development, proper security engineering planning, mechanisms and measures should be put in place and incorporated with various methodologies best suited for implementation, in order to assist with software development and provide a robust and secure end product.
	Siponen, Baskerville, and Kuivalainen (2015)	To incorporate automated techniques to ensure that secure programming practices are implemented to ease the burden by building efficient, effective, and secure systems	Although several issues of integrating security into agile are solved, those methods have many limitations. The combination of related methods can eliminate some weaknesses and improve the existing methods.
	Baca and Carlsson (2011)	To implement Microsoft SDL procedures to reduce the drawbacks associated with agile development	For a reasonable security practice, an organisation should implement an integrated approach to all processes, including agile development processes.
Spikes in agile development for testing	Hooda and Chhillar (2015)	Quality assurance of software applications by carrying out particular test techniques and optimising the processes of software testing.	Most software failures happen due to a lack of security and performance testing. Therefore, a proposed right mix of testing (functional, performance, and security) can be applied for better software quality, where the spike considers one of performance testing.
	Hellmann, Sharma, Ferreira, and Maurer (2012)	To integrate agile development testing in the SDLC	An analysis of the tools used for agile testing showed a focus towards unit and acceptance testing tools.

The use of cloud computing in organisations has brought changes in the way these organisations run their applications and store data. Cloud computing helps organisations manage large volumes of data and provide prompt responses to their users. Integrating agile spikes into cloud computing may provide a solution to the problems of quantifying risks and timing uncertainty [22].

G. *Agile Development in Internet of Things (IoT)*

In Internet of Things devices, customer responsiveness is considered the main factor, but with fast-growing technology, the responsiveness to the customers' responsiveness is considered the end solution for all associations. The changing requirements are potentially supported by agile approaches. However, the alignment of the agile framework is relevant to the value stream of the agile process [11]. Additionally, continuous improvement and the sustainability of practices are the major inputs needed for scaling through regulations; competition; and volatility, uncertainty, complexity, and ambiguity [1]. Furthermore, it is important to consider the involvement of spikes in agile development as a factor that can benefit the merge of Internet of Things during software development. Although agile development aims to deliver a high-quality product rapidly, the involvement of spikes may offer a wide possibility to reduce the risk in an agile development environment for internet of things.

IV. QUALITY IN AGILE SOFTWARE DEVELOPMENT

The agile processes are best known for delivering results in short time intervals; however, it is important to ensure that they are meeting the quality requirements of the particular project as well. Quality is important when it comes to software development because it determines customer satisfaction. The same is true in agile software development where the spike is incorporated in the fulfilment of some fundamental components involved in unit testing. For instance, testing may determine whether the assembling life cycle of an agile environment and its supportive components are complete or whether the incorporated techniques will provide good quality.

A. *Quality Assurance for Agile Software Development*

Quality assurance also involves the management of future risk, and the incorporation of spikes may create a platform on which to test the riskiness of software usage in the future. Two major characteristics of agile development are its ability to handle unstable requirements that are executed throughout the development life cycle and its ability to deliver a product in defined budget constraints and shorter time frames. Agility is related to strategy, release iteration, and continuous and daily working software. Agile development allows users to develop software products in small increments or releases, which are then approved by the customer. The spike solution is the operational prototype [36].

Software quality assurance is also used to govern the processes for building the desired quality into software products. Quality assurance is divided into two main types: dynamic and static [18]. The organisation, objectives, and selection of the specific technique depending on the nature and requirements of the software project. Additionally, the selection of these methodologies depends on the project criteria. The static technique includes the examination of project documentation by groups or individuals via different tools, such as project inspection of the requirements and reviewing the code technically. However, the dynamic technique includes the execution of code and is generally used in agile development and processes [18].

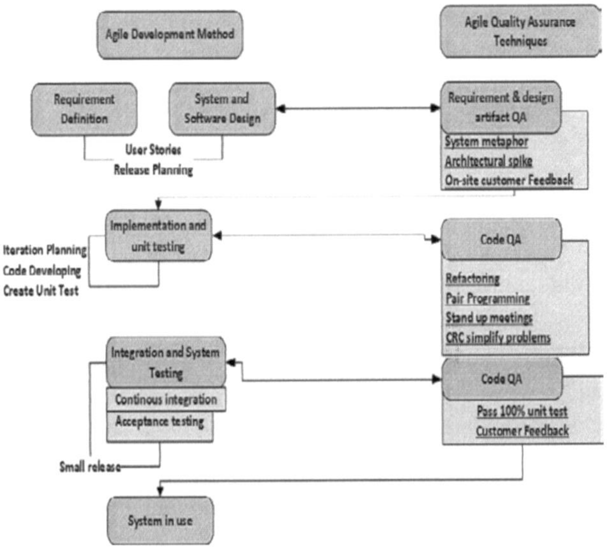

Figure 1. Quality Assurance in Agile Methods

In Figure 1, the generalised development life cycle approach of the agile methodology shows where some of the agile stages overlap one another. In agile development, some of the techniques have integrated both the quality assurance ability and agile functionality, which means the agile approaches have moved some of the quality assurance responsibilities to the developers.

In agile development, a small amount of output is sent for quality assurance in order to get fast feedback. The quality assurance practices and development practices integrate with one another to exchange the results quickly that helps in maintaining the processing speed. This approach enables two-way communication in agile development [18].

The architectural spike is a fixed variable/time scope PBI that is incorporated to inform the software team that more investigation is required for maximising velocity. The effective implementation of architectural spikes helps the software team get maximum estimates. The spikes are composed of a series of investigations that are created to find the solutions to maximum problems. The architectural spike technique is integrated to reduce the risks posed by XP [18][40].

B. *Testing in Agile Software Development*

In agile software development, testing is considered the cornerstone as most of the agile practices depend completely on effective software testing. The effectiveness and efficiency of the agile methodology help in determining agile software development outcomes. In agile development, the test plan is updated and written for every release. The agile test plan involves different testing types that are executed in a specific iteration, such as test results, test environments, infrastructure, and test data requirements. The general test plan in agile development includes the following: testing scope, new functionalities that need to be tested, types or levels of testing depending on complex features, performance and load testing, infrastructure consideration, risks or mitigation plan, resourcing, and milestones and deliverables [20].

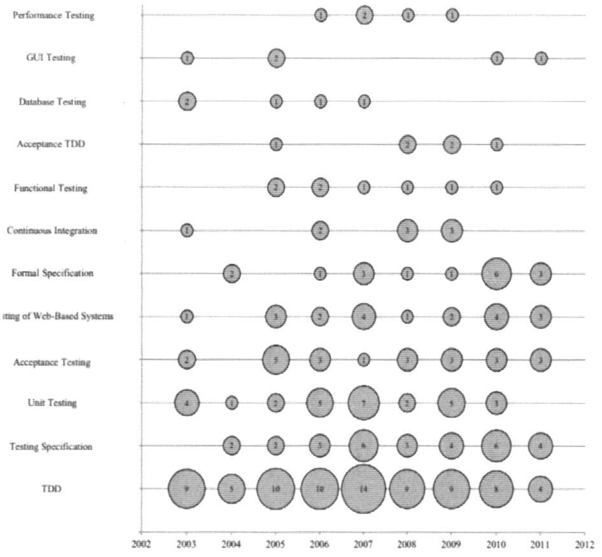

Figure 2. Testing Use over Time

Figure 2 provides a better understanding of how agile testing techniques are used over time. Interest in Test-Driven Development (TDD) continued to increase, highlighting its central role in agile testing. However, on the other side, the other agile testing use represents the "distinct spikes". For instance, there are gaps in performance, publication database record, acceptance, and graphical user interface (GUI) testing. This specific point highlights the subfields with respect to more distinct agile testing fields. For example, in agile development, the GUI testing was not included from 2006 to 2009; however, database testing interest was shown in the same time period [16].

Although TDD has been the most used testing method in recent years, there are other forms of agile testing that are regarded as more efficient by software developers; many developers suggest that TDD does not lead to an increase in quality or faster development [48][50]. Some of the new techniques include Acceptance Test-Driven Development (ATDD) and Behaviour-Driven Development (BDD). Even though these three agile testing methods are related, ATDD is primarily a communication tool for the three amigos (customer, developer and tester) to ensure that all requirements are properly defined. Unlike TDD, ATDD does not require test automation. Often, the tests that are used in TDD are derived from ATDD, and while the ATDD test should be understood by the customer, the TDD test does not need to be readable by the customer. The BDD goes a step further by combining practices found in TDD and ATDD. In BDD, tests are initially written but focused on describing behaviour rather than tests used in TDD to test a unit of implementation [47]. Exploratory testing is another agile testing method in which the test design and test execution phases occur simultaneously, while in session-based testing, although similar to exploratory testing, the software is tested comprehensively and in a more orderly fashion [48]. Furthermore, TDD has continued to mature over the years in its use and acceptance by software developers because writing the test first allows you really understand what you want to code, receive faster feedback, reduces the time spent on rework and debugging. TDD leads to a greater understanding of the software being developed. The rise of other testing methods, albeit similar to TDD, was hinged on the preference of developers for writing tests after the code was already written. This preference is reflected in Test Last Development (TLD) and Iterative Test Last (ITL) [47] [49]. The Incremental Test-last Development (ITLD) is another closely related process to TDD. Both testing methods only differ in the order of activities that are involved in each increment and follow the same iterative steps, such as decomposing the specifications into smaller programming tasks, testing, coding and refactoring. However, while TDD requires the test to be written before the code, ITLD goes for writing the code first before the test. When TDD and ITLD were compared via a simple greenfield task, the difference was not significant. It was concluded that TDD did not appear to improve external quality. Furthermore, it was discovered that when TDD was used for simple tasks it was more productive than ITLD. The productivity of TDD significantly dropped when applied to more complex brownfield tasks [50].

V. AGILE IT SECURITY IMPLEMENTATION

In all software products, there are various potential vulnerabilities that can cause a lot of damage. Therefore, software developers are required to develop more efficient and secure systems by conducting all the phases of the software development life cycle. Developers must consider and incorporate all the security aspects in each phase to ensure that there is no vulnerability. The security is considered the most important component when developing any software product. Agile IT security goes beyond safeguarding the software as it also focuses on efficiency in performing tasks. This is facilitated by involving spikes, for instance, which boosts the testing process to abolish uncertainty and inconsistencies, boosts the software life cycle and ability to function efficiently, and thus sorts security issues that might arise from unresolved complexities. Furthermore, the involvement of spikes covers issues or challenges that may arise as a result of software developers lacking knowledge regarding futuristic implications from a particular feature. Lack of knowledge about the implications of feature can leave developers unaware of which areas they need to cover to secure the software. The involvement of spikes covers this uncertainty, giving a boost to agile IT security [25].

To reduce the drawbacks associated with agile development, five-step models are considered the best solution. In the first phase, all the security activities are extracted from the existing guidelines and processes, and the agile activities are defined to measure their level of agility. The integration problems and security issues related to agile activities are handled by implementing algorithm techniques and strategies. This way, the agility reduction tolerance parameter and its optimum value are taken into consideration to ensure the system's security. It is important to include the latest security advancements in all the stages of the Software Development Life Cycle (SDLC) to develop an efficient software system. The Comprehensive Lightweight Application Security Process (CLASP) and the Microsoft Security Development Lifecycle (SDL) are considered the two main processes for improving and enhancing a software product's security. However, some disadvantages and advantages have been compared and analysed in order to identify potential vulnerable areas. With respect to the agile methodologies, the Microsoft SDL procedures are implemented [4].

VI. Conclusion and Future Work

This paper provides a critical review of the use of spikes in various agile software projects. Spikes has also been illustrated as playing a critical role in agile software development by minimising unforeseen risks and uncertainties in the development cycle. This can be achieved by getting the agile team to understand the risks involved in the software development cycle and finding a viable solution that guarantees the best output in the form of software. However, there were challenges experienced in gathering relevant data because there is no sufficient information to back up the quality and effectiveness of the software produced related to spikes. This has been warranted by the limited information available for study, more research and experiments need to be carried out to ascertain the nature and effectiveness of software produced since there is varying information.

Professionals and industry partners will be recruited to assist in the use of spikes in agile software development because they will play a critical part in the entire process. In this regard, some case studies will be used for authentication purposes and also further research employed in order to clearly showcase the spikes in agile software development in the future.

References

[1] M. Akem, "Agile and The Internet of Things (IOT)" [Online]. Available: https://www.projecttimes.com/articles/agile-and-the-internet-of-things-iot.html. [Accessed: 18-AUG-2019].

[2] A. Albadarneh, I. Albadarneh, and A. Qusef, "Risk Management in Agile Software Development: A Comparative Study," In 2015 IEEE Jordan Conference on Applied Electrical Engineering and Computing Technologies (AEECT), pp. 1-6. IEEE, 2015.

[3] T. Arndt, "Big Data and Software Engineering: Prospects for Mutual enrichment," Iran Journal of Computer Science., vol. 1, no. 1, pp. 3–10, 2018.

[4] D. Baca and B. Carlsson, "Agile Development with Security Engineering Activities," In Proceedings of the 2011 International Conference on Software and Systems Process, pp. 149-158. ACM, 2011.

[5] K. Beck, et al, "Manifesto for agile software development. 2001," [Online]. Available: http://www.agilemanifesto.org/. [Accessed: 12-SEP-2019].

[6] K. Beck and E. Gamma, *Extreme Programming Explained: Embrace Change*. Addison-Wesley Professional, 2000.

[7] J. Bergin, C. Kussmaul, T. Reichlmayr, J. Caristi and G. Pollice, "Agile Development in Computer Science Education: Practices and Prognosis," Proceedings of the 36th SIGCSE Technical Symposium on Computer Science Education, pp.130-131. ACM, 2005.

[8] BIGDSE '16, "Proceedings of the 2nd International Workshop on BIG Data Software Engineering," [Online]. Available: https://sse.uni-due.de/bigdse16/. [Accessed: 08-AUG-2019].

[9] D. Brown, *Agile User Experience Design: A Practitioner's Guide to Making it Work*. Newnes, 2012.

[10] B. Boehm, "Risk Management in Agile Software Development: A Comparative Study," IEEE Software, vol. 8, no. 1, pp. 32 - 41, 1991.

[11] B. Cheng, S. Zhao, M. Niu and J. Chen, "Agile IoT Service Communication and Orchestration Platform Using Event Driven SOA Paradigm," In IEEE INFOCOM 2018-IEEE Conference on Computer Communications Workshops (INFOCOM WKSHPS), pp. 1-2. IEEE, 2018.

[12] H-M. Chen, R. Kazman, S. Haziyev, "Agile Big Data Analytics Development: An Architecture-Centric Approach," In 2016 49th Hawaii International Conference on System Sciences (HICSS), pp. 5378-5387. IEEE, 2016.

[13] TS. Da Silva, MS. Silveira, F. Maurer and T. Hellmann, "User Experience Design and Agile Development: From Theory to Practice," Journal of Software Engineering and Applications, vol. 5, no. 10, pp. 743-751, 2012.

[14] A. Fuqua 2016, "What's A Spike, Who Should Enter it, And How To Word it?" [Online]. Available: https://www.leadingagile.com/2016/09/whats-a-spike-who-should-enter-it-how-to-word-it/. [Accessed: 23-SEP-2019].

[15] N. Grady, J. Payne and H. Parker, "Agile Big Data Analytics: AnalyticsOps for Data Science," In 2017 IEEE International Conference on Big Data (Big Data), pp. 2331-2339. IEEE, 2017.

[16] T. Hellmann, A. Sharma, J. Ferreira, and F. Maurer, "Agile Testing: Past, Present and Future," In Agile Conference (AGILE), pp. 55-63. IEEE, 2012.

[17] R. Hoda, J. Noble and S. Marshall, "Self-Organizing Roles on Agile Software Development Teams," In IEEE Transactions on Software Engineering, vol. 39, no. 3, pp. 422-444, 2012.

[18] M. Huo, J. Verner, L. Zhu, M. Babar , "Software quality and agile methods," In Proceedings of the 28th Annual International Computer Software and Applications Conference (COMPSAC), pp. 520-525. IEEE, 2004.

[19] Ibba 2019, "Agile methodologies and blockchain development," [online]. Available: https://iris.unica.it/handle/11584/260671#.XQx52RZKjIU. [Accessed: 29-AUG-2019].

[20] M. Isaacs, "What is Agile Testing? Process, Strategy, Test Plan, Life Cycle Example," [Online]. Available: https://www.guru99.com/agile-testing-a-beginner-s-guide.html. [Accessed: 12-AUG-2019].

[21] N. Jain and S. Dubey, "Agile Development Methodology with cloud computing," International Journal of Engineering and Computer Science, vol. 3, no. 4, pp. 5373-5378, 2014.

[22] S. Kalem, D. Donko and D. Boskovic, "Agile methods for cloud computing," In 2013 36th International Convention on

Information and Communication Technology, Electronics and Microelectronics (MIPRO), pp. 1079-1083. IEEE, 2013.

[23] R. Knaster and D. Leffingwell, *SAFe 4.5 Distilled: Applying the Scaled Agile Framework for Lean Software and Systems Engineering*. Addison-Wesley Professional, 2018.

[24] D. Larson and V. Chang, "A review and future direction of agile, business intelligence, analytics and data science," International Journal of Information Management, vol. 36, no. 5, pp. 700-710, 2016.

[25] J. Laskowski, *Agile IT security implementation methodology*. Packt Publishing Ltd, 2011.

[26] D. Leffingwell, *Agile software requirements: lean requirements practices for teams, programs, and the enterprise*. Addison-Wesley Professional, 2010.

[27] V. Lenarduzzi, M. Lunesu, M. Marchesi and R. Tonelli, "Blockchain applications for Agile methodologies," In Proceedings of the 19th International Conference on Agile Software Development: Companion, p. 30. ACM, 2018.

[28] G. Matharu, A. Mishra, H. Singh and R. Tonelli, "Empirical study of agile software development methodologies: A comparative analysis," ACM SIGSOFT Software Engineering Notes, vol. 40, no. 1, pp. 1-6, 2015.

[29] A. Moniruzzaman and S. Hossain "Comparative study on agile software development methodologies," Global Journal of Computer Science and Technology, vol. 13, no. 7, pp. 1-25, 2013.

[30] A. Moran, "Agile Big Data Analytics: AnalyticsOps for Data Science," In Agile Risk Management, pp. 33-60. Springer, Cham, 2014.

[31] I. Perera, "Impact of using agile practice for student software projects in computer science education," International Journal of Education and Development using ICT 5, vol. 5, no. 3, pp. 85-100, 2015.

[32] N. Rahman, D. Rutz and S. Akhter, "Agile development in data warehousing," In Principles and Applications of Business Intelligence Research, pp. 286-300. IGI Global, 2013.

[33] K. Rindell, S. Hyrynsalmi and V Leppänen, "Case Study of Agile Security Engineering: Building Identity Management for a Government Agency," International Journal of Secure Software Engineering (IJSSE), vol. 8, no. 1, pp. 43-57, 2017.

[34] K. Schwaber and M. Beedle, *Agile software development with Scrum*, vol. 1. Upper Saddle River: Prentice Hall, 2002.

[35] M. Siponen, R. Baskerville and T. Kuivalainen, "Integrating security into agile development methods," In Proceedings of the 38th Annual Hawaii International Conference on System Sciences, pp. 185a-185a. IEEE, 2005.

[36] I. Stamelos and P. Sfetsos, *Agile software development quality assurance*. Igi Global, 2007.

[37] Tanner, "Spikes Purpose and Usage," [Online]. Available: https://www.spikesandstories.com/spikes-purpose-and-usage/. [Accessed: 15-SEP-2019].

[38] C. Woodward, J. Montgomery, R. Vasa and A. Cain, "Agile development spikes applied to computer science education," In Proceedings of 2013 IEEE International Conference on Teaching, Assessment and Learning for Engineering (TALE), pp. 699-704. IEEE, 2013.

[39] M. Younas, I. Ghani, D. Jawawi and M. Khan, "A framework for agile development in cloud computing environment," Journal of Internet Computing and Services, vol. 17, no. 5, pp. 67-74, 2016.

[40] S. Ambler, *Agile modeling: effective practices for extreme programming and the unified process*. John Wiley & Sons, 2002.

[41] A. Solinski and K. Petersen, "Prioritizing agile benefits and limitations in relation to practice usage," software quality journal, vol. 24, no.2. pp.447-482, 2016.

[42] K. Schwaber and J. Sutherland, "Scrum Guide," [Online]. Available: https://www.scrumguides.org/docs/scrumguide/v2017/2017-Scrum-Guide-US.pdf. [Accessed: 30-SEP-2019].

[43] Eric, "How to use (and difference of) Spike vs Proof of Concept vs MVP," [Online]. Available: https://www.agileview.com.au/how-to-use-and-difference-of-spike-vs-proof-of-concept-vs-mvp/. [Accessed: 30-SEP-2019].

[44] L. Garland, "Spikes, POCs, Prototypes and the MVP," Medium, 2014. [Online]. Available: https://medium.com/studio-zero/spikes-pocs-prototypes-and-the-mvp-5cdffa1b7367. [Accessed: 03- OCT- 2019].

[45] The Interaction Design Foundation, "A Simple Introduction to Lean UX," 2019. [Online]. Available: https://www.interaction-design.org/literature/article/a-simple-introduction-to-lean-ux. [Accessed: 02- OCT- 2019].

[46] C. Schmidt, T. Kude, A. Heinzl and S. Mithas, "How Agile practices influence the performance of software development teams: The role of shared mental models and backup," Association for Information systems. 2014.

[47] L. Alberto, "Analysis of the impact of test-based development techniques (TDD, BDD, AND ATDD) to the software life cycle," [Online]. Available: https://iconline.ipleiria.pt/bitstream/10400.8/3699/1/Dissertation_2160085_LuisGomez.pdf. [Accessed: 04- OCT- 2019].

[48] L. Cisneros, C. Reis and M. Maximiano, "An Experimental Evaluation of ITL, TDD and BDD," In ICSEA 2018, The Thirteenth International Conference on Software Engineering Advances (pp. 20-24). ICSEA,2018

[49] A. Čaušević, D. Sundmark and S. Punnekkat, "Impact of test design technique knowledge on test-driven development: A controlled experiment" In International Conference on Agile Software Development, pp. 138-152. Springer, 2012.

[50] A. Tosun, et al, "An industry experiment on the effects of test-driven development on external quality and productivity," Empirical Software Engineering, vol. 22, no. 6, pp. 2763-2805, 2017.

[51] I. Hooda and R. Chhillar "Software test process, testing types and techniques," International Journal of Computer Applications, vol. 111, no. 13, pp. 10-14, 2015.

Graph-Based Analysis of the Architectural Restructuring Impact on Energy Efficiency

Basma khil
Faculty of Mathematical, Physical and Natural Sciences of Tunis
Tunis, Tunisia
Email: basma.khil@fst.utm.tn

Adel Khalfallah
Higher Institute of Computer Science
Ariana, Tunisia
Email: adel.khalfallah@isi.utm.tn

Samir Ben Ahmed
Faculty of Mathematical, Physical and Natural Sciences of Tunis
Tunis, Tunisia
Email: samir.benahmed@fst.utm.tn

***Abstract*—Software design patterns and refactoring are widely used in software engineering to enhance maintainability, reuse and productivity. However, recent empirical studies revealed the high energy overhead in these patterns. Our approach consists of automatically applying refactoring techniques, detecting and injecting design patterns during design level for better energy efficiency without impacting existing coding practices. Regarding that, refactoring techniques could help to tackle these issues considering that it is a method of changing the internal design of the system while preserving the external behavior. In this paper, we propose a graph transformation for refactoring, design pattern injection and furthermore rules to compute the total energy consumption and perform an initial evaluation of the energy efficiency.**

Keywords–Energy-efficiency; Software Architectures; Graph transformation rules; Energy consumption.

I. INTRODUCTION

Energy consumption has emerged as an important design constraint in software engineering. Information and Communication Technology (ICT) [1] and the Internet of Things (IoT) yield a huge potential increase in energy demand. These kinds of systems are mostly imposed by a restrict power budget. This is a problem that now looks to exceed many challenges and has been enlarged into a mammoth task. It takes into account the effects of hardware, devices, networks, drivers, operating systems, and applications on energy consumption. In this paper, we focus on applications and, particularly, on how we experiment with the effect of applying transformations activities at a design level which can be optimized in terms of energy consumption.

In searching generic transformation units, we worked on the original definition of standardized transformations such as the refactoring catalog. Refactoring is proven to improve the quality of a system. Thus, it can be a potential solution to increase software maintainability and re-usability. It is proven that software engineering best practices can improve software maintainability [1][2]. Hence, investigating refactoring activities to optimize energy consumption seems more and more trendy.

Some tentative proved that software engineering best practices can improve energy efficiency [3][4][5]. Notably, [6][7][8][9] focused on the impact of refactoring activities on energy consumption. Nevertheless, the available evidences are tried and tested in a limited number of refactoring techniques. Typically, they are applied in a code artifact, Whereas the most common approach used in software engineering makes a great emphasis on the use of modeling artifact [1]. Therefore, it is desirable to master the modeling in software architecture by working at a relevant level of abstraction. That gives rise to the idea of managing energy consumption since the phase architectural design.

The scope of this work lies at the design level. We aim to explore the effect of transformation activities on energy consumption. In particular, we propose a combinatorial approach based on graph transformations. Namely, we use metamodeling to represent the architectural design artifact, as well as graph transformation rules to explore the different alternatives induced by the design decisions and transformations.

The remainder of the paper is organized as follows: Section 2 surveys recent literature to have an overview of how software engineering researchers are tackling energy consumption issues. In Section 3, the current proposal is explained by a suitable process and with an adequate architectural metamodel. Sections 4 and 5 state the graph transformation rules. The first kind of rule embodies transformation activities. the other kind surveys their effect on energy consumption. In Section 6, a motivating scenario is presented to illustrate the proposal with a concrete example. Finally, Section 7 concludes this paper and gives avenues for future work.

II. RELATED WORK

The literature on the energy efficiency topic shows divergences: According to some works, the energy consumption in network infrastructure is predominant, whereas, for others, it is prominent in the terminals. Many experimental approaches specifically deal with identifying the parts of an application that mostly affect the total energy consumption [10] and try to minimize its consumption. For this purpose, some trials [11][12] optimized code to minimize power consumption.

Luo [13] proposed an ant colony algorithm for task scheduling to optimizing the energy cost. Liu [14] explored the non-dominant sorting genetic algorithm to bridge the trade-off between energy consumption and delay in task scheduling. However, scheduling tasks using only offline power consumption information cannot generate efficient schedules on account of the dynamic variation in energy consumption. Thus,[15][16] proposed a real-time monitoring and management system for energy consumption. However, there is further evidence that changes in architectural design tend to have a greater impact on energy consumption [17].

Other attempts rely on the quantitative evaluation of energy consumption of software systems at higher levels and in early stage in the software development process [18][19][20]. Some of these works proposed architecture description languages that support the analysis of power consumption at the design level [1][12][21]. Other implemented experimental solutions and tools to evaluate and monitor energy consumption. Seo has performed an energy consumption analysis for specific architectural styles [22] such as client-server. The works [23][24][25] propose an approach that predicts energy consumption using linear power models.

Other attempts aimed to evaluate the energy consumption of the Cloud Computing application and High-Performance Computing (HPC) systems. Previously discussed approaches focus on the energy consumption analysis at an architectural-level. Some of them do not take account of parametric dependencies between software components [24][25] while others percept the dependency between different energy concerns [26]. They specify the relationships between energy concerns under the modeled component. These relationships can then be used during the analysis phase to see how an energy concern (communication) can affect other energy concerns (for example, compression storage).

Recently, certain approaches take advantage of the positive effect of software engineering best practices on software quality [1][2]and on energy consumption to tackle trade-off between productivity and energy efficiency [3][4][6][7][8][9]. Some works prove that software engineering best practices can improve energy efficiency [3][4]. Others [6][7][8][9] focus on the impact of refactoring activities on energy consumption. The searchers experiment that idea in a code application such as Java, C and Android applications. However, these evidences are experimented in a limited number of refactoring techniques. Typically, they are empirical studies applied in a code artifact. However, it is desirable to work at a relevant level of abstraction and also manage the Global Software issues through modeling.

Our approach is involved in this area, it consists of applying refactoring activities by analyzing modeling artifacts and monitor the changes in energy consumption. That gives rise to the idea of managing energy consumption at architectural design. And follow the impact of refactoring on software consumption. Therefore Graph-based approaches seem very promising, due to their robust theoretical foundation.

III. Motivation

A major challenge that is currently faced in the design of applications concerns the optimal use of available energy resources. In particular, the IoT applications are imposed by the battery lifetime of the devices. The challenge is derived from the heterogeneity of the devices, in terms of their hardware and the provided functionalities. Several works in energy management are focusing their studies on the hardware side of computational systems. However, it is tempting to suppose that only hardware dissipates power, not software. Since energy consumption is the amount of energy used by devices or a built environment. The energy consumption varies according to the kind of device and the time that it remains in the operating modes. It is, therefore, necessary to think about saving energy, and that requires a careful choice of electrical appliances. Recently, the software engineering community started to carry out researches about estimations of energy consumption in software applications [12][17]. According to the authors,the software directs much of the activity of the hardware. Therefore, the software can have a substantial impact on the power dissipation of computational systems. They investigated the mixes of hardware-software designs to minimize energy consumption. However, these approaches were focused on low levels of software design, such as the number of execution cycles of a software, optimization of memory addresses. Other works analyze this issue from a different perspective [27] where energy management is discussed in higher levels of abstraction. Such levels are related to software requirement analysis, design and specification. We intend to approach this issue in design levels.

IV. Proposed Approach

The main contributions of this paper are defined as follows. First, it outlines an approach for modeling and injection of restructuring activities such as refactoring and ever more design patterns by analyzing UML diagrams. Second, a methodical analysis to assess the relative impact of that restructuring activity and expect the total energy consumption induced by the different components of an IoT application. Following that, we perform an analysis of the impact of refactoring activities on energy consumption and performance in software applications. We aim to take advantage of the formal foundations of graphs transformation.

A. The proposed method

In the thought of taking advantage of the formal foundation of graphs, we presented a graph-based transformation to introduce restructuring activities in the design of a new application or an existing one. Furthermore, we established sets of graph transformation rules to estimate the total energy consumed. We presented our graph-based system and then performed an exploratory analysis of the impact of design transformation on energy consumption and performance in software applications. In this area, graph-based approaches seem more promising due to their robust theoretical foundation. Consequently, graphs are well-known structures combining rigor with simplicity [28], which are beneficial in modeling design software systems.

B. Method process

In the exploratory study here reported we investigated the impact of software architecture restructuring with well-known transformation techniques on energy consumption. We consider design transformations activity as a set of graph transformations applied to a graph instance representing a given model. So, a given transformation recognition is provided by the mechanism of matching within graphs.

A graph transformation introducing a complex restructuring, such as a design Pattern, is composed of a sequence of graph transformation units. In searching for a generic transformation unit, we worked on the original definition of the refactoring catalog and the Elements Design Patterns (EDPs) defined by Smith [29]. They represent micro-transformations whose different combinations lead to the introduction of Design Patterns into models. So we built a library of the possible instantiations of each transformation such as Refactoring, EDP and intermediate pattern compositions. In practice, we used the toolset GROOVE to implement these transformations as graph transformation rules [11]. Also, we enrich our rule set by another kind of rules that compute the energy consumed under each stage in the entire application tasks. We will explain later in this article how to investigate the effect of refactoring transformation in energy efficiency by analyzing UML diagrams (class diagram) and not only existing code. Software optimizations and energy computing, in this context, have been discussed at three levels of granularity (Figure 1): Type graph, graph transformation rules and instance graph.

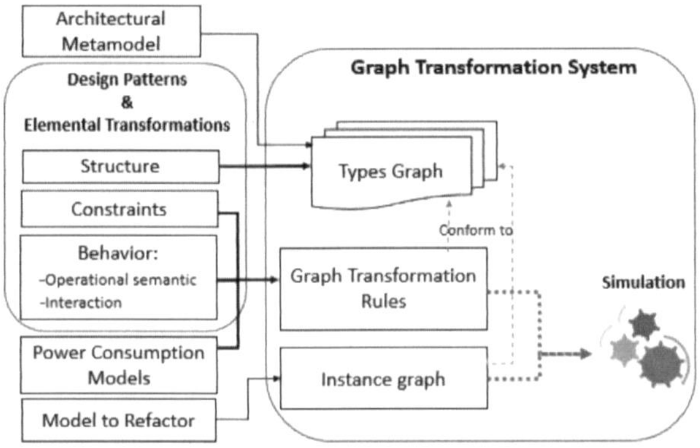

Figure 1. Graph transformation system.

We represent our architectural design as a graph, we identify and represent refactoring activity as graph transformation rules and then we formalize another cluster of rules to compute the energy consumption. The following section will detail every level individually.

V. META MODEL

To analyze the energy consumption of a software system, we propose the meta-model depicted in Figure 2. It includes the required artifacts, on the one hand, to describe the software architecture and on the other hand to assess the expected energy consumption.

Our model is based on the concepts of component-oriented architectures (CBSE) and service-oriented architectures (SOA). To analyze the expected energy consumption of so many alternative architectural solutions, we must define the elements of such a solution. As shown in Figure 2, the architectural aspect is represented by an architectural style element that includes a collection of homogeneous and heterogeneous components (elements and architectural constraints). An architectural element is composed, in turn, by other architectural elements, components that interact through connectors.

A component is defined as a set of interacting tasks and services to fill a role and communicate with the environment via two interfaces. Typically, connectors define abstractions that encapsulate the mechanisms of communication, coordination, and conversion (type, number, frequency, and order of interactions) between components. The component is also defined by a predefined set of tasks or roles. A task is a semantic entity of the basic unit of work (activity or role). It can be a task of calculation or storage, etc. It can be extended by others under spots. Sometimes the execution of a task is heavily dependent on other tasks (for example, remote storage of data depends on the communication problem). As a result, this information is defined by a reflexive relationship that reflects this dependency [30].

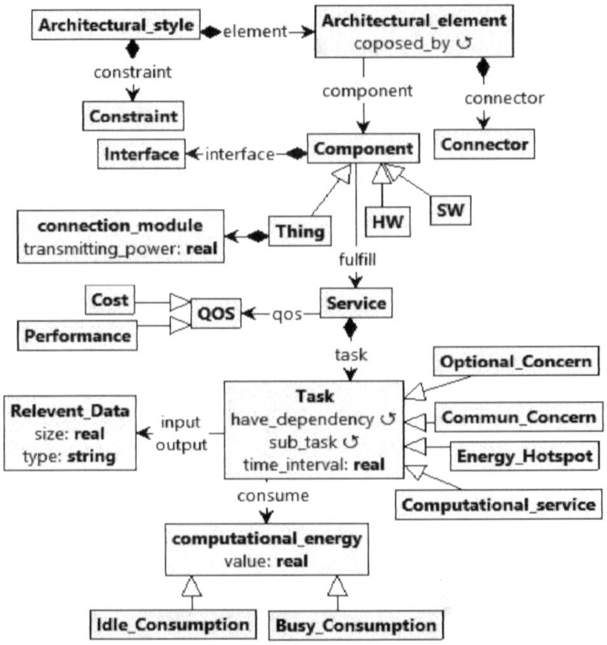

Figure 2. Component-oriented architecture as a graph.

To enlarge the scope of the current approach, in particular, tackling the artifacts involved with the IoT paradigm. the metamodel encompasses concepts related to a thing.

A Thing is organized into two categories (Figure 3):

- A physical thing is organized into a group of physical networked things, including devices, sensors, actuators, and even embedded devices.
- A virtual thing is organized into a virtual group of things in a network, including web services and programs.

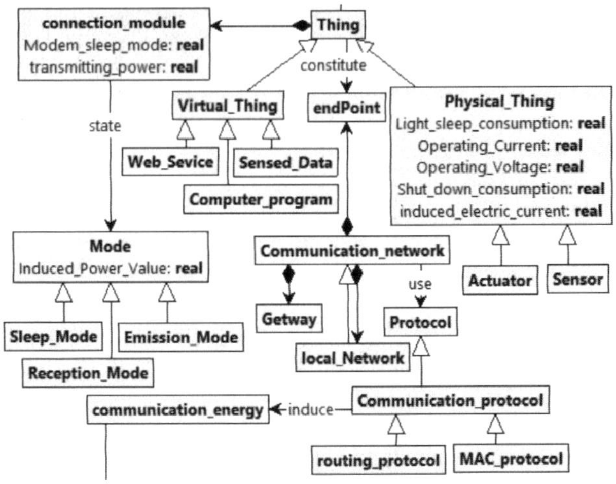

Figure 3. Meta-model of the entities types in IoT.

To analyze the expected energy consumption, it is required to discriminate the fields that affect the global consumption. They are mainly due to several operations such as computational tasks and data communication.

The Energy consumed by the processing unit is divided into two parts: the energy induced by computational tasks in the busy state and the energy consumed in the idle state. The first one is determined by the supply voltage and the total capacity switched likewise in the hardware level (sensors and actuators, etc.) and the software level (by running software program, services, etc.). The second one corresponds to the energy consumed when the calculation unit does not carry out any treatment. The communication energy can be divided into the reception energy, the energy of the emission and the sleep mode. This energy is determined by the amount of data to be communicated and the transmission distance, as well as by the physical properties of the communication module.

Another part of our meta-model is dedicated to representing power distribution infrastructure (see Figure 4). Power distribution infrastructure can be organized in a hierarchical manner [1]. Power distribution units distribute power to racks which in turn provide power to the connected devices.

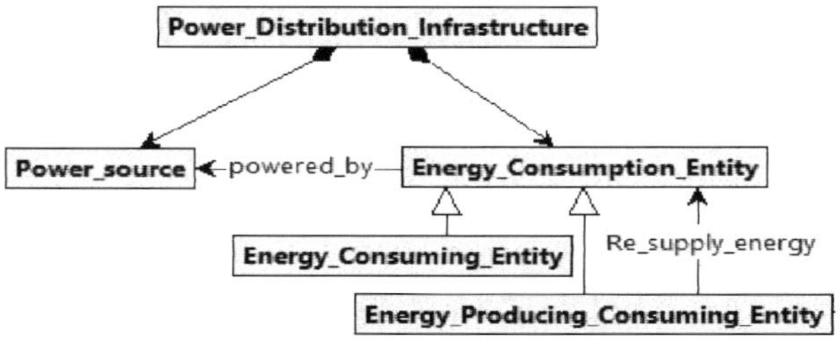

Figure 4. hierarchical of power distribution infrastructure.

In order to percept the dependency between different tasks, we add a reflexive link labeled as "have dependency". It specifies the relationships between energy concerns under the modeled component. Then, we classified tasks according to the well-known energy concerns hierarchy and activities more recurrent in a given application such as Store, Communication, Data Access, Data collect [31] (see Figure 5). That list will be augmented once there is new evidence about other energy hotspots.

There are many variabilities in how to design and implement concerns (e.g., the data could be stored locally or remotely, compress audio or video files). Additionally, these concerns could depend on each other. For instance, there are several concerns related to Communication, such as Data Access and Store. Due to that dependency, for every energy consumption concern cannot be analyzed on an isolated basis. Instead, a whole architecture should be analyzed taking into account these explicit dependencies modeled.

VI. Expected Energy Consumption Based-Graph Transformation Rules

Commonly, energy calculation is straightforward. The electrical energy is (in kilowatt-hour, kWh), found by multiplying the power use (in kilowatts, kW) by the number of hours during which the power is consumed.
Accurate the expected energy consumption characterization

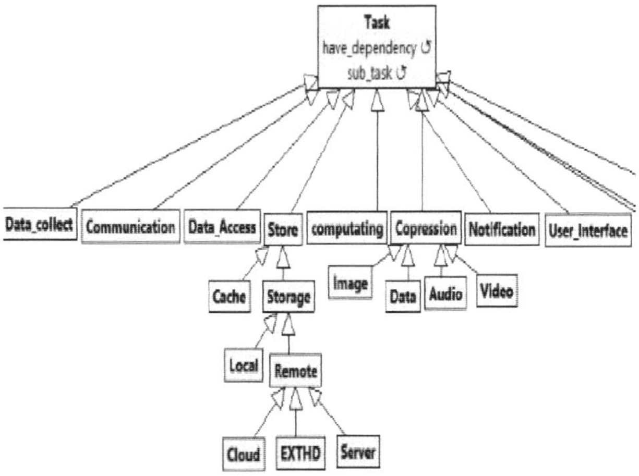

Figure 5. Relevant concerns in IoT applications.

is important in computing platforms, notably IoT based applications. To extend our approach on a large scale of IoT applications, we adopt an incremental scheme to quantify total energy consumption. We consider that the total consumption is evaluated by the sum of the energy consumption induced by the different tasks from the collection of the data, sending via the network until the processing of this data. The total spot is estimated and summarized over the period of real-time which is the typical IoT application architecture. Thus, the period T is outlined by three layers as follow:

- The first is the perception layer: It is defined by physical objects and sensor devices that collect and acquire data from the physical world. It consists of two parts: the detection devices and the wireless sensor network. The first includes sensor nodes and the Radio Frequency Identification (RFID) tag. The latter is a self-organized wireless network consisting of numerous sensor nodes distributed over a large area. These devices coordinate to monitor the state of the physical environment (M2M terminal and a sensor gateway). These devices monitor in a coordinated manner the state of the physical world. The collected information is then passed on to the transport layer.
- Transport layer is an intermediate layer: It enables the transfer of data received from the perception layer to the application layer through different networks as wireless or cable networks. There are various technologies used include infrared, 2G, 3G and Bluetooth, depending on the sensor devices. The collected data will be transferred across long distances and over a large area through different kinds of networks that employ different technologies and protocols.
- Application Layer: this part focuses on data processing and providing services for all user types. The transmitted data will be treated and managed by suitable management systems, Then various services will be provided to the target users.

Figure 6 displays how energy consumption at the global process of an IoT application is estimated. It is the sum of several contributions represented by different areas, called layers. A layer, Li, corresponds to the consumption of part of the system for task i. The energy consumption of the entire system is the addition of the energy consumption of each task. It essentially consists of applying estimation for each task of the system with the order of layers.

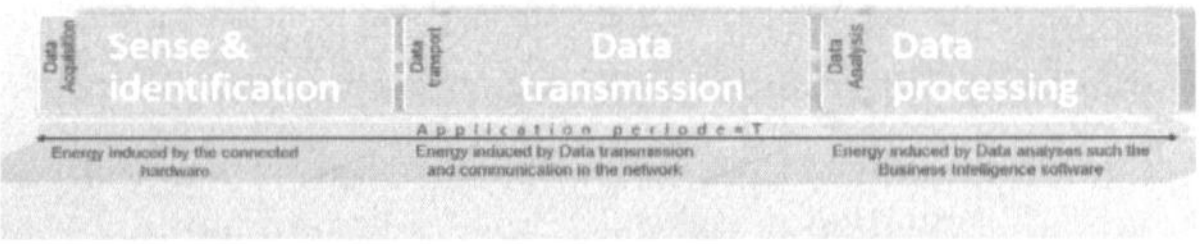

Figure 6. Energy consumption induced within IoT architecture.

Based on this assumption the power required can be broken down into three main blocks: power for data acquisition appointed as Pacq, power for data processing Pprc and power for data networking Pnet. Additionally, a tiny fraction is intended for system management tasks such as rising the system at periodic wake-ups or running a real-time operating system. The needs of these management tasks are gathered in this Psys contribution. The general formula (1) is expressed by the contribution of these elements together.

$$Ptot = Pacq + Pprc + Pnet + Psys \quad (1)$$

In order to estimate the power consumption, it is required to avail Power models. These models correlate energy consumption with measurable metrics. A wide variety of power models exist [20][32][33]. We establish a set of graph transformation rules implementing power consumption models as mentioned in Figure 1. Those rules enable computing energy consumption in the different layers (Figure 7). For instance, Figure 8 introduce the formula (1) as graph transformation rule.

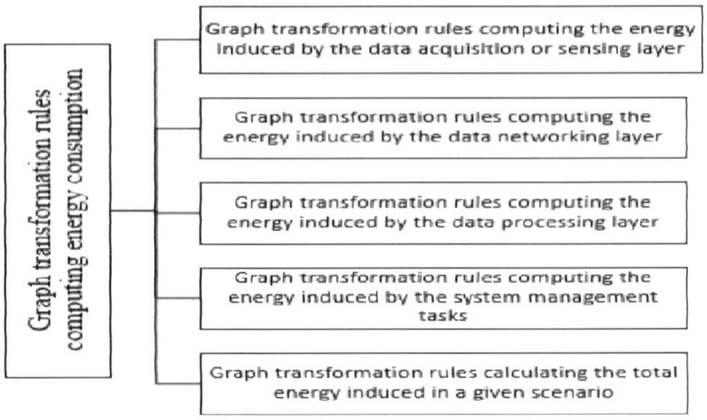

Figure 7. kinds of graph transformation rules computing energy consumption.

We start with exploring the energy consumed by the connected devices (sensor, actuator and computer program). Although software systems do not consume energy themselves, they affect the use of the hardware resulting in indirect energy consumption. Namely, it is required to inquire into the given software under execution, hardware platform and during a given time. The energy consumption E is an accumulation of power dissipation P over time (formula (2)). The energy E is measured in watts and power P is measured in joules, i.e.

$$E = P * t \quad (2)$$

For example, if a given task takes 15 seconds to be achieved and dissipate 5 watts, it consumes 75 joules of energy.

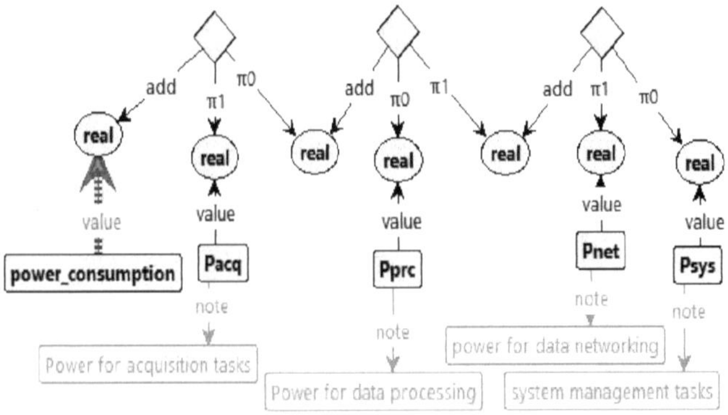

Figure 8. Computing total power consumption.

The display view of the corresponding rule (Figure 9) is composed of different kinds of nodes: the node depicted by a diamond stand for triple of data values. It states a multiplication operation for a pair of real values 0 and 1 which correspond respectively to power and time interval. The edge labeled as "mul" specifies the data node representing the result of the performed operation. Then the result will be attributed to a node typed as power consumption which is an element of the adopted meta-model. Note that the ellipses, typed as real, allow to handle unknown values and the values will only be established when matching the rule. It ensures the applicability of that rule in all cases of value. This rule calculates energy consumption by multiplying the power by the estimated time for such a task. After computing the energy consumption in each task alone, it is required to elaborate a rule that encompasses the total energy induced by a set of tasks, which collaborate to achieve a particular intent or service.

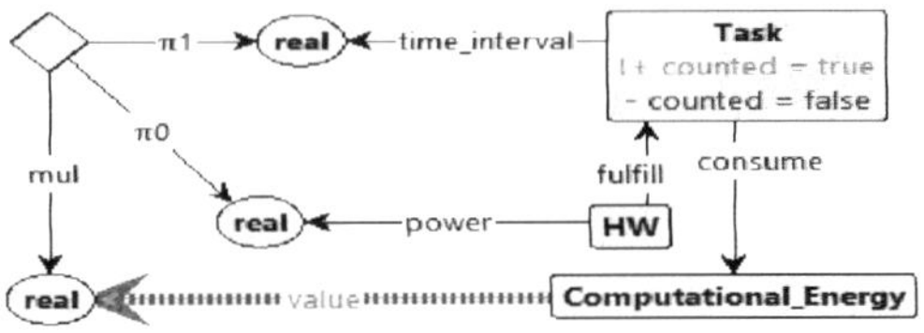

Figure 9. Graph transformation rule calculating energy induced by a set of tasks.

Figure 10 and Figure 11 depict graph transformation rules modeling Data Acquisition Energy.
Commonly, monitoring applications could be classified into two categories: regular sensing with a fixed acquisition time interval, and event-driven sensing characterized by stochastic distribution. In event-driven sensing, a random event triggers the acquisition of a collection of samples from the sensor. Thus, the energy consumption of the acquisition component

can be established as follow (4)[33].

$$E_{acq} = \begin{cases} E_{smp} * N & (Regular) \\ E_{smp} * N' * Pr(e) & (Event) \end{cases} \quad (3)$$

E_{smp} is the energy required to acquire one sample and N is the number of samples taken during one regular sensing interval. For event-driven sensing, Pr(e) is the probability of an event occurring in one sensing interval, and N' is the number of samples taken following the occurrence of an event.

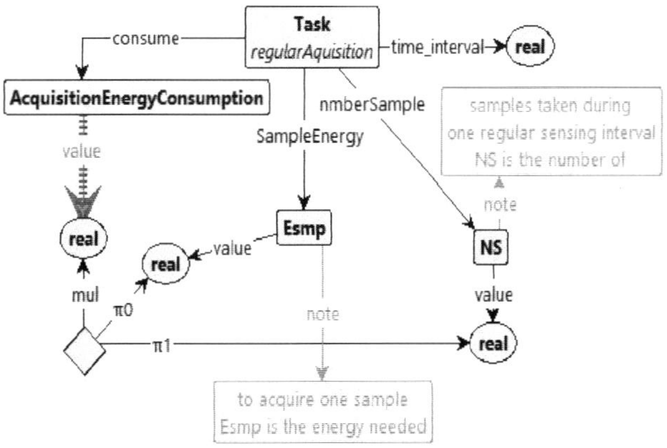

Figure 10. Graph transformation rule computing energy consumption of regular sensing

In our framework, the calculation is carried with graph transformation rules. For instance, the graph transformation rule (shown in Figure 10) calculates the energy consumed by the acquisition component during one regular sensing interval.

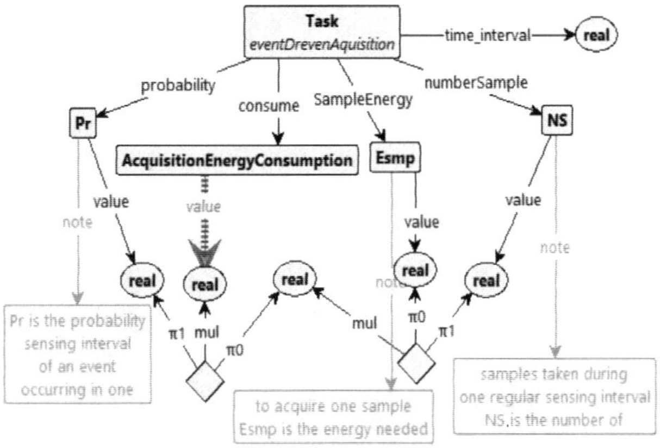

Figure 11. Graph transformation rule computing energy consumption of event-driven sensing

Figure 11 computes the energy consumed by the acquisition component in event-driven sensing.

VII. Elementary Transformations Based Graph Transformation Rules

In order to implement our approach, we build a library of combined graph transformation rules that incorporate restructuring activities and refactoring [34]. We take advantage of the formal specifications of refactoring techniques presented in the literature such as the refactoring catalog, EDPs catalog. Entire EDPs can be found in [29] with full definition and original explication. Please refer to that base document if necessary. Some refactoring operations are represented in TABLE I.

TABLE I. ELEMENTARY TRANSFORMATIONS INCLUDING THEIR ACTORS AND ROLES.

Elementary transformations	*tackled artifacts*	*Role*
Extract class	class	source class, new class
	field	moved fields
	method	moved methods
Extract interface	class	source classes, new interface
	field	moved fields
	method	moved methods
Inline class	class	source class, target class
Move field	class	source class, target class
	field	moved field
Move method	class	source class, target class
	method	moved method
Push down field	class	superclass, subclasses
	field	moved field
Push down method	class	superclass, subclasses
	method	moved method
Pull up field	class	subclasses, superclass
	field	moved field
Pull up method	class	subclasses, superclass
	method	moved method
Move class	package	source package, target package
	class	moved class

Every restructuring activity is associated with a graph transformation rule implemented using GROOVE, with the same name and the corresponding components. This part will depict some of the techniques formalized as graph transformation rules. Figure 12 represents an elemental transformation as graph transformation rule. It aims to create a class hierarchy once two classes have two attributes with the same names and the same types, and then pull up that attribute to the superclass. Figure 13 represents another elemental transformation as a graph transformation rule. It leads to pull up the other attributes to the superclass.

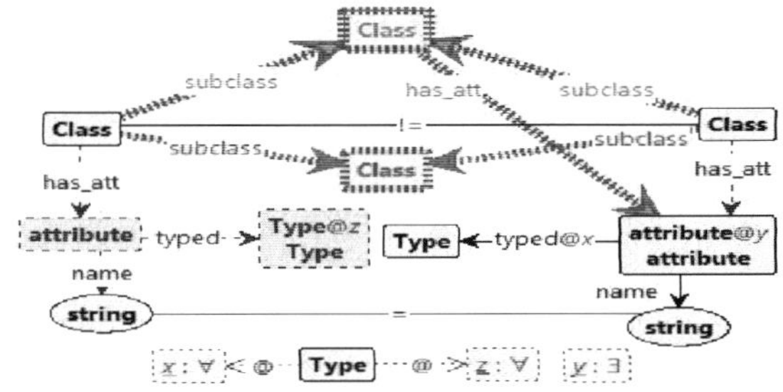

Figure 12. The transformation"pull up field" represented as graph transformation rule

Applying some of the elemental transformation techniques can impact energy consumption whether they can contribute to the design pattern injection. In particular when applying the technique 'Inline Method' can enhance performance and support power reduction for a specific application [35]. In the embedded systems, the 'Inline Method' may be useful (if it is small) since it can yield less code than the method call preamble and return. Extract Method and Extract Class can increase the energy consumption of mobile devices due to the increase of message traffic between the objects [6].

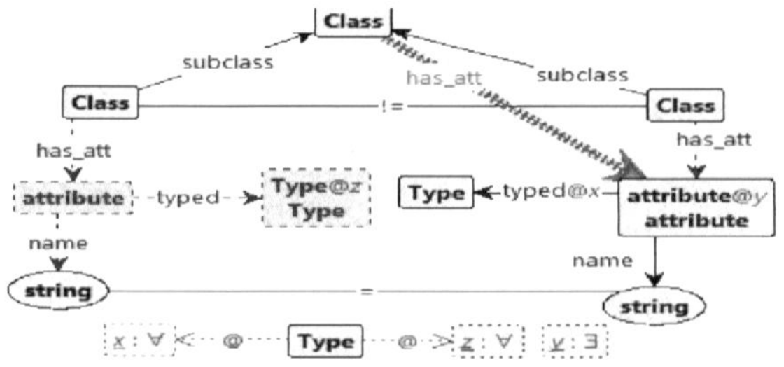

Figure 13. The transformation"Move field" represented as a graph transformation rule

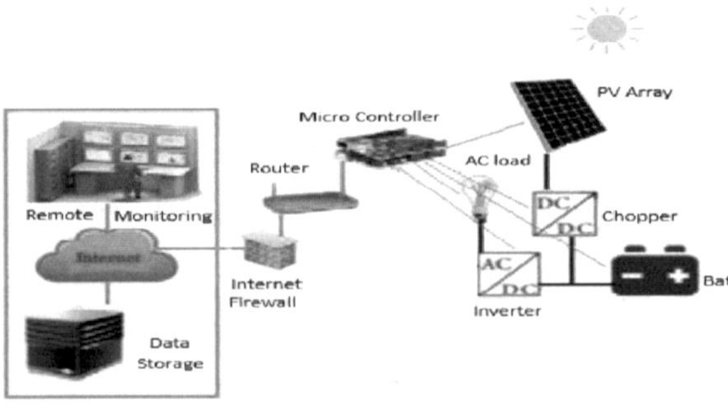

Figure 14. Architecture photovoltaic system based on IoT technology.

Additionally, applying a sequence of elemental transformations in particular orders could contribute to the injection of design patterns [36]. Thus, they can enhance energy efficiency corresponding that software engineering best practices can improve energy efficiency [3][4][5].

VIII. Motivating Scenario

We are investigating the validity of our approach in motivating scenarios in the scope of IoT. A focus is made on the use of IoT in the monitoring and remote control in the solar photovoltaic system accurately on the off-grid system installing. It is customary that this kind of electricity-management system includes a combination of a photovoltaic module, electric power converters and Storage devises to handle the intermittency of power output presented by renewables [37]. Besides, it contains power-conditioning equipment, including devices to limit current and voltage to maximize power output and convert direct-current to alternating current.
Availing the IoT technique, additional smart components enable to achieve energy efficiency in PV systems. That technology is used at all levels of the network such as production, distribution and consumption. It allows to:

- Real-time flow control: System-wide sensors instantly show electrical flows and consumption levels. Operators can then redirect energy flows according to demand.
- The integration of different types of renewable energies.
- More responsible management of consumption resources (scheduling): They provide useful information for the scheduling of household electricity supplies during the day in case of lack of energy.

IoT based photovoltaic system architecture can be established by three different layers as clearly depict in Figure 14. The PV system layer, gateway linkage layer and the remote control and monitoring layer. Figure 14 clearly depicted the IoT architecture for photovoltaic systems.

Although the performance and cost of each component of the PV System are important parameters to be considered before the design process, it is required to carry out optimizing in the software held in the system. thus, software design choice effects heavily global cost and performances. For the sake of enhancing performances and cost reduction for a prospective mini-grid architect, we undertake an analysis of various architectural solutions.

Our investigation is ongoing for identifying eligible tasks that constitute hotspot and undertake transformations and refactoring techniques. We are availing quality metrics measurement to access the impacts of applying restructuring activities and to make informed trade-off decisions between costs and QoS of offered services.

IX. Conclusion and Future Work

Energy-aware software development is a growing trend in computing. Indeed, the software developer community is paying more and more attention to energy-efficiency concerns. Refactoring can be a potential solution to many of the discussed challenges as architectural choices and design quality; it is proven to improve the quality of a system. However, the impact of design refactoring on energy efficiency has been scarcely investigated. In the exploratory study here reported, a graph-based approach is proposed to investigate the impact of refactoring on energy consumption on the design level, focusing on how we experiment with the effect of applying transformations activities at a design level, which can be optimized in terms of energy consumption. According to the literature, though refactoring is involved in the area of code re-engineering successfully there is huge potential for refactoring at the architectural level.

In further work, it is intended to develop a concept of following detailed refactoring techniques which include methods to identify architecture smells and to evaluate its effect in the consumption energy, apply suitable refactoring and test applied refactoring to guarantee less energy consumption of the system.

References

[1] G. Procaccianti, H. Fernández, and P. Lago, "Empirical evaluation of two best practices for energy-efficient software development," Journal of Systems and Software, vol. 117, 2016, pp. 185–198, ISSN: 0164-1212.

[2] F. A. Moghaddam, G. Procaccianti, G. A. Lewis, and P. Lago, "Empirical validation of cyber-foraging architectural tactics for surrogate provisioning," Journal of Systems and Software, vol. 138, 2018, pp. 37–51, ISSN: 0164-1212.

[3] A. Hindle, "Green mining: a methodology of relating software change and configuration to power consumption," Empirical Software Engineering, vol. 20, no. 2, 2015, pp. 374–409, ISSN: 1382-3256.

[4] A. R. Tonini, L. M. Fischer, J. C. B. de Mattos, and L. B. de Brisolara, "Analysis and evaluation of the android best practices impact on the efficiency of mobile applications," in Proceedings of the 3rd Brazilian Symposium on Computing Systems Engineering (SBESC) December 4–8, 2013, Niteroi, Rio De Janeiro, Brazil. IEEE, Dec. 2013, pp. 157–158, ISBN: 978-1-4799-3890-2.

[5] Linares-Vásquez et al., "Mining energy-greedy api usage patterns in android apps: an empirical study," in Proceedings of the 11th Working Conference on Mining Software Repositories(MSR) May 31 – June 01, 2014, Hyderabad, India. ACM, May 2014, pp. 2–11, ISSN: 978-1-4503-2863-0.

[6] R. Pérez-Castillo and M. Piattini, "Analyzing the harmful effect of god class refactoring on power consumption," IEEE software, vol. 31, no. 3, 2014, pp. 48–54, ISSN: 0740-7459.

[7] A. Vetrò, L. Ardito, G. Procaccianti, and M. Morisio, "Definition, implementation and validation of energy code smells: an exploratory study on an embedded system," in Proceedings of the 4th international conference on Future energy systems (e-Energy) May 21 – 24, 2013, Berkeley, California, USA. ThinkMind, May 2013, pp. 34–39, ISSN: 978-1-4503-2052-8.

[8] M. Gottschalk, J. Jelschen, and A. Winter, "Saving energy on mobile devices by refactoring." in Proceedings of the 28th International Conference on Informatics for Environmental Protection: ICT for Energy Effieciency, (EnviroInfo) September 10–12, 2014, Oldenburg, Germany,. BIS-Verlag, Sep. 2014, pp. 437–444, ISBN: 978-3-8142-2317-9.

[9] A. Rodriguez, M. Longo, and A. Zunino, "Using bad smell-driven code refactorings in mobile applications to reduce battery usage," in Simposio Argentino de Ingeniería de Software (ASSE) September 3–4, 2015, Rosario, Santa Fé, Argentina, Sep. 2015, pp. 56–68, ISSN: 2451-7593.

[10] G. Mouzon and M. B. Yildirim, "A framework to minimise total energy consumption and total tardiness on a single machine," International Journal of Sustainable Engineering.

[11] S. Hasan et al., "Energy profiles of java collections classes," in Proceedings of the 38th International Conference on Software Engineering (ICSE) May 14 – 22, 2016, Austin, Texas. ACM, May 2016, pp. 225–236, ISBN: 978-1-4503-3900-1.

[12] D. Li, S. Hao, J. Gui, and W. G. Halfond, "An empirical study of the energy consumption of android applications," in 2014 IEEE International Conference on Software Maintenance and Evolution (ICSME) Sep 28 – Oct 3, 2014, Victoria, British Columbia, Canada. IEEE, Sep. 2014, pp. 121–130, ISBN: 978-1-4799-6146-7.

[13] H. Luo, B. Du, G. Q. Huang, H. Chen, and X. Li, "Hybrid flow shop scheduling considering machine electricity consumption cost," International Journal of Production Economics, vol. 146, 2013, pp. 423–439, ISSN: 0925-5273.

[14] Y. Liu, H. Dong, N. Lohse, S. Petrovic, and N. Gindy, "An investigation into minimising total energy consumption and total weighted tardiness in job shops," Journal of Cleaner Production, vol. 65, 2014, pp. 87–96, ISSN: 0959-6526.

[15] M. Trejo-Perea et al., "Development of a real time energy monitoring platform user-friendly for buildings," Procedia Technology, vol. 7, 2013, pp. 238–247, ISSN: 1877-7058.

[16] R. Bayindir, E. Irmak, I. Colak, and A. Bektas, "Development of a real time energy monitoring platform," International Journal of Electrical Power & Energy Systems, vol. 33, no. 1, 2011, pp. 137–146, ISSN: 0142-0615.

[17] K. Grosskop and J. Visser, "Identification of application-level energy optimizations," Proceeding of ICT for Sustainability (ICT4S), vol. A4, 2013, pp. 101–107, ISBN: 978-3-906031-24-8.

[18] A. Noureddine and A. Rajan, "Optimising energy consumption of design patterns," in Proceedings of the 37th International Conference on Software Engineering-Volume 2 (ICSE) May 16 – 24, 2015,Florence, Italy. IEEE Press, May 2015, pp. 623–626, ISSN: 1558-1225.

[19] G. Procaccianti, P. Lago, and G. A. Lewis, "Green architectural tactics for the cloud," in Proceedings of the 2014 IEEE/IFIP Conference on Software Architecture (WICSA) April 7–11, 2014, Sydney, NSW, Australia. IEEE, Apr. 2014, pp. 41–44, ISBN: 978-1-4799-3412-6.

[20] C. Stier, A. Koziolek, H. Groenda, and R. Reussner, "Model-based energy efficiency analysis of software architectures," in Proceedings of the 9th European conference on software architecture (ECSA) September 7 – 11, 2015, Dubrovnik/Cavtat, Croatia. Springer, Sep. 2015, pp. 221–238, ISBN: 978-3-319-23727-5.

[21] V. De Maio, R. Prodan, S. Benedict, and G. Kecskemeti, "Modelling energy consumption of network transfers and virtual machine migration," Future Generation Computer Systems, vol. 56, 2016, pp. 388–406, ISSN: 0167-739X.

[22] C. Seo, G. Edwards, S. Malek, and N. Medvidovic, "A framework for estimating the impact of a distributed software system's architectural style on its energy consumption," in Proceedings of the 7th Working IEEE/IFIP Conference on Software Architecture (WICSA) February 18 – 21, 2008, Vancouver, BC, Canada. IEEE, Feb. 2008, pp. 277–280, ISBN: 978-0-7695-3092-5.

[23] A. Brunnert, K. Wischer, and H. Krcmar, "Using architecture-level performance models as resource profiles for enterprise applications," in Proceedings of the 10th international ACM Sigsoft conference on Quality of software architectures (QoSA) June 30 - July 04, 2014, Marcq-en-Bareul, France. ACM, Jul. 2014, pp. 53–62, ISBN: 978-1-4503-2576-9.

[24] R. N. Calheiros, R. Ranjan, A. Beloglazov, C. A. De Rose, and R. Buyya, "Cloudsim: a toolkit for modeling and simulation of cloud computing environments and evaluation of resource provisioning algorithms," Software: Practice and experience, vol. 41, 2011, pp. 23–50, ISBN: 978-1-60750-073-5.

[25] K. Kurowski et al., "Dcworms–a tool for simulation of energy efficiency in distributed computing infrastructures," Simulation Modelling Practice and Theory, vol. 39, 2013, pp. 135–151, ISBN: 978-3-642-40516-7.

[26] A. Memari, J. Vornberger, J. M. Gómez, and W. Nebel, "A data center simulation framework based on an ontological foundation," in Proceedings of the 28th International Conference on Informatics for Environmental Protection: (ICT) for Energy Effieciency, September 10-12, 2014, Oldenburg, Germany. BIS-Verlag, Sep. 2014, pp. 461–468, ISBN: 978-3-8142-2317-9.

[27] N. Amsel, Z. Ibrahim, A. Malik, and B. Tomlinson, "Toward sustainable software engineering: Nier track," in Proceedings of the 33RD international conference on software engineering (ICSE) May 21 – 28, 2011, Honolulu, Hawaii, USA. IEEE, May 2011, pp. 976–979, ISBN: 978-1-4503-0445-0.

[28] E. Biermann et al., "Emf model refactoring based on graph transformation concepts," Electronic Communications of the EASST, vol. 3, 2006, ISSN: 1863-2122.

[29] J. M. Smith, Elemental design patterns. Addison-Wesley, Apr. 2012, ISBN: 978-0321711922.

[30] M. Kim, H. Ahn, and K. P. Kim, "Process-aware internet of things: A conceptual extension of the internet of things framework and architecture," KSII Transactions on Internet and Information Systems (TIIS), vol. 10, 2016, pp. 4008–4022, ISSN: 1976-7277.

[31] N. Gamez, M. Pinto, and L. Fuentes, "Hadas green assistant: designing energy-efficient applications," arXiv preprint arXiv:1612.08095, vol. abs/1612.08095, 2016.

[32] X. Fan, W.-D. Weber, and L. A. Barroso, "Power provisioning for a warehouse-sized computer," in Proceedings of the 34th annual international symposium on Computer architecture (ISCA) June 9–13, 2007, San Diego, California, USA, vol. 35. ACM, Jun. 2007, pp. 13–23, ISSN: 0360–5442.

[33] B. Martinez, M. Monton, I. Vilajosana, and J. D. Prades, "The power of models: Modeling power consumption for iot devices," IEEE Sensors Journal, vol. 15, 2015, pp. 5777–5789, ISSN: 1558-1748.

[34] B. Babic, N. Nesic, and Z. Miljkovic, "A review of automated feature recognition with rule-based pattern recognition," Computers in industry, vol. 59, no. 4, 2008, pp. 321–337, ISSN: 0166-3615.

[35] W. G. da Silva, L. Brisolara, U. B. Corrêa, and L. Carro, "Evaluation of the impact of code refactoring on embedded software efficiency," in Proceedings of the 1st Workshop de Sistemas Embarcados (WESE) October 28 – 28, 2010, Scottsdale, Arizona, Oct. 2010, pp. 145–150, ISBN: 978-1-4503-0521-1.

[36] N. Zoubeir, A. Khalfallah, and S. Ahmed, "Graph-based decomposition of design patterns," International Journal of Software Engineering and Its Applications (IJSEIA), vol. 8, 2014, pp. 391–408, ISSN: 1738-9984.

[37] N. M. Kumar, K. Atluri, and S. Palaparthi, "Internet of things (iot) in photovoltaic systems," in Proceedings of the National Power Engineering Conference (NPEC) March 9–10, 2018, Madurai, India. IEEE, Mar. 2018, pp. 1–4, ISBN: 978-1-5386-3804-0.

On the Realization of Meta-Circular Code Generation: The Case of the Normalized Systems Expanders

Herwig Mannaert

Normalized Systems Institute
University of Antwerp, Belgium
Email: herwig.mannaert@uantwerp.be

Koen De Cock and Peter Uhnak

Research and Development
NSX BVBA, Belgium
Email: koen.de.cock@nsx.normalizedsystems.org

Abstract—**The automated generation of source code is a widely adopted technique to improve the productivity of computer programming. Normalized Systems Theory (NST) aims to create software systems exhibiting a proven degree of evolvability. A software implementation exists to create skeletons of Normalized Systems (NS) applications, based on automatic code generation. This paper describes how the NS model representation, and the corresponding code generation, has been made meta-circular, a feature that may be crucial to improve the productivity of the development of software for source code generation. The detailed architecture of this meta-circular code generation software is presented, and some preliminary results are discussed.**

Keywords–Evolvability; Normalized Systems; Meta-circularity; Automated programming; Case Study

I. INTRODUCTION

Increasing the productivity in computer programming has been an important and long-term goal of computer science. Though many different approaches have been proposed, discussed, and debated, two of the most fundamental approaches toward this goal are arguably automated code generation and homoiconic programming. Increasing the evolvability of Information Systems (IS) on the other hand, is crucial for the productivity during the maintenance of information systems. Although it is even considered as an important attribute determining the survival chances of organizations, it has not yet received much attention within the IS research area [1]. Normalized Systems Theory (NST) was proposed to provide an ex-ante proven approach to build evolvable software by leveraging concepts from systems theory and statistical thermodynamics. In this paper, we present an integrated approach that combines both Normalized Systems theory to provide evolvability, and automated code generation and homoiconic programming to offer increased productivity.

The remainder of this paper is structured as follows. In Section III, we briefly discuss two fundamental approaches to increase the productivity in computer programming: automatic and homoiconic programming. In Section III, we briefly present NST as a theoretical basis to obtain higher levels of evolvability in information systems. Section IV discusses the application of these fundamental concepts to the Normalized Systems code expansion in general and the Prime Radiant in particular. Section V elaborates on the declaration of both the various expanders generating the code artifacts, and the configuration parameters that control the expansion process. Finally, we discuss some results in Section VI and present our conclusion in Section VII.

II. AUTOMATIC AND HOMOICONIC PROGRAMMING

In this section, we briefly discuss two fundamental and long-standing approaches to increase the programming productivity: automatic and homoiconic programming.

A. Automatic or Meta-Programming

The automatic generation of code is nearly as old as coding or software programming itself. One often makes a distinction between *code generation*, the mechanism where a compiler generates executable code from a traditional high-level programming language, and *automatic programming*, the act of automatically generating source code from a model or template. In fact, one could argue that both mechanisms are quite similar, as David Parnas already concluded in 1985 that "automatic programming has always been a euphemism for programming in a higher-level language than was then available to the programmer" [2].

Another term used to designate automatic programming is *generative programming*, aiming to write programs "to manufacture software components in an automated way" [3], in the same way as automation in the industrial revolution has improved the production of traditional artifacts. As this basically corresponds to an activity at the meta-level, i.e., writing software programs that write software programs, this is also referred to as *meta-programming*. Essentially, the goal of automatic programming is and has always been to improve programmer productivity.

Software development methodologies such as *Model-Driven Engineering (MDE)* and *Model-Driven Architecture (MDA)*, focusing on creating and exploiting conceptual domain models and ontologies, are also closely related to automatic programming. In order to come to full fruition, these methodologies require the availability of tools for the automatic generation of code. Currently, these model-driven code generation tools are often referred to as *Low-Code Development Platforms (LCDP)*, i.e., software that provides an environment for programmers to create application software through graphical user interfaces and configuration instead of traditional computer programming. As before, the goal remains to increase the productivity of computer programming, though the realization of this goal is not always straightforward [4].

B. Homoiconicity or Meta-Circularity

Another technique in computer science aimed at the increase of the abstraction level, and thereby the productivity, of computer programming, is homoiconicity. A language is homoiconic if a program written in it can be manipulated as data using the language, and thus the program's internal representation can be inferred just by reading the program itself. As the primary representation of programs is also a data structure in a primitive type of the language itself, reflection in the language depends on a single, homogeneous structure instead of several different structures. It is this language feature that conceptually enables meta-programming to become much easier. The best known example of an homoiconic programming language is Lisp, but all Von Neumann architecture systems can implicitly be described as homoiconic. An early and influential paper describing the design of the homoiconic language TRAC [5], traces the fundamental concepts back to an even earlier paper from McIlroy [6].

Related to homoiconicity is the concept of a *meta-circular evaluator (MCE)* or *meta-circular interpreter (MCI)*, a term that was first coined by Reynolds [7]. Such a meta-circular interpreter, most prominent in the context of Lisp as well, is an interpreter which defines each feature of the interpreted language using a similar facility of the interpreter's host language. The term meta-circular clearly expresses that there is a connection or feedback loop between the activity at meta-level, the internal model of the language, and the actual activity, writing models in the language.

III. Normalized Systems Theory and Expansion

In this section, we introduce NST as a theoretical basis to obtain higher levels of evolvability in information systems, and its realization in a code generation or *expansion* framework.

A. Evolvability and Normalized Systems

The evolvability of information systems (IS) is considered as an important attribute determining the survival chances of organizations, although it has not yet received much attention within the IS research area [1]. Normalized Systems Theory (NST), theoretically founded on the concept of *stability* from systems theory, was proposed to provide an ex-ante proven approach to build evolvable software [8][9][10]. Systems theoretic stability is an essential property of systems, and means that a bounded input should result in a bounded output. In the context of information systems, this implies that a bounded set of changes should only result in a bounded impact to the software. Put differently, it is demanded that the impact of changes to an information system should not be dependent on the size of the system to which they are applied, but only on the size of the changes to be performed. Changes causing an impact dependent on the size of the system are called *combinatorial effects*, and are considered to be a major factor limiting the evolvability of information systems. The theory prescribes a set of theorems and formally proves that any violation of any of the following *theorems* will result in combinatorial effects (thereby hampering evolvability) [8][9][10]:

- *Separation of Concerns*
- *Action Version Transparency*
- *Data Version Transparency*
- *Separation of States*

The application of the theorems in practice has shown to result in very fine-grained modular structures within a software application. Such structures are, in general, difficult to achieve by manual programming. Therefore, the theory also proposes a set of patterns to generate significant parts of software systems which comply with these theorems. More specifically, NST proposes five *elements* that serve as design patterns [9][10]:

- *data element*
- *action element*
- *workflow element*
- *connector element*
- *trigger element*

Based on these elements, NST software is generated in a relatively straightforward way. First, a model of the considered universe of discussion is defined in terms of a set of data, task and workflow elements. Next, code generation or automated programming is used to generate parameterized copies of the general element design patterns into boiler plate source code. Due to the simple and deterministic nature of this code generation mechanism, i.e., instantiating parametrized copies, it is referred to as *NS expansion* and the generators creating the individual coding artifacts are called *NS expanders*. This generated code can, in general, be complemented with custom code or *craftings* to add non-standard functionality that is not provided by the expanders themselves, at well specified places (anchors) within the boiler plate code.

B. Variability Dimensions and Expansion

In applications generated by a Normalized Systems expansion process, we identify four variability dimensions, as visualized in Figure 1. As discussed in [11][12], the combination of these dimensions compose an actual Normalized Systems application codebase, and therefore determine how such an application can evolve throughout time, i.e., how software created in this way exhibits evolvability.

First, as represented at the upper left of the figure, one should specify or select the *models* or *mirrors* he or she wants to expand. Such a model is technology agnostic (i.e., defined without any reference to a particular technology that should be used) and represented by standard modeling techniques, such as ERD's for data elements and DFD's for task and flow elements. Such a model can have multiple versions throughout time (e.g., being updated or complemented) or concurrently (e.g., choosing between a more extensive or summarized version). As a consequence, the chosen model represents a first dimension of variability or evolvability.

Second, the *expanders* (represented by the big blue icon in the figure) generate (boiler plate) source code by instantiating the various class templates or *skeletons*, taking the specifications of the model as *parameters*. For instance, for a data element Person, a set of java classes PersonBean, PersonAgent, PersonView, PersonData, etcetera will be generated. This code can be considered boiler plate code as it provides a set of standard functionalities for each of the elements within the model, though they have evolved over time to provide standard finders, master-detail (waterfall) screens, certain display options, document upload/download functionality, child relations, etcetera. The expanders or template skeletons themselves evolve throughout time, as bugs of the previous version are solved and additional features (e.g., creation of a status graph) are provided. Given the fact that the application model is completely technology agnostic and can be used as argument

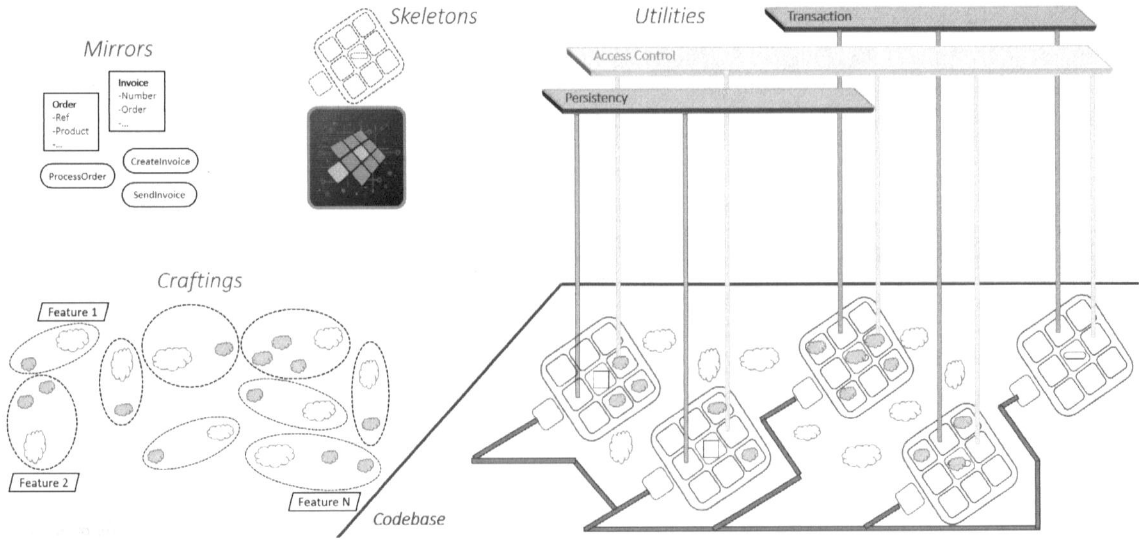

Figure 1. A graphical representation of four variability dimensions within a Normalized Systems application codebase.

for any version of the expanders, these bug fixes and additional features become available for all versions of all application models (only a re-expansion or "rejuvenation" is required). As a consequence, the expanders or template skeletons represent a second dimension of variability or evolvability.

Third, as represented in the upper right of the figure, one should specify *infrastructural options* to select a number of frameworks or *utilities* to take care of several generic concerns. These consist of global options (e.g., determining the build automation framework), presentation settings (determining the graphical user interface framework), business logic settings (determining the database used) and technical infrastructure (e.g., access control or persistency). This means that, given a chosen application model version and expander version, different variants of boiler plate code can be generated, depending on the choices regarding the infrastructural options. As a consequence, the settings and utility frameworks represent a third dimension of variability or evolvability.

Fourth, as represented in the lower left of the figure, "custom code" or *craftings* can be added to the generated source code. These craftings enrich (are put upon) the earlier generated boiler plate code and can be harvested into a separate repository before regenerating the software application (after which they can be applied again). This includes extensions (e.g., additional classes added to the generated code base) as well as insertions (i.e., additional lines of code added between the foreseen anchors within the code). Craftings can have multiple versions throughout time (e.g., being updated or complemented) or concurrently (e.g., choosing between a more advanced or simplified version). These craftings should contain as little technology specific statements within their source code as possible (apart from the chosen background technology). Indeed, craftings referring to (for instance) a specific GUI framework will only be reusable as long as this particular GUI framework is selected during the generation of the application. In contrast, craftings performing certain validations but not containing any EJB specific statements will be able to be reused when applying other versions or choices regarding such framework. As a consequence, the custom code or craftings represent a fourth dimension of variability or evolvability.

In summary, each part in Figure 1 is a variability dimension in an NST software development context. It is clear that talking about *the* "version" of an NST application (as is traditionally done for software systems) in such context becomes more refined. Indeed, the eventual software application codebase (the lower right side of the figure) is the result of a specific version of an application model, expander version, infrastructural options, and a set of craftings [12]. Put differently, with M, E, I and C referring to the number of available application model versions, the number of expander versions, the number of infrastructural option combinations, and crafting sets respectively, the total set of possible versions V of a particular NST application becomes equal to:

$$V = M \times E \times I \times C$$

Whereas the specific values of M and C are different for every single application, the values of E and I are dependent on the current state of the expanders. Remark that the number of infrastructural option combinations (I) is equally a product:

$$I = G \times P \times B \times T$$

Where G represents the number of available global option settings, P the number of available presentation settings, B the number of available business logic settings, and T the number of available technical infrastructure settings. This general idea in terms of combinatorics corresponds to the overall goal of NST: enabling evolvability and variability by *leveraging the law of exponential variation gains* by means of the thorough decoupling of concerns and the facilitation of their recombination potential [10].

IV. Toward Meta-Circular Expansion Control

In this section, we discuss the application of automatic programming and homoiconicity to the Normalized Systems expansion in general and the Prime Radiant in particular.

A. Phase 1: Standard Code Generation

The original architecture of the Normalized Systems expansion or code generation software is schematically represented in Figure 2. In the right part of the figure, the generated source

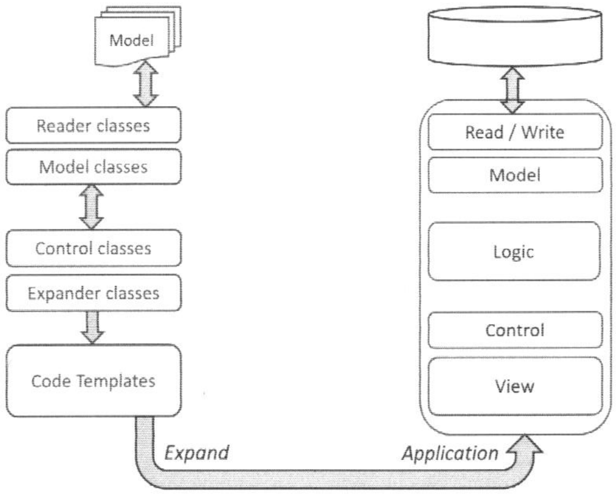

Figure 2. Representation of a basic code generator structure.

code is represented in blue, corresponding to a traditional multi-tier web application. Based on a *Java Enterprise Edition (JEE)* stack [9][12], the generated source code classes are divided over so-called layers, such as the logic, the control, and the view layer. On the left, we distinguish the internal structure of the expanders or the code generators, represented in red. This corresponds to a very straightforward implementation of code generators, consisting of:

- *model files* containing the model parameters.
- *reader classes* to read the model files.
- *model classes* to represent the model parameters.
- *control classes* selecting and invoking the different expander classes.
- *expander classes* instantiating the source templates, using the *String Template (ST)* library, and feeding the model parameters to the source templates.
- *source templates* containing the parametrized code.

B. Phase 2: Generating a Meta-Application

In essence, code generation models or meta-models — and even all collections of configuration parameters — consist of various data entities with attributes and relationships. As the Normalized Systems element definitions are quite straightforward [9][12], the same is valid for its metamodels. Moreover, one of the Normalized Systems elements, i.e., the data element, is basically a data entity with attributes. This means that the NS meta-models, being data entities with attributes, can be expressed as regular models. For instance, in the same way 'Person' and 'Invoice' can be NS data elements with attributes and relationships in an information system model, the NS 'data element' and 'task element' of the NS meta-model can be defined as NS data elements with attributes and relationships like any other NS model.

As the NS models can be considered a higher-level language according to Parnas [2], the single structure of its model data and meta-model language means that the NS model language is in fact homoiconic in the sense of [6]. This also enables us to expand or generate a meta-application, represented on the left of the figure in dark red, as represented in Figure 3. This NS meta-application, called the *Prime Radiant*,

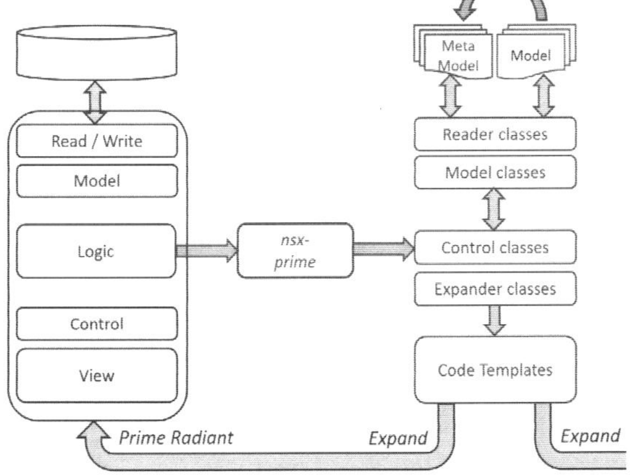

Figure 3. Expansion of a meta-application to define meta-models.

is a multi-tier web application, providing the functionality to enter, view, modify, and retrieve the various NS models. As the underlying meta-model is just another NS model, the Prime Radiant also provides the possibility to view and manipulate its own model. Therefore, by analogy to the meta-circular evaluator of Reynolds [7], the Prime Radiant can be considered as a *meta-circular application*.

For obvious reasons, the generated reader and model classes (part of the Prime Radiant on the left of Figure 3) slightly differ from the reader and model classes that were originally created during the conception of the expansion or code generation software (on the right of Figure 3. This means that, in order to trigger and control the actual expansion classes to generate the source code, an integration software module needed to be developed, represented in the middle of Figure 3 as *nsx-prime*. Though the Prime Radiant meta-application is auto-generated, and can therefore be regenerated or rejuvenated as any NS application, this *nsx-prime* integration module needed to be maintained manually.

C. Phase 3: Closing the Expander Meta-Circle

Though the original reader and model classes of the expander software differed from the generated reader and writer classes, there is no reason that they should remain so. It was therefore decided to perform a rewrite of the control and expander classes of the expander software (right side of Figure 3), in order to allow for an easier integration with the auto-generated reader and model classes (left side of Figure 3. Enabling such a near-seamless integration would not only eliminate the need for the reader and model classes of the expander software, it would also reduce the complexity of the *nsx-prime* integration component to a significant extent.

Originally, the refactoring was only aimed at the elimination of the reader and control classes of the original expander software. However, during the refactoring, it became clear that it became possible to retire the control and expander classes of the expander software as well. Indeed, by adopting a declarative structure to define the expander templates and to specify the relevant model parameters, both the control classes

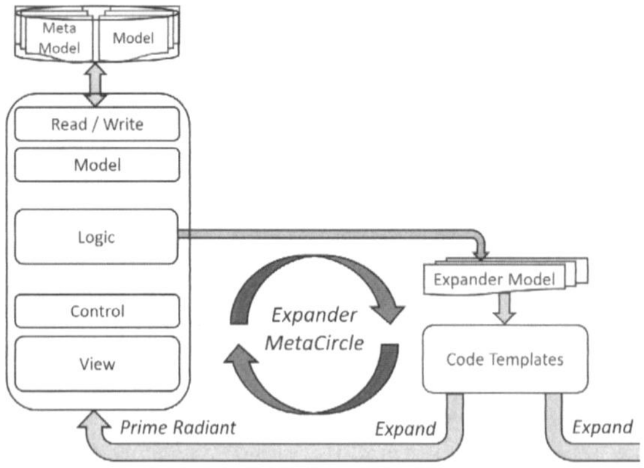

Figure 4. Closing the meta-circle for expanders and meta-application.

(selecting and invoking the expander classes) and the expander classes (instantiating and feeding the source templates) were no longer necessary. Moreover, as schematically represented in Figure 4, the refactoring also eliminated the *nsx-prime* integration module. As extensions to the meta-model no longer require additional coding various expander software classes (e.g., reader, model, control, and expander classes), nor in the nsx-prime integration module, one can say that the *expander development meta-circle* has been closed, as visualized in Figure 4. Indeed, expander templates can be introduced by simply defining them, and extensions to the NS meta-model simply become available after re-running the expansion or code generation on this meta-model.

V. Declarative Expansion Control Structure

In this section, we elaborate on the declaration of both the various expanders generating the code artifacts, and the configuration parameters that control the expansion process.

A. *Declarative Representation of Expanders*

The basic NS expander software currently consists of 181 individual expanders. Every expander is able to instantiate a specific template into a corresponding artefact, using the parameters of the model. An example of the definition of such an individual expander is shown below.

```
<expander name="DataExpander"
  xmlns="http://normalizedsystems.org/expander">
  <packageName>expander.jpa.dataElement</packageName>
  <layerType name="DATA_LAYER"/>
  <technology name="JPA"/>
  <sourceType name="SRC"/>
  <elementTypeName>DataElement</elementTypeName>
  <artifact>$dataElement.name$Data.java</artifact>
  <artifactPath>$componentRoot$/$artifactSubFolders$/
    $dataElement.packageName</artifactPath>
  <isApplicable>true</isApplicable>
  <active value="true"/>
  <anchors/>
  <customAnchors/>
</expander>
```

Such an expander definition in XML format contains the following information.

- The identification of the expander, name and package name, which also identifies in an unambiguous way the source code template.
- Some technical information, including the tier or layer of the target artifact in the application, the technology it depends on, and the source type.
- The name and the complete path in the source tree of the artifact that will be generated, and the type of NS element that it belongs to.
- Some control information, stating the model-based condition to decide whether the expander gets invoked.
- Some information on the anchors delineating sections of custom code that can be harvested and re-injected.

B. *Declarative Mapping of Parameters*

The internal structure of an NS element (data, task, flow, connector, and trigger element) is based on a detailed design pattern [8][9][10], implemented through a set of source code templates, each represented by an expander definition. During the actual expansion or code generation, for every instance of an NS element, e.g., a data element 'Person', the set of source code templates is instantiated, steered by the parameters of the model. The instantiation of an individual source code template for an individual instance of an NS element, is schematically represented in Figure 5, and contains the following aspects.

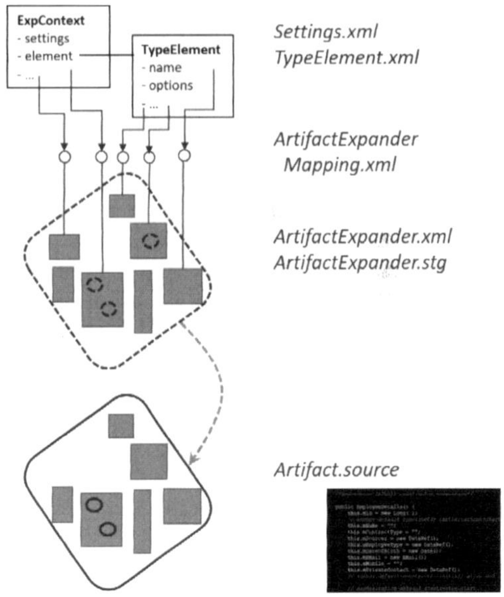

Figure 5. Expansion of a single artifact.

- The model parameters, represented on the top of Figure 5, consisting of the attributes of the element specification, e.g., the data element 'Person' with its attributes, and the options and technology settings. All these parameters are available through the auto-generated model classes, and may either originate from the Prime Radiant database, or from XML files.
- An individual source code template, having unique name that corresponds to the one of the expander definition as described above. Such a template, represented in the middle of Figure 5, contains various parameter-based conditions on the value and/or presence of specific parts of the source code.

- An instantiated source file or artifact, represented at the bottom of Figure 5, where the various conditions in the source code template have been resolved.

An important design feature is related to the mapping of the parameters from the model, to the parameters that appear in the source code templates and are thereby guiding the instantiation. In order to provide loose coupling between these two levels of parameters, and to ensure a simple and straightforward relationship, it was decided to implement this mapping in a declarative *ExpanderMapping* XML file. As the entire NS model is made available as a graph of model classes, the parameters in the templates can be evaluated in the NS model using *Object-Graph Navigation Language (OGNL)* expressions. These expressions are declared in the XML mapping file of the expander.

VI. Some Preliminary Results

The Normalized Systems expander software has been in development since late 2011. Over the years, it was used by several organizations to generate, and re-generate on a regular basis, tens of information systems [11][12]. During these years, and often on request of these organizations, many additional features and options were built into the source code templates. The overall refactoring was triggered by a concern over the growing size — and therefore complexity — of the control classes, but also motivated by a desire to leverage the implicit homoiconicity of the NS model to increase the productivity of improving and extending the expander software.

The complete refactoring was performed in six months by two developers. Afterwards, the 181 expanders were cleanly separated, and the software developers considered the expander codebase to be much better maintainable. Moreover, the learning curve for developers to take part in expander development was widely considered to be very steep, mainly due to the size and complexity of the control classes. After the refactoring, nearly all of the approximately 20 application developers of the company, have stated that the learning curve is considerably less steep, and that they feel comfortable to add features and options to the expander software themselves. As an additional result, we mention the fact that a junior developer has created in two months a new set of 20 expanders. This newly developed collection of expanders, targeted mainly at the development of REST services using Swagger, has already been successfully used in several projects.

VII. Conclusion

The increase of productivity and the improvement of evolvability are goals that have been pursued for a long time in computer programming. While more research has traditionally been performed on techniques to enhance productivity, our research on Normalized Systems has been focusing on the evolvability of information systems. This paper presented a strategy to combine both lines of research.

While the technique of automated programming or source code generation was already incorporated in our work on Normalized Systems, we have explored in this paper the technique of homoiconicity or meta-circularity to increase the productivity of the automatic or meta-programming. A method was presented to make the representation of the code generation models homoiconic, resulting in a considerable simplification of the expanders, i.e., the code generation software. Such a reduction of complexity could lead to a significant increase in productivity at the level of the development of the code generation software, and we have presented some very preliminary results that this is indeed the case.

This paper is believed to make some contributions. First, we show that it is possible to not only adopt code generation techniques to improve productivity, but to incorporate meta-circularity as well to improve the productivity of the code generation. Moreover, this is demonstrated in a framework primarily targeted at evolvability. Second, we have presented a case-based strategy to make a code generation representation homoiconic, and the corresponding application meta-circular. Finally, we believe that the simplified structure of the code generation framework improves the possibilities for collaboration at the level of code generation software.

Next to these contributions, it is clear that this paper is also subject to a number of limitations. It consists of a single case of making a code generation application meta-circular. Moreover, the presented results are very preliminary, and the achieved collaboration on code generation software is still limited to nearby colleagues. However, it is our goal to set up a collaboration of developers on a much wider scale at the level of code generation software, and to prove that this architecture can lead to new and much higher levels of productivity for developing automatic programming.

References

[1] R. Agarwal and A. Tiwana, "Editorial—evolvable systems: Through the looking glass of IS," Information Systems Research, vol. 26, no. 3, 2015, pp. 473–479.

[2] D. Parnas, "Software aspects of strategic defense systems," Communications of the ACM, vol. 28, no. 12, 1985, pp. 1326–1335.

[3] P. Cointe, "Towards generative programming," Unconventional Programming Paradigms. Lecture Notes in Computer Science, vol. 3566, 2005, pp. 86–100.

[4] J. R. Rymer and C. Richardson, "Low-code platforms deliver customer-facing apps fast, but will they scale up?" Forrester Research, Tech. Rep., 08 2015.

[5] C. Mooers and L. Deutsch, "Trac, a text-handling language," in ACM '65 Proceedings of the 1965 20th National Conference, 1965, pp. 229–246.

[6] D. McIlroy, "Macro instruction extensions of compiler languages," Communications of the ACM, vol. 3, no. 4, 1960, pp. 214–220.

[7] J. Reynolds, "Definitional interpreters for higher-order programming languages," Higher-Order and Symbolic Computation, vol. 11, no. 4, 1998, pp. 363–397.

[8] H. Mannaert, J. Verelst, and K. Ven, "The transformation of requirements into software primitives: Studying evolvability based on systems theoretic stability," Science of Computer Programming, vol. 76, no. 12, 2011, pp. 1210–1222, special Issue on Software Evolution, Adaptability and Variability.

[9] ——, "Towards evolvable software architectures based on systems theoretic stability," Software: Practice and Experience, vol. 42, no. 1, 2012, pp. 89–116.

[10] H. Mannaert, J. Verelst, and P. De Bruyn, Normalized Systems Theory: From Foundations for Evolvable Software Toward a General Theory for Evolvable Design. Koppa, 2016.

[11] P. De Bruyn, H. Mannaert, and P. Huysmans, "On the variability dimensions of normalized systems applications: Experiences from an educational case study," in Proceedings of the Tenth International Conference on Pervasive Patterns and Applications (PATTERNS) 2018, 2018, pp. 45–50.

[12] ——, "On the variability dimensions of normalized systems applications : experiences from four case studies," International journal on advances in systems and measurements, vol. 11, no. 3, 1960, pp. 306–314.

An Enhanced Fault Prediction Model for Embedded Software based on Code Churn, Complexity Metrics, and Static Analysis Results

Safa Omri
Karlsruhe Institute of Technology
Germany
Email: safa.omri@kit.edu

Carsten Sinz
Karlsruhe Institute of Technology
Germany
Email: carsten.sinz@kit.edu

Pascal Montag
Daimler AG
Boeblingen
Germany
Email: pascal.montag@daimler.com

Abstract—**Software systems evolve over time because of functionality extensions, changes in requirements, optimization of code, fixes for security and reliability bugs, etc., and it is commonly known that software quality assurance is thus a continuous issue and is often extremely time-consuming. Therefore, techniques to obtain early estimates of fault-proneness can help in increasing the efficiency and effectiveness of software quality assurance. The ability to predict which components in a large software system are most likely to contain the largest numbers of faults in the next release helps to better manage projects, including early estimation of possible release delays, and affordably guide corrective actions to the quality of the software. This paper extends our previous work, where we demonstrated that the combination of code complexity metrics together with static analysis results allows accurate prediction of fault density and to build classifiers discriminating faulty from non-faulty components. The extension presented in this paper augments our predictor and classifier with code churn metrics. We applied our methodology to C++ projects from Daimler's head unit development. In experiments to separate fault-prone from non-fault-prone components, our new approach achieved a classification accuracy of 89%, and the regressor predicted the fault density with an accuracy of 85.7%. This is an improvement of 7.5% with respect to the accuracy of fault density prediction, and an improvement of 10% to the accuracy of fault classification compared to our previous approach that did not take code churn metrics into account.**

Keywords–Software defects mining; static analysis tools; statistical methods; complexity metrics; churn metrics; fault proneness.

I. Introduction

Software plays an important role in automotive product development and in embedded systems in general. As such software is often safety-critical, considerable efforts have to be put into quality assurance. Increasing the effectiveness and efficiency of this effort hence becomes more and more essential.

It is generally acknowledged that software quality assurance is a pressing concern for embedded software development [1]. Given the size, complexity, time and cost pressure in automotive development projects, efficiency is of prime importance. Nowadays, quality assurance is overall the most expensive activity for nearly all software developing companies, since team members need to spend a significant amount of their time inspecting the entire software in detail rather than, for example, implementing new features. If bugs are detected, the fixing of those consumes further development time.

Numerous research studies have analyzed code churn as a variable for predicting faults in large software systems [2], [3], [4]. Code churn is a measure of the quantity of code modification occurring within a software component gradually. But not only code churn is an indicator of problematic code. In our previous work [5], we investigated whether defects detected by static analysis tools combined with code complexity metrics can be used as software quality indicators and employed these measures to build pre-release fault prediction models. We showed in a case study from the automotive domain that the combination of these two measures can be used to predict the pre-release fault density with an accuracy of 78.3%. We have also shown that this combination can be used to separate high and low-quality components with a classification accuracy of 79%.

High churn is typically related to more faults showing up in code that has actually been changed frequently. And studying these changes that take place during software evolution via code churn is also important. We thus make use of code churn to predict the fault density in software components. We have mined the version control database of a large software system to collect code churn variables. We create as well as validate a collection of relative churn variables as early indicators of software fault density. Relative churn variables are normalized values of the numerous measures acquired throughout the churn procedure [4].

In this article, we develop a prediction model based on the following hypothesis: the history of code changes between different releases (code churn) when combined with our two previous measures can improve the prediction accuracy of software faults density. Another contribution is to apply our prediction model to automotive software, where we obtain improved results compared to our previous approach.

The organization of the paper is as follows. After discussing the state of the art in Section II, we describe the design of our approach in Section III. Our results are reported and discussed in Section IV. Section V concludes and discusses future work.

II. Related Work

This section discusses the state of the art and the research results in software fault prediction techniques:

A. Faults, Bugs and Failures

In this work, we use the term *fault* to refer to a bug (an error) in the source code. A bug is a fault in a program which causes it to behave abruptly. We refer to an observable error at program run-time as *failure*. That is, every failure can be traced back to a fault, but a fault does not necessarily result in a failure. In recent years, researchers have learned to exploit the vast amount of data that is contained in software repositories such as version and bug databases [4], [6], [7], [8]. The key idea is that one can map problems (in the bug database) to fixes (in the version database) and thus to those locations in the code that caused the problem [9], [10], [11]. The focus of this work is these faults to obtain an early estimate of software component's fault-proneness in order to guide software quality assurance towards inspecting testing the components most likely to contain faults. Fault-proneness is defined as the probability of the presence of faults in the software. Past research on fault-proneness has focused on (i) the definition of code complexity and testing thoroughness metrics, and (ii) the definition and experimentation of models relating metrics with fault-proneness. Moreover, extracting data when mining the software repositories help to better identify the fault-proneness of software components.

B. Mining Software Repositories

Mining software repositories allows researchers to analyze the information produced throughout the software development process, such as source code, version control system's metadata, as well as issue reports [12], [13], [14]. With such evaluation, researches can empirically examine, understand, and also discover valuable and also actionable insights for software engineering. The extracted data when mining the software repositories help to understand the impact of code smells [15], [16], explore exactly how developers are doing code reviews [17], [18], [19], [20] as well as which testing practices they comply with [21]. Furthermore, historical information extracted from software repositories allows researchers to predict classes that are more susceptible to defects [11], [22], [23], [24], and also determining the core developers of a software team, e.g., to transfer knowledge [25]. Our basic hypothesis is that while these works used only the change and historical information from the source code, it is highly likely that these detected information from software repositories, combined with code complexity metrics and with static analysis faults would be a good indicator of the overall code quality, and help to enhance the fault prediction model presented in our previous work [5].

C. Fault Prediction

Fault prediction is an active research area in the field of software engineering. Many techniques and metrics have been developed to improve fault prediction performance.

Object-oriented metrics were initially suggested by Chidamber and Kemerer [26]. Basili et al. [27] and Briand et al. [28] were among the first to use such metrics to validate and evaluate fault-proneness. Subramanyam and Krishnan [29] and Tang et al. [30] showed that these metrics can be used as early indicators of externally visible software quality. D'Ambros et al. have compared popular fault prediction approaches for software systems [31], namely, process metrics [32], previous faults [33] and source code metrics [27]. Nagappan et al. [34] presented empirical evidence that code complexity metrics can predict post-release faults. They found that sets of complexity metrics are correlated with post-release defects using five major Microsoft products, including Internet Explorer 6.

Omri et al.'s work [5] builds on the study of Nagappan et al. [34] and focuses on pre-release faults while taking into consideration not only the code complexity metrics but also the faults detected by static analysis tools to build accurate pre-release fault predictors [5].

Furthermore, faults are closely related to changes made in the software systems and studying the changes that take place during software evolution via code churn is also important. Khoshgoftaar et al. [2] were among the first to use past changes for bug prediction. Their objective was to classify the modules as fault-prone or not. Therefore, they identified modules where debug code churn exceeded a threshold. They showed, by studying the change history of two consecutive releases of a large legacy software system of telecommunications, that a high code churn, i.e., a high amount of lines added and removed, is a good indicator of fault-prone modules. The system studied contain over 38,000 procedures in 171 modules. Ohlsson et al. [35], Graves et al. [3] studied the evolution of changes in the software systems to understand their relationship with software quality. Based on a study on eight large-scale open source systems (Eclipse, Postgres, KOFFICE, gcc, Gimp, JBOSS, JEdit and Python), Zimmermann et al. [8] mined the version histories and predicted the location of future changes in systems with an accuracy of 70%. Closely related to our study is the work performed by Nagappan and Ball [4] on predicting defect density in software systems using relative code churn metrics, i.e., code churn weighted by lines of code. They analyze different code churn measures in isolation, and show that relative code churn is better than absolute code churn values to predict defects at statistically significant levels. Their approach is similar to ours in the sense that we are also considering relative churn variables to predict fault potential. However, we focus on predicting fault density on an extended number of variables including code complexity metrics and the faults detected by static analysis tools.

To the best of our Knowledge, this work is the first to combine code churn metrics with code complexity metrics and with static analysis results to predict software defect density.

III. APPROACH

Our approach, represented in Figure 1, can be summarized in the following two steps:

A. Data Pre-Proprocessing

First, we collect the data required to train and test the fault prediction models (the regressor and the classifier) out of a git versioned software project. Git versioning allows us to capture the required data for all software releases. The data required to train our fault prediction models is:

1) **Independent variables**: The independent variables are the input variables to the prediction models. (a) *Static analysis faults*: we execute static code analysis on each component for each release. We define the static analysis fault density of a software component as the number of faults found by static analysis tools, per KLOC (thousand lines of code).

(b) *Code complexity metrics*: we compute different code complexity metrics for each of the components and for each release as describes in Table I. (c) *Code churn metrics*: we mine the git repositories databases to extract several code churn metrics (e.g, added LOC, removed LOC, etc., see Table I) for each release.

2) **Dependent variable**: The dependent variable is the output that will be predicted by our prediction models. We mine the git repositories using natural language processing techniques to parse and analyze commit messages mentioning bug fixes keywords (e.g, bug fix, bug fixing, etc.). Such bug fix commits are the indicator of the true known fault density of the software components for each release.

B. Model Training

We train different machine learning models to learn the fault densities of each software component based on the independent variables: (a) static analysis faults densities, (b) code complexity metrics, and (c) code churn metrics.

We split our data into two parts: (1) train data which accounts for 3 successive releases of all software components, and (2) test data representing the fourth release (the last release).

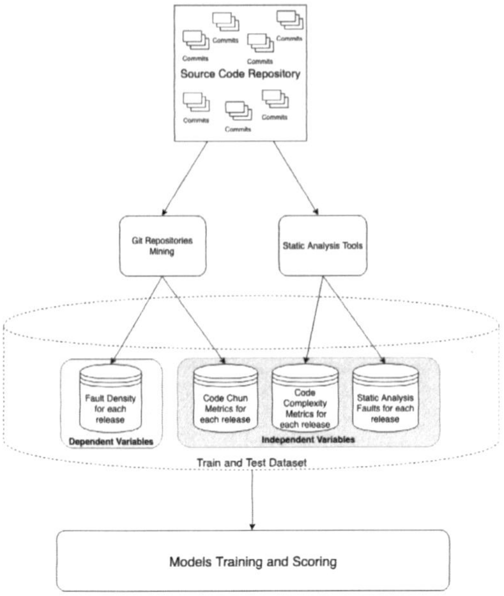

Figure 1. Overview of the fault prediction process

IV. EMPERICAL STUDY

In this section, we present the empirical study that we performed to investigate the hypotheses stated in Section I. In this section, we discuss the dataset, the statistical methods and machine learning algorithms we used, and report on the results and findings of the experiments. The experiment was carried out using 70 components of an automotive head unit control system (Audio, Navigation, Phone, etc.). The size of the code base analyzed is 28.71 MLOC (2,871 KLOC). All repositories use the object oriented language C++.

A. Data Preparation

The goal of this work is to come up with fault predictors that evaluate our hypothesis and enhance our prediction model built in our previous study [5]. The data required to build our fault predictors are:

1) Faults Data: We are interested, in this work, in faults that have been detected during the development and mentioned as bugfixes in git commits. For each component, we extracted all detected bugs through mining the git repositories. The extracted faults are then used to compute the **fault density**.

2) Static Analysis Fault Density: Moreover, we executed static analysis tools on each component and extracted the identified faults. These faults were then used to compute the **static analysis fault density**. We used commercial non-verifying static analysis tools in this study.

3) Code Complexity Metrics: We compute several code complexity metrics for each of the components. The code complexity metrics are represented in Table I. We limit our study to a set of selected metrics that have shown to provide significant quality indicators over a long period of time. Code complexity metrics have been shown to correlate with fault density in several case studies [28], [29], [30], and they have been proposed in different case studies to assess software quality [1], [34].

4) Code Churn Metrics: Software repositories contain historic information regarding the overall development of software program systems. Mining software databases is nowadays considered one of the most intriguing expanding areas within software engineering. Different recent works have used past changes as indicators for faults because faults that are introduced by recent changes and the more changes are done to a part of the source code the more likely it will contain faults[36]. Thus, we mine the software repositories databases to extract the churn metrics. We use these code churn metrics, as described in Table I to predict software fault density. This study builds on our work [5] and goes for faults collected through mining the git repositories of all software components, and takes into consideration not only the static faults and the code complexity metrics but also the code churn metrics to build accurate fault predictors.

5) Relative Code Churn Metrics: For each of the component, we compute a number of relative code churn metrics, as described in Table I. We show in this paper that using relative code churn as fault predictor is better than using (absolute) code churn predictors. Furthermore, combining relative code churn metrics with code complexity metrics and static analysis faults can accurately predict the fault density with a high degree of sensitivity. Our metric suite in this work is able to discriminate between fault and not fault-prone components with an accuracy of 89.0 percent.

B. Model Fitting and Regression Analysis

In this section we compare predictive models built using the different metrics presented in Table I in order to find the best model for accurate fault prediction. We fit several models to the absolute code churn data as well as the relative code churn data separately as predictors, with the fault density as the dependent variable. We tested our data on the four main regression models families (Generalized Linear models, Deep Learning Models, Random Forest Models and Boosted Models). The experiment

TABLE I. METRICS USED FOR THE STUDY

Metrics	Description
Static Analysis Fault Density	# faults found by static analysis tools per KLOC (thousand lines of code).
Code Churn Metrics	
Added LOC	# lines of code added
Removed LOC	# lines of code deleted
Modified Files	# files modified
Files count	# files compiled to create a software component
Developers	# developers
Relative Code Churn Metrics	
Added LOC / Relevant LOC	We expect the larger the proportion of added code to the Relevant LOC, the higher is the probability of the presence of faults in the software component.
Removed LOC / Relevant LOC	We expect the larger the proportion of removed code to the Relevant LOC, the higher is the probability of the presence of faults in the software component.
Modified Files / Files count	We expect the larger the proportion of files in a component that get modified, the higher is the probability of these files introducing faults.
Code Complexity Metrics	
Relevant LOC	# relevant LOCs without comments, blanks, expansions, etc.
Complexity	cyclomatic complexity of a method
Nesting	# nesting levels in a method
Statements	# statements in a method
Paths	# non-cyclic paths in a method
Parameters	# function parameters in a method

shows that boosted models are showing the best fitting and generalized accuracy. This result can be explained by the fact that the relation between the independent variables is highly non-linear. The boosted models include RGBoost (also known as regularized gradient boosting), Distributed Random Forests (DRF) as well as Gradient Boosting Machines (GBM). We will shortly explain the model that we used in this study to predict the fault density. RGBoost is a supervised learning algorithm that implements a process called boosting to yield accurate models [37]. Boosting refers to the ensemble learning technique of building many models sequentially, with each new model attempting to correct for the deficiencies in the previous model [38]. In tree boosting, each new model that is added to the ensemble is a decision tree. RGBoost provides parallel tree boosting that solves many data science problems in a fast and accurate way. For many problems, RGBoost is one of the best gradient boosting machine frameworks today [37]. Both RGBoost and GBM follows the principle of gradient boosting. There are, however, differences in modeling details. Specifically, RGBoost uses a more regularized model formalization to control over-fitting, which gives it better performance, especially when the correlation between the independent variables is non-linear. Distributed Random Forest (DRF) is a powerful classification and regression tool. When given a set of data, DRF generates a forest of classification or regression trees, rather than a single classification or regression tree [39]. As a measure of the regression fits, we compute R^2. R^2 measures the variance in the predicted variable that is accounted by the regression built using the predictors. As a measure of the unbiased error estimate of the error variance, we use the mean squared error (MSE). The regression model fit for absolute code churn metrics has an R^2 value of 0.473, an MSE value of 0.235. Nevertheless, using the relative code churn metrics as fault predictors shows a better fit; the R^2 value increases to 0.730, the MSE

TABLE II. REGRESSION FITS

		RGBoost		DRF		GBM	
		R^2	MSE	R^2	MSE	R^2	MSE
Predictors	Absolute Code Churn Metrics **alone**	0.473	0.235	0.325	0.337	0.592	0.195
	Relative Code Churn Metrics **alone**	0.730	0.113	0.651	0.267	0.694	0.221
	Relative Code Churn Metrics **Combined With** Code Complexity Metrics and Static Analysis Fault Density	**0.857**	**0.015**	0.683	0.103	0.784	0.067

decreases to 0.113. We then combined relative code churn metrics with code complexity metrics and with static analysis fault density as predictors for the fault density. Table II shows that when using the combination relative code churn metrics with code complexity metrics and with static analysis fault density as fault predictors, we obtain the best fit using the Regularized Gradient Boosting (RGBoost) model; the R^2 value increases to 0.857, the MSE decreases to 0.015. Therefore, we conclude that it is more beneficial to combine relative code churn metrics with code complexity metrics and static analysis fault density to explain software faults. The validation of the model goodness is repeated 10 times using the 10-fold cross-validation technique. A benefit of using ensembles of decision tree methods like regularized gradient boosting is that they can automatically provide estimates of feature importance from a trained predictive model, as presented in Figure 2.

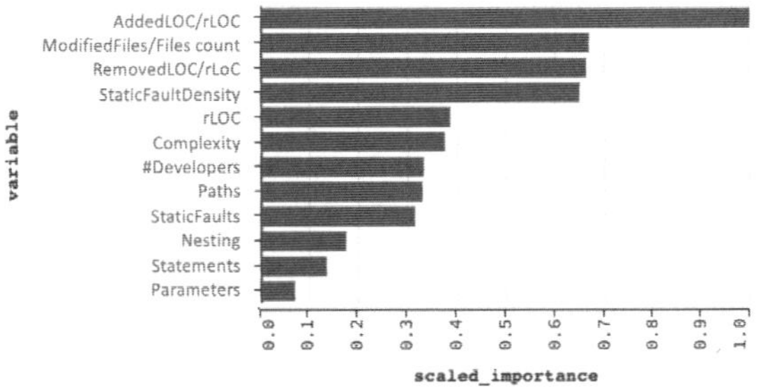

Figure 2. Variable Importances

C. *Fault-Proneness Analysis*

In order to classify software components into fault-prone and not fault-prone components, we applied several statistical classification techniques. The classification techniques include the same techniques that we considered for the regression; RGBoost, DRF and GBM. The independent variables for the classifiers are the relative code churn metrics combined with the code complexity metrics and the static analysis fault density. The dependent variable is the result of binarizing (i.e., fault-prone vs. not fault-prone) the fault density. A confusion matrix, as defined in Table III, is used to store the correct and incorrect decisions made by a classification model. For instance, if a component is classified as fault-prone when it is truly fault-prone, the classification is true positive (tp). If the component is classified as fault-prone when it is actually

TABLE III. COMPARING OBSERVED AND PREDICTED COMPONENT CLASSES IN A CONFUSION MATRIX. USED TO COMPUTE PRECISION AND RECALL VALUES OF CLASSIFICATION MODEL

		Observed class: fault prone	Observed class: non-fault prone
Predicted class	fault prone	True negative (TN)	False negative (FN)
Predicted class	non-fault prone	False positive (FP)	True positive (TP)

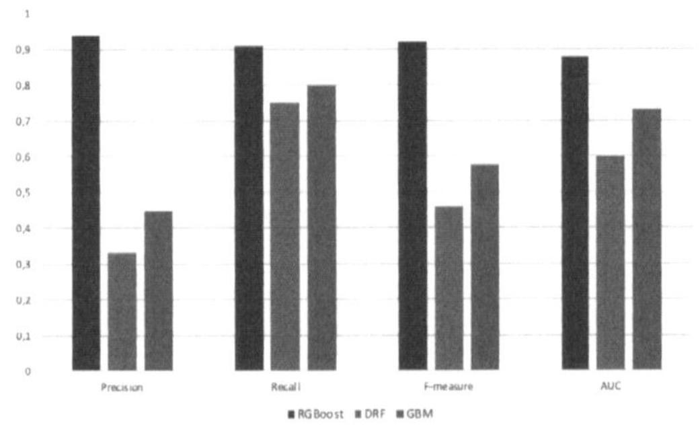

Figure 3. Classification performance of our approach

clean (not fault-prone), then the classification is a false positive (fp). If the file is classified as clean when it is in fact fault-prone, the classification is a false negative (fn). Finally, if the issue is classified as clean and it is, in fact, clean, the classification is true negative (tn). In order to compare the actual observed and predicted classes for each component, we categorized each predicted class into four individual categories as shown in Table III. As evaluation measures, we compute precision, recall, and F-measure defined as:

- Precision: how many of the components classified by our classifiers as fault-prone are actually fault-prone.
  $$precision = \frac{tp}{tp+fp}$$
- Recall: how many fault-prone components our classifiers were able to identify correctly as fault-prone.
  $$recall = \frac{tp}{tp+fn}$$
- F-measure: measures the weighted harmonic mean of the precision and recall.
  $$F\text{-}measure = 2 * \frac{precision * recall}{precision + recall}$$

All two measures are values between zero and one. A precision of one indicates that the classification model does not report any false positives. A recall of one implies that the model does not report any false negatives. The F-measure can be interpreted as a weighted average of the precision and recall, where an F-measure reaches its best value at one and worst at zero. Furthermore, we investigate the use of the area under the receiver operating characteristic (ROC) curve (AUC) as a performance measure for approach. The area under the ROC curve (AUC) equals the probability that the classifiers predict a randomly chosen true positive higher than a randomly chosen false negative. The larger the AUC, the more accurate is the classification model. As shown in Figure 3, the classification model which uses RGBoost as the classifier produced an impressive result with all four performance indicators (Precision, Recall, F-measure and AUC) being well above 0.9. Using DRF or GBM achieved very high recall, but at the same time it appeared to produce many false positives, and thus their precision is much lower than the precision produced by RGBoost. All studied classifiers achieved an AUC well above the 0.5 threshold; 0.89 for RGBoost, 0.6 for DRF and 0.73 for GBM.

D. Threats to Validity

The validity of credibility problems occur when there are mistakes in measurement. This is negated to an extent by the reality that the whole data collection procedure is automated through the version control systems through mining the git repositories. Nevertheless, the version control systems only documents data upon developer check-out or check-in of files. If a developer made several overlapping edits to a file in a single check-out/check-in period then a certain amount of changes will not be visible. Moreover, a developer may have a file checked out for a very long period of time throughout which few churns were made. These worries are reduced somewhat by the cross-check among the measures to recognize irregular values for any of the measures, as well as the significant dimension and diversity of our dataset. In our study, we give proof for utilizing all the relative code churn metrics rather than a subset of values or principal components. This study is particular and ought to be improved based upon further result.

V. Conclusion And Future Work

In this paper we verified the hypothesis that history of code changes between different commits and releases (code churn) when combined with static analysis fault density and code complexity metrics are a good predictor of pre-release fault density. Moreover, adding code churn metrics increases the prediction accuracy.

For future work we plan to further validate our study by analyzing additional software projects. Attributing fault density to smaller units of code (e.g., files, functions), we consider also an interesting direction of research. To achieve that it might be needed to take additional features of the source code, such as the abstract syntax tree (AST), control- and dataflow into account. For this, we also plan to train deep learning models to predict software faults not only on the component level, but also on the method level. We also plan the generalizability of the presented approach on different open source projects.

Acknowledgement

We would like to thank Steffen Görzig and Pascal Montag from Daimler AG for their support and for providing the data underlying our case study.

References

[1] R. Rana, M. Staron, J. Hansson, and M. Nilsson, "Defect prediction over software life cycle in automotive domain state of the art and road map for future," in 2014 9th International Conference on Software Engineering and Applications (ICSOFT-EA), Aug 2014.

[2] T. M. Khoshgoftaar, E. B. Allen, N. Goel, A. Nandi, and J. McMullan, "Detection of software modules with high debug code churn in a very large legacy system," in Proceedings of the The Seventh International Symposium on Software Reliability Engineering, ser. ISSRE '96. Washington, DC, USA: IEEE Computer Society, 1996, pp. 364–.

[3] T. L. Graves, A. F. Karr, J. S. Marron, and H. Siy, "Predicting fault incidence using software change history," IEEE Transactions on Software Engineering, vol. 26, no. 7, July 2000, pp. 653–661.

[4] N. Nagappan and T. Ball, "Use of relative code churn measures to predict system defect density," in Proceedings of the 27th International Conference on Software Engineering, ser. ICSE '05. New York, NY, USA: ACM, 2005, pp. 284–292.

[5] S. Omri, P. Montag, and C. Sinz, "Static analysis and code complexity metrics as early indicators of software defects," Journal of Software Engineering and Applications, vol. 11, no. 4, april 2018.

[6] A. Mockus, P. Zhang, and P. L. Li, "Drivers for customer perceived software quality," in ICSE 2005, 2005.

[7] T. J. Ostrand, E. J. Weyuker, and R. M. Bell, "Predicting the location and number of faults in large software systems," IEEE Trans. Softw. Eng., vol. 31, no. 4, Apr. 2005, pp. 340–355.

[8] T. Zimmermann, P. Weisgerber, S. Diehl, and A. Zeller, "Mining version histories to guide software changes," in Proceedings of the 26th International Conference on Software Engineering, ser. ICSE '04. Washington, DC, USA: IEEE Computer Society, 2004, pp. 563–572.

[9] D. Čubranić and G. C. Murphy, "Hipikat: Recommending pertinent software development artifacts," in Proceedings of the 25th International Conference on Software Engineering, ser. ICSE '03. Washington, DC, USA: IEEE Computer Society, 2003, pp. 408–418.

[10] M. Fischer, M. Pinzger, and H. Gall, "Populating a release history database from version control and bug tracking systems," in Proceedings of the International Conference on Software Maintenance, ser. ICSM '03. Washington, DC, USA: IEEE Computer Society, 2003, pp. 23–.

[11] J. Śliwerski, T. Zimmermann, and A. Zeller, "When do changes induce fixes?" in Proceedings of the 2005 International Workshop on Mining Software Repositories, ser. MSR '05. New York, NY, USA: ACM, 2005, pp. 1–5.

[12] K. K. Chaturvedi, V. B. Sing, and P. Singh, "Tools in mining software repositories," in Proceedings of the 2013 13th International Conference on Computational Science and Its Applications, ser. ICCSA '13. Washington, DC, USA: IEEE Computer Society, 2013, pp. 89–98.

[13] F. Z. Sokol, M. F. Aniche, and M. A. Gerosa, "Metricminer: Supporting researchers in mining software repositories," in 2013 IEEE 13th International Working Conference on Source Code Analysis and Manipulation (SCAM), Sep. 2013, pp. 142–146.

[14] A. Zaidman, B. V. Rompaey, S. Demeyer, and A. v. Deursen, "Mining software repositories to study co-evolution of production & test code," in Proceedings of the 2008 International Conference on Software Testing, Verification, and Validation, ser. ICST '08. Washington, DC, USA: IEEE Computer Society, 2008, pp. 220–229.

[15] S. M. Olbrich, D. S. Cruzes, and D. I. K. Sjoberg, "Are all code smells harmful? a study of god classes and brain classes in the evolution of three open source systems," in Proceedings of the 2010 IEEE International Conference on Software Maintenance, ser. ICSM '10. Washington, DC, USA: IEEE Computer Society, 2010, pp. 1–10.

[16] F. Palomba, A. Panichella, A. Zaidman, R. Oliveto, and A. De Lucia, "The scent of a smell: An extensive comparison between textual and structural smells," in Proceedings of the 40th International Conference on Software Engineering, ser. ICSE '18. New York, NY, USA: ACM, 2018, pp. 740–740.

[17] A. Bacchelli and C. Bird, "Expectations, outcomes, and challenges of modern code review," in Proceedings of the 2013 International Conference on Software Engineering, ser. ICSE '13. Piscataway, NJ, USA: IEEE Press, 2013, pp. 712–721.

[18] M. Beller, A. Bacchelli, A. Zaidman, and E. Juergens, "Modern code reviews in open-source projects: Which problems do they fix?" in Proceedings of the 11th Working Conference on Mining Software Repositories, ser. MSR 2014. New York, NY, USA: ACM, 2014, pp. 202–211.

[19] V. J. Hellendoorn, P. T. Devanbu, and A. Bacchelli, "Will they like this?: Evaluating code contributions with language models," in Proceedings of the 12th Working Conference on Mining Software Repositories, ser. MSR '15. Piscataway, NJ, USA: IEEE Press, 2015, pp. 157–167.

[20] P. Thongtanunam, S. Mcintosh, A. E. Hassan, and H. Iida, "Review participation in modern code review," Empirical Softw. Engg., vol. 22, no. 2, Apr. 2017, pp. 768–817.

[21] D. Spadini, M. Aniche, M.-A. Storey, M. Bruntink, and A. Bacchelli, "When testing meets code review: Why and how developers review tests," in Proceedings of the 40th International Conference on Software Engineering, ser. ICSE '18. New York, NY, USA: ACM, 2018, pp. 677–687.

[22] A. Bacchelli, M. D'Ambros, and M. Lanza, "Are popular classes more defect prone?" in Proceedings of the 13th International Conference on Fundamental Approaches to Software Engineering, ser. FASE'10. Berlin, Heidelberg: Springer-Verlag, 2010, pp. 59–73.

[23] M. D'Ambros, A. Bacchelli, and M. Lanza, "On the impact of design flaws on software defects," in Proceedings of the 2010 10th International Conference on Quality Software, ser. QSIC '10. Washington, DC, USA: IEEE Computer Society, 2010, pp. 23–31.

[24] L. Pascarella, F. Palomba, and A. Bacchelli, "Re-evaluating method-level bug prediction," in 2018 IEEE 25th International Conference on Software Analysis, Evolution and Reengineering (SANER), March 2018, pp. 592–601.

[25] A. Mockus, R. T. Fielding, and J. Herbsleb, "A case study of open source software development: The apache server," in Proceedings of the 22Nd International Conference on Software Engineering, ser. ICSE '00. New York, NY, USA: ACM, 2000, pp. 263–272.

[26] S. R. Chidamber and C. F. Kemerer, "A metrics suite for object oriented design," IEEE Trans. Softw. Eng., vol. 20, no. 6, Jun. 1994.

[27] V. R. Basili, L. C. Briand, and W. L. Melo, "A validation of object-oriented design metrics as quality indicators," IEEE Trans. Softw. Eng., vol. 22, no. 10, Oct. 1996, pp. 751–761.

[28] L. C. Briand, J. Wüst, S. V. Ikonomovski, and H. Lounis, "Investigating quality factors in object-oriented designs: An industrial case study," in Proceedings of the 21st International Conference on Software Engineering, ser. ICSE '99. New York, NY, USA: ACM, 1999.

[29] R. Subramanyam and M. S. Krishnan, "Empirical analysis of CK metrics for object-oriented design complexity: Implications for software defects," IEEE Trans. Softw. Eng., vol. 29, no. 4, Apr. 2003.

[30] M.-H. Tang, M.-H. Kao, and M.-H. Chen, "An empirical study on object-oriented metrics," in Proceedings of the 6th International Symposium on Software Metrics, ser. METRICS '99. Washington, DC, USA: IEEE Computer Society, 1999.

[31] M. D'Ambros, M. Lanza, and R. Robbes, "Evaluating defect prediction approaches: A benchmark and an extensive comparison," Empirical Softw. Engg., vol. 17, no. 4-5, Aug. 2012, pp. 531–577.

[32] R. Moser, W. Pedrycz, and G. Succi, "A comparative analysis of the efficiency of change metrics and static code attributes for defect prediction," in Proceedings of the 30th International Conference on Software Engineering, ser. ICSE '08. New York, NY, USA: ACM, 2008, pp. 181–190.

[33] S. Kim, T. Zimmermann, E. J. Whitehead Jr., and A. Zeller, "Predicting faults from cached history," in Proceedings of the 29th International Conference on Software Engineering, ser. ICSE '07. Washington, DC, USA: IEEE Computer Society, 2007, pp. 489–498.

[34] N. Nagappan, T. Ball, and A. Zeller, "Mining metrics to predict component failures," in Proceedings of the 28th International Conference on Software Engineering, ser. ICSE '06. New York, NY, USA: ACM, 2006.

[35] M. C. Ohlsson, A. von Mayrhauser, B. McGuire, and C. Wohlin, "Code decay analysis of legacy software through successive releases," in 1999 IEEE Aerospace Conference. Proceedings (Cat. No.99TH8403), vol. 5, March 1999, pp. 69–81 vol.5.

[36] S. Kim, T. Zimmermann, K. Pan, and E. J. J. Whitehead, "Automatic identification of bug-introducing changes," in Proceedings of the 21st IEEE/ACM International Conference on Automated Software Engineering, ser. ASE '06. Washington, DC, USA: IEEE Computer Society, 2006, pp. 81–90.

[37] T. Chen and C. Guestrin, "Xgboost: A scalable tree boosting system," in Proceedings of the 22Nd ACM SIGKDD International Conference

on Knowledge Discovery and Data Mining, ser. KDD '16. New York, NY, USA: ACM, 2016, pp. 785–794.

[38] J. H. Friedman, "Greedy function approximation: A gradient boosting machine," Annals of Statistics, vol. 29, 2000, pp. 1189–1232.

[39] M. Guillame-Bert and O. Teytaud, "Exact distributed training: Random forest with billions of examples," ArXiv, vol. abs/1804.06755, 2018.

Incorporating Petri Nets into DEVS Formalism for Precise System Modeling

Radek Kočí and Vladimír Janoušek

Brno University of Technology, Faculty of Information Technology,
IT4Innovations Centre of Excellence
Bozetechova 2, 612 66 Brno, Czech Republic
email: {koci,janousek}@fit.vutbr.cz

Abstract—**Modeling and simulation are part of software development because of their ability of system abstraction and validation. One of the research motivation is oriented towards more interactivity during system requirements modeling and a possibility to investigate models under real condition. To achieve this goal, the system has to be modeled precisely. There is a lot of suitable paradigms—the paper concentrates especially on Object Oriented Petri Nets (OOPN) and Discrete-Event Specification (DEVS) formalisms. OOPN constitute an abstract formalism allowing a natural description of parallelism, synchronization and non-determinism. The formalism of DEVS constitutes a basis for a theory of modeling and simulation and can be considered as a basic platform for multi-paradigm system design. Therefore, the formalism of OOPN has been incorporated to the formalism of DEVS.**

Keywords–Object Oriented Petri Nets; DEVS; modeling; simulation; interconnection.

I. Introduction

Modeling plays an irreplaceable role in the software community, but its meaning is perceived in different ways. Its primary task is to better present the domain problem solution, to facilitate understanding of domain elements and, thus, simplify the process of system analysis. In this understanding, the model usually takes the form of static figures, which are no longer used after analysis and design, eventually they serve only as a starting point for implementation. However, the implementation gradually moves away from these models and the resulting product no longer corresponds to these models. At this stage, tool-based testing or analysis cannot be provided because the used models do not have a sufficient level of precision in the specification of requirements. Some specified elements need to be verified at a later stage of development, or it is necessary to implement a prototype on which these actions can already be performed. Both approaches extend the time required to properly validate requests.

To model and analyze systems under real conditions during the process of creating requirements and design, it is desirable that these formal models can be linked to parts of the implementation that would be subject to the same way of running control. In order to accurately determine point the system diverts from expected behavior, we should be able to stop the simulation and analyze it. We need to have such formalisms that allow to control model execution.

The most widespread modeling tool is Unified Modeling Language (UML) and its variants or adds that refine models (e.g., Object Constraint Language—OCL [1]) to allow their simulation (e.g., Executable UML). Generally, these methods can be called executable modeling [2]. However, the used formalisms usually lack an inherent relationship between graphical representation of models and the precise specification of system behavior. There are approaches that attempt to describe selected UML models in a fully formal way, such as Foundational Subset for Executable UML Models (fUML) [3], [4], which can specify a part of UML models by formal description. On the other hand, this blurs the advantage of UML, namely graphic notation.

The concept of model based design and executable modeling is mainly applied to cyber physical systems [5] and is not very widespread for system design and implementation. This paper is a follow-up to the work on application of formal models for specification and design of software systems [6], [7], which concentrates on DEVS and Petri nets formalisms. DEVS is a systems specification formalism developed by B. Zeigler [8]. It constitutes a basis for theory of modeling and simulation and can be considered as a basic platform for multi-paradigm modeling and simulation [9]. Object Oriented Petri Nets (OOPN) constitute a formalism suitable for structure modeling with graphical notation [10].

If we want to integrate the created models into the real environment, we must have a suitably adapted interface to the system in which the considered real environment is implemented. Implementation means its simulation, control of simulated or real components, communication with a database or other systems, etc. The formalism of OOPN allow to incorporate executive code into a model—the code is placed in transition actions. Such a solution makes it very difficult to adopt already existing code, complicates the simulation and analysis of the model and may not be completely conformist from the designer's point of view. Another solution is to select the appropriate interface and delegate code execution to formalism, which allows direct code incorporation while adopting a run-time management method. DEVS is such a formalism, but it becomes less transparent for larger systems (there is no other form of graphical presentation other than blocks). Therefore, this paper deals with an incorporation of OOPN and DEVS formalisms.

The paper is organized as follows. First, we briefly present formalisms of OOPN and DEVS (Section II). Section III takes simulation control of both formalisms into account. Section IV deals with the problem of incorporating OOPN into DEVS-based framework. The OOPN and DEVS incorporation is demonstrated on simple example in Section V. At the end, we discuss results and benefits of presented solution.

II. USED FORMALISMS

This section briefly introduces formalisms of OOPN and DEVS that are taken into account in the paper.

A. Formalism of Object Oriented Petri Nets

Formally, an OOPN is a tuple $\Pi = (\Sigma, \Gamma, VAR, CONST, c_0, oid_0)$, where Σ is a system of classes, Γ is a system of objects, VAR is a set of variables, $CONST$ is a set of constants, c_0 is an initial class, and oid_0 is the name of an initial object instantiated from c_0.

Σ contains sets of structural elements, which constitute classes. It comprises classes $CLASS$, net elements (places P and transitions T), class elements (object nets $ONET$, method nets $MNET$, synchronous ports $SYNC$, negative predicates $NPRED$), and message selectors MSG. We denote $NET = ONET \cup MNET$.

A *class* is mainly specified by an object net (an element of $ONET$), a set of synchronous ports and negative predicates (a subset of $SYNC$ and $NPRED$), a set of method nets (a subset of $MNET$), and a set of message selectors (a subset of MSG) corresponding to its method nets, synchronous ports, and negative predicates. Object nets describe possible autonomous activities of objects, while method nets describe reactions of objects to messages sent to them from the outside. Synchronous ports are special transitions, which cannot fire alone but only dynamically fused to some other transitions.

Elements from $CLASS$ and NET describe a structure of simulation model and have to be instantiated to simulate the model. For example, the instance of initial class c_0 has to be created with the object identifier oid_0. At the same time, there are created instances of object net. If the message is sent to the object, an instance of the method net is created.

Let us define Γ as a structure containing sets of object identifiers OID, and method net instance identifiers MID. We denote $ID = OID \cup MID$. Object net is strictly connected with the class, so that we can identify its instance by object identifier. We also define universe U as the set of tuples of constants, classes, and object identifiers. The set of all bindings of variables used in OOPN is then defined as $BIND = \{b \mid b : \mathit{VAR} \longrightarrow U\}$.

A state of a running OOPN model has the form of *marking* of net instances. Marking is represented as the multiset of token elements. An element of transition marking has a form of cartesian product $ID \times T \times BIND$, where $nid \in ID$ represents the identifier of the method or object net instance, $t \in T$ is a static representation of transition in the net instance nid, and $b \in BIND$ is one element of bound variables. An element of place marking has a form of cartesian product $ID \times P \times U$, where $nid \in ID$ represents the identifier of the net instance, $p \in P$ is a static representation of place in the net instance nid, and $u \in U$ is one element of place content. A state s is then define as an item of multiset $s \in [(ID \times T \times BIND) \cup (ID \times P \times U)]^{MS}$.

Evaluation of transition fireability is based on high-level Petri net evaluation—a transition is *fireable* for some binding of variables, which are present in the arc expressions of its input arcs and in its guard expression, if there are enough tokens in the input places with respect to the values of input arc expressions and if the guard expression for the given binding evaluates to true.

B. Formalism of DEVS

DEVS is a formalism which can represent any system whose input/output behavior can be described as sequence of events. DEVS is specified as a structure

$$M = (X, S, Y, \delta_{int}, \delta_{ext}, \lambda, ta)$$

where

X is the set of input event values,
S is the set of state values,
Y is the set of output event values,
$\delta_{int} : S \longrightarrow S$ is the internal transition function,
$\delta_{ext} : Q \times X \longrightarrow S$ is the external transition function,
$Q = \{(s, e) \mid s \in S, 0 \leq e \leq ta(s)\}$ is the set of total states,
e is the time passed since the last transition,
$\lambda : S \longrightarrow Y$ is the output function,
$ta : S \longrightarrow {R^+}_{0,\infty}$ is the time advance function.

At any time, the system is in some state $s \in S$. If no external event occurs, the system is staying in state s for $ta(s)$ time. If elapsed time e reaches $ta(s)$, then the value of $\lambda(s)$ is propagated to the output and the system state changes to $\delta_{int}(s)$. If an external event $x \in X$ occurs on the input in time $e \leq ta(s)$, then the system changes its state to $\delta_{ext}(s, e, x)$.

This way we can describe atomic models. Atomic models can be coupled together to form a coupled model CM. The later model can itself be employed as a component of larger model. This way the DEVS formalism brings a hierarchical component architecture. Sets S, X, Y are obviously specified as structured sets. It allows to use multiple variables for specification of state and we can use input and output ports for input and output events specification, as well as for coupling specification. A lot of extensions and modifications of the original DEVS has been introduced, such as parallel DEVS [11] or dynamic structure DEVS [12] and a lot of simulation frameworks has been developed.

III. SIMULATION CONTROL

This section describes basic concepts of simulation control for OOPN and DEVS formalisms.

A. DEVS Simulation

DEVS simulation is a structure $SIM_D = (DM, \tau_D, D)$, where DM is a DEVS model, $\tau_D \in \mathbb{N}$ is a model time of DEVS simulation, and D is a set of *solvers*. DEVS model consists of coupled or atomic subcomponents, each such a component is controlled by its *solver*. The simulation of DEVS model is controlled by special *root solver*. The simulation control can be described as shown in Figures 1, 2, and 3.

$\tau_D \leftarrow 0$
$ta \leftarrow 0$
while $ta \neq \infty$ **do**
    call solver on $root\ model$
    $ta \leftarrow ta$ from $root\ model$
    if $ta \neq \infty$ **then**
        $\tau_D \leftarrow \tau_D + ta$
    end
end

Figure 1. DEVS Root Solver Control

The root solver (Algorithm 1) works in cycle until the time advance ta gets infinity. In each step, it calls a solver of root model and updates the model time τ_D. If there is no component which is able to do a step, the ta is set to infinity.

DM_i is a set of subcomponents of the component i
$ta = \infty$
foreach $m \in DM_i$ **do**
  call solver on m
  propagate event values from output ports of m to connected input ports of subcomponents from DM_i
  $t_m \leftarrow ta$ from component m
  $ta \leftarrow min(ta, t_m)$
end

Figure 2. DEVS Coupled Solver Control

The solver of coupled component (Algorithm 2) goes through all subcomponents. For each subcomponent, the solver calls a subcomponent solver and propagates event values from its output ports to input ports of connected subcomponents. At the end, the solver sets ta to be a minimum value of ta of all subcomponents.

m is an atomic DEVS model
if $ta = 0$ **then**
  execute the output function λ on m
  execute the internal function δ_{int} on m
else
  if *an external event* $x \in X$ *occurs* **then**
    execute the external function δ_{ext} on m
  end
end
$ta \leftarrow ta$ from component m

Figure 3. DEVS Atomic Solver Control

The solver of atomic component (Algorithm 3) tests two conditions. If its $ta = 0$, the output and internal functions are executed. If $ta > 0$ (the component waits for the event) and any external event occurs (an input port contains an event value), the external function is executed. Finally, a new value of ta is obtained.

B. OOPN Simulation

To simulate OOPN, we first extend previously established definitions. The system of objects $\Gamma = (OID, MID, PID, FTID)$ is extended to identifiers of place instances PID and fired transition instances $FTID$. We denote $ID = OID \cup MID \cup PID \cup FTID$. Let define a relation $@ \subseteq ID \times CLASS \cup NET \cup P \cup T$, which represent relationships *is an instance of*. For example, $(a, C1) \in @$ means that a is an instance of the element named `C1`. We will write this relation in the form `a@C1`. If the instance identifier is not important, we will type only `@C1`.

OOPN simulation is a structure $SIM_\Gamma = (\Pi, \tau_\Gamma, CAL)$, where Π is the system of OOPN classes and objects, $\tau_\Gamma \in \mathbb{N}$ is a model time, and $CAL = \{(t, e) \mid t \in \mathbb{N} \wedge e \in FTID\}^{MS}$ is a calendar represented by multiset of timed events.

The transition $t \in T$ can be fireable for any of possible bindings $\mathcal{P}(BIND)$. If the transition t is fired for the binding $b \in \mathcal{P}(BIND)$, three possibilities can occur—(a) the fired transition is completed immediately (it contains simple action), (b) the fired transition will wait for specified time, or (c) the fired transition will wait for called method finishing. The possibilities (b) and (c) imply that the *fired transition* $ft \in FTID$ is created.

Three kinds of events can occur during the simulation—fireable transition (it can be fired), fired transition (it can be complete, i.e., the method called from this transition finished), and timed fired transition (the transition waits for specified time). The first and second events are called *executable events* and the third one is called *timed event*.

Let define $objevents_\Gamma : OID \rightarrow \mathcal{P}(T \cup FTID)$ determining *executable events* over all nets of the object, ϑ determining a least time of event from the calendar, where

$$\vartheta(C) = \begin{cases} \infty, & C = \emptyset \\ t, & \exists(t, e) \in C \wedge \forall(t_i, e_i) \in C : t \leq t_i \end{cases}$$

and $events_\vartheta(C) = \{e \mid (t, e) \in C \wedge t = \vartheta(C)\}$ determining a set of *timed events* having least time in the calendar.

The simulation control is described in Algorithm 4. While there is possible to do a step ($activity = true$), the simulator calls one simulation step.

$activity \leftarrow true$
while $activity = true$ **do**
  call $step$
end

Figure 4. OOPN Simulation Control

The simulation step is described in Algorithm 5. First, it obtains a set of objects having at least one *executable event*. If this set in not empty, the simulator selects an event from each such an object and fires it. Firing events means that the transition is fired and completed, or the transition is only fired (so that the fired transition $ft \in FTID$ arises), or the fired transition is completed. Second, if the set of objects is empty, the simulator obtains a set of *timed events*. If this set is not empty, it sets a model time τ_Γ to the value of ϑ and releases all events waiting at the time ϑ. Releasing timed events means that they are removed from calendar and becomes *executable events*. Third, if there is no event in the calendar, the simulation is finished ($activity \leftarrow false$).

IV. Embedding OOPN into DEVS

There are several techniques to integrate various formalisms. The most common ones are *combination*, *mapping*, and *wrapping*. The combination derives *a new formalism* from already existing ones by their combination, e.g., DEV&DESS [13] or Hybrid Petri nets [14]. The *mapping* approach maps formalisms to supporting one so that just the supporting formalism is interpreted. The *wrapping* approach connects simulators of different formalisms so that each model is interpreted by its simulator and simulators communicate with each other by means of a compatible interface. It is advantageous if one of the formalisms can be use as a control simulator for all other formalisms. Since DEVS rigorously defines the component interface, it is very suitable to serve as a basic component

1 $objs = \{o \in OID \mid objevents_\Gamma(o) \neq \emptyset\}$
2 **if** $objs \neq \emptyset$ **then**
3   **foreach** $o \in objs$ **do**
4         $e \leftarrow$ select an item from $objevents_\Gamma(o)$
5   fire e
6   **end**
7 **else**
8     $ev = events_\vartheta(CAL)$
9   **if** $ev \neq \emptyset$ **then**
10         $\tau_\Gamma \leftarrow \vartheta(CAL)$
11   **foreach** $e \in ev$ **do**
12   release event e
13   **end**
14   **else**
15         $activity \leftarrow false$
16   **end**
17 **end**

Figure 5. The OOPN Simulation Step.

platform for multiparadigmatic simulations. Consequently, we have chosen *wrapping* to embed the OOPN formalism to the DEVS formalism.

A. Ports and Places Mapping

Set of input event values X and output event values Y used in the DEVS formalism can be specified as structured sets. It allows to use multiple variables for specification of state and we can use named input and output ports for input and output events specification, as well as for coupling specification. Let us have the structured set $X = (V_X, X_1 \times X_2 \times \cdots \times X_n)$, where V_X is an ordered set of n variables and $X_1 \times X_2 \times \cdots \times X_n$ denotes a value for each member from the set V_X. We can write the structured set as $X = \{(v_1, v_2, \ldots, v_n) | v_1 \in X_1, \ldots, v_n \in X_n)\}$. Members $v_1, v_2, \ldots, v_n$ are called *input ports* for the set X and *output ports* for the set Y.

DEVS components communicate each other through their ports—when a new object is placed to the output port of a component, it is carried to the appropriate input port of the connected component. The way how to relate DEVS with OOPN is to map ports and places.

Let $M_{PN} = (M, \Pi, map_{inp}, map_{out})$ be a DEVS component M which wraps an OOPN model Π, $c_0 \in CLASS$ is an initial class of the model Π, $oid_0 \in OID$ is an initial object of the class c_0, V_X is an ordered set of input ports of the model M, and V_Y is an ordered set of output ports of the model M. Let define $onet_\Sigma : CLASS \rightarrow ONET$ determining an object net of the class, $places_\Sigma : NET \rightarrow \mathcal{P}(P)$ determining a set of places of the net, and $place_\Gamma : ID \times P \rightarrow PID$ determining an instance of a place in the net. We divide places of object net of an initial class c_0 into two groups $P_{c0}^{inp}, P_{c0}^{out} \subseteq places_\Sigma(onet_\Sigma(c_0))$, where $P_{c0}^{inp} \cap P_{c0}^{out} = \emptyset$. Then we can define a mapping of OOPN places into DEVS ports as bijections $map_{inp} : P_{c0}^{inp} \rightarrow V_X$ and $map_{out} : P_{c0}^{out} \rightarrow V_Y$.

Informally, if an OOPN model is defined as a DEVS component, then an object net of initial class defines input and output places. The initial class is instantiated immediately the component is created, and the defined places serve as input or output ports of the component.

B. OOPN Simulation Control Adaptation

In addition to place mapping, the simulation control has to be adapted too. The OOPN simulator has to define functions ta, δ_{ext}, λ, and δ_{int}.

After each step, the simulator checks the time of the next step by the function *timeAdvance* ($t(a)$). It tests three conditions, as shown in Figure 6: (1) if there is at least one executable object, the advance time is 0; (2) if there is at least one timed event with activating time t, the time advance is a difference of t and current model time τ_Γ; (3) if there is at least one value in any place which is mapped as output port, the advance time is 0 (the output function has to be executed to propagate values from output ports); (3) otherwise, time advance is $infinity$.

if $\exists o \in OID : objevents_\Gamma(o) \neq \emptyset$ **then**
    return 0
else
    $t = \vartheta(CAL)$
    if $t \neq \infty$ **then**
        return $t - \tau_\Gamma$
    else
        if $\exists y \in V_Y : map_{out}^{-1}(y)$ *is not empty* **then**
            return 0
        else
            return ∞
        end
    end
end

Figure 6. timeAdvance ta

The external transition function δ_{ext} is described in Fugure 7. If the component, which wraps OOPN model, receives an external event (new data in its input ports), the function *extTransition* (δ_{ext}) is called. It takes values out from input ports and puts them into mapped places.

foreach $x \in V_X$ **do**
    $p = map_{inp}^{-1}(x)$
    $v \leftarrow$ a value from x
    if v *is not empty* **then**
        put v into a place $place_\Gamma(oid_0, p)$
    end
end

Figure 7. extTransition δ_{ext}

The output function λ is described in Figure 8. If the component, which wraps OOPN model, has any value to be put output ports, it takes values from mapped places and puts them into into appropriate output ports.

The internal function δ_{int} is described in Figure 9. It is modified simulation step from Figure 5. First, the model time τ_Γ is not updated directly by OOPN simulator (see the line 10 in Figure 5), but is set to the model time τ_D of DEVS root solver (see the line 1 in Figure 9). Second, the liveness of simulation is not tested by means of the attribute $activity$, but the function ta. Third, the simulation cycle is subordinate to DEVS root solver, so that the simulation control described in Figure 4 is not in use.

foreach $y \in V_Y$ **do**
  $p = map_{out}^{-1}(y)$
  $v \leftarrow$ a value from $place_\Gamma(oid_0, p)$
  if v *is not empty* **then**
    put v into an output port y
  end
end

Figure 8. outputFunction λ

$\tau_\Gamma \leftarrow \tau_D$
$objs = \{o \in OID \mid objevents_\Gamma(o) \neq \emptyset\}$
if $objs \neq \emptyset$ **then**
  foreach $o \in objs$ **do**
    $e \leftarrow$ select an item from $objevents_\Gamma(o)$
    fire e
  end
else
  $ev = events_\vartheta(CAL)$
  if $ev \neq \emptyset$ **then**
    foreach $e \in ev$ **do**
      release event e
    end
  end
end

Figure 9. intTransition δ_{int}

C. Controlling External Events

In the course of simulation, the events arise and are served inside the model. Nevertheless, DEVS components or OOPN objects can serve as interfaces to the outer world and the incidental events from the world can arise. DEVS controlling uses *se-message*—a mechanism for a notification of the root solver about a state event, which serves as a request for internal transition function. This mechanism is used especially in real-time simulations.

In addition to *internal events* (fireable transitions, fired transitions, and timed fired actions), the simulation of OOPN distinguishes *control event* (serving method nets instantiation and destroying) and *external event*. Because OOPN objects can communicate with objects from the outer world, OOPN is able to work with extended set of classes $ECLASS = CLASS \cup PCLASS$, where $PCLASS$ is a set of classes of product environment. Then, external event represents a message called from object $o@C$, where $C \notin CLASS$. If the message is received, the control event instantiates method net, consequently, new internal events arise, and a signal for starting simulation cycle in the case of $activity = false$ is generated. When the OOPN model is wrapped to DEVS component, the signal for simulation cycle is simply substituted for *se-message*.

V. Demonstration of OOPN embedding

We demonstrate embedding the OOPN formalism to the DEVS formalism on a simple example.

A. Model

The model consists of two atomic components $D1$ and $D2$. Each component has one input port inp and one output port $outp$ ($V_X = \{inp\}$ and $V_Y = \{outp\}$). Component ports are connected as shown in Figure 10 (on the left).

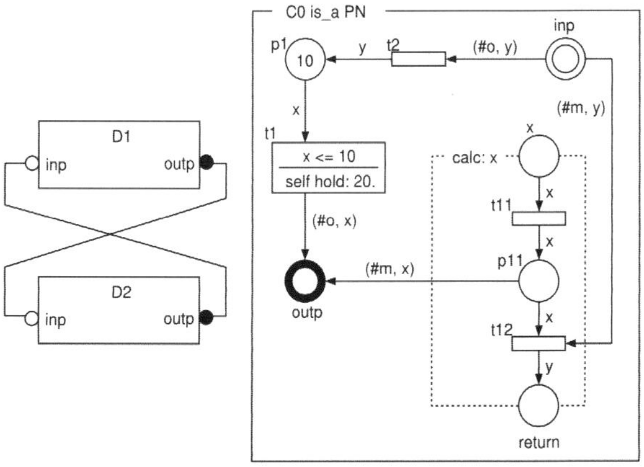

Figure 10. An OOPN-DEVS example.

The DEVS component $D2$ is atomic component, which gets a value x at its input port inp, and puts a value $x + 1$ to its output port $outp$. Formally, the component $D2$ defines following functions:

$$\begin{aligned} \delta_{ext}: &\quad x \leftarrow V_X(inp) \\ \lambda: &\quad x \neq \infty \implies V_Y(outp) \leftarrow x + 1 \\ \delta_{int}: &\quad x \leftarrow \infty \\ ta: &\quad \begin{cases} 0, & x \neq \infty \\ \infty, & x = \infty \end{cases} \end{aligned}$$

The DEVS component $D1$ wraps an OOPN model Π consisting of the class $C0$ (see the Figure 10 on the right). The OOPN class has an object net and method net $calc:$. The object net consists of places $p1$, inp, and $outp$, and transitions $t1$ and $t2$. The class $C0$ is an initial class c_0 of the model Π and oid_0 is an initial object. The input port inp is mapped to the place inp and the output port $outp$ is mapped to the place $outp$.

B. Simulation without External Events

First, we will investigate what happens if the model simulation starts and nobody will call the method $calc$: as an external event. Possible states of the object oid_0 are shown in Figure 11 in the form of place and fired transition marking—$p1(10)$ means a place $p1$ with one token a number 10, $@t1(x = 10)$ means a fired transition $t1$ with bound variable $x = 10$.

Simulation steps of components $D1$ and resp. $D2$ are shown in Figure 12 and 13, respectively. Rows represents component's simulation step, columns contain information about the step: i is step sequence number (over whole simulation), τ_D is model time, s is current state, $\frac{\lambda}{\delta_{ext}}$ represents results of stated functions, δ_{int} is a new state after executing the function δ_{int}, $event$ represents an event which has been fired (transition or fired transition with the binding), and ta is time advance after this step. Since the event, which has been fired, is relevant only for OOPN component $D1$, the column $event$ is not present for the component $D2$.

s	$object\ net\ oid_0$
s_0	$p1(10), inp(), outp()$
s_1	$p1(), inp(), outp(), @t1(x = 10)$
s_2	$p1(), inp(), outp(10)$
s_3	$p1(), inp(), outp()$
s_4	$p1(), inp(11), outp()$
s_5	$p1(11), inp(), outp()$

Figure 11. List of states of the initial object oid_0

There is a special sequence number $i = 0$ meaning initialization of components when only δ_{int} and ta are executed. The component $D1$ fires a transition $t1$ for bindings $x = 10$, switches to a state s_1, and its ta is 20, because the fired transition $@t1(x = 10)$ holds for 20 time units. The component $D2$ sets its internal variable $x = \infty$, stays in a state s_0, and produces $ta = \infty$ because there is no action to be done.

i	τ_D	s	$\frac{\lambda}{\delta_{ext}}$	δ_{int}	$event$	ta
0	0	s_0	$\frac{none}{none}$	s_1	$t1(x = 10)$	20
1	20	s_1	$\frac{none}{none}$	s_2	$@t1(x = 10)$	0
2	20	s_2	$\frac{Y(outp) \leftarrow 10}{none}$	s_3	–	∞
5	20	s_3	$\frac{none}{inp \leftarrow 11}$	s_4	–	0
6	20	s_4	$\frac{none}{none}$	s_5	$t2(y = 11)$	∞

Figure 12. Simulation step of the component $D1$

The next step $i = 1$ activates the component $D1$ for a time 20. It fires an event $@t1(x = 10)$, changes to a state s_2, and sets $ta = 0$ because the event put a value to the place $outp$ which is mapped to output port—the value has to be added to mapped output port in next step. Step $i = 2$ generates a value 10 in the output port $outp$, switches $D1$ to a state s_3, and sets $ta = \infty$ because there is no event.

i	τ_D	s	$\frac{\lambda}{\delta_{ext}}$	δ_{int}	ta
0	0	s_0	$\frac{none}{none}$	d_0	∞
3	20	s_0	$\frac{none}{x \leftarrow 10}$	d_1	0
4	20	s_1	$\frac{Y(outp) \leftarrow 11}{none}$	d_2	∞

Figure 13. Simulation step of the component $D2$

The value is propagated through connection $D1.outp \rightarrow D2.inp$ and the external function δ_{ext} is executed on $D2$ in step $i = 3$. It removes a value from input port inp, puts it in variable x, and sets $ta = 0$ because the component has to process this value in next step. The value is propagated through connection $D2.outp \rightarrow D1.inp$ and the external function δ_{ext} is executed on $D1$ in step $i = 5$. It removes a value from input port inp and puts it in the place inp. Step $i = 6$ carries the value from place inp to place $p1$ and sets $ta = \infty$ because there is no fireable transition (the condition $x <= 10$ in $C0.t1$ is not met).

VI. Conclusion

The paper raised a question of modeling systems in real environments and a need for incorporating executive code into system models. It also presented the solution based on a combination of Petri nets and DEVS formalisms. The presented solution makes it possible to associate the formal models described by High-level Petri nets (not just OOPN) with an executable code that is incorporated into DEVS formalism structures. DEVS formalism has the advantage of being an abstract concept that can be easily adapted to a particular environment due to the basic structures and principle of the simulator. In the future, we plan to fully incorporate DEVS formalism to the implementation of the software modeling tool.

Acknowledgment

This work has been supported by the internal BUT project FIT-S-17-4014 and The Ministry of Education, Youth and Sports of the Czech Republic from the National Programme of Sustainability (NPU II); project IT4Innovations excellence in science – LQ1602.

References

[1] J. Warmer and A. Kleppe, The Object Constraint Language: Getting your models ready for MDA. Longman Publishing, 2003.

[2] F. Ciccozzi, I. Malavolta, and B. Selic, "Execution of uml models: a systematic review of research and practice," Software & Systems Modeling, vol. 18, no. 3, 2018, pp. 2313–2360.

[3] S. Mijatov, P. Langer, T. Mayerhofer, and G. Kappel, "A framework for testing uml activities based on fuml," in Proc. of 10th Int. Workshop on Model Driven Engineering, Verification, and Validation, vol. 1069, 2013.

[4] S. Guermazi, J. Tatibouet, A. Cuccuru, E. Seidewitz, S. Dhouib, and S. Gérard, "Executable modeling with fuml and alf in papyrus: Tooling and experiments," in EXE@MoDELS, 2015.

[5] R. Manione, "A full model-based design environment for the development of cyber physical systems," Design, vol. 3, no. 1, 2019, pp. 1–30.

[6] R. Kočí and V. Janoušek, "The Object Oriented Petri Net Component Model," in The Tenth International Conference on Software Engineering Advances. Xpert Publishing Services, 2015, pp. 309–315.

[7] R. Kočí and V. Janoušek, "Specification of Requirements Using Unified Modeling Language and Petri Nets," International Journal on Advances in Software, vol. 10, no. 12, 2017, pp. 121–131.

[8] B. Zeigler, T. Kim, and H. Praehofer, Theory of Modeling and Simulation. Academic Press, Inc., London, 2000.

[9] D. Cetinkaya, A. V. Dai, and M. D. Seck, "Model continuity in discrete event simulation: A framework for model-driven development of simulation models," ACM Transactions on Modeling and Computer Simulation, vol. 25, no. 3, 2015, pp. 17:1–17:24.

[10] V. Janoušek and R. Kočí, "PNtalk: Concurrent Language with MOP," in Proceedings of the CS&P'2003 Workshop. Warsaw University, Warsawa, PL, 2003.

[11] A. Chow and B. Zeigler, "Parallel devs: a parallel, hierarchical, modular, modeling formalism," in Proceedings of the 30th conference on Winter simulation, 1994, pp. 716–722.

[12] F. Barros, B. Zeigler, and P. Fishwick, "Multimodels and dynamic structure models: An integration of dsde/devs and oopm," in Proceedings of the 30th conference on Winter simulation, 1998, pp. 413–420.

[13] B. Zeigler, "Embedding dev&dess in devs: Characteristic behavior of hybrid models," in DEVS Integrative M&S Symposium, 2006.

[14] H. Alla and R. David, Discrete, Continuous, and Hybrid Petri Nets. Springer, 2005.

Comparative Evaluation of Input Features Used for Deep Neural Networks to Recognize Semantic Indoor Scene from Time-Series Images Obtained Using Mobile Robot

Hirokazu Madokoro, Hanwool Woo, and Kazuhito Sato

Department of Intelligent Mechatronics
Faculty of Systems Science and Technology
Akita Prefectural University
Yurihonjo City, Akita, Japan
Email: madokoro@akita-pu.ac.jp

Abstract—**Human living indoor environments are changing continuously according to our various lifestyles and activities. Human-symbiotic robots require advanced capabilities of environmental understanding and adaptation. For robotic environmental adaptation, numerous machine-learning-based approaches have been proposed. Moreover, numerous types of features such as brightness, edges, texture, etc. have been used for learning networks. This study was conducted to evaluate combinations of supervised-learning-based indoor scene recognition methods and their input features. This paper presents a framework to provide image features of three types according to learning strategies. The experimentally obtained results evaluate using two open benchmark datasets revealed suitable combinations of input features including weights obtained from category maps of Counter Propagation Networks (CNNs) used for Deep Neural Networks (DNNs). We demonstrate a suitable combination of features from scene images used for semantic indoor scene recognition. Particularly, higher recognition accuracy is obtainable using original time-series images for learning with CNNs.**

***Keywords*–bags of features; category maps; convolutional neural networks; counter propagation networks; self-organizing maps; and semantic indoor scene recognition.**

I. INTRODUCTION

Human vision has a gazing mechanism that selects attention-gathering information from a huge amount of information: around 10^9 bit/s [1]. Treisman et al. defined visual saliency as a bottom-up target extracting mechanism based on physiological knowledge and perception with visual feature attention [2]. Koch et al. [3] proposed Saliency Maps (SMs) as a conceptual model of visual saliency. Subsequently, Itti et al. [4] implemented SMs as a computational model for computer-aided processing of images. Applications using saliency models have been proposed widely for computer vision, machine vision, robot vision, collision detection, autopilot, visual perception, and various recognition systems [5]. Using salient objects as visual landmarks in an environment is regarded as highly useful for semantic category recognition used as components that characterize a complex scene [6].

Human living indoor environments are changing continuously according to our various lifestyles and activities. Human-symbiotic robots must have advanced capabilities of environmental understanding and adaptation. Numerous machine-learning-based approaches have been proposed for the adaptation of robots in general environments [7][8][9]. In our earlier study, we proposed a supervised-learning-based scene recognition method using category maps [10]. Our experimentally obtained results revealed that category maps, which visualize relations among scene features, are beneficial for semantic scene recognition.

In conventional machine-learning-based methods, suitable combinational features are extracted in advance. Subsequently, the number of feature dimensions is set as equal using Bag-of-Features (BoF) representation methods. Recently, Deep Neural Networks (DNNs) of various models are fascinating because of their advanced classification and recognition accomplishments [11]. We contemplate that improved accuracy is obtainable for robotic scene recognition using DNNs. However, no scene recognition result has been reported for DNNs trained using weights extracted from category maps.

Saliency-based features are used widely for outdoor and indoor scene classification and for recognition tasks. In one earlier study of saliency-based object recognition, Shokoufandeha et al. [12] examined an SM Graph (SMG) that extracts object saliency regions in several scales using wavelet transformation. Walther et al. [13] produced a biologically plausible model based on SMs for detecting objects from natural scenes. They used a Scale-Invariant Feature Transform (SIFT) [14] descriptor for extracting and describing object features. For outdoor scene recognition, Agrawal et al. [15] described a method to specify accurate positions using cost effective sensors simultaneously combined with GPS. As a challenging reason for indoor scene recognition, Quattoni et al. [8] demonstrated that vast indoor scenes are characterized by objects. It is limited to scenes that are characterized by spatial properties.

Fornoni et al. [16] explained an image classification method based on saliency used for indoor semantic scene recognition. For their method, they used SIFT and Support Vector Machines (SVMs) [17] as a feature descriptor and as a classifier. Botterill et al. [18] proposed a real-time detection method of similar scenes for position estimation used for a mobile robot. They used low-dimensional codebooks combined with a rapid descriptor based on Speeded-Up Robust Features (SURF) [19]. Their method achieved not only rapid object extraction and recognition, but also position estimation in real time for 30 fps, which is an ordinary video frame rate.

For one earlier study using feature descriptors and DNNs, Sachdeva et al. [20] compared the respective accuracies of

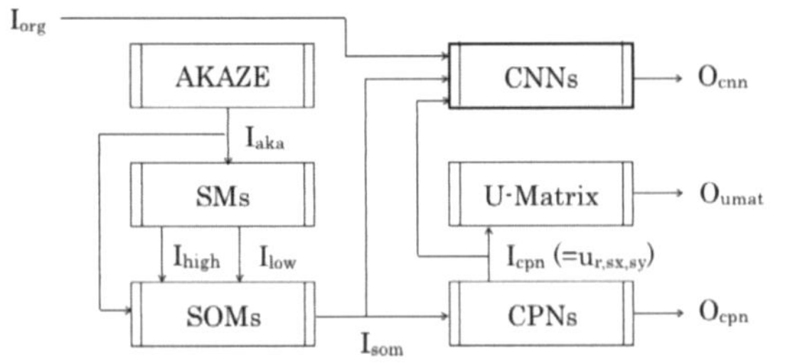

Figure 1. Whole system structure of our proposed framework including data flows among several algorithms.

their proposed model using SIFT and of Convolution Neural Networks (CNNs). They reported that CNNs, which learned using original images, achieved superior accuracy to those which learned using SIFT features with BoF. Mundher et al. [21] proposed a facial expression recognition method using fully connected CNNs combined with dense SIFT. The accuracy of their method was superior to that achieved using the conventional method using CNNs trained using original image features. Both results demonstrated a different tendency for selecting features from scene images used for learning data of CNNs. Actually, the main advances in semantic indoor scene relies on making use of state-of-the-art DNNs. However, we consider that the limitation of DNN-based approaches is inarticulate between input image features and recognition accuracies.

This study was conducted to evaluate combinations of machine-learning-based semantic indoor scene recognition methods and their input features. This paper presents a framework for providing image features of three types according to learning strategies. The experimentally obtained results evaluated using two open benchmark datasets revealed suitable combinations of input features including weights obtained from category maps used for DNNs. We demonstrate a suitable combination of features from scene images used for learning data of CNNs.

The rest of the paper is structured as follows. Sections II and III present our proposed method and an experimental setup including benchmark datasets and evaluation criteria, respectively. Subsequently, Section IV presets evaluation experimental results with discussion. Finally, Section V concludes and highlights future work.

II. Proposed Method

A. Whole architecture

Our proposed supervised-learning-based semantic indoor scene recognition method comprises the following six steps:

1) description of Accelerated KAZE (AKAZE) features,
2) selection of salient regions using SM,
3) generation of BoF using Self-Organizing Maps (SOMs),
4) creation of category maps using Counter Propagation Networks (CPNs),
5) extraction of category boundaries using U-Matrix,
6) and recognition of semantic scenes using DNNs.

Figure 1 depicts the whole system architecture of our proposed framework including data flows among the respective algorithms used for the system. First, local features are extracted from an original input image I_{org} using AKAZE [23] for feature description. Subsequently, high-saliency or low-saliency regions are divided using SMs. Herein, I_{aka} and I_{sm} respectively denote AKAZE features and an image mask of SMs. AKAZE features on high saliency regions I_{high} and those on low saliency regions I_{low} are defined as

$$I_{high} = I_{org} \wedge I_{aka} \wedge I_{sm}, \tag{1}$$

$$I_{low} = I_{org} \wedge I_{aka} \wedge \overline{I_{sm}}. \tag{2}$$

Our method adopts SOMs [24] for BoF. Subsequently, codebooks are created from I_{aka}, I_{high}, and I_{low}. Letting I_{som} a be histogram of SOMs as codebooks, then using I_{som} as input features, category maps are created with CPNs [25]. Letting I_{cpn} be weights of CPNs, then category boundaries are extracted from I_{cpn} using a U-Matrix. For the comparison of recognition accuracies, I_{org}, I_{som}, or I_{cpn} are used as input features for CNNs.

B. AKAZE descriptor

For conventional generic object recognition, SIFT [14] has been used widely for use as an outstanding descriptor of local features. Actually, SIFT descriptors are robust for rotation, scale, position, and brightness changes not only from a static image, but also from dynamic images. Alcantarilla et al. [22] proposed KAZE using nonlinear scale space as a feature that exceeded the SIFT performance. Moreover, they proposed Accelerated-KAZE (AKAZE) [23], which accelerated construction of nonlinear scale spaces of KAZE. In contrast to SIFT, AKAZE was demonstrated as being approximately three times faster, although maintaining equivalent performance and accuracy. Therefore, we use AKAZE, which is suitable for indoor environments where environmental changes occurred frequently.

C. SMs

Briefly, the procedures of SMs include the following five steps. First, a pyramid image is created from I_{org}. Second a Gaussian filter is applied to the pyramid image. Third, images of the respective components of color phase, brightness, and direction are created. Fourth, Feature Maps (FMs) are created as visual features of each component with center-surround and normalization operations. Finally, SMs are obtained from a Winner-Take-All (WTA) competition for the linear summation of FMs.

D. BoF

For this study, we used SOMs to create codebooks. Fig. 2 presents our codebook creation procedure from I_{aka} as BoF. The following is the SOM learning algorithm.

Let $x_p(t)$ be output from the input layer unit p $(1 \leq p \leq P)$ at time t. As input features, I_{aka}, I_{high}, and I_{low} are given to $x_p(t)$. Let $w_{p,q}(t)$ be a weight from p to mapping layer unit q $(1 \leq q \leq Q)$ at time t. Herein, P and Q respectively denote the total numbers of input layer units and mapping layer units. Before learning, $w_{p,q}(t)$ are randomly initialized. Using the Euclidean distance between $x_p(t)$ and $w_{p,q}(t)$, a winner unit $c_q(t)$ is sought for the following.

$$c_q(t) = \underset{1 \leq q \leq Q}{\operatorname{argmin}} \sqrt{\sum_{p=1}^{P} (x_p(t) - w_{p,q}(t))^2}. \tag{3}$$

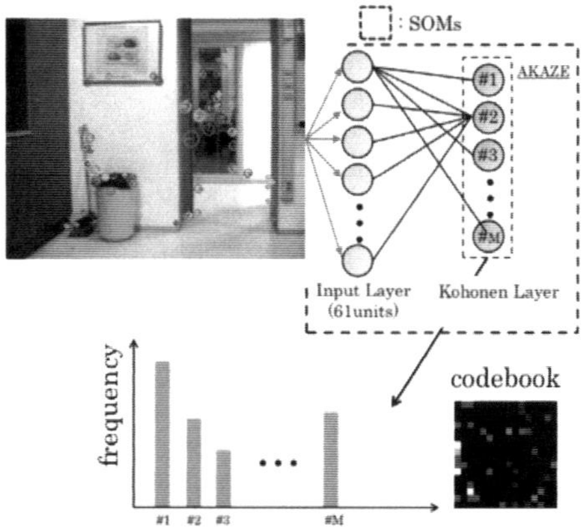

Figure 2. Codebook creation procedure using SOMs from I_{aka} as BoF.

A neighborhood region $\psi_{som}(t)$ is set from the center of c_q as the following.

$$\psi_{som}(t) = \lfloor \psi_{som}(0) \cdot Q \cdot \left(1 - \frac{t}{Z_{som}}\right) + 0.5 \rfloor, \quad (4)$$

where Z_{som} is the maximum learning iteration. Subsequently, $w_{p,q}(t)$ in $\psi_{som}(t)$ is updated as

$$w_{p,q}(t+1) = w_{p,q}(t) + \alpha(t)(x_p(t) - w_{p,q}(t)), \quad (5)$$

where $\alpha(t)$ is a learning coefficient that is decreasing according to the learning progress.

After learning, test data are entered to the input layer. A winner unit is used for voting to create a histogram as a codebook: I_{som}. We obtained I_{som} of two types: a 1-Dimensional (1D) codebook using a 1D category map and a 2D codebook using a 2D category map. For creating I_{som}, the index of the mapping layer is changed to qx and qy.

E. CPNs

We create a category map using CPNs. For learning CPNs, I_{som} are entered to the input layer of CPNs as input features. Let $y_r(t)$ be output from the input layer unit r $(1 \leq r \leq R)$ at time t. Let $w_{r,s}(t)$ be a weight from r to Kohonen layer unit s $(1 \leq s \leq S)$ at time t. Herein, R and Q respectively denote the total numbers of input layer units and Kohonen layer units. Before learning, $w_{r,s}(t)$ are initialized randomly. Using the Euclidean distance between $y_r(t)$ and $w_{r,s}(t)$, a winner unit $c_s(t)$ is sought for the following.

$$c_s(t) = \underset{1 \leq s \leq S}{\operatorname{argmin}} \sqrt{\sum_{r=1}^{R} (y_r(t) - u_{r,s}(t))^2}. \quad (6)$$

A neighborhood region $\psi_{cpn}(t)$ is set from the center of c_s as the following.

$$\psi_{cpn}(t) = \lfloor \psi_{cpn}(0) \cdot S \cdot \left(1 - \frac{t}{Z_{cpn}}\right) + 0.5 \rfloor, \quad (7)$$

where Z_{cpn} stands for the maximum learning iteration. Subsequently, $u_{r,s}$ and $v_{s,k}$ in $\psi_{cpn}(t)$ is updated as shown below.

$$u_{r,s}(t+1) = u_{r,s}(t) + \beta(t)(y_r(t) - u_{n,m}(t)), \quad (8)$$

Figure 3. Brightness changes in daytime (upper) and nighttime (lower) with similar positions.

$$v_{s,k}(t+1) = v_{s,k}(t) + \gamma(t)(z_l(t) - v^j_{n,m}(t)), \quad (9)$$

where $\beta(t)$ and $\gamma(t)$ are learning coefficients that decrease along with learning progress.

As a learning result, $u_{r,s}$ is used for the input to CNNs. We defined this interface as I_{cpn}.

F. U-Matrix

For this study, we used a 2D Kohonen layer. The unit index s is extended to sx and sy. Category boundaries are extracted from $u_{r,sx,sy}$ using U-Matrix. Based on metric distances between weights, U-Matrix visualizes the spatial distribution of categories from similarity of neighbor units [26]. On a 2D category map of square grids, a unit has eight neighbor units except for boundary units. Assuming U as the similarity calculated using a U-Matrix, then for the component of the horizontal and vertical directions, $U_{h\pm}$ and $U_{v\pm}$ are defined as shown below.

$$U_{h\pm} = \sqrt{\sum_{r=1}^{R} (u_{r,sx,sy} - u_{r,sx\pm1,sy})^2}, \quad (10)$$

$$U_{v\pm} = \sqrt{\sum_{r=1}^{R} (u_{r,sx,sy} - u_{r,sx,sy\pm1})^2}. \quad (11)$$

For the components of the diagonal directions, $U_{d\pm}$ are defined as the following.

$$U_{d\pm} = \frac{1}{2}\sqrt{\sum_{r=1}^{R} (u_{r,sx,sy\pm1} - u_{r,sx\pm1,sy})^2} \quad (12)$$

$$+ \frac{1}{2}\sqrt{\sum_{r=1}^{R} (u_{r,sx\pm1,sy} - u_{r,sx,sy\pm1})^2} \quad (13)$$

G. DNNs

Numerous DNN frameworks are provided. For this study, we used VGG-16 [28] that composed 13 convolutional layers and three fully connected layers. As a mechanism to reduce errors, VGG-16 includes a batch normalization algorithm in each convolutional layer [27]. For general object position identification and classification, VGG-16 demonstrated superior results in large-scale image competitions [28].

III. Experimental Setup

A. Benchmark datasets

Quattoni et al. presented large-scale indoor scene recognition datasets [8]. The database includes 67 indoor categories that collectively include 15,620 images. Although the numbers of images vary among the categories, each category has at least 100 images. Images were obtained using a monocular camera. Therefore, the datasets comprise dispersed images. For a real-world robotics application, it remains a challenging task for a mobile robot to move 67 different places [29].

For this study, we used two open benchmark datasets that comprised time-series images obtained using mobile robots. The first dataset is KTH-IDOL2 [30], which comprises time-series images used for indoor robotics navigation and vision-based position estimation. Indoor scenes are of five categories: a printer area (PA), a corridor (CR), a one-person office (EO), a kitchen (KT), and a two-person office (BO). The image resolution is 320 × 240 pixels. This dataset includes some object changes because images were obtained at time intervals of up to six months in the same environment. Moreover, rotated images were obtained at PA and KT for providing diverse visual information.

The second dataset includes place recognition datasets [29] that comprise time-series images obtained using a monocular camera on a mobile robot. This dataset includes 17 scene categories: 11 categories at York University and the remaining 6 categories at the Coast Capri Hotel. For this study, the York University sub-dataset and the Coast Capri Hotel sub-dataset are abbreviated respectively as YUSD and CHSD. The respective resolutions of the images are 640 × 480 pixels.

As common features of both datasets, two robots of different heights were used for image data acquisition. We used images obtained using a higher robot. Both datasets include diverse image appearances with positional shifts because the robot moved a previously setting route with manual operation. Moreover, images are obtained in daytime and nighttime. Fig. 3 shows brightness changes with similar positions. For this study, we used the both illumination condition images.

B. Evaluation criteria

As evaluation criteria, recognition accuracy R is defined as

$$R = \frac{S_{test}}{N_{test}} \times 100, \qquad (14)$$

where N_{test} and S_{test} respectively denote the numbers of test images and of correct recognition images. For this study, we used Leave-One-Out Cross-Validation (LOOCV) [31] to evaluate the capability of generalization.

IV. Evaluation Experiment using CPNs

A. Saliency for recognition

We evaluated the relations between recognition accuracy and input features of three types: I_{aka}, I_{high}, and I_{low}. Fig. 4 depicts results obtained from a comparison of the recognition accuracy for KTH-IDOL2. The mean recognition accuracies of I_{aka}, I_{high}, and I_{low} were, respectively, 67.8%, 59.3%, and 61.2%. The recognition accuracy of I_{aka} was 8.5 percentage points higher than that of I_{high} and 6.6 percentage points higher than that of I_{low}. This result revealed that I_{aka} was the highest among three feature patterns.

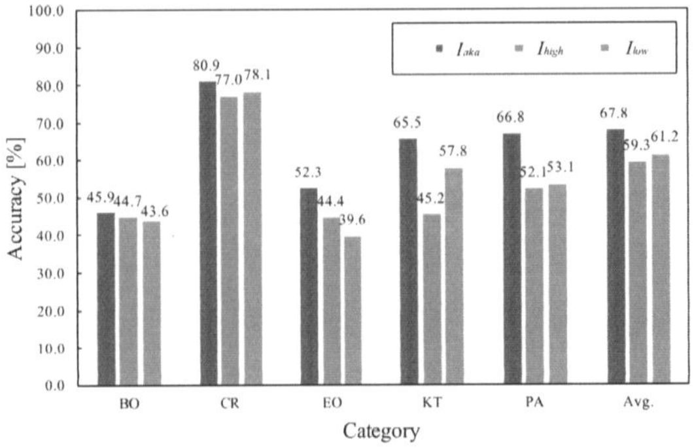

Figure 4. Recognition accuracy in each category for KTH-IDOL2.

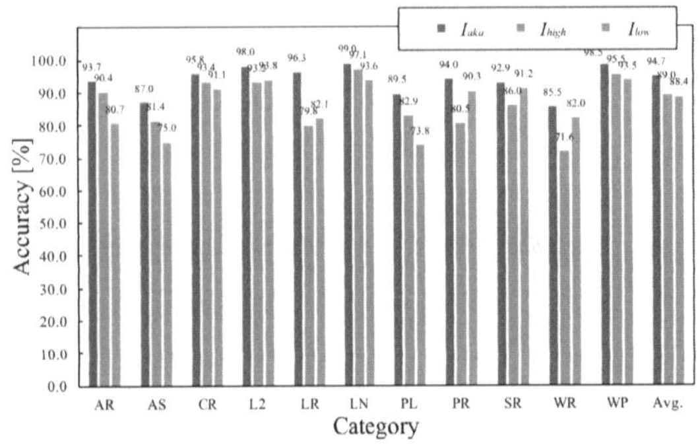

Figure 5. Recognition accuracy in each category for YUSD.

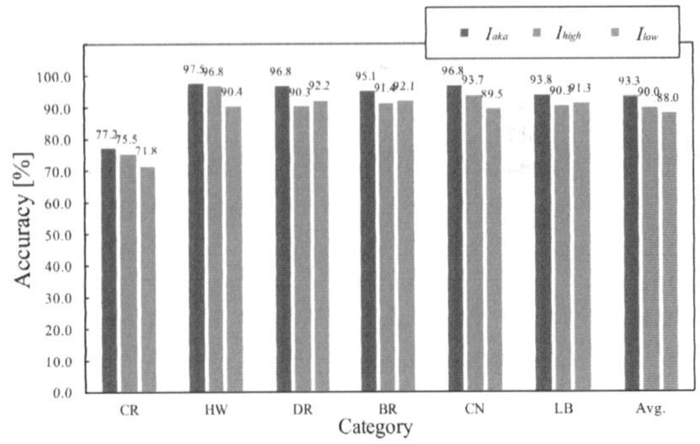

Figure 6. Recognition accuracy in each category for CHSD.

Fig. 5 presents results obtained from a comparison of the recognition accuracy for YUSD. The mean recognition accuracies of I_{aka}, I_{high}, and I_{low} were 94.7%, 89.0%, and 88.4%. The recognition accuracy of I_{aka} was 5.7 percentage points higher than that of I_{high} and 6.3 percentage points higher than that of I_{low}. This result revealed I_{aka} as the highest among three feature patterns.

Fig. 6 presents results obtained for comparison recognition accuracy for CHSD. The mean recognition accuracies of I_{aka}, I_{high}, and I_{low} were 93.3%, 90.0%, and 88.0%. The recognition accuracy of I_{aka} was 3.3 percentage points higher than that of I_{high} and 5.5 percentage points higher than that of I_{low}. Results demonstrated that I_{aka} was the highest among three feature patterns. We obtained the similar tendency for input features. Results also demonstrated that saliency-based

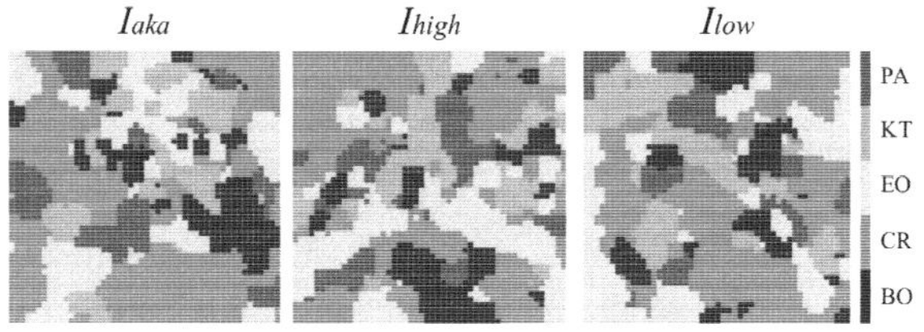

Figure 7. Results of category maps for KTH-IDOL2.

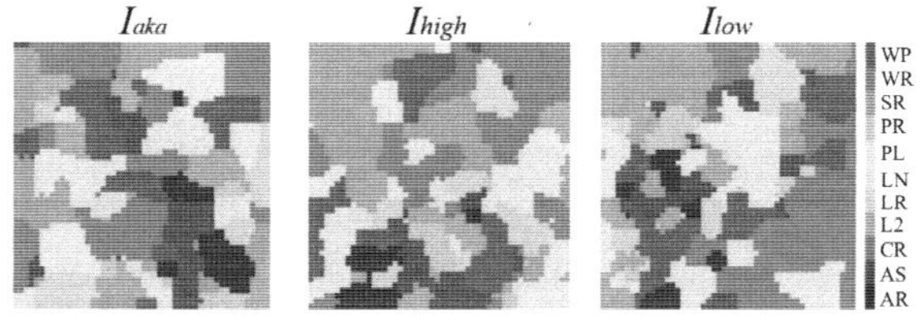

Figure 8. Results of category maps for YUSD.

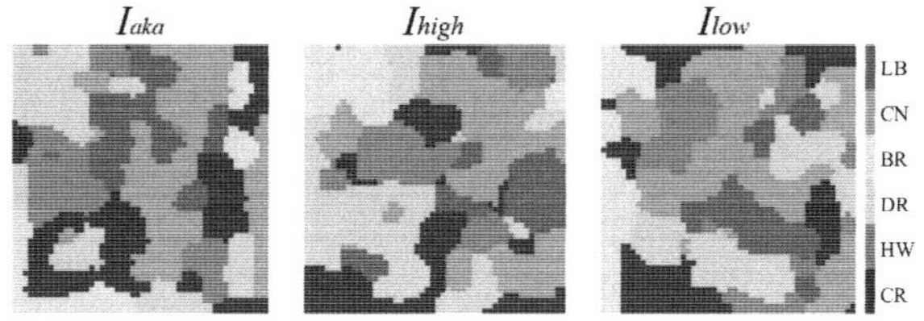

Figure 9. Results of category maps for CHSD.

features dropped recognition accuracy.

B. Category maps

Fig. 7 portrays category maps created from KTH-IDOL2. Unit color patterns correspond to scene category labels. For all feature patterns, scene categories were divided into several independent clusters. Clusters of various shapes and sizes were mixed on the category maps. Moreover, independent clusters consisting of a single unit exist in the maps. Particularly, PA, CR, EO, KT, and CR of I_{aka} respectively comprised 9, 12, 14, 16, and 15 clusters. The CR clusters are larger than those of other categories.

Fig. 8 portrays category maps created from YUSD. As an overall tendency, similar categories are divided into independent clusters that depict scene diversity. Comparison with the result of KTH-IDOL2 reveals that clusters are gathered to particular locations, with few independent units. Fig. 9 displays some category maps created from CHSD. Although positions and sizes differed among categories, the cluster distribution tendency was similar to those of results presented in Fig. 8. The experimentally obtained results revealed that category maps with numerous clusters reflected the complexity of indoor scenes.

C. Category boundary extraction

For analyzing the category relation, we extracted category boundaries using U-Matrix, which calculated the similarity of neighbor units based on the distance of weights between category map units. For enhancing category boundaries, we used the representative automatic image thresholding method reported by Otsu [33]. U-Matrix boundaries are depicted using temperature colors, with high temperature portrayed as red according to the distances among weights.

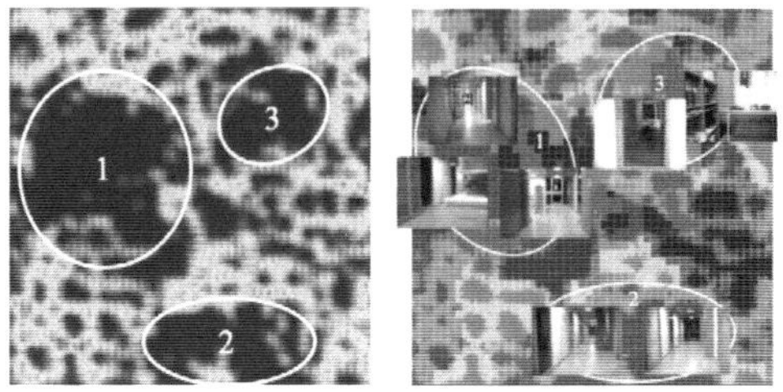

Figure 10. Boundary extraction results and category representative images obtained using U-Matrix.

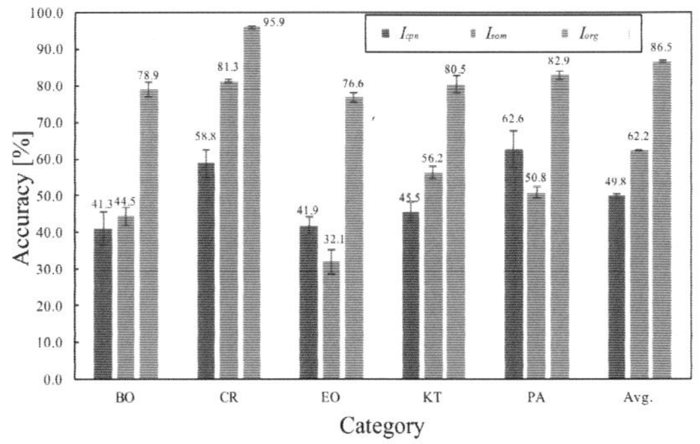

Figure 11. Recognition accuracies and comparison results obtained for each input feature.

The left panel of Fig. 10 depicts boundary extraction results for the results depicted in Fig. 7(a). The category map included three independent regions and several slight regions. For the three independent regions, we assigned labels as Boundaries 1–3 according to the order of sizes. The right panel of Fig. 10 portrays a category map with superimposed boundary extraction results and category representative images. Numerous units were labeled to CR in Boundary 1, especially gathered PA images. In Boundary 3, labels were mixed with all categories.

D. Evaluation Experiment using CNNs

For this evaluation experiment, we used KTH-IDOL2 alone because we obtained sufficient recognition accuracies in place recognition datasets using CPNs.

For learning and validation of CNNs, we used input image features of three types: I_{cpn}, I_{som}, and I_{aka}. Fig. 11 presents results obtained from comparison of the respective scene categories. The mean recognition accuracies of I_{cpn}, I_{som}, and I_{aka} with LOOCV were, respectively, 49.8%, 62.2%, and 86.5%. Comparison of the three results indicates the following I_{aka} obtained the highest recognition accuracies in all categories. Regarding details of respective categories, recognition accuracies of I_{som} in BO, CR, and KT were 3.2, 22.5, and 10.7 percentage points higher than those of I_{cpn}. By contract, recognition accuracies of I_{cpn} in EO and PA were, respectively, 9.8 and 11.8 percentage points higher than those of I_{som}.

V. CONCLUSION

For semantic indoor scene comprehension when used for a mobile robot, we evaluated combinations of supervised machine-learning-based methods and input features using AKAZE, SMs, SOMs, CPNs, U-Matrix, and DNNs. After optimizing the parameters and input features, we conducted two experiments using CPNs and CNNs as a recognizer using open benchmark datasets comprising time-series images The experimentally obtained results obtained using CPNs revealed that the mean recognition accuracy of I_{aka} was higher than those of I_{high} and I_{low} in all categories. Several clusters were created on category maps with designated complexity of scenes. The experimentally obtained results obtained using CNNs revealed that higher recognition accuracy was obtainable using original time-series images for learning.

For our future work, we expect to improve the recognition accuracy to reduce false recognition around scene-switching zones. The relation between processing time and recognition accuracy must be assessed with an assumption of adaptation to the real environment. Moreover, future studies must assess recognition when using cameras with spherical lenses. Furthermore, we will implement our proposed framework to a human-symbiotic robot for the conduct of evaluation experiments in an actual environment.

REFERENCES

[1] K. Koch et al., "How Much the Eye Tells the Brain," *Current Biology*, vol. 16, pp. 1428–1434, 2006.

[2] A.M. Treisman and G. Gelade, "A Feature-Integration Theory of Attention," *Cognitive Psychology*, vol. 12, no. 1, pp. 97–136, 1980.

[3] C. Koch and S. Ullman, "Shifts in Selective Visual Attention: Towards the Underlying Neural Circuitry," *Human Neurobiology*, vol. 4, no. 4, pp. 219–227, 1985.

[4] L. Itti, C. Koch, and E. Niebur, "A Model of Saliency-Based Visual Attention for Rapid Scene Analysis," *IEEE Trans. Pattern Analysis and Machine Intelligence*, vol. 20, no. 11, pp. 1254–1259, 1998.

[5] A. Borji and L. Itti, "State-of-the-Art in Visual Attention Modeling," *IEEE Trans. Pattern Analysis and Machine Intelligence*, vol. 35, no. 1, pp. 185–207, 2013.

[6] H. Madokoro, K. Sato, and N. Shimoi, "Semantic Indoor Scene and Position Recognition Based on Visual Landmarks Obtained from Visual Saliency without Human Effects," *Robotics*, vol. 8, no. 1, pp. 1–24, 2019.

[7] C. Siagian and L. Itti, "Rapid Biologically Inspired Scene Classification Using Features Shared with Visual Attention," *IEEE Trans. Pattern Analysis and Machine Intelligence*, vol. 29, no. 2, pp. 300–312, 2007.

[8] A. Quattoni and A. Torralba, "Recognizing Indoor Scenes," *Proc. Computer Vision and Pattern Recognition*, pp. 413–420, 2009.

[9] A. Torralba, K.P. Murphy, W.T. Freeman, and M.A. Rubin, "Context-Based Vision System for Place and Object Recognition," *Proc. IEEE International Conference Computer Vision*, pp. 1023–1029, 2003.

[10] H. Madokoro, Y. Utsumi, and K. Sato, "Unsupervised Indoor Scene Classification Based on Context for a Mobile Robot (in Japanese)," *Journal of the Robotics Society of Japan*, vol. 31, no. 9, pp. 918–927, 2013.
[?] S. Lazebnik, C. Schmid and J. Ponce, "Beyond Bags of Features: Spatial Pyramid Matching for Recognizing Natural Scene Categories," *Proc. Computer Vision and Pattern Recognition*, pp. 2169–2178, 2016.

[11] A. Krizhevsky, I. Sutskever, and G. Hinton, "ImageNet Classification with Deep Convolutional Neural Networks," *Advances in Neural Information Processing Systems*, vol. 25, pp. 1097–1105, 2012.

[12] A. Shokoufandeh, I. Marsic, and S.J. Dickinson, "View-Based Object Recognition Using Saliency Maps," *Image and Vision Computing*, vol. 17, pp. 445–460, 1999.

[13] D. Walthera and C. Koch, "Modeling Attention to Salient Proto-Objects," *Neural Networks*, vol. 19, no. 9, pp. 1395–1407, 2006.

[14] D.G. Lowe, "Object Recognition from Local Scale-Invariant Features," *Proc. IEEE International Conference Computer Vision*, vol. 2, pp. 1150–1157, 1999.

[15] M. Agrawal and K. Konolige, "Real-time Localization in Outdoor Environments using Stereo Vision and Inexpensive GPS," *Proc. 18th International Conference on Pattern Recognition*, pp. 1063–1068, 2006.

[16] M. Fornoni and B. Caputo, "Indoor Scene Recognition using Task and Saliency-driven Feature Pooling," *Proc. British Machine Vision Conference*, pp. 1–12, 2012.

[17] C. Cortes and V. Vapnik, "Support-Vector Networks," *Machine Learning*, vol. 20, no. 3, pp. 273–297, 1995.

[18] T. Botterill, S. Mills, and R. Green, "Speeded-up Bag-of-Words algorithm for robot localisation through scene recognition," *Proc. 23rd International Conference Image and Vision Computing*, pp. 1–6, 2008.

[19] H. Bay, T. Tuytelaars, and L.V. Gool, "Surf: Speeded Up Robust Features," *Proc. European Conference on Computer Vision*, pp. 404–417, 2006.

[20] V. Sachdeva et al., "Performance Evaluation of SIFT and Convolutional Neural Network for Image Retrieval," *(IJACSA) International Journal of Advanced Computer Science and Applications*, vol. 8, no. 12, pp. 518–523, 2017.

[21] M. Al-Shabi, W. P. Cheah, and T. Connie, "Facial Expression Recognition Using a Hybrid CNN–SIFT Aggregator," *Proc. International Workshop on Multi-disciplinary Trends in Artificial Intelligence*, pp. 139–149, 2017.

[22] P.F. Alcantarilla, A. Bartoli, and A.J. Davison, "KAZE Features," *European Conference on Computer Vision*, pp. 214–227, 2012.

[23] P.F. Alcantarilla, J. Nuevo, and A. Bartoli, "Fast Explicit Diffusion for Accelerated Features in Nonlinear Scale Spaces," *British Machine Vision Conference*, pp. 1–12, 2013.

[24] T. Kohonen, "Self-Organized formation of Topologically Correct Feature Maps," *Biological Cybernetics*, vol. 43, no. 1, pp. 59–69, 1982.

[25] R. H. Nielsen, "Counterpropagation networks," *Applied Optics*, vol. 26, pp. 4979–4983, 1987.

[26] A. Ultsch, "Clustering with SOM U C," *Proc. Workshop on Self-Organizing Maps*, pp. 75–82, 2005.

[27] S. Ioffe and C. Szegedy, "Batch Normalization: Accelerating Deep Network Training by Reducing Internal Covariate Shift," *Proc. the 32nd International Conference on International Conference on Machine Learning*, vol. 37, pp. 448–456, 2015.

[28] K. Simonyan and A. Zisserman, "Very Deep Convolutional Networks for Large-Scale Image Recognition," *Proc. 3rd IAPR Asian Conference on Pattern Recognition*, pp. 730–734, 2015.

[29] R. Sahdev and J.K. Tsotos, "Indoor Place Recognition System for Localization of Mobile Robots," *Proc. 13th Conference on Computer and Robot Vision*, pp. 53–60, 2016.

[30] J. Luo, A. Pronobis, B. Caputo, and P. Jensfelt, "The KTHIDOL2 Database," *Technical Report CVAP304, KTH Royal Institute of Technology, CVAP/CAS*, 2006.

[31] R. Kohavi, "A Study of Cross-Validation and Bootstrap for Accuracy Estimation and Model Selection," *Proc. Fourteenth International Joint Conference on Artificial Intelligence*, vol. 2, no. 12, pp. 1137–1143, 1995.

[32] H. Madokoro, N. Shimoi, and K. Sato, "Adaptive Category Mapping Networks for All- Mode Topological Feature Learning Used for Mobile Robot Vision," *Proc. 23rd IEEE International Symposium on Robot and Human Interactive Communication*, pp. 678–683, 2014.

[33] N. Otsu, "A Threshold Selection Method From Gray-Level Histograms," *IEEE Trans. System, Man, and Cybernetics*, vol. 9, no. 1, pp. 62–66, 1979.

[34] H. Madokoro and K. Sato, "Visualizing Support Vectors and Topological Data Mapping for Improved Generalization Capabilities," *Proc. IEEE World Congress on Computational Intelligence*, pp. 4226–4232, 2010.

Re-Planning of Bus Timetable Based on Route Search Log to Get on Now

Toshihiko Sasama†‡, Bhattacherjee Rupali†, Takao Kawamura†‡, Kazunori Sugahara†‡
†Graduate School of Sustainability Science,
‡Cross-informatics Research Center,
Tottori University
4-101 Tottori City, Tottori 680-8552, Japan
e-mail: sasama@tottori-u.ac.jp, m19j4063h@edu.tottori-u.ac.jp, kawamura@tottori-u.ac.jp, sugahara@tottori-u.ac.jp

Abstract—**There are many web services developed for public transport recently. We developed the "Busnet" in 2006, which is a path planning system for route buses and trains in Tottori prefecture, Japan. This system search includes about 8,500 bus stops and stations and about 1,000 route search requests per day. These route searches of recent years show that people used the Busnet for searching "Now". As smartphone users increased, make plan for tomorrows is in a minority, and route search results have a lot of waiting time for riding because the number of bus is small. Then we get the direct data of waiting time from this search log. In this paper, for reducing these waiting times, we consider the possibility to propose a plan to remake bus timetable that mean to shift departure time of each bus, from analysis of this daily route search log. As a result, to shift median value of each bus's waiting times reduced average of waiting times by 5 minutes, otherwise, results in some conditions using Genetic Algorithm (GA) are reduced or increased by few minutes.**

Keywords-Busnet; route search; log analysis; optimization; genetic algorithm.

I. Introduction

Public transport systems are important for people who do not have a car, such as children and old people. However, in rural area, bus services and trains become unprofitable and as a result some lines are abolished or the number of buses decreased. This causes inconvenience and no one use buses, making it further unprofitable. For these reasons, we need to improve the convenience of using buses and stop the decline of bus usage.

The "Busnet" is a path planning web service system for buses and trains in Tottori prefecture, Japan for improving convenience [1]. It collaborates with bus companies and has some feature functions. One function is the Global Positioning System (GPS) tracing [2]. Each bus driver has a smartphone and enters a route-ID that is specified by each bus company when starts running on the route. A smartphone sends latitude and longitude using browser and JavaScript code to the server, and the Busnet plots real time bus positions on map web pages. From bus timetable information and nearest bus stop information, this system calculates delays of buses every minute and provides this information to the end users. Other functions are to generate index for route search to shorten search time, to mount a touch screen computer terminal in front of the station for visitors to introduce our service and try it out.

The last function of this system is the web view for smartphones. In the first place we generate only character (no-image and no-Cascading Style Sheets (CSS)) Hyper Text Markup Language (HTML) to access from old mobile phones. As android phone becomes popular, we generate and distribute search tools of android application [3][4]. However, due to performance improvements of smartphones and development of JavaScript and CSS library, we drop android only application, and rebuild web pages that can be used on any computer and mobile Operating System (OS) using responsive web design. From this system log, most users access from smartphones, and in many searched requests "departure time" was set to the current time. This can be interpreted as meaning users searching on their smartphone for the next arriving bus, in other words, that is the log of waiting time to get on. Previously scheduling was based on indirect data, such as ride number survey or questionnaire. In this paper, based on these actual usage data, to reduce waiting time we propose time shift plan of each bus. If one bus schedule shifts forward to reduce some user's waiting time, other users will miss the bus and need to wait for the next bus, and this causes the need to shift the next bus in order to reduce waiting time of these users. In some cases, it is better that the previous bus schedule shift backwards so passengers get on early without changing the schedule of the following bus. To optimize such complex combinations, we try to use Genetic Algorithm (GA).

The rest of this paper is organized as follows. Section II describes the analysis results of the recent route search log. Section III describes the proposal re-planning of bus schedule using the result presented in Section II. Finally, Section IV draws the conclusion and acknowledgement.

II. Statistical Data of Route Search Log

Some results of this system's log analysis were reported at academic workshop. From route search log we found some trends, for example, tourists use it to make plans ahead of time, and local people use it for daily routine. Moreover, most users, about 60%, are smartphone users, not desktop PC and notebook PC. In many cases, about 90%, departure and destination search parameters are bus stops and some landmark, which are probably used by tourists. One can set latitude and longitude as departure or destination in place of a landmark, however these are rare cases. So, one common usage for this system users is to check departure time (= waiting time) using a smartphone while heading to the target bus stop. In rural areas, it is normal the number of buses is 1/hour, and the average of waiting time to get on the bus is about 15 minutes.

III. TIME SHIFT OF BUS SCHEDULE

In some cases, this system shows transfer routes. To simplify the problem, we consider the first transfer landmark as destination in this experiment and consider the request that get on near time from near bus stop.

Fig.1 shows each day's average waiting time of 2019/9/2(Mon) ~ 9/4(Wed) that is labeled "base". It used cleaned logs of smartphones access only, searching from current time ±60 minutes, a bus waiting time of 60 minutes or less, fixed departure is a bus stop, and destination is a bus stop without a stopover (it is not a tourist spot, and not a landmark after transfer). Three columns of Table. 1 show the number of logs when cleaned under the above conditions. For example, on 9/2, 867 requests are arrived totally to the system and the system showed the resultant routes to each request. 593 requests in total requests are from mobile phone users and as shown in Colum (3') 474 busses are examined in this work. These 474 busses are chosen to have same departure and destination bus stops as the resultant route and to have around 60 minutes departure time. Here, the length of the gene in GA search method can be set to 474. A code number of each gene corresponds shifting departure time of each bus. By using GA method, the proposed system tried to find the optimum departure time with the probability of the existence of multiple users on the same bus is about 50%. It means half buses can be scheduled thinking only one user in a plan, and half buses need shared scheduling.

In Fig.1, labeled "median" shows the set shift time to waiting time's median value of each bus. When nobody gets on it, we set shift time to 0. Waiting time's average is under 6 minutes. It is the best in this figure. Situations of others are as follows. GA(15): a code range is ±15 minutes, a mutation rate is 0.1%, a population size is 10, a generation limit is 100, used alternating swap method and discrete generation model, and in fitness evaluation, max waiting time limited to 60 minutes, and when no bus exists to get on is evaluated as this limited max, too. GA(60): same parameters of GA(15) but a code range is ±60 minutes, a population size 50, and a generation limit is 500. GA(max): same parameters of GA(15) but a code range is -1 * max waiting time of that bus ~ 30 minutes. It is better than GA(15) or GA(60). GA(15) and GA(60) are worse than "base".

From results of GA(15) and GA(60), changing a population size and a generation limit are not expected to have effects. From other results adjusting a code range is expected to have effects.

TABLE I. NUMBER OF EXTRACTED LOGS

Date	(1) Search count	(2) Search from mobile	(3) Search forward in 60min (Fitness evaluation)	(3') Bus count around time (Genes length)
9/2	867	593	242	474
9/3	782	463	207	442
9/4	2097	490	250	461

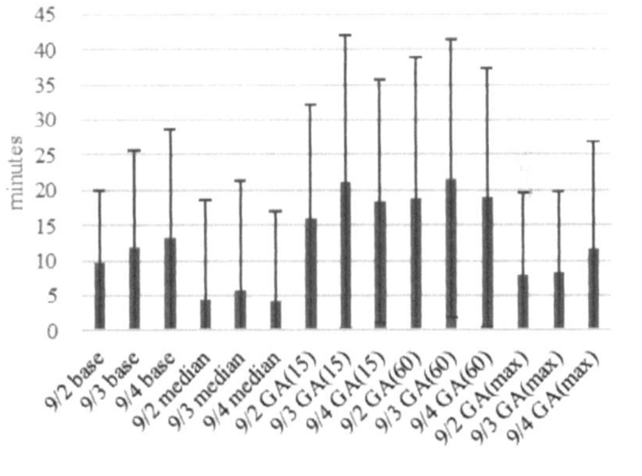

Figure 1. Waiting time's average and standard deviation.

IV. CONCLUSION

In this paper, we selected route search log of web service that a user wants to get on instantly from some bus stop using a smartphone, and we defined it as real waiting time of bus users. Based on it, we proposed new service timetable with shifting departure time according to the GA outputs which makes users convenient with small waiting times. On one day data sets, these were real and small data sets, the set shift time to waiting time's median reduced the average to 5 minutes, and GA optimizations were worked in some code patterns, and were unusable in some cases.

In future work, we need to evaluate large data sets, such as weeks or months that have transfers, many code patterns, analysis of complex combination, and other machine learning optimizations such as neural networks.

ACKNOWLEDGMENT

This work was supported by JSPS KAKENHI Grant Numbers JP17K01256, JP17K06600.

REFERENCES

[1] Nihon Trip LLP, *Busnet.* [Onnline]. Available from: http://ikisaki.jp, 2006 [retrieved: 10, 2019]

[2] M. Ito, T. Kawamura, and K. Sugahara, "Development of an Automatic Vehicle Location System Using Smartphones," IEICE Trans. Japan, vol. J96-D, no 10, pp.2327-2339, 2013.

[3] H. Shibata, M. Ito, T. Kawamura, and K. Sugahara, "Promotion of the Use of Public Transport with Social Media on a Mobile Application," Proceedings of the 10th Asia Pacific Conference on Computer Human Interaction (APCHI 2012), pp. 743-744, 2013.

[4] M. Taketa, M. Ito, T. Kawamura, and K. Sugahara, "Development of Optimized User Interface of Public Transit Navigator for a Smartphone," International Journal of Computer, Electrical, Automation, Control and Information Engineering, vol. 5, no. 11, pp. 1342-1346, 2011.

Statistical Processing of Delay Time of Public Secondary Traffic and its Application to the Operation Plan

Rupali Bhattacherjee†, Toshihiko Sasama†‡, Takao Kawamura†‡ and Kazunori Sugahara†‡

†Graduate School of Sustainability Science, Tottori University

‡Cross-informatics Research Center, Tottori University

4-101 Tottori City, Tottori 680-8552, Japan

email: †m19j4063h@edu.tottori-u.ac.jp, ‡{sasama, kawamura, sugahara}@tottori-u.ac.jp

Abstract— **We have developed and maintained a system called "Busnet" with the aim of contributing to improve the convenience of using public transportation from the standpoint of information engineering. The Busnet is a system that enables route search as its basic function and has a function as a bus location system that shows the position of the running bus. In this paper, we report on a system that grasps the bus operation status by statistically processing the bus location system's log data of the Busnet combining with the weather conditions such as snowfall.**

Keywords-Busnet; Location log data; Statistical processing.

I. INTRODUCTION

In recent years, the declining birthrate and aging population in Japan have become a social problem. In addition, depopulation of local cities is a major issue in close connection with the declining birthrate and aging population. Furthermore, the increase in the number of elderly people living alone is also a problem. These problems are urgent issues for local cities to take measures, and they become a major issue related to the survival of the local city itself. Therefore, although various measures have been taken in local cities, the present situation is that the results have not been achieved easily.

Tottori prefecture, where we live, locates in the Chugoku region of the western end of Honshu, Japan. It is a local city located about a couple of hours away by railroad from Osaka, the second largest city in Japan, and is one of the most decentralized prefectures.

In Tottori prefecture, we are actively working on various problems that occur with depopulation. Maintenance of public second transportation, such as route buses is one of the serious problems for such local cities. As depopulation progresses, the number of public transportation users decreases, and it makes difficult to maintain the number of routes and the busses. When the number of busses decreases, convenience for users decreases. This causes a continuous decrease in the number of users. Therefore, the prefecture provides many subsidies to bus operators and manages to maintain them, but it is financially difficult.

The development of motorization, such as private cars, can be cited as a cause of the decrease of the number of public transportation users. However, traffic accidents caused by elderly people driving cars have not decreased. It is difficult to think of a society that relies on the driving of its own private car, especially in a single living family. From this point of view, we believe that public transportation maintenance by local government such as prefectures and cities is essential to the functioning of an aging society.

II. BUSNET SYSTEM

As a member of a university located in Tottori Prefecture, we have developed and maintained a system called "Busnet" with the aim of contributing to the maintenance of such public transportation from the standpoint of information engineering. The Busnet is a system that uses route search as its basic function and has a function as a bus location system that shows the current locations of the running buses. Several systems have been developed so far for bus and railway route search systems, and many systems are available even today. However, the Busnet system has various functions based on the characteristics of the route bus and are used by many general users. The biggest feature of Busnet is not to show the transfer between bus stops, but to give a route using public transport between the departure point and the destination point including walking route. Bus location function is also one of the biggest features of Busnet. To realize the bus location function, about 300 smart phones are equipped in all buses, and by using their GPS functions the location data of current buses are transferred into a server computer. The bus position information stored on the server will be used for various purposes as log data of location system. In this paper, based on these log data, we analyze travel situations of the route buses in the past and constructed a system to estimate the future travel situations depending on weather information.

III. LOG DATA ANALYSIS OF BUSNET SYSTEM

About 300 smartphones are equipped in all local busses to realize the bus location function in the Busnet and transmit their current positions about every 20 seconds. On the server, location information of latitude and longitude of all bus stops, route information of each bus, operation timetable, etc., are stored. From the location information sent from each bus and the data on the server, it is possible to know which bus has passed through which bus stop, or the delay status of each bus.

There are 315 bus routes data and 8178 bus stops data stored on the Busnet server, and the log data recorded in one day is about 130 Mbytes. In addition, it is necessary to respond to changes in bus service routes and changes in bus stops locations for update of the schedule several times each year. This paper is based on three years of data, about 150 Gbytes.

The operation status of the buses is determined by obtaining the delay time at the bus stop of each bus. Since travel data from the bus is sent about every 20 seconds, these are not always sent from the bus stop locations. For this reason, data pairs before and after the actual bus stop are extracted from the log data, and the passage time at the bus stop position is calculated by linear interpolation from the transmission time and the latitude / longitude value. By comparing this value with the operation timetable on the server, the delay status of each bus can be determined.

Figures 1 and 2 show examples of the delay situation obtained by using proposed system. Figure 1 shows the delay situation of the all bus stops in the prefecture at 10:00 am on November 23, 2016 and Figure 2 shows the situation on February 10, 2017. In these figures, the bus delay time at each bus stop is indicated by a colored circle. It is green when the delay time is short and red when it is long, i.e., more than 30-minutes delay. Although Figure 1 shows the delay situation in the absence of snow even in winter, it can be seen that green circles are displayed at almost all location. On the other hand, in Figure 2, it can be seen that there are several delays mainly at bus stops in the mountains area due to snow. The delay time at each bus stop at a certain time indicates the delay time of the bus that passed immediately before the specified time. Considering the bus stops included in many bus routes, the delay time differs depending on the travel route of the passed bus. That is, the bus traveling in the urban area does not have a large delay time, but in the case of a bus traveling in the mountain area, the delay time tends to be long. In this system, in consideration of these, it is devised so that not only specification of date and time but also specification of bus route etc., can be considered to obtain past delay situation.

IV. Conclusion

This paper reports the construction of a system that calculates the delay time of a route bus in a specific time zone at a specific bus stop based on data from the past three years. By using the results obtained by the proposed method together with weather information and learning by various AI methods, it is possible to estimate the delay information of the future bus. Predicting bus delays based on the weather at that time provides useful information to the users. In addition, indicating how much delay has occurred in which regional bus route during snowfall based on past results is important information for route managers such as prefecture road staffs and bus companies. This will give useful information in deciding which road to manage intensively.

Acknowledgment

This work was supported by JSPS KAKENHI Grant Numbers JP17K01256, JP17K06600.

References

[1] Nihon Trip LLP, *Busnet*. [Online]. Available from: http://ikisaki.jp, 2006 [retrieved: 10, 2019]

[2] H. Shibata, M. Ito, T. Kawamura, and K. Sugahara, "Promotion of the Use of Public Transport with Social Media on a Mobile Application," Proceedings of the 10th Asia Pacific Conference on Conputer Human Interaction (APCHI 2012), pp. 743-744, 2013.

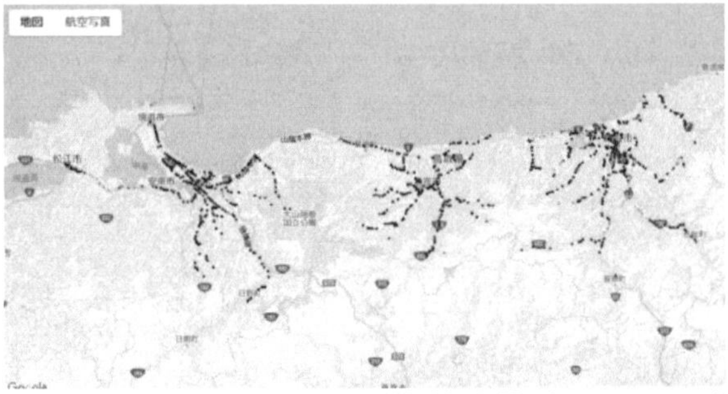

Figure 1. Bus delay on November 23, 2016 (Not in snow season)

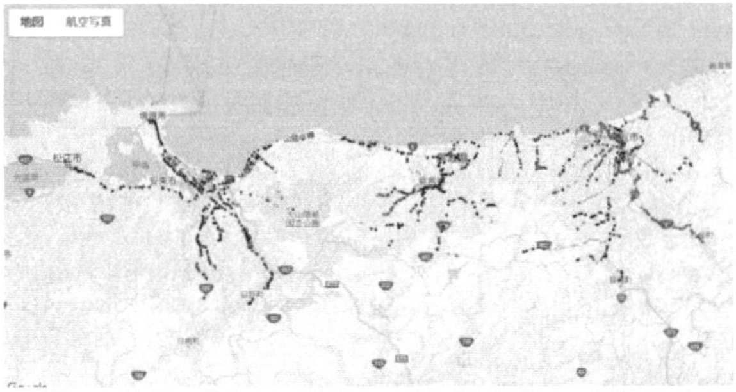

Figure 2. Bus delay on February 10, 2017 (Snowfall time)

Computer Analysis of World Chess Championship Players

Oscar Romero
Universitat Politecnica de Valencia
Valencia, Spain
E-mail: -oromero@dcom.upv.es

Lorena Parra
Universitat Politecnica de Valencia
Valencia, Spain
E-mail: -loparbo@doctor.upv.es

Jose Fernando Cuenca
Chess24
Madrid, España
E-mail: -Jose.fernando.cuenca@gmail.com

Jaime Lloret
Universitat Politecnica de Valencia
Valencia, Spain
E-mail: -jlloret@dcom.upv.es

Abstract— **In some sports, it is difficult to know who has been the best winner of the world championship. In athletism, it is not so difficult because world records clearly state which is the best mark. Nevertheless, in the case of chess, it is challenging to know who has been the best world chess championship player. Nowadays, it is well known that many chess engines can beat the best chess players in the world, so we can use it for comparison purposes. In this paper, we use one of the best chess engines, Stockfish 10, in order to know which world chess championship player is the best of all time. We have compared their moves during the world championship with the ones suggested by the chess engine in each game. Results show how good each one of them was, compared with Stockfish 10, which player obtained the greatest percentage of best moves during their games, how the quality of their moves evolved during the games and the average percentage of best moves throughout the games.**

Keywords-Chess; Computer Analysis; World Chess Championship.

I. INTRODUCTION

Chess is a strategy board game that involves two players. It is one of the most popular strategy games played across the globe. Modern chess is based on the rules adopted in Spain in the 15th century [1]. It is played on a checkered board with 64 squares and includes 6 different types of pieces. Each player starts with 16 pieces and the player who has the white pieces starts the game by moving first. The number of game states that can be reached through a legal play was estimated to be around 10^{46} [2]. Because of its complexity, chess has been used as a testbed for most of the Artificial Intelligence (AI) systems.

It 1947, Alan Turing designed a program to play chess for the first time in history. Since 1950, different programs have been developed to play chess. Different strategies have been applied to improve their results. While in 1960 chess programs only can beat amateur players, in 1990 those programs have become powerful and can win chess masters [3].

In the last decades, chess players have evolved and improved using chess programs to practice and learn. The Elo is a method used to calculate the skills of a chess player. The best players can foresee the development of a game 10 to 15 moves to decide the best strategy [4]. The current world champion (since 2013), Magnus Carlsen, has an Elo rating of 2882 [5]. On the other hand, the current versions of the best chess programs have more than 3400 [6].

In 2006, Guid and Bratko used CRAFTY, a chess program, to evaluate the quality of chess players regardless of the game score [7]. They evaluate players of the World Chess Championships (WCCs). CRAFTY calculates the best move for each given position and compare the move that did the players with the best move and assign an average error to each player. Their results were strongly criticized because some of the best players as Fischer were placed as weaker than players who only won the WCC one year. On the other hand, their results were disputed as the engine used to calculate the best moves was considered weaker than most of the analyzed players.

In this paper, we are going to analyze the performance of all chess players in the WCC, like the work presented by M. Guid and I. Bratko in 2006, but using a stronger engine. Our hypothesis is that the results obtained in the past were skewed by the used engine. Nowadays, computers are more powerful and probably the best move calculated in the past will be something different than the best move calculated in this paper. Therefore, the average error for each player may be different. We use all the games of the WCC, from 1886 to 2018, and the chess engine is configured with a depth of 28. A total of 20 computers were used to calculate the average error of each player and some other parameters. Then, the results of the average error or each player are compared. Finally, our results will be compared with the results obtained in the past to evaluate the ranking of best chess players according to their average error change.

The remaining of this paper is structured as follows. Section 2 describes the related work. Section 3 details the material and methods utilized. The results are shown in Section 4. Finally, Section 5 presents the conclusion and future work.

II. RELATED WORK

In this section, we are going to summarize the papers which deal with the topic of chess, algorithms and AI.

Guid and Bratko compared the quality of different chess players of the WCC [7]. They used the CRAFTY program. CRAFTY evaluated the individual move realized by each player. They used the games played in the WCC from 1886 to 2006. CRAFTY used a depth of 12 moves in the analyses. The parameters used to compare the players were the average error, % of blunders, complexity expected error, % of best moves and difference between best moves. Their results showed that Capablanca was the best player and Fischer was the one with the highest difference between best moves.

Ribeiro et al. [4] in 2013 used CRAFTY (Elo rating of 2950) to evaluate the white player advantage move-by-move. They used 73,444 high-level chess matches available in Portable Game Notation (PGN) Mentor. CRAFTY calculated de advantage in terms of the number of remaining pieces and its placement. A positive value indicated that the white player has an advantage, while the negative value indicated that is the black player who has the advantage. Their results included the advantage, mean of advantage and variance of advantage along with the game in each match. They compare the data from different periods, 1857-1918, 1919-1949 and 1950-2011 to evaluate the changes in the chess players. Their results suggested that the opening stage of a match is becoming longer and pointed out that this might be related to a collective learning process.

On the other hand, many authors used chess to test and train AI systems. One example is the work proposed by Vázquez-Fernández et al. in 2011 [8]. They proposed a method for tuning the weights of the evaluation function of chess based on evolutionary programming. They used 10 different players and 6 training games. They used as "theoretical" values: 100 (pawn (fixed value)), 300 (knight), 330 (bishop), 500 (rook) and 900 (queen). As mobility, a weight of 10, and bounds of [0,300], was used. After 50 generations, the weight changed to 100 (pawn), 310.89 (knight), 325.32 (bishop), 514.92 (rook), 841.61 (queen) and 5.62 (mobility). Finally, their engine was tested playing 10 games with a human player. It is important to note that, in this paper, the Elo of the used engine was 1463. The Elo of the human who played with the engine was 1737.

One year later, Vázquez-Fernández et al. [3] presented how their engine reaches an Elo ranking of 2425 after readjusting the weights. Moreover, they used the Hooke-Jeeves algorithm [9] in order to pursue the adjustment of the weights according to the best virtual players.

In 2014, Vecek et al. [10] presented a comparison between different evolutionary algorithms. They proposed to use Chess Rating System for Evolutionary Algorithms (CRS4EAs) instead of the typical Null Hypothesis Significance Testing (NHST). They claimed that NHST was often misused and misinterpreted. The CRS4EAs was planned as a tournament in which the algorithms are the players and the solutions of algorithms as the game outcome. A total of 15 evolutionary algorithms were tested. The best evolutionary algorithm according to CRS4EAs was the jDE/rand/1/bin (it was the second according to NHST). According to the positions, 9 out of 15 obtained the same position with both methods. Their results revealed that CRS4EAs is comparable with NHST, but it is easier to use and it is less sensitive to outliers.

In recent years, machine learning techniques have been applied to strategy games, and then, trying to play better than static algorithms. Alphago Zero was developed to play go, a simple game, with simple rules, but with many possible moves. It is an artificial intelligence, based on deep learning and neuronal networks. After a deep training, it was able to win the best human player on year 2016. In chess, several artificial intelligences have been developed. One of the most important is Leela Chess Zero (LCZero), also based on neuronal networks. After an intense training, it became the champion in Top Chess Engine Champion (TCEC) season 15, in May 2019, where Stockfish, one of the best static algorithms, obtained the second position. Recently, Stockfish has been improved and it is the current TCEC champion, season 16, celebrated on October 2019. This time, LCZero was in second position. Probably both of them will be improved again, and perhaps they will get an ELO above of 4000 very soon.

III. TEST BENCH AND METHOD

In this work, we have evaluated all players in all world chess championships, from 1886 to 2018. Today, there are chess engines that play clearly better than the best human players. Thus, using one of those chess engines we can evaluate a human player. For this analysis, we get the score of each move and compare it with the best move obtained by the engine to get the human player error. From the information provided by the chess engine, we can extract additional information such as if the human selected the first, second, etc. best move.

A. *Test Bench*

The chess engine selected for this study is Stockfish 64 bits Version 10, one of the strongest engines in early 2019. We have created a program, using the Universal Chess Interface (UCI) protocol to communicate with the chess engine. The feature of the computers used to perform the test was intel i5, 8th Gen, at 2.8 GHz. One of the most important parameters to configure the engine is the depth. We used a depth of 28 in order to meet the time requirements (2 hours for 40 minutes plus 1 hour every new 20 moves, or 90 minutes plus 30 seconds every move) for each game taking into account the computer features. The chess engine and computer features provide us a good rating, and clearly, this engine beats the Crafty engine used in [7]. We tested other depths, like 29 and 30, but the results were similar, although they needed very much more calculation time. Then, with a depth of 28 and the used hardware, the average move evaluation time was 3 minutes per move or 5 hours per game. There was also the option to set up a fixed time per move or game, but obviously this would provide different results in different computers, or even in the same computer, because the actual time used by the engine would depend on the load of the computer, that may vary for different reasons (status of Operative System, running processes, RAM memory, etc.).

When our program is analyzing a game, it evaluates the human player move, and it compares with the best move given by the engine. Then, the difference will be the error made by the human, if ever. Also, the program will tell us if the human-made the best, the second-best, etc. move.

In total, near 1000 games were analyzed, employing almost 5000 hours by the 20 computers with exactly the same features, for 10 days.

For the analysis, some situations have been taking into account. The first moves have been widely studied, and chess players usually play opening books. The evaluation of these first moves would not add too much information to this study. Thus, we decide to start the analysis from move number 7, that is, we have not evaluated the first 12 moves (6 from the white and 6 from the black).

Another important decision is when to stop the analysis of a game. There may be a moment that the evaluation of the position is high (either positive por white pieces or negative por black pieces) before the end of the game. Under this situation, the white player may not play the best move, for example, because it may take a lot of time to find it, and it may be enough with a weaker move, fast to calculate, and good enough to keep the big advantage. We selected the limit of 2 white pieces (-2 for black pieces). On the other hand, if white player is losing, even for more than 2 (white position evaluation lower than -2) we will continue analysing the game, because the player will try to play the best move, trying not to lose the game (the same for black pieces with a score of 2 or more).

In other studies like [7], complexity had been analyzed. But in this paper, we are focused on the evaluation of each player, regardless of complexity, present material, or type of opening, for example. To get good results in all these situations is part of the skill of the player. In this way, blunders are also evaluated, when it may cause draw or lose a game. Not to make blunders is also part of the skill of the player.

IV. RESULTS

In this section, we have analyzed the average error for each player (compared with the move suggested by Stockfish version 10), the percentage of best moves performed during the game, the evolution of each player along the games (from past to present), for those that have played more than one world chess championship, and the average of best moves vs number of moves.

A. *Average error*

The average error is the difference between the evaluation of the human player and the best move provided by the chess engine. The formula used is

$$\text{Mean error} = \frac{\sum|\text{best move evaluation} - \text{player move evaluation}|}{\text{number of moves}} \quad (1)$$

Figure 1 shows the average errors for all players in all world championships. As expected from the results in the last years, Magnus Carlsen is the top one chess player. Other present players like Caruana and Karjakin show good performance. Famous players like Kasparov, Karpov, and Fischer, although not in the top five, show good results, with an error average lower than 0.11.

Figure 2 shows the comparison of the results from this study and results from [6], thus, showing the world champions up to 2006. Results are similar, but the study of 2006 is giving in general higher average error, the mean average error of players was 0.143 according to the results of 2006 and 0.14 according to results of 2019.

It is interesting to discuss the evaluations for very important players like Kasparov, Fischer, where the difference between both studies is almost 30%, and also Karpov, with a difference of 16%. According to this study, that is more precise than the previous one, these three players have a good rating, as they have shown in their tournaments. On the other hand, players like Lasker and Smyslov had an over-evaluation in the past, and the new study shows that they have actually a lower play strength.

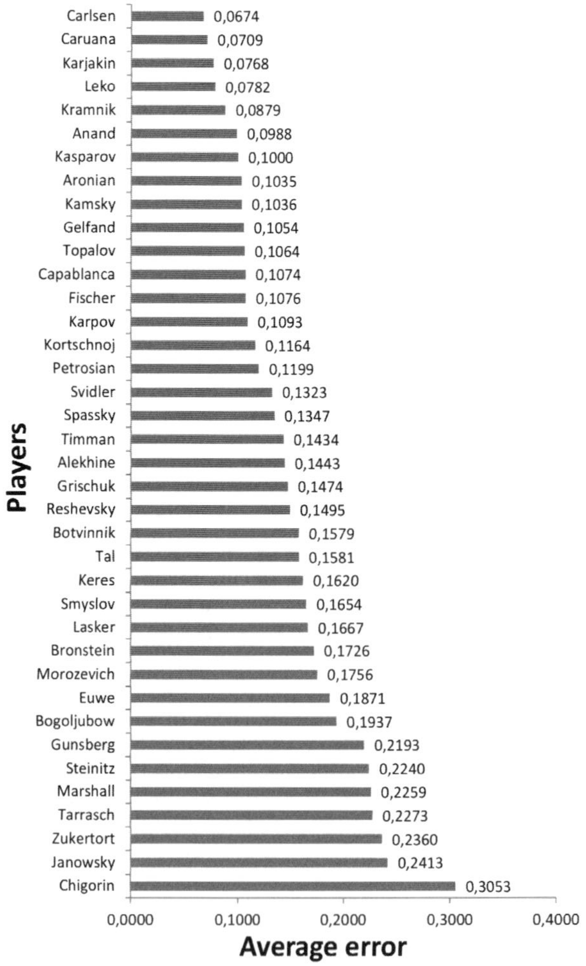

Figure 1. Comparison of players in terms of average error.

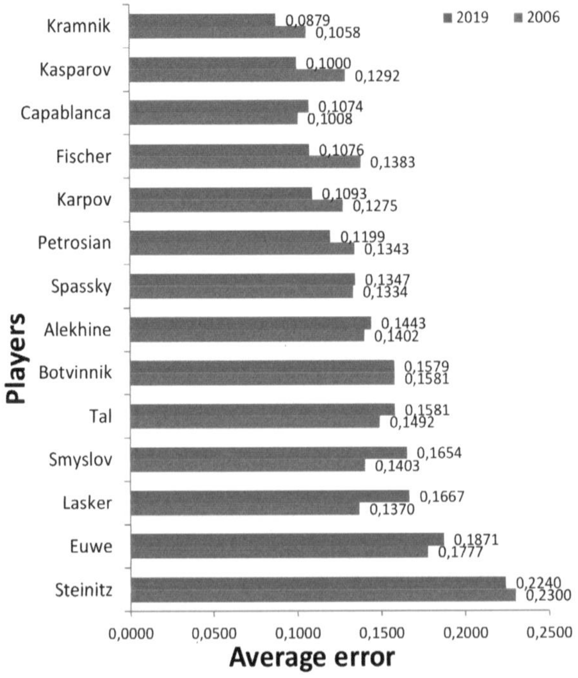

Figure 2. Comparison of average errors calculated in 2006 [7] and 2019.

B. Player evolution along games over the time

The quality of a player may change with time. In this subsection, we show the evolution of some players along the time, showing how the average error changes with the games played along the time. In this section, we have analyzed only those players who have played the world chess championship more than one time in order to have enough games for this analysis.

Figure 3 shows the average error evolution of some players along with their participation in world championships. The figure is divided into different periods, a) presents the data from WCC champions between 2000 and 2018 with the 3 champions of this period (Carlsen, Anand, and Kramnik). Note that even that the first played WCC by Anand was in 1996, he is included in this graphic. Carlsen, see Figure 3 a), although starting with a good average error in his first WCC, shows a general improvement along with his participation in four WCCs. Kramik and Anand had their best result in the second played WCC. The most relevant issue is that all of them have average errors lower than 0.105 between 2000 and 2018 (the average error of 0.12 of Anand corresponds to the WCC in 1996), and the variations in their average errors are minimum (lower than 0.025).

Figure 3 b) represents the average errors of players between 1980 to 1996 with the 4 champions of this period (Kasparov, Karpov, Spassky, and Botvínnik). There were other WCC champions in this period who only played one WCC and are not included. Kasparov had the best performance in his first WCC, Karpov, and Spassky had their best results in the second year and Botvinnik in ninth WCC. During this period, the average error of the players, 0.12, is higher than in the current period and their variations of the average error were higher than nowadays. Botvinnik is the player who had higher variations, his worst results were found in his fourth WCC.

The last period is represented in Figure 3 c) and corresponds to the campions of the oldest WCCs (1886 to 1946). During this period, the players had even higher variations than in the previous periods. The best results of Alekhine, Capablanca, Lasker, and Steintz were in their first, second seventh and fifth WCC respectively.

Apparently, there is no general trend that confirms that the more time a player plays in the WCC, the better he plays chess.

C. Percentage of "best moves"

Figure 4 shows the percentage of the best move selected by the players. Famous world champions like Kasparov, Carlsen, Karpov, and Fischer have similar rate choosing the best move, but none of them are in the top five. Other famous players from the past, like Capablanca, Lasker or Steinitz have 50% or less of rating for selecting the best move.

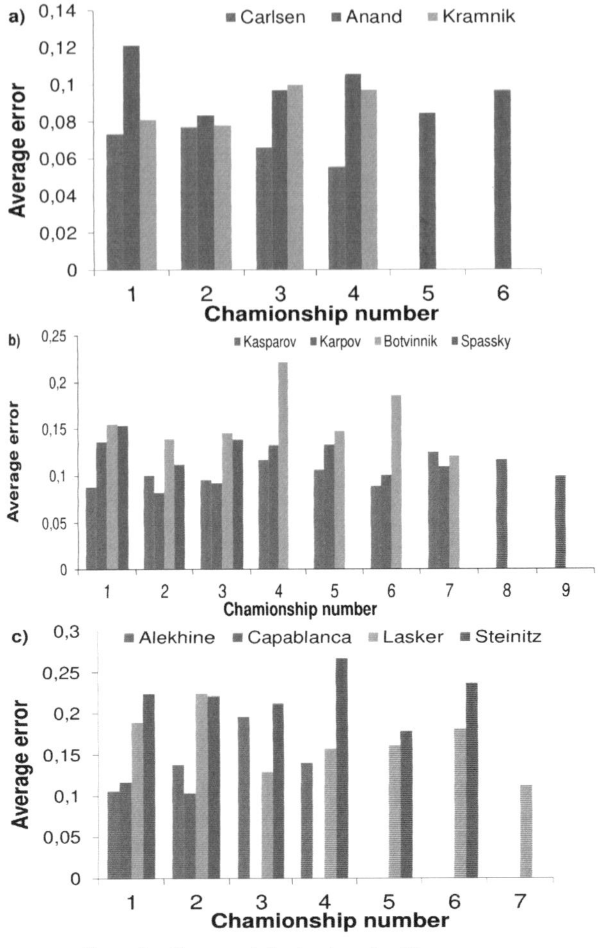

Figure 3. Player evolution by championships.

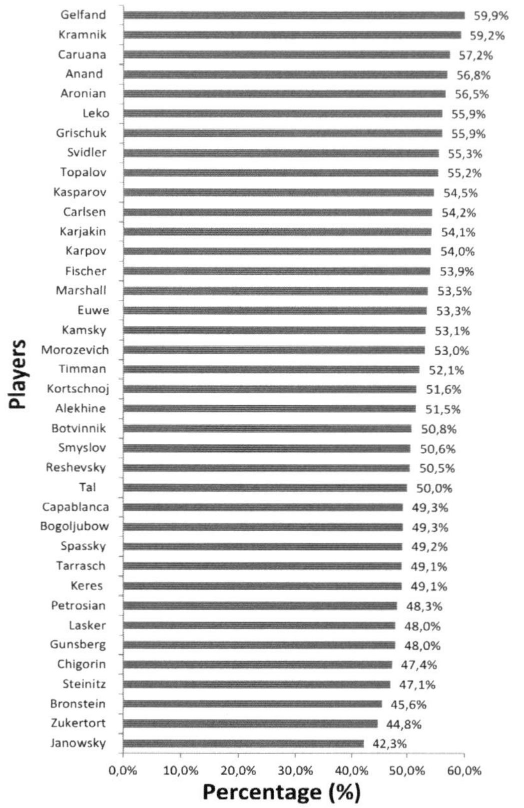

Figure 4. Percentage of best move of different players.

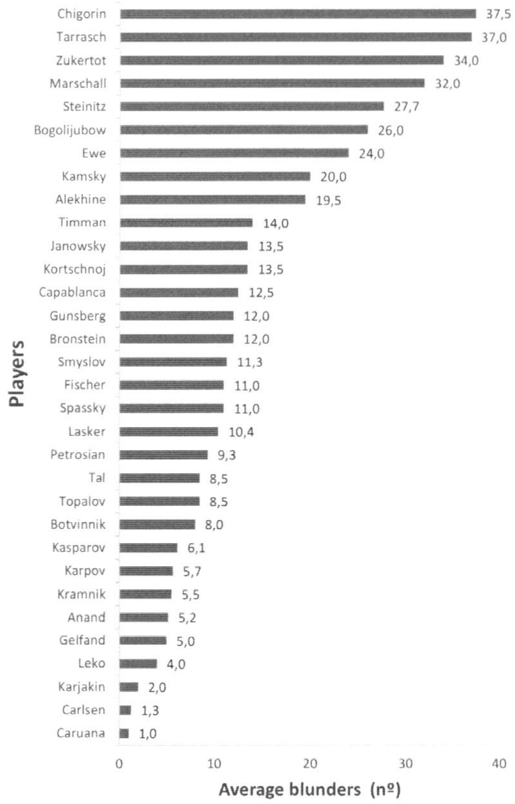

Figure 5. Comparison of average blunders played.

Carlsen, who is the current world champion, won 4 WCC and achieved the highest Elo in history. He has only 54.2% of best moves. He is placed in the 11th position behind some players who only played one WCC and never won the championship as Gelfand, Leko, or Aronian. Nonetheless, it is important to note that sometimes, the difference between the first and the second-best move are small and has almost no impact on the results of the game.

D. *Average of blunders*

The number of average blunders played by each one of the analyzed players is presented in Figure 4. For this analysis, we consider the WCC with only two players. A move is considered as a blunder when causes that white player has a score lower than 2 or black player has a score higher than -2.

While in the previous section, we saw how very famous players, such as Carlsen, Karpov or Kasparov, appeared in relative bad positions; when we analyze the data of blunders the results change, see Figure 5. The most recent WCC champions: Carlsen, Anand, and Kramnik, appear in the top seven positions. In their WCCs all of them played few blunders: 1.3, 5.1 and 5.5 blunders as average in all WCC respectively. It is relevant that Caruana is the player with the lowest average. Nonetheless, in the specific WCC that Caruana and Carlsen played, Carlsen had not played any blunder.

Some of the most famous champions, such as Kasparov and Karpov appears in the 9th and 10th position, with 5.5 and 6.1 average blunders per WCC. Meanwhile, other famous players from the past, like Alekhine, Capablanca, Lasker or Steinitz are in worse positions 24, 20, 12, and 28, with more than 10 average blunders in each WCC.

E. *Average of "best move" vs "number of move"*

Finally, we are going to evaluate the performance in terms of best move versus played move of different WCC players along with the game. Since in other section we pointed that the players were obtaining better performances in the last evaluated period of the history of WCC, 2000 to 2018, we are going to compare the players with best performances in this period: Kramik, Anand, Carlsen, and Caruana. As we may expect due to the time control at move 40, many players make mistakes in moves near move number 40, for example, in moves from 35 to 39. Then, along next moves, the quality of moves increases, but only for a short number of moves. Figure 6 shows how some players make mistakes again starting around move number 45. Then, we will compare the performance from move number 7 to move number 45, and from move 7 until the end.

The situation along a game, like beginning moves, ending, time left, may affect the capacity of the player to select the next move. Figure 6 shows if the players have selected the best move, second, etc, depending on the number of the move. Carlsen has a good rating, with an average around of second-best move, an average of 2.15 with standard deviation of 0.36 for moves 7 to 45. Only for very long games, he may make a bad selection move, such as in moves near number 60 or more than 70. Kramnik, also shows good rating, around second best move, average of 1.96 with standard deviation of 0.40 for moves 7 to 45 although not reaching long games. Anand has an average of 2.11 with standard deviation of 0.39 for moves 7 to 45. His results are similar to the observed results with Carlsen. On the other side, Caruana (who only played one WCC and did not win) is the one who has the highest variability in terms of best move versus played move, average of 2.09 with a standard deviation of 0.84 for moves 7 to 45. Thus, the player who played the best moves more times is Kramnik followed by Anand, Carlsen, and Caruana.

If we consider the whole game, moves 7 until the end, the results slightly change and the order of players who had the best average of best move versus played move is not maintained. The new order is Kramnik, Anand, Caruana, and Carlsen. The averages changed and, in most cases, the averages increased, which means that after long games the players selected worse moves. However, Kramnik had better average when we consider the entire game, 1.88. Thus, we can affirm that Kramnik had better performances in the endgame than the other players.

V. CONCLUSION AND FUTURE WORK

In this paper, we have compared the performance of WCC players with is Stockfish 64 bits Version. Our study was based on the presented results in 2006 [7] and we have compared our findings with their outputs.

When we compared the average error of different players, the best player was Magnus Carlsen, the current WCC champion. Nonetheless, some famous champions such as Kasparov and Karpov were not in relevant positions attending to these parameters. Other parameters such as the percentage of best move and average of blunders were used to compare players. While percentage of best moves gave similar punctuations to players with different quality and Elo, the ranking by average of blunders offered more accurate results. Finally, we have evaluated the average of best move versus played move of best players from 2000 to today.

As future work, we will increase the complexity of our analysis including other factors as stages. We will also include statistical analysis in order to add more value to our results. Moreover, we will analyze the performance of the players based on their or her physical condition.

REFERENCES

[1] J. L. Cazaux and R. Knowlton, "A World of Chess: Its Development and Variations Through Centuries and Civilizations", McFarland & Company, 2017.

[2] V. Janko and M. Guid, "A program for Progressive chess," Theoretical Computer Science, 644, 2016, pp. 76-91.

[3] E. Vázquez-Fernández, C. A. C. Coello, and F. D. S. Troncoso, "Assessing the positional values of chess pieces by tuning neural networks' weights with an evolutionary algorithm;" In 2012 World Automation Congress (WAC 2012), 24-28 June 2012, Puerto Vallarta, Mexico, pp. 1-6.

[4] H. V. Ribeiro, R. S. Mendes, E. K. Lenzi, M. del Castillo-Mussot, and L. A. Amaral, "Move-by-move dynamics of the advantage in chess matches reveals population-level learning of the game," PLoS One, 8(1), 2013, pp 1-7.

[5] Fide Ranking. Available at: https://ratings.fide.com/card.phtml?event=1503014. Last access 11/10/2019

[6] Ranking. of chess programs. Available at: https://ccrl.chessdom.com/ccrl/4040/. Last access 11/10/2019

[7] M. Guid and I. Bratko, "Computer analysis of world chess champions," ICGA Journal, 29(2), 2006, pp.65-73.

[8] E. Vázquez-Fernández, C. A. C. Coello, and F. D. S. Troncoso, "An evolutionary algorithm for tuning a chess evaluation function". IEEE Congress of Evolutionary Computation (CEC 2011), 5-8 June 2011, New Orleans, USA pp. 842-848.

[9] O. Tolga Altinoz, A. Egemen Yilmaz, Multiobjective Hooke–Jeeves algorithm with a stochastic Newton–Raphson-like step-size method, Expert Systems with Applications, Volume 117, 1 March 2019, pp. 166-175.

[10] N. Veček, M. Mernik, and M. Črepinšek. "A chess rating system for evolutionary algorithms: A new method for the comparison and ranking of evolutionary algorithms" Information Sciences, 277, 2014, pp. 656-679.

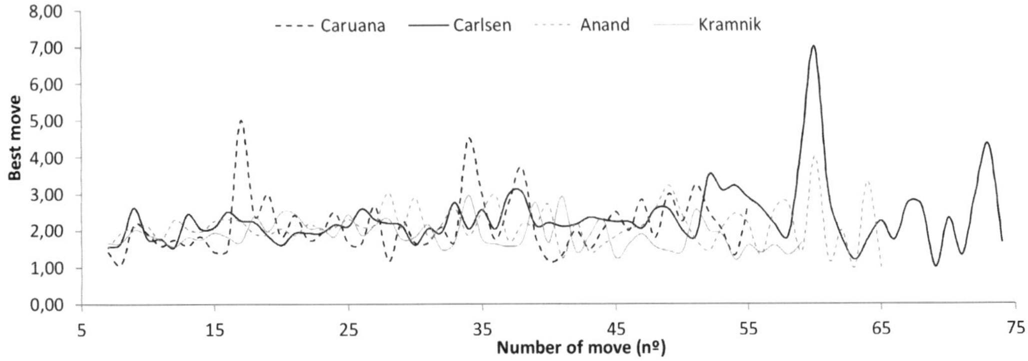

Figure 6. Comparison of the best move versus the played move.

A Proposal of Descriptive Pattern for Maintainability Requirements

Yuki Sanomachi
Shibaura Institute of Technology
Tokyo, Japan
e-mail: ma18051@shibaura-it.ac.jp

Tsuyoshi Nakajima
Shibaura Institute of Technology
Tokyo, Japan
e-mail: tsnaka@shibaura-it.ac.jp

Abstract—**To clearly define quality requirements is crucially important for developing high quality systems and software. Unlike usability and security requirements, maintainability requirements often come from developers themselves. Therefore, their descriptive patterns have not been discussed so much in spite of their importance. This paper proposes a descriptive pattern for maintainability requirements based on the quality requirements framework in the ISO/IEC 25030:2019. The proposed descriptive pattern covers maintainability requirements using all the measures in ISO/IEC 25023 and enables machine checking their correctness and unambiguity.**

Keywords-quality requirements; maintainability; SQuaRE; standardization.

I. INTRODUCTION

Information and Communication Technology (ICT) systems have been used in various places and situations, and therefore, their failures can have a large impact on the society. Therefore, it is required not only to fit them to various needs and usage scenes, but also to ensure their quality through careful consideration on social impact [1].

Development of a quality ICT system is required to meet its quality requirements as well as its functional ones. Quality requirements cover many views of the target system, among which quality views related to system behavior, such as usability and Security. These have been discussed thoroughly in separate communities to standardize manners to write their quality requirements.

In contrast, quality views related to the internal structure of the system, such as maintainability and portability, are not properly discussed with respect to standardization and the manner in which they are specified.

In the systems and software engineering field, the reality is that quality requirements are specified in a variety of manners, most of which are not properly written without being separated from functional requirements [2].

ISO/IEC 25000 series (SQuaRE: Systems and software Quality Requirements and Evaluation) are developed to provide a framework for quality definition and evaluation, including quality models and measures, which cover an exhaustive set of quality views. In addition, ISO/IEC 25030: 2019 [3] in the SQuaRE series provides a framework for defining quality requirements using the quality models and measures.

In this paper, we propose a descriptive pattern for specifying maintainability requirements based on the specification format defined in ISO/IEC 25030:2019. The proposed descriptive pattern covers various kinds of maintainability requirements and enables machine checking their correctness and unambiguity.

In this paper, Section II describes the related work, and then, Section III proposes a descriptive pattern for maintainability. Section IV gives a qualitative evaluation of the proposed pattern. Section V summarizes this paper and gives future work.

II. RELATED WORK

ISO/IEC 25010 [5] defines the product quality model with eight quality characteristics. Maintainability is one of them, which provides five sub characteristics: modularity, reusability, analyzability, modifiability, and testability, whose definitions are shown in TABLE 1.

TABLE I DEFINITIONS OF SUB－CHARACTERISTICS OF MAINTAINABILITY [5]

Sub-characteristic	Definition
modularity	degree to which a system or computer program is composed of discrete components such that a change to one component has minimal impact on other components
reusability	degree to which an asset can be used in more than one system, or in building other assets
analyzability	degree of effectiveness and efficiency with which it is possible to assess the impact on a product or system of an intended change to one or more of its parts, or to diagnose a product for deficiencies or causes of failures, or to identify parts to be modified
modifiability	degree to which a product or system can be effectively and efficiently modified without introducing defects or degrading existing product quality
testability	degree of effectiveness and efficiency with which test criteria can be established for a system, product or component and tests can be performed to determine whether those criteria have been met

ISO/IEC 25023 [6] product quality measures provides 86 quality measures corresponding to quality sub characteristics, including 13 measures for maintainability characteristic. Japan Users Association of Information Systems (JUAS) published a guideline which defines their own quality measures other than those of ISO/IEC 25023 [4]. These give recommendation on what measures should be used for maintenance requirements. However, these do not guide how to define maintenance requirements themselves. Therefore, there are needs for descriptive patterns to guide it.

ISO / IEC 25030: 2019 [3] provides the following specification format for specifying quality requirements.

- **Target entity:** *Components of the system*
- **Selected characteristic:** *modularity*
- **Quality goal with conditions:** *Reducing the coupling between any two of components*
- **Quality measure:** *(MMo-1-G) coupling of components*
- **Target value:** *1*
- **Acceptable range of values:** *0,98 – 1,00*

It is recommended to use this format for specifying not only the scope and goal of the quality requirement, but also quality measures with its target value and acceptable range of the value.

III. Descriptive Pattern for Specifying Maintainability Requirements

In this paper, we propose a descriptive pattern for maintainability requirements with the aim of standardizing the manner to specify them. We set the following four requirements for the descriptive pattern:

(1) The descriptive pattern for specifying maintainability requirements shall cover all types of maintainability requirements with as few descriptive patterns as possible.
(2) Maintainability requirement statements conformed to the pattern shall be natural to readers.
(3) Maintainability requirement statements conformed to the pattern shall prevent from ambiguities.
(4) The pattern shall enable machine checking correctness and unambiguity for maintainability requirement statements.

In order to create the descriptive pattern of the maintainability requirements, we did the following analysis:

i. Create a table of maintainability measures merging those from the ISO/IEC 25023 and JUAS guidelines.
ii. Extract what achievement to be measured in the corresponding quality sub characteristic as the "quality goal".
iii. Parameterize the quality measure so that it 2can be limited to the appropriate level of application. The parameters include:
   - Scope of the target entity
   - Criteria for the evaluation
   - Context for application (evaluation period, subjects, etc.)
iv. Create descriptive patterns and try using them to write requirement statements.

As a result of the above analysis, we propose the following descriptive pattern for maintainability requirements.

In order to *Quality goal*, *quality measure* shall be [greater | smaller] than *Target value*.

Quality goal = [improve | increase | suppress | decrease] *Attribute* of *Target entity*] | *Outcome of use*

The two rows of *Quality goal* and *Quality requirement statement* are added to the original table of quality measures to be TABLE 2. In TABLE 2, for example, if *Quality goal* is "increase the independency of system components," *Quality measure* is "the coupling of components," and *Target value* is "99.0%"," the quality requirement statement goes to:

In order to increase the independence of system components, the coupling of components shall be greater than 99.0 %.

IV. Evaluation

All the maintainability requirements in TABLE 2 can be specified naturally using the proposed descriptive pattern. This proves to meet the requirements (1) and (2).

Quality requirement statements conformed to the proposed descriptive pattern have all the items of the specification format in ISO/IEC 25030:2019, which is designed to prevent the quality requirement statements from being ambiguous, which meets the requirement (3).

SE Suite [7] is a tool for describing, checking, and evaluating quality in requirement specifications, and consists of the following three tools:

- Requirements Quality Analyzer (RQA),
- Requirements Authoring Tool (RAT)
- Knowledge Manager (KM)

RQA provides a checking function for general requirement statements with designated descriptive patterns. We can use this tool to implement machine checking maintainability requirements using the proposed description pattern and vocabularies defined in KM. SE Suite can check the following points:

- whether the statement is syntactically correct or not
- whether terms are defined or not
- whether relationship between terms are appropriate or not
- whether the context of application of the quality measure is appropriate or not
- whether the range of the quality measure is appropriate or not

Figure 1 shows an example of checking layers of SE Suite for the maintainability requirement statement using the proposed pattern.

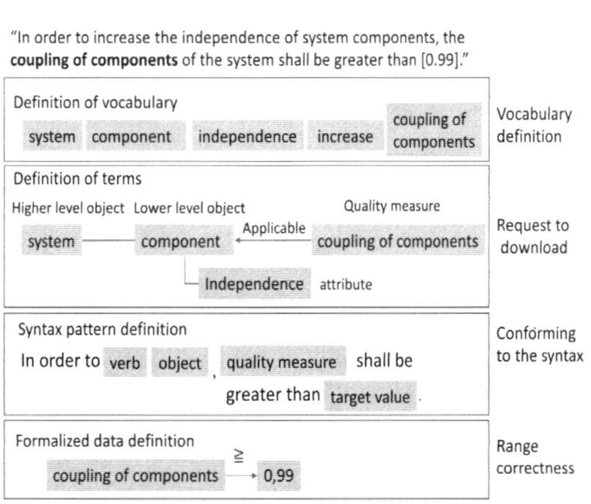

Figure 1 Checking layers of SE Suite for the maintainability requirement statement using the proposed description pattern

By implementing the description pattern proposed with SE suite, it is mechanically possible to detect errors, omissions, and ambiguities in the requested sentences.

This shows that the proposed description pattern meets requirements (4).

V. CONCLUSION AND FUTURE TASKS

In this paper, we proposed a descriptive pattern for maintainability requirements, which proves to cover various types of them. Using SE Suite, this pattern enables a variety of checking for maintainability requirement statements.

The proposed descriptive pattern can be applied to all the maintainability measures defined in ISO/IEC 25023 and JUAS, but it may not be limited to them. On the contrary, the single pattern might not be enough to specify some other maintainability requirement statements. Therefore, we should consider quantifying quality attributes, such as target question metrics (GQM). The proposed pattern should be examined to write more examples of maintainability requirements, which strengthen our belief on the proposed pattern to meet the requirements for it.

ACKNOWLEDGMENT

This research was conducted as a project of "International standardization for quality model and evaluation of system and software (Japan Standards Association)" as a part of the industrial standardization promotion business of Ministry of Economy, Trade and Industry, FY2019.

REFERENCE

[1] Information-technology Promotion Agency Japan, " Information system failure status", 2018, pp. 1–3.

[2] J. Eckhardt, A.Vogelsang, and D. Méndez Fernández, "Are non-functional requirements really non-functional? an investigation of non-functional requirements in practice", Proc. International Conference on Software Engineering(ICE16), ICE Press, Nov. 2016, PP. 832-842, doi:10.1145/2884781.2884788.

[3] ISO/IEC Software Engineering, ISO/IEC25030 Software Product Quality Requirements and Evaluation (SQuaRE) Quality requirements framework, 2019.

[4] JUAS ed, "A guideline for specification of non-functional requirements (UVC project II)", 2008, pp. 89–100.

[5] ISO/IEC Software Engineering, ISO/IEC25010 Software Product Quality Requirements and Evaluation (SQuaRE) System and software quality models, 2011.

[6] ISO/IEC Software Engineering, ISO/IEC25023 Software Product Quality Requirements and Evaluation (SQuaRE) Measurement of External Quality, 2016.

[7] The REUSE Company.Systems Engineering Suite, https://www.reusecompany.com/systems-engineering-suite, (accessed 2019-11-17).

TABLE II PROPOSED DESCRIPTIVE PATTERN FOR MAINTAINABILITY REQUIREMENTS AND ITS APPLICATION TO QUALITY MEASURES

Quality sub-characteristic	Quality goal	Quality measure	Measurement function	Quality requirement statement
Modularity	Increase the independence of system components.	Coupling of components	X=A/B A=Number of components which are implemented with no impact on others B = Number of specified components which are required to be independent	In order to increase the independence of system components, the coupling of components of the system shall be greater than [target value].
	Increase module cohesion	Cyclomatic complexity adequacy	X = 1– A/B A = Number of software modules which have a cyclomatic complexity score that exceeds the specified threshold B = Number of software modules implemented	In order to increase module cohesion, the cyclomatic complexity adequacy should be greater than [target value].
Reusability	Increase the number of reusable components (or modules).	Reusability of assets	X = A/B A = Number of assets which are designed and implemented to be reusable B = Number of assets in a system	In order to increase the number of reusable components (or modules), the reusability of assets (applicable range, criteria for being an asset, Criteria for reusability) shall be greater than [target value].
	Improve coding quality of modules	Coding rules conformity	X = A/B A = Number of software modules conforming to coding rules for a specific system B = Number of software modules implemented	In order to improve coding quality of modules, the coding rules conformity (scope, coding code) shall be greater than [target value].
Analyzability	Increase the adequacy of data used to trace causes of the system failures	System log completeness	X=A/B A = Number of logs that are actually recorded in the system B = Number of logs for which audit trails are required during operation	In order to increase the adequacy of data used to trace causes of the system failures, the system log completeness shall be greater than [target value].
	Improve the accuracy and efficiency of identifying causes of the system failure.	Diagnosis function effectiveness	X=A/B A = Number of diagnostic functions useful for causal analysis B = Number of diagnostic functions implemented	In order to improve the accuracy and efficiency of identifying causes of the system failure, the diagnosis function effectiveness shall be smaller than [target value].
		Diagnosis function sufficiency	X=A/B A = Number of diagnostic functions implemented B = Number of diagnostic functions required	In order to improve the accuracy and the efficiency of identifying causes of the system failure, the diagnosis function sufficiency shall be greater than [target value].
	Improve the readability of the program.	Program source comment rate	X=A/B A = Implemented comment rate B = Comment rate defined by the organization	To improve the readability of the program, the program source comment rate (application range) shall be more than [target value].
Modifiability	Improve the accuracy and efficiency of system correction.	Modification correctness	X = 1 – (A/B) A = Number of modifications that caused an incident or failure within a defined period after being implemented B = Number of modifications implemented	In order to increase the accuracy and efficiency of system correction, make modification correctness (target period) less than [target value].
		Modification capability	X=A/B A = Number of items actually modified within a specified duration B = Number of items required to be modified	In order to improve the accuracy and efficiency of system correction, the modification capability shall be smaller than [target value].
	Improve the appropriateness of system modification management.	Change Content Documenting Rate	X=A/B A = Number of features documented and subject to review B = Number of functions with program change	In order to improve the appropriateness of system modification management, the change content documentation rate shall be greater than [target value].
Testability	Increase the sufficiency of functions to support test execution.	Test function completeness	X=A/B A = Number of test functions implemented as specified B = Number of test functions required	In order to increase the sufficiency of the function to support test execution, the test function completeness shall be greater than [target value].
	Increase the possibility of independent testing.	Autonomous testability	X=A/B A = Number of tests that can be simulated by stub among the tests which depend on other systems B = Number of tests which depend on other systems	In order to increase the possibility of independent testing, make autonomous testability more than [target value].

A SysML-based Approach to Requirements Traceability using BPMN and DMN

Corina Abdelahad and Daniel Riesco
Departamento de informática
Universidad Nacional de San Luis
San Luis, Argentina
e-mail: cabdelah@unsl.edu.ar, driesco@unsl.edu.ar

Carlos Kavka
Research and Development Department
ESTECO SPA
Trieste, Italy
e-mail: kavka@esteco.com

***Abstract*—Model-based system engineering is a well-established methodology where the use of models has a central role. One of its main contributions is to support the documentation of the requirements and decisions that are taken during the design process. In particular, requirements traceability, or in other words, the capability to follow the life-cycle of the requirements, plays an important role in this methodology. Of course, system engineers' work in this area is supported by the use of standards. One of the most used standards in this domain is Systems Modeling Language (SysML), which being defined as an extension of the well-known and widely-used Unified Modeling Language (UML) standard, supports the definition and specification of requirements and their relations with the other components of the whole system. The main goal of this paper is to present an extension of SysML for requirements traceability particularly useful in the design of systems where decision-making activities are essential. The proposed extension to SysML, defined by following its standard extension mechanism, supports the association of processes and decision-making activities to system requirements, greatly improving their traceability. Processes and decision-making activities are defined in terms of the widely-used Business Process Model and Notation (BPMN) and Decision Model and Notation (DMN) standards, respectively. Our contribution is illustrated by means of a small case study.**

Keywords-SysML; BPMN; DMN; requirements traceability.

I. INTRODUCTION

Abstraction is one of the main tools used by engineers to deal with complexity, permitting them to focus only on the information that is considered significant or relevant. Based on it, Model-Based Systems Engineering (MBSE) is a successful methodology for the design of complex systems, which emphasizes the use of models when performing systems engineering activities [1]. These models, which can be executable or not, are used to describe the structure and the behavior of the systems.

With the evolution of systems engineering, the need for a consistent standard modeling language arose. International Council on Systems Engineering (INCOSE) together with the Object Management Group (OMG) [2] defined SysML, a general-purpose modeling language based on UML, which can be used for specifying, analyzing, designing, and verifying complex systems, including hardware, software, information, personnel, procedures, and facilities [4]. SysML is based on the so-called four pillars, which give the possibility to view a system from four different perspectives: Requirements, Structure, Behavior and Parametrics, each one of them defined in terms of diagrams [3]. Requirements modeling [20] is implemented in terms of the requirement diagram, which allows for capturing, analyzing and maintaining traceability of requirements in the modeled system. Structure modeling has a block definition diagram as the main diagram, representing structural elements (blocks) with their properties, relationships, and composition. Behavior modeling has different kinds of behavior diagrams like activities diagram, state machine, and sequence diagram. Parametric modeling has a parametric diagram that can be used to identify the system constraints [4]. In SysML, requirements can be related to other requirements, as well as to other model elements via one or more relationships, making possible the traceability of requirements. Furthermore, SysML can be integrated into other tools including spreadsheets and design and simulation software, such as Matlab or Modelica [19], enabling requirements verification.

The specification of business processes also followed the same path requiring standards for its definition. In particular, the Business Process Management Initiative (BPMI) together with the OMG developed the widely used BPMN notation for modeling business processes [5]. BPMN defines an abstract representation for the specification of business processes, which can include human intervention or not. BPMN couples an expressive graphical representation with a rigorous Extensible Markup Language (XML) encoding of processes and the interactions among them, supporting not only modeling activities but also process execution by using appropriate BPMN engines. Since many activities within a business process involve decision-making, the OMG defined recently the DMN standard for the elicitation and representation of decision models, effectively separating decision logic and control flow logic in business processes [6]. DMN was designed to be usable alongside the standard BPMN. At present, many companies have adopted BPMN not only because of its popularity, but because it is strongly related to DMN. This standard is already receiving adoption in the industry, with many tools being developed to assist users in modeling, checking, and applying DMN models.

As the main contribution, this work presents an innovative approach to enhance requirements traceability in the context of MBSE, by combining SysML, BPMN and DMN. This approach can help systems engineers to improve the design of requirements, to understand and cover their different views, improving maintenance and verification activities while contributing to refine the level of detail of the models.

The rest of this paper is organized as follows: Section II introduces related work, while Section III summarizes the basic concepts used in this paper. Section IV addresses the proposed approach with a case study presented in Section V. Section VI shows the conclusion.

II. RELATED WORK

Several works in the field of software engineering are related to the concept of requirements traceability using SysML. For example, the authors in [7] show how requirements traceability for mechatronic design can be achieved using MBSE and SysML. SysML is used for linking system requirements to the system elements of the different domain models while guaranteeing the traceability. This paper presents a case study of a mechatronic system in order to show this traceability.

In [8], a solution for SysML model verification and validation in an industrial context is presented. The authors provide a method and a list of the existing challenges; besides that, they show experimental results. A case study is presented, verification rules are in Object Constraint Language (OCL), while the validation rules are in a formal text format evaluated by a script. The authors mention that the verification of these rules ensures a certain degree of traceability.

In [9], an approach to construct true model-based requirements in SysML is presented. This approach proposes that every requirement can be modeled as an input/output transformation. This proposal uses SysML behavioral and structural models and diagrams, with specific construction rules derived from Wymore's mathematical framework for MBSE and taxonomies of requirements and interfaces. The authors consider that this proposal provides several benefits, including traceability, and improved precision over the use of natural language.

In [10], the authors propose a model-based approach to automotive requirements engineering for the general development of vehicles of passengers. The SysML requirement element is extended, through stereotype, to functional and non-functional requirements. The paper validates the advantages that include classified and modeled requirements graphically, as well as their relationships that are explicitly mapped. This article presents a case study that shows the proposed extension and the performed requirements traceability.

In [11], the authors propose a model-driven requirement engineering approach for the embedded software domain. This approach is based on UML, MARTE and SysML standard notations, which are integrated in order to improve requirements specification and traceability. MARTE is used to allow domain-specific non-functional requirements to improve the software specification and SysML is combined with UML/MARTE models to support requirements management, to follow their changes. The approach is illustrated by means of a case study.

In [12], the authors propose a metamodel, which establishes the traceability links among the requirement model, the solution model and the verification and validation model for embedded system design. This approach enables traceability of requirements by considering heterogeneous languages for modeling and verifying real-time embedded systems. A case study illustrates the approach with the use of languages such as SysML, MARTE, SIMULINK, among others.

However, to the best of our knowledge, no research work about requirements traceability has considered the decision requirement, a kind of requirement that involves decision making. This requirement appears in the decision requirement diagram, which represents human decision making or automated decision making within a process. The main motivation of this work is the need to provide support to decision requirements, by offering adequate tools to the system engineers that improve the design and handling of these types of requirements. Considering this, the approach presented in this paper is a step forward to support decision requirements, completing the different system engineering views by combining of SysML, BPMN and DMN.

III. BASIC CONCEPTS

This section presents the basic concepts on which the proposed approach is based. Section A introduces traceability related concepts in SysML, Section B describes the SysML requirements diagram and block definition diagram used in the approach. Section C shows some concepts about DMN and its relationship with BPMN.

A. *Traceability in SysML*

In [13], INCOSE indicates that "requirements traceability refers to the ability to describe and follow the life of a requirement in both a forward and backward direction along the design stages". Traceability plays an important role as part of any MBSE methodology [1]. MBSE emphasizes the use of models to perform the systems engineering activities, as mentioned before. In fact, "MBSE is the formalized application of modeling to support system requirements, design, analysis, verification and validation activities beginning in the conceptual design phase and continuing throughout development and later life cycle phases" [14].

Modeling with SysML allows good traceability because it defines relationships between requirements and among other modeling elements [15]. Figure 1 describes the approach in which SysML accomplishes traceability by means of the 4 pillars presented in Section I. This figure shows the system model as an interconnected set of model elements. The arrows that cross the pillars, as seen in Figure 1, illustrate how the different elements belonging to the different types of diagrams that participate in the pillars are related, supporting requirements traceability.

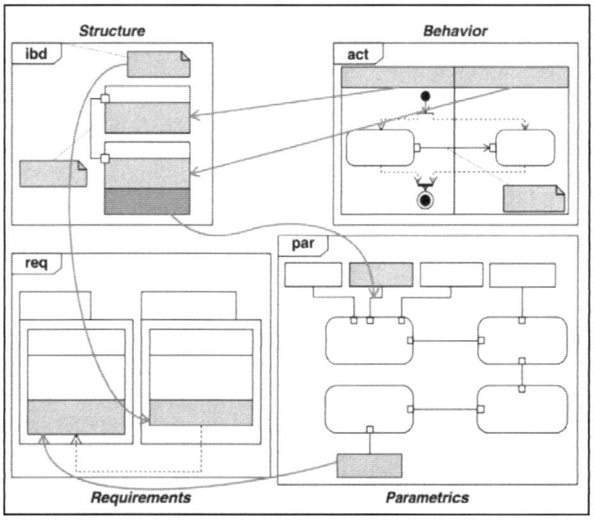

Figure 1. A system model example in SysML where requirements traceability is indicated with the connecting arrows (from [3]).

B. SysML Requirements diagram

In SysML, the requirements diagram shows the set of requirements and the relationship between them. A requirement specifies a function that must be satisfied or a condition that a system must achieve. Requirements modeling provides a bridge among different SysML diagrams because a requirement can appear on other diagrams to show its relationship to other modeling elements. The relationships that allow relating requirements with other requirements or with other modeling elements are [4]:

- Containment: a relationship which is used to represent how a compound requirement can be partitioned into a set of simpler requirements (denoted graphically with a circle containing a + symbol).
- «deriveReqt»: a relationship which describes that a requirement is derived from other requirement.
- «satisfy»: a relationship that describes that a design element satisfies a requirement. Usually, a requirement is satisfied by a block.
- «verify»: a relationship that connects a test case with the requirement that is verified by that test case.
- «refine»: a relationship which specifies that a model element describes the properties of a requirement in more detail.
- «trace»: a general-purpose relationship between a requirement and any other model element.

The requirements are related to the blocks through the relationship «satisfy», as mentioned before. The block definition diagram captures the relation between blocks, such as a block hierarchy. Since the activities can be seen as a block, they can have associations between each other, including composition associations. Activities in block definition diagrams appear as regular blocks, except for the «activity» keyword [4].

SysML enables characterization of any type of requirements for the system, including user, technical or others. A modeler can then define relationships between the specified requirements, providing the opportunity to create traceability among them. There is also an opportunity to create traceability from the logical and structural architecture design to their requirements, one of the most critical activities in systems engineering [16].

C. BPMN and DMN

The OMG provides the DMN notation for modeling decisions, which is not only understandable to stakeholders but it is also designed to be used in conjunction with the BPMN standard notation [6].

DMN provides constructs to both decision requirements and decision logic modeling. For decision requirements modeling, it defines the concept of Decision Requirements Graph (DRG) depicted with the Decision Requirements Diagram (DRD). This latter shows how a set of decisions depends on each other, on input data, and on business knowledge models. A decision element determines an output from the inputs, using decision logic, which may reference one or more business knowledge models. This denotes a function encapsulating business knowledge, e.g., as business rules, a decision table, or an analytic model. A decision table is a representation of decision logic, based on rules that determine the output depending on the inputs [6]. Decision-making modeled in DMN may be mapped to BPMN tasks or activities (Business Rules) within a process modeled with BPMN. The combined use of both thus provides a graphical language for describing decision-making, i.e., the BPMN tasks involving a decision can invoke a DMN decision model.

IV. MBSE AND REQUIREMENTS TRACEABILITY WITH SYSML

In this section, our contribution of traceability of requirements using SysML, BPMN, and DMN is detailed. Section A presents an extension to SysML for BPMN tasks while Section B describes details on the proposed approach for requirements traceability.

A. SysML extensions for BPMN tasks

In order to support the modeling of BPMN tasks in SysML, the element of SysML block diagram must be extended through stereotypes. The stereotypes are one of the extensibility mechanisms of UML, therefore also of SysML, that enable to extend its vocabulary allowing the creation of new kinds of building blocks that are derived from existing ones but specific to a problem [17]. Stereotypes are shown as text strings surrounded by the symbols "« »" [18]. The stereotypes change or add semantics to a base SysML element.

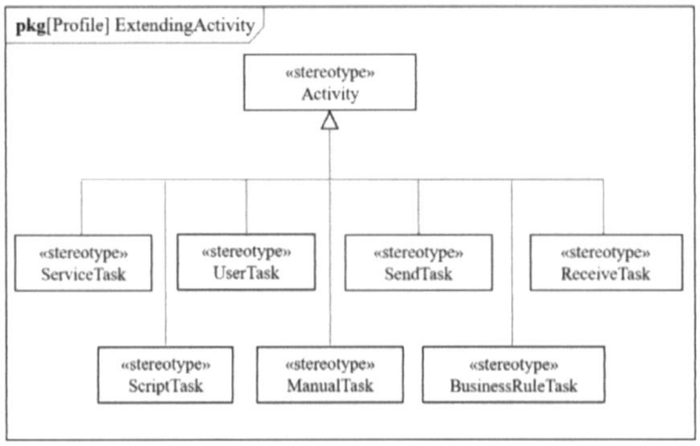

Figure 2. Extension of the SysML «Activity» stereotype.

Figure 2 shows the proposed extension of the SysML «Activity» stereotype in order to support all types of BPMN tasks [4].

This extension consists of the following stereotypes:

- «serviceTask»: represents a task that uses a web service or an automated application.
- «sendTask»: represents a simple task that is designed to send a message to an external participant.
- «receiveTask»: represents a simple task that is designed to wait for a message to arrive from an external participant.
- «userTask»: represents a task where a person performs the task with the assistance of a software application.
- «manualTask»: represents a task that is expected to be performed without the aid of any business process execution engine or any application.
- «scriptTask»: represents a task executed by a business process engine.
- «businessRuleTask»: represents a task that involves decision-making.

The business rule task was defined in BPMN as a placeholder for (business-rule-driven) decisions, being the natural placeholder for a decision task [6].

B. Requirements Traceability using SysML and BPMN-DMN

The interaction between the process and the decision models plays a crucial role because a decision can affect the process behavior or flow [5]. Therefore, it is important that decision-making must be considered as a requirement that should be performed and satisfied.

The approach will be illustrated with an example intended to carry out the traceability of the requirements through forward engineering, mainly focusing on those requirements involved in the decision-making activities, with the aim of integrating and covering their different views.

As it was mentioned before, the SysML requirement diagram has several relationships used to connect requirements. For example, Figure 3 presents a SysML

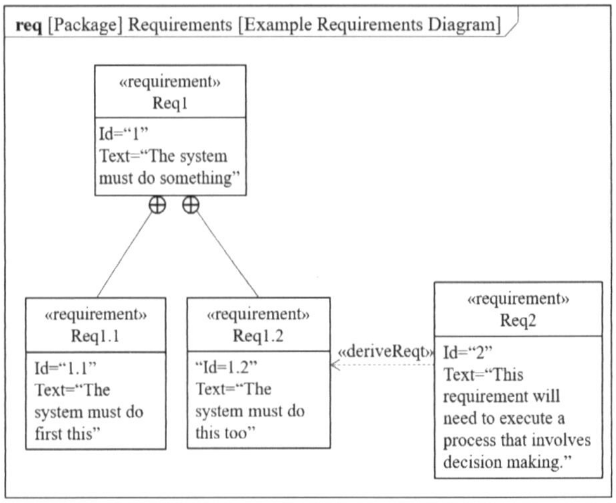

Figure 3. An example of a requirements diagram.

requirements diagram labeled "Example Requirements Diagram", which shows the relationship between requirements. In particular, it can be observed that the requirement with *id="2"* has a relationship with the requirement with *id="1.2"* through the «deriveReqt» relation. This relation specifies that the requirement with *id="2"* is derived from the requirement with *id="1.2"*.

Requirements can be related to other requirements and to other modeling elements through a specific set of relationships as mentioned before. Relationships between requirements and other modeling elements can appear on various types of diagrams. Figure 4 presents an example of a «satisfy» relationship between a *SimAct* activity and the *Req2* requirement which appears in the requirement diagram presented in Figure 3. The interpretation of this «satisfy» relationship is that the design of the activity depends on the requirement, meaning that if the requirement changes, the design of the activity must be changed.

Once the main requirements have been captured, the elements responsible to satisfy those requirements are modeled through a block definition diagram. As previously mentioned, activities can be seen as a block, except for the «activity» keyword [4]. This later provides a means for representing activity decomposition. Figure 5 shows an example of decomposition of the *SimAct* activity which was presented in Figure 4 by using the stereotypes proposed in Section IV-A. The block definition diagram shown in this figure indicates that the *SimAct* is an activity composed of other activities, including *Task 1*, *DecisionMaking Task* and *Task 2*, all these activities being of BPMN activity types.

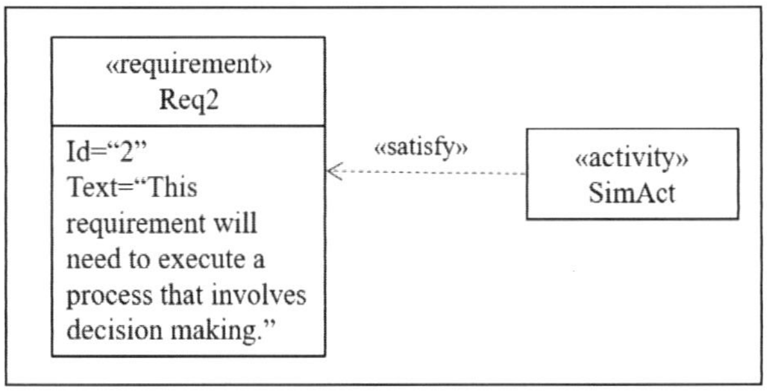

Figure 4. Example of a «satisfy» relationship between an Activity and a Requirement.

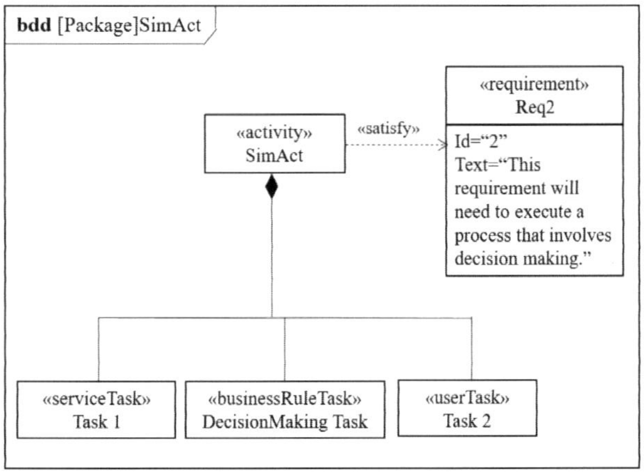

Figure 5. Block definition diagram with activities as blocks.

Finally, in order to cover the different views of the requirements, a BPMN model is constructed and associated to *SimAct* activity in order to show its behavior, as can be seen in Figure 6. In this figure, the activities that compose *SimAct,* which were modeled in Figure 5, are explicitated in BPMN format.

To conclude, the decision model related to the business rule task is built, since when BPMN and DMN are used, the BPMN tasks (business rule) have a link associated to the decision model, as mentioned in Section III-C. The *DecisionMaking Task* can then be implemented in terms of the associated decision requirements diagrams and decision tables.

V. CASE STUDY

To demonstrate our approach, we conducted a case study that includes the partial modeling of a Biodiesel Distiller and its requirements management. This case study illustrates how to carry out the traceability of the requirements through forward engineering.

Biodiesel is a type of biofuel that is similar to petroleum-based diesel, which can replace fossil fuel diesel. It is a sustainable fuel that is produced from fatty acids derived from animals such as beef fat, pork fat, chicken fat; and vegetable oils such as corn oil and cooking oil like those from restaurants that have already been used and disposed of. These oils are converted to diesel fuel through a chemical process.

Distilled biodiesel is a clean fuel that has been purified through the process of distillation. Biofuel distillation is a method that consists of taking a biofuel and removing particles and impurities within the liquid through an evaporation and condensation process.

The requirements diagram in Figure 7 illustrates the breakdown of the Biodiesel Distiller's requirements into a hierarchy of more refined requirements. This diagram named "Biodiesel Distiller Requirements Diagram" shows the relationship between its elements. In particular, it can be observed that the requirement *Initial Statement* is partitioned into a set of simpler requirements: *Generate Biodiesel*, *Heat Exchanger*, *Boiler*, *Biodiesel Properties* and *Distill Water*.

Once the main requirements of *Biodiesel Distiller* have been captured, the elements responsible to satisfy them are modeled through a block definition diagram. As previously mentioned, activities can be seen as a block and as a set of requirements that can be related to other requirements and to other modeling elements through a specific set of relationships. Figure 8 illustrates how the *Generator* activity satisfies the *Generate Biodiesel* requirement which appears in the requirement diagram presented in Figure 7, also showing how the *Machine* activity is composed.

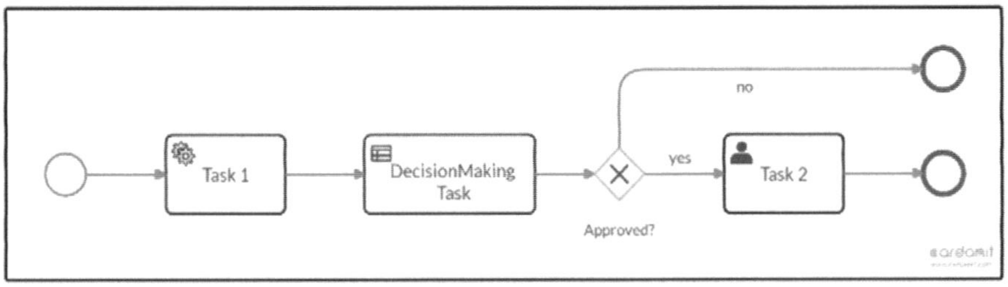

Figure 6. BPMN diagram of SimAct.

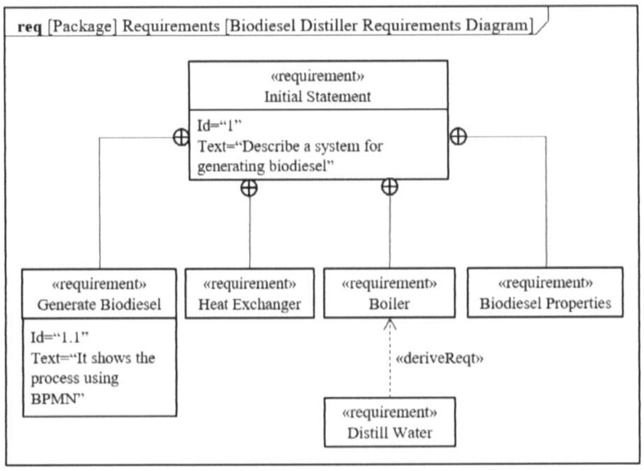

Figure 7. Requirements diagram: *Biodiesel Distiller Requirements Diagram*.

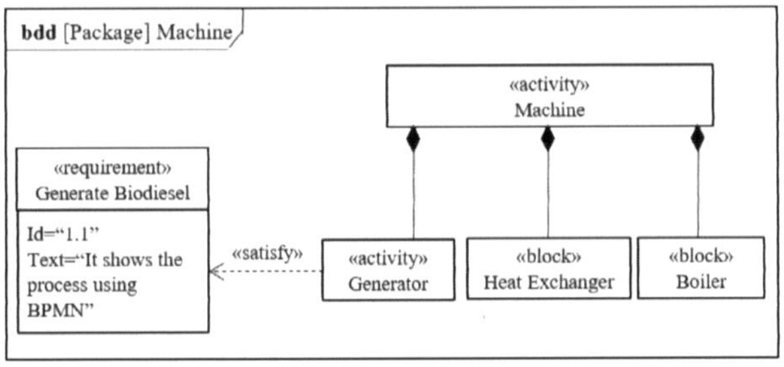

Figure 8. *Generator* activity satisfies the *Generate Biodiesel* requirement.

Continuing with the approach, Figure 9 illustrates the decomposition of the *Generator* activity by using the stereotypes proposed in Section IV-A. The block definition diagram shown in this figure indicates that the Generator is an activity composed of other activities such as: *Choose method* business rule, which involves decision-making, *Prepare reactors* activity, *Notify* user task, *Heat Water* service task, *Separate materials* service task, *Decant* activity and *Washing by decanting* service task, all these activities being of BPMN activity types.

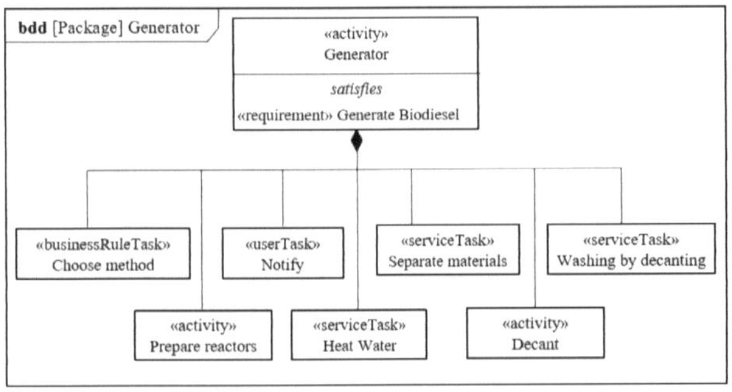

Figure 9. Decomposition of the *Generator* activity.

Following the approach presented in this work, a BPMN model is constructed in order to cover the different views of the requirements. This model shows the process which is carried out to generate biodiesel associated with the *Generator* activity. Its behavior can be observed in Figure 11.

To conclude, the decision model related to the business rule task is built. To prepare the reactors, the type of method to be used must be known and this depends on the type of material that will be used for the generation of biodiesel. The materials can be beef fat, pork fat, chicken fat, and vegetable fat. In the case of study, this decision making is shown in terms of the decision table as shown in Figure 10.

U	material	Method
	Text [beef, pork, chicken, vegetable]	Text [M1,M2,M3,M4]
1	beef	M1
2	pork	M2
3	chicken	M3
4	vegetable	M4

Figure 10. Decision table to *Choose method*.

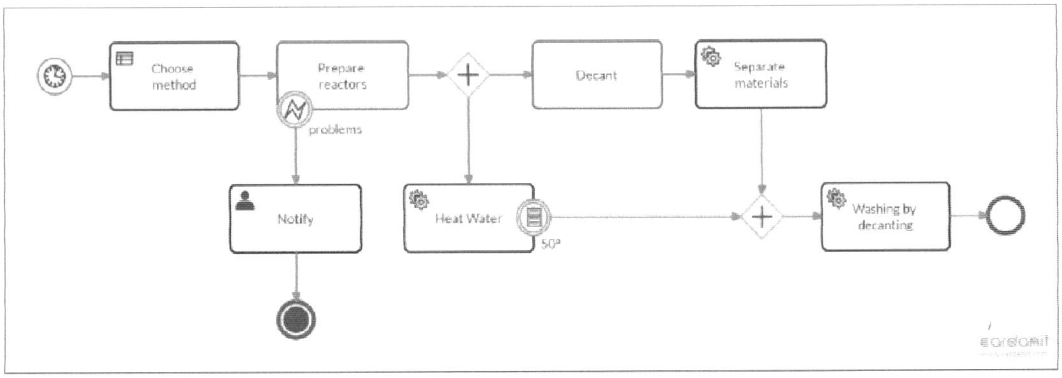

Figure 11. BPMN model of *Generator*.

VI. Conclusion

Requirements traceability is the capability to follow the life-cycle of the requirement playing an important role in model-based system engineering where the use of models has a central role. SysML is a general-purpose modeling language, based on UML, which enables traceability because it defines relationships between requirements and other modeling elements. The approach presented in this paper has as the central proposition to consider the decision-making activities that participate in a process as a decision requirement and through traceability, reaching its decision logic. The combination of SysML and BPMN-DMN is interesting because the use of SysML in the industry grows day by day. Not less important is the fact that SysML is a well-defined standard. The combination of all these standards is a step forward that enhances the modeling of the different views of the system to be built including also decision requirements. The approach forces us to define new stereotypes in SysML to support all types of BPMN tasks. An example and a case study have been provided to show how traceability of a decision requirement can be performed by combining SysML and BPMN-DMN. This approach seeks to integrate and cover the different views of the decision requirements, helping systems engineers to improve the design of them.

In future work, we will consider analyzing the link between the relationships in the requirements diagram and the DMN decision requirements diagram.

References

[1] J. Jacobs and A. C. Simpson, "Towards a process algebra framework for supporting behavioural consistency and requirements traceability in SysML, " in Proceedings of the 15th International Conference on Formal Engineering Methods (ICFEM 2013), ser. Lecture Notes in Computer Science. Springer, vol. 8144, pp. 266-281, 2013.

[2] OMG https://www.omg.org/ [retrieved: October, 2019]

[3] S. Friedenthal, A. Moore, and R. Steiner, "A Practical Guide to SysML The Systems Modeling Language", Burlington: Morgan Kaufmann/OMG, Elsevier, 2008.

[4] SysML https://www.omg.org/spec/SysML/1.5 [retrieved: October, 2019]

[5] OMG document number: "Business process model and notation". formal/13-12-09 [retrieved: October, 2019]

[6] Decision Model and Notation https://www.omg.org/spec/DMN/1.2/ [retrieved: October, 2019]

[7] E. J. Vidal and E. R. Villota, "SysML as a Tool for Requirements Traceability in Mechatronic Design". In Proceedings of the 2018 4th International Conference on Mechatronics and Robotics Engineering. ACM, pp. 146-152, 2018.

[8] R. Baduel, M. Chami, J. M. Bruel, and I. Ober, "SysML Models Verification and Validation in an Industrial Context: Challenges and Experimentation". In European Conference on Modelling Foundations and Applications. Springer, Cham, pp. 132-146, 2018.

[9] A. Salado and P. Wach, "Constructing True Model-Based Requirements in SysML". Systems, vol. 7, no 2, pp. 19, 2019.

[10] K. Gruber, J. Huemer, A. Zimmermann, and R. Maschotta, "Integrated description of functional and non-functional requirements for automotive systems design using SysML", 2017 7th IEEE Int. Conf. on System Engineering and Technology (ICSET), pp. 27-31, Oct 2017.

[11] M. R. S. Marques, E. Siegert, and L. Brisolara, "Integrating UML, MARTE and SysML to improve requirements specification and traceability in the embedded domain". In 2014 12th IEEE International Conference on Industrial Informatics (INDIN). IEEE, pp 176-181, 2014

[12] H. Dubois, M. A. Peraldi-Frati, and F. Lakhal, "A model for requirements traceability in a heterogeneous model-based design process: Application to automotive embedded systems". In 2010 15th IEEE International Conference on Engineering of Complex Computer Systems. IEEE, pp. 233-242. 2010

[13] INCOSE https://www.incose.org/ [retrieved: October, 2019]

[14] T. Weilkiens, "Systems engineering with SysML/UML: modeling, analysis, design" Elsevier, 2011.

[15] O. C.Z. Gotel and A. C.W. Finkelstein, "An Analysis of the Requirements Traceability Problem", Proc. IEEE Int. Conf. on Requirements Engineering, pp. 94-101, April 1994.

[16] http://www.omgsysml.org/INCOSE-OMGSysML-Tutorial-Final-090901.pdf [retrieved: October, 2019]

[17] UML 2.4 "Infrastructure Specification" https://www.omg.org/spec/UML/2.4.1/ [retrieved: October, 2019]

[18] G. Booch, J. Rumbaugh, and I. Jacobson, "The Unified Modeling Language User Guide" Addison-Wesley. 1999.

[19] Modelica: https://www.modelica.org/ [retrieved: October, 2019]

[20] P. Spoletini and A. Ferrari. "Requirements elicitation: a look at the future through the lenses of the past". In 2017 IEEE 25th International Requirements Engineering Conference (RE). IEEE. p. 476-477, 2017.

Alignment of Test Driven Development and Relative Correctness-based Development

Marwa Benabdelali

Université de Tunis
Institut Supérieur de Gestion de Tunis
Bardo, Tunisia, Lab. RIADI-GD
Email: marwa.benabdelali@yahoo.com

Lamia Labed Jilani

Université de Tunis
Institut Supérieur de Gestion de Tunis
Bardo, Tunisia, Lab. RIADI-GD
Email: lamia.labed@isg.rnu.tn

Abstract—**Deriving programs by reliability enhancement is the aim of a program development process based on relative correctness as presented in previous studies. In fact, it is clear that nowadays we do not develop programs from scratch but we exploit existing ones and try to modify and adapt them according to a given specification. On the other hand, the practice of agile methods is increasingly widespread in software development. In this paper, we are interested in the relation between Test Driven Development and Reliability Enhancement Development. Test Driven Development as a software engineering methodology is built upon eXtreme Programming. It emphasizes a test first approach, which differs from the traditional software development cycle and produces better software quality. Relative correctness is a formal model that permits to verify that a program P is more-correct than a program P'. This is the core of a development process based on reliability enhancement. We align the two processes, compare them and show that : 1)Test Driven Development is an instance of reliability enhancement development process and 2) Test Driven Development iteration can be used as a mean to transform a program P to another program P' that is more-correct than P according to a given specification R.**

Keywords–Reliability enhancement; Relative correctness; Specification; Test Driven Development.

I. INTRODUCTION

Software maintenance and evolution are known to require a lot of effort and, to cope with this, developing reusable assets turns out to be an interesting approach as it allows to reduce the time and cost for software development. In this context, Test Driven Development (TDD) and Relative Correctness-Based Development (RCBD) aim at managing software quality by means of incrementally developing assets (i.e., test cases and specifications) to guarantee that previously added behaviors still persist after changes and refinements. RCBD [1] proves its worth as a rigourous theoretical framework that derives programs by successive correctness enhancing transformations rather than deriving programs by successive correctness preserving transformations [2][3][4]. Whereas correctness preservation is the prevailing paradigm in programs construction, correctness enhancement seems to be a promising tentative for constructing correct and reliable programs and it formally models a wide range of software activities, as programs repair, evolution, etc. In this paper, we are specifically working on TDD and show that is an instance of RCBD. On the other hand, we use TDD iterations as a means for transforming one program P into another more correct program according to a given specification R. Indeed, we discuss that despite the fact that the program construction process using TDD is different to that of RCBD, the results obtained by both processes are the same, where we obtain a sequence of programs that are respectively more-correct with respect to a specification.

The paper is structured as follows; Section 2 briefly introduces some relational mathematics that we use throughout the paper to represent specications and programs. Section 3 presents the concept of relative correctness as a formal and generic model that allows the construction of reliable and correct programs. Section 4 aligns the TDD process and that of RCBD. Section 5 presents with an illustrative example the TDD as a strategy to derive reliable programs by correctness enhancement. Section 6 summarizes our findings and presents some perspectives on this work.

II. MATHEMATICAL BACKGROUND

In this paper, we use relational mathematics [5] to represent specifications and program functions. We represent sets in a program-like notation by writing variable names and associated data types (sets of values); if we write S as: $x : X; y : Y$; then, we mean to let S be the cartesian product $S = X \times Y$; elements of S are denoted by s and the $X-component$ of s is denoted by $x(s)$ and the $Y-component$ of s is denoted by $y(s)$. When no ambiguity arises, we may write x for $x(s)$, and x' for $x(s')$.

Given a program p that operates on a space called S and all the elements of S are called the *states* of p that are usually denoted in lower case s. We let P be the function of p that is represented as the set of pairs (s,s') such that if the program p starts the execution in state s then, it terminates in state s'. A relation R on a set S is a subset of the cartesian product $S \times S$; given a set of pairs (s,s') in R, we say that state s' is an image of state s by R.

Relations on S include the identity relation $I = \{(s,s')|s' \in S\}$, the empty relation $\phi = \{\}$ and the universal relation $L = S \times S$. As for operations on relations, they include the set theoretic operations of intersection $(R \cap R')$, difference$(R \setminus R')$, complement$(\bar{R})$, and union$(R \cup R')$. They also include the converse of a relation $\widehat{R} = \{(s,s')|(s',s) \in R\}$, the product of two relations (R o R') or (RR', for short) $=\{(s,s')|\exists s'' : (s,s'') \in R \wedge (s'',s') \in R'\}$ and the domain of a relation $dom(R) = \{s|\exists s' : (s,s') \in R\}$.

A relation R is *symmetric* if and only if $R = \widehat{R}$, *antisymmetric* if and only if $R \cap \widehat{R} \subseteq I$ and *asymmetric* if and only if $R \cap \widehat{R} = \phi$. A relation R is *transitive* if and only if $RR \subseteq R$ and *reflexive* if and only if $I \subseteq R$. A relation R is *partial ordering* if and only if it is *reflexive*, *antisymmetric*, and *transitive*. A relation R is *deterministic* if and only if $\widehat{R}R \subseteq I$ and *total* if and only if $I \subseteq \widehat{R}R$. A relation R is a *vector* if and only if $RL = R$. Vectors are used to represent subsets of S. A relation R *refines* relation R' ($R' \sqsupseteq R$ or $R \sqsubseteq R'$) if and only if $RL \cap R'L \cap (R \cup R') = R'$.

Definition 1. *Program P on space S is correct with respect to a specification R if and only if P refines R ($(R \cap P)L = RL$).*

Note that RL refers to the domain of the specification R that represents the initial states for which candidate programs must behave according to R. And the relation $(R \cap P)L$ refers to the set of initial states on which the behavior of P satisfies specification R. This set is denoted the *competence domain* of P with respect to R.

III. Program Construction by Relative Correctness

Whereas the traditional approach that preserves correctness is the dominant paradigm in program construction, the issues become no longer to develop program from scratch but rather to achieve a satisfactory reliability threshold with respect to a given specication. Being in this context, RCBD has proven its value as an alternative approach to the traditional refinement-based process of successive correctness-preserving transformations starting from the specification and culminating in a correct program (Figure 1). Where in the left side, program construction is done by correctness preserving transformations starting from a correct specification until obtaining a correct program. In the right side, an abort program is transformed to a more correct program according to a specification R. Then, series of similar transformations are done to obtain more and more correct programs (by correctness enhancement transformations). The process stopped when a correct program is completely derived.

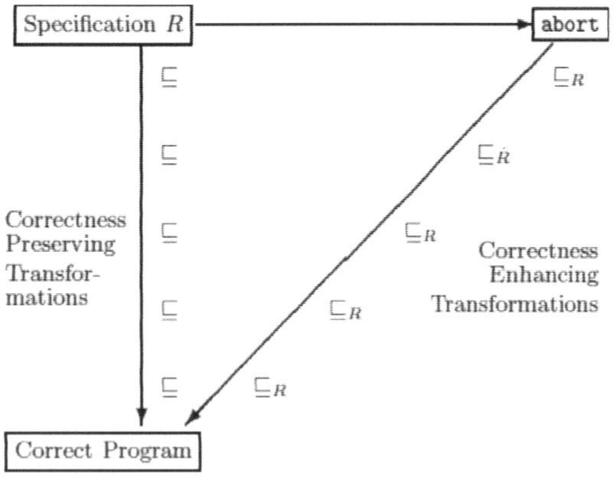

Figure 1. Program derivation process [1].

The concept of relative correctness was introduced in [1] as the property of a program to be more correct than another program with respect to a specification. We say that program P refines program P if and only if P is more-correct than P with respect to a specification.

Definition 2. *Due to [1] given two programs P_0, P_1 and a specification R; we say that P_1 is more-correct than P_0 if and only if P_1 obeys R for a larger set of inputs than P_0. This relation is denoted by $P_0 \sqsubseteq_R P_1$ which is equivalent to the relation: $(R \cap P_0)oL \subseteq (R \cap P_1)oL$. Also, we say that P_1 is strictly more-correct than P_0 with respect to R if and only if $P_0 \sqsubset_R P_1$ which is equivalent to the relation $(R \cap P_0)oL \subset (R \cap P_1)oL$.*

The relation $(R \cap P_0)oL$ refers to the *competence domain* of P_0 with respect to R (denoted by CD_{P_0}) which is the initial states on which the behavior of P_0 satisfies specification R. Relative correctness of P_1 over P_0 with respect to R simply means that P_1 has a larger competence domain than P_0.
To illustrate this definition; Let S be the space defined by $\{0, 1, 2, 3\}$ and let R be the following specification on S:
$R = \{(0,1),(0,2),(1,2),(1,3),(2,0),(2,2),(3,1),(3,2),(3,3)\}$.
We consider the following candidate programs:
$P_0 = \{(0,0),(0,1),(0,2),(1,0),(1,1),(2,0),(2,1),(2,3),(3,0)\}$.
$P_1 = \{(0,0),(0,1),(1,0),(1,2),(1,3),(2,0),(2,3),(3,0)\}$.
$CD_{P_0} = (R \cap P_0) = \{(0,1),(0,2),(2,0)\}$
$(R \cap P_0)oL = \{0,2\} \times S$
$CD_{P_1} = (R \cap P_1) = \{(0,1),(1,2),(1,3),(2,0)\}$
$(R \cap P_1)oL = \{0,1,2\} \times S$
Hence P_1 is more-correct than P_0 with respect to R. And we say that $P_0 \sqsubseteq_R P_1$.

IV. Test Driven Development as an Instance of Relative Correctness-Based Development

TDD [6] is considered to be one of the most effective development approaches that is derived from the agile software development methodology called eXtreme Programming (XP) [7]. It depends on a short development life cycle where the developer incrementally writes unit tests before any program code and is considered as a set of iterations where from one iteration to another we go from a program P to program P' that is more correct. TDD process revolves around five steps: 1) Write the first test. 2) Run the test and confirm that it cannot pass without any implemented code. 3) Write enough code to make test pass. 4) Run the test on the previous code and confirm the test pass else the code must be modified until the test pass. 5) Refactor which means to improve the code while keeping the same functionalities. The cycle must be repeated until all the specification functionalities are implemented and therefore we obtain a correct program that meets the specification.

TDD and RCBD are both programs derivation approaches. Despite the fact that their derivation processes are different, both processes give as a result a sequence of programs that are respectively more correct with respect to the specification. So, our aim is to align the TDD process with that of RCBD and formally validate that TDD is an instance of RCBD.
As shown in Figure 2, using series of test data specifications $\sum_{i=1}^{n} T_i$, we create a list of programs $\sum_{i=1}^{n} P_i$ such as each P_i is an upgrade of P_{i-1}. We assume that the T_i's have disjoint domains. Let R_i be the sequence of relations defined for $0 \leq i \leq n$ by:
$R_0 = \phi$, for $1 \leq i \leq n$: $R_i = \cup_{k=1}^{i} T_k$.
By this definition, and by virtue of the hypothesis that the T_i's have disjoint domains, for $1 \leq i \leq n$, we can write: $R_i = R_{i-1} \sqcup T_i$.
According to this formula, each step of TDD can be modeled as an instance of program upgrade. Indeed, if we let P_0 be $\{$abort$\}$ and we let P_i be the program derived at phase i by upgrading P_{i-1} with specification T_i , then, we can prove by

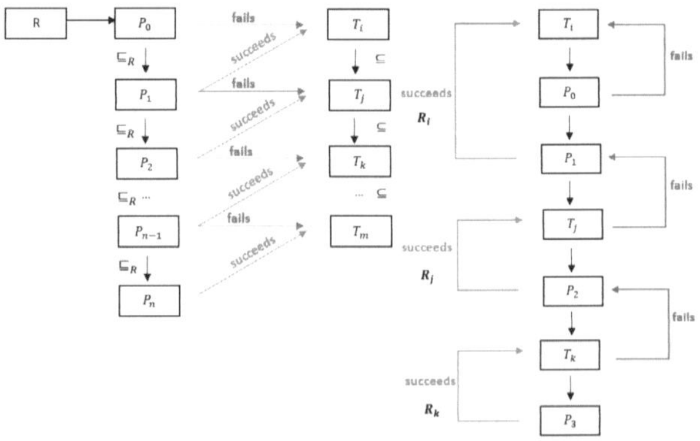

Figure 2. Alignment of Test Driven Development with relative correctness.

induction that for all i, $0 \leq i \leq n$, P_i is correct with respect to R_i. The following proposition provides that if we rename R_n as R and we let Q_i be the pre-restriction of P_i to the domain of R_i , then $\{Q_i\}$ forms a sequence of increasingly correct programs with respect to R.

Proposition 1. *We consider a space S and a non-empty test data specifications T_i on S, $1 \leq i \leq n$, for some $n \geq 1$ such that $T_iL \cap T_jL = \phi$ for any $i \neq j$. We define a set of specifications $\{R_i\}$ by:*
$R_0 = \phi$, for $1 \leq i \leq n$: $R_i = \cup_{k=1}^{i} T_k$
And we let $\{P_i\}$, for $1 \leq i \leq n$, be a set of programs such that for all i, P_i is correct with respect to R_i. Further, we let $\{Q_i\}$ be the set of programs defined by: $Q_i = P_i \cap R_iL$. Then, for all i, $0 \leq i \leq n$, Q_{i+1} is more-correct than Q_i with respect to R_n.

Proof: We rename R_n as R and we resolve to prove that for all i between 0 and $n-1$, $Q_{i+1} \sqsupseteq_R Q_i$.
To this effect, we must show that the competence domain of Q_i is a subset of that of Q_{i+1}:
$(Q_i \cap R)L$
$=$ {Definition of Q_i}
$(P_i \cap R_iL \cap R)L$
$=$ {By construction of R, R_i}
$(P_i \cap R_i)L$
$=$ {By definition 1}
R_iL
$\subset$ {By construction of R_i, and hypothesis that $T_i \neq \phi$}
$R_{i+1}L$
$=$ {By definition 1}
$(P_{i+1} \cap R_{i+1})L$
$=$ {By construction of R, R_{i+1}}
$(P_{i+1} \cap R_{i+1}L \cap R)L$
$=$ {Associativity, Commutativity, Definition of Q_{i+1}}
$(Q_{i+1} \cap R)L$ ■

Therefore, TDD can be seen as an instance of RCBD. However, the main difference between both development processes is that in the TDD process the specification is not known in advance but is built progressively alongside the program.

Test-driven development with the support of relative correctness offers the possibility to have a formal way for verifying to what extend sufficiently reliable programs are generated. On the other hand, deriving programs by relative correctness can use test-driven development iterative steps as a strategy for transforming one program to another more reliable one.

V. Test Driven Development iteration as a transformation strategy for Relative Correctness-based Development

Despite that program derivation by relative correctness is a promising tentative for constructing reliable programs, we argue that this latter process is not efficient as program derivation by refinement calculus which is older, matter and based on set of strong rules and sophisticated guidelines for program transformations. For that, we tried in [8] to find some mechanisms and scenarios for program transformation in the relative correctness- based reliable program construction approach. The first scenario is *domain enlargement* in which we keep the same program functionalities and at each transition from one program to another, we increase the domain of the program $(dom(P))$ with respect to the domain of the specification $(dom(R))$. The second scenario is a *particular case* in which the program does something else but in some particular cases, it does what the specification R requires, so it suffices to generate such program from P to P'. The third scenario is *changing behavior* where the behavior of the program changes depending on the type of input data, hence the next generated program P' adds code for a new type of input in addition to the existing ones in program P. And the last and fourth scenario is *improve program functionality* in which from one program to another, we add a little bit of code to the program compared to his predecessor until we reach an absolutely correct program with respect to R or we reach a sufficiency reliability threshold. With these four scenarios, we can also resort to the reuse-based development with the *reusable programs stored in a repository* in which we start with an abort program that never run successfully and then, we search in the repository for programs that are more correct according to the specification R by competence domain calculations.

Being in the context of program repair and as a tentative for program derivation mechanism by relative correctness, the authors in [9] present a generic algorithm that proceeds by successive removed fault as the relative correctness rises with each fault removal until reaching a correct program according to a given specification. This algorithm is based on the availability of a patch generator and focuses on the patch validation steps. The algorithm takes as input; a program P on space S, a test data set T as a subset of S, a specification R on S, and the domain of the specification R $(dom(R))$. And depending on patch generator, it returns as output either an absolutely correct program P' with respect to R, or a strictly more-correct program P' than P with respect to R or a message indicate that is impossible to more enhance correctness of P with respect to R.

Another tentative for program derivation mechanism by relative correctness is based on mutation testing [10] that allows gradually repairing an incorrect program by removing its faults one by one. Indeed, the derivation process starts by a faulty program P and repeatedly applying *muJava* to generate mutants.Then, taking mutants which are found to be *strictly* more-correct as base programs and recursively repeating the process until reached a correct program according to given specification R. Hence the transition from faulty program P to these generated mutants represents a fault removal and falls in the program repair activity.

Remaining in program derivation strategies by relative correctness, an iteration in the Test Driven Development process can be a mechanism that guides and defines the derivation of reliable program by exploring the unit test notion which is the center of TDD (development process in table I). Indeed, we start from an abort program (P_0) that never run successful with respect to R (we reuse programs that dont response to the specification or we evolve existing programs). We create a first test (t_0), run it on the abort program and confirm its failure else we rewrite it. then, we create enough code for P_1 to make t_0 pass. We create t_1 code that must integrate the t_0 code, we run it on P_1 and we confirm its failure else we rewrite it. Then, we create P_2 to make t_1 pass and here we check correctness enhancement from P_1 to P_2 by ensuring that $CD_{P_1} \subseteq CD_{P_2}$ which means that P_2 refines P_1. Therefore, we write $P_1 \sqsubseteq_R P_2$. Note that for P_0 and P_1 we may calculate their competence domains but is not necessary to ensure that$CD_{P_0} \subseteq CD_{P_1}$ because P_0 is an abort program that never meets the specification R. To create P_n programs, we need T_{n-1} tests. Table I shows a comparison between the TDD process phases and those of RCBD phases and a highlight of TDD process contribution to RCBD. Indeed, what we have done is to draw inspiration from TDD approach to construct programs using the concept of relative correctness. To summarize the derivation process, at each transition from one program to another we use the notion of test and for each program created,we must ensure that it refines his predecessor so we ensure that $CD_{P_i} \subseteq CD_{P_{i+1}}$. When we create a program to make the test pass, we obtain a part R_i of the specification R and at the end of the derivation, R is constructed by the union of all the R_i.

TABLE I. PROGRAM CONSTRUCTION PROCESSES.

	Test Driven Development process	Relative correctness process	Relative correctness process using TDD
1	Write first test.	Write an abort program.	Create an abort program and a first test.
2	Run test and assure its failure because code has not yet implemented.	Create the next program using a derivation mechanism.	Run the test on the abort program and confirm its failure else rewrite it.
3	Write enough code to makes test pass.	Calculate the function and the competence domain of the program.	Create the first program to make the test pass.
4	Run test on code and confirm its success else rewrite the code until the test pass.	Ensure that $CD_{P_i} \subseteq CD_{P_{i+1}}$.	Calculate the function and the competence domain of the program.
5	Refactor.	Repeat the cycle from the second step until reach correct or reliable program according to the specification.	Create the second test, run it on the first program and confirm its failure else rewrite it.
6	Repeat the cycle from the beginning until reach correct program according to the specification.		Create the second program to make the second test pass and ensure that $CD_{P_i} \subseteq CD_{P_{i+1}}$.
7			Repeat the cycle from the third step until reach correct program or satisfactory reliability threshold.

As an illustration of the TDD strategy, we conduct a simple empirical experimentation using *java* language and *Junit* [11] as a testing frameworks. *Junit* is the most popular testing frameworks for *Java* language used by developers to implement unit testing. It is based on assertions that test specific functionality in the code. The choice of this one is because it is suitable to be used with test driven development and eXtreme Programming.
What we are going to do is to follow the construction strategy presented above to derive either correct or reliable programs according to given specification.

As a hypothesis, we suppose that test cases constitute the specification that is known in advance in the approach of deriving programs by relative correctness (see proposition 1). Let S be the space defined by the integer variable x and the integer array TAB.
and let R be the following specification on S:
$R = \{(s,s')|((\forall i : 0 \leq i \leq N : x' \geq TAB[i]) \wedge (\exists i : 0 \leq i \leq N : x' = TAB[i]))\}$.
The specification mandates that x be assigned the largest integer value in TAB.
For the first step, we create P_0 as an abort program, create a test T_0 and run P_0 on this test. As a better example of an abort program would be one that throws an exception or one that does not exist at all, as is the case in traditional Test Driven Development. Therefore, its competence domain is the empty set. Indeed, it does not meet any functionality of the specification R. We create the test T_0 and run it on the abort program.

```
T0: import junit.framework.*;
public class TestMax extends TestCase {
public TestMax(String name) {
super(name);}
public void test0() {
assertEquals(200,
Max.maxval(new int[ ] {200, 50, -2, 80, 0 }));}}
```

Obviously, the console display the red bar which shows that the abort program (P_0) fails to meet the test T_0. To make the later pass, we need to create enough code for P_1:

```
P1: public class Max {
public static int maxval(int[] tab) {
int max = tab[0];
return max;}}
```

The function of this program and its competence domain are given as:
$P_1 = \{(s,s')|((\forall i : 0 \leq i < N : TAB[0] \geq TAB[i]) \wedge (x' = TAB[0]))\}$
$CD_{P_1} = (R \cap P_1)oL$
$= \{(s,s')|(\forall i : 0 \leq i < N : TAB[0] \geq TAB[i])\}$.
Indeed, this is the competence domain of P_1 with respect to R: which is the arrays that contain the largest value in index 0.
We run P_1 on T_0. As shown in Figure 3, the console displays the green bar which means that the P_1 succeeds to to meet the test T_0.We may end the derivation at this stage to obtain therefore a reliable program according to R but in order to obtain an absolute correct program we continue the derivation process.

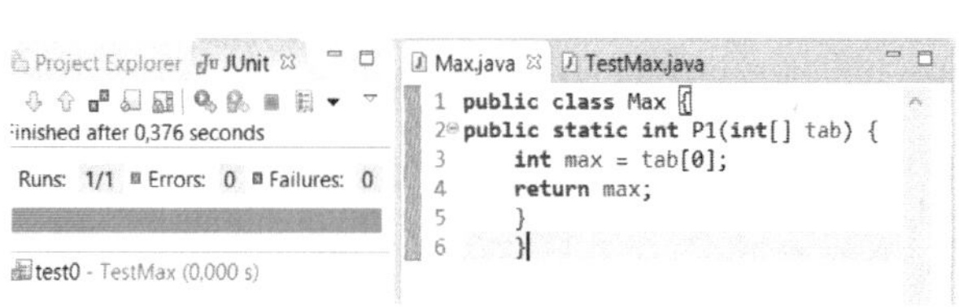

Figure 3. Green bar T_0.

For the next step, We create the test T_1 and we run it on the previous program (P_1).
We assume that $T_0 \subseteq T_1$.

```
T1: import junit.framework.*;
```

```
public class TestMax extends TestCase {
public TestMax(String name) {
super(name);}
public void test1() {
assertEquals(200,
Max.maxval(new int[ ] {200, 50, -2, 80, 0 }));
assertEquals(200,
Max.maxval(new int[ ] {50, -2, 80, 200, 0}));}}
```

As the execution result, the console displays the red bar (Figure 4) which shows that P_1 fails to meet the test T_1.

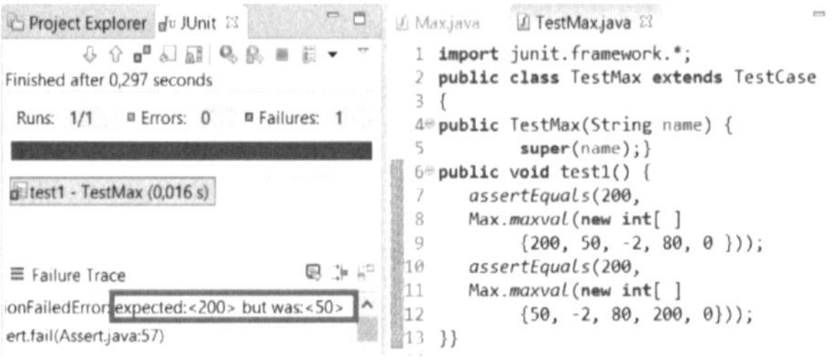

Figure 4. Red bar T_1.

As we previously did, we create enough code for program P_2 to pass the test T_1.

```
P2: public class Max {
public static int maxval(int[] tab) {
int index, max = 0;
for (index = 0; index < tab.length-1; index++){
if (tab[index] > max) {
max = tab[index];}}
return max;}}
```

The function of this program and its competence domain are given as:
$P_2 = \{(s,s')|((\forall i : 0 \leq i < N : x' \geq TAB[i]) \wedge (\exists i : 0 \leq i < N : x' = TAB[i]))\}$
$CD_{P_2} = (R \cap P_2)oL$
$= \{(s,s')|(\forall i : 0 \leq i < N : x' \geq TAB[i])\}$.
Indeed, this is the competence domain of P_2 with respect to R: which is the arrays that contain the largest value in any index except the last index.
We run P_2 on T_1. The console displays the green bar (Figure 5) which means that the P_2 succeeds to to meet the test T_1. We confirm that $CD_{P_1} \subseteq CD_{P_2}$ means that $P_1 \sqsubseteq_R P_2$.

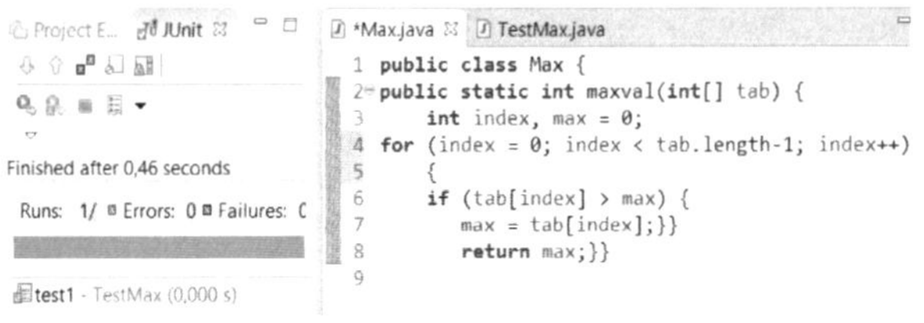

Figure 5. Green bar T_1.

At this derivation stage, we may end the derivation, hence we obtain a reliable program according to the specification R but we continue the derivation process until we reach an absolute correct program.
we create a test T_2 and we run it on the previous program. We assume that $T_1 \subseteq T_2$.

```
T2: import junit.framework.*;
public class TestMax extends TestCase {
public TestMax(String name) {
super(name);}
public void test2() {
assertEquals(200,
Max.maxval(new int[ ] {200, 50, -2, 80, 0 }));
assertEquals(200,
Max.maxval(new int[ ] {50, -2, 80, 200, 0}));
assertEquals(200,
Max.maxval(new int[ ] {50, -2, 80, 0, 200}));}}
```

As a result of running P_2 on T_2, the console displays the red bar (Figure 6) which shows that P_2 fails to meet the test T_2. indeed, P_2 returns the maximum value that exists in any index expect the last index of tab however, T_2 tests on the maximum value that exist in any index.

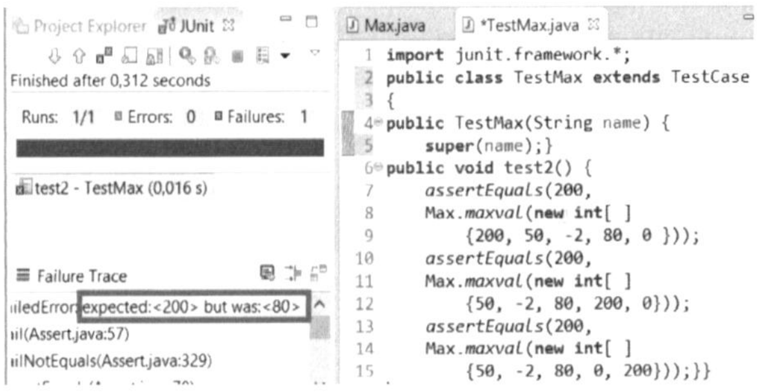

Figure 6. Red bar T_2.

As a solution to make the previous test pass(T_2), we create a program P_3.

```
P3: public class Max {
public static int maxval(int[] tab) {
int index, max = 0;
for (index = 0; index < tab.length; index++){
if (tab[index] > max) {
max = tab[index];}}
return max;}}
```

The function of this program and its competence domain are given as:
$P_3 = \{(s,s')|((\forall i : 0 \leq i \leq N : x' \geq TAB[i]) \wedge (\exists i : 0 \leq i \leq N : x' = TAB[i]))\}$.
$CD_{P_3} = (R \cap P_3)oL = RL = S$
The competence domain of P_3 is R. Therefore, P_3 is correct according to R. We run P_3 on T_2. The console displays the green bar (Figure 7) which means that P_3 succeeds to meet the test T_2.

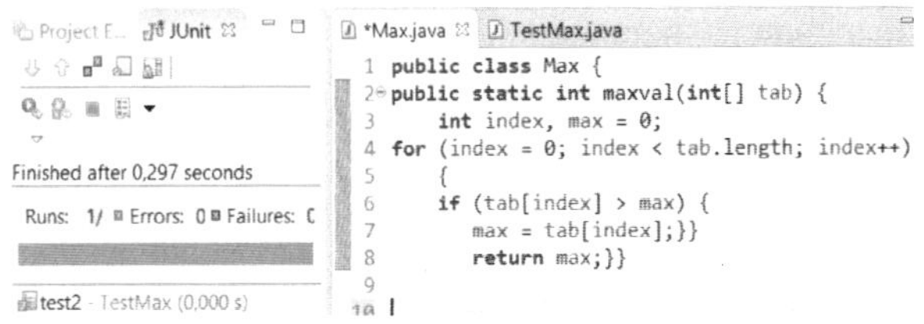

Figure 7. Green bar T_1.

At this derivation stage, we obtain a correct program that meets all the functionalities mandates by the specification

R. Therefore, we do have: $CD_{P_1} \subseteq CD_{P_2} \subseteq CD_{P_3}$. Hence $P_1 \sqsubseteq_R P_2 \sqsubseteq_R P_3$.

VI. Conclusion

TDD has received considerable individual attention since XPs introduction. Many recent researchers works show that Test Driven Development gives rise to defect reduction and quality improvement in academic and professional environments. On the other hand, RCBD seems to be adequate to do almost the same thing as Test Driven Development but in a formal manner. In this work, we showed formally that TDD is an instance of RCBD and also a TDD iteration (testing, coding, refactoring) can be an adopted strategy in the transformation process of Relative Correctness Enhancement. This is also a way to validate formally each TDD iteration. As near future work, we are going to test the RCBD on real cases where the transformation from one program to another is done according to the TDD iteration strategy.

References

[1] N. Diallo, W. Ghardallou, J. Desharnais, and A. Mili, "Program derivation by correctness enhacements," in Proceedings 17th International Workshop on Refinement, Refine@FM 2015, Oslo, Norway, 22nd June 2015., 2015, pp. 57–70, URL: https://doi.org/10.4204/EPTCS.209.5/ [accessed: 2019-08-04].

[2] R.-J. Back, "On the Correctness of Refinement Steps in Program Development," Ph.D. dissertation, 1978.

[3] C. Morgan, Programming from specifications, ser. Spectrum Book. Prentice Hall, 1990, URL: https://books.google.tn/books?id=95dQAAAAMAAJ/ [accessed: 2019-08-03].

[4] R. Back and J. von Wright, Refinement Calculus a Systematic Introduction. Springer-Verlag New York, 1998.

[5] C. Brink, W. Kahl, and G. Schmidt, Eds., Relational Methods in Computer Science. Berlin, Heidelberg: Springer-Verlag, 1997.

[6] K. Beck, Test Driven Development. By Example (Addison-Wesley Signature). Addison-Wesley Longman, Amsterdam, 2002.

[7] K. beck, Extreme Programming Explained: Embrace Change. Boston, MA, USA: Addison-Wesley Longman Publishing Co., Inc, 2000.

[8] M. Benabdelali, L. L. Jilani, W. Ghardallou, and A. Mili, "Programming without refining," in Proceedings 18th Refinement Workshop, Refine@FM 2018, Oxford, UK, 18th July 2018., 2018, pp. 39–52, URL: https://doi.org/10.4204/EPTCS.282.4/ [accessed: 2019-08-04].

[9] B. Khaireddine, A. Zakharchenko, and A. Mili, "A Generic Algorithm for Program Repair," in 2017 IEEE/ACM 5th International FME Workshop on Formal Methods in Software Engineering (FormaliSE), May 2017, pp. 65–71.

[10] N. Diallo, W. Ghardallou, and A. Mili, "Program repair by stepwise correctness enhancement," in Proceedings First Workshop on Pre- and Post-Deployment Verification Techniques, PrePost@IFM 2016, Reykjavík, Iceland, 4th June 2016., 2016, pp. 1–15, URL: https://doi.org/10.4204/EPTCS.208.1/ [accessed: 2019-08-06].

[11] K. Beck, JUnit - pocket guide: quick lookup and advice. O'Reilly Media, 2009.

Modeling and Verification of Car Parking System

Hadiqa Alamdar Bukhari
School of Electrical Engineering and Computer Science
National University of Sciences and Technology (NUST)
Islamabad, Pakistan
hbukhari.bese16seecs@seecs.edu.pk

Dr. Sidra Sultana
School of Electrical Engineering and Computer Science
National University of Sciences and Technology (NUST)
Islamabad, Pakistan
sidra.sultana@seecs.edu.pk

***Abstract*— Formal modeling and verification help in achieving safety related concerns in real time systems. Car parking system is modeled and verified in this paper to ensure the non-collision and the parking of a car which is both time and space efficient. A detailed simulation of the model is presented and described.**

Keywords-Uppaal; system verification; system modeling; car parking.

I. INTRODUCTION

Metropolitan cities are dealing with increasing traffic and in turn an increase in parking garages. With the increase in the use of automated systems and the introduction of Internet of Things, more cities are making use of smart car parking systems to deal with the common problem of finding a vacant parking space. Smart car parking systems deal with directing cars to an empty parking spot all the while keeping a record of which parking spots are free.

Car parking systems are safety critical and need to be modeled and verified before they are put into use. A single mistake may lead to damage of a person's car and waste of time due to an inefficient system [1]. These systems are incredibly complex and make use of expensive hardware. Therefore, it is essential that such systems are properly modeled, tested and verified on software before they are implemented on hardware [2]. System verification is of paramount importance [3] and advancements in technology have allowed us to optimize and check the safety of a system on a computer before it is constructed in the real world.

In this paper we modeled the car parking system using Uppaal model checker. The verified model with the timed automata can be used to implement a real time car parking system. We verified the safety, deadlock freeness, reachability, liveness, mutual exclusion, utility and fairness, which Uppaal's inbuilt verification module allowed us to do easily [4].

Following the introduction, in Section II a literature review is given where other similar projects are discussed. In Section III the system overview consisting of a model for car and a model for lane is described and the timed automata of these two models are also shown. The details of the Uppaal model checker and reasons behind why it is used are also discussed in this section. In Section IV system is verified and the verification properties are described. Finally, in Section V the conclusion and further improvements to the system are detailed.

II. LITERATURE REVIEW

A number of different car parking systems have been made in the past. In this section we will be discussing a few of these systems.

In [5], a car parking system is developed where the presence of a car causes the gates of a parking lot to open and the number of cars in the parking lot are displayed on an LCD. Here the authors focused mainly on the hardware aspects and the modeling and simulation were done on hardware rather than software.

In [6], a similar system to [5] is developed but the car is allotted the closest parking spot by judging the distance of the car from the entrance or exit of the parking lot. The authors in [7], aim to use an RFID and an infrared sensor based parking system. Here hardware modules are used to verify the correctness of the system which can be more expensive than using a modeling and verification software. In our project we significantly cut costs by modeling and verifying our system on the Uppaal model checker instead.

In [8], a web application based car parking system is made where a camera is used to check the availability of a parking spot and if a parking spot is free the user is notified. In [9], the authors have described a mobile application system that uses infrared sensors to find and allocate a parking spot.

In the above mentioned works, modeling and verification of the system was highly dependent on hardware modules. Hardware is not as reliable however, and it can be very hard to check all the verification properties on it. We chose to use Uppaal model checker in our project to ensure that all verification properties like reliability or deadlock freeness etc. are fulfilled.

In [10], the authors used Vienna Development Method-Specification Language (VDM-SL) to develop and verify a graph-based model. This model is used to find nearest empty parking spots. This is the most relevant project however, the simulator which we have used in our project, Uppaal is more versatile than VDM-SL and can be used to understand the traces to further correct the model, or to draw conclusions [11].

III. SYSTEM MODELING

In this section we give a system overview. Details on the Uppaal model checker are given and the timed automata of car parking system is detailed.

A. *System Overview*

As shown in Fig. 1, we modeled two automata, one for the car and one for the street on which the car looks for a parking space.

The cars can move on a street with two lanes and their sensors query a parallel automaton that models the street layout. The car looks for a free parking space and if there is one present on either lane, it moves into the available parking space and performs parallel reverse parking. After 40 seconds the cars can move out of the parking space and move forward to the end of the street. The street is 5 meters long and it has 2 suitable parking spaces in each lane. Two cars cannot park in the same parking spot at once.

The parallel automata communicate through shared channels. The cars can park multiple times in the street so long as there is a parking space available and the end of street has not been reached. The car can go back to the start of the street after it exits the street as well.

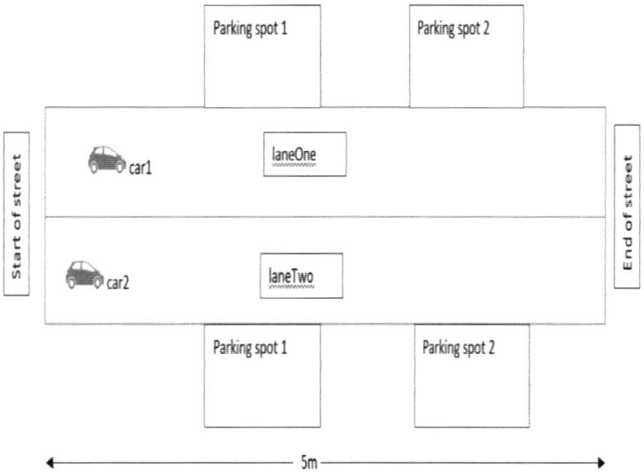

Figure 1. System state diagram.

B. *Uppaal*

We used the Uppaal model checker which is an integrated tool environment that gives us the ability to model and verify the behaviour of a system [12]. Uppaal is a very powerful tool since it can handle real time issues and transitions. Bounded liveness can be expressed and verified in Uppaal which is something that many model checkers do not provide. Also, Uppaal has an easy to use interface which makes it easier to model and execute a system.

Moreover, Uppaal displays the sequence diagram of the system as it is being executed so every state can be checked and the user can see of the states are being changed in the same sequence as intended. There are also a lot of projects which have been tested by Uppaal which further provided me with the confidence to use it as the model checker and verifier for this project [13].

C. *Timed Automata*

The Uppaal model checker was used to develop and test the model of a car which enters the parking system. As shown in Fig. 2, a car has four possible states, start, find_parking_spot, park and exit_street. A car can alternate between these four states.

For a car to transition from one state to another it must first fulfill the transition condition. As the car transitions from one state to another the position of the car which is stored in the car_pos variable is incremented. The car_pos variable helps detect the end of street.

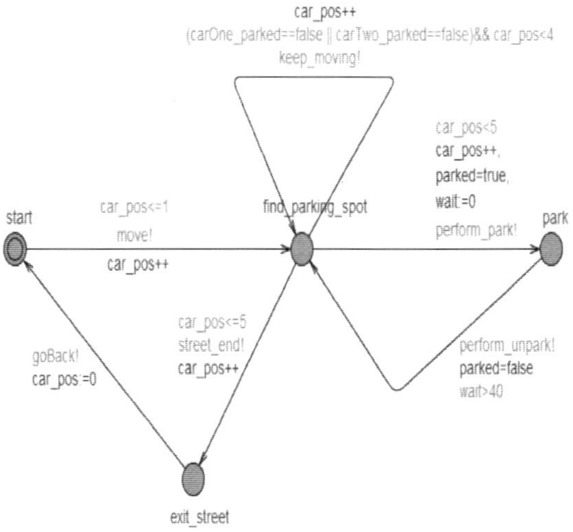

Figure 2. Model for car.

We also created a model for the lanes on which the cars can park. Each lane will have two parking spots as shown in Fig. 2. There are eight possible states in a lane. Similar to Fig. 1, the transition condition must first be fulfilled to transition from one state to another. A street_len variable is incremented whenever a car moves through the street. The street length is 5 meters.

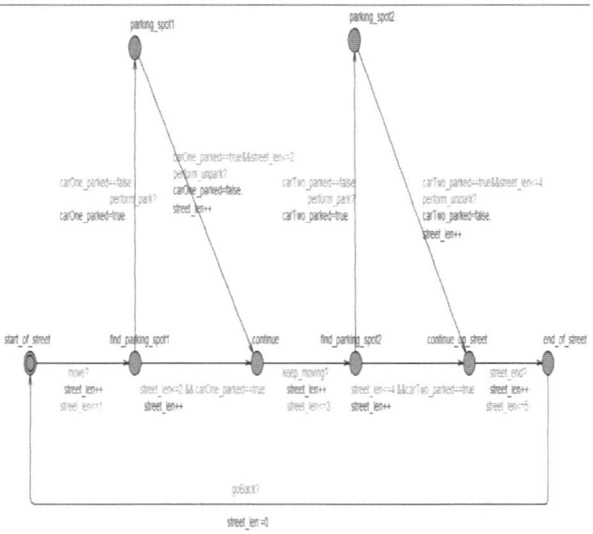

Figure 3. Model for lane.

The sequence diagram displayed in Fig. 4 shows the order in which states are executed and what triggers them. The states and transitions of the whole system are also displayed.

The sequence diagram can also be used to check the correctness of the system. In case of a deadlock, we can track the point at which deadlock occurs and can therefore, correct it.

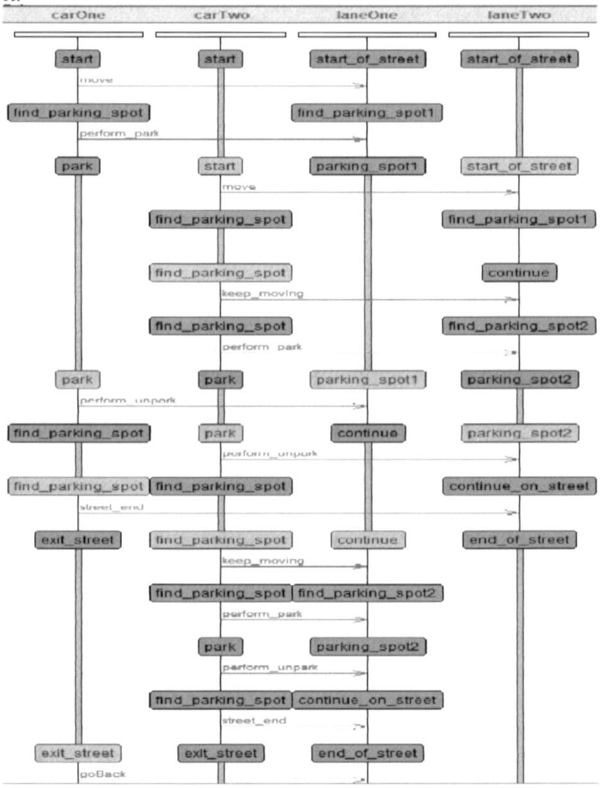

Figure 4. Sequence diagram

IV. System Verification

The system was verified using the Uppaal model checker to ensure the safety, reachability, liveness, utility, deadlock freeness and fairness of the system.

A. *Deadlock freeness*

- There are no deadlocks in the system at all.
  A[] not deadlock
- There are no deadlocks when the cars reach the end of the street.
  A[](deadlock imply (laneOne.end_of_street and laneTwo.end_of_street))

B. *Safety*

- Car one cannot take up 2 parking spaces in lane one as it would cause no other car to park in lane one and if a car tries to park in lane one it would crash into car one.
  A[]((laneOne.parking_spot1 and carOne.parked==true)imply not(laneOne.parking_spot2 and carOne.parked==true))
- Car one cannot take up 2 parking spaces in lane two as it would cause no other car to park in lane two and if a car tries to park in lane two it would crash into car one.
  A[]((laneTwo.parking_spot1 and carOne.parked==true)imply not(laneTwo.parking_spot2 and carOne.parked==true))
- Car two cannot take up 2 parking spaces in lane one as it would cause no other car to park in lane one and if a car tries to park in lane one it would crash into car two.
  A[]((laneOne.parking_spot1 and carTwo.parked==true)imply not(laneOne.parking_spot2 and carTwo.parked==true))
- Car two cannot take up 2 parking spaces in lane two as it would cause no other car to park in lane two and if a car tries to park in lane two it would crash into car two.
  A[]((laneTwo.parking_spot1 and carTwo.parked==true)imply not(laneTwo.parking_spot2 and carTwo.parked==true))

C. *Reachability*

- Car one exits the street infinitely often.
  E<> (carOne.exit_street)
- Car two exits the street eventually.
  E<> (carTwo.exit_street)

D. *Liveness*

- Car one or car two or both must always be looking for a parking space for the system to stay alive.
  E<> ((carOne.find_parking_spot and carTwo.park) or (carTwo.find_parking_spot and carOne.park) or (carOne.find_parking_spot and carTwo.find_parking_spot))

E. *Mutual exclusion*

- Car one cannot be parked in lane one and lane two at the same time.
  A[]((laneOne.parking_spot1 and carOne.parked==true)imply not(laneTwo.parking_spot1 and carOne.parked==true))
- Car two cannot be parked in lane one and lane two at the same time.
  A[]((laneOne.parking_spot1 and carTwo.parked==true)imply not(laneTwo.parking_spot1 and carTwo.parked==true))
- Car one cannot be at the start and the end of the street at the same time.
  A[]((carOne.start and laneOne.start_of_street)imply not(carOne.start and laneOne.end_of_street))

- Car two cannot be at the start and the end of the street at the same time.
  A[]((carTwo.start and laneOne.start_of_street)imply not(carTwo.start and laneOne.end_of_street))

F. *Utility*

- If carOne enters the street, it eventually parks on the street.
  E<> (carOne.start imply carOne.park)
- If carTwo enters the street then it eventually parks on the street.
  E<> (carTwo.start imply carOne.park)

G. *Fairness*

- Neither car one nor car two waits for longer than 40 seconds to unpark.
  A<> (carOne.wait<=40 and carTwo.wait<=40)
- Cars cannot drive on the street for longer than the length of the street.
  A[] (laneOne.street_len<6 and laneTwo.street_len<6)

Some of the verified properties are displayed in Fig. 5.

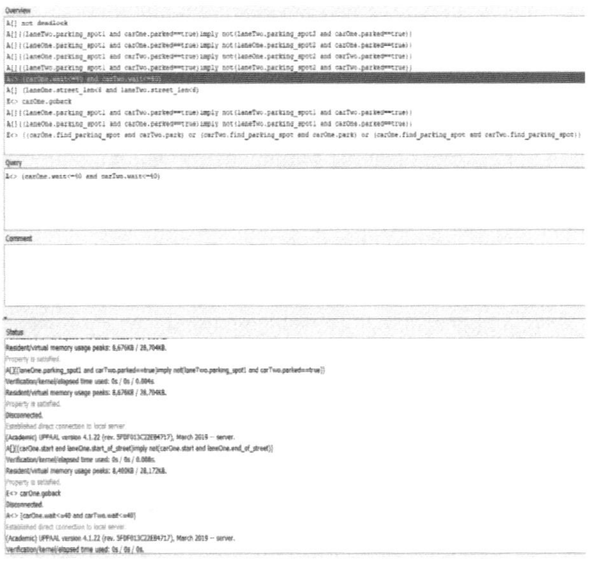

Figure 5. Results of the uppaal model checker

V. CONCLUSION AND FUTURE WORK

In this paper, an effective methodology for the modeling and verification of the car parking system was shown. The safety properties were verified using Uppaal and the stability of the real time automata was checked through the model checker as well. The car and lane models communicate effectively through common channel.

Most of the existing smart car parking systems are tested using hardware simulations which do not always ensure the correctness of the system. On the other hand, we have made use of formal modeling and verification techniques to prove that our model is correct.

For the time being we have developed a simple car parking system which is implemented in the real world scenario using the Uppaal model checker. To further improve our work, the system can be extended to accommodate a greater number of cars, lanes and parking spots. Moreover, a module can be added to find out and direct the car to the closest parking spot.

REFERENCES

[1] M. Jaffar-ur Rehman, F. Jabeen, A. Bertolino and A. Polini, "Testing software components for integration: a survey of issues and techniques", Software Testing, Verification and Reliability, vol. 17, no. 2, pp. 95-133, 2007.

[2] P. Upadhyay, "The Role of Verification and Validation in System Development Life Cycle", IOSR Journal of Computer Engineering, vol. 5, no. 1, pp. 17-20, 2012.

[3] M. Latuszynska, "Problems of verification and validation of computer simulation models", STUDIA INFORMATICA, pp. 27-40, 2013.

[4] G. Behrmann, A. David, K. Larsen, P. Pettersson and W. Yi, "Developing UPPAAL over 15 years", Software: Practice and Experience, vol. 41, no. 2, pp. 133-142, 2011.

[5] M. Ahmed and W. G. Wei, (2014). "Study on Automated Car Parking System Based on Microcontroller", International Journal of Engineering Research & Technology, vol. 3, no. 3, pp. 256-258, January 2014.

[6] S. Ghosh, S. Prusty and P. B. Natarajan, "Design and Implementation of Smart Car Parking System Using LabVIEW", International Journal of Pure and Applied Mathematics, vol. 120, pp. 329-338, October 2018.

[7] M. Sabnam, M. Das, P. A. Kashyap, "Automatic Car Parking System", ADBU Journal of Engineering Technology, vol. 4, no. 1, 2016.

[8] A. Ahad, Z. Khan, and S. Ahmad, "Intelligent Parking System", World Journal of Engineering and Technology, vol. 4, no. 2, pp. 160-167, May 2016.

[9] J. D. Bachhavl, Mechkul, "Smart Car Parking System", International Research Journal of Engineering and Technology (IRJET), vol. 4, no. 6, pp. 3036-3038, June 2017.

[10] S. Latif, H. Afzaal and N. A. Zafar, "Modelling of Graph-Based Smart Parking System Using Internet of Things", International Conference on Frontiers of Information Technology (FIT), pp. 7-12, 2018.

[11] "Formal Methods in the Teaching Lab Examples, Cases, Assignments and Projects Enhancing Formal Methods Education", Formal Methods Europe Subgroup on Education, Hamilton, ON, Canada, 2006, pp. 61-62

[12] M. P. Júnior and G. V. Alves, "A Study Towards the Application of UPPAAL Model Checker", 3rd Workshop-School on Theoretical Computer Science, pp. 5-8, September 2015.

[13] A. Hessel, K. Larsen, M. Mikučionis, B. Nielsen, P. Pettersson and A. Skou, "Testing real-time systems using UPPAAL", Formal Methods and Testing. pp. 77-117, January 2018.

International Academy, Research, and Industry Association (IARIA)
412 Derby Way
Wilmington, DE 19810

ISBN 978-1-7138-0058-3

9 781713 800583

5th International Seminar on Science and Technology (ISSTEC 2025)

BIO Web of Conferences Volume 226 (2026)

Yogyakarta, Indonesia
23 September 2025

edp sciences